The Gospel according to Matthew

By the author

Earliest Records of Jesus
First Epistle of Peter
St. Paul and His Letters
The Epistle to the Philippians

The Gospel according to Matthew

TRANSLATION, INTRODUCTION AND COMMENTARY

by

FRANCIS WRIGHT BEARE

*Professor Emeritus of New Testament Studies
in Trinity College, University of Toronto*

1817

HARPER & ROW, PUBLISHERS, SAN FRANCISCO
Cambridge, Hagerstown, New York, Philadelphia
London, Mexico City, São Paulo, Sydney

This work was first published in England under the title
The Gospel According to St. Matthew.
The Gospel According to Matthew. Copyright © 1981
by Francis Wright Beare. All rights reserved. Printed in
Great Britain.

For information address Harper & Row, Publishers, Inc.,
10 East 53rd Street, New York, NY 10022. Published
simultaneously in Canada by Fitzhenry & Whiteside,
Limited, Toronto.

FIRST U.S. EDITION

LC 81-47837
ISBN 0-06-060731-9
81 82 83 84 85 10 9 8 7 6 5 4 3 2 1

Contents

Acknowledgement

The author and publisher acknowledge with thanks the generous support of Trinity College, Toronto.

Preface

This commentary is an independent study of the Gospel according to Matthew, pursued unremittingly over a period of fifteen years. It was prompted in the first instance by the realization that this Gospel, though its narrative is almost wholly taken over from Mark, is not properly understood if it is looked upon as a revised edition of Mark with important supplementary matter added. The structure of Matthew is not determined by the narrative, but by the succession of great discourses, and the Markan narrative is only one of several elements which Matthew has built into his own highly original presentation of Jesus, the gospel of the kingdom, and the church. The aim of the work is not to analyse the component elements in themselves—Mark, Q, M, and so forth—nor to go into the history of the 'forms' of sayings and anecdotes in their pre-literary transmission, but to bring out the significance of Matthew as an evangelist, an author, even in some sense a theologian, and so to look upon his work in its totality. The mosaic is more than the *tesserae* that have gone into its making.

No major commentary on Matthew has appeared for many years now. In English, there have been many short commentaries, some of them excellent in relation to their limitations of space, but there has been nothing at all comprehensive since the important work of A.C. McNeile, first published in 1915. Archdeacon Allen's edition in the *ICC* is several years older still. In German, the work of Lohmeyer was planned on the model of the Meyer-Kommentar, and was actually published (incomplete) as a *Sonderband* in the Meyer series. In French, we have a very valuable edition by P. Bonnard of Lausanne in the *Commentaire du Nouveau Testament*, but this too is of limited scope. In the years that have passed since the appearance of the McNeile commentary, we have had the *Formgeschichte* (M. Dibelius) with its revolutionary consequences for our entire understanding of the Gospels; the 'post-Bultmannian' attempt to revive the 'quest of the historical Jesus' in a new form (following the recognition that the old 'quest' of Schweitzer's famous work had ended in failure); and in respect of Matthew, a number of monographs and special studies of outstanding importance (Bornkamm, Davies, Kilpatrick, Stendahl, Strecker, and Trilling, to mention only a few). The time has surely come when the attempt should be made to study the Gospel in its wholeness, taking into account the manifold studies that have been offered to us over these two generations.

Matthew has given us a grim book, singularly lacking in those notes of joy that sound through the writings of Luke. The Christ that he presents is on the whole a terrifying figure. It is Matthew above all who has inspired the Christus Pantocrator of Byzantine domes and apses. There is little trace here of a gospel of grace abounding to the chief of sinners. Over the centuries, his book has been perhaps the most influential of all the New Testament writings, and the influence has not been entirely for good—it has contributed greatly to that kind of legalism which deprives the spiritual life of the spontaneous joy that truly belongs to the gospel. His work needs to be read and studied not as a sufficient guide to Christian living and understanding, in itself; but as one aspect of the much more comprehensive presentation given by the corpus of New Testament writings of which it forms a part. It is significant that the church preserved four Gospels, rejecting all attempts to combine them into one, in a Diatessaron, or to select one above the others as sufficient in itself; and that from very early times, it canonized the apostolic writings and treated them as possessing equal authority with the Gospels in the concert of sacred scriptures. Such diversity and balance is necessary now as always.

This commentary would not have been completed without the encouragement and invaluable assistance of my wife Marianne, an accomplished New Testament scholar in her own right, and an experienced editor. To her I owe an immense debt of gratitude.

Trinity College,   Frank W. Beare
The University of Toronto

Abbreviations

ATR	*Anglican Theological Review*
AV	*Authorised Version* of the Bible
BDF	Blass and Debrunner, translated by Funk, *Greek Grammar*, see Bibliography
BETL	*Bibliotheca Ephemeridum Theologicarum Lovaniensium*
BZ	*Biblische Zeitschrift*
CBQ	*Catholic Biblical Quarterly*
CNT	*Commentaire du Nouveau Testament*
ET	English translation
HST	*History of the Synoptic Tradition*, by R. Bultmann, see Bibliography
IB	*Interpreter's Bible*, 12 volumes
ICC	*International Critical Commentary*
IDB	*Interpreter's Dictionary of the Bible*, 4 volumes
IG	*Inscriptiones Graecae*
JBL	*Journal of Biblical Literature*
KJV	*King James Version* of the Bible
L & S	Liddell & Scott, *Greek–English Lexicon*, see Bibliography
LXX	Septuagint
MT	Massoretic Text (Hebrew Bible)
NEB	*New English Bible*
NTD	*Das Neue Testament Deutsch*
NTS	*New Testament Studies*
RNT	*Regensburger Neues Testament*
RSV	*Revised Standard Version* of the Bible
SNTS	Society of New Testament Studies
TS	*Theological Studies*
UBS	United Bible Societies
W.-W.	Wordsworth, J. and H.J. White, *Novum Testamentum Latine* (1889–); Editio Minor, ed. H.J. White, 1911
ZNTW	*Zeitschrift für die neutestamentliche Wissenschaft*

Introduction

I   THE GREEK TEXT OF THE GOSPEL

The Greek text which has been used as the basis of the translation and commentary is that of the third edition of *The Greek New Testament* (1975), edited for the United Bible Societies (UBS) by Kurt Aland, Matthew Black, Carlo M. Martini, Bruce Metzger, and Allen Wikgren.

This edition contains in its *apparatus criticus* 185 sets of variant readings in the Gospel of Matthew. Comments on these and a certain number of other readings are discussed, on behalf of the editorial committee, by Professor Bruce Metzger, in *A Textual Commentary on the Greek New Testament* (United Bible Societies, London and New York, 1971).

For the purposes of this edition, which was prepared primarily for the use of translators in the service of the Bible Societies, the variants cited are limited to those which affect the translation into another language. A much greater range of variants is offered, in condensed form, in the twenty-sixth edition of the Nestle *Novum Testamentum Graece* (1979), in which the Greek text is edited by the same team as the UBS text; the apparatus, recast and greatly enlarged, was prepared by K. Aland and Barbara Aland. The text itself is identical with that of the UBS text, except for some details of orthography and punctuation. The same text is printed also in the ninth edition of the *Synopsis Quattuor Evangeliorum*, edited by K. Aland (1976), with an apparatus akin to that of Aland's twenty-fifth edition of the Nestle text.

In these two editions, there are more than two hundred sets of variants given in the first five chapters of Matthew alone, and over a thousand for the Gospel as a whole. Even this is no more than a selection of the more important variants. For a fuller presentation of the evidence we must still turn to Tischendorf's eighth *Editio Critica Major* (Leipzig, 1869–72), and to the edition of the Westcott and Hort text by S.C.E. Legg (Oxford, 1940). The latter was intended to be a 'new Tischendorf', but it was marred so by inaccuracy as to make it unreliable. For all its deficiencies, it is the most complete depository of the evidence as yet available. For the Gospel of Matthew it offers at least ten times as many variants as the latest Nestle-Aland edition. There is also a very full citation of evidence in the great edition of Hermann von Soden, *Die Schriften des Neuen Testaments in ihrer ältesten erreichbaren Textgestalt hergestellt* (Teil II, Text mit Apparat, Göttingen, 1913). Unfortunately, it is very difficult to use, mainly because von Soden invented for it a completely new set of sigla for all the manuscripts.

The Oxford text, edited by A. Souter (*Novum Testamentum Graecum*, 1910 and 1947) was not prepared on scientific principles, but was an attempted reconstitution of the text adopted by the English Revisers of 1881. At best it was a nineteenth-century text, and decidedly inferior to the Westcott and Hort Text which was published in 1881. The Revisers were sufficiently under the spell of the *Textus Receptus* that they allowed it to prevail against the principles of Westcott and Hort in too many instances; and the Souter text is the least satisfactory of all modern printed editions.[1] Besides that, this century has brought to light many important documents which were not available to Westcott and Hort or to the Revisers.

Even in 1947 Souter was able to cite only three papyri for Matthew. All are fragmentary, and include verses from chapters 1, 20, 21, 25, and 26; for chapter 26, 52 verses are represented, at least partially, but for the others the amount of text varies from 6 to 18 verses per chapter. Aland, in his latest editions of the Nestle text, includes readings from 15 papyri, varying in date from *c.* AD 200 to the seventh century, and containing parts of thirteen chapters.

Many vellum manuscripts of importance have also been discovered during the past century, and indeed in the last three decades. More important, the whole theory of the text has had to be revised through the study of the early papyri, with their evidence for the state of the text at a time much earlier than any of the vellum manuscripts, of which only two can be dated in the fourth century, and none earlier (apart from fragments of a few lines each). In this respect, the UBS and Nestle-Aland texts have virtually displaced

[1] See the incisive remarks of Kurt Aland in his article 'The Present Position of New Testament Textual Criticism' in *The Gospels Reconsidered* (Oxford, Blackwell, 1960), pp.1–15. A paragraph on the Souter edition concludes with the words: 'Such a reconstruction is an interesting experiment, but as a printed edition it can only do harm in practical use, for example among students' (p.4).

all others for serious study. Those of Merk and Bover, for instance, are no longer being published. We have a new *Textus Receptus*.

Two more ambitious enterprises are under way, with international co-operation. The International Project to Create a Critical Apparatus for the Greek New Testament plans to reprint the old Stephanus edition of the *Textus Receptus* with a very full apparatus. A second project, directed by Kurt Aland at the Institut für neutestamentliche Textforschung of Münster-in-W., proposes to construct a new critical text, as the base for a full apparatus.

II GENERAL CHARACTER OF THE WORK

The Gospel according to Matthew may be described as a manual of instruction in the Christian way of life, which the author sees as the fulfilment in Jesus Christ of the revelation of God given to Israel and preserved in the sacred scriptures. The instruction is gathered around the story of Jesus, who by his words and deeds has inaugurated the 'kingdom of heaven' (literally, 'of the heavens')—the reign of God on earth. The people of Israel, which traces its history back to the patriarchs, beginning with Abraham, has been the precursor and in a sense the historical locus of that Kingdom. Under God, its rule was committed to the famed King David and to his successors in the royal line; and Israel's hope centred in the expectation of a great 'son of David' who would rule in righteousness and peace for ever. The promises made in ages past through the prophets have now been fulfilled in the person of Jesus, the long-awaited 'Messiah', who is born 'son of David', but is made known to his followers as 'son of the living God'. In his life and death, all has come to pass in accordance with the prophetic scriptures—'all this took place to fulfil what the Lord had spoken by the prophet' (Mt.1:22). After his resurrection from the dead, he has revealed himself to his disciples as the one to whom all authority has been given, in heaven and on earth, and has commissioned them to make disciples of all the nations, baptizing them in his name (and with that, in the name of the Father and the divine Spirit also), and teaching them to keep all his commandments. He has come as Israel's Messiah, but he transcends all traditional categories. He is the Pantocrator, the ruler of the universe.

The story of Jesus is seen as the fulfilment of the destiny of Israel. But Israel has rejected its own Messiah; and as a consequence the Kingdom has been taken away from her and given to a 'nation' which will render to God the honour due to him (Mt.21:43). Israelites, though historically 'the sons of the kingdom', will see people coming from east and west to have part with the patriarchs in the kingdom of heaven while they themselves are cast out (Mt.8:11). The promises made to Israel are now inherited by the church of Christ's foundation, which is not limited to the racial community of Israel but is open to all who do the will of God, the heavenly Father (Mt.12:50; etc.). This is the one condition for entrance into the kingdom of heaven, and it is indispensable, as much for Israelites as for others. The scrupulous adherence to the law of Moses, as practised by the scribes and Pharisees, is not sufficient: 'Unless your righteousness exceeds that of the scribes and Pharisees, you will never enter the kingdom of heaven' (Mt.5:20). Profession of faith in Jesus as Lord will not suffice, for 'not everyone who says to me, "Lord, Lord", shall enter the kingdom of heaven, but only the one who does the will of my Father in heaven' (Mt.7:21).

Clearly enough, this is all based upon a highly developed Christology. The dogmatic conceptions of Christian faith shine through the Matthaean portrait of the Jesus who once lived on earth as a Jewish teacher and prophet. And with that the ancient mythology of Israel as the chosen people of the one living and true God has been transposed into a mythology of the Christian Church as the universal society created by Jesus, as the community of faith in the same God, and of obedience to his commandments as interpreted and applied through Jesus. The central concern of the evangelist, however, is not with the mythological structure (which he takes for granted), but with the moral requirements of the kingdom of heaven as they have been set forth by Jesus in his teaching. The law of Moses has not been abolished, but fulfilled (Mt.5:17); and though it is reinterpreted and deepened in the primacy given to love, we are bound to ask whether Matthew has not rabbinized the teachings of Jesus and paved the way for a new legalism. 'Matthew drew around the figure of Jesus the mantle of a lawgiver'. (W.D. Davies, *The Setting of the Sermon on the Mount*, 1964, p.415.) Has he thereby 'decked his Lord in an alien garb'? (*ibid.*)

For the story of the ministry of Jesus, against which the teaching is presented, Matthew is almost wholly dependent on the narrative of Mark. The few additional anecdotes which he offers are without exception legendary. But the narrative itself has become in Matthew little more than a setting for a series of 'discourses', or more exactly, collections of sayings of Jesus organized by the evangelist to show how Jesus with sovereign authority has laid down the laws which govern life in the kingdom of heaven. The stories are of interest to him partly as vehicles of teaching and partly as evidence that Jesus is indeed the promised Messiah—he does what the prophets have foretold that the Messiah would do, he suffers as it has been written of him, and he teaches in the manner that the prophets have pictured the Messiah as teaching. (Mt.12:17–21; 26:24, 31, 54, 56; etc. 'All this has taken place, that the scriptures of the prophets might be fulfilled.') The elements of human interest and of the picturesque, abundant in Mark, are reduced and all but eliminated. The fundamental structure of this Gospel is not the narrative, but the five principle collections of sayings. (See Section V, below, page 19.)

III   AUTHORSHIP AND MILIEU

Like all the Gospels, this is an anonymous work. The name of Matthew was attached to it quite early in the second century, and it has even been suggested that it may have been published (pseudonymously) under that name. (G.D. Kilpatrick, *The Origins of the Gospel according to St. Matthew*, Oxford, 1946, pp.138ff.) This was done, whether at or soon after its first publication, with the intention of attributing it to the Matthew whose name appears in all four lists of the 'apostles' which are given in the New Testament (Mt.10:3; Mk.3:18; Lk.6:15; Acts 1:13). But the dependence of the book upon documentary sources is so great as to forbid us to look upon it as the work of any immediate disciple of Jesus. Apart from that, there are clear indications that it is a product of the second or third Christian generation. The traditional name of Matthew is retained in modern discussion only for convenience.

The time and place of writing cannot be determined except within very broad limits. Such 'traditions' as we possess are nothing more than second-century guesses. We are dependent upon such hints as the book itself offers incidentally; and upon the way in which we understand its relationship to the other Gospels, especially Mark, and to the developing history of the Christian church in its contacts and conflicts with the organized Judaism of the period. It is generally agreed that it was written after the fall of Jerusalem to the armies of Titus (AD 70); and the widespread acquaintance with it which is exhibited in all the Christian literature of the second century makes it difficult to place its composition any later than the opening decade of that century. If the Sermon on the Mount can be regarded as in any sense 'the Christian answer to Jamnia . . . a kind of Christian mishnaic counterpart to the formulation taking place there' (Davies,

Setting, p.315), this would indicate a date of a few years before or after the turn of the century.

The place at which this Gospel was published is also uncertain. As it reflects a deep concern with the relations between the church and Judaism, it must have originated in an area where church and synagogue were in continual contact and conflict, and where Jewish influence was sufficiently strong to bring serious trouble to the communities of Christian believers. Christian preachers must expect to be haled before the local *sanhedrin*, to be flogged in the synagogue, and to be forced to flee from one town to another under the stress of persecution (Mt.10:17, 23). Christians and Jews appeal to the same holy scriptures; according to Matthew, Jesus had explicitly declared that he had not come to abolish the law and the prophets, and that not one iota, not even one small stroke of a letter, would pass away, until heaven and earth passed away (Mt.5:17f.). But Jews who became Christians, like Matthew himself, differed sharply from the accepted understanding of the Jewish law as it was taught by the scribes; and above all, in the overriding significance which they attached to Jesus as the Messiah to whom was given all authority in heaven and on earth (Mt.28:18), Christian Jews effectively ceased to be the people of a book in the way that the Jews were. Matthew appears not to have realized how great the difference was, in his eagerness to claim for Christianity the whole inheritance of Israel. But in any case he writes in and for a community in which the relationship with Judaism is of crucial importance; and this suggests a community which lives in a predominantly Jewish environment— either Palestine itself or the adjacent regions to the north where there was a large Jewish population.

It has long been conjectured that the book was produced at or in the neighbourhood of Antioch on the Orontes, the place of the first mission which carried the gospel message to Gentiles, and where 'the disciples were first called Christians' (Acts 11:26). The extraordinary influence which the work achieved within a few decades would certainly lead us to believe that it was sponsored by a Christian community of exceptional importance; and as it is hard to think of Jerusalem as its place of origin, it is certainly tempting to think of Antioch. That city had been the scene of the activities of Paul and Barnabas, following the unknown missionaries who established the church there; and it had sponsored their mission to Cyprus and Asia Minor (Acts 13:14) and received their report when they returned (14:26f.). It had been visited by Peter (Gal.2:11ff.); and in the early second century its bishop Ignatius was one of the most distinguished leaders of the church at large. Such hesitation as is felt over an Antiochene origin is occasioned by the complete lack of evidence of any acquaintance with the letters of Paul on the part of Matthew; and his total divergence from Paul's doctrine of a manifestation of the righteousness of God in Christ *apart from law* (χωρὶς νόμου — Rom. 3:21). These considerations, together with some slight hints which are given in the Gospel itself, have led Professor Kilpatrick to favour one of the cities of Phoenicia, perhaps Tyre or Sidon, though he is prepared 'to rest content with the general suggestion of Phoenicia as the place of origin' (*Origins*, pp.131–134).

Although the author is unknown, and the community in which he worked uncertain, he reveals something of himself in his way of ordering his materials, and reflects something of the conditions of his community in his references to its difficulties and its shortcomings and the tasks which it is called to undertake. He shows the influence of professional training as a Jewish 'scribe', schooled in the methods of interpretation of the sacred scriptures which had been developed by the teachers of Judaism (later to be called 'rabbis'). To this he has added a wide knowledge of the teachings of Jesus concerning the kingdom of God; it is often suggested that he describes himself in the words which he ascribes to Jesus as a picture of the Christian teacher. 'Every scribe who has been trained for the kingdom of heaven is like a householder who brings out of his storehouse what is new and what is old' (Mt.13:52). He has the scribe's unshakeable conviction of the divine authority of the holy scriptures, and he employs the methods of the schools in applying phrases—with no regard for their context or for the meaning which they had for the original writer and his readers—to persons and to situations of his own age. For him, this means that he applies them to the person of Jesus and to the events of his earthly life. He introduces materials of a midrashic nature, such as we find in abundance in the rabbinical documents. (These are of a somewhat later time, it is true, but they represent a literary and pedagogical tradition which was formed much earlier.) Most important is his adaptation of the radical demands of Jesus to the practical necessities of existence in the world of human life on earth. He provides a *gemara* to the sayings of Jesus, in something comparable to the way in which the later rabbis built up the Talmud by adding their *gemara* to the Mishnah (compiled *c.* AD 175–200).[2]

---

[2] See the admirable remarks of W.D. Davies on 'M and Gemara' (*Setting*, pp. 387–401). Cf. his comments on the parallels between Matthew's handling of the traditions about Jesus and the kind of instruction given in the Dead Sea Scrolls.

His citations from the scriptures are generally given in the words of the Septuagint—the Greek translation, begun in the third century BC at Alexandria in Egypt and completed before the end of the second century—but he sometimes changes it to a more exact rendering of the Hebrew, and sometimes he gives his own version of the Hebrew text. His use of the Old Testament raises many problems, which will be discussed as they arise; for the moment, we are concerned only to note that they show his competence in Hebrew and his confidence in his authority to interpret the ancient scriptures and to apply them to current questions.

This Gospel was prepared in the first instance for the use of a Christian community, and although the author does not tell us where it is or give any direct information about its numbers or its methods, he gives occasional indications of its structure and circumstances. We can see, for instance, that it is engaged in sharp conflict with Pharisaic Judaism, and that it has reason to fear that its missionaries will be persecuted and forced to flee from city to city (10:17–23). If it is enjoined to acknowledge the teaching authority of the scribes (and Pharisees), because they 'sit in Moses' seat' (23:2), this can only mean that they still think of themselves as observant Jews. He has no need to explain Jewish customs to them, as does Mark (cf. Mt.15:1 with Mk.7:1–4; about the ritual washing of hands before meals). He assumes that they will feel burdened in conscience if they are obliged to flee from danger on the sabbath (24:20). Since the Gospel was composed for them in Greek, we must conclude that they were Greek-speaking, like most of the Jews in the Roman Empire outside of Palestine. If they were residents of Syria or Phoenicia, they probably spoke Aramaic as well; we may think of them as a bilingual community.

The community was probably urban, rather than rural, though the indications of this are relatively slight. The word πόλις ('city') is used twenty-six times in Matthew, as compared with eight times in Mark; and the word κώμη ('village') is found only three times in Matthew as against seven instances in Mark (Kilpatrick, *Origins*, pp.124f.). It might be suggested, also, that only a city man would be likely to think that the presence of weeds in a field of grain must be due to the nefarious work of an enemy; a man of the soil would not

'Like the Essenes, the Church had to introduce regulations to meet the actualities of its present existence. It had, in short, to develop an interim-ethic. . . . One way in which Matthew did this was to modify the absolute demands of Jesus by means of gemaric additions to these, which reduced what was originally radical to the regulatory'. (*ibid.*, p. 221.)

expect to find a field free of weeds. (Mt.13:28; there is reason to hold that the allegorical exposition of the parable in vv. 37ff. is a construction of the evangelist, and that the parable itself has been adapted, if not wholly created, by him, with a view to the 'explanation').

There are some indications that the church for which this Gospel was written was relatively wealthy. The concern for the poor is less emphasized than in Mark, and it lacks the proletarian sympathies of Luke. The poor who are pronounced blessed in Matthew are defined as 'the poor in spirit' (Mt.5:3; cf. Lk.6:20); 'it is a spiritual condition and not material poverty that is blessed' (Kilpatrick, *Origins*, p.125). The very word πτωχός ('poor') occurs only five times in Matthew as compared with ten in Luke; and the rich man is told to sell what he has and give to the poor, *if he wants to be perfect* (Mt.19:21—a provision found only in Matthew). Further, the terms for 'money' and the names of coins are much more varied in Matthew, and higher sums are mentioned. Matthew alone uses the word χρῦσος ('gold'), and he alone speaks of the double drachma, the stater, and the talent. The talent could amount to seventy-five pounds of gold; in the parable of the 'talents', the parallel in Luke speaks of 'minas'—coins worth only the hundredth part of a talent (Mt.25:14ff.; Lk.19:11–17). Matthew and his church were evidently capable of thinking in terms of large amounts of money. In another parable, we hear of a man who owes ten thousand talents (18:24). This does not prove that they were accustomed to handling such immense sums themselves. They can, however, imagine that Jesus might find it necessary to charge his emissaries to 'acquire no gold or silver or copper to carry in [their] belts' (10:9), where Mark speaks only of copper and Luke of silver (Mk.6:8; Lk.9:3). As it is highly unlikely that the actual disciples of Jesus were ever in a position to acquire gold coins, we must suppose that the phrase in Matthew reflects the situation of a community which could provide its missionaries with gold as well as copper and silver coins for their journeys if it wished—in short, a fairly affluent group.

The organization of the community is not clearly defined. It has no presiding officer. The word ἐπίσκοπος (bishop) is never used, nor is there any hint of such an office. Elders are indeed mentioned, but only as members of the Sanhedrin, and as linked with the chief priests in conspiracies against Jesus (16:21; 21:23; 26:3, etc.); in one instance (15:2) they are the makers of the oral tradition. 'Deacon' (διάκονος) is used only in its ordinary sense of 'servant'. It is assumed that there are Christian scribes, trained for the kingdom of heaven, with stores of learning to dispense (13:52); and the prophecy of 23:34 indicates that the community is served by 'prophets' and 'wise men' as well as scribes. Christ has sent them, but nothing is said of their qualifications or functions—only that the Jewish authorities will kill and crucify some of them, and that others will be scourged in the synagogues and driven from town to town. Matthew is chiefly concerned that such leaders as the community has shall not play the master but devote themselves to service, should think of themselves as slaves of their brethren (20:25ff.). They must not pass their time in revelry, or treat their 'fellow slaves' brutally (24:45–51). They are not to claim titles of honour for themselves, such as 'rabbi', or 'father', or 'master' (23:6–10).

Matthew looks upon the apostle Peter as the rock on which Christ has promised to build his church (16:18); but the power of 'binding' and 'loosing' which was given to him is now exercised by the church (18:18); there is no thought that it has been inherited by another individual or by a college of office-bearers. The congregation itself is to act as a court for the discipline of recalcitrant members (18:17). As a last resort, they may excommunicate the one who refuses to listen to admonitions, but only after every effort has been made to restore him by private remonstrance and entreaty (cf. Gal. 6:1). Whatever judgement they make will be ratified in heaven, for Christ himself is present when they meet in his name, and God will give effect to their prayers (18:18–20). There is no provision for an appeal to a supervising official or to a higher court. Even this authority to exercise discipline is to be exercised subject to the rule of unlimited forgiveness, to be granted over and over, even to seventy-seven times (18:22ff.).

But the community is not to attempt to purge its membership, to make itself a society of the pure. The evangelist has no illusions about its moral qualities. There are weeds among the wheat, but the task of removing unworthy members is to be left for the judgement of Christ when he comes as Son of man at the end of the age. Then 'the Son of man will send out his angels, and they will gather out of his kingdom all causes of sin, and those who act lawlessly, and will throw them into the fire of the furnace . . . . Then the righteous will shine forth like the sun in the kingdom of their Father' (13:37–43). As long as the present age endures, the church is a mixed body, not a community of the perfect. Its members are strictly charged not to sit in judgement on one another, for their own faults are too great; their function is not to judge but to forgive (7:1–5). Among them are some who call Jesus 'Lord', but are not doing the will of his Father in heaven; and they will not enter the kingdom of heaven, even though they claim to have done mighty works in his name, and prophesied and cast out demons (7:21–23). Even among the leaders there are 'false prophets' who 'come in sheep's clothing, but inwardly are ravening wolves' (7:15); they will 'lead many astray' (24:11). Membership in the church is not a guarantee of admission into the kingdom of heaven, any more than descent from Abraham was for Jews (3:7–9). The duty of the Christian is to see that he himself is faithful and obedient, so that at the Last Judgement he may inherit the Kingdom, and enter into the joy of his Lord (25:21, 23, 31).

IV   THE NARRATIVE

The narrative framework of this Gospel is not of an essentially biographical and historical nature. The writer is primarily concerned with the life and faith of the church of his own time, with the responsibilities laid upon it, and with the conduct required of all who profess faith in Jesus and hope for eternal life in the kingdom of heaven. His interest in the past is dominated by its bearing upon the present. Jesus is depicted, from birth to death and resurrection, not alone in his historical character as a man who lived in Palestine in the early decades of the first century, but also, and above all, as the Lord who teaches and governs his church in the present time, as the Risen One to whom is given all authority in heaven and on earth. The whole story is seen in a double perspective. The anecdotes which make it up are formally presented as incidents in a life lived seventy years earlier, but they are at the same time images of the Jesus who lives and speaks to the disciples and the crowds of Matthew's own time. Details of place and time are of no real interest. They are given, for the most part, in vague terms; and in an order which has little to do with succession in time. The story of the leper, for instance, is told immediately after the Sermon on the Mount (8:1–4), and is placed during the descent of Jesus from 'the mountain' of the Sermon. But this 'mountain' is not a particular geographical location, and this 'sermon' was not delivered at one time and place; and the healing of the leper is set at its close, not because of any recollection or record that it took place then and there, but because it 'gives the best follow-on from the Sermon on the Mount which immediately precedes' (A. Farrer, *St. Matthew and St. Mark*, Westminster, 1954, p.45). In the Sermon, Jesus has insisted that the law must be fulfilled; in the healing, he instructs the healed leper to go and show himself to the priest, and make the offering, as is required in the law of Moses (Lev.14). On a wider scale, the whole series of healing miracles which are recounted in chapters 8 and 9 are brought together in this place as the complement to the Sermon; the Messiah of the word (the Sermon) reveals himself as also the Messiah of the deed (the Miracles).[3] The two collections, one of words, one of deeds, fit together like the two leaves of a diptych. And the words and the deeds are alike presented not simply or primarily as records of the past but as instruction for the present, for Jesus still teaches with authority and still acts with healing power in his church.

The double perspective in which Jesus is presented is extended to all the others who appear in the narrative. The people with whom Jesus has to do are at once the hearers—followers, interested crowds, enemies—whom he encountered during his earthly life, and are at the same time figures of the people with whom Matthew has to do—the church, the people to whom it proclaims its message, and its opponents.

The disciples are under one aspect the immediate followers of the man of Nazareth, who left home and business to cast in their lot with him, and at the same time they are 'stylized' as figures of the Christian believers of Matthew's church; there is little interest in them as individuals. The questions which they put to Jesus may or may not be based upon a tradition of questions actually put to Jesus two or three generations before; they are in any case given a place in the Gospel because they are questions to which the Christians of Matthew's day are seeking an answer. The opponents of Jesus— scribes and Pharisees in particular—are not to be seen as historical persons in their individual characters, though of course Jesus *was* questioned and criticized by scribes and Pharisees. But in Matthew they are much more types or figures of the Jewish rabbis and synagogue authorities with whom Matthew was in conflict in his own day. No attempt is made to differentiate among them; they are depicted, as a class, all alike in their hypocrisy (see esp. chap. 23)— though the vigour of the denunciations is partly due to the apprehension of Matthew that the same spirit may show itself in the lives of members of the Christian church; the disciples are warned to 'beware of the leaven of the Pharisees and Sadducees' (16:11).

This evangelist is not preparing a record for the archives. His primary aim is not to give exact information, but to provide practical guidance for the Christians of his own time, and for their leaders. Some of his scenes are artificially constructed settings for sayings of

---

[3] Cf. J. Schniewind, *Das Evangelium nach Matthäus* (8th edn., Göttingen, 1956).

Jesus, and are to be regarded rather as a sketch of typical circumstances under which a saying may have been uttered than as a plain account of how and when and where the words came to be spoken. Particular incidents are arranged without concern for the order in which they actually occurred; they are grouped around common themes, sometimes even around a single word. The order is pedagogical and literary, not chronological. We would have to agree with the late T.W. Manson, that 'if we think in terms of strict historical documentation these early Christians were guilty of tampering with the evidence' (*Ethics and the Gospel*, London, 1960, p. 92). We must learn not to look to them for 'strict historical documentation'.

This is not to say that the whole story is fictional. There is a nucleus, not inconsiderable, of recollections of the apostles and other hearers of Jesus and spectators of his actions. But these recollections were not committed to writing, except in fragmentary fashion, for some decades after his death; and they were subject to all the hazards that attend oral communications. Much was lost, for stories were passed along, and words were repeated, only as they were felt to be relevant to the situation and needs of new audiences and changing times. Much was added, both in story and in saying, by unwitting transference from stories and sayings of other persons, and by the imaginative reconstructions of Christian teachers.[4]

The story of the public ministry of Jesus as recounted by Matthew is almost entirely derived from Mark. In all probability, he had no other framework of events to guide him. There is reason to believe that Mark was the first Christian writer to attempt to weave the scattered anecdotes about Jesus into a continuous narrative, and Matthew had no more exact information about the movements and activities of Jesus which might have enabled him to arrange the anecdotes in a more reliable order. In any case, he is not really interested in establishing an historical sequence. Such few changes as he makes in the Markan order are dictated solely by literary and pedagogical considerations.

The narrative, constructed by Mark and followed in broad outline by Matthew, brings Jesus before us unheralded on the banks of the river Jordan, somewhere in Judaea, with the note that he has come from Galilee to be baptized by the prophet John, popularly known

---

[4] Such reconstructions continue to be made to this day, in sermons and Sunday School lessons, though of course they are not likely to be given a place in 'Gospels'. They do, however, get into modern 'lives of Jesus'—even those written by competent scholars. The insatiable desire to know more about Jesus is met with an irrepressible urge to say more than we know.

as 'the Baptist'. Apart from an encounter between Jesus and the devil (obviously mythical in character), nothing more is reported about him until the arrest of John and his imprisonment by Herod in the fortress of Machaerus on the Dead Sea. There is no indication of the time that may have elapsed since the baptism—for some weeks or months or even years Jesus is lost to view as completely as in the years between the settlement of the family in Nazareth (Mt. 2:21— not mentioned in Mark) and his appearance in the Jordan valley among the crowds attracted by John. The story resumes, after this gap, with the statement that when Jesus heard that John had been arrested, he returned to Galilee and settled in Capernaum, on the lake; and began a preaching ministry, with the proclamation: 'Repent! for the kingdom of heaven is at hand.'

In the Matthaean story, still following Mark, Jesus spent the following months, or years—the passage of time is not noted— moving about in Galilee from village to village, preaching in the synagogues, and healing the sick and infirm. He was accompanied by four fishermen—Peter and Andrew, James and John—and by an increasing number of followers who flocked to him from all parts of the Holy Land and beyond. How they and these 'great crowds' supported themselves from day to day is not indicated. It is obvious that shelter and food and drink could not be provided for any long time for 'great crowds'. It is not possible to trace the routes followed by Jesus, but there are indications that the group carried on its activities mainly around the shores of the lake of Galilee. Capernaum, Bethsaida, and other places on the lake are mentioned, and several times we hear of a boat which provides a means of transport from one shore to the other and occasionally serves Jesus as a pulpit from which he addresses the crowds standing on the shore. After a time, Jesus makes a trip into the regions north of Galilee—the neighbourhood of Tyre and Sidon, and the foothills of Mt. Hermon (the villages of Caesarea Philippi). After this, he and his disciples gather again in Galilee and begin to make their way to Jerusalem, travelling down the east bank of the Jordan and crossing at Jericho, where for the first time (in the Markan—Matthaean story) they enter Judaea, now governed by a Roman prefect, Pontius Pilate. The scene is thus set for the crucifixion. Conflict with the Jewish authorities becomes acute: the Sanhedrin suborns one of his disciples to betray him into its hands, and then turns him over to the Romans, with the accusation that he is a pretender to the throne of Israel (though the charge is not precisely formulated in Mark or in Matthew); and Pilate, though beset with misgivings and aware that such evidence as was offered was not sufficient to prove that Jesus was guilty as charged, bows to pressure and sentences him to death. Less than a week has passed since Jesus entered Jerusalem for the first time, and now he has been executed as a criminal, in company with criminals. His disciples have forsaken him and fled to seek safety for themselves; but a wealthy man of Arimathaea named Joseph, said by Matthew to have been 'made a disciple' of Jesus, (27:57 ἐμαθητεύθη τῷ Ἰησοῦ) undertakes the responsibility of the burial. Of Jesus' own followers, two women from Galilee alone have remained till the last to watch the burial. (In Mark it is said of him only that he was 'a respected member of the Sanhedrin, who was looking expectantly for the kingdom of God'—Mk.15:43; cf. Lk.23:50f.)

The death of Jesus took place on a Friday, and nothing more transpired until the sabbath was over. Early on the Sunday morning, the two women who had watched the burial went to the tomb. According to Mark, they brought spices with them to anoint the body of Jesus, which had been buried in haste without any preparation except wrapping in a shroud; Matthew thinks it enough to say that they went 'to see the tomb'. They found it empty, and were greeted by an angel, who told them that Jesus had risen from the dead, and was going to Galilee where they would see him; they were to carry this message to his disciples. The Markan story ended with this, on the strange note that the women were frightened and told nothing to anyone; but Matthew adds that as they were hurrying to the disciples with their great news, Jesus met them and charged them again to tell his disciples to go to Galilee where they would see him.

This is a meagre enough story, but even in Mark it includes elements of fancy, and further fictional details are added by Matthew. It is of course possible that Jesus never visited Jerusalem during the period of his public ministry until he went up with his disciples on the journey that ended in his crucifixion—but it cannot be regarded as probable. In the Gospel of John, most of the scenes are laid in Jerusalem with only occasional visits to Galilee. The Markan-Matthaean narrative outline is simply discarded and replaced by one which describes the movements of Jesus in quite different terms.

The date of the crucifixion is as uncertain as the date of the birth of Jesus. All forms of the tradition mention Pontius Pilate as the Roman governor of Judaea who passed sentence on him, but Pilate's term of office lasted for ten years (26 to 36), and the Gospels give no indication of how long he had been governing Judaea when Jesus was brought before him. Various attempts have been made to work back from the time of Paul's conversion (itself uncertain), to determine the year within that period in which the 15th Nisan—the date of the Passover—fell on a Friday. No firm results can be obtained in either way. The chronology of Paul's career is itself too uncertain to provide any assistance towards determining the date of the crucifixion; and while all four Gospels set the event on a Friday, it is the 15th Nisan in the Synoptics, but in John it is the 14th Nisan (Jesus dies before the Passover begins). The date has been calculated as early as 28 and as late as 33; it falls within this six-year period.

The narrative in its entirety is a collection of anecdotes which for some years circulated singly, without indications of time or place, often without any mention of names (apart from the name of Jesus himself), and unconnected with one another. Where our Gospels give indications of time or place, these are generally the work of an editor—either the evangelist himself or the compiler of one of his sources. Even when they are found, they are generally vague and little more than attempts to create a link between episodes which may have been transmitted without any connection between one and another. We hear of Jesus passing through grainfields (12:1), and then that 'he went on from there and entered their synagogue' (12:9), with no hint as to where that synagogue and those grainfields were located; and a few verses later, we read that 'he went on from there' (12:15). The next reference to his movements comes at the beginning of the parable chapter (13:1), and tells us that 'on that same day Jesus went out of the house and sat beside the lake'. But this seemingly precise reference is an editorial touch inserted by Matthew; for in Mark, his source, we are told only that 'he began again to teach by the lake'. All this is typical, and is enough to show that the evangelist is not really concerned with topography or with temporal succession, and the tradition does not provide him with the means of marking the course of events.

The incidents which make up the Matthaean narrative are taken almost entirely from Mark, from the appearance of John the Baptist (where Mark begins) to the arrival of Jesus in Jerusalem. Over this area, there are thirty-seven anecdotes in Matthew, and thirty-two of these are drawn from Mark. All but five of them are set down in the same order as in Mark, and the five which are shifted are arranged to make part of the sequence of miracle-stories (chaps. 8, 9), whereby Matthew presents Jesus as thaumaturge ('Messiah of the Deed') to follow his presentation of Jesus as teacher ('Messiah of the Word') in the Sermon on the Mount (chaps. 5, 6, 7). Only two Markan anecdotes are omitted (Mk. 7:31–37 and 8:22–26), and the former is replaced by a generalizing account of multiple healings. In the Passion Narrative, Matthew follows Mark more closely than ever, with small but seemingly deliberate alterations of wording; there is only one trifling omission (Mk.14:51), and no additions that are not manifestly legendary. In short, the Matthaean narrative is no more than a retelling of that of Mark.

Matthew systematically abbreviates nearly all the Markan anecdotes, often cutting them drastically at the expense of much of the colour and vividness of Mark. Every detail that does not contribute to the essence of the story is ruthlessly pruned away. This is particularly conspicuous in the story of the exorcisms in the Gadarene country (8:28—34; seven verses in place of Mark's twenty); in the 'sandwiched' stories of the resuscitation of the ruler's daughter and the stopping of a haemorrhage (9:18—26; nine verses in place of Mark's twenty-three); and in the story of the healing of the epileptic boy (17:14—21; eight verses in place of Mark's sixteen). This has the effect of focusing attention almost exclusively upon Jesus—upon his authority, his words, his call for faith. The words of the Healer are given a greater proportion of space; in some cases, even when the narrative element is reduced to the minimum, the evangelist adds sayings of Jesus which are not found in the Markan version.

The increased proportion of sayings within the narrative sections adds to the effect of the enormous increase of teaching materials in the tradition to direct attention even more to the Matthaean emphasis on the picture of Jesus as Teacher or Lawgiver and the diminished attention to his role as Thaumaturge or Healer.

V   THE SAYINGS OF JESUS: THE DISCOURSES

The public ministry of Jesus lasted for at the very least several months, probably for more than a year, and possibly for between two and three years. However short it may have been, he undoubtedly said many more things than are preserved in the pages of Matthew, more than are to be found in all the Gospels together. Jesus preached many times in synagogues, in the streets, on the lake shore, and sometimes in the open fields. The sermons were not written down, either by Jesus or by his disciples. In many cases we are told only the theme of his proclamation: 'Repent, for the kingdom of heaven is at hand' (Mt.4:17). The theme is stated more fully by Mark: 'The time is fulfilled, and the kingdom of God is at hand. Repent, and believe in the gospel' (Mk.1:15). Luke gives us a few sentences—

they can be read aloud in less than a minute—from a sermon delivered in his home village of Nazareth on a text from Isaiah (Lk.4:21:27). This is exceptional: for most of his sermons we have not even a text. And many of the sayings in Matthew are not set in any sermon, but pronouncements made in response to questioners or critics, or at a dinner table in the presence of a small group of guests. Obviously, these are not more than random samples of his talk; no one will imagine that we are told about every encounter with individuals or with little groups. It is clear, then, that Matthew is far from offering anything like a complete repertoire of all that Jesus said.

The store of sayings available to him included no more than a fraction of what Jesus had once said. Much was either not recalled by his listeners or was lost beyond recovery with the passage of the years. That any were preserved at all depended upon the memories of his disciples and others who had heard him speak, and after that upon the fidelity with which they were passed on by a second generation who received them from the original hearers and repeated them to others. We cannot tell how soon written collections were made or who made them. There is nothing in the letters of Paul, the only literature that survives from the first Christian generation, to suggest that he ever heard of such a collection. He never quotes Jesus directly, though he occasionally appeals to directions given by him (1 Cor.7:10f.), which he distinguishes from an application made by himself (1 Cor.7:12—'to the rest I say, not the Lord'). Some short collections, already committed to writing, were available to Mark, perhaps thirty years before Matthew; and a much more extensive collection, generally known as 'Q' (for the German *Quelle*, 'source'— it may be that a number of sources are represented by this symbol), was available to Matthew and Luke; and this may go back in part to written collections produced in the forties or fifties. But the oral tradition was still living when the evangelists wrote, and we even find a bishop of the second century telling us that he prefers 'the living and abiding voice' to anything that he finds in documents (Papias, Bishop of Hierapolis in Asia, *c.* AD 140). At all events, the entire tradition was transmitted by word of mouth for a significant number of years before any of it was published in writing; and this oral transmission did not come to an end when it was partially incorporated into written Gospels. The story of the Woman Taken in Adultery is an example of one such fragment of tradition. It was not taken up by any of the evangelists, but it remained available for later copyists; some of them placed it in the fourth Gospel (Jn.7:53—8:11, or at the end of the last chapter), while others placed it in the Gospel of Luke, after 21:38.

For some years, then, the tradition of the sayings of Jesus was carried by word of mouth. At the beginning they would be transmitted in Aramaic, and some of the written sources used by our evangelists may originally have been written in that language. It is probable that Jesus himself spoke to the people in Aramaic, not in Greek. Many of the sayings in our Greek Gospels show clear signs of translation from Aramaic, and even of mistranslation—so much so that a great Semitist like Professor C.C. Torrey could hold that the four Gospels in their entirety were composed in Aramaic.[5] As a general theory this has not found wide acceptance; but there are certainly passages which read in Greek like literal renderings of an Aramaic original. The familiar title 'Son of man' is a literal rendering of an Aramaic expression meaning simply 'a human being' (an individual specimen of the genus 'man'). In Greek it is simply unintelligible.

Everything in the Gospels, then, so far as it rests upon the reminiscences of eye-witnesses and hearers of Jesus, passed through a certain period of oral transmission, and still bears the marks of that early usage even after its incorporation into a written record. The shape and the significance of his sayings were altered to some extent by translation from Semitic phrases into Greek. The Semitic languages have nothing corresponding to the systems of tense, voice, and mood of the Greek verb. There is an almost complete absence of subordinate clauses in the Semitic languages; there is a tendency to link clause to clause by a simple 'and' (*parataxis*), instead of using a participle or a relative pronoun (*hypotaxis*). There are many other differences of linguistic structure, far too many to be discussed here—see M. Black in *An Aramaic Approach to the Gospels and Acts* (3rd edn., Oxford, 1967). Some of the characteristic Semitic locutions (including parataxis) happen to coincide with Greek popular speech of the period, and it is not so much their appearance as their frequency that betrays the Semitic turn of phrase that lies behind them.

Difficulties of a different order arise in the realm of vocabulary. It is a common experience of translators who are attempting to render the Bible into the language of their converts that the language does not possess any real equivalent for some terms of cardinal

---

[5] See *Our Translated Gospels* (1935), preceded by *The Four Gospels: A New Translation* (1933). 'Most of his examples of mistranslation . . . are open to grave objection'. (M. Black, *Aramaic Approach*, p. 5.)

importance in biblical thought. The scholars who translated the books of the Old Testament into Greek (mainly from Hebrew but partly from Aramaic) to make the Septuagint had made great strides in providing Greek renderings for Semitic terms. Sometimes they were very bold; they created in large measure a Greek vocabulary for the use of the early Christians. We owe to them, for instance, the use of the Greek νόμος for the Hebrew *Torah*, both of them rendered by 'law' in English and by *lex* in Latin. But Torah has a much wider range of significance than the Greek word *nomos*. The Torah *par excellence*, the Five Books of Moses, is by no means all 'Law' (or *nomos*, or *lex*); it contains myths of the creation, the fall, and the flood; sagas of the patriarchs; the story of Moses and the narrative of the exodus from Egypt and the forty years of journeying through the wilderness and the mountains. *Nomos*, on the other hand, has in some respects a wider range of meanings than *Torah*; and has no trace of a notion of a 'law' received from God and resting on his sole will. The same might be said of the choice of δικαιοσύνη ('justice', or 'righteousness') to render the Hebrew *tsedeq* or *tsedaqah*, and of countless other terms of the religious vocabulary. The Greek terms had to be stretched far beyond their normal range of meaning. (See C.H. Dodd, *The Bible and the Greeks*, 1935, Part I, 'The Religious Vocabulary of Hellenistic Judaism', pp. 1–95.)

Even with the Septuagint to help them, the translators of the sayings of Jesus from Aramaic into Greek were faced with unimaginable difficulties. The early church was not in a position to create anything like the staffs of skilled translators that work for the Bible Societies of our day. Papias remarks that 'Matthew compiled the *logia* in the Hebrew language, and everyone translated them as best he could' (by 'Hebrew' he almost certainly meant Aramaic; and by the *logia* he means the sayings of Jesus). Not many take Papias seriously, and those who do interpret him in different ways; but when he says that 'everyone translated them as best he could', he describes exactly how the Aramaic words of Jesus were sporadically, and almost at haphazard, turned into Greek—everyone translating them as he went along, whenever he wanted to tell Greek-speaking people, who had no knowledge of Aramaic, about Jesus. There was no formal collection of the sayings in Aramaic, and no 'Authorized Version' of them in Greek. The notion that the tradition was somehow 'guarded' by the apostles is altogether untenable.

Far from there being any general collection, the evidence shows beyond dispute that the sayings circulated at first as single sentences, or at most a series of brief sentences linked by a word which they have in common; the longer parables, amounting almost to short stories, would require several sentences each from the outset. The assembling of larger units was the work of the evangelists themselves, or of compilers of earlier sources which they employed. This association of sayings in groups as, for instance, in the Sermon on the Mount or in the sequences of parables (Mk.4; Mt.13; Mt.21: 28—22:15) carried with it a certain element of re-interpretation. As the Pontifical Biblical Commission remarks, 'Since the meaning of a statement also depends on the sequence, the Evangelists, in passing on the words and deeds of our Saviour, explained these now in one context, now in another, depending on [their] usefulness to the readers.' ('Instruction on the Historical Truth of the Gospels'— Rome, *Osservatore Romano*, May 14, 1964, IV.1, as translated by J.A. Fitzmeyer, *Theological Studies*, Vol. 25, No. 3, Sept. 1964, p.401.)

We must now observe that the sayings of Jesus were generally passed on with no indication of when they were first spoken, or where, or to what audience. The missionary or the teacher would as often as not imagine a setting and so create a little narrative framework. A saying such as 'I came not to call righteous people but sinners' (Mt.9:13b; cf. Mk.2:17b; Lk.5:32), clearly is a response to critics who took objection to the kind of people with whom Jesus associated; but the particular setting which makes it a response to 'the Pharisees' (Matthew), 'the scribes of the Pharisees' (Mark), or 'the Pharisees and their scribes' (Luke), and lays the scene at a dinner party—all this could well be the creation of a story-teller, perhaps Mark, perhaps an unknown predecessor. Again, Professor Jeremias has shown that many of the parables were originally told as a retort to opponents, but have been transposed into a lesson in the duties or attitudes of disciples. 'Many parables which the primitive Church connected with the disciples were originally addressed to a different audience, namely, to the Pharisees, the scribes, or the crowd.' (*Parables of Jesus*, rev. edn., London, 1963, p. 38.) It must be added that often the original setting of the parable is lost beyond recovery, and more or less plausible settings have been created for it; as had no doubt been done by Christian teachers and preachers, who made use of it in discourse as being fitted to the instruction of their hearers.

A good example may be seen in the parable of the Lost Sheep. Jeremias points out that in Luke the parable is spoken by way of response to the Pharisees and the scribes when they complain, 'This man receives sinners and eats with them'. (Lk.15:2.) This is substantially the same criticism that we find in Matthew 9:11 (cf. Mk. 2: 16; Lk. 5:30), where it is answered with the saying, 'I came not to call righteous people, but sinners.' Jeremias assumes that Luke has preserved the original setting, but it may very well be a creation of the evangelist. In Matthew the setting and the point made by the parable are totally different. It is built into a discourse addressed to the disciples as responsible leaders of the Christian community, and its point is to impress upon them that they must care for every single member of the flock of God, however unimportant he may be. 'It is not the will of your heavenly Father that one of these little ones should perish' (Mt. 18:14). There is no trace of the emphasis of the Lukan version: 'There will be more joy in heaven over one sinner who repents than over ninety-nine righteous people who need no repentance' (Lk. 15:7). The situation suggested by Luke may seem more plausible in relation to the actual historical situation of Jesus; but it may for all that be the product of his imagination, not a genuine tradition of the original setting.

Jeremias, like C.H. Dodd, is confident that he can recover the original setting, and with it the original significance of the parable as first uttered by Jesus, even when he feels obliged to reject every setting given in the Gospels as incompatible with the conditions of Jesus' earthly life. But it must be said that the efforts of a modern scholar to reconstruct for a parable (or a saying) some situation in the life of Jesus which has simply not been preserved in any form of the tradition as known to us are not likely to be more successful than the efforts of the evangelists and those who transmitted the tradition before it was written down at all. They are bound to be conjectural, and Professor P. Bonnard, in approaching the interpretation of the Matthaean parables, tells us that 'our first task is not to understand hypothetical parables that may have been pronounced by Jesus in such and such a situation of his life, but to look into the sense which Matthew attributed to them in the situations which he himself faced, in the place where we find them today in this Gospel.' (*L'évangile selon saint Matthieu*, Neuchâtel, 1963, p.189.) To go behind the Matthaean parables to the primitive church is in some degree possible; but it ought to be recognized that 'the return to Jesus from the primitive church' (Jeremias, *Parables*, chap. II), in the attempt to recover 'the original meaning' given to them in the utterance, is as much the following of a will-o'-the-wisp as 'the quest for the historical Jesus' has turned out to be. ('At the end of this research on the life of Jesus stands the recognition of its own failure' —G. Bornkamm, *Jesus of Nazareth*, ET, 1960, p.13.)

Jeremias lists ten 'laws of transformation' which operated in the shaping of the transmission of the parables as they passed from their original life-setting in the activity of Jesus to a different setting— even a variety of different settings—in their usage in the primitive church (*Parables*, pp.113f.). These and similar laws have also operated in the transmission of the sayings generally. In the most recent studies, attention is focused on the fact that they receive a third setting in the handling of the evangelist. This was clearly brought out by W. Marxsen in his book, *Der Evangelist Markus* (1956, p.12), and by H. Conzelmann in *Die Mitte der Zeit* (1954); these two works mark the real beginning of the method of 'redaction criticism' (*Redaktionsgeschichte* is Marxsen's term). Within a few years, it was given authoritative expression and sanction in Roman Catholic circles in the 'Instruction on the Historical Truth of the Gospels' which we have mentioned above, page 23. It urges the interpreter to 'pay diligent attention to the *three* stages of tradition by which the doctrine and the life of Jesus have come down to us' (VI.2, Fitzmyer); the role of the evangelists is described in section IX.

The distinction between the first two 'stages of tradition' has long been recognized. In the words of J. Jeremias,

as they have come down to us, the parables of Jesus have a double historical setting. (1) The original setting . . . is some specific situation in the pattern of the activity of Jesus. (2) But subsequently, before they assumed a written form, they 'lived' in the primitive church. . . . It is important to bear in mind the difference between the situation of Jesus and that of the primitive church. In many cases it will be necessary to remove sayings and parables of Jesus from their setting in the life and thought of the primitive church, in the attempt to recover their original setting in the life of Jesus. (*Parables*, p. 23; cf. C.H. Dodd, *Parables of the Kingdom*, rev. edn., 1961, pp. 103–105.)

The more recent criticism insists more strongly than ever that we must also pay attention to the third stage, the work of the evangelists individually, in which the diverse elements of the tradition, already modified in oral use in the previous decades, are made to take their place in a more or less comprehensive account of the ministry and teaching of Jesus in its entire significance, and so are presented in relation to what must be called a unified and distinctive *theological* conception of the ultimate significance of Jesus for Christian faith and understanding. Studies in redaction criticism accordingly become studies in the *theology* of Matthew, of Luke, or of Mark. John is not alone among the evangelists as a creative theologian.

We have now to observe that besides modifying the sayings of Jesus which he received from tradition, partly by the selection which he made from the available store, partly by the interpretation which he imposed upon them by arrangement and context, Matthew also added to them sayings which can hardly be attributed to the historical person of Jesus in any form, even after allowance is made for changes occasioned in preceding oral transmission. Among these we may distinguish (i) sayings which may have originated as utterances of Christian prophets, given as words of the risen Christ; (ii) sayings derived from other sources, as from the preaching of John the Baptist, the deliverances of other Jewish teachers, or even sentences from the Old Testament; and (iii), most surprising of all to readers of our time, sayings of Matthew's own composing.

It is evident that a number of sayings which Matthew gives us as utterances of Jesus in his earthly ministry can be understood only when they are seen to be utterances of the risen Christ. This applies, for instance, to the saying, 'Where two or three are gathered in my name, there am I in the midst of them' (Mt. 18:20). There is nothing to suggest that little groups met in the name of Jesus during his days on earth, or that he could be present in more than one place at any time. Omnipresence belongs to the risen Christ; it is not a property of human nature as such but of the glorified humanity of Christ risen and ascended. And meetings of groups in his name begin when his followers have learned to know him as the Lord. Indeed, the assurance is given in the context of action to be carried out by 'the church' for the discipline of recalcitrant members (18:17ff.). A.C. McNeile remarks (*Matthew, ad. loc.*) that 'it is probable that behind the section lie some genuine sayings; but in its present form it belongs to a date when the Church was already an organized Body'; but he makes no attempt to discuss how these hypothesized 'genuine sayings' may have been framed or in what context. We cannot claim certainty, but it is at least possible that sayings like these were first uttered *ad hoc* by Christian prophets, mediating the will of Christ to his followers. R. Bultmann, who holds that many sayings originated in this way, asks 'whether it was originally intended to ascribe such prophetic sayings to Jesus. They could very easily have gained currency at first as utterances of the Spirit in the Church.' (*History of the Synoptic Tradition*, ET, 1963, p.127.)

Sayings from John the Baptist and other Jewish teachers and from the Old Testament came quite easily to be attributed to Jesus in the oral tradition of the church. The tradition was not in the hands of scholars or bookish persons who would take care to verify their references; and there is a tendency in all traditions to attribute to famous teachers sayings which were in fact coined by others, or were simply floating maxims. We are actually told that 'later sayings from the Christian tradition were put into the mouth of Mohammed' (Bultmann, *HST*, p.101, n.2). T.W. Manson pointed to a number of sayings of Jesus in Matthew which appeared to be transferred to him from John the Baptist (*Sayings*, pp. 25f., 190, 238). It is not easy to determine with certainty whether any given saying of Jesus is transferred to him from a Jewish sage or actually framed by himself; but we must agree with Bultmann that a number of sayings 'are hardly if at all characteristic of a new and individual piety in Judaism, but are observations on life, rules of prudence and popular morality, sometimes a product of humour or scepticism, full of sober popular morality, and even of a naif egoism' (*HST*, p.104). Do we find anything characteristic of Jesus in the advice not to take a seat at the head table, for fear that the host may embarrass you by sending you to a less dignified place in the banqueting-hall (Lk.14:8—10)? The numerous sayings of Jesus which are closely paralleled in utterances of Hillel and other Jewish sages may of course have been repeated by Jesus, but there is the distinct possibility that some of them have been transferred to him in the Christian tradition.

Touching the third category of sayings, it may seem strange and indeed unwelcome to us to learn that Matthew should not shrink from attributing to Jesus sayings which are demonstrably of his own composing. But Jeremias, in his careful examination of the Matthaean interpretation of the parable of the Tares (13:36—41) and that of the Seine-Net (vv.49f.) demonstrates that this is precisely what the evangelist has done here (*Parables*, pp.81—85). T.W. Manson long since argued that the parable of the Tares itself, and not merely the interpretation of Matthew, is a creation of Matthew built on the base of Mark's parable of the Seed Growing Secretly (Mk.4: 26—29; *Sayings*, p.193). Matthew exercises a creative freedom which goes far beyond editorial re-arrangements. Fr. Green holds that 'Mt.'s larger additions all arise out of Markan contexts, and in many cases can be explained as midrashic elaborations of them.' (*Matthew*, p.15; and see his succinct remarks on *midrash*, pp.10ff.)

Matthew has arranged most of the sayings of Jesus in the form of five discourses. The first and most familiar of these is what is called the Sermon on the Mount, which occupies three entire chapters (chaps. 5, 6, and 7). The scene is set on 'the mountain', and the audience consists of the disciples of Jesus and the 'great crowds' which have been drawn to him from all parts of the Holy Land—

'from Galilee and the Decapolis and Jerusalem and Judaea and from beyond the Jordan' (4:25). The second discourse is a charge to the twelve disciples, who are now designated 'the twelve apostles' (10: 2–4); it occupies the remainder of chapter 10. The third is not given as a single sustained discourse; there are changes of scene and of audience. It begins with Jesus teaching from a boat by the shore of the lake, as he speaks to the 'great crowds' that have gathered there (13:1–2), but after the telling of a single parable he is pictured as in converse with his disciples, to whom he explains his reason for speaking in parables, and gives an allegorical interpretation of the parable of the sower, which is clearly not meant for the crowds, for it has not been given to them 'to know the secrets of the kingdom of heaven'. There has, however, been no intimation of a change of place, and after the interpretation of the first parable has been given, Jesus is again found addressing the crowds, telling them three more parables (vv.34f.). At this point, 'he left the crowds and went into the house' (v.36), and there he speaks to his disciples, giving them an allegorical interpretation of the parable of the weeds among the wheat (vv.37–43) and continuing with three more parables, the last with an allegorical interpretation appended. Despite the changes of scene and of audience, this collection of parables, which occupies nearly the whole of chapter 13, is intended to be taken as a unit of instruction. The fourth discourse, like the second, is given to the disciples alone, with no indication of the time or place; it has been described as a brief manual of church order (*Gemeindeordnung*), intended chiefly for those who hold positions of leadership in the church; it is found in chapter 18. The fifth, like the first, occupies three entire chapters (chaps. 23, 24, 25); like the third, it is broken by changes of scene and of audience. It begins with a long section addressed to the crowds and to the disciples (23:1), apparently in the temple. As Jesus is leaving the temple, he predicts that it will be torn down stone by stone (24:1f.). The scene then shifts to the Mount of Olives, and the audience consists of the disciples alone (v.3). The next section is apocalyptic in character; convulsions in nature and in society, persecutions, apostasies in the church, and the profanation of the temple are foretold as signs of the close of the age and the glorious coming of Jesus as the Son of man (vv.3–35). But the time is not known, and the remainder of the discourse is given to warnings of the need to be always on the watch, prepared at every moment for the decisive event. The theme is now: 'Watch, therefore, for you know neither the day nor the hour.' (25:13; cf. 24:36, 44.) At the conclusion of the entire discourse, Jesus gives his unforgettable vision of the Last Judgement, when all the nations are gathered before the glorious throne of the Son of man to hear their final destiny, which he will pronounce on the basis of their treatment of the destitute and the oppressed (25:31–45).

Each of these five collections of sayings is followed by a formula which runs: 'When Jesus had finished (all) these sayings' (7:28; 19:1; 26:1), with appropriate variations according to the subject of the discourse (11:1—'had finished instructing his twelve disciples'; 13:53—'had finished all these parables'). The evangelist thus marks off his Gospel into five 'books', perhaps to suggest that he is thinking of the law delivered by Christ as given in a new Pentateuch, like the five books of Moses. The parallel with Moses ought not to be pressed too far (W.D. Davies, *Setting,* II.1, pp.14–25), but the formulas cannot be dismissed as insignificant. They are conspicuous markings, designed by the composer of the Gospel himself, and they must be taken to underline the areas of his book which he intends the reader to distinguish.

It must be remembered that an ancient writer did not have at his disposal the methods of modern book-planning. His manuscript was written, and copied by scribes for the use of others, without any division into chapters, paragraphs, or sentences, or even the separation of words, and there was seldom any attempt at punctuation. We may note the remarks of Sir Frederic Kenyon:

The lack of assistance to readers, or of aids to facilitate reference, in ancient books is very remarkable. The separation of words is practically unknown, except very rarely when an inverted comma or dot is used to mark a separation where some ambiguity might exist. Punctuation is often wholly absent, and is never full and systematic. (*Books and Readers in Ancient Greece and Rome* 2nd edn., Oxford, 1951, p. 67.)

If a writer, then, wanted to bring the attention of his readers to the significant divisions in his text, he could only do so by putting a sentence into the text of his work. And these five formulas are by far the most conspicuous indications that Matthew offers, to indicate the way in which he has organized his work.

These five discourses were never delivered in anything like the form which has been given to them by the evangelist. Every one of them 'is an agglomeration put together by the editor of the Gospel' (B.H. Streeter, *The Four Gospels*, London, 1926, p.165). The materials which they contain were of many different origins and came into the hands of the evangelist through many different channels and after a long history of transmission, primarily oral, but in part documentary. Jesus himself left nothing in writing, and gave no commandment to his disciples to make written records of his words and deeds. They were sent out to preach, not to write memoirs. From the beginning, they would tell stories about him, and would recall and repeat such of his words as would serve to instruct their converts in the ways of God, as they exhorted and encouraged and charged them 'to lead a life worthy of God, who [had] called [them] into his own kingdom and glory' (1 Thess.2:11). They would also find in them the kind of sayings that would help them in controversy with their opponents, and others that would determine their ways of worship and their exercise of authority.

None of this, however, would require the systematic recital of long discourses—nor could a long discourse be remembered without the aid of a written record. At first, the sayings of Jesus (and the stories of Jesus) were brought forward piecemeal, in accordance with the requirements of the situation. There was no need to recall the time and place where something had been said, or even to remark on the audience. Words which Jesus had spoken to opponents could be adapted and treated as addressed to the disciples (and through them to the church). From time to time the store of sayings kept in memory came to be supplemented by new sayings shaped by teachers of the church, in part at least by prophets speaking 'in the Spirit', which were regarded as words spoken by the risen Jesus.[6] The five 'discourses' of this Gospel are all put together out of fragmentary materials of these varying origins. 'We must also realize', to quote again from the late T.W. Manson, 'that the five great discourses . . . are not shorthand records of addresses delivered by the Prophet of Nazareth on specified dates at specified places' (we might add, 'or before specified audiences'). 'They are systematic presentations of the mind of Christ on various matters of great moment to his Church.' (*Ethics and the Gospel*, p. 46.) The words are, at least in great part, the words of Jesus; but the systematic presentation is the work of Matthew.

VI   THE TEACHING OF THE EVANGELIST

The teaching of Matthew is presented to us chiefly in the form of sayings of Jesus. Most of them are gathered into five great collections,

---

[6] See my article, 'Sayings of the Risen Jesus in the Synoptic Tradition: An Inquiry into their Origin and Significance', in *Christian History and Interpretation: Studies Presented to John Knox* (Cambridge, 1967), pp. 161–181.

ordered by the evangelist into discourses delivered by Jesus at specific times in his ministry, and in specific places; but some are given as responses made by him to hostile critics or to friendly questioners. A certain number are embedded in anecdotes which are preserved for the sake of a pronouncement of Jesus, or formed to make a plausible setting for the saying. But as we have seen, all these sayings have been transposed into a body of instruction given by the risen Christ who is now worshipped in his church, to bring out their significance for the Christian believers of Matthew's time. The evangelist is not preparing records for the archives, but setting before his readers the way that leads to life and warning them against the danger of taking the broad way that leads to destruction (Mt. 7:13–14). He is not an historian or a biographer, nor is he to be regarded as a theologian, but as a pastor and teacher with essentially practical concerns.

To some degree, Matthew has rabbinized Jesus; there is room for disagreement over how far he has thus distorted the whole picture. Beyond all question, he does not give a balanced or anything like a complete presentation of what Jesus actually taught. This was not his purpose, and in any case, he was not in a position to carry out such a purpose if he had so much as entertained it. He stands at two generations removed from the age of Jesus' ministry, and he works in a very different environment. The tradition about Jesus had not been preserved unimpaired through all the changes of time and place. Jesus himself committed nothing to writing, and gave no instruction to his disciples to write down anything that he had said. From the beginning, his sayings were passed on by those who heard them—the apostles and others—not in stereotype, but with free adaptation to the needs of the people to whom they ministered, and 'with that fuller understanding which they enjoyed, having been instructed by the glorious events of the Christ and taught by the light of the Spirit of Truth' (from the 'Instruction' [Fitzmyer], cited above, page 23). Sayings were used by the apostles, and by countless others as time went on, in contexts quite unfamiliar to Jesus, and to hearers of different regions and of different tongues—people not at all like the Galilean villagers with whom Jesus had mainly to do. Many of the sayings had been reshaped to accommodate them to the understanding of these different hearers, and many had ceased to be used in the teaching and preaching and been lost for good and all. Matthew in turn contributed to this ongoing process, by selecting and organizing these elements of tradition as they came to him, and presenting them in the light of his own understanding of the Christian faith and life.

His teaching, accordingly, although stemming from what was remembered of the teaching of Jesus of Nazareth, is so deeply affected by the mutations of the tradition through two generations of transmission, and by his own concern to focus on the way of righteousness, the way of life, that it is impossible to distinguish clearly between what may be confidently ascribed to Jesus, what has been contributed by the transmitting church, and what is due to Matthew as interpreter. There is no means at our disposal for constructing an 'objective' historical definition of the teaching of Jesus such as would enable us to judge how faithfully the teaching given in Matthew represents the teaching once given by Jesus. We must be content to take note of the substance of Matthew's teaching without making vain attempts to uncover some nucleus which might be regarded as pure and unalloyed teaching of Jesus. (See the remarks, more cautiously phrased, of Pierre Bonnard, *Matthieu*, p. 11.)

The doctrine of Matthew is rooted and grounded in his Jewish inheritance. Like Jesus himself, this evangelist was born and reared in Judaism; unlike Jesus he was trained in the scribal methods of interpretation of the scriptures, and in many ways he shares the Pharisaic outlook, despite the bitter invectives which he hurls against 'scribes and Pharisees' (chap. 23) as if they formed one monolithic mass doomed to perdition. Like them, he holds that the law given through Moses is inviolable, so long as heaven and earth remain (5:18). Unlike them, he rejects the authority of the oral law, the accumulated tradition of interpretation and application of the Mosaic code, affirming that the scribes and Pharisees make the law itself null and void by the tradition (15:1–9). More than that, he brings a profound modification in the approach to the law, even while affirming its continuing validity to the last syllable. The tradition of the scribes is radically rejected; it is now the law as 'fulfilled' and interpreted by Jesus which demands our obedience. Whoever hears and obeys the words of Jesus is like a man who builds his house upon a rock—it will stand solid against all the storms that beat against it; whoever fails to do what Jesus has said is like a man who builds his house upon sand—it will come down in ruins when it has to face winds and floods (7:24–27). Moreover, the substance of the law and of the whole scripture can be summed up in the Golden Rule: 'Whatever you wish that others would do to you, do so to them' (7:12). When Jesus is asked by a scribe, 'Which is the greatest commandment in the law?' he replies, 'You shall love the Lord your God with all your heart, with all your soul, and with all your mind; this is the great commandment, the first of all. The second is like it:

"You shall love your neighbour as yourself." The whole law, and the teaching of the prophets, hang on these two commandments' (22: 34–40). Everything in the way of statutes, everything in prophetic teaching, is to be understood in the light of the overriding primacy of love—love to God, first of all; and co-ordinated with that, the love of one's neighbour. In the same spirit, in the dialogue with the rich ruler, Jesus completes a list of commandments chosen from the familiar ten, by adding as the climax of all, 'You shall love your neighbour as yourself' (19:18f.; deliberately added by Matthew to the Markan form, Mk.10:18f.). Finally, when the risen Jesus commissions his disciples to make disciples of all the nations, he charges them to teach their converts to observe all that he himself has taught (28:19f.). Nothing is said of observance of the Mosaic law. There is a tacit repudiation of the demand that in the Christian church, Gentile converts must be circumcised, and charged to keep the law of Moses (Acts 15:5).

The Jewish inheritance of Matthew is not limited to the scriptures of the Old Testament. Some of his principal themes developed in the Judaism of the last few centuries before Christ, which is represented for us chiefly by the apocalyptic literature. This is most familiar to us in the book of Daniel, which attained its present form in the time of the Maccabees (167–163 BC). It is the only work of Jewish apocalyptic which has attained canonical status; but among the Jews even Daniel was not counted among 'The Prophets', but among 'The Writings' (Heb. *Kethubim*, Gk. *Hagiographa*). Some others are classified among the Apocrypha of the Old Testament, and others more generally among the numerous Pseudepigrapha (R.H. Charles, ed., *The Apocrypha and Pseudepigrapha of the Old Testament in English*, 2 vols., 1913). For Matthew, the book of Daniel is fully authoritative; his thought of Jesus as 'the Son of man' derives from Daniel's vision of a heavenly being of human appearance—'one like a son of man'—who appears before the throne of God in heaven, and is given 'dominion and glory and kingdom, that all peoples, nations, and languages should serve him' (Dan.7:14; cf. vv.18, 27).

In Matthew, 'the Son of man' is one of the chief titles of Jesus, and the 'Kingdom' is clearly the central theme. The association of the two is found in Daniel, not in any of the more ancient scriptures.

The kingdom of heaven (literally, 'of the heavens') has the same meaning as 'the kingdom of God', as it is always called in the rest of the New Testament, 'the heavens' being simply a circumlocution adopted in Jewish usage to avoid speaking directly of God. The

Matthaean form is the only one that is used in the rabbinical literature (all later than the Gospels). It is probable that Jesus himself used this peculiarly Jewish manner of speech, and that the phrase is a literal translation of the common rabbinic expression *malkuth shamayim*. In Aramaic, as in Hebrew, the word for 'heaven' has no singular, so that the plural has to serve both for 'heaven' and 'heavens'. God dwells in the heavens, and the place of his abode is used by metonymy for him who dwells there. 'Kingdom of God' will then have been adopted to make the expression more intelligible to Gentile readers. But Matthew is not rigid in the matter; on occasion he also speaks of 'the kingdom of God'. In either form, the term did not mean very much to Gentile readers, and as a consequence it quickly disappears from the Christian vocabulary, even within New Testament times. It hardly ever occurs in the letters of Paul; and even the Gospel of John abandons it, after a passing mention in the dialogue with Nicodemus (Jn.3:3, 5), in favour of 'life', 'eternal life'. The Jesus of John does not come to proclaim a 'gospel of the Kingdom', but to bring life and light. For him, the Kingdom is wholly spiritual; it cannot be entered, it cannot even be seen, except through regeneration by the Spirit; and when Jesus before Pilate speaks of his own role as king, it is to declare flatly, 'my kingdom is not of this world' (18:36). For Paul too it is spiritually conceived: 'The kingdom of God is not food and drink, but righteousness, peace, and joy in the Holy Spirit' (Rom.14:17—the only mention it receives in the great epistle to the Romans). 'Flesh and blood' does not inherit it; 'this mortal nature must put on immortality' (1 Cor. 15:50, 53). Even in Matthew, there are traces of this tendency to spiritualize, in that 'to have eternal life' (19:16) is taken up in the same anecdote by the traditional 'to enter the kingdom of heaven' (vv. 23f.).

The Old Testament does not at any point speak of 'the kingdom of God' (or 'of heaven'), though the writers often speak of God as King. In the vision of Daniel, 'kingdom' is used by itself, and it is given to the mysterious figure 'like a son of man', who is a kind of heavenly counterpart of 'the saints of the Most High' (7:13). It is bestowed by God in heaven, but it is exercised on earth, in history. 'The kingdom and the dominion and the greatness of the kingdoms *under the whole heavens* shall be given to the people of the saints of the Most High; their kingdom shall be an everlasting kingdom, and all dominions shall serve and obey them' (v.27). Daniel thinks of the glorious destiny of Israel, the people of God; Matthew sees this destiny as fulfilled in Jesus as 'the Son of man', after the Kingdom is taken away from Israel and transferred to the Christian church, 'a nation producing the fruits of it' (21:43).

The word rendered 'kingdom'—whether the Greek βασιλεία or the Hebrew *malkuth* (Aramaic *malkutha*)—has a double sense. It may be used of the realm ruled by the king, or of the sovereign power, the kingly rule, which he exercises. Both senses are found in the Gospels, but it generally has the spatial meaning. People may be *cast out* of the kingdom; the supreme end of life is to *enter* the kingdom. It can be represented figuratively as a great house or palace with doors which can be shut to exclude those who wish to enter (23:13); it has keys which can be entrusted to a disciple of Jesus (16:19). On the other hand, some key passages require the meaning 'kingly rule', as, for instance, 'the kingdom of heaven is at hand', the ascription 'yours is the kingdom', or 'the kingdom of God has come upon you', or again, 'before they see the Son of man coming in his kingdom'. It should be kept in mind that these two thoughts are held in suspension in the one phrase, and it is not always easy to see which element should be given the greater emphasis.

In Matthew, the word βασιλεία, 'kingdom' occurs nearly sixty times, compared with less than twenty occurrences in Mark; in the two Gospels, all but five of these instances bear upon the kingdom of God (of heaven), or of Christ. In Matthew, the theme is sounded first by John the Baptist, in his proclamation: 'Repent! for the kingdom of heaven is at hand'—the very words that afterwards are spoken by Jesus at the commencement of his public ministry in Galilee (3:2; 4:17). It has been argued that in Mark the words should be rendered 'the kingdom of God has arrived, is here'. This is made the key to the thesis of Professor C.H. Dodd, that Jesus teaches 'realized eschatology', first promulgated in his book *The Apostolic Preaching and its Developments* (1936), and applied systematically to the interpretation of the parables in *The Parables of the Kingdom* (1936; rev. edn., 1961). The perfect ἤγγικεν in itself permits the interpretation 'has arrived', in place of 'has come here, is at hand', but it is certainly not so understood by Matthew, for he would not hold that the Kingdom was inaugurated by the preaching of John the Baptist before Jesus appeared on the scene. For him, it is a future expectation, announced by John and then by Jesus as near at hand, to be inaugurated only when he comes as Son of man in his glory, attended by hosts of angels (24:30; 25:31).

The Sermon on the Mount is penetrated throughout by the doctrine that the kingdom of heaven is the fulfilment of hope and longing, the sum of blessedness. It is for the poor in spirit, the meek, those who mourn, who hunger and thirst for righteousness, the pure in heart, the persecuted. Wealth cannot purchase an entrance—'it is hard for a rich person to enter the kingdom of heaven' (19:23f.). It is not a reward for virtue or for any kind of human achievement. The righteousness of the scribes and Pharisees, scrupulous as it may be, will not suffice to gain them an entrance (5:20). Eminence in religious leadership confers no prescriptive right to an entrance; priests and elders in the temple are warned: 'The tax collectors and harlots go into the kingdom of God before you' (21:31), because they refused to believe and repent at the preaching of John the Baptist.

Jesus goes about 'preaching the gospel of the kingdom' (4:23; 9:35), commissions his disciples to make this the theme of their proclamation (10:7), and foretells that 'this gospel of the kingdom will be preached throughout all the world as a testimony to all the nations' (24:14), before the end comes. Many of his parables are devoted to showing what the kingdom of the heavens is like, but from these we could not deduce with certainty a doctrine of the Kingdom (Allen, *Matthew*, p. lxx). At most, they throw light upon a number of aspects of the meaning. Jesus, as Matthew portrays him, is not concerned to give definitions, to clarify people's ideas, but to move them to action. He bids all who hear to 'seek first God's kingdom and righteousness', before even the primary needs of food and clothing, let alone the stultifying pursuit of riches (6:33 [19–34]). The Kingdom cannot be defined in ways that would make it intelligible to disinterested observers: its 'mysteries' are unfolded only to the disciples, who have ears to hear and eyes to see; to others this knowledge is not granted (13:11, 16); it is 'hidden from wise and prudent people, and revealed to babes' (11:25f.; cf. 1 Cor.1:18–21; 2:6–10).

Jesus had proclaimed that 'the kingdom of heaven is at hand'; and his followers continued to live in hope and expectation of the arrival of the Kingdom within that generation (16:28; 24:34). The expectation now was linked more and more with the coming of Jesus, crucified, dead, and buried, but raised from the dead to sit at the right hand of God, given the name that is above every name. All authority in heaven and on earth has been committed to him, and he is always present with his disciples, till the end of the age (28:18–20; cf. 18:20). At the end, he will come as Son of man to gather together his elect, and to cast out of 'his kingdom' every alien element; 'then shall the righteous shine forth like the sun in the kingdom of their Father'; they will 'inherit the kingdom prepared for them from the foundation of the world'; they will enter 'into eternal life' (13:41–43; 25:34, 46).

In the interim, 'they were expecting the kingdom of God; it was the church that came' (A. Loisy). In Matthew there are already traces of a tendency to think of the church as the present form of the Kingdom, so far as it can be realized in this age, in history. The Kingdom, as in the judgement scenario of chapter 25 (vv. 31–46), is tacitly identified with the abode of the blessed after death, and its essential meaning spiritualized as 'life eternal'. It may also be said that the expectation of the Parousia, the coming of Jesus as Son of man in glory, though still very much alive, is accompanied by the faith in Jesus as ever-present, governing the life of his church in the present age. Thoughts of the church are scarcely veiled in the application of some of the parables—the parable of the Tares as interpreted (13:24–30, 37–43); the parable of the Talents, which deals with the responsibilities of the followers of Christ in the present age—its climax, of course, is in the judgement which is to be passed at the return of the absent master; and again, the 'keys of the kingdom of heaven' which are entrusted to Peter, named the Rock on which Christ will found his *church*, certainly symbolize the exercise of authority in the church that is to be, not in a heavenly realm or in any future kingdom. In the present age, so long as the world that we know endures, the community of the kingdom—the church—gathers in good and bad. The righteous are inextricably intermingled with the lawless, as in a field which bears a plentiful growth of weeds among the wheat. The community must be on its guard against false prophets, who come in sheeps' clothing, but inwardly are ravening wolves (7:15); they prophesy in the name of Jesus, cast out demons in his name, and in his name perform miracles, but they will not enter the kingdom of heaven, for in the Judgement none are admitted but those who do the will of the Father in heaven (7:21–23). The church, then, is not the ultimate form of the kingdom of heaven, but its temporal expression. Membership in the church no more guarantees final acceptance into the kingdom of heaven than descent from Abraham (cf. 3:7–10). It will be purged, but the purging is not the function of the church, nor can it be done in the present age. The weeds and the wheat must be allowed to grow together until the harvest, which is the end of the age, and then angels sent by the Son of man will make the separation.

Though the conception of God's rule on earth, the coming of his Kingdom, is rooted in the Jewish world of thinking, it no longer carries the slightest overtone of national privilege for Israel. The

Israelites may be called 'the sons of the kingdom'—its natural heirs—but they are warned that 'many will come from east and west to sit at table with Abraham, Isaac, and Jacob in the kingdom of heaven, while the sons of the kingdom will be thrown into the outer darkness' (8:11f.). In Jewish expectation, the hope of the Kingdom was inseparable from the freeing of the nation from a foreign yoke, the establishment of Jerusalem as the capital of the world. The prophetic scriptures, indeed, love to paint the future in terms of a reign of righteousness and peace, but they do not succeed in extricating it from the trammels of national triumph. When the saints of the Most High receive the kingdom, 'all dominions shall serve and obey them' (Dan.7:27; cf. v.14). The same thought of national triumph goes back far beyond the apocalyptic writings to the great classical prophets. Not only is Israel delivered from the power of her enemies; but they in their turn become subject to her.

> Aliens shall stand and feed your flocks,
> foreigners shall be your ploughmen and vine-dressers;
> .... You shall eat the wealth of the nations,
> and in their riches you shall glory. (Isa.61:5f.)

The God of the Kingdom is the God of Israel; he is the One (Mt.19:17), the living God (16:16), the God of Abraham, Isaac, and Jacob (22:31f.), the God who created man in the beginning, male and female, and ordained that they should be joined together in the indissoluble union of marriage (19: 4–6). He is the God who gave the law through Moses, and who spoke through the prophets (1:22, and often). The Kingdom is his kingdom, but he is never called King; at most, he is sometimes figured by an earthly king in parables (18:23; 22:2). But far more often he is called Father. In his own prayers, Jesus addresses him as 'Father', and teaches his disciples to invoke him as 'Our Father'. In all, God is called Father no less than forty-five times in this Gospel. This is far different from Jewish usage; in the Shemoneh Esreh, for instance, God is invoked as 'Our Father' in only two of the nineteen benedictions (5, 6), and in both it is paralleled by 'our King', and he is called 'King' in eight of the benedictions. In the entire Psalter, God is called Father only twice. Nor can Matthew's usage be regarded as common to the Synoptic tradition as a whole; for in the Gospel of Mark 'Father' is used of God only four times, and in Luke only seventeen (in John, where Father is used more frequently even than in Matthew, the sense is not at all the same). In Matthew, Jesus frequently speaks of God as 'Father in heaven', or 'heavenly Father' (ὁ πατὴρ ὁ ἐν τοῖς οὐρανοῖς, thirteen times; ὁ πατὴρ ὁ οὐράνιος, seven times). The latter expression is never used by any other New Testament writer, and the former only once (Mk.11:25; v.26 is not found in the best witnesses, and is to be regarded as spurious). These phrases do not occur anywhere in the Old Testament or in later Jewish writings.

As Father in heaven, God has revealed the truth of Jesus to Peter (16:17). He forgives, and requires that those whom he has forgiven shall show the same spirit of forgiveness to others (6:14); he will not forgive, and will punish most severely, any who refuse to grant forgiveness to others (6:15; 18:35). He is concerned for the 'little ones'; their angels are constantly in his presence, and it is not his will that a single one of them should perish (18:10, 14). He answers our prayers, and can be counted on, more surely than any human father, to give good things to those that ask him (7:7–11); to the followers of Jesus, if only two of them are agreed about any request, he will grant it (18:19). The disciples of Jesus are called to be perfect, as their father in heaven is perfect, in loving their enemies and praying for those that persecute them (5:44f.); they are his sons, in so far as they reflect his character in their conduct. The supreme requirement for all is that they should do his will; it is in this that they are acknowledged by Jesus as his brother, and sister, and mother (7:21; 12:50). There is no suggestion that the fatherhood of God has as its corollary the brotherhood of man—the world of mankind contains many 'sons of the devil' (13:38f.).

It is recognized by Paul, likewise, that it is only Christians who have the right to invoke God as Father. This is a privilege conferred in baptism, when God sends the Spirit of his Son into our hearts (Gal.4:4–6; cf. Rom.8:14–16).

In the imagery of Daniel's vision (chap. 7), the kingdom is given to 'one like a son of man', a mysterious figure which comes 'with the clouds of heaven' and is presented before the throne of God in heaven, pictured as 'an ancient of days' (that is, a very old man). This 'one like a son of man' is not conceived as an individual person. Like the four surrealist animal figures (vv. 3–7), which turn out to be symbols of four world empires, this figure is the symbol of a community. The 'one like a son of man' is interpreted for the seer (by a heavenly attendant spirit) as 'the saints of the Most High' (vv.16–22, 27)—the holy community of Israel. It is a communal symbol, not intended to suggest an individual being who will come down to earth. In Matthew, as in the usage of the Gospels generally, it has become a symbol of Jesus, peculiarly fused with the notion of 'Messiah'. It is not possible to show that there was any preparation whatever in Jewish apocalyptic for this development; if there is any pre-history of the Son of man—Messiah fusion, it cannot be traced in any literature known to us. All that we can do is to examine how it is used by Matthew.

The title 'Son of man' is used in all the Gospels as a title of Jesus, but it is never used by anyone but Jesus himself. Except for a single passage in Acts, where it is placed on the lips of Stephen at the time of his martyrdom (Acts 7:56), it is not used elsewhere in the New Testament. It is not used exclusively of Jesus' coming in glory at the end of the age, to inaugurate the Kingdom (as in 13:40; 16:27f.; 24:27, 30, 37, 39, 44; 25:31). In some of these sayings, the identification of Jesus with the apocalyptic 'Son of man' is not explicit; it is possible to interpret them as implying not that Jesus himself returns to earth to fulfil the glorious role of 'Son of man', but that the Son of man, a heavenly being who will come as judge at the end of the age, will determine the fate of individuals in accordance with the response of each to the earthly Jesus. But it is hazardous to go behind Matthew and the other Synoptic evangelists, and to conjecture that these sayings have initially meant something of which the evangelists are quite unconscious. There can be no question that in their understanding every mention of the Son of man is a reference to Jesus. It remains open to question whether the term was used in this apocalyptic sense by Jesus, or indeed whether it was used by him in any sense whatever.

But the title is used in a number of contexts in which it bears upon Jesus in his activity on earth, or in his betrayal, his death, and his resurrection; and in a few instances it seems to be no more than a surrogate for the personal pronoun and is occasionally equivalent to the generic 'man'. In the story of the paralytic (9:1—8), Jesus demonstrates his authority to forgive sins by healing the sufferer: 'that you may know that the Son of man has authority on earth to forgive sins' (v.6). Obviously, the thought would be the same if the text read 'I have authority' instead of the circumlocution; but in the reaction of the crowds, 'they glorified God, who had given such authority to *men*.' Again, in the story of the confession at Caesarea Philippi (16:13ff.), Jesus begins with the question, 'Who are people saying that the Son of man is?' This is Matthew's own rephrasing of the question which is given in Mark in the words, 'Who are people saying that I am?' (Mk.8:27; retained in Lk.9:18.) In the very next pericope, Matthew reverses the process: where Mark tells us that 'he began to teach them that the Son of man must suffer many things . . .' (Mk.8:31), Matthew replaces this by the wording, 'Jesus began to show his disciples that *he* must go to Jerusalem and suffer many things . . .' (16:21).

In the predictions of the passion, Jesus consistently speaks of himself as 'the Son of man' (17:22f.; 20:18; 26:2; cf. 17:12); and he uses it again in speaking of his resurrection (17:9; 12:40). In one passage, he speaks as if there were prophecies in the scriptures about the tragic fate of 'the Son of man' (26:24). This can only be taken to mean that Matthew interprets various passages which speak of the sufferings of various figures of the Old Testament as applying to Jesus as Son of man, even though the title is not to be found in such contexts (Ps.22, etc.).

There is little formal teaching on the doctrine of the Person of Christ in Matthew. Jesus is presented as the Messiah of Israel, the Son of David of whom the prophets have spoken. Traditional Jewish notions of the Messiah are totally abandoned, except for his descent from David; in fact, they are formally combated. Jesus rejects as a temptation of the devil any thought that he should seek to win the glory of the kingdoms of the earth (4:8–10); he is not sent to lead his people in victorious armed conflict with the Roman oppressor who holds sway over their land. His function is to 'save his people from their sins'—that is the meaning of his name Jesus (1:21). By divine revelation it is made known to his disciples that he is 'the Messiah, the Son of the living God' (16:16f.). He is recognized by the demons as Son of God (8:29), but they are forbidden to make him known; God himself, speaking in 'a voice from heaven', acknowledges that Jesus is his 'beloved Son' (3:17; 17:5). His disciples are moved to worship him as Son of God, when they witness his power to walk on the waters of the lake while the winds are high, and to save Peter from sinking (14:33). But they are forbidden to make him known as Messiah (16:20), or to tell of his transfiguration into his glorious heavenly form until he is raised from the dead (17:9). During his ministry his Messianic dignity and his unique relationship to God are hidden. He is known in his true being only to the Father, and 'no one knows the Father except the Son and any one to whom the Son chooses to reveal him' (11:27). His function is 'not to be served, but to serve, and to give his life as a ransom for many' (20:28). This is a hard lesson for his disciples to learn; they cannot accept the thought that he, whom they know as Messiah and Son of the living God, 'must . . . suffer . . . and be killed, and on the third day be raised'; but when Peter gives voice to their horror at the very idea, Jesus warns him sternly that he is siding with Satan (16:22f.).

The title Κύριος ('Lord') is seldom given to Jesus in Matthew. Except in the vocative, where it is generally honorific (as in common Greek usage), not cultic, it usually refers to God, following the practice of the LXX translators; in LXX, it renders the Hebrew title Adonai, 'Lord', which had been substituted for the sacred name Yahweh, by then regarded as ineffable. (In Hebrew manuscripts, the consonants of Yahweh [YHWH] continued to be written, but the vowels of Adonai were added, to indicate that Adonai should be read.) It is unlikely that Jesus was called 'the Lord' in his lifetime on earth, but within the first generation of the church, this became his principal title, while 'Christ' became a proper name, often coupled with the personal name Jesus, as the original sense of 'Messiah' faded—it had little meaning for non-Jews—while 'the Lord' was widely used as a cult title; cf. Paul's remark, 'there are many "gods" and many "lords"' (1 Cor. 8:5). But for Christians there could be only one Lord, Jesus Christ, as for them there was only one God, the Father (v. 6). To Paul and to the churches of the Gentiles in general the basic confession is, 'Jesus is the Lord', and he will affirm that 'the word of faith' which he preaches can be summed up as teaching that 'if you confess with your lips that Jesus is Lord, and believe in your heart that God has raised him from the dead, you will be saved' (Rom. 10:8f.). The Jesus of Matthew, on the other hand, warns his hearers that 'not every one who says to me, "Lord, Lord" shall enter the kingdom of heaven, but only those who do the will of my Father who is in heaven' (7:21).

To address a person as *Kyrie*, in Greek, does not ordinarily mean that you regard him as a divine being, any more than our 'Sir' indicates that he is a knight. Jesus is addressed as Kyrie, but so is Pontius Pilate (27:63), who was certainly not worshipped as a god by the chief priests and Pharisees. Yet Matthew imposes a remarkable limitation on its use in addressing Jesus; he confines it to disciples and those who ask his aid. Even Judas is not allowed to address him as Kyrie, but only as Rabbi (26:25, 49). Scribes and Pharisees do not address him as Kyrie, but as Teacher (διδάσκαλε). It is apparent from this that Matthew feels that there is something more than ordinary courtesy involved when Jesus is addressed as Kyrie— it verges on the Christian cultic sense of 'Lord Jesus'. Only when they appear before him for judgement do the condemned call him Kyrie (7:22; 25:44), and then it is to hear him pronounce their doom.

But in all his work, Matthew lays stress on the practical aspect of the supreme greatness of Jesus, on its significance for the direction of human life, rather than on the nature of his relationship to God. He is the one who must be obeyed, whose words must be heard and 'done'—made the foundation of life. It is to him that all must render account at the Day of Judgement, and all will be judged on the basis of how they have responded to him by doing the will of his Father in heaven. Professions of faith in him, even if they are accompanied with evidence of miracles done in his name, will avail nothing (7:21f.). If they have ministered to human need—the want of food, drink, and clothing; imprisonment, sickness, the loneliness of the stranger in a strange land—he will take it as service to himself; if they have neglected such responsibilities (for others) he will take it as neglect of him (25:31–46). He will disown those who have disowned him on earth, and will acknowledge as faithful those who have acknowledged him on earth (10:32f.).

In this Gospel, the theme of Judgement is all-pervasive. Jesus is not always involved; it is God, the Father in heaven, who refuses forgiveness to those who refuse to forgive others (6:15; 18:35). But judgement is unquestionably the principal function of Jesus—not indeed in his earthly ministry, but in his glorious coming as Son of man. And the punishment of the damned is described in far more vivid terms than the bliss of the blessed. They are not only excluded from the kingdom of heaven, but are cast into the outer darkness, where nothing is heard but weeping and gnashing of teeth, while the blessed enjoy the festive banquet with Abraham, Isaac, and Jacob (8:11f.). They are sent to suffer eternal punishment, in 'the eternal fire prepared for the devil and his angels' (25:41, 46), while the blessed inherit the kingdom prepared for them from the beginning of the world, in 'eternal life' (vv.34, 46). The good and faithful slaves are invited to 'enter into the joy' of their Lord (25:21,23) while the wicked and slothful slave is condemned to the outer darkness (v.30). Darkness and fire are the lot of the damned—above all, the figure of the Gehenna of fire, the furnace of fire, is mentioned again and again.

The emphasis on Judgement is so pronounced as to cast a sombre pall over the picture of Jesus, in striking contrast to the note of Joy that is sounded over and over in the Gospel of Luke. The Jesus of Matthew provides the fundamental lineaments of the formidable Christus Pantocrator who frowns upon us from the cupolas of Byzantine churches. The terrors of the Day of Judgement hang perpetually over the heads of Matthew's readers.

In Matthew, it must be said that there is little trace of a gospel of 'grace abounding for the chief of sinners'. The name of Jesus is explained as meaning that 'he shall save his people from their sins' (1:21); but in the story of the ministry, his power to save is shown chiefly in the healing of disease and the exorcism of demons (8:13; 9:21f.; etc.) and in rescuing from danger (8:25; 14:30). The doctrine that his death is an atonement for sin is no more than adumbrated in two sayings: the declaration that 'the Son of man came not to be served but to serve, and to give his life as a ransom for many' (20:28), and the words that accompany the giving of the cup in the narrative of the institution of the Eucharist, 'This is my blood of the covenant which is poured out for many for the forgiveness of sins' (26:28). It is not developed; in fact, apart from these two sayings, the *theologia crucis* is almost as totally lacking as in the Gospel of Luke.

VII   THE QUESTION OF SOURCES

The Gospel of Matthew was published around the turn of the first century, some seventy years after the crucifixion (see sec.III, p.7). From what sources did its author derive such information as he is able to give us about Jesus of Nazareth and how was it transmitted during the intervening years?

We have to keep firmly in mind that Jesus himself left nothing in writing and did not commission his followers to make records of his words and deeds for the use of future generations. For some years, his sayings and the stories of his deeds were preserved only in the memories of those who had heard and seen him, and were transmitted to others by word of mouth. The oral tradition was still very much alive in the time of Matthew. We do not know just when anything of this was committed to writing; we can only say that it is likely that notes of some kind were prepared for the use of teachers and preachers as they moved from place to place to spread the gospel message. It is not too bold to conjecture that the need of written materials increased as the mission spread beyond the ranks of the Jewish people into areas of Gentile population, and especially to Greek-speaking people who would not be acquainted with the Aramaic of Palestine;[7] the missioners would need translations of such elements of the tradition as they wished to use in their preaching and teaching. It is not unlikely that some of the material would

---

[7] The common language of Palestine was Aramaic, from the sixth century BC, after the capture of Jerusalem by Nebuchadnezzar (587 BC) and the ensuing Exile. Hebrew appears to have survived principally as a literary language, like Latin in mediaeval Europe. From the time of Alexander (late fourth century BC), Greek largely superseded Aramaic for official purposes, and was the

be committed to writing within the first decade of the church's activities, though no written sources have been found of so early a date.

It is generally held that the Gospel of Mark represents the first attempt to compose a connected account of the ministry of Jesus, and that this book was published towards the year 70, not long before or after the fall of Jerusalem to the Romans under Titus. Mark then provided the first written source for Matthew, and the only one that has survived. The Markan narrative is taken over almost in its entirety by Matthew, with striking abbreviation. In addition to Mark, the comparison with Luke has led most scholars to hold that he made use of a second source, commonly designated by the symbol Q (*Quelle*, 'source'), which was also employed by Luke. There is wide acceptance of this Two-Document Hypothesis, and it will be found that in the great majority of articles and monographs it is taken for granted.

The priority of Mark has never been totally accepted. Until recent times, Roman Catholic scholars held to the ancient theory, which goes back at least to Augustine, that Matthew was the first to write a Gospel, that he wrote it in Aramaic, and that Mark was dependent upon Matthew, and not vice versa. This theory was actually prescribed by the Pontifical Biblical Commission in a formal pronouncement (19 June 1911). This pronouncement is no longer held to be binding on scholarly investigators, and ever since the publication of the papal bull *Divino Afflante Spiritu* (1943), nearly all scholars of the Roman church have come to hold to the priority of Mark, and to affirm that our Matthew is not a translation of a supposititious 'Aramaic Matthew', but a work based almost entirely on Greek sources (including Mark and Q). There is no longer any confessional difference in the approach to this question. Some Roman Catholics still maintain the priority of Matthew (Dom B.C. Butler, *Originality*; in French, notably L. Vaganay, *Le problème*

---

principal language of the Greek cities of the Decapolis. The Roman occupation under Pompey (63 BC) inevitably brought with it a certain amount of Latin, but official documents were as a rule published in Greek, as in the centuries of Ptolemaic and Seleucid domination. But Aramaic continued to be the language of the masses, and 'Jesus must have conversed in the Galilean dialect of Aramaic, and His teaching was probably almost entirely in Aramaic' (Black, *Aramaic Approach*, p.16).

There has been much debate on the question; the most satisfactory account of the linguistic situation is that given by J.A. Fitzmyer in his article 'The Languages of Palestine in the First Century AD' (*CBQ* 32, 1970, pp. 501–531).

synoptique, X. Leon-Dufour, and others), and so do some Protestants (Adold Schlatter, *Matthäus*, and throughout his life; W.R. Farmer, *The Synoptic Problem*, see below, and others). But among scholars of all confessions there is an overwhelming majority in favour of the priority of Mark, so that V. Taylor was able to assert, as 'significant of the stability of critical opinion', that 'in a modern commentary it is no longer necessary to prove the priority of Mark' (*Mark*, p.11).

On the other hand, it is evident that there is extensive disagreement over the validity of the Q hypothesis. A certain number of scholars prefer to explain the non-Markan parallelisms between Matthew and Luke on the theory that Luke had read Matthew and employed him as his source for these passages. This was the view of J.H. Ropes of Harvard (*The Synoptic Gospels*, 1934), and of M.S. Enslin (*Christian Beginnings*, 1938); and it was argued forcefully by Austin Farrer in his essay 'On Dispensing with Q', in the volume of *Studies in Memory of R.H. Lightfoot* (1955). More recently, it was supported by W.R. Farmer, *The Synoptic Problem* (1964). But the arguments against such dependence of Luke on Matthew are hard to combat. This theory would require us to imagine that Luke, having the structured Sermon on the Mount of Matthew before him, discarded great parts of it and scattered the remainder over six different chapters; and that he presented as a declaration of 'the wisdom of God' a saying which he found attributed directly to Jesus in his Matthaean source (Lk.11: 49–51; Mt.23:34–36). In these and many other passages, the similarities and differences between the two evangelists are much more plausibly explained on the hypothesis of the independent use of a common source—that is to say, Q. It remains possible that Q is not to be understood as a more or less fixed unitary source, but as the aggregate of a number of sources which have been used by Matthew and Luke independently of one another.

Against all these attempts to dispense with Q, it must be remarked that there are numerous efforts to investigate Q on the principles of redaction criticism, as a relatively stable document which may reveal the leading ideas and methods of its compiler. A review of recent literature (to 1970) is given by M. Devisch in his paper, 'Le document Q, source de Matthieu. Problématique actuelle' (*L'Evangile selon Matthieu: Rédaction et Théologie* ed. M. Didier, *BETL*, XXIX, 1972, pp. 71–97). Research along this line is being actively pursued by a number of American and German scholars; see the article by R.D. Worden, 'Redaction Criticism of Q: a Survey' (*JBL*, 94, 1975, pp.532–546).

Acceptance of the Two-Document Hypothesis leaves with us the problem of enquiring into the source, or sources, of the considerable amount of Matthew which has no parallel in either Mark or Luke. Sometimes the symbol M is used to refer to all this material; or (perhaps more often) M is made to stand for a document containing discourse material peculiar to Matthew. It is so used, for instance, by G.D. Kilpatrick (*Origins*, chap.2, 'The Documentary Sources'), and is taken for granted by W.D. Davies (*Setting*, pp.387–401; and see the general index under M). T.W. Manson warns against too much reliance on the source M, as reflecting the 'Jewish-Christianity' of the opposition to Paul in the Jerusalem church and elsewhere, and as adulterated by touches of the teaching of John the Baptist (*Sayings*, p.26). But once it is recognized that the materials peculiar to Matthew are at least in part of his own composition (note especially the remarks of J. Jeremias on the 'interpretation' of the parable of the Tares (*Parables*, pp.82f.), and that all of it has been shaped in keeping with his overall editorial and theological intention, it becomes extremely difficult to distinguish effectively between what Matthew received from tradition (oral or written) and what he himself framed, largely in the way of midrashic elaboration and interpretation. The integrity of M, even in the delimited sense suggested by Kilpatrick (*Origins*, p.35), seems to dissolve. And if the peculiar materials are in significant degree the work of Matthew himself, we must consider the possibility, even the likelihood, that these materials give us the primary key to the understanding of his mind, and are not to be regarded as representing the unwary retention of elements which he found in some source and was reluctant to discard, even if they were not wholly in accord with his general conception of Jesus and his teaching. This would appear to be substantially the position taken in the commentary of Fr. H.B. Green in the New Clarendon Bible (1975), and more radically by M.D. Goulder in his Speaker's Lectures, published in 1974 under the title *Midrash and Lection in Matthew*.

The interest of scholars in source criticism faded in the years after the first world war, largely as a result of the rise of form criticism, for which 'it is a matter of indifference in what source any particular unit happens to be found' (Bultmann, *HST*, p. 3). Anton Fridrichsen noted with relief that 'the mania for source analysis has been abandoned', and regards this as one of the 'permanently acquired results' of form criticism, even in its earliest days (*The Problem of Miracle*, ET 1972 [from the original French edition of 1925], p.163, n.5). For redaction criticism, also, the question of sources is of subordinate interest, since the primary concern is to study the Gospel in its ultimate form as the work of an author and theologian. The Two-Document Hypothesis and the general results of form criticism are taken more or less for granted in these studies, and recent challenges to the prevailing hypothesis are left unheeded, without any evidence of a desire to take them seriously.

A word may be said about two of the recent challenges, even though they do not appear to be acquiring any general support. First of all we have the attempt to revive the hypothesis of J.S. Griesbach, the scholar to whom we owe the current use of the terms 'synopsis' and 'synoptic' in the literary criticism of the Gospels. Griesbach held that Luke made use of Matthew, and that Mark made up his Gospel by combining selected pericopes from Matthew and Luke in turn, discarding the greater part of both. No satisfactory explanation seems to be offered, or to be possible, to account for the production of such a limited work. If the churches already possessed Matthew and Luke, how could they be interested in another Gospel which lacked the genealogy and infancy stories, the massive teaching of the Sermon on the Mount, and so many of the great parables (the Good Samaritan, the Prodigal Son, the Marriage Feast, the Talents, etc.)? The revival of this theory is promoted in our day principally by W.R. Farmer (*The Synoptic Problem*, 1964), and by Dom B. Orchard (*Matthew, Luke, and Mark: the Griesbach solution to the Synoptic Problem*, Vol.I of three, 1976). Secondly, we may mention the complex theory of literary relationships propounded by M.-E. Boismard in a commentary based on P. Benoit's *Synopse des Quatre Évangiles en français* (Vol.I, 1965; Boismard's commentaries in Vols. II, 1972, and III, 1977). Boismard postulates no less than four pre-Markan sources (A,B,C, and Q), and a succession of editors. See the discussion of this novel theory in my article 'On the Synoptic Problem: a New Documentary Theory' (*ATR* Supplementary Series No.3, March 1974, pp.15–28).

Questions of source criticism receive only sporadic attention in this commentary. A comprehensive survey of modern critical opinion is given by the late Josef Schmid is his *Einleitung in das Neue Testament* (1973; published as the 6th 'völlig neu bearbeitete' edition of the classic Wikenhauser introduction). See the section 'Die synoptische Frage', pp.272–290. There is nothing comparable to it available at this time in English, but treatments will be found in all the standard Introductions and biblical encyclopaedias. But the decline of interest in these problems of literary relationship which set in with the rise of form criticism continues, and very little success has attended efforts to reawaken it. Nearly all scholars would agree with Philipp Vielhauer that 'there is no alternative to it [the Two-Document Hypothesis] worth mentioning, even though counter-theories are not wanting' (*Geschichte der urchristlichen Literatur*, 1975, p.269).

Bibliography

Titles may be abbreviated in references in the text and the notes, as Allen, *Matthew, etc.*

1 COMMENTARIES ON THE GOSPEL OF MATTHEW

Allen, W.C. *A Critical and Exegetical Commentary on the Gospel according to S. Matthew*, 3rd edn., 1912 (*ICC*)

Benoit, P. *L'Évangile selon saint Matthieu*, 1961

Bonnard, P. *L'Évangile selon saint Matthieu*, 1963 (*CNT* I) [2nd edn., 1970, not available to me]

Gaechter, P. *Das Matthäusevangelium*, 1963

Green, H.B. *The Gospel according to Matthew*, 1975 (*The New Clarendon Bible*)

Grundmann, W. *Das Evangelium nach Matthäus*, 3rd edn., 1972 (Theologischer Handkommentar I)

Klostermann, E. *Das Matthäus-Evangelium*, 2nd edn., 1927

——— *Origenes Matthäus Erklärung*, 3 vols., 1935–41 (Die Griechischen Christlichen Schriftsteller der ersten drei Jahrhunderte, 40–41)

Lagrange, M.-J. *Évangile selon saint Matthieu*, 1927 (Etudes Bibliques)

Lohmeyer, E. *Das Evangelium des Matthäus* [posthumously published], ed. W. Schneemelcher, 1958 (Meyer-Kommentar, Sonderband)

McNeile, A.C. *The Gospel according to St. Matthew*, 1915

Reuss, J. (ed.) *Matthäus-Kommentare aus der griechischen Kirche, aus Katenenhandschriften gesammelt*, 1957

Schlatter, A. *Der Evangelist Matthäus: Seine Sprache, sein Ziel, seine Selbständigkeit* [1929], 6th edn., 1963

Schmid, J. *Das Evangelium nach Matthäus*, 5th edn., 1965 (*RNT* I)

Schniewind, J. *Das Evangelium nach Matthäus*, 8th edn., 1956 (*NTD* 2)

Schweizer, E. *The Good News according to Matthew*, ET D.E. Green, 1975 (from *NTD* 2, 13th edn., 1973)
Wellhausen, J. *Das Evangelium Matthaei*, 2nd edn., 1914

2 OTHER COMMENTARIES

Barrett, C.K. *The Gospel according to John* [1955], 2nd edn., 1978
Beare, F.W. *The First Epistle of Peter*, 3rd edn., 1970
Bernard, J.H. *A Critical and Exegetical Commentary on the Gospel according to St John*, 2 vols., 1928 (*ICC*)
Bultmann, R. *The Gospel of John: A Commentary*, ET G.R. Beasley-Murray et al., 1971 (from the 10th edn. of the Meyer-Kommentar, 1941, as printed in 1964, with supplement of 1966)
Creed, J.M. *The Gospel according to St. Luke*, 1930
Haenchen, E. *Der Weg Jesu: Eine Erklärung des Markus-Evangeliums und der kanonischen Parallelen*, 1966
Hering, J. *La première épître de saint Paul aux Corinthiens*, 1949 (*CNT* VII)
Lightfoot, R.H. *St. John's Gospel: A Commentary* [posthumously published], ed. C.F. Evans, 1907
Loisy, A. *Les Évangiles Synoptiques*, 2 vols., 1907
Moore, G.F. *A Critical and Exegetical Commentary on Judges*, 1895 (*ICC*)
[Strack, H.L. and] P. Billerbeck *Kommentar zum NT aus Talmud und Midrasch*, 6 vols., 1922–1961, cited as Billerbeck, *Komm.*
Swete, H.B. *The Gospel according to St. Mark* [1898], 3rd edn., 1909
Taylor, V. *The Gospel according to St. Mark*, 1955

3 GREEK TEXTS OF THE NEW TESTAMENT

Aland, K., M. Black, C.M. Martini, B. Metzger and A. Wikgren, (eds.) *The Greek New Testament*, 3rd edn., 1975 (United Bible Societies)
——— *Synopsis Quattuor Evangeliorum*, 9th edn., 1976
Legg, S.C.E. *Novum Testamentum Graece secundum Textum Westcotto-Hortianum: Evangelium secundum Matthaeum*, 1940
(Nestle, Eberhard and Erwin) *Novum Testamentum Graece*, now edited by K. Aland et al. (editors of The Greek New Testament of the United Bible Societies), 26th edn., 1979, apparatus criticus prepared by K. Aland and Barbara Aland

Soden, H. von,   *Die Schriften des Neuen Testaments in ihrer ältesten erreichbaren Textgestalt hergestellt*, 4 vols., 2nd edn., 1911–13

Souter, A.   *Novum Testamentum Graece: Textui a retractoribus Anglis adhibito brevem adnotationem criticam subjecit*, 1910; 2nd edn., 1947

Tischendorf, C.   *Novum Testamentum Graece: Editio Critica Octava Major*, 2 vols., 1869–72

4   GENERAL

Bacon, B.W.   *Studies in Matthew*, 1930

BDF *see* Blass and Debrunner

Beare, F.W.   *The Earliest Records of Jesus*, 1962

Benoit, P., M.-E. Boismard, et al. *Synopse des Quartre Evangiles en français*, 3 vols., 1965–77; Vol. II, *Commentary on the Synoptic Gospels and the Johannine Parallels*, M.-E. Boismard, 1972

Black, M.   *An Aramaic Approach to the Gospels and Acts*, 3rd edn., 1967

Blass, F., and A. Dubrunner, ed.; ET R.W. Funk [BDF], *A Greek Grammar of the New Testament and Other Early Christian Literature* (from the 9th–10th German edn.), 1961

Blinzler, J.   *Der Prozess Jesu: Das römische und das jüdische Gerichtsverfahren gegen Jesus Christus auf Grund der ältesten Zeugnisse dargestellt*, 3rd edn., 1960

Bornkamm, G., G. Barth, and H.J. Held   *Auslegung und Überlieferung im Matthäusevangelium*, 1960
   ET: *Tradition and Interpretation in Matthew*, 1963

——— *Jesus of Nazareth*, ET, 1960 (from the German 3rd edn., 1959)

Brown, R.E.   *The Birth of the Messiah: A Commentary on the Infancy Narratives in Matthew and Luke*, 1977

Bultmann, R.   *History of the Synoptic Tradition* [*HST*], ET John Marsh, 1963

——— *Theology of the New Testament*, ET K. Grobel, 2 vols., 1951/55

Burkill, T.A.   *New Light on the Earliest Gospel*, 1972

——— *Mysterious Revelation*, 1963

Burrows, M.   *The Dead Sea Scrolls*, 1956

Butler, Dom C.   *The Originality of St. Matthew: A Critique of the Two-Document Hypothesis*, 1951

Charles, R.H.   *The Apocrypha and Pseudepigrapha of the Old Testament in English*, 2 vols., 1913

——— A Critical and Exegetical Commentary on the Revelation of St. John, 2 vols. 1920 (ICC)

Conzelmann, H.   Die Mitte der Zeit, 1954

Cullmann, O.   Peter: Disciple-Apostle-Martyr, ET F.V. Filson, 1953

Cumont, F.   Lux Perpetua, 1949

Daube, D.   The New Testament and Rabbinic Judaism, 1956

Davies, W.D.   The Setting of the Sermon on the Mount, 1964

(Dehn, G.)   Festschrift für Günther Dehn, ed. W. Schneemelcher, 1957

(Deissmann, A.)   Festgabe für A. Deissmann, 1927

Dibelius, M.   Botschaft und Geschichte, ed. G. Bornkamm, 2 vols., 1953, 1956

——— Die Formgeschichte des Evangeliums, 3rd edn., 1959 (references in the commentary are made to this edition); ET B.L. Woolf, From Tradition to Gospel (based on the German 2nd edn., 1933), 1934

Didier, M., ed.   L'Évangile selon Matthieu: Rédaction et Théologie, (XXIX BETL), 1972

Dodd, C.H.   The Apostolic Preaching and its Developments, 1936

——— The Bible and the Greeks, 1935

——— The Fourth Gospel, 1953

——— Historical Tradition in the Fourth Gospel, 1963

——— The Parables of the Kingdom, rev. edn. 1961

——— Studies in the Gospels, ed. D.E. Nineham, 1955

(Dodd, C.H.)   Christian History and Interpretation, Studies in Honour of C.H. Dodd, ed. W.R. Farmer, et al., 1956

Dupont, J.   Les Béatitudes, 2 vols., 1954; 2nd edn., 1969

Enslin, M.S.   Christian Beginnings, 1938

(Enslin, M.S.)   Understanding the Sacred Text, ed. J. Reumann, 1972

Farmer, W.R.   The Synoptic Problem: A critical review of the literary relationships between Matthew, Mark, and Luke, 1964

Farrer, A.   St. Matthew and St. Mark, 1954

Fohrer, G.   History of Israelite Religion, 1968; ET D.E. Green, 1972

Fridrichsen, A.   The Problem of Miracle in Primitive Christianity, 1925; ET R.A. Harrisville and J.S. Hannan, 1972

Gerhardsson, B.   Memory and Manuscript: Oral Tradition and Written Transmission in Rabbinic Judaism and Early Christianity, 1961 (see the critical remarks of W.D. Davies, 'Reflections on a Scandinavian Approach to "The Gospel Tradition" ', in his Setting of the Sermon on the Mount, Appendix XV, pp.464–480)

Goulder, M.B.   *Midrash and Lection in Matthew*, 1974
Grant, F.C.   *The Earliest Gospel*, 1943
Gundry, R.H.   *The Use of the Old Testament in St. Matthew's Gospel, with special reference to the Messianic hope*, 1975 (SNTS Supplement 18)
Hare, D.R.A.   *The Theme of Jewish Persecution of Christians in the Gospel according to St. Matthew*, 1967 (SNTS Monograph Series 6)
Hastings Dictionary of the Bible, rev. edn., ed. F.C. Grant and H.H. Rowley, 1963
Hennecke, E.   *New Testament Apocrypha*, 2nd edn., ed. W. Schneemelcher, ET R.McL. Wilson et al.; vol. I, *Gospels and Related Writings*, 1963
Hummel, R.   *Die Auseinandersetzung zwischen Kirche und Judentum im Matthäusevangelium*, 1963
Jeremias, J.   *The Parables of Jesus*, rev. edn., 1963; ET S.H. Hooke from the German 6th edn., 1962
Johnson, Marshall D.   *The Purpose of the Biblical Genealogies*, with special reference to the genealogies of Jesus, 1969 (SNTS Monograph Series, 8)
Jülicher, A.   *Die Gleichnisreden Jesu*, 2 vols, 1899; 2nd edn., 1910
Kenyon, Sir F.C.   *Books and Readers in Ancient Greece and Rome*, 2nd edn., 1951
Kilpatrick, G.D.   *The Origins of the Gospel according to St. Matthew*, 1946
Kingsbury, J.K.   *Matthew: Structure, Christology, Kingdom*, 1975
——— *Parables of Matthew in Matthew 13: A Study in Redaction Criticism*, 1969
Kittel, G. and G. Friedrich (eds.)   *Theologisches Wörterbuch zum Neuen Testament*, 10 vols., 1933–1979. ET G.W. Bromiley, *Theological Dictionary of the New Testament*, 10 vols., 1964–1976
Klein, G.   *Die zwölf Apostel: Ursprung und Gestalt einer Idee*, 1961
(Knox, J.)   *Christian History and Interpretation: Studies Presented to John Knox*, 1967
Kümmel, W.   *Introduction to the New Testament* (17th edn. of the Feine-Behm *Einleitung*), ET H.C. Kee, 1975
Lake, K., and R.J. Foakes-Jackson   *The Beginnings of Christianity*, 5 vols., 1920–1923
Liddell, H.G. and R. Scott [L&S]   *A Greek-English Lexicon*, rev. H.S. Jones, 2 vols., 1925–1940
(Lightfoot, R.H.)   *Studies in the Gospels: Essays in Memory of R.H. Lightfoot*, ed. D.E. Nineham, 1955

Loisy, A. *The Birth of the Christian Religion*, ET L.P. Jacks, 1948

Lowe, J. *The Lord's Prayer*, 1962

Manson, T.W. *Ethics and the Gospel*, 1960

—— *The Sayings of Jesus*, 2nd edn., 1949

Marxsen, W. *Der Evangelist Markus*, 1956; ET, *Mark the Evangelist*, R.A. Harrisville, 1969

Massaux, E. *Influence de l'Évangile de saint Matthieu sur la littérature chrétienne avant saint Irénée*, 1950

Metzger, B.M. *A Textual Commentary on the Greek New Testament*, 1971

Meye, R.P. *Jesus and the Twelve: Discipleship and Revelation in Mark's Gospel*, 1968

Moore, G.F. *Judaism in the First Centuries of the Christian Era; The Age of the Tannaim*, 3 vols., 1927–1930

Moule, C.F.D. *The Birth of the New Testament*, 1962

Moulton, J.H., et al. *A Grammar of New Testament Greek*, 4 vols., 1906–76; Vol.I., *Prolegomena*, J.H. Moulton [1906], 3rd edn., 1908; Vol.II, *Accidence and Word-Formation*, W.F. Howard, 1919; Vol.III, *Syntax*, N. Turner, 1963; Vol.IV, *Style*, N. Turner, 1976

Mowinckel, S. *He that Cometh*, 1951; ET G.W. Anderson, 1954

Neirynck, F. *The Minor Agreements of Matthew and Luke against Mark*, 1974 (*BETL* 37)

Nilsson, M. *Geschichte der griechischen Religion*, 2 vols., 2nd edn., 1955–1961 (Handbuch der Altertumswissenschaft)

—— *Greek Folk Religion*, 1940

—— *Greek Piety*, 1948

Orchard, Dom B. *Matthew, Luke, and Mark: The Griesbach Solution to the Synoptic Problem*, 3 vols., projected; Vol.I, 1976

Pittenger, N. *Rethinking the Christian Message*, 1956

(Quasten, J.) *Kyriakon: Festschrift Johannes Quasten*, ed. P. Granfield and J.H. Jungmann, 2 vols., 1970

Rigaux, B. *Témoignage de l'évangile de Matthieu (Vers une histoire de Jesus, II)*, 1967

(Robert, A.) *Mélanges bibliques rédigés en l'honneur de André Robert*, 1957

Ropes, J.H. *The Synoptic Gospels*, 1934

Schmid, J. *Einleitung in das Neue Testament*, 1973 (published as the 6th edn. of A. Wikenhauser's *Einleitung*, but actually a radically new work)

Schmithals, W. *The Office of Apostle in the Early Church*, 1961; ET J. Steely, 1969

Schürer, E.   *The History of the Jewish People in the Age of Jesus Christ (175* BC — AD *135)*, New English Version, rev. and ed. G. Vermès and F. Millar, Vol. I, 1973

Smith, M.   *Tannaitic Parallels to the Gospels*, 1951 (JBL Monograph Series 6)

Soiron, Th.   *Die Logia Jesu*, 1916

Stendahl, K.   *The School of St. Matthew and its Use of the Old Testament*, 1954; 2nd edn., n.d. [1967]

Strecker, G.   *Der Weg der Gerechtigkeit: Untersuchung zur Theologie des Matthäus*, 2nd edn., 1966

Streeter, B.H.   *The Four Gospels: A Study of Origins*, 1924

Suggs, M.J.   *Wisdom, Christology, and Law*, 1975

Taylor, V.   *The Formation of the Gospel Tradition*, 1935

——— *The Life and Ministry of Jesus*, 1955

——— *The Names of Jesus*, 1953

Torrey, C.C.   *The Four Gospels: A New Translation*, 1933

——— *Our Translated Gospels*, 1935

Trench, R.C.   *Notes on the Parables of Our Lord*, 1906

Trilling, W.   *Das wahre Israel*, 1959; 2nd edn., 1964

Trocmé, E.   *La formation de l'évangile selon Marc*, 1963; ET P. Gaughan, 1975

Vaganay, L.   *Le problème synoptique*, 1954

Weiss, J.   *A History of Primitive Christianity*, ET Four Friends (F.C. Grant et al.), 1937

Wellhausen, J.   *Einleitung in die drei ersten Evangelien*, 2nd edn., 1911

Wikenhauser, A.   *Einleitung in das Neue Testament*, 2nd edn., 1956; ET J. Cunningham, 1958; 6th edn., see under J. Schmid

(Wikenhauser, A.)   *Synoptische Studien Alfred Wikenhauser dargebracht*, ND [1953]

(Willoughby, H.-R.)   *Early Christian Origins: Studies in honour of H.-R. Willoughby*, ed. A. Wikgren, 1961

Windisch, H.   *The Meaning of the Sermon on the Mount*, ET S.M. Gilmour, 1961

Winter, P.   *On the Trial of Jesus*, 1961; 2nd edn., ed. T.A. Burkill and G. Vermes, in *Studia Judaica I,* 1973

5   ARTICLES

I have renounced, somewhat reluctantly, any attempt to list even selected articles on the Gospel of Matthew from learned journals, Festschriften, and Acta (such as the papers included in the five volumes of addresses delivered at the successive Oxford Congresses of New Testament [lately, Biblical] Studies). Not only are the numbers overwhelming, but they continue to be produced by scores in every year that goes by.

Virtually all important articles, as well as books and reviews, are listed within a year or two of publication in the *Elenchus Biblio-graphicus Biblicus*, edited by P. Nober for the Biblical Institute Press at Rome. Each annual volume contains several pages of listings under *Matthaeus*; and to this must be added a larger number under *Vita Christi* (from thirty to fifty pages) which will often work with Matthaean materials.

Still more extensive listings, though limited to articles from periodicals, are given in the annual volumes (from 1954) of the *Internationale Zeitschriftenschau für Bibelwissenschaft und Grenz-gebiete*.

For a much more extensive bibliography, see W.D. Davies, *The Setting of the Sermon on the Mount*, pp. 481–504.

Translation
and Commentary

Prelude
The Nativity of Jesus

Mt. 1:1–2:23

Matthew begins his Gospel with a genealogical table in which he traces the descent of Jesus from Abraham through David and his successors in the royal line of Israel, the people of God. The last figure in the list, before Jesus himself, is Joseph, the husband of Mary the mother of Jesus, even though the following section will make it clear that Joseph is not in fact the father of Jesus. It would be wrong to conclude, as is often done, that the two sections are not related—that the genealogy has been constructed independently of the nativity story and in ignorance of the belief that Jesus was born of a virgin. On the contrary, since Matthew himself believes that the mother of Jesus was a virgin at the time of his conception and of his birth, and also regards it as essential that Jesus should be the legitimate heir to the Davidic monarchy, he can establish the Davidic lineage of Jesus only by postulating his adoption into the royal line. Such an adoption, to be valid, could only be made by one who himself stood in the line of succession to the throne. For the purposes of the evangelist, therefore, it is necessary to establish the Davidic ancestry of Joseph. The genealogy actually paves the way for the nativity story. When Joseph obeys the command of the angel and takes his betrothed Mary to his home, he thus accepts as his own the child that has been conceived in her womb, and thereby gives him a legitimate place in the Davidic line. The Messiah must be 'a son of David', if he is to inherit the kingship.

1   THE GENEALOGY OF JESUS *1:1–17*

¹ The book of the genealogy of Jesus Christ, son of David, son of Abraham.

² Abraham begot Isaac, Isaac begot Jacob, and Jacob begot Judah and his brothers. ³ Judah begot Phares and Zara by Tamar, Phares begot Hesrom, Hesrom begot Aram, ⁴ Aram begot Aminadab, Aminadab begot Naasson, Naasson begot Salmon, ⁵ and Salmon begot Boes by Rahab. Boes begot Obed by Ruth, and Obed begot Jessai, ⁶ and Jessai begot David the king.

David begot Solomon by the (former) wife of Ourias, ⁷ and Solomon begot Roboam, Roboam begot Abia, Abia begot Asaph, ⁸ Asaph begot Josaphat, Josaphat begot Joram, Joram begot Ozias, ⁹ Ozias begot Joatham, Joatham begot Achaz, Achaz begot Hezekias, ¹⁰ Hezekias begot Manasse, Manasse begot Amos, Amos begot Josias, ¹¹ and Josias begot Jechonias and his brothers at the time of the deportation to Babylon.

¹² After the deportation to Babylon Jechonias begot Salathiel, Salathiel begot Zorobabel, ¹³ Zorobabel begot Abioud, Abioud begot Eliakim, Eliakim begot Azor, ¹⁴ Azor begot Sadok, Sadok begot Achim, Achim begot Elioud, ¹⁵ Elioud begot Eleazar, Eleazar begot Matthas, Matthas begot Jacob, ¹⁶ and Jacob begot Joseph the husband of Mary, from whom was born Jesus who is called Christ.

¹⁷ So there were fourteen generations in all from Abraham to David, and from David to the deportation to Babylon fourteen generations, and from the deportation to Babylon until the Christ fourteen generations.

That the genealogy is artificial hardly needs to be demonstrated. No ancient society kept records which extended unbroken over so long a period as extends from Abraham to Christ. The greater part of the list is drawn by Matthew from the first three chapters of 1 Chronicles; this provides the names as far as Zorobabel (*Heb*. Zerubbabel); from that point on, the Chronicler continues with the descendants of Hananiah, the second son of Zerubbabel (Abioud is not mentioned), and we have no means of knowing where Matthew found the remaining names in his table. In the Lukan genealogy of Jesus (Lk. 3:23–38, proceeding in the reverse sequence, from Joseph to Adam, and so to God), the list includes eighteen names between Zerubbabel and Joseph where Matthew gives only nine; and all the names over this stretch are different, even to those of the father and grandfather of Joseph.

But Matthew adds a further touch of the artificial, in that he divides his list into three periods of fourteen generations each, with intermediate dividing points at the establishment of the monarchy under David and its temporary overthrow at the deportation to

Babylon. But he is able to arrive at this neat scheme of three equal periods only by doing violence to his sources. His second group (from David to the deportation) has been reduced to fourteen by the omission of three names from the Chronicler's list between Joram and Ozias (Uzziah); and in the third group we can make up the count of fourteen only by including Jeconiah a second time or by counting in the Virgin at the end, in addition to Joseph. It is clear that he attaches great significance to the number fourteen, and the most probable explanation for this is that he sees in it a mystical meaning. Fourteen is the sum of the numerical values of the three letters that make up the name of David in Hebrew (*daleth, waw, daleth* = 4 + 6 + 4). In his mind, this number reflects the thought that in Jesus the promises of God to Israel are brought to fulfilment, and that the appointed channel of fulfilment is the Davidic monarchy in the person of the 'son of David' who will be acknowledged also to be the Son of God. This kind of number symbolism has no longer any appeal to us, but it is not unusual in the world in which Matthew lived.[1]

The genealogy, in accordance with Jewish custom, is reckoned in the male line, but Matthew mentions four of the mothers—Tamar, Rahab, Ruth and 'the wife of Ourias' (Bathsheba). Each of these marks a certain irregularity in the line of descent. Tamar was not the wife of Judah, but the widow of two of his sons, whom she married in succession without bearing children to either of them; when Judah failed to give her his third son in marriage, in keeping with the levirate law, she entrapped him by putting on the garments of a harlot and offering herself to him by the roadside (Gen. 38). Rahab was an alien, a harlot of Jericho who gave shelter to the Hebrew spies (Josh. 2). (The Old Testament makes no mention of a marriage to Salmon, or of children; later Jewish traditions make her a wife of Joshua.) Ruth was another alien, a Moabite woman who became a proselyte to Israel after the death of her first husband; according to the law, no Moabite could ever be admitted to the holy community of Israel, not even after ten generations (Deut. 23:3). The wife of Uriah was seduced by David while her husband was away, fighting David's battles; after his death, which was most shamefully contrived by David, she was married to the king and remained his principal

[1] Johnson, Marshall D., *The Purpose of the Biblical Genealogies, with Special Reference to the Genealogies of Jesus*. SNTS Monograph Series, 8. Cambridge, 1969.

Hood, Rodney T., 'The Genealogies of Jesus', in (Willoughby, H.R.) *Early Christian Origins*, ed. A.K. Wikgren, Chicago, 1961, pp. 1–15.

wife until his death (2 Sam.11; 1 Ki.1,2). Many commentators are persuaded that these names are introduced with an apologetic motive, to discount the effect of Jewish slanders on the legitimacy of Jesus and the chastity of his mother, but the force of the suggestion is diminished by the observation that all but Rahab are taken directly from Matthew's source (1 Chron.2:4; 3:5). It is perhaps significant, for Matthew, that all four of them are aliens—Canaanite, Moabite, Hittite—the royal line did not hold to the laws of racial purity. Is there some hint that the community to be founded by the Messiah will not restrict its membership to the race of Israel?

Strange though it may seem to modern commentators, no moral stigma was attached to these women in Jewish tradition. In Aramaic Targums, in various midrashim, in the Talmud, and in synagogue poetry, Tamar is not represented as an alien or a sinful woman, but as one whose whole action was governed by the divine purpose in Israel's history. She desired the grace, which was accorded to her, of a place in the line of descent which was to lead on to David and eventually to the Davidic Messiah (Renée Bloch, 'Juda engendra Phares et Zara de Tamar', in *Mélanges bibliques rédigés en l'honneur de André Robert* (Paris, 1957), pp. 381–89). Rahab actually finds a double place in the honour rolls of the Christian church; as an example of faith (Heb.11:31), and as one who was 'justified by her works' (Jas.2:25). These Christian writers are undoubtedly drawing upon Jewish tradition. There is reason to believe that in traditions known to Matthew, Ruth and Bathsheba were similarly lauded.

Verse 1 may be taken as a heading for the genealogy (so in *NEB*: 'A Table of Descent', and in *RSV*: 'The book of the genealogy'). It seems likely, however, that it is intended to be at the same time the title of the entire Gospel. The phrase βίβλος γενέσεως suggests the title of the first book of the Bible, given in LXX as Γένεσις (whence our *Genesis*), and conveys the thought that this will be the story of the New Creation. John makes the same point by opening his Gospel with the words ἐν ἀρχῇ, taken directly from the LXX of Genesis 1:1, and giving a literal rendering of the accepted Hebrew title of the book, *b'rēshīth*. It will be noted that 'the book of the generations of Adam' (Gen.5:1—in LXX, ἡ βίβλος γενέσεως ἀνθρώπων: 'the book of the genesis of men') is followed by a combination of genealogy and narrative.

The name Ἰησοῦς is used in LXX as the rendering of 'Joshua', but it is formed upon an abbreviated form of the Hebrew name (*Y'shua* for the older *Y'hoshua*—'Yahweh saves'), which came into use in Persian times and was abandoned after the first century AD, when 'the name "Jesus" became unspeakable for Jewry' (Schlatter). The Hebrew name is rendered Joshua in English.

χριστός (verbal adjective from χρίζω—'anoint') is the Greek rendering of the Hebrew *Mashiah*, the Greek transliteration Μεσσίας (whence the Latin *Messias* and our 'Messiah') is affected by the Aramaic form of the participle. The rite of anointing, in Israel, marked the investiture with the sacral kingship. The king of Israel is 'the Lord's Anointed'; his person is inviolate—it is a *religious* offence to strike at him; and he is the bearer of the divine blessing for his people, which enables him to lead them to victory over their enemies and to assure their general prosperity and well-being (1 Sam. 10:1; 26:9ff., etc.). In the Judaism which developed after the Babylonian Captivity, when the monarchy had ceased to exist, 'the Messiah' came to be used of the King that was to be, whenever it should please God to 'restore the kingdom to Israel' (Acts 1:6). The hope of restoration took many different forms, but it was frequently associated with the belief that the King-to-be would be a scion of the royal line of David—a 'son of David'. This did not carry with it any thought that he would be a divine being who would come down from heaven. He would be a monarch of earthly race who would receive the fulness of the divine blessing and so fulfil the ideals and hopes that had been disappointed in all his predecessors. It is unlikely that Jesus himself ever claimed to be the Messiah, or thought of his mission in anything like the traditional Messianic categories; but the title was certainly attributed to him by his disciples as soon as they were convinced that he had risen from the dead. To Matthew, it is of cardinal importance; the demonstration that Jesus is indeed the Messiah, though his own people have repudiated him, is one of the main themes of his entire Gospel.

As 'Son of David', then, Jesus fulfils all the promises that God had made through the ancient prophets for the restoration and blessing of Israel under the rule of a future descendant of David, the legitimate heir of the divinely ordained monarchy. As 'Son of Abraham', Jesus fulfils the promise made to the founder of the holy community that he would be 'the father of a multitude of nations', and that in him 'all the families of the earth' would be blessed (Gen.17:6; 12:3; cf. Gal. 3:8,15–18,29).

The genealogy as a whole stresses the continuity between the mission of Jesus and the history of Israel, and paves the way for the doctrine that the church which Jesus will found (Mt.16:18) is the true Israel of God and the heir of all the promises.

2   THE ANNUNCIATION TO JOSEPH *1:18–25*

¹⁸ This is how the birth of Jesus Christ came about. Mary his mother was betrothed to Joseph, and before they took up life together it was found that she was with child, by the Holy Spirit. ¹⁹ Joseph her husband, being a righteous man and having no wish to expose her to open shame, resolved to divorce her without publicity. ²⁰ But when he had formed this plan, an angel of the Lord appeared to him in a dream and said: 'Joseph, son of David, do not fear to take Mary your wife to your home, for that which is conceived in her is formed by the Holy Spirit. ²¹ She will bear a son, and you will give him the name Jesus, for he shall save his people from their sins.' ²² All this came about in order that the word spoken by the Lord through the prophet might be fulfilled—the word which declares:

> ²³ Behold, the virgin shall conceive and bear a son,
> And they shall give him the name Emmanuel

(which means, in translation, 'God with us'). ²⁴ When he awoke from his sleep, Joseph did as the angel had charged him, and took Mary to his home as his wife. ²⁵ And he had no conjugal relations with her until she bore a son; and he named him Jesus.

The final entry in the genealogical table is conspicuously different from all that precedes it. In place of the regular ἐγέννησεν ('begot'), with Joseph we find the phrase, in itself enigmatic, which describes him as 'the husband of Mary, of whom was born Jesus, who is called Christ' (v.16). In the pericope which follows it is made clear that while Mary was the mother of Jesus, Joseph was not his father, yet there was no unchastity involved. The disquietude of Joseph over the discovery of Mary's pregnancy is dispelled by the assurance that 'that which is conceived in her is of the Holy Spirit' (v.20). The part of Joseph is to give Mary's child his place in the Davidic succession by proceeding with the marriage (taking her to his home as his wife), and so making Jesus legally his son and heir. It is not precisely an adoption, but rather an acknowledgement of a child born in wedlock. Jesus inherits his title 'son of David' by this action of Joseph.

The story presupposes the contemporary Jewish marriage customs. Although Matthew speaks of Joseph and Mary as 'husband' and 'wife', he explicitly states that as yet Mary was 'betrothed' (μνηστευθείσης, v.18) to Joseph, but that they had not yet 'come together' (συνελθεῖν) —that is, he had not yet completed the marital procedure by taking her to his home (παραλαβεῖν, παρέλαβεν, vv.20,24). In Jewish law, betrothal was as binding as marriage and could not be dissolved except by the same documentation as divorce. With the betrothal, the woman passed from the authority of her father to that of her husband, and he could at any time take her from her parents' home to his own. This taking home of the bride was regarded as the completion of the marriage.

It is often felt that the genealogy of Joseph is irrelevant to the matter, if he was not believed to be the father of Jesus, and that it must have been composed independently of the narrative of the miraculous conception by people to whom the latter story was unknown. But this is to make the error of interpreting an ancient story in terms of modern ideas. The Jewish law and custom of the first century are presupposed throughout. Descent was not traced in the female line, and the mother could not transmit to her child the crown rights of the house of David, even if Davidic descent were claimed for her. The doctrine of the virgin birth, therefore, actually requires that the place of Jesus in the Davidic succession should be secured through adoption or acknowledgement by one who was himself a 'son of David'. The genealogy and the story of the miraculous conception, accordingly, are not incompatible with one another, but complementary.

In keeping with his intention of affirming the place of Jesus in the royal line of inheritance, Matthew fixes our attention on Joseph, and on Joseph as 'son of David'. The severe economy of the narrative is characteristic of this evangelist. He strips away everything that would be extraneous to his main purpose. For this, the spiritual experience of Mary, however interesting it might be in itself, is irrelevant. His readers, we must recall, did not have in their hands the Gospel of Luke with its beautiful story of the Annunciation of the Blessed Virgin; and we have no need to conjecture that it was known to him or to them. If their traditions included anything about the Virgin beyond her name, they had no bearing upon the theme with which the evangelist is dealing, and he passes them over in silence.

VERSE 18: 'Before they came together'—not primarily of sexual intercourse, but of the commencement of life together when Joseph would bring her to his home from that of her parents. There was apparently no further ceremony of marriage, after the betrothal. The point is to make it clear that Joseph was not the father of Mary's child (cf. v. 25).

εὑρέθη—literally, 'was found'. As in French *se trouver*, no thought of 'finding' is involved, and there is no need to ask who first learned of her situation. The Matthaean story does not presuppose the annunciation of the Virgin, as recounted by Luke. The introduction of the phrase 'of the Holy Spirit' at this point anticipates the revelation that is to be made to Joseph by the angel (v. 20).

VERSE 19: δίκαιος, 'just'. It is not easy to understand what Matthew means by 'just' in this context. The word translates the Hebrew *tsadiq*, and with its cognate δικαιοσύνη (Heb. *tsedeq*, or *ts'daqah*—'righteousness' or 'justice') is one of the key terms of the Matthaean vocabulary. It is scarcely capable of carrying the sense of 'kind' or 'merciful'. The unwillingness of Joseph to expose Mary to public shame (δειγματίσαι) is represented—and this is what makes the difficulty—as a function of his 'justice' or 'righteousness', not of his kindness. There is no suggestion that *although* he is a just man he is unwilling to stigmatize her; it is precisely by virtue of his righteous character that he shrinks from exposing her. Yet this unwillingness is not to be attributed to any notion that her conception of a child is due to a miraculous act of divine grace. Since he plans to divorce her at all events, he must be taking it for granted that she is guilty of unchastity. According to the law, if a woman was found guilty of premarital sexual intercourse (with another than her affianced husband) she was to be stoned to death at the door of her father's house (Deut. 22:21). There is no evidence that this penalty was imposed at the time of the Gospel, but a public repudiation would certainly bring lasting shame upon the woman. Viewing the situation as he did, Joseph would be no more than fulfilling his legal duty by charging Mary openly with infidelity and repudiating her.

The unusual expression, then, is a preliminary indication that the 'just man', in Matthew's thought, is not coldly insistent on the prescriptions laid down in the law. The true 'righteousness'—that which 'exceeds the righteousness of the scribes and Pharisees' (5:20) —is expressed in love, given without discrimination to deserving and undeserving alike (5:44–48), and is summed up in conduct based on the Golden Rule (7:12). The 'just' man is merciful, as God is merciful.

VERSE 20: Revelation in dreams is widely known in the ancient world, both in Israel and in the surrounding paganisms. In the temples of Isis, an interpreter of dreams (ὀνειροκρίτης) was regularly found as a member of the temple staff, and at the shrines of Asklepios medical advice was given by the god in dreams to patients who slept in the precincts. Papyrus documents of Hellenistic times tell how Sarapis appeared in dreams to order the construction of temples for his worship; and in the well-known novel of Apuleius, *The Golden Ass*, Osiris appears in dreams both to his priest and to the candidate for initiation to appoint the time and the mode of the novice's admission. In much earlier times, manuals of interpretation ('dream books') were composed in Babylonia and in Egypt. But the background of the Matthaean dream revelations is to be sought primarily in the Old Testament, though there (apart from the apocalyptic visions of the book of Daniel) it is usually God himself who appears in the dream; sometimes the dream visitant is first called an angel and afterwards identifies himself as God (Gen. 31:11, 13). In Greek and Latin literature, the dream figure is usually a deity, but often enough it is an image of a deceased person—as Patroclus appears to Achilles (Homer, *Iliad* 23.65f.) and Palinurus the steersman to Aeneas (Virgil, *Aeneid* 6, 337–83), to plead for the rites that will enable them to find rest among the dead. Matthew is using an imagery, and moving within a realm of notions that were common to the people of his age. The 'angel', however, does not appear in the classical literatures of Greece and Rome. In Israel, the developed doctrine of angels (as distinct from the isolated appearances of the *malach*—'angel of the Lord'—who is often a manifestation of Yahweh himself)[2] belongs to the post-exilic period and owes much to Persian influence. Still more, the later doctrine is developed in relation to the belief in the absolute transcendence of Yahweh, which sets him so completely above the human condition that it is impossible to think of him as communicating directly with mortal men. He must employ intermediaries, and in the New Testament writings he does not speak directly to men but deals with them through angels, who communicate his will or intervene to deliver his servants from danger. On great occasions, however, his voice is heard from the heavens (the Baptism) or from an over-shadowing cloud (the Transfiguration). But the ministry of angels declines in significance as the church of Christ comes to know her risen Lord as forever present in her midst and in the hearts of believers, and to experience his Spirit as guiding 'into all the truth' (Jn. 16:13) and as governing all her activities (Acts 13:2,4, and frequently). The new life initiated through Christ is 'the dispensation of the Spirit' (2 Cor. 3:8).

VERSE 21: The meaning of the name is not to be found in the

---

[2] 'He is always a subordinate minister of Yahweh, although he often appears to be practically identical with Yahweh, so that "angel of Yahweh" and "Yahweh" are mutually interchangeable. In other instances he comes close to the ancient Near Eastern notion of the heavenly vizier who carries out on earth the will of the supreme god at his behest.' Georg Fohrer, *History of Israelite Religion*, ET D.E. Green (Nashville: Abingdon, 1972), p. 174.

Greek Ἰησοῦς ('Jesus'), but in the Hebrew name Joshua which it renders (see on 1:1). 'Since such a play was not possible in Aramaic, a Hebrew original must underlie the verse.' (McNeile, *loc. cit.*) R. Bultmann argues from this that Matthew made use of a Semitic *Grundlage* for the story, but that it cannot have contained the theme of a virgin birth 'unheard of in a Jewish environment', and he asserts roundly that 'the idea of a divine generation from a virgin is not only foreign to the OT and to Judaism, but is completely impossible' (*HST*, p. 291, with n.1). This element must therefore have been added in the Hellenistic recasting of the story. He suggests that in the original form of the story, the angel simply informed Joseph that his son would be the Messiah. It is certain that the particular idea of a virgin birth of the Messiah is not found in Judaism, and indeed there is no trace of the notion of a virgin mother in the stories of miraculous births, following upon a divine promise, in any of the OT stories. But it must be observed that the Hellenistic (and earlier Greek) stories of the birth of a hero by divine generation by no means suggest a *virgin* birth: Zeus, Apollo, Poseidon, or whatever God it may be, is pictured as having sexual intercourse with the maiden of his choice. Often enough he rapes her against her will; the legend of Ion is typical of many more (Euripides, *Ion*, 437–40, 'He (Apollo) takes virgins by force, betrays them, begets sons secretly and cares not if they die'). It is not easy to see how the Matthaean story could have been reshaped to its present form under such influences as these. It is something new in Judaism but is not, for all that, Hellenistic in spirit.

In his article entitled 'Jungfrauensohn und Krippenkind' (1932; republished in *Botschaft und Geschichte* 1 (1953), 1–78), Dibelius tells us that 'if we are to speak of a *Vorgeschichte* of the Christian idea, our questions must be addressed first of all to Hellenistic Judaism' (p. 25). He speaks primarily of the Lukan annunciation story (Lk. 1:26–38), but with reference to Matthew he seems to have in mind mainly the use of the Septuagint—ἡ παρθένος, 'the virgin', as the rendering of the Hebrew *ha'almah* 'the young woman'. He is far from suggesting that the translation gave rise to the story, though he admits that it may have played some part in the emergence of the Christian idea ('it cannot with any certainty be excluded'). But he remarks that the emphasis in the Matthaean narrative is not on the virginity of Mary (as in Luke, esp. in 1:34) but on the miraculous conception of the child in her womb.

The promise of salvation which is carried in the name Jesus is defined in spiritual terms, as salvation from sin. There is an implicit repudiation of the notion that the function of the Messiah is to win an earthly dominion for Israel, or to deliver the nation from subjection to an alien power. His salvation is in the first instance for 'his people' (σώσει τὸν λαὸν αὐτοῦ), that is, Israel, the *laos* that God has formed for himself, to show forth his praise (Isa.43:21). In Hebrew religious thought, it is God who 'will redeem Israel from all his iniquities' (Ps.130:8); 'Israel is saved by the Lord with everlasting salvation' (Isa.45:17). It will become clear as the Gospel story develops that 'Israel' is no longer to be defined in racial or national terms, but that the salvation which God brings through Israel's Messiah is for all mankind. (We must observe that in the body of the Gospel, the function of saving from sin is not emphasized.)

VERSE 22: We now encounter for the first time a formula which Matthew will use, with variations, no less than ten times. In eight of them it begins with a purpose clause—ἵνα (three times ὅπως) πληρωθῇ τὸ ῥηθέν (1:22; 2:15; 2:23; 4:14; 8:17; 12:17; 13:35; 21:4); in the other two it makes the affirmation τότε ἐπληρώθη τὸ ῥηθέν (2:17; 27:9). They differ in important respects from the other citations of Scripture in this Gospel. (F.C. Grant lists 61, in his article 'Matthew, Gospel of' (*IDB* III, pp. 307–11), calls them 'the sixty-one most obvious examples', and remarks that Matthew's collection of OT oracles 'is much fuller than that of any other evangelist—or any other writer in the NT'.) They frequently depend on a combination of the LXX text with the Hebrew, but often 'they show deviations from all Greek, Hebrew and Aramaic types of text known to us, while at the same time they intermingle influences from these' (Stendahl, *School*, p. 97). Here τὸ ῥηθέν ('that which was spoken') was spoken 'by the Lord' (ὑπὸ Κυρίου); in all the other instances it is 'that which was spoken through (διά) the prophet'; and in most of the passages the name of the prophet is given, sometimes erroneously (27:9, 'Jeremiah' by mistake for 'Zechariah').

The citation here, from Isa.7:14, depends for its relevance upon the Greek of the LXX, which rendered the Hebrew *ha'almah* ('young woman') by ἡ παρθένος ('virgin'). In Isaiah, the oracle does not predict a miraculous birth from a virgin, nor does it bear upon the birth of a Messiah in an age still more than seven centuries in the future. It is an assurance to King Ahaz, terrified as he is by the threat of an invasion from the north, that the danger is negligible. The two hostile kings are scornfully described as 'these two smouldering stumps of firebrands' (Isa.7:4, *RSV*), who pose no threat to the king of Israel. The oracle is given as a sign to him; a child will be conceived and born—obviously in the near future—and before he is

out of the nursery the two threatening kingdoms will have lost all
their power. 'Before the child knows how to refuse the evil and
choose the good, the land before whose two kings you are in dread
will be deserted' (v.16). The whole passage bears upon the troubles
of the late eighth century BC, not upon a future Messianic epoch.
The name Immanuel does not carry any implication that the child
who bears it is divine. In the original oracle, it is to be given by way
of a thankful acknowledgement that God has made his presence
known among his people by removing the danger that has threatened;
in the Matthaean passage, it does not convey the doctrine that Jesus
is himself divine, but the conviction of the evangelist that in Jesus,
God is again manifesting his presence in Israel by sending a deliverer.

   The verse of Isaiah shows a number of variant readings in the
principal LXX manuscripts, some of which are probably assimilations
to the text of Matthew's citation. For ἕξει (Aleph, AQ), Codex B
reads λήμψεται; and for καλέσουσιν (undoubtedly an assimilation)
B and A read καλέσεις ('thou shalt call'). The reading of Aleph,
καλέσει ('she shall call') is in accord with the Hebrew (*qereth*). The
generalizing plural 'they shall call' is an Aramaizing equivalent of the
passive, 'he shall be called'.

3   A CYCLE OF INFANCY LEGENDS *2:1–23*

The Matthaean infancy narratives are variations on ancient themes
of myth and legend which recur widely in the Near and Middle East.
The discovery of the child, and his miraculous escape from the
enemies who threaten his life—these are the primary motifs of the
stories in themselves; and they are crossed by the theological pre-
occupations of the evangelist—the fulfilment of prophecy, the
rejection of the Saviour by the rulers of Israel and his acknowledgement by strangers to the covenants of promise, harbingers of the
Gentiles who will be gathered into the church that is to be. The
ancient themes appear in a form familiar to us in the story of Moses,
and it is this that is the immediate model of the Gospel tales; the
experiences of the leader of the Exodus are, as it were, recapitulated
in the great Redeemer who will bring about the final deliverance of
the people of God from the dominion of darkness and will transport
them into his kingdom of love. There is no point in debating the
historicity of such a chain of stories; whatever significance they
possess does not lie in any possible kernel of historical fact which
may be embedded in them, but in the purpose which they are
intended to serve as they are understood by Matthew.

None of the four stories that make up the cycle has any relationship to the cycle found in the Gospel of Luke, nor is it possible to work the two cycles into a common narrative framework.

The Coming of the Astrologers 2:1–12

[1] After Jesus had been born in Bethlehem of Judaea (it was in the days of Herod the king), astrologers from the east arrived in Jerusalem, asking, [2] 'Where is the child that has been born as king of the Jews? We observed his star at its rising, and we came to worship him.' [3] When Herod heard this he was deeply shaken, and all Jerusalem shared his dismay. [4] He convoked a meeting of all the chief priests and scribes of the people and questioned them about the place where the Messiah was to be born. [5] They responded, 'In Bethlehem of Judaea, for so it is written through the prophet:

[6] You, Bethlehem, land of Judah,
>   Are by no means least among the governors of Judah;
> For from you there shall come forth a ruling prince
>   Who will be the shepherd of my people, Israel.'

[7] Herod then summoned the astrologers to meet him secretly and got precise information from them of the time when the star first appeared. [8] He sent them on to Bethlehem with the charge, 'Go and make a careful search for the child, and when you find him, send back word to me, so that I too may go and worship him.'

[9] When they had heard these words of the king they went on their way. The star which they had observed at its rising now led them on until it stood still over the place where the child was, and [10] when they saw the star again, they were filled with the greatest joy. [11] They went into the house and there they saw the child with Mary his mother, and they fell prostrate before him in worship; and they opened their caskets and offered him gifts—gold, frankincense, and myrrh. [12] But as they were given a warning in a dream, bidding them not to turn back to Herod, they took another route for the return to their own country.

The actual birth of the child is not recounted in this Gospel. It is anticipated in the story of the annunciation to Joseph, and it is mentioned as already over in the story of the astrologers. Joseph is the centre of attention in the first story; in the second he is not so much as mentioned, and the attention is directed chiefly to the conflict between the true and the false king. Even the presence of Mary is incidental to the approach of the worshippers to the child king.

It is not an outright historical impossibility that a company of magians from the East came to Jerusalem about the time of the birth of Jesus. Three ancient writers tell us of the visit of such a company to the court of Nero in AD 66,[3] and there is no imperative need to dismiss as absurd the notion that others may have come to the court of Herod the Great some sixty-five years earlier. It is more difficult to suppose that they had read in the heavens the signs of the birth of a great ruler, that their astrological lore had sufficed even to indicate to them that he would be born as King of the Jews, and that their purpose was to worship at his cradle. The credibility of such a story depends upon the value which the reader is prepared to attach to the prognostications of astrologers and to the belief that astrology is an exact science. Such a belief was widely held in the world of that time, not as a superstition of the ignorant, but as the firm faith of educated and influential men—mathematicians, philosophers, and rulers. Astrology was a dominant influence on the minds of men, and was to retain its dominance until modern times. It always had its charlatans, as it has to this day; but in those times it commanded the services of astronomy, mathematics, and philosophy, and was the real religion of many of the most elevated and clear-minded spirits. But it was always a pseudo-science, for it depended upon the theory that the earth is the centre of the universe, and that the planets are living powers, mighty spirit-beings which have the moral characteristics of the gods of the old mythology whose names they bear. It is quite silly for anyone who does not share these beliefs to put any faith in astrology. And it would be equally absurd to suppose that magians of the first century were any more able to read in the stars the signs of coming events in human history on earth than are the columnists who give advice in our own newspapers from day to day to those born under a particular sign of the Zodiac.

It is permissible, but it is not by any means necessary, to postulate a nucleus of bald fact in the story of a visit of Magi to the court of Herod. In a work which was not composed until some years after the death of Nero, this element is sufficiently accounted for as a reflection of the visit of Tiridates and his associates to the court of the Roman Emperor, the more so as Nero's visitors also 'returned to their own country by another way'. The rest of the Matthaean tale is built around a number of traditional motifs of a mythology which may rightly be called international, interwoven with early Christian

---

[3] Suetonius, *Nero* xii; Pliny, *His. Nat. XXX.* 6; Dio Cassius, *Hist.* lxiii.7.

theological presuppositions which give it a distinctive emphasis. The basic theme is the Discovery of the Child, which comes before us in another form in the story of Moses (Ex.11:1–10), but is far older in both Babylonia (the legend of Sargon I) and in Egypt (the finding of Osiris—in this case, it is true, not as a child, but as a dismembered corpse). The discovery of a new star which is interpreted as heralding the birth of a great man is almost a standard feature of Hellenistic legends; perhaps the most familiar is found in the stories of Mithridates of Pontus. The threat to the life of the Child is another very ancient mythological theme; in the Osiris myth, the life of the child Horus is threatened by Set; and in Babylonia the infant Sargon is miraculously preserved from the murderous assaults of his enemies. The Moses story is the immediate inspiration of the Gospel tale, but it in its turn is but a Hebrew reproduction of a much more ancient pattern.

Without making any claim to historicity for the story, it is reasonable to suppose that there may lurk within it some popular remembrance of an appearance of Halley's comet, which was visible in Palestine only a few years before the birth of Jesus. The word ἀστήρ, 'star', is in fact used in Greek of comets also. Père Lagrange was greatly attracted by the suggestion that the star of the Magi was a comet, especially after he witnessed the appearance of Halley's comet in 1910 in the east, and saw it again on 20 January of the following year in the west. He felt that the date of its appearance at that epoch (October of 12 BC) was too early for the birth of Jesus (though in fact there is no compelling reason against supposing such a date for the Nativity); and was therefore inclined to ask if the astronomers could not tell us of another comet which may have appeared a few years later. If we are not thinking of strict historical fact, but of the growth of legend into a form which it assumed two or three generations afterwards, the matter of a few years' difference in dating is negligible. That a comet—or any kind of star, for that matter—should move in such a way as to guide travellers from Jerusalem to Bethlehem, a matter of five or six miles, is indeed inconceivable, let alone that it should hover 'above the place where the child was' (ἐπάνω οὗ ἦν τὸ παιδίον). The comet of 12 BC is indeed said to have given the people of Rome the impression that it was hovering over the city for some time.[4] This is still far removed from the notion of its coming to rest over a particular house!

VERSE 1: The name 'Jesus' picks up the closing verse of chapter 1,

[4] Dio Cassius, *His..* liv.29: τότε ἄστρον ὁ κομήτης ὠνομασμένος ὑπὲρ αὐτοῦ τοῦ ἄστεως αἰωρηθεὶς ἐς λαμπάδας διελύθη.

where this name is given to the child in keeping with the angel's command (1:21). The story itself rests upon the theme that Jesus is the Messiah (Christ), the promised king of Israel. It assumes that the identification of one who has been 'born king of the Jews' with the Messiah is self-evident, and also that the place of his birth can be learned from the ancient scriptures.

'In the days of Herod the king' is a Semitic form of expression (Hos.1:1; Amos 1:1; etc.). Herod was recognized as 'rex socius' by the Romans in 44 BC and died in 4 BC. His 'days' as king, accordingly, extended over a period of forty years, so that the phrase does not give anything like a precise dating for the birth of Jesus, and Matthew provides no other means of arriving at a correct date. Even 25 December, celebrated as the day of his birth, is not fixed by any kind of chronological data, but is the transference to Jesus (in the fourth century) of the birthday of the Unconquered Sun (*dies natalis solis invicti*) from the festival inaugurated at Rome by the Emperor Aurelian in AD 274.

'In Bethlehem of Judaea', so called to distinguish it from another Bethlehem in Galilee, is also given as the birth-place of Jesus in the Lukan narrative (Lk.2:4—7), but this is the only point of contact. In Matthew, Jesus is born at Bethlehem because that is where Joseph and Mary were living; in the Lukan story, they live at Nazareth, and have come to Bethlehem (in the last days of Mary's pregnancy) only because they were obliged to report there for the census ordained by Augustus Caesar and administered by Quirinius, the legate of Syria. (This census took place in AD 6, after Archelaus had been deposed and his tetrarchy of Judaea put under the rule of Quirinius.) Similarly, there is no suggestion in Matthew that Jesus was born in a stable or laid in a manger; when the astrologers find him, he and his mother are in a house, and the reader would naturally assume that it is their own house.

'Then a star, called the comet, riding high above the very city, was divided into torches.'

See also Servius on *Aeneid* ii.801 (in Lagrange, *ad loc.*, p. 28), and Lagrange's comment: 'Mais certainement la vue de la comète qui les avait pour ainsi dire devancés en Occident et qui paraissait suspendue au-dessus de Bethléhem était un signe plus significatif qu'ils etaient arrivés que la disparition de Venus au matin quand Enée vint chez les Laurentes.' And following:

'Il en est de ce signal un peu comme de la voie lactée qui servait de guide aux pèlerins du moyen age et qu'on nommait pour cela le chemin de saint Jacques. Elle ne dispensait pas de toute autre information; tout cela doit s'entendre positis ponendis, l'écrivain ne mettant en relief que le phénomène céleste qui sert de signe' (p. 29).

Matthew is not interested in geography or chronology. If he mentions Bethlehem, it is because he is persuaded that the Messiah *must* be born there to fulfil a prediction made in the prophetic scriptures of Israel. If he mentions Herod, it is not for the sake of a dating, but that he may serve as the false king who trembles at the thought of the coming of the true king, and resorts to desperate measures to eliminate him as a threat to his power.

μάγοι ἀπὸ ἀνατολῶν—the *magoi* from the east are undoubtedly introduced in the character of astrologers, perhaps from Iran, but more likely from Arabia, the source of gold, frankincense, and myrrh, at least according to Hebrew poetic convention (Isa.60:6; Cant.3:6,; etc.; cf. Lagrange *ad* 1,11). The early iconographic tradition represents them uniformly as Persians. 'But attempts to determine the country intended are guesses' (McNeile).

VERSE 2: ἐν τῇ ἀνατολῇ—'at its rising', not 'in the east'; the change from the plural (ἀνατολῶν) of verse 1 is decisive for the meaning here. The moment of a star's appearance above the horizon was of prime importance in astrology. Probably it is assumed that the star appeared at the precise moment of the Saviour's birth (or conception).

ὁ τεχθεὶς βασιλεύς—the one who is king by right of birth, in contrast to the Idumaean usurper who won his kingship by force and guile and by his agility in keeping on the right side of the Roman overlords, no matter who was victorious in the civil wars.

VERSE 3: ἐταράχθη—the verb means literally to 'shake, stir up, throw into turmoil', as of the wind shaking trees, or Poseidon whipping up a stormy sea. Metaphorically, it can be used of any kind of mental or spiritual turmoil. Here it suggests above all fear, with overtones of fury. 'All Jerusalem' shares the fear, rather than the fury; or it may be simply that the citizens are excited and unsettled by the mere suggestion that the Messiah has been born. It is more probable that the evangelist intends to suggest that Jerusalem and the king are united in hostility and fright. The rejection of Jesus in the fulness of his manhood (Mt.27:20–25) is foreshadowed in the reaction of the city to the news of his birth.

VERSE 4: 'The chief priests'—the term includes the high priest in office, his deposed predecessors, and members of the greater priestly families. There was only one High Priest in Israel, and the title ἀρχιερεύς properly belongs to him alone. The more extended use is found also in Josephus.

'Scribes of the people' is an unusual expression; 'elders of the people', on the other hand, occurs in Matthew four times (21:23;

26:3,47; 27:1). The 'people' (λαός) is not the populace in a general sense, or the commons of Israel in contrast to the ruling classes, but the community considered in its religious significance as the 'people of God'. The scribes, in Jewish terminology, were not calligraphers, or town clerks (as in civil usage), but the 'professional exponents and teachers of the law in post-exilic Judaism' (M. Black, *IDB, ad voc.*). It was they, rather than the priests, that would be counted upon to give an authoritative answer to the king's question about the birthplace of the Messiah, if this were indicated in the scriptures. For this there would be no need for a general convocation—one qualified scribe could give the traditional answer.

The oracle of Micah (actually the work of an unknown prophet of a much later era) promises that from the insignificant clan of Ephrathah (which included Bethlehem) would come forth a ruler who would 'stand and shepherd his flock in the name of Yahweh'. It is, accordingly, a Messianic prophecy, and hints that the promised one will be of the Davidic family, but not specifically that Bethlehem will be his birth-place.

VERSE 5: 'It is written'—the wording of the 'formula quotations' cannot be followed, for the scribes cannot speak of a fulfilment of the oracle, since they have no knowledge that the birth of Messiah has taken place. But 'through the prophet' has the same force—the oracle is given by God, and the prophet is merely his mouthpiece.

VERSE 6: The citation is drawn in part from Micah 5:2, and in part from 2 Sam.5:2, but it agrees with neither the Hebrew text nor the Septuagint. In the last line, the change is merely a shift from the second person to the third; the more striking feature of it is that words addressed (in the story of 2 Sam.) to David are transferred to the 'ruling prince' (ἡγούμενος) of the oracle of Micah, who is clearly taken to be the Messiah. The phrases from Micah are much more radically altered. The words γῆ Ἰούδα ('land of Judah') are not found in LXX nor are they represented in the underlying Hebrew. In the second line, Matthew introduces the strong negative οὐδαμῶς ('by no means'), and this actually reverses the meaning of the Hebrew (and of LXX). For 'clans' ('thousands') he has substituted 'rulers'. This change cannot be explained at all from the LXX (χιλιάσιν), but reflects a variant reading in the Hebrew text—the substitution of *'alluphē* ('chieftains') for *'alphē* 'thousands', 'clans'. The result is that a text which read 'little though you are among the thousands (clans) of Judah' is transformed into 'you are by no means least among the governors of Judah'. The third line in

Matthew's citation drastically simplifies LXX (which itself gives a literal rendering of the Hebrew), by omitting μοι ('for me') and substituting the participle ἡγούμενος ('governing', 'ruling prince') for the cumbersome infinite clause of LXX τοῦ εἶναι εἰς ἄρχοντα ἐν τῷ Ἰσραήλ—'to be a leader in Israel'. The fourth line is then added, from 2 Sam.5:2, to indicate the function of the 'ruling prince' in terms of the charge laid upon David by the Lord; in sense this is equivalent to Micah 5:4 which Matthew does not use.

The Hebrew text known to Matthew certainly read Bethlehem, as did LXX. But it is far from certain that the Jews of the time commonly held that the Messiah would be born in Bethlehem, even though the Targum of Micah (*c.* AD 300) renders 'from you Messiah shall come forth before me'. The general Jewish view then and later seems to have been that which is voiced in John 7:27: 'When the Messiah appears, no one will know where he comes from' (cf. Origen, *Contra Celsum* i.51). Since both Matthew and Luke, in wholly independent cycles of infancy narratives, place the birth of Jesus in Bethlehem, it is evident that this was a widespread tradition among Christians; but it cannot be claimed that the tradition was based upon a prior Jewish belief that there the Messiah must be born. If it is not based upon the facts of the case (which is not inconceivable, but improbable), it may well have been an inference from the accepted fact that 'our Lord is sprung from Judah' (Heb.7:14), coupled with the tendency to imagine that the Messiah Son of David must recapitulate the experience of his famous ancestor.

VERSE 7: 'Secretly'—the point of the secrecy is not obvious. If 'all Jerusalem' is in a turmoil over the news that astrologers are in town seeking a newborn Messiah, and if the assembled chief priests and scribes have pointed to Bethlehem as the place of his birth, what purpose can be served by secrecy in the meeting between Herod and the visitors? Perhaps it carries a hint of dark designs brewing in the mind of Herod.

ἠκρίβωσεν . . . τὸν χρόνον, κτλ.—Herod 'secured accurate information of the time'. Exactitude of observation was essential in all astrological calculations, and the precise moment of the heliacal rising of a star was of particular importance. For Herod, such astrological precision was not necessary; he wants to know the age of the child, on the supposition that the star made its first appearance at the moment of his birth, or of his conception. The story does not tell us what answer he received, but perhaps his later action in arranging for the murder of all the infants of the region 'of two years and under' is intended to suggest that it was nearly two years since the rising of the star was observed. The iconography depicts the child as old enough to sit up on his mother's lap to greet the visitors.

VERSE 8: πορευθέντες, ἐλθών—the two participles, almost superfluous, reflect a common Hebraic usage. The use of ἐλθών in this way is particularly frequent in Matthew (cf. ἐλθὼν ἐστάθη (v.9), ἐλθὼν κατῴκησεν (v.23, and again 4:13), etc.).

VERSE 9: The sight of the star would indicate that the astrologers travelled by night, but for the few miles from Jerusalem to Bethlehem such guidance would not be needed, and it is hard to imagine how a star could give any kind of guidance over such a short distance (ten kilometres), or how it could be imagined as standing still over a little village, and even over a particular cottage. It is peculiar, also, that this star moves in a southwesterly direction (leading them on from Jerusalem to Bethlehem), whereas the (apparent) movement of all the stars in the sky is from east to west. J. Schmid (*Matthäus, ad loc.*) remarks that the evangelist thereby 'excludes any kind of natural interpretation', and that 'the star can therefore not be employed for dating'.

VERSE 11: πεσόντες—'falling down' (they worshipped him). The participle emphasizes that this was the true oriental *proskynēsis*, prostration before the king, or the god. (cf. Dan.3:5—'You are to fall down and worship the golden image.') The attempt of Alexander to induce his Macedonians to adopt this Persian custom before him was greeted with scorn. The iconography does not make use of this form of adoration, but generally depicts the Magi, in Persian dress, running forward with small boxes in their hands, in which their gifts are contained.

θησαυρούς—not 'treasures', but the boxes or caskets in which the precious things were contained. (The Protevangelium of James, a second-century infancy Gospel, uses the word πήρα, 'wallet'.)

Gifts of gold and incense are mentioned in the Old Testament as proper to Arabia (Isa.60:6, etc.), and this has led commentators to suggest that the astrologers are thought by the teller of the story to come from Arabia. But gold, incense, and myrrh would be appropriate gifts for a king, whatever the home of the visitors might be.

Nothing is said in the story of the number of Magi, nor is it suggested that they were kings. The number three was probably suggested by the three gifts, and the tradition that the worshippers were kings was perhaps suggested in the first instance by Old Testament passages, such as Isa.60:3, coupled with verse 7, and Psalm 72:10.

VERSE 12: χρηματισθέντες—the verb is generally used of an

oracle given by a god to a worshipper who sleeps in the temple after making his petition. From this custom comes the Vulgate rendering *responso accepto*. Here, as again in verse 22, there is no mention of an angel as the medium of the revelation, nor is God named, but the thought is none the less of a divine intervention.

δι' ἄλλης ὁδοῦ—'by another way'. Much speculation was devoted to imagining the route taken by the Magi on their return. Probably it means no more, to the evangelist, than that they did not return by way of Jerusalem, as they had come. From Bethlehem they could cross the lower Jordan by bridge, or cross the Dead Sea by boat, but legendary imagination was not so easily satisfied and invented extensive tours by land and sea. Meanwhile Herod waits in vain for the astrologers to bring him their information, and while he waits, the Holy Family is given time to escape from danger.

The Flight into Egypt 2:13–15

¹³ After they had gone, an angel of the Lord appeared in a dream to Joseph, to tell him: 'Get up, take the child and his mother and escape to Egypt, and stay there until I tell you; for Herod is going to search for the child, to murder him.' ¹⁴ He rose, took the child and his mother by night, and left for Egypt, ¹⁵ and lived there until the death of Herod; this took place to fulfil the word spoken by the Lord through the prophet: 'Out of Egypt I called my son.'

Egypt and Israel were bound together by geography and history. Egypt had been 'the house of bondage' (Ex.20:2), and God made himself known as the Redeemer of his people when he delivered them. The commandments of the law were grounded on this deliverance, and the young Israelite was taught by his father that 'we were Pharaoh's slaves in Egypt; and the Lord brought us out of Egypt with a mighty hand' (Deut.6:21). But Egypt was also a land of refuge for Israelites who were driven into exile or sought escape from danger at home. Jeroboam fled to Egypt when Solomon planned to execute him (1 Ki.11:40); the prophet Uriah escaped to Egypt when Jehoiakim threatened his life, but he was brought back and put to death (Jer.26:20–23); and Jeremiah himself was carried off into Egypt against his will by a group of Judaean warriors who feared Babylonian vengeance for the murder of the governor Gedaliah (Jer.41:1–2; 43:1–7); centuries later the high priest Onias III fled to Egypt and built a temple in Heliopolis (169–168 BC). The Egypt of the Ptolemies, which controlled Palestine for more than a century after the death of Alexander, was far more friendly to the Jewish people than the Seleucids of Syria.

The story is introduced by Matthew primarily to provide a setting for the citation from Hosea (11:1). There is no reason to suppose that it has any historical basis. Matthew gives the text in the form which it has in the Hebrew; in LXX it reads very differently—ἐξ Αἰγύπτου μετεκάλεσα τὰ τέκνα αὐτοῦ, 'I summoned his children out of Egypt'. In Hosea, the words are an appeal to the ancient deliverance as the ground of Yahweh's appeal to Israel for a renewed loyalty. 'When Israel was a child I loved him, and out of Egypt I called my son. . . . I led them with cords of compassion, with the bands of love' (v.1,4). There is no hint of a reference to the future, or to the career of a Messiah. But Matthew, like all the Jewish interpreters of his time, is not concerned with an historical interpretation. He thinks of Jesus as recapitulating in his person the experiences of his people; he is as it were the embodiment of Israel, and its history is treated typologically. There is something also of the typology of Jesus as the new Moses, whose life is threatened by the tyrant king.

The Massacre of the Infants 2:16–18

[16] When Herod saw that the astrologers had made mock of him, he fell into a furious rage. He sent his men to kill all the children of two years old and under in Bethlehem and all its environs, in keeping with the time that he had ascertained from the astrologers. [17] Thus the word was fulfilled which was spoken through the prophet Jeremiah:

[18] A voice was heard in Ramah,
  wailing and loud lamentation—
Rachel weeping over her children,
  and refusing to be comforted, for they were no more.

Again we have a story which appears to have been developed as a setting for the oracle. Such a massacre is indeed quite in keeping with the character of Herod, who did not hesitate to put to death any who might be a threat to his power, even if they were his own sons. Augustus is said to have made the grim pun that it was better to be Herod's pig (ὗς) than his son (υἱός).

VERSE 18: The words of Jeremiah (31:15) picture 'Rachel', at her tomb in Ramah (about five miles north of Jerusalem) weeping as she watches the columns of captives ('her children') marching along the road into exile, under the guard of the victorious Assyrians, after the fall of the (northern) Kingdom of Israel (2 Ki.17:6). At some later time a tradition arose that she was buried near Bethlehem, by the road to Jerusalem, and this site became a place of pilgrimage. This later tradition is followed by Matthew, and Rachel becomes for him the representative of the mothers of Bethlehem, weeping for their slaughtered infants. The historical background of the Jeremiah passage is wholly lost.

The citation does not agree exactly either with the Hebrew text or with LXX. It appears to be an independent translation of the Hebrew, abbreviated, and possibly influenced by some form of LXX. The relationship with LXX is complicated by the striking differences of text in Greek manuscripts; the text of Codex Alexandrinus stands closer to MT than does that of Codex Vaticanus, and thus has more points of contact with the Matthaean form of the citation. The most significant feature in Matthew is the use of τέκνα, 'children', for the υἱοῖς, 'sons' (Heb. *baneyha*) of the LXX manuscripts, which in this respect are more faithful to the Hebrew. (In LXX, the passage is found in Jer.38:15.)

The Return to the Land of Israel 2:19–23

[19] When Herod died, an angel of the Lord appeared in a dream to Joseph in Egypt and said to him, [20] 'Rise, take the child and his mother and go to the land of Israel, for those who sought the life of the child are dead.' [21] And he rose, took the child and his mother, and went into the land of Israel. [22] But as he heard that Archelaus was reigning in Judaea in succession to his father Herod, he was afraid to go there; but in obedience to an oracle given him in a dream he went on into the district of Galilee [23] and settled there in a city called Nazareth, so that the word spoken through the prophets might be fulfilled: 'He shall be called a Nazarene.'

Herod the Great died in the year 4 BC. The story gives no indication of the age of Jesus and no suggestion of how long the Holy Family stayed in Egypt. Josef Schmid reckons that 'several months at least passed between the coming of the Magi and the death of Herod . . . thus the stay of the Holy Family in Egypt lasted a corresponding length of time.' Père Lagrange is content with 'at least one month', and tells us that 'nothing indicates that the flight into Egypt lasted any longer than that.' In fact, nothing indicates how long it lasted, if it ever took place. Any such calculation, of course, is pointless once it is recognized that we are dealing with legendary materials which lack any trustworthy historical base.

'The land of Israel' was the usual Jewish term for Palestine—a term charged with religious sentiment and the sense of a communal history and destiny under God. It would include Galilee as well as Judaea, and its mention prepares the way for settlement in another place than Bethlehem.

Some time went by after the death of Herod before the question of the succession was finally settled at the court of Augustus. The land was divided between three sons of Herod. Archelaus, who had been designated by Herod himself as his principal successor, was allowed to take over Judaea, with Samaria and Idumaea, but without his father's title of king—he was designated ethnarch. He was promised the title of king if he proved worthy of it. His half-brothers Antipas and Philip were each given the title of tetrarch, and the remainder of Herod's domains were divided between them. Galilee and Peraea were given over to Antipas (called 'Herod' in the later Gospel story); and the north-easterly regions, largely occupied by Gentile populations, were allotted to Philip. Archelaus was indeed a savage ruler and under him the land was continually in an uproar, so that after ten years Augustus sent him into exile in Gaul and put his part of 'the land of Israel' under military government, headed by a Roman prefect. Still, it is hard to say how Joseph knew that he would turn out to be so ferocious, and what reason he might have had for supposing that Antipas would be any less fearsome. But Matthew is not really interested in the moral character of the two rulers. He must bring Jesus to Nazareth—the tradition was fixed on the fact that it was there that he was brought up—and he has Joseph decide for Nazareth not out of any regard for the qualities of the tetrarch but in obedience to an oracle given to him in a dream. This move also, like the flight into Egypt and the return, is made under the direction of God.

The story ends with another of the formula citations so characteristic of Matthew. In this one case, however, it is impossible to find such a citation in any scripture known to us. The broadness of the reference ('through the prophets') is itself an indication that the evangelist did not know just where such words could be found. Jerome pleads that 'in calling on "the prophets" in the plural, he indicates that he has not taken over the words from the scripture, but the sense of them.' (Lagrange, *ad loc.*) But it is still hard to say where he found such a sense, even in different words, anywhere in the scriptures.

On the philological difficulty raised by the use of the adjective Ναζωραῖος, see the article by G.F. Moore in Appendix B to the first volume of 'Prolegomena' of *The Beginnings of Christianity* (ed. K. Lake and R.J. Foakes-Jackson (1920), pp.426–432) under the title 'Nazarene and Nazareth'.

An extensive bibliography covering the discussion is given in the Bauer-Arndt-Gingrich lexicon, *ad voc.* Ναζωραῖος. A brief recent treatment by M. Black (*Aramaic Approach*, pp. 197ff.) brings up again the denial that Ναζωραῖος can be derived from Ναζαρεθ; but the philological difficulties seem to have been adequately dealt with years earlier by Moore (see above) and by Adolf Schlatter (*Der Evangelist Matthäus*, pp.49f.).

A

Preparation for the Public Ministry

Mt. 3:1-4:22

At this point, Matthew takes up the Markan narrative. He tells us nothing of the life of the Holy Family in Nazareth, of the schooling of Jesus, or of his experiences in childhood and youth. He does not even indicate how many years have gone by since Joseph brought Mary and the child back from Egypt and settled with them in the Galilean village. It is only in Luke that we are told that Jesus was now 'about thirty years of age' (Lk.3:23) and that John the Baptist had begun his preaching 'in the fifteenth year of Tiberius Caesar' (Lk.3:1). This has been variously calculated as falling in 26/27 or 27/28 or 28/29 of our era, and there is no hint of how long it was after that before Jesus came down from Nazareth to seek baptism at his hands. We can guess only vaguely that between twenty-five and thirty years have been passed over in silence. As in Mark, Jesus is brought upon the scene unheralded, and apparently unknown except to his family and the inhabitants of Nazareth, where he had grown up.

Building on the opening scenes of the Markan narrative, Matthew now frames an introduction to his own account of the public ministry. This section falls into three parts, as follows:

1. Preparation of the People: the Ministry of John the Baptist 3:1–12
     John Calls Israel to Repentance 3:1–6
     John Rebukes the Leaders of Israel 3:7–10
     John Proclaims the Coming of a Greater One 3:11–12
2. Preparation of Jesus 3:13–4:11
     Jesus is Baptized 3:13–17
     Jesus is Tempted 4:1–11
3. Preparation for the Mission 4:12–22
     Jesus Moves to Capernaum 4:12–17
     Jesus Calls his First Disciples 4:18–22

1 PREPARATION OF THE PEOPLE: THE MINISTRY OF
JOHN THE BAPTIST 3:1–12

John Calls Israel to Repentance 3:1–6

¹ In those days John the Baptist made his appearance, preaching in
the wilderness of Judaea ² on the theme: 'Repent, for the kingdom
of heaven is at hand.' ³ For this is he of whom the prophet Isaiah
spoke when he wrote:

> A voice of one who cries in the wilderness,
> 'Prepare the way of the Lord!
> Make his paths straight!'

⁴ This John wore a cloak of camel's hair with a leather belt around
the waist; his food was locusts and wild honey. ⁵ Jerusalem and all
Judaea began to go out to him, and all the region of the Jordan,
⁶ and they were being baptized by him in the Jordan River, making
confession of their sins.

VERSE 1: 'In those days' is a vague connecting phrase with no
chronological significance; at least, it means 'in the days of which
we are about to speak', not 'in the days of which we have just
spoken'. A similar lack of concern for precise dating has been seen
in the placing of the birth of Jesus 'in the days of Herod the King'
(2:1), which covered a period of forty years.

John the Baptist is introduced as one whose name will be familiar
to everyone, so that the evangelist feels no need to give any information about him. According to Luke, he was the son of a Jewish
priest named Zacharias and his wife Elizabeth (Lk.1:5–7,24f.,
57ff.), who lived in 'the hill country of Judah' (vv.39–40), and
before his appearance as a public preacher, he lived for some time
'in the wilderness' (v.80). This has led to the conjecture that he may
have been brought up in the Qumran community, but the words of
Luke suggest rather that he lived as a solitary ascetic—nothing
more definite can be said. The Lukan story of his birth was probably
derived from the circles of his followers who cherished their
traditions about him and embellished them with legendary features,
which have been carried over into the work of the Christian
evangelist; the relationship of Elizabeth to Mary the mother of Jesus
(Lk.1:36–56) may be a fancy of Luke himself.

The designation 'the Baptist' would not be applied to him until after he had been carrying on his ministry for some time; in Luke, he is called simply 'John the son of Zacharias'. 'The Baptist' is a nickname by which he came to be generally known among the people as they heard of the strange rite which he administered to those who responded to his summons to repentance; Mark calls it 'a baptism of repentance for the forgiveness of sins' (Mk.1:4). Matthew makes no mention of the forgiveness of sins as the effect or purpose of John's baptism, but when he tells us that those whom he baptized in the Jordan confessed their sins, he probably implies that God's forgiveness is granted to those who make their confession. This would be in keeping with a doctrine often put forth in the Old Testament, as for instance in Psalm 32:5—'I said, "I will confess my transgressions unto the Lord"; then you forgave the guilt of my sin.' It is expressed still more directly in Proverbs 28:13—'He who conceals his transgressions will not prosper, but he who confesses and forsakes them will obtain mercy.' In the books of the Law it is prescribed or assumed that the confession is accompanied by sacrifice (Lev.5:5f.; Num.5:7f.; etc.), but there is obviously no question of the offering of a sacrifice in connection with the Johannine rite.

'The wilderness of Judaea' ordinarily means the rugged and inhospitable wasteland west of the Dead Sea; here it must be taken to include at least the lower reaches of the Jordan valley. The words 'of Judaea' are an addition made by Matthew; in Mark it is simply 'the wilderness', and probably anticipates or reflects the words of Isaiah which are about to be cited. It is not to be supposed that John did his preaching in one area and led the people to another place for the baptism. 'The wilderness' as such is hardly the place for a preacher to attract great crowds. It is perhaps for that reason that Luke has changed the picture. In his account, 'the word of God came to John . . . in the wilderness; and he *went into* all the region about Jordan, preaching . . .' (Lk.3:2f.).

VERSE 2: The theme of John's preaching is given by Matthew in the very words which he will later attribute to Jesus (4:17). He calls his hearers to repent, and lends urgency to his appeal by the proclamation that 'the kingdom of heaven is at hand.'

The Greek verb μετανοέω, 'repent', means literally to change one's mind, and does not always imply that one feels remorse about one's former attitude, or that one has been guilty of a moral offence. The moral content which it carries in the New Testament derives principally from the Hebrew verb *shub*—'turn', or 'return'. In LXX this verb is usually rendered by a compound of the Greek verb στρέφω, 'turn'. It means a reversal of one's whole course of life, a complete change of direction. A man recognizes that he has been sinning against the Lord, and he turns in his tracks; he 'returns' to the Lord. The appeal of the prophets is often made in these terms; it is summed up in the words of the Lord: 'I have sent to you all my servants the prophets . . . , saying, "Turn now every one of you from his evil way, and amend your doings"' (Jer.35:15). The great prophet of the Exile takes up the same plea:

> Let the wicked forsake his way,
> and the unrighteous man his thoughts;
> let him return to the Lord, that he may have mercy on him,
> and to our God, for he will abundantly pardon. (Isa.55:7)

In the same spirit, the repentance for which John calls means not merely a change of outlook, but the turning to God in obedience, showing itself in action.

Matthew does not feel it necessary to explain what 'the kingdom of heaven' means, for he knows that his readers, like the hearers of John's preaching, are well acquainted with the expression. It belongs to the religious vocabulary of the later Judaism. He does not attempt to define it, but simply records John's proclamation that it is 'at hand'. This is the new note, which will be taken up by Jesus. It is this nearness that lends urgency to the summons to repent. John sees the Kingdom under its aspect of judgement. For all the hope and glory that it may hold for Israel, it will be a fearful day of reckoning for all who have been unfaithful and disobedient. This will be made explicit in his words of rebuke to the scribes and Pharisees who come to his baptism (vv.7–11).

VERSE 3: The citation from the book of Isaiah is based upon the LXX, and it is only in that form that it could suggest the wilderness preaching of John. The Greek version runs:

> A voice of one who cries in the wilderness,
> 'Prepare the way of the Lord,
> make straight the paths of our God.'

In the Hebrew original, the phrase 'in the wilderness' is not attached to the 'voice', but to the road that is to be built; and it is paralleled in the second line by 'the desert'. It runs:

> A voice cries,
> 'In the wilderness prepare the way of the Lord,
> make straight in the desert a highway for our God.' (Isa.40:3)

We are probably to understand that the voice of the crier is heard in

Jerusalem (v.2). The thought, accordingly, is not at all of *preaching* in the wilderness, but of building a new highway there—across the desert (to provide for the return of the exiles from Babylonia to Jerusalem). 'The Lord' here renders the divine name Yahweh, and it is paralleled in the second line by the words 'our God'. But once Matthew, like Mark, has taken 'the Lord' to be a reference to Jesus, 'the Lord' of Christian faith, he must reconstruct the second line to omit the reference to 'our God', and for that he substitutes the pronoun 'his'. Thus the whole sentence, in disregard of its original meaning, is interpreted as a prophecy of a wilderness preacher who is sent to prepare the way for Jesus.

The application of these words to John the Baptist shows again how little our evangelists, and the early Christian teachers in general, were interested in the intrinsic, historical meaning of the words which they cited. (This is equally true of the Jewish teachers of the time, and is not very different from the way in which many Greek philosophers and historians interpreted passages from Homer.) They sought for an application that would give the sacred words relevance to their own situation, regardless of what they may have meant to the Hebrew writer and to his contemporaries. They were persuaded that the Old Testament in all its parts was written with Christ and the gospel in view, and they applied its words in ways that seem strange, arbitrary, and even perverse to us. But we must not judge them by our standards of scholarly investigation; they used the methods of their own time. Scientific exegesis and historical criticism in anything like our sense was quite unknown to them.

VERSE 4: The camel's hair cloak and the leather belt are not merely marks of simplicity in dress; they are the sign of John's vocation as a prophet (Zech.13:4). More particularly, the words echo the description of Elijah which was given to King Ahaziah: 'He was wearing a garment of haircloth, with a leather belt about his waist.' This was all the information that the king needed; he said at once: 'It is Elijah the Tishbite' (2 Ki.1:8).

The expectation of a return of Elijah had become an established tradition and an accepted element in scribal teaching about the coming of the Messiah, and we are told that Jesus himself taught his disciples that Elijah had already come in the person of John (Mt.17: 10–13). This tradition appears to go back to an oracle in the book of Malachi: 'Behold, I send you the prophet Elijah before the great and terrible day of the Lord comes' (4:5). It is mentioned again in the great tribute to Elijah in the book of Ecclesiasticus (48:10).

The diet of John, 'locusts and wild honey', points to the austerity of his life. Locusts are still used for food, and 'wild honey' (the honey of wild bees) was to be found in hives among the rocks. John lived on the meagre fare which the desert provided; unlike Jesus, who was accused of drunkenness and gluttony, he came 'neither eating nor drinking', and people thought him mad (Mt.11:18).

VERSE 5: According to Mark, John's preaching attracted 'all the Judaean countryside and all the people of Jerusalem' (Mk.1:5). Matthew adds to this, 'all the region about the Jordan'. 'All' is of course an exaggeration—most people would not join the pilgrimage to the Jordan, but there were probably large throngs from time to time. The region about the Jordan would include the eastern part of Samaria, a corner of Galilee, and a strip east of the river. These lands were all under the rule of the tetrarch Antipas, the second son of Herod the Great, who later had John thrown into prison and beheaded. There is no indication of how word of his mission came to the ears of Jesus in Nazareth, or of what impelled him to leave home and to make the journey to the scene of John's mission.

Jerusalem and all Judaea were by this time governed by Pontius Pilate, and there is no suggestion that John's activities ever came to his notice. He would hardly have failed to be concerned about a movement which drew any considerable numbers of the restive population of Jerusalem and Judaea to the Jordan, in response to a preacher of the imminent coming of the kingdom of God. It is probable, then, that John's greatest influence was felt in the regions governed by Herod Antipas.

VERSE 6: If John came to be called 'the Baptist', it must be because the rite which he administered caught the people's imagination. It is far from clear what this rite meant to John and to those who responded to his preaching, and we are not told what actually took place. The baptism was undoubtedly an immersion, and it was accompanied by a confession of sins, but there is little more that we can say about it. The Jewish historian Josephus, viewing it from the outside, seems to think of it as a simple ablution, but he is far from understanding that John was calling sinners to repentance. 'John was a pious man,' he writes, 'and he was bidding the Jews who practised virtue and exercised righteousness towards each other and piety toward God, to come together for baptism. For thus, it seemed to him, would baptismal ablution be acceptable, if it were used not to beg off from sins committed, but for the purification of the body when the soul had previously been cleansed by righteous conduct' (*Ant.* xviii.5.2). The Gospels take the very different view that the baptism was not for the virtuous and godly, but for the sinful and disobedient. The chief priests and the elders did not respond to him, and he scorned the pious professions of the scribes and Pharisees, but 'the tax collectors and the harlots believed him' (Mt.21:23–32). Those who responded to his appeal did not profess righteousness and piety, but confessed their sins.

But how did they make their confession, and in what way were they baptized? It is most unlikely that personal and individual confessions were made to John, or that he led people one by one into the river, as the iconography pictures him. Perhaps no words of confession were spoken, the acceptance of baptism being a confession in itself; perhaps the candidates entered the river in groups, and immersed themselves as John stood by. It is worth noticing that Luke can describe the baptism of Jesus without so much as mentioning the presence of John. 'When all the people were baptized,' he writes, 'and Jesus also had been baptized and was praying . . .' (Lk.3:21).

But was the rite more than a symbol of the washing away of sin? Did it have a positive effect, as a rite of admission to the kingdom of heaven, which John declared was near at hand? Or was it conceived, as the contrast with a 'baptism with wind and fire' would suggest, as the way now open for escape from 'the wrath to come' (vv.7,11)? Is it to be understood as an 'eschatological sacrament', as is held now by most commentators, following Albert Schweizer?

John Rebukes the Leaders of Israel 3:7–10

[7] When he saw many Pharisees and Sadducees coming to his baptism, he said to them, 'Spawn of vipers! Who warned you to flee from the wrath to come? [8] Bring forth fruit, then, that will give proof of your repentance. [9] Do not presume to say to yourselves, "We have Abraham as our father"; for I tell you, God can raise up children to Abraham out of these stones. [10] The axe is already laid at the root of the trees, and every tree that does not bring forth good fruit is chopped down and thrown into the fire.'

This passage is found almost word for word in the Gospel of Luke (3:7–9). The only significant change is in the introductory sentence. In Luke, the Pharisees and Sadducees are not mentioned; the scathing rebuke of John is addressed 'to the multitudes that came out to be baptized by him'. The linking of Pharisees and Sadducees is peculiar to Matthew, who uses the phrase five times; it never occurs elsewhere in the New Testament except in Acts 23:7, where members of the two parties are pictured as breaking into open dispute (*stasis*) in the Sanhedrin. In fact they were deeply divided in almost every respect, and it is not at all likely that such of their number as might be interested would join together in an approach to John. We must therefore hold Matthew responsible for linking them together here (and also in 16:1–12 [four times]; cf. Mk.8:11–15). It is possible that Luke has kept more closely to the wording of the source, but he too may have altered it. We cannot be any more sure that John addressed these rebukes to the multitudes than that he directed them at the Pharisees and Sadducees.

In any case, the words cannot be taken as a verbatim report, nor is it certain that they were all spoken at the same time and to the same people. As with the discourses of Jesus, they are probably a selection and compilation from a larger stock of sayings of John that were transmitted in the bands of his disciples. This selection and grouping was clearly made in the source which lay before Matthew and Luke; that is, in an earlier Christian document. They are far from giving an adequate summary of the substance of John's teaching, and we have no means of supplementing it from other sources. The Christian writers were not interested in the teaching of John except in so far as it was related to the message of Jesus, and to their own controversy with the Jewish leadership of their time. If they have given us these sayings, it is not out of any desire to preserve them as words of John, but only because they gave vigorous expression to Christian criticisms of Judaism. For Matthew, the active leaders of the Jewish communities which he knew were above all the Pharisees. Luke is not involved in the same struggle with Jewish opposition, and he sees in the words a criticism of the Jewish masses in general, not especially of their leaders.

VERSE 7: 'Spawn of vipers!' It must be admitted that this vicious epithet is more likely to have been spat out at leaders than at the whole audience. The viper (ἔχιδνα) is a poisonous snake (cf. Acts 28:3); the religious leaders are accused of poisoning the people committed to their charge. 'Who has warned you?'—an odd question, seeing that it is John himself who has been giving the warning. Perhaps the emphasis should be placed on the word 'you'. But it still seems strange that they should be rebuked for heeding the warning, no matter from whom it came. 'The wrath to come' (τῆς μελλούσης ὀργῆς) is a way of speaking of the punishments which God will inflict at the day of judgement (cf. Zeph.1:15: 'a day of wrath is that day'); Paul will speak of 'Jesus, who rescues us from the wrath to come' (ἐκ τῆς ὀργῆς τῆς ἐρχομένης—1 Thess.1:10). We thus learn indirectly that John's message carries the urgent warning that the coming of the kingdom of heaven is not all joy and peace; it comes also as judgement on evil.

VERSE 8: 'fruit' (in Luke's text, 'fruits') is used as a figure for 'good deeds'. If the repentance is genuine, it will show itself in a change of conduct; cf. Mt.7:16ff.

VERSE 9: Another trifling change is seen in the Lukan version— 'do not begin' (μὴ ἄρξησθε) for 'do not presume' (μὴ δόξητε). John warns against religious complacency, the confidence that racial privilege, descent from Abraham, assures them of entrance into the kingdom of heaven, as members of the 'chosen people'.

VERSE 10: The axe laid to the root of the trees marks where the woodsman is about to make his first cut; it indicates that he is not planning a pruning operation, but the destruction of the trees that are not producing good fruit. There is a strong emphasis on the word 'already' (ἤδη), which is set at the beginning of the sentence (in Greek). The threat of national disaster is not to be postponed; the end is near.

John Proclaims the Coming of a Greater One 3:11–12

[11] 'I am baptizing you with water, in token of repentance, but he who is coming after me is mightier than I—I am not fit to carry his sandals; he will baptize you with the Holy Spirit and with fire. [12] His winnowing shovel is in his hand, and he will clear his threshing floor. He will store his wheat in the granary, and will burn the chaff with fire unquenchable.'

VERSE 11 is 'attached unsuitably to the rebuke to the religious leaders' (McNeile). In Mark, where the invective of vv.7–10 does not appear, the prophecy of the greater one to come and the contrast of the two baptisms is all that is given of the preaching of John (Mk.1: 7f.). This was undoubtedly the centre of interest in John for Christians.

The contrast between a baptism with water, administered by John, and a baptism 'with the Holy Spirit and with fire', to be brought by the mysterious 'mightier' one who is to come, is certainly understood by Matthew—and by the three other evangelists also—as a contrast with Christian baptism. It is probable also that the phrase 'Holy Spirit' is a Christian interpretation of John's words, which changes the sense of his prediction radically. In Greek, the word πνεῦμα means in the first place 'wind' or 'breath' (it is defined by Aristotle as 'air in motion'), and even in its relatively late use in the sense of 'spirit' it retains something of the older physical meaning. In the Gospel of John (20:22), the disciples receive the Spirit when Jesus breathes upon them; and in the imagery of the Pentecost scene, the coming of the Spirit is attended by a sound 'like the rush of a mighty wind' (Acts 2:2). The double sense of the word is played upon in the dialogue with Nicodemus (Jn.3:5–8). It is probable that the word 'holy' is a Christian intrusion into a saying that warned originally of a baptism 'with wind and fire'. This sense is actually presupposed by the following verse, where the function of the wind is to separate the chaff from the wheat, and the function of the fire is to burn the chaff. This suggests that in this passage the baptism of John is viewed as a mild purification, while the mightier one to come after him will initiate a far more drastic purification by wind and fire.

Rites of purification by water are of course prescribed in the sacred law of Israel for the removing of all manner of ritual defilements, and ablutions of various kinds are known to virtually all religions. The figures of wind and fire as instruments of divine judgement are used by many of the Hebrew writers, though they apply most often to historical national disasters, interpreted as punishments inflicted by God, not to the Last Judgement or to the purification of souls. In certain passages, however, both wind and fire are used as symbols of general judgement, without historical reference of any kind. 'The wicked . . . are like the chaff which the wind drives away. Therefore the wicked will not stand in the judgement' (Ps.1:4f.); or again, 'The day comes . . . when all the arrogant and evil-doers will be stubble; the day comes that will burn them up, says the Lord of hosts' (Mal.4:1). But far more frequent are the passages which threaten historical judgements upon nations—upon Gentile peoples, but also upon Israel and Judah, as in Amos 1 and 2, with the repeated threat: 'I will send a fire' (upon Damascus, Gaza, Tyre, Teman (Edom), Ammon, Moab, and Judah); or the warning to Judah: 'I will scatter you like chaff, driven by the wind from the desert' (Jer.13:24); or again, Ezekiel's oracle against the Ammonites: 'I will blow upon you with the fire of my wrath; and I will deliver you into the hands of brutal men. . . . You shall be fuel for the fire' (Ezek.21:31f.). But the figures of wind and fire are not linked, nor is there any parallel use of water. The notion of a triple purification, by water, wind, and fire, recalls rather certain Hellenistic doctrines of the destiny of the soul and its liberation from the pollutions and impurities which it has contracted in its contact with the flesh and the life of earth. The cosmology of the age had brought with it a transference of Hades (Sheol) from the dark realms under the earth to the starry sky. The soul does not descend but mounts towards its true home in the heavens. 'The atmosphere (between the earth and the sphere of the moon) became the first abode of the soul, and there it was punished and purified by being washed with rain, burned with fire, and agitated with wind' (M.P. Nilsson, *Greek Piety* (Oxford, 1948), p. 101). The wide acceptance of this doctrine is shown by its presence in Cicero and Virgil, in learned notes of ancient scholars (scholiasts), and in early Christian writers, such as Clement of Alexandria. And it was not limited to the speculations of theologians. It was expressed also in cult, notably in the cult of Dionysus. The devotees were subjected to 'fumigations by torch and sulphur, to ab-lutions, and then to a "ventilation", to the end that they, purified by fire, by water, and by air, might be spared like trials in another life' (F. Cumont, *Lux Perpetua* (Paris, 1949), p. 209). It is difficult not to feel that there is some relationship between these ideas and practices of the contemporary paganism and the association of the three elements of purification and punishment in the passage before us.

The mightier one of whom John speaks was naturally understood by the Christians as Jesus, and they would be quite prepared also to accept John's self-depreciation—'I am not fit to carry his shoes'— as a perfectly proper acknowledgement of his inferiority to Christ. But it is doubtful if the words would originally suggest a human figure at all. Certainly they can never have been meant as a reference to God himself; no Jewish prophet could have made any such comparison of himself with God; but he may well have been thinking of a supernatural being. The terms of self-depreciation are remark-ably strong, especially in the form which they take in all the other Gospels—not of 'carrying' sandals but of (stooping down and—Mk.) 'loosing the thong' of the sandals. The full force of such words is felt when we learn that the disciple of a rabbi ought to do anything for his master that a slave would do, except take off his shoes; John confesses himself unworthy to perform even this servile task for the 'mightier one'. (D. Daube, *The New Testament and Rabbinic Judaism* (London, 1956), p. 266.) Mere superiority in strength is not enough to call for such abject humility; it supposes an exalted rank, above any conceivable earthly character, even the Messiah. Again, this would be quite acceptable to Mark and to the church for which he wrote, for to them Jesus was indeed a more than human figure. But can we assume that John anticipates the Christology of the church?

VERSE 12: After the harvest was gathered, the reaped grain was laid on a threshing floor in the open air, and threshed with flails to separate the grain from the straw. The winnowing was the final step. The straw was removed from the floor and tied in bundles for burning; then the grain was tossed in the air with a winnowing shovel or fan (πτύον), so that the wind might blow away the chaff. If the harvester has the fan *in his hand*, it is because he is ready to begin this last stage of the process. Like the axe laid at the foot of the trees, it is another symbol of the imminence of the final judgement. The burning of the chaff is anomalous, and is added to provide a function for the fire as well as the wind. The words make it clear that the mightier one of whom John speaks comes as the divine agent of judgement, and that the day of judgement—primarily upon Israel, perhaps (in John's thought) also for the world—is at hand. This is the only clue that the texts give to indicate what the coming of 'the kingdom of heaven' meant to him. If it meant more than that, in terms of ultimate blessing, our sources do not tell us so.

At this point, Luke adds a few sentences of specific counsel which John gave to 'the multitudes', to tax collectors, and to soldiers (Lk.3:10–14). In these sayings there is no hint of the eschatological emphasis. He also tells us that John 'evangelized the people with many other exhortations' (3:18)—a reminder, if that were needed, that John's preaching is recorded only in part.

2 PREPARATION OF JESUS 3:13–4:11

Jesus is Baptized 3:13–17

13 Then Jesus made his appearance, coming from Galilee to the Jordan, to John, to be baptized by him. 14 John tried to prevent him, saying, 'I need to be baptized by you, and do you come to me?' 15 But Jesus answered him, 'Let it be so now, for it is fitting for us to fulfil all righteousness in this way.' Then John consented. 16 And when Jesus had been baptized, he went up at once from the water; and now the heavens were opened and he saw God's Spirit descending like a dove and alighting upon him; 17 and a voice from heaven, saying, 'This is my beloved Son, in whom I am well pleased.'

VERSE 13: The arrival of Jesus is announced in the same terms as the appearance of John. 'In those days' (3:1), here 'then', he 'comes on the scene'—or, as we have put it, he 'makes his appearance'. παραγίνεται is the historic present, much favoured by Mark (151 instances), but generally avoided by Matthew, except for the third person of λέγω, 'say'. In these two places (3:1,13) he actually substitutes it for Markan aorists, and in this part of his Gospel, he uses it with surprising frequency (seven instances in the section 3:1–4:11 out of a total of twenty-seven in his entire Gospel [apart from λέγει, λέγουσιν]; most of the others are found in parables). Allen suggests that 'this would be explicable if the editor were following a source of which the use of the historic present was a marked feature' (*Matthew*, p. ix).

The same verb (in the aorist παρεγένετο) is used of the arrival of the Magi in Jerusalem. It does not occur again in this Gospel, and is sparsely used in the remainder of the New Testament, except in Luke and Acts; but it occurs with great frequency in LXX. It appears to carry a certain atmosphere of formality and solemnity, sometimes of an appearance before a king or a judge, sometimes of the coming of God or of his angel, or of the arrival of a prophet to speak for God (1 Sam.13:10).

VERSE 14: Mark has told us only that Jesus 'came . . . and was baptized' (Mk.1:9); Matthew amplifies this by affirming that he came to the Jordan with this in mind (τοῦ βαπτισθῆναι—infinitive of purpose). This raises the problem—does Jesus like the others acknowledge the need of repentance, of a radical change in his own life and in his relationship with God? To Matthew, it was impossible to imagine any such thing. He tries to provide an answer to the difficulty by devising the little dialogue with John. There has been nothing to suggest that John had any prior knowledge of Jesus. In the account of Luke, the two were said to be cousins, and John responded to the presence of Jesus even while they were both in the womb (Lk.1:36,41), but there is nothing to indicate that Matthew ever heard of this. So far as Matthew's story goes, Jesus was unknown to John when he arrived on the banks of the Jordan. But John, with prophetic insight (?), recognizes the superior status of the stranger, and seeks to restrain him from offering himself for baptism. The imperfect διεκώλυεν has *conative* force (BDF § 326), he 'tried to hold him back'. His words: 'I have need to be baptized by you' are probably not meant to suggest that he sees in Jesus the one who is to baptize with the Holy Spirit, but rather that Jesus is better qualified than he to administer a baptism of repentance.

VERSE 15: The answer of Jesus indicates that for him the acceptance of baptism is not a confession of sins, but a fulfilment of righteousness. 'It is fitting for us'—John, as well as Jesus, is complying with the divine will in this act—John by administering, Jesus by accepting, the baptism. The expression 'to fulfil all righteousness' is characteristic of Matthew. The 'righteousness' which is thus fulfilled is not to be interpreted in Pauline terms, as 'the righteousness of God' which is reckoned to the man of faith, apart from the works of the law (Rom.3:21ff.; 4:1ff.; Phil.3:9f.; etc.). It is the 'righteousness' demanded by the Sermon on the Mount, which is fidelity to the commandments of God as the Christ of the Sermon will interpret them—a righteousness which must exceed the righteousness of the scribes and Pharisees (Mt.5:20). The emphasis is on man's fulfilment of his duty to God, not (as in Paul) on the gift of grace.

VERSES 16–17: With these verses we are brought into the realm of myth, even though it is generally held that the baptism of Jesus by John is itself historical (this is none the less open to question). In any case, the evangelist's chief interest lies much less in the baptism as such than in the mythical events attached to it—the opening of the heavens, the descent of the Spirit, the voice from heaven, and the words of revelation.

It is widely held that the story is based upon a communication made by Jesus himself to his disciples at some later time, to let them know what his baptism by John had meant to him. It is hard to imagine any particular circumstances in which he might have felt the need to make such a revelation. Nowhere in the Gospels are such self-revelations of personal spiritual experiences attributed to Jesus, and there is no real justification for looking upon this story as an exception. Whether it reflects an inward experience of Jesus or not, the primary question it raises for us is that of its meaning to the evangelist, and what he intended to convey to his readers. It is apparent from his entire Gospel that he was not bent upon preserving biographical anecdotes merely for the sake of their human interest. Granted that he did not invent the story, but took it over from Mark, it remains true that he gave it a place in his Gospel, and thereby indicated that he saw it in something of continuing significance for the church.

This significance may probably be seen as twofold. First, it is an initial revelation to the reader—not to Jesus or to John and the crowds that have come to his baptism—that Jesus is the Son of God. Secondly, it is given as the prototype of Christian baptism, the rite by which every Christian becomes a member of Christ's church. 'The church consisted of the baptized; she must know how baptism originated' (Schlatter, *Matthäus*, p. 52). In coming to baptism, the Christian believer follows in the footsteps of Jesus, and he receives 'the Spirit of adoption', by which he becomes a son of God. As Paul

will put it, 'You are all sons of God through faith in Jesus Christ;
all of you who were baptized into Christ have put on Christ . . . God
sent forth his Son . . . that we might receive adoption as sons' (Gal.
3:26f.; 4:5; cf. Rom.8:14f.).

It is tempting to suppose, as modern commentators often do, that
the baptism was of decisive importance to Jesus: in it he underwent
an experience which awakened him to a consciousness of his unique
relationship to God, and of his vocation as Israel's Messiah. It may
safely be said that no such idea was in the mind of any of the
evangelists; it is a conjecture inspired by a modern desire to enter
into the psychology of the religious experience of Jesus. The texts
themselves afford no basis for theories of this type. We are not given
the slightest hint of how the mind of Jesus worked, and there is no
flicker of a suggestion of an inward development. The student may
speculate as much as he pleases, but the tradition with which he is
dealing shows no sign of interest in such things; and in interpreting
an ancient text, the primary task is to discern what the writer intends
to say, and how it would be understood by those for whom he
wrote.

The imagery reflects the old naive conception of the universe.
'The heavens' form a solid firmament, and above it is the abode of
God; they must be 'opened' if the Spirit of God is to 'descend', and
the voice (of God) to be heard. The descent 'as a dove' suggests that
the Spirit takes visible form, as Luke makes clear by his interpretative
addition 'in bodily form'. It is doubtful if any of the evangelists
thought of a vision and audition experienced inwardly by Jesus,
though the wording of Mark might be so taken. In Matthew, the
Markan phrase, 'he saw the heavens opening', becomes more
'objective'—'behold, the heavens were opened'; and the words of
the voice from heaven, which are given by Mark in the second person
('you are'), as if addressed to Jesus, are transposed into the third
person in Matthew ('this is'), making them more specifically a general
proclamation. But these changes have little real significance. Our
distinction of subjective and objective is not made by any of our
evangelists. It is worth noticing, however, that none of them suggests
that any effect was produced upon the bystanders; it is not said
that they 'marvelled' or that 'they were astonished' or that they
'gave glory to God' or that they 'went away and spread his fame'—
phrases that are often used to describe the reaction of the crowds to
miracles (Mt.9:8,33; 15:31; etc.).

VERSE 17: The words spoken by the voice from heaven begin as
if to cite a 'decree of the Lord', which bears in the first instance

upon the promise of world sovereignty to the King of Israel. It represents the King, either at his coronation or at an anniversary celebration, declaring that the Lord has recognized, or adopted, him as his son, and assures him that he will subdue all his rivals with violence, and extend his rule to the ends of the earth. The passage runs:

> I will declare the decree of the Lord;
> > He said to me, You are my son,
> > today I have begotten you.
> Ask of me, and I will make the nations your heritage,
> > and the ends of the earth your possession.
> > > You shall break them with a rod of iron,
> > > and dash them in pieces like a potter's vessel. (Ps.2:7–9)

The phrase 'You are my son' is all that is given here (in Mark it appears in this precise form, but Matthew has transposed it into the third person, 'this is my son'). The remainder of the declaration is taken, with striking alterations, from a declaration by God about one whom he addresses as 'my servant' (or, 'slave'). The Hebrew text is translated as follows:

> Behold my servant, whom I uphold,
> > my chosen, in whom my soul delights;
> I have put my spirit upon him,
> > he will bring forth justice to the nations. (Isa.42:1)

In LXX, this is rendered very differently; it might be translated as follows:

> Jacob is my servant, I will come to his aid;
> > Israel is my chosen, I have accepted him.
> I have put my spirit upon him,
> > he will bring forth judgement to the nations.

But Matthew knows, or at least quotes, the passage in a quite different Greek rendering, which appears to be related to the Targum and to the Peshitta. This is how he cites it in 12:18:

> Behold, my servant whom I have chosen,
> > my beloved with whom my soul is well pleased.
> I will put my Spirit upon him,
> > and he shall proclaim justice to the Gentiles.

In this form, the second line is very close to the wording of the second part of the baptismal proclamation. A rendering of this type has been fused with the declaration of Psalm 2, to make the composite affirmation: 'You are my son, my beloved, with whom my soul is well pleased.' Such a combination of texts is often found in rabbinic teaching, especially in a triple grouping of one sentence from the Law, one from the Prophets, and one from the Writings. This particular combination is probably to be regarded as 'a Christian hymnic translation coined *ad hoc*' (Stendahl, *School*, p. 144). The adjective ἀγαπητός, 'beloved', and the verb εὐδόκησα, 'well pleased', are not found in any Greek version known to us, but they occur again in Matthew's longer citation from Isaiah 42 (Mt.12:18ff.), where they may have been introduced under the influence of this passage (Stendahl, *loc.cit.*). It is perhaps more likely that the evangelists have had before them an independent Greek version.

The use of 'beloved' (ἀγαπητός) in combination with 'Son' is reminiscent of the Septuagintal form of the words used of Isaac in the story of Genesis 22. Here the Hebrew *yachid*, properly 'only', is three times rendered in LXX by the Greek ἀγαπητός. Thus the Lord says to Abraham, 'Take your beloved son, (λάβε τὸν υἱόν σου τὸν ἀγαπητόν) whom you love, Isaac' (Gen.22:2). So, again, in verses 12 and 16, we find the same rendering (in the genitive): 'You did not spare your beloved (Heb., "only") son.' It is not impossible that there is an overtone here, in the words of the voice from heaven, of the sacrifice of the only, the beloved Son of God—a hint that in the baptism he is being called not only to kingship, but to death.

We have still to enter into the difficult question of the meaning to be attached to 'son' in this context. In Hebrew usage it does not carry any metaphysical content; it bears upon status and function. In Psalm 2, when the Lord says to the king of Israel, 'You are my son', there is no suggestion that the king is, or that he now becomes, a divine being. He is being commissioned to act as God's vicegerent, to overcome his enemies and gain sovereignty over the nations as the representative of God. In other passages, Israel as the redeemed community is called God's son (Hos.11:1—'When Israel was a child, I loved him, and out of Egypt I called my son'). The title can be given to Israelites both collectively and individually, as in Psalm 82: 'I [God] said, "you are gods, sons of the Most High, all of you"' (v.6; cf. Jn.10:34ff.). It is a way of expressing privilege or status, but is far from asserting that they are divine beings; they are immediately reminded that they are mortal ('nevertheless, you shall die like men'—v.7). The declaration, 'You are my Son', and even 'You are my beloved Son', is not an affirmation of the divinity of Jesus, but an appointment to office, perhaps even to sacrifice and to service.

In a Greek context, the words would have a different sense, and this is not easy to determine, for in Greek usage the title could have a wide variety of meanings. We must keep in mind, also, that in the Greek world there was nothing like the same conception of divinity. Israel acknowledged only one God, the living and true God; Greece knew countless gods, great and small; and many of them were the fathers of human sons by human mothers, or the mothers of human sons by human fathers. In Hellenistic times, it was no great thing to be a 'son of god'—every monarch of the Middle East, every little kinglet claimed the title for himself. In early Christian times, every Roman emperor called himself, on public documents, 'son of god' (θ εοῦ υἱός), and 'the Lord' (ὁ κύριος); and a cult was offered to him. In every city there were temples of the imperial cult, and priests to serve them. Apart from kings and emperors, the Hellenistic world witnessed the appearance of quite a number of 'divine men' (θεῖοι ἄνδρες) who 'claimed to be sons of (a) god or were regarded as such, and some of whom were cultically worshipped' (R. Bultmann, *Theology of the New Testament* I, p. 130). In a different realm, there were theosophical speculations which developed the theme that by regeneration, through enlightenment, involving an awakening to the knowledge of God and of the self, a human being may become a 'son of God' (*Hermetica*, XIII.14). And in a Jewish writing much influenced by Greek thought, the just man (ὁ δίκαιος) holds himself to be 'God's son' (υἱὸς θεοῦ—Wisdom 2:18).

It is clear, then, that 'the expression "son of God" might suggest to various classes of readers . . . a wide variety of ideas. It might suggest a man of god-like character or power, a prophet or initiate, the Messiah of the Jews, or a supernatural being mediating the knowledge of the supreme God' (C.H. Dodd, *Fourth Gospel*, p. 253). If to Mark, who gives us our earliest documented form of the baptism story, and to Matthew and Luke, who draw upon his work, it will have suggested in the first instance the Jewish Messiah, it may still have carried with it overtones of one or other of these Greek ideas. The initial application of the combined sayings to Jesus is likely to have taken place in Hellenistic circles of early Jewish Christianity, rather than in an early Palestinian church unaffected by Hellenism (Bultmann, *HST*, pp. 250f.). Seen from the Jewish viewpoint, the declaration that Jesus is God's Son would not be an ontological affirmation (bearing upon the essential nature of Jesus as divine, as in the later Greek creeds), nor should it be interpreted as 'adoptionist' in the technical theological sense (that Jesus now becomes God's Son by adoption); for there is no reason to think that the pronouncement by the divine voice is taken to effect a change in the relationship of Jesus to God. It would be understood rather as a declaration of fact—that Jesus is the Son who will act with the Father's authority and exercise the Father's power on earth.

Jesus is Tempted 4:1–11

[1] Then Jesus was led up by the Spirit into the wilderness to be tempted by the devil. [2] He fasted forty days and forty nights, and afterwards he became hungry. [3] The tempter now made his approach and said to him, 'If you are the Son of God, command these stones to become loaves of bread.' [4] Jesus answered, 'It is written,

'Man shall not live by bread alone,
but by every word that proceeds from the mouth of God.'

[5] Then the devil transported him to the holy city and set him on the pinnacle of the temple, [6] and said to him: 'If you are the Son of God, cast yourself down, for it is written,

He shall give command to his angels about you,
and On their hands they will bear you,
lest you strike your foot against a stone.'

[7] Jesus said to him, 'Again it is written, "You shall not tempt the Lord your God."'

[8] Again, the devil transported him to a very high mountain, and showed him all the kingdoms of the world and their splendour, [9] and said to him, 'All these things will I give you if you fall down and worship me.' [10] Then Jesus said to him, 'Begone, Satan! for it is written,

The Lord your God you shall worship,
and him alone you shall serve.'

[11] Then the devil left him, and now angels made their approach, and waited on him.

The story of the temptation continues to move in the realm of myth which was introduced in the aftermath of the baptism. Apart from Jesus, there are no human actors. He is moved by the Spirit which descended on him in the baptism; he encounters the devil; and at the end he is attended by ministering angels. The references to place are imaginary and symbolic. The 'very high mountain' from which all the kingdoms of the world can be exposed to view is not to be found in Palestine or anywhere on earth. The temple exists, of course, and its 'pinnacle', but we are not to suppose that Jesus is magically carried about—transported by Satan—first to the roof of the temple in

Jerusalem, and then to a very high mountain. The 'wilderness' is probably no more to be taken literally than the mountain peak, the pinnacle of the temple, and the transportation from place to place. The evangelist makes no attempt to bring Jesus back to the Jordan valley, and tells us nothing of where he spent the time between the encounter with Satan and the return to Galilee, after hearing of John's arrest (v.12). The wilderness is probably to be taken symbolically as the habitation of Satan, and the Spirit leads Jesus there to challenge the devil on his own ground. The 'mighty one' finds his house invaded by one stronger than he, who will bind him and be able to 'plunder his house' (Mt.12:29).

What we have before us in this pericope is a dramatic dialogue in three acts. The dialogue is central; the scenery is nothing more than a setting for the debate. It would be absurd to think of the discussion between Jesus and the devil as the record of an actual conversation, begun in the wilderness, continued on a pinnacle of the temple, and finished on a mountain top. The debate is a literary device for expounding the nature of the perils that beset the soul, and the way in which they are to be surmounted.

There are, however, different ways of understanding the temptations that are here envisaged. The first question is whether we are meant to think of them as 'Messianic', or as generally human. Is the basic idea that Jesus is tempted to attain his Messianic ends by false means, or is it that Jesus is tempted to fail in the radical obedience to God that is the duty of every human soul? There is the further question of whether we may think of this whole story as emanating in the first instance from Jesus, however greatly altered in the process of transmission; or whether it is the creation of a Christian teacher of the first or second generation. If Jesus be regarded as the ultimate author, are we then to think of the temptations as suddenly assailing him during a period of retreat immediately following his baptism, or as revealing the kind of temptations which beset him repeatedly, or continually, through the whole course of his ministry?

The temptation story in Matthew appears in Luke also, in a closely related form. The terms of the debate are virtually the same in the two versions, though the order of the temptations is changed. The second temptation of the Matthaean narrative stands in the third and final place in Luke; and Matthew's third temptation is placed second. This makes it impossible for the dismissal of Satan to follow the encounter on the mountain (the 'high mountain' is not mentioned by Luke), and the Lukan conclusion is therefore given differently. (The devil departs from Jesus 'till the appointed time' [ἄχρι καιροῦ], after he had 'ended every temptation'—Lk.4:13). In Luke, the temptation is not so closely linked with the baptism of Jesus, for the genealogy is interposed (Lk.3:23—38); the connection is retained less directly by a double reference to 'the Spirit' and to the influence of the Spirit (Lk.4:1). 'Full of the Spirit' (which had come upon him in the baptism), Jesus 'returned from the Jordan' as if to go back to Galilee, but in fact he 'was led ($\mathring{\eta}\gamma\epsilon\tau o$, impf.) for forty days in the wilderness, being tempted by the devil.' That is, Luke thinks of the leading by the Spirit and the tempting by the devil as going on continuously throughout the forty days. Within the dialogue between Jesus and the devil, the differences from Matthew are mainly verbal. For 'these stones . . . loaves of bread' Luke writes 'this stone . . . a loaf of bread.' The Matthaean form would suggest a miracle to satisfy the needs of multitudes; while Luke's words suggest rather the little needed to satisfy his own hunger. The 'high mountain' is not mentioned in Luke; he says only that 'the devil took him up' (high in the air above the temple?), and adds the phrase 'in a moment of time' (after 'showed him all the kingdoms of the world'), perhaps to suggest a flash of vision. There are also some slight differences in the extent of the citations of scripture, though they are taken entirely from LXX, and they both make the same alteration of phrasing, in the temptation to worship the devil, from 'You shall fear the Lord' (LXX) to 'You shall worship the Lord.'

All this shows clearly enough that Matthew and Luke have drawn upon a common written source, which contained an account of the debate, and that they have provided independently an introduction and a conclusion. These are also independent of the Markan story, though that may have supplied Matthew with the mention of angels (not in Luke), and perhaps with the wilderness setting. Mark says nothing of a fast, and suggests that the temptations were continuous through the forty days—this may have affected the Lukan introduction, but not the Matthaean. But Mark is not the primary source for either Matthew or Luke, in this pericope, even for the introduction. The dialogue surely had some kind of introduction and conclusion in the source which supplied it to Matthew and Luke, but we have no means of determining how much of it is retained in either of our Gospels.

VERSE 1: 'Jesus was led up' ($\mathring{\alpha}\nu\acute{\eta}\chi\vartheta\eta$). This marks a certain softening of Mark's 'the Spirit drove him out' ($\alpha\mathring{v}\tau\grave{o}\nu\ \mathring{\epsilon}\kappa\beta\acute{\alpha}\lambda\lambda\epsilon\iota$), which 'appears to indicate strong, if not violent, propulsion' (V. Taylor, *St. Mark, ad* 1:12). If this insists too strongly on the original sense of the verb ἐκβάλλω (though it is fully justified in Markan usage), we must at least attach significance to the fact that in Matthew Jesus is the acting subject, not the object, in this movement into the wilderness. 'The power of the Spirit does not infringe upon the personal nature of the inward life; Jesus remains master of his will and consciousness.' (Schlatter, *Matthäus, ad. loc.*) Yet Jesus is not the subject in the displacements, he is transported by Satan!

ὑπὸ τοῦ πνεύματος—the absolute use of the term, 'the Spirit', was avoided by Matthew in his version of the story of the baptism, where he replaced it by the more Jewish expression 'God's Spirit', πνεῦμα θεοῦ. This absolute usage is distinctively Christian. In Greek religious thought there is nothing remotely comparable to the notion of such a divine 'spirit'; and in Jewish usage it is always 'spirit of God', or 'spirit of the Lord' (of Yahweh); or it has some other determinative (his spirit, your spirit, a spirit of wisdom, etc.).

'The wilderness'—the wasteland on either side of the Jordan, imagined as the abode of evil spirits and of their chief, the devil. Mark tells us that 'he was with the wild beasts' (demons?), but this theme is not taken up by Matthew.

πειρασθῆναι—'to be tempted', the infinitive of purpose, Matthew is alone in stating that Jesus went into the wilderness with the express purpose of challenging Satan, as it were, on his own ground.

'The devil' (ὁ διάβολος, 'the slanderer') was adopted in LXX to render the Hebrew 'the Satan' (from a Hebrew root meaning 'to accuse', or 'to act as an adversary'). The 'Satan' of the Old Testament is not a mighty adversary of God and man, nor even an evil being; he is a functionary in the divine court, who acts subject to God's authority (Job 1:6–12;2:1–7). In later times, he assumes the features of the Iranian counter-deity, Angra Mainyu (Ahriman), the opponent of the supreme God Ahura Mazda (Ormuzd); and in the New Testament he is the mighty prince of evil, master of hordes of demons, the arch-enemy of God and man. Many different names are given to him in later Jewish writings and in the New Testament—Asmodeus, Beliar, Beelzebul, etc. (see art. 'Satan', by T.H. Gaster, in *IDB* IV, pp. 224–28). In this passage he is called 'the tempter' (vs.3), 'the devil' (vss.5.8), and again he is addressed as 'Satan' (vs.10); Luke writes 'the devil' throughout; in Mark, it is always 'Satan'.

There is no doubt that the early Christians, like most of the Jews of the time, believed that there was such a mighty spirit of evil; nor can we question the fact that Jesus himself shared these beliefs. None the less, we must recognize that this is a mythical conception that has lost appeal to the minds of men; we cannot ourselves accept it without falling victims to superstition.

VERSE 2: 'Fasted'—only Matthew uses the cultic term; Luke writes 'he ate nothing.' Mark makes no suggestion that he went without food, or became hungry; when he tells us that 'the angels served him', he probably means that they supplied him with food throughout the forty days.

'Forty days and forty nights'—Mark and Luke speak only of 'forty days'. Fasting as a religious practice in antiquity, as in Islam today, meant abstinence from food throughout the day, but not through the night. The Matthaean addition may simply enhance the severity of the fast undertaken by Jesus, but more probably it is a recollection of the experience of Moses: 'he was there with the Lord forty days and forty nights; he neither ate bread nor drank water' (Ex.34:28; cf. Deut.9:9,25).

Both Matthew and Luke, though in different words, place the onset of hunger after the forty days are over. This is not the normal experience of those who go without food—the hunger is sharpest in the early stages. But the mention of hunger serves to give a point of contact for the first temptation, to turn stones into bread.

VERSE 3: 'Made his approach'—the verb $\pi\rho o\sigma\acute{\epsilon}\rho\chi o\mu\alpha\iota$, here its aorist participle $\pi\rho o\sigma\epsilon\lambda\vartheta\acute{\omega}\nu$, is used with extraordinary frequency by Matthew, and with a force which I have attempted to suggest by the awkward phrase 'make approach'. It seems intended to convey the thought that all who come near to Jesus show respect, voluntarily or involuntarily, and do him a kind of homage. The verb occurs in this Gospel no less than fifty-two times, more than three times as often as in all the other Gospels taken together (five times in Mark, ten in Luke, and only once in John). In at least seven instances, Matthew introduces a form of this verb where it was not found in the Markan parallel; and in several more, in passages found in Luke but not in Mark, the Lukan parallel does not use it. Jesus is the subject in only two of the fifty-two instances; and it is significant that in both of these, it is the glorified Jesus (transfigured, risen) that 'approaches' others. In every other instance, it is others who 'make their approach' to Jesus. The indications are that Matthew wants to emphasize that no one approaches Jesus casually. Here even 'the tempter' makes a ceremonial 'approach', as do the angels in verse 11. It is used alike of friends and foes, of people who come seeking help and of those who come to challenge his authority or to criticize his actions, of disciples and also of scribes and Pharisees, and of Judas at the betrayal.

This apparent overuse of the word cannot be ascribed to mere carelessness, for Matthew is a meticulously careful writer. He seems to have adopted it deliberately to enhance the majesty of Jesus; he compels the respect of friends and enemies, even of devils and angels.

All this recalls the ceremonious way in which disciples, opponents, rival teachers, and even *devas* approach the Buddha. Visakha, a laywoman, 'sat down at a respectful distance'; Devadatta, an ambitious rival, 'got up, saluted the Lord, and spoke'; the venerable Malunkyaputta, a solitary ascetic, 'arose from his seclusion and drew near to where the Blessed One was; he greeted the Blessed One respectfully and sat down respectfully at one side, and . . . spoke to the Blessed One.' (Countless examples will be found in collections of Buddhist scriptures.) The Buddhist formulas are more varied— naturally enough, for they do not reflect the idiosyncrasies of a single writer—but they show the same desire to indicate the imposing dignity of the World-Saviour.

'If you are the Son of God'—Jesus is tempted to doubt the truth of the declaration made by the voice from heaven at the baptism. He is invited to seek external confirmation by performing a miracle. This is akin to the repeated demand for 'a sign' (12:38ff.; 16:1–4) which Jesus refused with the words: 'An evil and adulterous generation seeks for a sign, but no sign shall be given it.'

VERSE 4: The answer of Jesus indicates that the maker of the temptation story has in mind the experience of Israel in the wilderness as it is interpreted in the book of Deuteronomy. There it is explained that hunger was one of the means that God used to test the will of the people to obey him. 'He humbled you and caused you to hunger . . . that he might make you know that man does not live by bread alone, but that man lives by everything that proceeds from the mouth of the Lord' (Deut.8:3; in LXX 'by everything' is rendered 'by every word', and 'God' replaces 'the Lord'; the text is cited according to the LXX). In the passage of Deuteronomy, the scene is 'the wilderness', and Israel is led by God; in the Gospel, Jesus is led by the Spirit. In the Old Testament passage, it is God who tests Israel; in the Gospel it is Satan who acts as the tempter. But this reflects the tendency in Judaism to refrain from attributing to God anything like an incitement to wrongdoing. A remarkable instance of this, which is relevant to the interpretation of the Gospel story, is the change made by the Chronicler (about 400 BC) in the earlier account of how David took a census of Israel and Judah, and was severely punished for it by God. In the initial story, we are told that 'the anger of the Lord was kindled against Israel, and he incited

David against them, saying, "Go, number Israel and Judah"' (2 Sam. 24:1). In the later version, we find instead: 'Satan stood up against Israel, and incited David to number the people' (1 Chron.21:1). For the Gospel writer it would be unthinkable to imagine that God himself would tempt Jesus; but he would certainly hold that Satan unwittingly executes the purpose of God, in testing the Son's acceptance of the will of the Father.

There is no suggestion that Jesus refuses to perform a miracle that would be solely for his own benefit. It is wholly a matter of complete submission to the will of God. He will not seek to escape from the ordeal of hunger by the use of powers which the evangelist certainly believes him to possess, but which he will exercise only in accordance with the will of God.

It will be observed that the reply of Jesus is not based upon any claim of Messiahship; it is *man* (ὁ ἄνθρωπος) who is not to live by bread alone, but by every word that proceeds from the mouth of God.

VERSE 5: Strangely enough, the narrator pictures Jesus as the object of the devil's action: the devil 'transports' (παραλαμβάνει αὐτόν) him and 'set' him (literally 'caused him to stand'—ἔστησεν αὐτον). In the realm of myth, however, it is perhaps not surprising that we should find magic. Of course it is assumed that the devil has supernatural powers; the strangeness lies only in the thought that he is able to use them upon Jesus.

'The pinnacle'—probably refers to a conspicuous architectural feature of the temple, but we have no means of identifying it more precisely. The continuation of the story implies that it is some kind of protuberance that overhangs space, high enough that a leap from it would endanger life. Although no spectators are mentioned, the narrator must none the less be thinking of a public display. If it were only a matter of a daring leap into space to test the willingness of God to provide supernatural protection against an act of folly, there were plenty of precipitous heights available in the wilderness; the transfer to the temple presupposes a mass demonstration (Lagrange). Again the temptation is introduced by the instigation of doubt— 'if you are the Son of God'. But there is no suggestion that the temptation has anything to do with the work of Messiah. The passages which the devil cites are not addressed to any Messiah, but to the devout Israelite who has 'made the Lord (his) refuge', and who 'dwells in the shadow of the Most High' (Ps.91:1—10). The protection which the angels are to provide, in keeping with the charge which God has laid upon them, is pictured in terms of aid to a traveller walking along a rough and rocky path—the angels will hold him up to keep him from tripping over a stone. So far as the Psalm goes, there is no thought of a fall from a cliff, let alone a leap from a dizzy height. But Satan is no more interested in the original setting of a text than a rabbi or an evangelist. Indeed, the use of Scripture in this debate, on both parts, is like nothing so much as the way in which a pair of rabbis would proceed in a disputation. How can it be imagined that Jesus resorted to such a way of unfolding his own mind? This debate is the creation of someone who was trained in the methods of the rabbinical schools.

The reply of Jesus again points up the relationship of his temptation with the experience of Israel in the wilderness. It is taken from the book of Deuteronomy (6:16,LXX) which continues, 'as you put him to the test in the Temptation' (ἐν τῷ πειρασμῷ; Heb. 'at Massah'). This refers to an incident of the journey, when the people were on the verge of stoning Moses because of the lack of water, and he brought forth abundant supplies from a rock which he struck with his rod (Ex.17:1–7; cf. Num.20:2–13). The complaints of the people are interpreted as a 'tempting' of God. They 'put him to the test'. The story is the basis of a warning against repeating the offence, given in the final charge of Moses which is cited here from Deuteronomy, and taken up in the familiar words of the *Venite*:

> O that today you would hearken to his voice!
> Harden not your hearts, as at Meribah,
> as in the day at Massah in the wilderness,
> when your fathers tested me,
> and put me to the proof . . . (Ps.95:7b,8)

The theme, then, is still that of the contrast between the Israel which failed in its duty, and Jesus who made the response of total obedience and trust. Jesus will not test the good will of God by demanding proofs.

It will be felt that the nature of this temptation is very peculiar indeed. Certainly it is not a common temptation of man; no one will be tempted to throw himself down from a dizzy height unless he is under the influence of drugs, or otherwise out of his mind. But can we then suppose that such a temptation ever so much as flashed through the mind of Jesus, or (still more unthinkable) that it recurred to him again and again? How then can we imagine that Jesus himself is the author of this dramatic dialogue, at whatever far remove?

VERSE 8: In this third temptation (the second, in the Lukan order), there are greater differences between the two versions than in the other two. The reply of Jesus (v.10) is given in the same words, except for a transposition of phrases, but it is preceded in Matthew by the words of dismissal—'Begone, Satan!'—which anticipate the rebuke to Peter at the scene in Caesarea Philippi (16:23), when he remonstrates with Jesus over the prediction of the passion. But the most striking differences are in the description of the action, and in the Lukan supplements to the words of Satan. Where Matthew says that Satan 'transports' Jesus (again, παραλαμβάνει) to a very high mountain, Luke has only the participle ἀναγαγών, 'leading him up', with no indication of place. This is incoherent, for the two parties have last been pictured as standing on the pinnacle of the temple. It is hardly possible to accept the suggestion of McNeile, that Luke describes 'an exaltation into a state of spiritual vision'. It looks rather like an infelicitous attempt to avoid the intrusion of the fairy-tale mountain. The secondary character of the Lukan version reveals itself still more clearly in his misplacing of the words 'and the glory of them' (καὶ τὴν δόξαν αὐτῶν), which are clearly appropriate following 'all the kingdoms of the world' (Matthew), but come in very awkwardly after 'all this authority' (τὴν ἐξουσίαν ταύτην ἅπασαν), where Luke has set them. Luke also adds the words 'in a moment of time'; this makes it explicit that he thinks of an instantaneous mental perception. A further difference is seen in Luke's insertion of the claim of Satan that 'it [all this authority] has been delivered to me and I give it to whom I will.' In the view of Luke, this is not a false claim; it is in fact implicit in the offer of universal dominion. It is the expression of early Christian political theory, which looked upon the kingdoms of the world as the sphere of evil powers, and their rulers as agents of Satan, exercising their authority under him. He is the real 'ruler of this world' (Jn.14:30). There is another change, merely verbal, in the wording of the promise: 'all these things will I give you' (Matthew) becomes 'all [this authority] will be yours' (Luke).

The prospect of 'all the kingdoms of the world and their glory' presents worldly dominion under the enticing aspect of 'glory'. There is, however, no thought that the rule over the world is an *unworthy* ambition, for the evangelist certainly holds that Jesus is destined to universal sovereignty. This is the common Christian belief: 'for he must reign until he has put all his enemies under his feet' (1 Cor. 15:25). This is predicted of the king whom God has owned as his 'son' (Ps.2:7f.; cf. comment on 3:17, *supra*).

VERSE 9: The temptation is not to entertain a false ambition, but to seek a desirable end by unholy means. The worship of Satan has a twofold bearing. Most directly, it suggests the adoption of the methods commonly used by rulers to gain dominion—force, guile, and bribery, all the devices of power politics. There is probably a secondary thought of the basic theme of the entire narrative—the contrast between the failure of Israel to maintain its fidelity to God, and the response of Jesus in obedience complete and unwavering. For the worship of Satan certainly carries the suggestion of idolatry, and in this also Israel had proved unfaithful. When Moses came down from the mountain with the tables of the law, he found the people offering worship to a golden calf which they had made.

VERSE 10: The reply of Jesus is again drawn from the last charge of Moses in the book of Deuteronomy. The words are cited in the LXX version, with two slight changes. The ancient text runs: 'You shall fear the Lord your God, and him shall you worship.' (Deut. 6:13,LXX.) In the temptation story, the verb 'worship' is substituted for 'fear' in the first clause, to echo the demand for worship made by Satan; and in the second clause, the word 'alone' is added. This sums up the sense of the original charge, which insists on the exclusive claims of the God of Israel. It continues, 'You shall not go after other gods, or the gods of the peoples who are round about you; for the Lord your God in the midst of you is a jealous God.' (vv.14f.) Israel had already offended (Ex.32), by making and worshipping a golden calf ('gods of gold', v.31). Jesus will not be enticed to worship any other than God even by the most stupendous bribe.

Accordingly, this temptation is not peculiarly 'Messianic'. Jesus will put the solemn warning to his disciples: 'What shall it profit a man if he gain the whole world and lose his (true) life?' (Mt.16:26).

3   PREPARATION FOR THE MISSION 4:12–22

Jesus Moves to Capernaum 4:12–17

¹² When he heard that John had been arrested, he returned to Galilee. ¹³ He now left Nazareth and made his home in Capernaum by the sea, in the territory of Zebulun and Naphtali, ¹⁴ that what was spoken by the prophet Isaiah might be fulfilled:

¹⁵ Land of Zebulun and land of Naphtali,
  On the road by the sea, across the Jordan,
  Galilee of the Gentiles—
¹⁶ the people who sat in darkness
  have seen a great light,
  and for those who sat in the region and shadow of death
  light has dawned.

[17] From that time Jesus began to preach, with the proclamation: 'Repent! for the kingdom of heaven is at hand.'

VERSE 12: The connection with the temptation story is very loose—one might say non-existent. There is no attempt to suggest what Jesus did with himself after the dismissal of Satan or where he spent his time until he received word of the arrest of John; there is not even a hint of how long it was before the news came. The Fourth Gospel describes a ministry of Jesus in the Jordan area while John is still active (Jn.1:35–51), a brief visit to Galilee (2:1–12), and a renewed period of activity in the south (2:13–4:2) which was attended by great success (3:26ff.; 4:1). Professor Dodd has argued that John here draws upon 'a tradition with a genuine historical content' (*Historical Tradition*, p. 289; see the entire chapter on 'The Baptist in the Fourth Gospel and in the Synoptics', pp. 288–301). There is room for this in the gap which Matthew leaves between the temptation and the return to Galilee. But it is clear that Matthew himself knows nothing of any such activity. He not only attaches the return to Galilee to the news that John has been arrested, but he plainly indicates that Jesus did not begin to proclaim his message until after he had settled in Capernaum. It is almost as if he felt that the era of 'the law and the prophets' had come to an end with the removal of John from the stage, and that this is the signal for the new era to begin, with the entrance of Jesus upon his public ministry (cf. Mt.11:11–14).

VERSE 13: Matthew alone tells us of a definitive move from Nazareth, from the home of Jesus' childhood and youth where his mother and his brothers and sisters were still living (Mt.13:55), to Capernaum. To our evangelist, this change of abode is not an incidental item of topographical interest. It is a fulfilment of prophecy, and it establishes Jesus in a region where a mission to Israel can be carried on in an environment which includes Gentiles. It is a foreshadowing of the great Gentile mission that is to come. There is perhaps also a suggestion of the breaking of family ties. Not merely is the time of tutelage over, and the security of the family circle renounced, but the service of the kingdom of God takes precedence over the closest domestic bonds of affection. Jesus will express this clearly when he turns aside the request of his mother and brothers to see him, asking, 'Who is my mother? and who are my brothers?' and answers his own question by pointing to his disciples and saying, 'Here are my mother and my brothers! For whoever does the will of my Father in heaven is my brother and sister and mother' (Mt.12:48–50; cf.10:37; 19:29).

If Matthew takes the trouble to tell us that Capernaum is 'on the sea', and 'in the territory of Zebulun and Naphtali', it is not for the sake of geographical precision, but to provide a point of attachment for the citation which he wishes to introduce. 'The sea' is actually a lake (the lake of Galilee), and of course the city could not be located in the territory of two tribes; it was in the lands of Naphtali (as was Nazareth also), and Zebulun lay to the west. By the time of Matthew, the tribal areas had long since ceased to be of any importance; they were of no more than antiquarian interest. The tribes of the north, after the Assyrian conquest, were scattered and lost all remaining identity as tribes, in the conglomerate masses of the Assyrian provinces.

In the time of Isaiah, the tribes were still to be found in the areas of their ancient settlement, and the oracle which he delivers looks back to the recent Assyrian conquest; but this historical reference is entirely lost from view in Matthew. In the Hebrew text—much distorted in LXX—the (prose) note which forms a preface to the oracle runs: 'In the former times he brought into contempt the land of Zebulun and the land of Naphtali, but in the latter times he will make glorious the way of the sea . . .' (Isa.8:23, in MT). All that remains of this in Matthew is 'land of Zebulun and land of Naphtali', and 'way of the sea'. The 'way of the sea' meant in Isaiah the road from Damascus to the Mediterranean, which passed through the territories of Zebulun and Naphtali; the promise that 'He [i.e., God] will make glorious' this way, means that those areas will be delivered from their present state of distress, in subjugation to Assyria. They are 'beyond the Jordan' only to one travelling from the east (Damascus, etc.); to a Palestinian, Galilee was 'on this side of the Jordan'.

VERSES 15–16: These verses constitute the oracle proper. The Hebrew text would run:

> The people who walked in darkness have seen a great light;
> those who dwell in a land of the shadow of death,
> on them light has shone. (Isa.9:2, MT)

('Shadow of death'—the Hebrew phrase is a metaphor for 'impenetrable darkness'; cf. Ps.23:4, where it pictures a valley so deep that the sun never touches its floor.) For 'walked', Matthew has substituted 'were seated' (perhaps to assimilate it to the following sentence). For the verb 'has shone', he uses ἀνέτειλεν, 'has risen'—the verb which commonly refers to the rising of the sun. The LXX rendering treats 'land of Zebulun, the land of Naphtali' as a vocative, and turns the first verb into an imperative (ἴδετε, 'see'), as if to invite the two lands to open their eyes to a 'great light' which the prophet sees on the horizon; and it turns the second verb into a future (λdμψeι—'will shine'). Matthew, then, seems to have made his own translation from the Hebrew, with some recollection of the LXX. In any case, he wants his readers to think of the coming of Jesus as the dawn of hope for a nation sunk in gloom. The oracle is applied to the circumstances of the ministry of Jesus, and its original reference to the hope of deliverance from Assyria is of no interest. Those who have been sitting in darkness are the Jewish people of the first Christian century, not the tribesmen of the eighth century BC, and the great light that has risen upon them is Jesus.

It may well be that Matthew has in mind the rest of the oracle, which sees the hope of deliverance in an heir to the throne who has just been born, or (more likely) in a king who has just ascended the throne.

> For to us a child is born,
> to us a son is given;
> and the government will be upon his shoulder,
> and he will be called,
> 'Wonderful in counsel, divine in might,
> a father forever, a beneficent prince.' (Isa.9:6)

On this, see the notes of R.B.Y. Scott, in *IB*, vol. V, pp. 231–34; cf. Virgil, *Eclogue IV*, called the 'Messianic eclogue'.

VERSE 17: The text of the first preaching of Jesus is given by Matthew in the words that he has used for the proclamation of John: 'Repent! for the kingdom of heaven is at hand.' It is often suggested that Matthew has transferred to John the words which his sources attributed to Jesus, but it is possible that he is here following the oral tradition of his own church. However much he makes use of Mark as a principal source, we cannot suppose that he heard of John and his preaching for the first time when a copy of Mark came into his hands. In fact, Mark records no words of John's preaching; he tells us only that he was 'preaching a baptism of repentance for the remission of sins' (1:4), and he does not so much as suggest that John made any prophecy about the coming of the Kingdom. He goes on to call the message of Jesus 'the gospel of God', and sums up its content in the words: 'The time is fulfilled, and the kingdom of God is at hand. Repent, and believe in the gospel!' Contrary to his usual practice, Matthew abbreviates these words—elsewhere, even when he is drastically reducing the narrative element in a story, he gives the words of Jesus in full, as he finds them in Mark, and at times he even expands them by the introduction of other sayings from different contexts. If he works so differently here, it is surely because he wishes to emphasize the continuity of the preaching of Jesus with that of John. When the great 'voice crying in the wilderness' has been silenced, the greater successor takes up the same proclamation.

Jesus Calls his First Disciples 4:18—22

[18] As he walked by the lake of Galilee, he saw two brothers, Simon who is called Peter, and Andrew his brother, casting a net in the lake; for they were fishermen. [19] He said to them, 'Come with me, and I will make you fishers of men.' [20] They at once left their nets and followed him. [21] Going on from there he saw two more brothers, James the son of Zebedee and John his brother, in the boat with their father Zebedee, mending their nets. He called them; [22] and they at once left the boat and their father and followed him.

This double story is taken over by Matthew without substantial change. As in Mark, it is introduced immediately after the statement of the theme of Jesus' first preaching. Such changes as Matthew makes are little more than verbal—he adds a phrase here and there, omits the reference to workers employed by Zebedee (Mk.1:20), and makes a few minor alterations of order. His main addition is the remark that Simon was also called Peter.

The story is told with the utmost simplicity, but it raises a number of questions which are not easy to answer. As it stands, the story would suggest that Jesus is out for a stroll on the lakeshore when he happens upon some fishermen who have never laid eyes on him before, calls upon them to join him, with the promise that he will make them 'fishers of men'; and they leave their work and their property on the spur of the moment and go off in his company.

It is obvious that things did not happen so abruptly as this, but Mark and Matthew seem to have felt no need to ask whether anything had taken place to prepare the fishermen to make this drastic decision, or to suggest what might have paved the way. The readers of these Gospels, of course, would know the names of Peter and Andrew, James and John, as apostles. Perhaps Mark—and Matthew after him—felt that it was enough to give this brief account of the moment at which they left home and kindred to join Jesus in his ministry. Zebedee, the father of James and John, is mentioned;

but nothing is said of the family of Peter and Andrew. We will be told later that the mother-in-law of Peter lives in his house (Mt.8:14), but even then his wife is not mentioned; and we never hear anything about relatives of Andrew other than his brother Peter. The absence of all such detail throws the emphasis all the more heavily upon the thought that the apostolate to which Christ calls these men requires the sacrifice of everything that has occupied them.

Luke and John do not take up this account of the calling. Luke gives us a completely independent story, in the form of an epiphany; he places it at a later stage, after Jesus has been engaged in his activities of preaching and healing for a considerable time (Lk.5: 1:11). Simon Peter had already heard him preach in the synagogue of Capernaum, and had taken him home to see his sick mother-in-law (Lk.4:38f.). In the Gospel of John, the time and the circumstances are totally different. The scene is not even laid in Galilee, but in Judaea on the banks of the Jordan, where John the Baptist is working. John points out Jesus to two of his own disciples, and they forthwith begin to follow Jesus. One of them turns out to be Andrew, and Andrew brings his brother Simon to Jesus, who confers on him the name of Peter. They are not even said to be fishermen, and there is no promise that they will become 'fishers of men' (Jn.1:35–42). This is not to be understood as a preliminary experience which might prepare the brothers for a later call by the lake of Galilee. It has no importance for the Markan-Matthaean story, which would indeed lose its force if any such psychological interpretation of their instant response were implied (see C.K. Barrett, *St. John* (London, 1955), p. 149).

B

Opening of the Public Ministry:
Initial Successes

Mt. 4:23-11:1

The preparations are complete, and Jesus is ready to commence his public ministry. Designated as Messiah and Son of God in his baptism, proved faithful in temptation, established in a base of operations at Capernaum, and attended by a group who have abandoned home and business to follow him, he moves about Galilee from village to village, preaching, teaching, and healing. His fame spreads like wildfire, even beyond the bounds of Galilee, and attracts great crowds. His teaching is set forth in a collection of sayings which the evangelist presents in the form of a sermon delivered on a mountain. It makes a powerful impression on the crowds, and after he comes down from the mountain they continue to follow him, but they no longer play any role in the story (they are mentioned only twice in the next two chapters). This first Matthaean account of the teaching of Jesus is complemented by a sequence of miracle stories arranged in three groups of three stories each, with non-miraculous anecdotes to divide the groups. The great Teacher reveals himself as also the healer of disease and the vanquisher of demons: the Messiah of the Word is at the same time the Messiah of the Deed. These two parts are bound together formally by the literary device of inclusion —the repetition of parallel phrases at the beginning and the end (4:23 and 9:35). The third part of this division follows up the tale of success: the crowds indicate to Jesus a need and an opportunity. He enlists assistants, and commissions twelve of his disciples as apostles, to share his mission to Israel. His second great discourse is cast in the form of a mission charge to these twelve.

This second main division of the Gospel may be broadly outlined as follows:

Prelude: First Mission Tour in Galilee: Gathering of the Crowds 4:23—25

I   The First Major Discourse: The Sermon on the Mount 5:1—7:29

II A Sequence of Miracle Stories 8:1—9:35

III The Second Major Discourse: The Mission Charge 9:36—11:1

PRELUDE: FIRST MISSION TOUR IN GALILEE: GATHERING
OF THE CROWDS
Mt.4:23–25

²³ He went about all Galilee, teaching in their synagogues, preaching the gospel of the Kingdom, and healing every disease and every infirmity among the people. ²⁴ His fame spread throughout all Syria, and they brought him all the sick—people afflicted with various diseases and pains, demoniacs, epileptics, and paralytics—and he healed them. ²⁵ Great crowds followed him from Galilee and the Decapolis and Jerusalem and Judaea and from beyond the Jordan.

The paragraph is constructed out of materials provided by Mark. Matthew recasts a brief Markan statement about Jesus' first preaching tour (Mk.1:39), and adds to it the substance of a later Markan description of the crowds that gathered from all parts of the country as they heard of the miraculous healings (Mk.3:7–10). In Matthew it is put together here to serve as a framework for the Sermon on the Mount (not found in Mark). The crowds provide the audience for the sermon.

VERSE 23: 'All Galilee'—the boundaries of the district known as 'Galilee' fluctuated a great deal in pre-Christian times but were relatively fixed after 63 BC when Pompey took control of Palestine for the Roman Republic. It lay between the Jordan valley on the east and the coastal plains of southern Phoenicia to the west, covering an area of some seven hundred square miles. Matthew does not attempt to give anything like an itinerary, or to indicate how much time was given to this first preaching tour. According to all the Synoptic Gospels Jesus spent almost the whole of his ministry in Galilee, and when specific localities are mentioned, they are nearly always on or near the lake of Galilee. Occasionally Jesus goes by boat to the eastern shore of the lake, where he would still be in the territory ruled by Herod Antipas; once he goes north into the Lebanese foothills, the district of Caesarea Philippi (Mt.16:13); and once into Phoenicia ('the district of Tyre and Sidon'—15:21); and he does not journey southwards to Jerusalem until the last days, when he goes to his crucifixion (Mt.19:1; Lk.9:51). The Fourth Gospel abandons this general framework, and pictures Jesus as carrying on a general ministry in the south, much of it in Jerusalem and its environs, with occasional visits to Galilee, which is made the scene of only two episodes (2:1–12; 4:43–54)—a third, the miracle of the loaves, is laid on the eastern shore of the lake (6:1). The

Synoptic framework is the creation of Mark, and is artificial—there was nothing in the tradition to guide him in discovering the order of the episodes. Matthew and Luke followed him (in the main) because they had no other guide. If John has made such a different arrangement, it is perhaps because he had at his disposal a number of stories which were transmitted with a local reference (Bethany, Mount of Olives, the portico of Solomon, etc.), or a connection with a festal season (which would be celebrated at Jerusalem—Passover, Dedication); but there is no reason to suppose that his general arrangement is any less artificial than that of Mark. We are on slippery ground when we try to use these materials, with or without harmonization, as biographical sources. It is quite arbitrary to affirm that 'Jesus . . . does not continue the work of the Baptist and his followers in the Jordan valley, but starts his own work in Galilee' (G. Bornkamm, *Jesus of Nazareth*, p. 54). This is what we are told by Mark, and it is repeated (without any other grounds) by Matthew and Luke; but John tells us exactly the contrary—and he may be right. We simply cannot be sure, for we have not the materials needed for settling the question.

'Teaching in their synagogues'—the population of Galilee was mixed, as is indicated by the phrase 'Galilee of the Gentiles', and it is probable that Jews did not constitute a majority. Greek was spoken as freely as Aramaic, in some of the towns Greek was perhaps the more prevalent (see the article of J.A. Fitzmyer, 'The Languages of Palestine in the First Century AD, *CBQ* Vol. 32, No. 4, (Oct., 1970), pp. 501–31). If Jesus taught in the synagogues, however, he would not find Greek-speaking people before him (though some of his hearers may have been bilingual); he would give his teaching in Aramaic. Matthew perhaps is hinting, by his use of this phrase, that Jesus from the beginning felt that he 'was not sent but to the lost sheep of the house of Israel' (Mt.15:24). The worship of the synagogue included the reading and exposition of the scriptures, and any male Jew of thirty years of age or over was competent to fulfil such functions. Jesus held no office.

'Teaching . . . preaching . . . healing'—Matthew puts before us a threefold activity. The 'teaching' will be set out in the three chapters which he gives to the Sermon on the Mount (chaps.5–7); the preaching proclaims 'the gospel of the Kingdom'—that is, the assurance that 'the kingdom of the heavens' is at hand, and the urgent summons to repentance (v.17); the ministry of healing will be illustrated by the narrative of chapters 8 and 9. 'Every' disease and 'every' infirmity is hyperbolical, like the 'all' of 'all Galilee'.

VERSE 24: 'All Syria'—again hyperbolical. The name Syria, applied by the Greeks and Romans to the land of the Aramaeans (through a confusion with Assyria) was used with some vagueness of the whole area between the Euphrates and the Mediterranean, from Egypt to Cilicia. Matthew is probably thinking primarily of the regions around Damascus, Antioch on the Orontes (farther north), and perhaps the Phoenician coastal territories (Ptolemais, Tyre, and Sidon). We may be given a hint of the place of origin of this Gospel (G. Kilpatrick, *Origins*, p. 131).

VERSE 25: 'Great crowds followed him'—hardly to be taken literally, as if Jesus moved from place to place at the head of a disorganized rabble from all over the country. Crowds of four and five thousand, besides women and children, are mentioned as participating in the miraculous feedings (Mt.14:21; 15:38), but it is quite inconceivable that anything like such numbers of people could have accompanied him as he went through 'all Galilee'—even if by a succession of miracles they could be provided with food and drink, it is not likely that the authorities would have looked kindly on such a march. 'Follow' is probably meant to suggest something of a response of hope, if not altogether the dedication of the apostles who left all and 'followed' him. These 'crowds' (ὄχλοι) become a standing feature of Matthew's story; they are mentioned by him no less than forty-nine times. They 'were characterized from the beginning by their acceptance of Jesus' message and his authority as prophet of God' (P.S. Minear, 'The Disciples and the Crowds in the Gospel of Matthew', *ATR*, Supplementary Series No. 3 (March, 1974), p. 30). At this point they are brought on the scene to provide an audience for the great sermon, not a cortège. The regions from which they come are listed, with some surprising differences from the Markan list (Mk.3:8); Idumaea is omitted, the 'great crowd from around Tyre and Sidon' becomes 'all Syria', and the Decapolis is added. The following of Jesus includes seekers from all parts of the land of Israel and beyond. The Decapolis is a loose federation of ten cities with the autonomous administration of the Greek *polis*, situated mainly east of the Jordan, and largely Greek-speaking, with pagan religious institutions; and of course Syria was pagan territory, though with some Jewish settlements in the south. The audience of the first sermon is representative of the future expansion of the church into the Gentile world, though it is cast in terms that belong to the religious inheritance of Israel.

I THE FIRST MAJOR DISCOURSE: THE SERMON
    ON THE MOUNT
    Mt.5:1—7:29

THE SCENE AND THE AUDIENCE *5:1—2*

¹ Seeing the crowds, he went up on the mountain, and when he had seated himself, his disciples came to him, ² and he opened his mouth and gave them this teaching: . . .

The setting on the mountain is formal, with no topographical significance. We are not told where the mountain is; in Luke, the corresponding sermon is delivered by Jesus after he has come down from the mountain to 'a level place' (Lk. 6:12, 17), and he does not seat himself but stands. The audience also is differently described. Matthew mentions only his disciples, but he probably means us to understand that the disciples form an inner circle, and that the 'great crowds' from all parts of the land (4:25) make up most of the audience. In Luke, there is 'a great crowd of his disciples' (Matthew has spoken of only four, up to this point) and 'a great multitude of people from all Judaea and Jerusalem and the seacoast of Tyre and Sidon' (Lk.6:17); but the words are addressed primarily to the disciples.

VERSE 1: 'Seated himself'—the custom of the Jewish teacher; cf. Lk. 4:20. Despite that, he is said to stand for the Lukan sermon—on a level place, great crowds could not hear a seated speaker beyond the first few rows.

VERSE 2: 'He opened his mouth'—an expression found here and there of a person beginning to speak (Job 3:1; Dan.10:16; Ps.78:2; etc.). Here it adds a certain solemnity.

The teaching which follows is not the report of a sermon actually delivered by Jesus of Nazareth to a single audience, whether on a mountain or on a plain. It is a compilation of sayings, uttered at different times and places, sometimes to individuals or to small groups rather than to 'great crowds'. Matthew has made use of an earlier compilation, which has been laid under contribution by Luke also (Lk.6:20—49). The Lukan version too begins with a sequence of Beatitudes, ends with the parable of the Two Houses, and includes many of the sayings that we find in Matthew's sermon, with some variations in order. To this common base, Luke has added little but the small section of four Woes (6:24—27—a counterpart to his four Beatitudes). But in Matthew this core is greatly expanded. In an important section, Jesus' attitude to the Law of Moses is stated, first positively (5:17—19 [20]), then in contrast with his own teachings in six Antitheses (5:21—48); of this, Luke includes most of the substance of the sixth antithesis (on the theme 'Love your enemies'

—vv.43–48), but without casting it into the antithetical form (Lk.6:32–36). No part of chapter 6 is paralleled in the Lukan sermon, but parallel materials are distributed through other chapters of Luke's Gospel (chaps. 11,12,16). Parts of chapter 7 appear in the Lukan sermon also (6:31,37–42,43–45,46,47–49); other parts find Lukan parallels in other chapters of his Gospel, scattered in different contexts (Lk.11:9–13; 13:23–27).

Somewhere in the background of the two versions of this 'sermon', there lies an earlier collection of sayings of Jesus, almost certainly closer to the Lukan form than to the Matthaean in content. Similarities of structure and coincidences of wording are sufficient to show that they have a common ancestor; differences are so great as to indicate that it is some degrees removed; the two evangelists have not drawn upon an immediately proximate source. While retaining substantial elements of the more distant ancestor, it has passed through different channels of transmission. Luke's four Beatitudes, for instance, cannot well be regarded as derived from Matthew's sequence of (seven or) eight, nor Matthew's as an expansion of Luke's four, though they leave the impression that Matthew has reinterpreted those which are paralleled in Luke. But the remainder of the Matthaean 'sermon' is drawn from a number of different sources, and Mark is not one of them. They have then been supplemented by interpretative comments which are, in all likelihood, introduced by Matthew himself (see, for example, the comments on 5:23–26; 6:7–15).

The literary problems are complex, as will appear when we examine them in detail. But it is evident that the discourse as it stands is a compilation made by Matthew, largely from earlier written sources, partly from independent sayings which he has arranged in order at his own discretion, and partly of editorial contributions which he has framed himself and has not hesitated to attribute to Jesus. The real audience with which Matthew is concerned is not the four fishermen who have been called as disciples, nor the 'great crowds' which have come to him from all over the land, but the Christian believers of his own time; and the speaker is the risen Christ, who here makes his mind known to them on matters of lasting interest and importance in their lives and in the life of the church.

1 EXORDIUM TO THE SERMON 5:3–16

The sermon in Matthew opens with a sequence of eight beatitudes; in Luke, with a sequence of four. In Matthew, they are all cast in the third person; in Luke, they are given in the second person (Blessed are you), as if meant specifically for the 'great crowd of his disciples', without the generalized character that they have in Matthew. Three of the Lukan four are represented in the Matthaean sequence, though with a different emphasis; the fourth is taken up by Matthew also, but made the opening of a new section, cast in the second person throughout, in which Jesus no longer speaks in general terms of moral character, but of the situation of his disciples in relation to the world in which they live (vv.11—16).

All the beatitudes, and indeed the entire sermon, take it for granted that attainment of entrance to the kingdom of heaven is the supreme goal of life, and that there is no serious alternative. Such an assumption could be made only in a Jewish community. Greek thought could not possibly state the end in anything like these terms.

The Blessed Life 5:3—10

3 Blessed are the poor in spirit,
   for theirs is the kingdom of heaven.
4 Blessed are those who are mourning,
   for they shall be comforted.
5 Blessed are the gentle,
   for they shall inherit the earth.
6 Blessed are those who are hungering and thirsting for righteousness,
   for they shall be satisfied.
7 Blessed are the merciful,
   for they shall obtain mercy.
8 Blessed are the pure in heart,
   for they shall see God.
9 Blessed are the peacemakers,
   for they shall be called sons of God.
10 Blessed are those who are persecuted for the sake of righteousness,
   for theirs is the kingdom of heaven.

Beatitudes are found frequently in the Old Testament, and occasionally in Greek literature. In the Hebrew scriptures they are put in the form of the construct *'ashrē*, and are not so much pronouncements as exclamations: 'O the happiness of 'the man who . . .' (Ps.1:1, and often; or 'those who', or 'all who', Ps.84:4, etc.). Sometimes they are put in the third person, singular or plural; sometimes in the second person, as in the Lukan parallel, and in verse 11 of this chapter (cf. Deut.33:29). In the Old Testament such beatitudes are not found in sequences of more than two.

In selecting the Greek adjective μακάριος to render the Hebrew

'ashrē, the LXX translators intended to suggest a happiness which
flows from a right relationship with God. Though it had come to be
used without religious overtones, it still carries some flavour of the
old μάκαρες, which Homer uses of the gods—he often calls them
simply οἱ μάκαρες, 'the blessed ones'. Aristotle insists that it means
more than εὐδαίμων, 'fortunate'; μακαριότης, 'blessedness' belongs
to the gods alone. Those who are called 'blessed' in these beatitudes
are not fortunate, in any ordinary sense of the word. They may be
poor, hungry and thirsty, mourning, persecuted—but they are none
the less 'blessed'. This is a blessedness which does not require ease
and comfort; it is independent of circumstances. It is illumined by
the assurance of a glorious future, of life in the kingdom of heaven
which more than compensates for any present misfortunes. In the
soaring thought of Paul, earthly hardships are not to be compared
with the glory that is in store for the Christian believer—they even
enhance it. 'This slight momentary affliction is preparing for us an
eternal weight of glory beyond all comparison' (2 Cor.4:17).

This blessedness is not something that can be attained by any
'pursuit of happiness'; nor by any kind of social reconstruction that
can be made the basis of political programmes. Jesus is not represented as an advocate of social and economic reform, or political
revolution. The satisfactions promised to the blessed are not of their
achieving; they are the gift of God. In the Lukan version of the
beatitudes, the Kingdom brings a reversal of condition—the
Kingdom is for the poor, while the rich can expect nothing; those
who now weep will laugh, while those that now laugh will mourn
and weep; those who hunger will be satisfied, while those that are
now full will go hungry (6:21f.,24f.). This reversal of fortunes is a
favourite theme of Luke; as in the *Magnificat* (Lk.1:51—53) and in
the parable of Dives and Lazarus (16:19—25). But even in Luke there
is no hint that Jesus encourages his followers to take action to bring
such changes about. He does not enlist people for a crusade; he calls
them to repentance.

The eight beatitudes are arranged in a formal structure of couplets,
in each of which the first line states one aspect of the life that is
blessed and the second gives a corresponding aspect of the blessedness which is theirs. In all, the blessedness consists in participation
in the kingdom of the heavens, and the entire sequence is bound
together by this theme. It is not that the poor in spirit and the
persecuted are assured of the Kingdom, while the mourners, the pure
in heart, the peacemakers and so forth receive a variety of different
blessings. Those who are blessed are not various types; they are the

same people, described in a variety of ways, and the rewards of life in the Kingdom are shared by all—to be admitted to the kingdom of heaven means to be comforted, to have the deepest longings amply satisfied, to be acknowledged as sons of God, and to see him.

There is one striking variation in the arrangement which must be noticed. In all the Latin versions, verse 5 precedes verse 4, instead of following it, as here. This brings together the blessing on the 'poor in spirit' and that on the 'gentle'; and these two expressions mean substantially the same thing. This order is preferred by Tischendorf and Bover (though all other modern editors print the beatitudes in the order given here), and by many distinguished commentators, especially among the Roman Catholic scholars (Lagrange, Benoit, Dupont). It is well supported by manuscript, versional, and patristic testimony; it is the reading of the great bilingual D (Codex Bezae) in Greek as well as in Latin; by the Alexandrian minuscule 33, and several of the Caesarean group; and is supported by the Old Syriac (Curetonian) and by Syrian fathers who use the Diatessaron. This makes it certain that both readings were known in the second century. They are not omitted in any of the witnesses known to us.

The variation in order has led many scholars to hold that the blessing on the 'gentle' is an interpolation, and that the sequence as it left the hand of Matthew included only seven beatitudes (Wellhausen, T.W. Manson, Lagrange, Bultmann, J. Schmid, Dodd, and many others). We would then have another example of Matthew's predilection for the number seven—seven Woes in chapter 23; seven petitions in the Lord's Prayer; three groups of twice seven in the genealogy; seven parables in the collection of chapter 13; the charge to forgive not seven times but seventy-seven times (18:21). And it is observed that fluctuations of order in the witnesses is itself evidence of some weakness in the attestation (T.W. Manson, *Sayings*, p. 152). It is recognized by all that the beatitude is based on Psalm 37:11 as rendered in LXX (Ps.36:11).

The question is examined with great thoroughness by Dom J. Dupont (*Les Béatitudes*, chap. VI, pp. 251—57); he comes to the conclusion that the beatitude was framed by Matthew himself and inserted in the Latin order, as a new explanation of the beatitude on the 'poor in spirit'.

VERSE 3: 'Poor in spirit'—a difficult phrase, apparently an interpretative recasting of the simple 'poor', retained in the Lukan version. Matthew wishes to make it clear that Jesus is speaking of a spiritual condition, not of material poverty. The simple word 'poor' might suggest that Jesus is speaking as a social and economic agitator.

In Hebrew usage 'the poor' had developed into a virtual synonym for 'devout', 'faithful'. This was partly caused by the feeling that the wealth and power had become concentrated more and more in few hands, and that the privileged classes often oppressed and defrauded the poor, and despised them. As early as the eighth century, Amos denounces their rapacity: 'they sell the righteous for silver, and the needy for a pair of shoes, . . . trample the heads of the poor into the dust of the earth, and turn aside the way of the afflicted' (2:6f.; cf. 4:10f.; 8:4–6). He declares that the religious practices of such people are mere show, and God will not accept them. The same note is sounded by Micah (3:1–3, etc.), Isaiah, and others. The poor suffer at the hands of the wealthy, but they put their hope in the Lord, and he is attentive to their cry. It is this aspect of their poverty that Matthew desires to stress. The poor know that they are helpless; they cry all the more earnestly: 'Incline your ear, O Lord, and answer me, for I am poor and needy' (Ps.86:1); they receive the assurance of God's care and protection: 'This poor man cried and the Lord heard him and delivered him out of all his troubles' (Ps.34:6); 'I will give great thanks to the Lord . . . for he stands at the right hand of the needy to save him' (Ps.109:30f.).

The Semitic phrase that stands behind the Greek πτωχοὶ τῷ πνεύματι has never been found in any Jewish writing of any period until quite recently; it has turned up in one of the Qumran scrolls in the form *'anawe ruach*. This does not lessen the probability that Matthew's phrase is his own interpretative modification of the basic 'poor' (*'anawim* alone).

In a sermon preached in the synagogue in Nazareth, according to Luke, Jesus read a passage from the book of Isaiah, and declared that it spoke of his own mission (Lk.4:17–19).

> The Spirit of the Lord God is upon me,
> because he has anointed me
> to preach good news to the poor. (Isa.61:1)

In both Gospels, the sermon opens with 'good news for the poor'—theirs is the kingdom of heaven (in Luke, of God).

The second clause of the oracle (not cited by Luke) runs, 'to bind up the broken-hearted'; and this theme is restated in verse 2b—'to comfort all who mourn.' This now becomes the theme of Matthew's second beatitude (third in Luke).

VERSE 4: Those mourning will be comforted. This is the first aspect of meaning of life in the kingdom of heaven. The passive, as frequently, is a Semitic paraphrase for 'God will comfort them.' The

Matthaean phrasing is more in keeping with the words of the oracle than Luke's 'you will laugh.' The mourning is not to be limited to grief over one's sins. Although the thought is primarily eschatological, it is already fulfilled in Christian experience. God 'comforts us in all our affliction, so that we may be able to comfort those who are in any affliction' (2 Cor.1:4).

VERSE 5: In this verse, the saying of Psalm 37:11 is made into a beatitude by adding μακάριοι to the rendering given by LXX (Ps.36: 11 in LXX). Here the Hebrew 'anawim has been rendered πραεῖς, instead of the more usual πτωχοί; and the Hebrew yîr'shû, 'shall possess' by κληρονομήσουσιν, 'shall inherit'. In the Psalm, the promised possession is 'the land'—that is, the land of Israel; now controlled by 'evil-doers' (v.1), its future possession is assured to the 'poor'. In the New Testament, the 'inheritance' has been spiritualized, and widened; it is no longer the region promised to Abraham and his descendants (Gen.13:14f.); it is 'an inheritance imperishable . . . reserved in heaven for you' (1 Peter 1:4). 'The earth', not just 'the land' is the regenerated universe of the kingdom of heaven. The clause may have been framed by Matthew himself; wherever it originated, it is in substance a paraphrase of the first beatitude. πραΰς does not mean 'poor'—it is a second attempt to bring out the spiritual sense of 'anawim, modifying it as in the 'poor in spirit' of verse 3. The beatitude is a doublet of the first. πραΰς means not 'meek', but 'gentle' or 'mild' (Latin Vulgate, *mitis*).

VERSE 6: As in verse 3, Matthew brings out the spiritual sense of the beatitude, which in Luke reads simply, 'Blessed are you that are hungry now.' He interprets it in terms of the hunger and thirst of the soul for God. Amos foresees a time of famine in the land, 'not a famine of bread, nor a thirst for water, but of hearing the words of the Lord' (8:11); and in the Psalms we often find the longing for God expressed in terms of thirst: 'My soul thirsts for God, for the living God' (Ps.42:2; cf. Ps.63:1; 143:6; and Isa.55:1).

'For righteousness'—that is, for the fulfilment of God's will in themselves and in all the earth; even more, for the dawn of the day when God's purpose of blessing will be realized in the establishment of his Kingdom. It is an error to import into this passage the Pauline doctrine of the righteousness of God which is given to faith and is not a righteousness of our own (Phil.3:9).

Righteousness is one of the key words in Matthew. Jesus demands of his followers a righteousness which will exceed the righteousness of the scribes and Pharisees (5:20), and an entire section of the sermon (5:21—48) will be devoted to an exposition of how this higher righteousness goes beyond the strict requirements of the Law. 'Righteousness is the ideal of Old Testament and late Jewish piety. It consists in nothing else than living in conformity with the will of God' (J. Schmid, *Matthäus, ad loc.*).

VERSE 7: 'Mercy', 'merciful', and 'show mercy' (ἔλεος, ἐλεήμονες, ἐλεέω) often have the broad sense of 'generous', etc.; with particular reference to the giving of alms—so the cognate ἐλεημοσύνη in 6:2–4. In the context of the beatitudes, however, the words mean primarily 'forgiveness', 'forgive', etc. The passive ἐλεηθήσονται, 'they will receive mercy' means 'God will show mercy to them.' This is another way of unfolding the blessings of the kingdom of heaven; God grants his forgiveness to those who forgive others.

The sentiment is again an expression of Jewish piety, which has many parallels in the ancient scriptures and in the sayings of rabbis. In the Wisdom of Ben-Sirach, for instance, the sage declares:

Forgive your neighbour the wrong he has done,
and then your sins will be pardoned when you pray. (Ecclus. 28:2)

From Rabbi Gamaliel II, a contemporary of Matthew, we have the saying: 'So long as you are merciful, the Merciful One is merciful to you.'

Divine forgiveness of our sins is linked inseparably with our forgiveness of the wrongs done to us by others. It is echoed in the fifth petition of the Lord's Prayer: 'Forgive us our debts as we also have forgiven our debtors' (Mt.6:12), and this is driven home by the warning which follows the Prayer, in Matthew: 'For if you forgive men their trespasses, your heavenly Father also will forgive you; but if you do not forgive men their trespasses, neither will your Father forgive your trespasses' (6:14f.; cf. Mk.11:15).

In the Gospels generally, as in the rabbinical writings, the correlation between God's forgiveness of our sins and our forgiveness of others is expressed in such a way as to suggest that our willingness to forgive others is the *condition* of God's mercy to us. In other New Testament writings, the emphasis is radically shifted, in that God's forgiveness of us is the *motive* for our forgiveness of others. We are urged to forgive, as we have been forgiven, not in order that we may win forgiveness. This is most beautifully expressed in the plea of the writer of Ephesians:

'Be kind to one another, tenderhearted, forgiving one another, just as God, for Christ's sake, has forgiven you. Be imitators of God, as (his) beloved children' (Eph.4:32—5:1). This is the distinctively *Christian* emphasis. It is brought out vividly in the parable of the

Unforgiving Slave (Mt.18:23—35), especially in the rebuke administered by the king: 'You wicked servant! I forgave you all that debt
because you besought me; and should not you have had mercy on
your fellow slave, as I had mercy on you?'

VERSE 8: The beatitude of the pure in heart recalls the words of
the Psalmist:

> Who shall ascend the hill of the Lord?
> and who shall stand in his holy place?
> He who has clean hands and a pure heart,
> who does not lift up his soul to what is false,
> and does not swear deceitfully. (Ps.24:3f.)

Ritual purifications are not enough. The multitude of laws defining
'uncleanness' and the prescriptions for purification, which often had
no relation to moral offences, often led people to suppose that if
only the rites of purification were duly performed they need not be
concerned too much about morality. Prophets like Isaiah had long
since warned their people against such delusions; sacrifices and
offerings are an abomination to the Lord if they are not accompanied
by repentance and uprightness of conduct.

> What to me is the multitude of your sacrifices?
> says the Lord.
> I have had enough of burnt offerings and rams
> and the fat of fed beasts . . .
> When you come to appear before me,
> who requires of you
> this trampling of my courts?
> Bring no more vain oblations . . .
>
> Even though you make many prayers I will not listen—
> your hands are full of blood.
> Wash yourselves, make yourselves clean;
> remove the evil of your doings
> from before my eyes;
> cease to do evil,
> learn to do good;
> seek justice,
> correct oppression . . . (Isa.1:11—17)

There is greater difficulty about the promise: 'they shall see God',
for it was generally believed that no one could see God and live.
When Isaiah sees the Lord, he cries: 'Woe is me! for I am lost . . . for
my eyes have seen the King, the Lord of hosts' (Isa.6:5). The saying
in the prologue of the Fourth Gospel expresses the general

conviction: 'No one has ever seen God' (Jn.1:18); God is 'the King of kings and Lord of lords, who . . . dwells in unapproachable light, whom no one has ever seen or can see' (1 Tim.6:15f.). In the developed mystical theology, the vision of God becomes the symbol of the ultimate blessedness, but this is a relatively late development and should not be read back into the beatitude. In the Jewish context, to 'see God' is to appear in his presence, to enjoy unbroken communion with him. In the beatitude, it is another way of bringing out the meaning of the assurance that 'theirs is the kingdom of heaven.'

VERSE 9: The peacemakers are those who are not merely of a peaceable disposition in themselves, but who actively promote peace. God is himself the author of peace, and the great Deliverer of Israel is given the title 'the Prince of peace'. Christ 'is our peace', and 'he came and preached peace' (Eph.2:14–17), and 'we have peace with God through our Lord Jesus Christ' (Rom.5:1).

The passive ('shall be called') again stands for the active 'God will call them his sons.' They manifest his own nature and share his action in bringing peace. In calling them his sons, God recognizes in them their likeness to their heavenly Father. They enter the kingdom of heaven as the acknowledged children of its Ruler.

'Persecuted for righteousness' sake'—this beatitude is again a generalization, probably framed by Matthew himself, on the basis of a saying such as is addressed to the disciples in the following verses and is paralleled in the fourth of the Lukan series (Lk.6:22f.). It does not speak of the moral characteristics of those who are blessed, like all that go before, but of the treatment which they receive at the hands of others. In form, it corresponds to the first of the sequence, echoing the assurance that 'theirs is the kingdom of heaven.' This repetition indicates that the two verses (3 and 10) are the beginning and the end of a balanced series; it is the rhetorical device of 'inclusion'. The poor in spirit, who hunger and thirst for righteousness, who are merciful and pure in heart, and makers of peace, are persecuted because of the very virtues which show that the Kingdom with all its blessings is to be theirs.

The disciples do not encounter persecution for their faith during the lifetime of Jesus, but they know that John the Baptist has been thrown into prison because of his zeal for righteousness; in days to come they will face the hostility of the authorities, both civil and religious.

Despite the parallels, the Lukan beatitudes reflect an outlook quite different from that of the Matthaean sequence. In Luke, all the beatitudes describe the outward circumstances of the blessed: poverty, hunger, grief, persecution; and in the promised Kingdom these circumstances are reversed. In Matthew, the emphasis is on the moral and spiritual qualities of those who receive the Kingdom. These qualities are not to be taken separately, as if one might be admitted for his purity of heart and another for his hunger for righteousness. They are to be taken together—it is the same people who are described in all the beatitudes, in different facets of their character; those who are poor in spirit, mourning, and meek are also pure in heart, peacemakers, and subject to persecution.

All these sayings are expressions of simple Jewish piety. There is nothing distinctively Christian about them. Jesus speaks to Jewish hearers in terms that are entirely familiar to them; and Matthew passes the words on to Christians of a later generation as the validation by the church's Lord of Israel's purest moral ideals. That is not to say that they reflect the common attitude of the Jews of the time; far from it. The land as a whole was seething with unrest under a foreign yoke, and any leader who promised a hope of ousting the Roman occupying forces and regaining the independence of the nation could readily gain supporters. The poor in spirit, the peacemakers, the merciful were not the stuff of a war of independence. Those who thirsted for the liberation of their people and their land could not listen patiently while Jesus spoke of the blessedness of those whose hunger and thirst was for righteousness, for purity of heart, and while he affirmed that the kingdom of heaven, God's kingdom, was for the meek, the peacemakers, the persecuted. Many were passionately convinced that the triumph of God's cause was bound up with the restoration of an independent Jewish state under its own rulers, and hoped that this end might be achieved as in the days of the Maccabees, by armed conflict.

Jesus decisively rejects all such aspects of the hope of Israel; to this all the Gospels bear clear and explicit testimony. There is no place for ideas of national aggrandizement. The Kingdom is not restricted to Israel, and will not be made to triumph by force of arms. He does not speak of political programmes or of social and economic reforms. His concern is not with how the Kingdom is to be established, but with how people may enter, or inherit it. This is the theme of the beatitudes, and of the entire sermon. 'Seek first God's kingdom and righteousness' (6:33); 'Strive to enter by the narrow gate . . . for the gate is narrow and the way is hard that leads to life, and those who find it are few' (7:13f.).

Blessedness in the Service of Jesus 5:11–16

¹¹ Blessed are you, when they revile you and persecute you and accuse you falsely of all manner of evil, for my sake. ¹² Be joyful, be exultant, for a rich reward is yours in heaven; the prophets before you were persecuted in the same way.

¹³ You are the salt of the earth. But if the salt loses its savour, how can it be restored? It is then good for nothing but to be thrown out, to be trampled under foot.

¹⁴ You are the light of the world. A city cannot be hidden when it is built upon a mountain, ¹⁵ nor do we light a lamp and put it under a tub; we set it on the lampstand, and it gives light to all that are in the house. ¹⁶ So you must let your light shine among men, so that they may see your good works and give glory to your Father who is in heaven.

In the eight beatitudes of the sequence which we have studied, Jesus has spoken in general terms of the character of those who have part, or are to have part, in the kingdom of heaven. Now he takes up the theme of the blessedness of 'those who are persecuted for righteousness' sake', and applies it directly to his hearers, who are addressed as committed disciples, ready to suffer for his sake. It is framed now in the second person, like all the Lukan beatitudes ('Blessed are you'), and it closely resembles the fourth of the Lukan series (Lk. 6:22) in substance, though the wording is surprisingly different. In Luke, there is no mention of persecution; he speaks of hatred and of exclusion and of 'casting out your name as evil'—words which are not found in Matthew at all; and 'for my sake' is given in the form 'for the sake of the Son of man'. In both Gospels, the rhythmic structure of the initial sequence (three in Luke, eight in Matthew) is abandoned for this beatitude, which would seem to indicate that it was transmitted as a separate saying in the oral tradition.

In both its forms, but especially in that of Matthew, the beatitude seems to reflect the experience of the followers of Jesus after his death. John had indeed been thrown into prison, and Jesus may well have realized that there was trouble in store for him and for his disciples, so that he must warn them and encourage them to bear it with joy and hope. Yet the Gospels do not suggest that during the period of his ministry they encountered the hatred and ostracism (Luke), the reviling and slander and outright persecution (Matthew), which is envisaged here. Certainly this was the common experience of the church in the years that lay ahead, and both Luke and

Matthew give to the words of Jesus a new emphasis to point their relevance to the condition of the people for whom their Gospels were written. The specific mention of *persecution* in Matthew is clear evidence of such a pointing; it must be an interpretative addition introduced by Matthew into the substance of his source, for Luke was not the man to eliminate such a word if he found it before him. Matthew, even more clearly than Luke, sees the disciples constantly in a double perspective; he sees in them the figure of the Christian believers of his own time; and he thinks of Jesus as speaking beyond his immediate hearers to the church of the generations to come.

VERSES 13—16: 'You are the salt of the earth . . . you are the light of the world.' In the context, the words are meant for the blessed who are reviled and persecuted for the sake of Jesus, those who hear his words and are assured that 'theirs is the kingdom of heaven.' In this form, they reflect the editorial reshaping of Matthew, giving the evangelist's interpretation of sayings about 'salt' and 'light' which are found without such an application in Mark and Luke (Mk.9:50; Lk.14:34—'Salt is good; but if salt has lost its taste, how shall its saltness be restored? It is fit neither for the land nor for the dunghill; people throw it away'; in Mark, the question is followed by the injunction: 'Have salt in yourselves, and be at peace with one another'; and Mk.4:21; Lk.8:16, on setting the lamp on the lampstand). Salt and light are among the simplest necessities of life. If Matthew, in bold metaphors, applies them (as words of Jesus) to the disciples and hearers, it is not to congratulate them but to warn them that their essential character and privilege as members of the kingdom of heaven is not for their own enjoyment but for the benefit of others, and for the glory of God the Father in heaven.

The words, in this Matthaean form, can hardly be taken as a record of words spoken by Jesus of Nazareth, either to the crowds who have come to him 'from Galilee and the Decapolis and Jerusalem and Judaea and from beyond the Jordan' (4:25), or to the few who can already be called 'his disciples' (5:1). We take them rather as expressing the mind of Christ as it was understood by the evangelist and put into language that reflects his conception of the mission of the church of his time. He sees this anticipated in the mission of Jesus, and traces its inspiration and outlook back to the teaching given by Jesus in the days of his flesh. The church is seen by him as no mere sect, formed to purify and sanctify the life of Israel (salt) or to bring light to the dark condition of Judaism. Though it suffer abuse and persecution, it is a source of blessing to all mankind—the salt of *the earth*, and the light of *the world*. Matthew is well aware that Jesus himself restricted his own mission to Israel, and responded to appeals from Gentiles only under a kind of compulsion (8:5–13; 15:21–28), but he perceives that the effects of his work are not destined to be limited to Israel. By placing these words at the beginning of Jesus' ministry, Matthew foreshadows the charge that will be given by the risen Christ: 'Go into all the world and make disciples of all nations' (28:19). 'The calling of the disciples has no limits; they are sent to mankind' (A. Schlatter, *Der Evangelist Matthäus*, p. 146). The kingdom of heaven, the reign of the God who made the world, cannot be locally or racially circumscribed, and those who enter it are called to serve it in its fulness.

Jesus speaks here to his disciples of 'your Father who is in heaven'. He will also speak of 'my Father who is in heaven', and he will teach them to pray to God as 'our Father in heaven'. Sometimes the phrase is varied by the use of the adjective οὐράνιος 'heavenly'—'your heavenly Father'. It is striking that even though he speaks of 'the kingdom of God' (or 'of heaven'), he does not dwell on the thought of God as King, but speaks most naturally of him as Father. In keeping with this, the peacemakers are called 'his sons' (5:9), and we are bidden to love our enemies and pray for those who persecute us, that we may be sons of our Father who is in heaven (5:44f.). Jesus owns as his mother and brother and sister 'whoever does the will of my Father who is in heaven' (12:50). And he charges his followers: 'Be perfect, as your heavenly Father is perfect (τέλειος).' As Father in heaven, God is the pattern of character and conduct for his children, and his will is their law.

As Father in heaven, he 'will forgive your trespasses, if you forgive men their trespasses' (6:14), but he will withhold his forgiveness from those who withhold forgiveness from others. There are terrible punishments in store for the unforgiving, and it is still 'the heavenly Father' who metes them out. 'So will my heavenly Father do to you, if you do not forgive every man his brother, from your hearts' (18:35). But the emphasis is above all on the *graciousness* of the heavenly Father. If earthly fathers know how to give good gifts to their children, 'how much more will your Father who is in heaven give good things to those who ask him!' (7:11). Little ones must not be despised, 'for I tell you that in heaven their angels always behold the face of my Father who is in heaven', and 'it is not the will of my Father in heaven that one of these little ones should perish' (18:10, 14). And he will grant the prayers of his people. 'If two of you agree on earth about anything they ask, it will be done for them by my Father who is in heaven' (18:19). It remains true that the test of life is obedience to his will, not the profession of loyalty to Jesus. 'Not every one who says to me "Lord, Lord" shall enter the kingdom of heaven, but he who does the will of my Father who is in heaven' (7:21). And when we pray to him as 'our Father in heaven', the prayer that his Kingdom may come means that his will is to be done in heaven and on earth.

All these thoughts lie behind the charge to the followers of Jesus to let their light shine—to live a life of such manifest goodness that 'they may see your good works and glorify your Father who is in heaven.' Jesus does not promote his own glory, nor does he bid his followers seek glory for themselves. Their lives are to be lived in such a way that they will be a constant testimony to others of the glory of the heavenly Father.

2   FULFILMENT OF THE LAW AND THE PROPHETS *5:17-19*

[17] Do not think that I came to abolish the Law and the Prophets; I did not come to abolish, but to fulfil. [18] I tell you truly: until heaven and earth pass away, not one iota, not one stroke, shall pass away from the Law, until all be fulfilled. [19] So whoever sets aside one of the least of these commandments and teaches others to do so shall be called least in the kingdom of heaven; but whoever keeps them and teaches others to keep them shall be called great in the kingdom of heaven.

Matthew here brings together three sayings of Jesus which were transmitted separately in earlier tradition. The first and the third have no parallel in any other Gospel; the second is introduced by Luke in a different context and with some not unimportant differences of wording (Lk.16:17—'It is easier for heaven and earth to pass away than for one stroke of the Law to be dropped').

In Matthew's arrangement, the sayings are linked to make an uncompromising statement of Jesus' fidelity to the Law of Moses, the code of commandments which were the traditional base of Israel's life as the people of God. They are framed to meet the accusation of opponents that the teaching of Jesus is destructive of all that was most cherished in the spiritual inheritance of Israel. There can be no doubt that many religious leaders seriously believed this. They accused his disciples of violating the law of the sabbath, of laxity in observance of the fasts, and of failure to perform the ritual ablutions ('washing of hands') prescribed by 'the tradition of the elders' (Mt.15:2) if not by the written Law. Here Matthew represents Jesus as refuting such charges without qualification; he affirms that the Law remains in force to the last dot on the last 'i'.

'The Law and the Prophets'—a way of referring to the sacred scriptures of Israel. 'The Law' was written in the five books ascribed to Moses, which we often call the Pentateuch (a Greek, not Hebrew, term). Critical study has shown that they took shape over some centuries and reached their present form not earlier than the fifth century BC, nearly a thousand years after the time of Moses; but Jesus and the early Christians take for granted the current Jewish belief that 'the Law was given through Moses' (Jn.1:17) and commonly speak of it as 'the Law of Moses.' 'The Prophets' formed the second principal division of the sacred scriptures; it included four books which we still think of as prophetic literature (Isaiah, Ezekiel, Jeremiah, and the 'Book of the Twelve Prophets' [the 'minor prophets', in our terminology]); but it also included a number of books which we look upon as historical literature, but which the Jews called 'the Former Prophets' (Joshua, Judges, 1 and 2 Samuel, and 1 and 2 Kings). Besides these the Jews of Jesus' time made use of a large number of other sacred books, which they called simply 'the Writings'. These had not yet attained an assured position, and the collection had no fixed limits. It included all the other books which go to make up our own Old Testament—the Psalms and the Proverbs; the book of Daniel; the historical books of Ezra, Nehemiah, and Chronicles; and several others (Ruth, Job, Lamentations, etc.). There were a number of other writings, some composed in Greek, which were venerated in some circles and were included in the scriptures of the early church (most of these are found in our so-called 'Apocrypha'), but they were rejected by the synagogue authorities in the decisions which were made about the end of the first Christian century.

Jesus speaks here, then, of 'the Law and the Prophets', but the teaching which follows is concerned only with the Law, and with the Law as 'commandments'. For Jews, the Law was primary, the Prophets secondary in importance. Among the Christians, on the other hand, the ancient Scriptures came to be understood primarily as prophetic, as divinely given predictions of Christ and the church of Christ; and even 'the Law' came to be regarded less as a code of commandments than as a testimony to what God was to do through Christ. So in the Gospel of Luke, when the risen Jesus appeared to the two disciples at Emmaus, 'beginning with Moses and all the prophets, he interpreted to them in all the scriptures the things concerning himself' (Lk.24:27; cf. v.44—'everything written about me in the Law of Moses and the prophets and the psalms must be fulfilled'). But in our passage the words of Jesus are not concerned with the Law as prophecy, but with the Law as commandments. Matthew, as he gathers together the teaching of Jesus about character and conduct, places at the head of his collection a group of sayings which bear upon the question of the relationship of this teaching to the inherited tradition of Israel, the Law.

This was a burning question for the early church, as we can see from the early chapters of Acts and from the letters of Paul. The apostles and other missionaries at first confined their preaching to Jews (note especially Acts 11:19), and even when it was agreed that Gentiles might be admitted to the church through baptism (Acts 11:18), there was a strong party (described as 'some believers who belonged to the sect of the Pharisees'—Acts 15:5) which insisted that such converts must be circumcised and charged to keep the law of Moses. Paul fought them all his life, maintaining that the demand for circumcision and submission to the Law meant nothing less than a relapse into slavery (Gal.3:23–4:7). He will even say: 'You are severed from Christ, you who would be justified by law; you have fallen away from grace' (Gal.5:4); and he will write to the Romans: 'If it is the adherents of the law who are to be the heirs [of the promise made to Abraham and his descendants], faith is null and the promise is void' (Rom.4:14; cf.6:14—'you are not under law but under grace').

It is not surprising that the authenticity of all three sentences in Matthew 5:17–19 should be challenged. The saying of verse 18, in particular, could easily have been framed within the ranks of the Palestinian party of Jewish Christians who were determined to maintain the rite of circumcision and to impose the obligation to observe the Law upon Christian believers. The difficulty lies in discovering what meaning these words can have had for Matthew, when he sets them at the head of a long series of antitheses in which Jesus first cites a provision of the Law, and then sets over against it his own pronouncement, 'You have heard that it was said to the men of old . . . but I say unto you.' Matthew felt no obligation to reproduce everything that he found in his sources, and we must suppose that he did not find this saying so completely incompatible with the pronouncements of Jesus which follow, as it seems to us. Whatever Jesus may have said, Matthew could not but know that the law of circumcision (Gen.17:9–14) was effectively annulled in Christian practice; that the food laws were no longer generally observed by Christians; and that Peter as well as Paul would 'live like a Gentile and not like a Jew' (Gal.2:14—precisely in the context of the food laws). Heaven and earth had not passed away, but it was abundantly evident that few Christians held that the Law was still valid for them to the last dot over the 'i'.

There can be little doubt that verse 18, with its insistence of the continuing validity of the Law even in its most minute provisions, was formulated in the course of debate in the early days of the church—debate not between Christians and Jews, but between Christians who accepted the kind of freedom from the Law which is most radically defended by Paul, and Christians who held to a rigorous observance of all that the Law required. Verse 19 is a polemic against those who claim such freedom for themselves, and especially against Christian teachers like Paul who teach such a way of life. It has even been held that it is an attack upon Paul himself (Manson, *Sayings*, pp. 25,154; Johannes Weiss, *History of Primitive Christianity* (1937) Vol. II, p. 753). We must in any case take note that Matthew himself reports that when Jesus is asked the question: 'Who is greatest in the kingdom of heaven?' he does not reply, 'Whoever keeps the Law, even to its least important commandment, and teaches others to do so'; but he calls a child to him, and says: 'Truly, I say to you, unless you turn and become like little children, you will never enter the kingdom of heaven. Whoever humbles himself like this child, he is the greatest in the kingdom of heaven' (18:1—4). And with this we may compare his word to the disciples: 'Whoever would be great among you must be your servant' (20:26).

VERSE 17: 'Do not think that I came to abolish the Law and the Prophets; I came not to abolish but to fulfil.' This opening declaration can hardly have been made apart from the recognition that some people had begun to think that the teaching of Jesus was destructive of basic Jewish tradition. 'There was no point on which devout Palestinian Jews were more sensitive than on any attempt to tamper with the Law, which was for them something given by God Himself, and therefore perfect and irreformable' (T.W. Manson, *Sayings*, p. 153). It is most unlikely that the charge of tampering with, or of abolishing, the Law was made at the very beginning of Jesus' ministry, and Jesus would not reply to such a charge before it was made. If the words are his, they could hardly be called for until a later stage of his mission, when the 'scribes and Pharisees' were beginning to take a hostile attitude to him. Even then, the words 'I came' imply a claim of Messianic status, and indeed of heavenly origin, on the part of Jesus; for they carry the sense 'I came down to earth'—'I came from heaven.' There is a high christological claim for Jesus here, and we may well question whether Jesus himself ever spoke of his mission in terms like these. R. Bultmann admits that 'there are no possible grounds for objecting to the idea that Jesus could have spoken in the first person about himself and his coming; that need be no more than what befits his prophetic self-consciousness. Yet as individual sayings they rouse a number of suspicions' (*HST*, p. 153). But the question of authenticity is not of primary importance; whether Jesus stated his position in precisely this form of words or not, the saying is a faithful statement of his fundamental attitude. He holds consistently that the Law was given to Israel by God, and that it retains its validity for him and for those who would follow him. If a man would 'enter into life' he must 'keep the commandments' (Mt.19:17). Only if the principle is applied in the minute way which is demanded in verses 18 and 19 may we feel that he is misrepresented. And Matthew himself brings a broadly different interpretation of how the 'fulfilment' of the Law is accomplished, when he sums up the basic teaching of Jesus in the words of the Golden Rule. 'Whatever you wish that men would do to you, do so to them; for this is the law and the prophets' (7:12).

3 THE HIGHER RIGHTEOUSNESS EXPOUNDED IN SIX ANTITHESES
5:20–48

A Higher Righteousness Required 5:20

[20] For I tell you, unless your righteousness far exceeds that of the scribes and Pharisees, you will never enter the kingdom of heaven.

The affirmation that the Law must be held valid and scrupulously obeyed to its most minute detail would seem to imply that Jesus approves of the scribes and Pharisees, for they were the very people who devoted themselves most conscientiously to ordering their lives in keeping with all that the Law commanded. Now he warns his disciples that this is not enough for men who hope to enter the kingdom of heaven. Of them is required a righteousness that far exceeds the righteousness of the scribes and Pharisees. Are we to take this in the sense that the disciples of Jesus are to outdo the Pharisees in painstaking adherence to the prescription of the Law? Or is there behind these words a hint that the kind of righteousness which can be defined in terms of strict obedience to the Law is intrinsically incapable of commending a man to God?

Scribes and Pharisees are grouped together as practising a righteousness which falls short of what is required of those who would enter the kingdom of heaven. Here, as elsewhere in his Gospel, Matthew leaves the impression that they formed a single party in Israel. They are, however, quite different. There were scribes in Israel long before anyone ever heard of Pharisees, and they did not constitute a sect but a profession, distinguished by competence in the interpretation of the Law. Some scribes might belong to the sect of the Pharisees, but not many Pharisees would have anything like the professional training of the scribes.

The scribes were men of learning, the scholars of Israel, and their dominant concern was the study of the Law, written and oral. But in Israel, the only law was 'the Law of the Lord'—the Law which had been given by God through Moses at Mount Sinai (this was the established faith of the Jewish people). The written Law was contained in the five books of Moses; the oral Law was also regarded as given to Moses, though it was not put in writing but transmitted by word of mouth from scribe to disciple. It was required of the disciple, therefore, that he should memorize accurately what his master taught in order that he might himself pass on faithfully the body of legal lore which took shape as 'the tradition of the elders' (Mt.15:2). The most extreme methods of interpretation were employed to find a meaning in the written Law that would confirm the rulings established in the oral tradition, but in theory these rulings were also given by revelation, through Moses. Accordingly, all law in Israel was looked upon as *religious* law, and the scribes, the acknowledged experts in the understanding of the Law, were religious leaders, even though the functions of priesthood were no part of their office. At the time of Jesus, they were laymen with professional qualifications; towards the end of the century, as the priesthood declined in importance after the destruction of the Temple (AD 70), they came to be ordained as 'rabbis', each rabbi ordaining his own disciples as they became qualified under his guiding hand. The oral Law itself now began to be codified in written form as *Mishnah*, and towards the end of the second century the Mishnah of Rabbi Judah the Prince was formulated and won acceptance as the authoritative compendium of the tradition preserved by the scribes.

The Pharisees were a society of laymen, drawn from all classes of the population, without hereditary distinctions (like the priests) or professional attainments (like the scribes). We do not hear of them until the second century before Christ, and the origins of the sect are wrapped in obscurity. To some degree, they may be regarded as continuing the tradition of the *Hasidîm* ('the pious') who emerge in the time of the Maccabees, 'mighty warriors of Israel, every one who offered himself willingly for the law' (1 Macc.2:42). They took a strong stand against the attempts of the Seleucid rulers of the land, especially Antiochus IV Epiphanes (175–164 BC), to impose Greek customs and Greek religious rites upon the people of Judaea. The name 'Pharisees' is used of them by the Jewish historian Josephus (late first century AD) in speaking of their opposition to the Hasmonean ruler John Hyrcanus (134–104 BC). They were ready to fight to preserve the faith of Israel against foreign efforts to subvert it, but they were equally hostile to an independent Jewish state which would be secular. They made it their aim to bring all life in Israel, private and public, under the rule of the sacred Law.

The name itself is generally taken to be derived from the Hebrew *parash*, 'separate', so that they would be known as 'the separated ones'. This leaves room for differences of understanding what particular kind of separateness was meant; but it is perhaps best taken in the sense that they kept themselves apart from all that might cause them to incur defilement, moral or ceremonial. To them it would be an offense to eat with Gentiles, or with 'tax collectors and sinners.' They reproached Jesus for what they looked upon as unseemly rashness: 'This man receives sinners and eats with them' (Lk.15:2), and they asked his disciples: 'Why does your teacher eat with tax collectors and sinners?' (Mt.9:11.) In the same spirit they attacked Peter, after he visited the household of the Roman centurion Cornelius, with the challenge: 'Why did you go to uncircumcised men and eat with them?' (Acts 11:3.) The Jewish historian Josephus gives us the view of a Greek (Nicholas of Damascus, who did not admire them) in a description of them as 'a body of Jews who profess to be more religious than others, and to explain the laws more accurately' (*Jewish War* I.5.2). They organized themselves in groups for the study of the Law, and in rabbinic writings they are often called *habherîm*, 'companions'. They sought to put into practice the teaching of the scribes, and to bring the Law to bear upon the vastly changed conditions of the national life.

As the late Professor T.W. Manson insisted, 'We do the scribes and Pharisees a monstrous injustice if we imagine that they did not conscientiously strive to carry out what was for them a divinely appointed way of life. Indeed if any criticism is to be made, it is that they were too conscientious; that in their zeal for the minutest details of Law and tradition they were apt to lose sight of the larger moral purposes which the Law as a whole was meant to serve' (*Sayings*, p. 162). If Jesus calls upon his disciples for a righteousness that far exceeds the righteousness of the scribes and Pharisees, his words actually presuppose a general agreement that the scribes and Pharisees are precisely the people who were most esteemed for their scrupulous fidelity to the Law. Even their high standards of conduct are not high enough for those who aspire to the kingdom of heaven.

Exposition of the Higher Righteousness

The pronouncement of verse 20 stands as a heading for a series of antitheses (vv.21–48) which serve as concrete illustrations of the righteousness required of the disciples, which far surpasses the righteousness of the scribes and Pharisees. Jesus takes for his point of departure six provisions of the Law of Moses, and then declares with Messianic authority that none of them goes far enough. The commandment which forbids murder is extended to condemn the hatred which contains in itself the seeds of murder; the prohibition of adultery carries with it the condemnation of the lustful look which is a token of the will to commit adultery. There are six of these antitheses in all. They are each prefaced by the formula (with inconsequential variations of wording): 'You have heard that it was said to the men of old . . . but I say unto you.' But before we proceed to examine them severally, we must take note that in each case they are accompanied by a series of comments, or elaborations, which go beyond the terms of the antithesis, and these extensions are probably the work of Matthew himself. Sometimes his additions are sayings of Jesus which are found elsewhere in the Gospels in a different context, and sometimes even with a different sense. Sometimes they are better understood not as sayings of Jesus himself (though Matthew presents them as such), but as Christian interpretations or even modifications of the absolute demands of Jesus, intended to adapt them to the practical possibilities of the human condition. The sayings of Jesus are absolute, in the sense that they state the will of God for man without concern for the possibilities of human nature or the ambiguities of moral choice in a world that is far removed from the perfection of the kingdom of heaven. The Christian teacher soon recognized that he must help deal with 'the actualities of existence in this world. The ethic of crisis had to be adapted to the humdrum affairs of life.' (Davies, *Setting*, p. 387.)

And so Matthew reflects in some of his additions to the basic antitheses something of the development that had already taken place in the oral tradition of the teaching of Jesus, by which 'these *radical* words began to take on a *regulatory* character, that is, they became used as guides for the actual business of living.' (*ibid.*)

This will not apply to all the supplementary material in this section. A good deal of it is to be seen simply as part of Matthew's editorial grouping together of sayings, without concern for their original context, in a *topical* arrangement, bringing together sayings which he regarded as having a bearing upon the same general theme.

The formula 'You have heard . . . but I say unto you' is not found in any of the other Gospels, and it occurs nowhere else in Matthew. It is probable, however, that he did not frame it himself, but found it in one of his sources. A literary analysis of the passage leads to the conclusion that his series of six antitheses is an enlargement of an earlier series of three; and he has then used the heading to group other sayings with these in the same antithetical form, as further illustrations of the meaning of the higher righteousness. It is generally agreed that the earlier series consisted of the first, the second, and the fourth of those given by Matthew in the sentences which follow:

You have heard that it was said to the men of old, 'You shall not kill; and whoever kills shall be liable to judgement.' But I say to you that every one who is angry with his brother shall be liable to judgement (vv.21,22a).

You have heard that it was said, 'You shall not commit adultery.' But I say to you that every one who looks at a woman lustfully has already committed adultery with her in his heart (vv.27f.).

Again you have heard that it was said to the men of old, 'You shall not swear falsely, but shall perform to the Lord what you have sworn.' But I say to you, Do not swear at all (vv.33,34a).

The First Antithesis 5:21–26

[21] You have heard that it was said to the men of old, 'You shall not kill; and whoever kills shall be liable to judgement.' [22a] But I say to you that every one who is angry with his brother is liable to judgement.

First supplement: [22b] Whoever says 'Raca!' to his brother shall be liable to the Sanhedrin, and whoever says to his brother 'Fool!' shall be liable to the Gehenna of fire.

Second supplement: [23-24] So if you are offering your gift at the altar, and there remember that your brother has something against you, leave your gift there before the altar and go away; first be reconciled to your brother, and then come and offer your gift.

Third supplement: [25-26] Make an agreement quickly with your accuser, while you are in the street with him, lest he hand you over to the judge, and the judge to the guard, and you be thrown into jail. I tell you truly, you will not get out until you have paid back the last penny.

'You have heard'—through the reading of the Scriptures in the synagogue services. There was not much private reading in the ancient world, and many of the hearers of Jesus would never have learned to read and write; besides, when every copy of a book had to be made by hand, costs were high, and the poor of the land, who formed most of the audience, could hardly afford to buy a leather scroll of the Law for themselves. 'The men of old' means the generation which received the Law through Moses at Sinai. The citation which Jesus makes is a commandment of the Decalogue, so that we cannot suppose that he is talking only of the oral Law, 'the tradition of the elders'. He begins with the very heart of the written Law, the Ten Commandments. The point of his pronouncement is that the prohibition of murder goes beyond the overt act to the inward disposition, and men are judged (by God) not merely by what they do, but for what they are. Any court of law, in Israel as elsewhere, can take cognizance only of the act; it can deal with murder, but not with hatred. The saying of Jesus points beyond any earthly tribunal to the ultimate judgement of God; it is before this Judge that men will be called to answer for the sin of hatred.

The first supplement is conceived in a quite different spirit; it looks very much like a fragment of a rule of discipline for a community. It has even been suggested that it might have been formulated by someone who had felt the influence of the Qûmran sect, whose Dead Sea Scrolls have come to light in recent years. In their *Manual of Discipline*, gradations of punishment are prescribed for various offences which may be committed by a member of the community against his fellows. In particular, there is a little section which deals with angry words. The terms 'Raca' and 'More' (Fool) are not mentioned, but the rule uses more general expressions, 'one who speaks with a stiff neck', or 'speaks in anger' or 'haughtily', or 'one who vilifies unjustly his fellow' (see Davies, *Setting* pp. 237–

38; for a translation of the *Manual*, see Millar Burrows, *The Dead Sea Scrolls* (1956), pp. 371–89; esp. section III, 'The Rules of the Order', pp. 376–84). The initial words of Jesus do not seem to allow for such calculations of less or more serious offences, since they put murder and anger on the same footing as violations of the sixth commandment.

The meaning of 'Raca' is not certain; it is not Greek, but a transliteration of an Aramaic word, obviously an insult. Perhaps it does not differ greatly in meaning from 'More', the vocative of the Greek word for 'fool'; but as it is used here it implies that the second is a more deadly insult than the first. 'Sanhedrin' is a Hebrew (and Aramaic) transliteration of the Greek word *synedrion*, 'session' or 'council'; it was used of all manner of local councils in Jewish localities, but especially of the Great Sanhedrin in Jerusalem, composed of priests, elders, and scribes (cf. Mk.14:53), with the High Priest presiding. 'Gehenna' is a Greek transliteration of the Hebrew *Gē'-hinnom*, 'valley of Hinnom' (frequently 'valley of Ben-Hinnom'), a deep gully south of Jerusalem which was execrated because it was the place of the cremation of children in sacrifice to gods of Canaan (Jer.32:35; 2 Ki.23:10). In later times it became the symbol of the hell of fire in which sinners were to be consumed; this idea appears for the first time in the second century BC, in Jewish literature. Hell was a Greek invention; the notion of the punishment of evil men in the after-life was promoted by no less an authority than Plato (see M. Nilsson, *Greek Folk Religion* (1940), pp. 118–20; more fully in his *Geschichte der griechischen Religion*, Bd. II, 'Die hellenistische und römische Zeit', 2nd. ed. rev. (1961), pp.304f., 549f., and see Index under 'Unterweltsstrafen'). The Greeks, of course, had no thought of any survival of the physical frame of the individual; the body did not survive death. But for Jews, the notion of a 'naked soul' was abhorrent, if not utterly inconceivable; the after-life is conceived in terms of a resurrection of the body, and the body suffers along with the soul in hell. In a rabbinical treatise, probably of the third century AD (*Tosephta* 'Sanhedrin' 13.2), the Jewish belief is expressed in these words:

The wicked of Israel in their bodies, and the wicked of the nations of the world in their bodies go down to hell and are punished in it for twelve months. After twelve months their souls become extinct, and their bodies are burnt up, and hell casts them out, and they turn to ashes, and the wind scatters them and strews them beneath the feet of the righteous (translated in G.F. Moore, *Judaism*, vol. II (1928), p. 387).

It is this imagery which is used in our passage; the judgement of God takes effect in the sentencing of sinners to a fiery hell. The same image is used several times in Matthew; in Mark it occurs in a single passage (9:43,45,47, paralleled in Mt.5:29—30); and we find it once only in Luke (12:5, paralleled in Mt.10:28). Elsewhere it is not used at all in the New Testament except for one verse in the Epistle of James, and there it does not refer to punishments in the after-life (Jas.3:6—'the tongue, the world of iniquity . . . which sets on fire the cycle of nature and is itself set on fire by Gehenna'). The idea of a fiery hell is of course introduced in other forms, especially in the book of Revelation, which pictures 'a lake of fire and sulphur' into which the devil and those who have served him are thrown at the Last Judgement, to be 'tormented day and night for ever and ever' (Rev.20:10—15). And in the scene of the judgement of the nations, which forms the conclusion of the last of the great discourses of Jesus as constructed by Matthew, the sentence of damnation is put in the words: 'Depart from me, accursed, into the eternal fire prepared for the devil and his angels,' and they 'go away into eternal punishment' (Mt.25:41,46).

Whatever the origin of the saying, it is patently absurd to threaten men with the judgement of the Sanhedrin for one insult ('*Raca*'), and with 'the hell of fire' for another ('*More*'—fool). How could such a saying ever have found acceptance in the tradition of Jesus' words at all? We have seen that they are foreign to the context in which Matthew has placed them. We may raise the further question of whether this imagery of a hell of fire was employed by Jesus at all. Apart from Matthew's Gospel, it finds almost no echo in the Synoptic tradition, and there is no trace of it in the Gospel of John. For Matthew, it seems to have had a morbid fascination. We find it brought forward in a different way in his interpretation of the parable of the Tares in the Wheat (Mt.13:37—43), which is almost certainly the work of Matthew himself (Jeremias, *Parables*, pp.81—85). Here the burning of weeds after they have been separated from the wheat at the harvest is treated allegorically as signifying the burning of evil-doers, after they have been separated from the righteous at the close of the age. 'Just as the weeds are gathered and burned with fire, so will it be at the close of the age. The Son of man will send his angels, and they will gather out of his kingdom all causes of sin and all evil-doers, and throw them into the furnace of fire; there men will weep and gnash their teeth' (vv.40—42). The same figure is used by him again in his interpretation of the parable of the fishing net, where the figure of 'burning' is quite inappropriate (unsaleable fish are not burned). In the parable, the fishermen sorted the fish and *threw away* the bad; in the interpretation, the sorting is again allegorized as 'the close of the age', when the angels 'separate the evil from the righteous, and throw them into the furnace of fire; there men will weep and gnash their teeth' (Mt.13:47–50). This interpretation must also be regarded as the work of Matthew. We may remark that the words 'weeping and gnashing of teeth' are found with one exception (Lk.13:28, parallel to Mt.8:12), only in Matthew, who uses them six times.

It can scarcely be doubted that Jesus warns men of the danger of punishments in the after-life, but he seldom mentions the nature of such punishments. Most frequently, he speaks of disowning and rejection at the judgement: 'I never knew you; depart from me, you evil-doers' (Mt.7:23); and of exclusion from the kingdom of heaven —of the shutting of the door against those who do not come in time, or who are found unworthy (Lk.13:25). His emphasis is on the glorious destiny that may be missed, not on the sufferings to be inflicted. The 'hell of fire' and the 'weeping and gnashing of teeth' may have been used by him as figures of the endless and vain remorse of those who realize too late that they have missed their opportunity of eternal blessedness.

The second Matthaean supplement turns from the negative—the warning against anger—to the positive counterpart, the active search for reconciliation. It suggests that where there is hostility between man and man, it is vain to offer worship to God. It is striking that Jesus does not speak of seeking reconciliation with one who has offended you, but with one who 'has something against you'. He does not ask whether you are really to blame; there is no need of fixing the blame before you seek to make friends. In the very act of offering your gift at the altar, you are to break it off and straighten out the trouble with your brother before you come back to God's altar to make your gift.

The third supplement is a parable which follows up the theme of reconciliation. Here we have pictured a man who is being hauled to court for the recovery of a debt. He is advised to settle out of court. On the surface, this looks like a bit of prudent advice, such as a lawyer frequently gives to his client to this day. Rather than risk the consequences of an action which may go against you—in this case, it is assumed that the man is actually in debt and that the creditor will win his case—it is better to come to an agreement. The situation leaves no room for delay; the man and his accuser are actually 'in the street', that is, on the way to court, and agreement must be reached at once. It is taken for granted that a man may be imprisoned for debt, and kept in jail until the debt is paid.

The same parable is found also in Luke, but in a very different context (Lk.12:58–59). There it is clearly taken as a warning to prepare for the judgement. Sin is often thought of as a debt which man has incurred, as in the words of the Lord's Prayer: 'Forgive us our debts, as we also have forgiven our debtors' (Mt.6:12). The point of the parable, in Luke, is the urgency of coming to a settlement with God before it is too late. In Matthew's version, it is transferred to the relations between man and man, and so made to serve as a plea to seek reconciliation with one whom we have offended, without delay. The urgency of seeking reconciliation with God falls into the background; with a certain infelicity, the accuser is imagined as a human creditor, and reconciliation becomes little more than common prudence. Are we to seek reconciliation with a brother simply because we fear that he may invoke the whole rigour of the law against us? It is scarcely possible to imagine that Jesus himself offered this rather sordid motive as a ground for urgency in the search for reconciliation. See the remarks of C.H. Dodd on this passage (*Parables*, pp. 105–08).

The Second Antithesis 5:27–30

²⁷You have heard that it was said, 'You shall not commit adultery.' ²⁸But I say to you that every one who looks at a woman to desire her has already committed adultery with her in his heart.

Supplement: ²⁹If your right eye causes you to sin, pluck it out and throw it away; it is better that you lose one of your members than that your whole body be thrown into hell. ³⁰And if your right hand causes you to sin, cut it off and throw it away; it is better that you lose one of your members than that your whole body go into hell. ['Hell' in these verses is in Greek *Gehenna*.]

The basic antithesis extends the seventh commandment in the same way as the first has dealt with the sixth commandment. The prohibition against the act is extended to include the inward disposition which reveals the essential character as much as the act itself. The warning of judgement is not expressed but is implied; God knows the hearts of men and his judgements are not made on the evidence of outward acts alone.

It may be noted that 'woman' here means specifically a married woman (since it is a question of adultery); and that the Decalogue itself forbids such desire: 'You shall not covet your neighbour's wife' (Ex.20:17). In the Greek translation, the verb 'covet' is rendered by ἐπιϑυμέω, and it is this verb that is used again in the antithesis ('to desire her').

If this is to be taken as a 'demand' of Jesus, then it must be said that he is demanding the impossible, for it is the universal experience that the sexual impulses are uncontrollable. Like Paul, we can 'delight in the law of God in our inmost self,' and yet find 'another law in our members, at war with the law of our mind and making us captive to the law of sin which dwells in our members' (Rom.7:22–23). There is surely an underlying thought here that when we judge others we condemn ourselves. We all stand in need of God's forgiveness, and we cannot hope to overcome the evil in us but by divine grace.

Such considerations as these have led to the classic Lutheran interpretation of the Sermon, widely accepted in Protestant theology, as intended to drive men to despair, to recognize their complete inability to attain to such a standard of life and conduct as is here set before them, and so to learn that they are wholly dependent on the saving work of Christ, that they may be justified by faith alone, without the works of the Law. This is, in effect, to impose a Paulinizing interpretation on the Sermon. It may well be that Paul has penetrated into the significance of Jesus more deeply than Matthew, but it is more than doubtful that Matthew himself intended his readers to entertain any such understanding of the teaching which he has presented in the Sermon. For him, it seems clear that Jesus is a lawgiver, of supreme authority, and that he lays commands upon men which are intended to be obeyed. Our primary task must be to discern, if we can, how Matthew understands the demands of Jesus. This does not prevent us from going on to ask if he has fully appreciated the deeper implications of the teaching.

In the supplement to this antithesis, Matthew has made use of a pair of sayings which are found in Mark (9:43,45,47) in a different context, attached to a warning against causing anyone who believes in Jesus to sin. 'Whoever causes one of these little ones who believe in me to sin, it would be better for him if a great millstone were hung round his neck and he were thrown into the sea' (v.42). Mark mentions first the offending hand, then the foot, and last of all the eye. Since Matthew has spoken of the lustful *look*, he finds it appropriate to mention first the eye, even 'your right eye,' that causes you to sin. No one will suppose that Jesus (or the evangelist) means the words to be taken literally. He is not advising any kind of self-mutilation. It is a forceful image of the drastic effort that must be made 'to tame the natural desires and passions at all costs' (Manson, *Sayings*, p. 157). The figure is carried over into the threat of hell; it is not to be supposed that Jesus thinks of men entering the world of the dead with the physical disabilities which they have suffered in life. Matthew has not included Mark's mention of the offending foot; and he has dropped Mark's gruesome description of hell as the place 'where their worm does not die, and the fire is not quenched' (Mk.9:48). He does mention the foot in the second use of the same passage, where he is keeping to the Markan context (Mt.18:8–9).

The Third Antithesis 5:31–32

[31] It was also said, 'Whoever divorces his wife, let him give her a certificate of divorce.' [32] But I say to you that every one who divorces his wife, except on the ground of unchastity, makes her an adulteress; and whoever marries a divorced woman commits adultery.

This is the only one of the six antitheses which does not begin with the phrase 'You have heard'. When the question is raised again (Mt.19:3–9, paralleled in Mk.10:2–12), the command is specifically ascribed to Moses (vv.7,8). The reference is to Deut.24:1–4. This passage does not in fact lay down the command that the husband who divorces his wife must provide her with a certificate. It takes this procedure for granted, and goes on to prescribe that if she marries again and is again divorced (under the same form—the second husband 'dislikes her and writes her a bill of divorce'—v.3), then the first husband 'may not take her again to be his wife, after she has been defiled' (v.4). All that can be said is that 'Moses' (that is, the Law ascribed to him) does not forbid divorce, but is concerned only with the case of a wife who has been divorced twice. It is not even said that she may not marry a third time, but only that her first husband may not remarry her. More than that, it supposes that she has been guilty of some 'indecency' in her first marriage. The second husband may divorce her simply because he 'dislikes her'; but of the first it is said, 'if she finds no favour in his eyes because he has found some indecency in her' (v.1). This is probably the clause that has led Matthew to insert his exception to the rule of Jesus—'except on the ground of unchastity'.

This antithesis is really a supplement to the second, giving a new definition of adultery, extending it to include remarriage after divorce. In the parallel passages, there are some wide variations in the way that the law against divorce is framed.

In Mark and in Luke no exception is made. In Mark, after making his response to the Pharisees (10:2—9), Jesus is questioned by his disciples, in the house, and he declares to them: 'Whoever divorces his wife and marries another commits adultery against her; and if the woman who has divorced her husband marries another, she commits adultery' (vv.11f.).

Neither of the other evangelists makes any reference to the case of a woman divorcing her husband, which was not possible under Jewish law.

Luke, who does not make use of the setting of a debate with the Pharisees, introduces here the provision that 'he who marries a woman divorced from her husband commits adultery' (Lk.16:18). This has been used by Matthew here in 5:32b, and is not repeated in 19:9.

Neither Luke nor Matthew speaks of the husband committing adultery against his wife. Here again Mark has used language which would be impossible in a Jewish setting; in Jewish law, the adulterer committed an offence against the husband of the unfaithful wife, not against his own wife. In keeping with this Jewish approach, Paul charges the Thessalonians 'that no man transgress, and wrong his brother in this matter' (1 Thess.4:6).

Only Matthew mentions any exception to this stringent rule— 'except for unchastity' (19:9), 'except on the ground of unchastity' (5:32), and only he adds the curious statement that the husband who divorces his wife 'makes her an adulteress'. This peculiar saying is perhaps best understood as applying to the remarriage of the wife; the first husband, in divorcing her, is held to be responsible for creating a situation in which she cannot remarry without committing adultery. Nothing is said at this point about the case of the husband who remarries after divorce.

The sayings of Jesus about divorce must be understood in the first instance in the context of scribal debate. The two great schools of the period took different positions. The school of Shammai was much the more rigorous; it maintained that a man 'must not divorce his wife unless he has found in her a matter of shame'; the rival school of Hillel held that he could divorce her for the merest trifle, 'even if she has burnt his food in cooking it' (*Mishnah*, 'Gittin', ix.10). The debate was over the causes for which divorce might be allowed; both schools take for granted that divorce is permissible and that the decision rests with the husband. The handling of the material in Matthew suggests that Jesus takes the side of the school of Shammai. But the tradition indicates that the exception introduced by Matthew is secondary, and that Jesus is not interested in the conditions which may justify divorce. He admits that the law of Moses allows for divorce, but he holds that this was a concession made in recognition of the hardness of men's hearts. Looking back to the story of creation (itself a part of the Law of Moses), he reminds his questioners that 'in the beginning it was not so' (Mt.19:8). 'Have you not read that he who created them from the beginning made them male and female, and said, "For this reason a man shall leave his father and mother and be joined to his wife, and the two shall become one flesh"? . . . What therefore God has joined together, let no man put asunder' (Mt.19:4–6). This goes far beyond the debates of the schools, and looks upon marriage as ideally, in the primal design of God (and so in the kingdom of heaven), the indissoluble union of one man and one woman.

Here again we have an absolute saying, which makes no allowances for the realities of human character ('the hardness of your hearts'). But there is no room to hold that Jesus intended such sayings to be taken as legislation, even for his followers, much less for the state. The Matthaean addition reflects again the tendency to translate such absolute declarations of the unconditioned will of God into regulations for conduct in an imperfect society.

The Fourth Antithesis 5:33–37

[33] Again you have heard that it was said to the men of old, 'You shall not swear falsely, but shall perform to the Lord what you have sworn.' [34] But I say to you, Do not swear at all.

Supplement: [Do not swear at all] either by heaven for it is God's throne, [35] or by earth, for it is his footstool, or by Jerusalem, for it is the city of the great King. [36] And do not swear by your head, for you cannot make one hair white or black.

[37] Let your word be 'Yes, Yes' or 'No, No'; anything more than this comes from the evil one.

In this instance, Jesus does not cite directly any clause of the Law, but puts into his own words the substance of several passages which bear in part upon perjury and in part on failure to perform a vow that has been made to God. The prohibition of perjury is perhaps expressed most clearly in Leviticus 19:12, in the words: 'You shall not swear by my name falsely, and so profane the name of the Lord.' This is a particular application of the third commandment, 'You shall not take the name of the Lord your God in vain' (Ex.20: 7). The performance of vows is dealt with very fully in Numbers 30:2–15. Most of this passage is devoted to stating circumstances under which a vow or pledge taken by a woman may or may not be binding (if she is still in her father's house, it is not binding unless the father consents to it; if she is married, it is void if her husband disapproves). The basic principle is stated at the beginning (v.2): 'When a man vows a vow to the Lord, or swears an oath to bind himself by a pledge, he shall not break his word; he shall do according to all that proceeds out of his mouth.' There is a similar provision in Deuteronomy 23:21–23, which begins with the words: 'When you make a vow to the Lord your God you shall not be slack to pay it; for the Lord your God will surely require it of you.'

In the primary saying of Jesus, two matters are combined: an oath taken to confirm the truth of a statement, and a vow made to the Lord. The supplementary comment bears only upon the former of these—a statement made under oath. It then goes on to mention a number of forms of oath; a man swears 'by heaven', 'by earth', 'by Jerusalem', 'by my head'. The first three are forbidden on the ground that they are equivalent to invoking God himself; the third on the strange ground that you cannot change the colour of your hair! Nothing is said of whether the statement to which you have sworn is true or false—the only matter with which the Mosaic Law is concerned. In the Psalms, the blessing of the Lord is assured to 'the man who does not lift up his soul to what is false, and does not swear deceitfully' (Ps.24:4), 'who swears to his own hurt and does not change' (Ps.15:4). The taking of oaths is not only allowed; it is actually commanded. 'You shall fear the Lord your God . . . and by his name you shall swear' (Deut.10:20). The Lord himself swears in confirmation of his promises (Gen.22:16; Deut.8:18, and frequently; cf.Heb.6:13).

It is clear that in this antithesis, Jesus rejects an explicit provision of the Law. This would appear to be irreconcilable with the assertion that 'till heaven and earth pass away, not an iota, not a dot, shall pass away from the Law' (5:18); and that 'anyone who annuls one of the least of these commandments shall be called least in the kingdom of heaven' (5:19).

The last sentence of the supplement suggests that the word of a truly honest man is all that is needed. Perhaps there is some thought that the taking of oaths carries the implication that we cannot trust people to tell the truth if they do not support it with an oath.

The passage finds an echo in the Epistle of James. 'Above all, my brethren, do not swear, either by heaven or by earth or with any other oath, but let your yes be yes and your no be no, that you may not fall under condemnation' (James 5:12). This is probably what is meant by the peculiar wording found in Matthew, where the sentence reads literally: 'Let your word be "Yes, Yes," "No, No."' When you say 'Yes' or 'No', you are saying unequivocally what you mean, and there is no need to confirm it with an oath of any kind.

There is some discussion of oaths in the rabbinical writings, but swearing is never totally forbidden. The stress is on taking oaths in no casual way, and on keeping them faithfully.

The Fifth Antithesis 5:38–42

38 You have heard that it was said, 'An eye for an eye' and 'a tooth for a tooth.' 39 But I say to you, Do not resist one who is evil, but if anyone strikes you on the right cheek, turn to him the other also; 40 and if any one would sue you and take your coat, let him have your cloak as well; 41 and if any one forces you to go one mile, go with him two miles.

42 Give to any one who begs from you, and do not refuse any one who would borrow from you.

The *lex talionis* (retaliation in kind, a penalty proportioned to the offence) as it is cited here is extracted from a longer catalogue of injuries which is given in Exodus 21:22. 'If any harm follows, then you shall give life for life, eye for eye, tooth for tooth, hand for hand, foot for foot, burn for burn, wound for wound, stripe for stripe.' In this passage, it is attached to the particular case of hurt done to a woman with child in the course of a fight ('When men strive together, and hurt a woman with child, so that there is a miscarriage'—v.22). In Leviticus it is applied more generally. 'When a man causes a disfigurement in his neighbour, as he has done it shall be done to him, fracture for fracture, eye for eye, tooth for tooth; as he has disfigured a man, he shall be disfigured' (Lev.24: 19f.). Another application is made in Deuteronomy 19:16–21, which prescribes that a false witness shall suffer the punishment that he intended to bring upon his brother. Similar provisions are included in other ancient law codes of the Near East and also of Rome (the Twelve Tables).

All these provisions have to do with the public administration of justice; the appropriate punishment is to be administered by judges or by the community. Jesus applies the principle to private vengeance. The *lex talionis* was in its time a social advance of great magnitude; it put an end to the vendetta, the blood feud, which allowed unlimited retaliation for an injury done to a member of the family or tribe, so that an entire group could be wiped out before the demands for vengeance were satisfied. By the *lex talionis* the injury done by a man to his neighbour was brought within the domain of public law, and the penalty was limited to the equivalent of the injury suffered. The law sounds savage, but it was actually a softening of the primitive fierceness of the feud, which set no limits to the revenge that the group might take against the offender and all his family or tribe. The words of Jesus, however, are not concerned with public law, but with private vengeance. It is not enough to limit revenge to the imposition of the same injury; Jesus declares that we must take no revenge at all. This is the force of the saying, 'Do not resist him who is evil'; it means substantially, 'Do not seek revenge of any kind against one who has done you a wrong.' The follower of Jesus must not let his conduct be determined by the conduct of those who treat him badly.

The thought goes beyond the counsel of non-retaliation. Far from hitting back, Jesus bids us accept—even invite?—a second blow. Like the sayings about plucking out an eye and cutting off a foot (vv.29,30), this is best taken as an exaggerated way of insisting that we must not return evil for evil, blow for blow: it is better to endure more blows than to fight back. No special motive for such patience is suggested; there is no hint, for instance, that the attacker may be moved to feel shame. All is concentrated on the response of the man attacked. It is presupposed that the attack is unprovoked and unjustified, and that the man attacked might have the right to defend himself; he is not to stand on his rights, but to act as befits a disciple of Jesus, a member of the kingdom of heaven, who will not be moved to hostility by any wrong done to his person.

A second saying applies the same principle to legal proceedings; now the wrongdoer does not make a physical attack but uses the machinery of the courts to possess himself of your property. Perhaps the procedure for the recovery of a debt is meant to be understood. The Law provided that a creditor might not keep overnight a cloak given in pledge. 'When you make your neighbour a loan of any sort . . . if he is a poor man, you shall not sleep in his pledge; when the sun goes down, you shall restore to him the pledge, that he may

sleep in his cloak and bless you.' (Deut.24:10,12f.; cf. Ex.22:25f.)
The Law does not specifically say that you may not keep his undergarment (χιτών—'coat', in *RSV*), so the creditor seizes that, leaving
you with the cloak (ἱμάτιον). If this happens, you are charged not
merely to give up the undergarment but to let your creditor have
your cloak as well. Taken literally, this would mean that you would
be left naked; ἱμάτιον and χιτών are all the clothing that a man
wears; and a poor man (he must be very poor if he has to give his
clothing in pledge for a loan) would not have a second outfit. If the
words are to be taken literally, they would mean that one was left
to go out into the street naked, or not go out at all. This must be
regarded as another gigantic exaggeration by way of illustration of
the principle that the disciple of Jesus must not stand upon his
rights, but give more than strict justice would demand of him. In
the same spirit, Paul deprecates lawsuits among Christians. 'To have
lawsuits with one another at all is a defeat for you. Why do you not
rather suffer wrong? Why not rather be defrauded?' (1 Cor.6:7.) For
the Apostle, it is still worse when Christians take their case before
a pagan court (vv.1–6).

A third illustration is taken from the custom of the requisition of
service by the soldiery. A man might be required to let soldiers have
the use of an ass to carry the baggage of troops on the march, in
which case he would have to go along or risk the loss of his animal;
or he might be compelled to carry things on his own back. (In the
story of the crucifixion, a man passing by the marchers on the way
to Golgotha is compelled to carry the cross of Jesus—27:32.) This
must have been a common experience in Roman-occupied Palestine,
and would of course arouse deep resentment. When this happens to
you, says Jesus, you must not only do what the soldiers require of
you, but even more. It goes without saying that you do what you are
compelled to do; without compulsion you give more service than is
demanded of you. Again there is no thought of what effect this will
have on the soldiers; it is put forward as the action and attitude
appropriate to those who seek the kingdom of heaven.

The fourth saying has only the loosest connection with the theme
of non-retaliation. Neither the beggar who asks you for money nor
the would-be borrower who wants a loan can be regarded as having
done you a wrong. It would appear to be a separate saying, which is
a restatement of the Mosaic Law on loans. In Luke's form of the
saying, Jesus speaks of a loan that may never be repaid. 'If you lend
to those from whom you hope to receive, what credit is that to you?
Even sinners lend to sinners, hoping to receive as much again. . . .

Do good, and lend, expecting nothing in return' (Lk.6:34f.). This is still more closely in keeping with the provisions of the ancient Law. Loans must be made to a brother who is in need, without interest (Ex.22:25; Lev.25:36f.), and in Deuteronomy it is specifically stressed that you must not refuse the loan when the year of release (every seventh year) is near, the time when all loans were to be cancelled. 'If there is among you a poor man, one of your brethren . . . you shall not harden your heart against your poor brother, but you shall open your hand, and lend him sufficient for his need, whatever it may be. Take heed lest there be a base thought in your heart, and you say "The seventh year, the year of release is near," and your eye be hostile to your poor brother, and you give him nothing, and he cry unto the Lord against you, and it be sin in you' (Deut.15:7—9).

The Sixth Antithesis 5:43—48

[43] You have heard that it was said, 'You shall love your neighbour and hate your enemy.' [44] But I say to you, Love your enemies and pray for those who persecute you, [45] so that you may be sons of your Father who is in heaven; for he makes his sun rise on the evil and on the good, and sends rain on the just and on the unjust. [46] For if you love those who love you, what reward have you? Do not even the tax collectors do the same? [47] And if you salute only your brethren, what more are you doing than others? Do not even the Gentiles do the same? [48] You, therefore, must be perfect, as your heavenly Father is perfect.

Different manuscripts and versions add one or more of several clauses after 'love your enemies'. Sometimes it is 'bless those who curse you' or 'do good to those who hate you', or both; these words appear to be transferred, in copying, from Luke 6:27—28. Sometimes the same kind of transfer has led to a change of 'those who persecute you' to 'those who abuse you'; and sometimes a scribe has conflated the two readings, to give 'pray for those who abuse you and persecute you.' It is not at all unusual, in the manuscripts of the Gospels, to find that scribes mix their texts in this way, remembering the wording of a parallel passage in one of the other Gospels and harmonizing the two.

The commandment 'You shall love your neighbour' is found in Leviticus 19:18. It is not followed by any charge to 'hate your enemy'. This clause is not part of the citation but may be taken as a fair enough summary of the sense in which the love of your neighbour was commonly understood. In the Leviticus passage, the charge to 'love your neighbour as yourself' is given with specific reference to fellow Israelites; it is preceded by the words: 'You shall not take vengeance or bear any grudge against the sons of your own people.' Any such limitation is foreign to the teaching of Jesus; when the question is raised ('And who is my neighbour?'—Lk.10:29—in connection with the interpretation of this very passage), Jesus replies with the parable of the Good Samaritan, and the counter-question, 'Which of these three . . . proved neighbour to the man who fell among the robbers?' (v.36.)

There are passages in the Old Testament which at least encourage a deadly hatred of enemies. The invading Hebrews are charged not only to dispossess the nations of Canaan, but to exterminate them. 'When the Lord God gives them over to you, and you defeat them, then you must utterly destroy them; you shall make no covenant with them and show them no mercy' (Deut.7:2); even more strongly: 'In the cities of these peoples that the Lord God gives you for an inheritance, you shall save alive nothing that breathes' (Deut.20:16). A Psalmist will even say, sure that God will commend him: 'Do I not hate them that hate thee, O Lord? . . . I hate them with perfect hatred' (Ps.139:21f.). In the time of Jesus, the community of Qumran still makes it a duty 'to hate all the sons of darkness, each according to his guilt in vengeance of God' (Burrows, *Dead Sea Scrolls*, p. 371). The same *Manual of Discipline* gives 'the regulations for the way of the wise man in these times, for his love together with his hate, eternal hate for the men of the pit in a spirit of conceal-ment' (p. 384). A midrashic comment (*Sifra* on Lev.19:18) interprets the command to love your neighbour as meaning: 'You shall not take vengeance or cherish anger against the sons of your people, but you may take vengeance and cherish anger against others.' Seeing that Luke does not set the command of Jesus to 'love your enemies' in any kind of contrast to Jewish Law or traditional interpretation, we may well hold that it is Matthew who has framed this antithetical introduction, and added to the commandment a summary statement of the manner in which it was generally taken by Jewish interpreters. He thus throws into high relief the radical difference in the attitude of Jesus. The love of his followers must be given to all alike, not in proportion to their friendliness or hostility or out of consideration for anything but what belongs to the nature of a son of God.

The words of Jesus were initially those of a Jewish teacher speak-ing to Jews in the Palestine of the early first century. The land of their fathers was occupied by the Romans. A Roman prefect governed Judaea under the Roman legate of Syria; a tetrarch of Idumaean descent (Herod Antipas) governed Galilee under the Roman overlords; the tax collectors were Jewish, but the taxes went mainly to Rome and were exacted rapaciously (they were farmed out to Roman capitalists, who counted on making exorbitant profits); and foreign troops from many parts of the Roman Empire were at the disposal of the authorities—they were often needed to crush revolts. It is against this background of a people restive under its alien masters that Jesus pronounces the words: 'Love your enemies.'

In Matthew's church the situation was no longer the same. His book was written in and for a community which was not in fact or in ideal a community of Jews, and the 'enemy' was not the Roman power, but the Jewish religious leadership which he calls 'the scribes and Pharisees' (23:34). It is they who are described as 'those who persecute you'. There is for him no background of national hostility against alien overlords. The words of Jesus are now brought to bear upon the personal reaction of Christian believers to persecutors. They have already been charged not to resist, not to retaliate for any wrong they may suffer. Now this passive endurance of wrong is extended to the positive command to love the wrongdoer, and to pray for him even when he persecutes you for your faith. As in verse 11, the mention of persecution, in place of the 'hatred' and 'cursing' and 'abuse' which are alone found in the Lukan parallel (Lk.6:27f.), reflects the altered situation. Persecution, as we have remarked before, does not come upon the followers of Jesus during his life-time; it comes soon and persistently after his death.

But it is clear that these words have a wider import and go beyond any local or temporal situation. Hatred is always to be encountered, and it is always to be met with love. And this command to love your enemies is not based upon any hope that you may dispel the hatred of your enemy by your response of love. It is grounded wholly upon the nature of God, 'your Father who is in heaven'. If you are to be true to him, if you are to show that you are truly counted among the children of such a Father, then you must like him be good to all, without discrimination, for he 'makes his sun rise on the evil and on the good, and sends rain on the just and on the unjust,' or as it is put in Luke's Gospel, 'he is kind to the ungrateful and the selfish' (Lk.6: 35). From children of such a Father, something more is expected than the ordinary response of man to man in human society—to love those that love you, to give a kind word to your brethren. Even the tax collectors, whom you despise, and the Gentiles, to whom you feel so superior, can match that kind of conduct. If that is as far as you go, 'what more are you doing than others?' or, as it is put in the Lukan parallel, 'what credit is that to you? For even sinners do the same' (Lk.6:33). The conduct of the child of God must be marked by something distinctive, by a goodness that is not determined by the attitude of others, but by the nature of God. 'You, therefore, must be perfect, as your heavenly Father is perfect.'

The charge to be perfect as God is perfect is to be understood as a summing up of all that has been said under the heading, 'Love your enemies.' The perfection meant in this context is the completeness of love—a love which is not measured and limited by the character of those with whom we have to do, but is poured out in keeping with the love of God. In Luke, or in the tradition employed by Luke, some difficulty was found with this understanding of the word 'perfect' (τέλειος which usually means 'mature'), and the word 'merciful' (οἰκτίρμων) was substituted for it (Lk.6:36). This is not very appropriate, for the context has not been concerned with showing mercy, but with the much broader thought of manifesting love. Both words are attempts to render the Hebrew word *tam*, or *tamim*, which is applied to Noah ('perfect in his generation'—Gen. 6:9), to Job ('perfect and upright, one who feared God, and turned away from evil'—Job 1:8); it is given in the charge to Abraham ('walk before me, and be perfect'—Gen.17:1), and in a command to the Israelite ('You shall be perfect before the Lord your God'—Deut.18:13, in connection with warnings not to follow the 'abominable practices' of the nations then living in Canaan). In *RSV* the word is usually translated 'blameless'. But the Hebrew word which lies behind it means basically 'complete', 'possessing integrity'. The words should not be interpreted as demanding our best human effort to attain the unattainable, but rather our 'total engagement' (Bonnard), without half-measures or reserves.

4   THE HIGHER RIGHTEOUSNESS ILLUSTRATED UNDER THREE ASPECTS OF PIETY *6:1–18*

Introductory: Modes and Motives 6:1

[1] Take care not to act out your righteousness in the public view, so that it may be noticed by people; for then you will have no reward from your Father who is in heaven.

The theme is still 'righteousness'—the righteousness exceeding that of the scribes and Pharisees which is required of all who hope to enter the kingdom of heaven. It is no longer developed in relation to specific commandments of the Law, as in the Antitheses. The word δικαιοσύνη is now used in the concrete sense of religious observances such as were practised by the devout Jew, and the emphasis is laid primarily on the mode of the action and on its real motive. There must be nothing ostentatious, no public exhibition of piety; and there must be no motive of winning admiration, but only of pleasing God and seeking no reward except that which he may give. Deeds done to impress others, to win a reputation for outstanding godliness, are not of any value in the eyes of God. Actions good in themselves can be a form of self-seeking, if they are done to win approval and admiration from other people. Such a motive is far removed from the spirit of letting your light shine for all to see 'so that they glorify your Father who is in heaven'; it is more like seeking the spotlight, so that the observers may glorify you.

This opening sentence states the general principle. It is now to be illustrated under three aspects—almsgiving, fasting, and prayer—by way of example. Other pious practices are to be looked upon in the same light.

First Example: Almsgiving 6:2—4

[2] Thus, when you give alms do not sound a trumpet before you, as the hypocrites do in the synagogues and in the streets, so that they may be glorified by the people. Truly I tell you, they have received their reward. [3] But when you are giving alms, do not let your right hand know what your left is doing, [4] so that your alms may be given in secret; and your Father who sees in secret will reward you.

It is by no accident that the giving of alms is chosen as the first example of 'righteousness', for in Jewish parlance generally, ἐλεημοσύνη, 'almsgiving', had come to be used virtually as a synonym for δικαιοσύνη, 'righteousness'. In the LXX, the Hebrew word ts'daqah, 'righteousness', is often rendered ἐλεημοσύνη, though never with the specific sense of 'almsgiving'. But in the later Jewish literature, the equation becomes more pronounced. Tobit is told by the angel Raphael that 'almsgiving delivers from death and will purge away every sin. Those who perform deeds of charity and righteousness will have fulness of life' (Tob.12:9). Here 'almsgiving' is set in synonymous parallelism with 'deeds of charity and righteousness'. In the Law, care for the poor is looked upon as a prime duty of the Israelite (Deut.15:7–11; etc.). The Jewish communities had developed a highly organized system of aid to the poor in the time of Jesus, and alms were received in the Temple and in the synagogues. The figure of sounding a trumpet is clearly enough used in the sense of self-advertisement; but it is perhaps given an additional pertinence from the fact that in the Temple the six receptacles placed for the depositing of alms were in the form of trumpets; and it appears that in the synagogue service of the sabbath a trumpet was sounded at the time of the collection. Alms could of course be given in the streets, to beggars, especially to the disabled and the blind (cf. Mk.10:46ff.; Acts 3:1–10). There was no comparable tradition of almsgiving in any form of paganism; neither Greek shrines nor oriental temples were expected to take any responsibility for relief of poverty. The grain ration distributed to the Roman proletariat was never regarded as in any sense a service to Jupiter or to any other god; it was simply a means of appeasing urban unrest.

Our saying builds upon the well-established Jewish tradition, and there is no suggestion that Jewish almsgiving was niggardly, or that the followers of Jesus should give more generously than others. The saying, 'It is more blessed to give than to receive', cited as a word of 'the Lord Jesus' (Acts 20:35), is wholly in the Jewish tradition.

VERSE 2: 'Hypocrites'—the Greek ὑποκριτής is the ordinary word for 'actor' in the theatre, and in itself carried no suggestion of humbug. It can also be used of an 'interpreter' (of dreams, or of riddles), and of an orator, still in a good sense. The bad sense, of one who makes a pretence of virtue, develops out of the notion of 'actor'. On the stage, the actor plays the part assigned to him and wins applause for the excellence of his acting; but if the man who professes to be pious is merely playing a part, and hoping for applause, he is a humbug. This is the sense of the word here. It is above all the hope of winning applause that is stigmatized.

The word is prominent in the Matthaean vocabulary; it is used fourteen times in his Gospel (against only once in Mark, three times in Luke, and never in the rest of the New Testament). Any kind of pretence in religious professions or in moral conduct is abhorrent to him. It is one of his blanket charges against the Pharisees, frequently against scribes and Pharisees together (15:7; 22:18; seven times in chap.23). As a blanket charge, it is as unjust as the same condemnation that is often levelled against Puritans, Methodists, or 'the Victorians'. The Pharisees are not mentioned here, or in verses 5 and

16, though Matthew probably has them especially in mind. He is still concerned to show how the righteousness of those who hope for the kingdom of heaven is to exceed that of the scribes and Pharisees.

In all fairness, it must be said that the teachers of the Pharisees were equally opposed to ostentation. A saying of Rabbi Eliazar (early second century) runs: 'He who gives alms in secret is greater than Moses our teacher' (*Baba Bathra* 6b).

'They have received'—the Greek verb ἀπέχουσιν, though used in the present tense, has the sense of a perfect. It is a familiar term of commerce; countless receipts (for taxes, or for the repayment of a loan) begin with the word ἀπέχω; occasionally ἀπέχομεν or ἀπέχουσιν, equivalent to our 'Paid', or 'Payment Received'. The account is settled in full; these 'hypocrites' have got what they wanted, the applause of their fellow citizens, and have nothing to expect from God.

VERSES 3–4: The saying cannot, of course, be taken literally; the left hand cannot be ignorant of what the right hand is doing. The sense is, 'Far from seeking publicity for your generosity, give so quietly that even your next-door neighbour does not know of it.' Your Father in heaven sees what you do, however secretly you go about it, and he will reward you.

There is no thought here of doing the deed for its own sake, or for your own satisfaction. All through the New Testament there is the assurance that goodness does not go unrewarded; only the rewards are not given in material goods or in anything that can be measured by earthly standards. 'God rewards those who seek him' (Heb.11:6), and his rewards are eternal, and in comparison with them, all that the world can offer is trifling. The world may reward our faithfulness with suffering, but even of Jesus it is written that he *'for the joy that was set before him* endured the cross, despising the shame' (Heb.12:2). But the divine 'reward' belongs to no temporal frame of things. 'We look not to the things that are seen but to the things that are unseen; for the things that are seen are transient, but the things that are unseen are eternal' (2 Cor.4:18). Again, under the figure of the life of the Christian believer as a race, Paul reminds us that the runners in the stadium contend for a prize, but for a prize— a wreath ('crown', στέφανος, of wild olive, celery, etc.)—that is itself perishable, while the wreath which the Christian seeks to win is imperishable (1 Cor. 9:24–26; cf. Phil.3:14). To do our duty without any thought of reward is a noble thought, it may be; but does it rest upon a notion of individual moral autonomy which is incompatible with the nature of a servant of God?

Second Example: Prayer 6:5–15

⁵ When you pray, you must not be like the hypocrites, for they love to stand praying in the synagogues and at the corners of the avenues, so that they may be noticed by people. I tell you truly, they have received their reward. ⁶ But you, when you pray, go into your room, shut the door, and pray to your Father who is in the secret place. Your Father, who sees in the secret place, will reward you.

⁷ Again, when you pray do not babble on like the Gentiles; they think that they will be heard for their many words. ⁸ Do not be like them; for your Father knows what you need before you ask.

⁹ This is the manner, then, in which you are to pray:

Our Father in Heaven,
Your Name be sanctified
¹⁰ your Kingdom come,
your will be done
on earth as in heaven.
¹¹ Give us today bread sufficient for us;
¹² forgive us for our offences
as we now forgive those who have offended against us.
¹³ Do not bring us under trial,
but deliver us from the evil one.

¹⁴ For if you forgive others for their offences, your heavenly Father will forgive you; ¹⁵ But if you do not forgive others, neither will your heavenly Father forgive you.

This second example begins, like the first and the third, by a contrast between the desire for general admiration and the disinterested aim to please God (vv.5–6). But this is followed by a series of supplements. First, there is a contrast not with those who exhibit their piety to win public admiration, but with 'the Gentiles' whose prayers are verbose and largely meaningless (vv.7–8); then comes a model prayer, generally known as 'the Lord's Prayer' (vv.9–13); and finally a brief commentary—as it were, a footnote—on one petition of that prayer (vv.14–15). Matthew takes occasion to develop the theme of 'prayer' by assembling a series of passages that go beyond the pattern of 'righteousness' of his opening verse.

VERSE 5: The emphasis is not on 'standing' in prayer, any more than on praying in itself. It was the general Jewish custom to stand for the prayers in the synagogues or anywhere else, though there is plenty of evidence for kneeling also (Dan.6:10). The stress is on the verb φιλοῦσιν ('love') together with the motive, 'that they may be noticed by others' (literally, 'by men', not by God). Prayer in the synagogue was a communal action, but was led by a member of the congregation, usually an elder, and no fault could be attached to him for accepting the task on occasion. Prayer 'at the corners of the avenues' (πλατειῶν, the 'broad' ways) suggests that a place is deliberately chosen because it is conspicuous; one is sure to be seen by many people. Again, a Jewish setting is presupposed; in other ancient societies, as in our own, people were not more highly esteemed if they were seen to be diligent in their devotions.

VERSE 6: Not a prohibition of participation in public prayers, in the synagogue or the Temple (or, in a Christian setting, in church). Even for private devotions, the words are not to be taken *au pied de la lettre*; they are simply a vivid way of insisting that any thought of display, to build up a reputation for piety, is out of the question. Jesus himself goes out 'to a lonely place' to pray (Mk.1:35; cf. Lk. 6:12), but he is also pictured as praying in the presence of his disciples, and presumably others (Lk.11:1; Mt.11:25f.). In the Gospel of John, he prays openly at the grave of Lazarus (Jn.11:41f.), and in the presence of his disciples (at the Last Supper, chap.17). But there is surprisingly little mention of the praying of Jesus in the Gospels; it is brought into the story by Luke more than by any of the other evangelists. In the Old Testament, Daniel goes into his house, 'where he had windows in his upper chamber open towards Jerusalem,' and makes his accustomed prayers three times a day, despite the royal decree forbidding it (Dan.6:10); but this was not to avoid being seen. He was in fact seen by his enemies, and his conduct reported to the king (vv.11f.). And it is of course quite possible to pray openly, in the public view, with no thought of what people may think; the Muslim rolls out his small prayer rug wherever he may be at the appointed hours, as unselfconsciously as the peasant uncovers his head at the ringing of the Angelus.

'Your Father who is in the secret place'—τῷ πατρί σου τῷ ἐν τῷ κρυπτῷ—is a variation on the distinctively Matthaean phrase 'your Father who is in heaven'. The companion expression, 'your Father who sees in the secret place' has been used in verse 4; cf. the similar phrases in verse 18. The thought that God is everywhere present is not a new doctrine; it is a frequent theme in the Psalms, and finds beautiful expression especially in Psalm 139, verses 7–12.

VERSES 7–8: The two following verses break away from the pattern. The bad example to be avoided is no longer that of the hypocritical worshipper of the God of Israel, but the follies of the devotees of false gods. In typical Jewish fashion, they are grouped together as 'the Gentiles'. Just as the Greeks spoke of all other nations as βάρβαροι (our 'barbarians'), even though they knew that the civilization of Egypt and of Babylonia was far older than their own; so the Jews thought of all the rest of mankind collectively as 'the Gentiles', though they could hardly fail to know that the religions which they practised were as diverse as their languages. The Greeks themselves worshipped many gods, and all the Semitic cults were quite different, to say nothing of the peculiar religion of Egypt. But the Jews were not in the least interested in these differences; people who worshipped the many gods and lords worshipped nullities, 'vanities', (and there was no inclination to distinguish between one false god and another, or to do justice to any values that might be found in them)—they were all dismissed as 'Gentiles'.

VERSES 7—8: The verb βατταλογέω, here rendered 'babble', is apparently an onomatopoetic formation. Its origin and precise meaning are unknown. The βαττα-prefix is perhaps a Semitic borrowing (Aramaic *baṭṭal*, 'futile'), combined with the Greek λογ- (λέγω, λόγος). Schlatter, however, holds that such hybrid Graeco-Semitic formations do not exist, and qualifies the derivation from *baṭṭal* as 'fantastic'. He seeks to relate the ending -λογέω to λέγω in the sense of 'collect', and the prefix to the Greek βατός, 'bramble', to give the meaning, 'gather twigs of bramble'—a totally unprofitable task. The 'vain repetitions' of *AV* is generally rejected, but seems to be supported by *L&S*, where it is taken to be a vagrant form of the onomatopoetic verb βατταρίζω, 'stutter' or 'stammer' — to say the same thing over and over. It is virtually equivalent in sense to πολυλογία of the next clause, as if to stress the *multitude* of words.

Possibly Matthew (Jesus?) recalls the mocking description of the supplications of the priests of Jezebel's Baal, with their day-long continuance and their complete futility (I Ki.18:26—29). It must be said that such Greek prayers as have come down to us were neither meaningless nor lengthy; the beautiful prayer of Socrates at the close of the *Phaedrus* is perhaps not typical; but the prayers in Homer are pithy, and very much to the point, and those of the characters in the dramas are full of meaning. In some of the Syrian cults, with which Matthew might be more familiar, there was a good deal of ecstatic utterance, which must have seemed gibberish to outsiders. There is no suggestion that Jewish prayers were meaningless.

The injunction to avoid multiplying words is not based on the fact that your prayers are offered to the only true God, not to the impotent gods of 'the Gentiles', but on the conviction that the true God is our Father, who knows our needs before we voice them, and will not refuse good things to his children when they ask for them (cf.7:11). His knowledge of us is total; he does not need to be informed. The thought of God's omniscience is well established in Jewish piety. 'Even before a word is on my tongue, O Lord, you know it altogether' (Ps.139:4). This is not taken to mean that we should not ask God for all that we need. On the contrary, Jesus encourages his disciples to pray, and even to pray with persistence, undiscouraged by an initial lack of response (see esp. the parable of the Importunate Widow, Lk.18:1–7). Paul exhorts his converts to pray without ceasing (1 Thess.5:17), and bids them 'in everything by prayer and supplication with thanksgiving let your requests be made known to God,' in the assurance that he 'will supply every need of yours according to his riches in glory in Christ Jesus' (Phil. 4:6,19).

This warning against the wrong kind of praying, introduced as a supplement to the warning against ostentation and the desire to win a reputation for piety, is now itself supplemented by a model prayer for the disciples of Christ to use. The Matthaean setting is obviously artificial. A more plausible setting is suggested in Luke, where it is said that Jesus gave this prayer in response to a direct request made by the disciples: 'Lord, teach us to pray, as John taught his disciples' (Lk.11:1). It is evident that the Prayer was widely used in the early church, and in this devotional use there would be no mention of the circumstances in which it was first spoken by Jesus. The Lukan setting is plausible enough—it was not uncommon for Jewish teachers to compose forms of prayer for their disciples—but it is none the less a framework devised by Luke, not a fragment of the tradition as transmitted. A comparison of the two versions of the Prayer, along with references to it in other Christian writings, shows clearly that it was not memorized verbatim, but adapted with considerable freedom to the manner in which it was used. The Lukan form is shorter and simpler, and is generally taken to be nearer to the original; but this is a hazardous conclusion. In Luke it runs:

Father,
Let your Name be sanctified;
Let your Kingdom come.
Give us each day sufficient bread for us;
Forgive us our sins, for we also forgive every one
who is indebted to us;
And do not bring us under trial. (Lk.11:2–4)

It will be noticed that here 'Father' is used alone, without the familiar 'our' and 'in heaven'. This at least seems to be the original form, for Jesus himself addresses God simply as 'Father' in his own prayers (Mk.14:36; Mt.11:25f.; etc.), and Paul indicates that the convert at his baptism learned to say 'Abba, Father,' probably along with this Prayer (Gal.4:6; Rom.8:15f.). The Matthaean form looks like a liturgical elaboration; it is also in line with the phrasing of rabbinical prayers. More striking is the fact that the petition, 'Let your will be done' (with the supplementary, 'as in heaven, so upon earth') is not found at all in Luke. This clause too may be secondary, whether Matthaean or pre-Matthaean, designed to make explicit the essential meaning of the petition, 'Let your Kingdom come.' The last Matthaean petition is also missing in Luke, who has nothing corresponding to 'Deliver us from the evil one.' The remaining differences may be no more than translation variants, arising from independent renderings of the Aramaic of Jesus. The doxology, now so widely used, is not found in the Greek text of either of these Gospels. It occurs in the *Didache* (mid second century?), but is not found in any Greek manuscript of Matthew earlier than the fifth century; and where it occurs in early patristic writings and in versions, there is a good deal of variation in the wording. (It is not found in the Latin Vulgate [W.-W., Oxford, 1911; J. Bover, Madrid, 1950] and in most Old Latin witnesses.) There can be no doubt that it is a liturgical addition, not an integral part of the Prayer. There is evidence that in the second century, some manuscripts of Luke read, 'Let your Holy Spirit come upon us and cleanse us', in place of 'Let your name be sanctified.' This was the reading known to Marcion (*c.*150) and taken as correct by Tertullian (*c.*200). This looks very much like a form adapted for use in the baptismal service.

Such variations as these tell strongly against any theory that the words of Jesus were committed to memory and that there was any great concern to preserve them exactly. It is highly unlikely that Jesus ever intended his disciples to store up his precise words as the *talmidim* of a rabbi were expected to do. The tradition of his sayings was not stereotyped. His pervasive influence was by no means bound to the letter of what he had said so many years before. In fact, it is very difficult to imagine how the transmission of the tradition could be controlled, in the charismatic society of early times.

For a careful examination of the views of some recent Scandinavian scholars, see W.D. Davies, in a long Appendix to his *Setting of the Sermon on the Mount* (pp.464–80).

The Prayer falls into two major divisions: the first three petitions have to do with the action of God in its cosmic dimension, the remaining four with his care for his people, individually and, even more, in the community of his church.

VERSES 9–10: The first three petitions are closely related. The sanctifying of God's name is one significant aspect of the coming of his Kingdom, and it is when his Kingdom is fully established—his sovereignty universally accepted—that his will is to be done on earth as it is in heaven. Despite the passives ($\dot{\alpha}\gamma\iota\alpha\sigma\theta\dot{\eta}\tau\omega$, $\gamma\epsilon\nu\eta\theta\dot{\eta}\tau\omega$) and the intransitive ($\dot{\epsilon}\lambda\theta\dot{\alpha}\tau\omega$), the prayer is for God to act to bring these things to pass. Only God can sanctify his name; only God can bring in his Kingdom on earth; only God can create an order in which his will is done by all his creatures, on earth as in heaven.

The 'name' of God means God himself as revealed. The Old Testament prophets charge that God's own people profane his name when they are unfaithful and disobedient, when they indulge in the sexual profligacies of the Canaanite shrines on the 'high places' or 'under every green tree', when the rich cheat the poor and the strong oppress the weak (Amos 2:7; Jer.3:6; Ezek.23:37–39). God is holy and his name is holy; and in his Law he charges his people to be holy as he is holy. 'You shall keep my commandments and do them; I am the Lord. And you shall not profane my holy name, but I will be hallowed among the people of Israel; I am the Lord who sanctify you' (Lev.22:31f.; and indeed the whole book of Leviticus is devoted to the theme).

The worship of other gods, the participation in heathen cults, and all kinds of oppression and violence in Israel have profaned the name of their God among the Gentiles; and in the end he will act to sanctify his great name, to vindicate his holiness, first by the punishments which he brings upon his people, and ultimately by forgiveness and restoration, by which the nations will learn to honour him. His name will be great among the Gentiles, not alone in Israel. This thought is especially developed by Ezekiel; and it is made clear that this sanctifying of the name of God, this vindication of his holiness, is to be accomplished by God himself—not by his people, but in spite of their gross and repeated failure to live as he has commanded.

Thus says the Lord God:

It is not for your sake, O Israelites, that I am about to act, but for the sake of my holy name, which you have profaned among the nations to which you came. I will sanctify ['hallow', NEB; 'vindicate the holiness of', RSV] my great name . . . and the nations will know that I am the Lord . . . when I shall be sanctified in you before their eyes. (Ezek.36:22f.)

The theme is sustained throughout this chapter and the next. As it goes on, God's action in sanctifying his name is linked with the ultimate blessing of Israel, restored, purified, and in unbroken communion with God, and in the enjoyment of unlimited prosperity; it is linked also with the acknowledgement of his holiness by all the nations (36:25–38). Ezekiel sees Israel as it were raised from the dead (37:1–14—a passage which was inevitably interpreted by Christians as a foreshadowing of the Christian faith in personal resurrection); and at the last it introduces the assurance of a people reunited under one king—a David still to come; and of a covenant of peace which will be everlasting (37:24–28).

The Christian interpretation of course goes beyond what the petition could mean to Jewish hearers of the time of Jesus, but not beyond what it would mean to Matthew and the Christians of his time. But its fundamental sense is constant. It asks God to accomplish what he has promised for the end-time—forgiveness and redemption, and the revelation of God to all mankind.

The petition 'Let your Kingdom come' is closely related to that for the sanctifying of God's name. It carries no implication of 'realized eschatology', or of any significant role of Jesus in the coming of the Kingdom; it does not even imply that the Kingdom is 'at hand'. In the early church, the hope of the coming of the Kingdom came to be conceived more and more in terms of the coming of the risen and glorified Jesus to establish it. So the visions of the Apocalypse of John culminate in the picture of the 'new heavens and new earth', where 'the throne of God and of the Lamb' will be found; and finally the Seer prays, 'Amen. Come, Lord Jesus.' In the Didache we again find a similar linking of the coming of Jesus with the coming of the Kingdom, in the prayer, 'Remember your church, O Lord . . . and gather it together in holiness from the four winds to your kingdom which you have prepared for it. . . . Let grace come and this world pass away. Amen, come, Lord' (*Maran, atha*, Aramaic).

The third petition, 'Let your will be done', is not so much a further request as an indication of the sense which Matthew takes to be central to the sanctifying of God's name and the establishment of his Kingdom. In all likelihood, it is not an integral part of the original Prayer. It is totally lacking in the version known to Luke—he would not have removed such words as these, if they had been in the tradition that came to him. It has even been suggested that Matthew has transferred them from the prayer offered by Jesus in Gethsemane (Mt.26:42; not in Mark or Luke). It is perhaps more likely that Matthew has introduced the phrase into the Markan story of the

Agony in the Garden in a conscious reminiscence of his own reshaping of the Lord's Prayer. Here, though, the thought of resignation, of accepting calamity without rebelling, because God wills it (as, for instance, in Acts 21:14), is not in view. The tragic circumstances of personal experience are not envisaged, but only God's unchallenged sovereignty in the Kingdom that is to come. Where his kingly rule is wholly accepted, it means perfect obedience to him— his will is done.

These first three petitions, or these two with the third attached as an interpretation of the second, bear upon the hope of the future. We pray for the fulfilment of God's declared purpose for the world and for all people. We pray in the faith that the future is in God's hands, and that he who holds the future in his hands is our Father in heaven, who will not refuse the petitions of his children. He has promised, and he will be faithful to his promise.

God is not dependent upon us, upon our prayers or our co-operation. Yet he calls upon us as his children to have part in his work, assured that our labour is not in vain (1 Cor.15:58). It is he that has made us, and not we ourselves; and it is he that will sanctify his name, cause his Kingdom to come and his will to be done 'as in heaven, so also upon earth.'

'As in heaven, so also on earth'—this clause may be taken as attached especially to the third petition, in the sense that God's will is now perfectly done in heaven, and we pray that it may be done with the same completeness on earth. But it is more likely that the combination of 'heaven' and 'earth' is used here, as it is generally in the Hebrew scriptures, as a way of speaking of the entire created universe. When God is acknowledged as 'Maker of heaven and earth', it means that he has made all things. And it is not to be taken for granted that 'heaven' is here understood as the sphere of holiness made perfect, even though it is the abode of God. In the thought of the New Testament, there is rebellion in heaven also, and the purpose of God in Christ is not only the redemption of mankind, but the reconciliation of all things 'whether on earth or in heaven' to himself (Col.1:20). The Christian is challenged to 'put on the whole armour of God', precisely because the enemies against whom he must wrestle are not creatures of flesh and blood, but 'the spiritual hosts of wickedness in the heavenly places' (Eph.6:11f.). Heaven and earth alike are to pass away, 'but according to his promise we wait for new heavens and a new earth in which righteousness dwells' (2 Pet.3:13).

All such language reflects conceptions of the universe and of its material and spiritual components which are far removed from anything in our own ways of thinking. They use an imagery of a universe of which earth is the centre, and the heavens are a canopy above the earth, or—in the more sophisticated theories of astrology— a series of spheres surrounding it. These heavens of astrology were populated by innumerable spirits—the stars were 'visible gods' (even Plato can speak of them so, though he was no astrologer), and the planets were the powerful rulers of the seven spheres. Centuries before, many Israelites had come to worship 'the sun and the moon and all the host of heaven' (Jer.8:2; cf. 2 Ki.21:3–5; Deut. 17:3); and in an apocalyptic picture of the divine judgement, it is said that 'on that day the Lord will punish the host of heaven, in heaven, and the kings of the earth, on the earth' (Isa.24:21). We need not suppose that this astrological lore is in the mind of Jesus (or of Matthew), but we must recognize that he speaks the common language of the first century, and that in that language 'heaven' can be conceived as a theatre of evil as well as of good.

The essentially Jewish character of these first three petitions is seen at once by a comparison with Jewish prayers which were used in worship in New Testament times and are still in general use today. 'May his great name be magnified and sanctified in the world which he has created according to his will. May he cause his kingdom to rule and his redemption to shoot forth, and may he bring near his Messiah and redeem his people in your life and in your days, and in the life of all the house of Israel, speedily, and at a near time.' This ancient prayer, the *Qaddish*, links the sanctifying of the name and the establishment of the Kingdom as in the Lord's Prayer. It includes a note of urgency ('in your days . . . speedily, at a near time') which is not taken up in the Prayer of Jesus.

VERSES 11–13: The four petitions of the second part of the prayer no longer bear upon the future consummation but on the action of God in our lives here and now, from day to day. The Jewish character is no less pronounced. There is not a single clause that is without parallels in Jewish prayers known to us. We pray that God will provide for our needs, both material and spiritual.

VERSE 11: The word ἐπιούσιον, here rendered 'sufficient', has generally been translated 'daily', but its meaning is uncertain. No instance of its use has ever been found in Greek literature or in the non-literary documents such as papyri and inscriptions. (A single occurrence cited as from a papyrus is more than dubious; the papyrus in question is no longer to be found, and its editor indicates that he restored it by conjecture—most of the space was occupied by a lacuna.) Origen, perhaps the most widely read man of his age, tells us that he had never encountered it anywhere else. It is, undoubtedly, an attempt at rendering an Aramaic expression into Greek, but it is impossible to be sure what the Aramaic actually was. Our familiar 'daily bread' has been constant in English translations from Tyndale to *RSV* and *NEB*, except for the Rheims translation of 1582. This was made from the Vulgate of Jerome, who took the unusual adjective to be derived from ἐπί + οὐσία and interpreted it as referring to the 'supernatural' bread of the Eucharist. A number of modern scholars take it to mean 'of tomorrow'. Jerome informs us that in the apocryphal 'Gospel of the Nazarenes', the Aramaic word *mahar*, 'to-morrow', was used; but this may itself be a stab at rendering Matthew's Greek, and perhaps even 'the earliest attempt to explain it' (P. Vielhauer, in Hennecke, *New Testament Apocrypha* I, p.142). This interpretation would be justified if the peculiar ἐπιούσιος could be taken as formed on the common everyday participle. ἐπιοῦσα, usually in the dative τῇ ἐπιούσῃ (ἡμέρᾳ), 'on the next day', 'on the morrow'. But these -ιος endings are generally formed upon nouns, not upon adjectives. Debrunner (BDF, § 123 [1]) admits somewhat gingerly that this 'is perhaps to be considered'. The chief objection to it remains, even if the formation be grammatically admissible; that is, that it is completely irreconcilable with the injunctions against concern for to-morrow and its needs which will come a few paragraphs on (vv.25–34).

The proposal to understand the word as 'sufficient' requires us to suppose that the underlying Aramaic has been misunderstood, and to conjecture an original that carried the sense given in the Syriac Peshitta, which reads 'bread of our necessity' (Allen, *ad loc.*). The great Syrian Ephraem (fourth cent.) exhorts his readers, 'Let the bread of the day suffice for you, as you have learned in the Prayer.' Moreover, this interpretation is in keeping both with the rest of the Gospel teaching, and with the Old Testament wisdom. 'Feed me with the food that is sufficient for me' (Prov.30:8). It likewise reflects the lesson of the manna (Ex.16:4).

The familiar rendering 'daily' may derive from Jerome's rendering of the same word in the Lukan parallel, *cotidianum* (Lk.11:3,Vg.).

The σήμερον, 'today', of Matthew is represented in Luke by the distributive τὸ καθ' ἡμέραν, 'day by day'. This is no more than a translation variant, possibly affected by the language of Exodus 16:5.

It is surprising that the otherwise unknown word ἐπιούσιον established itself so firmly in the Greek text of the Prayer, and that no other Greek rendering has survived. Aramaic was very widely spoken in the churches of Syria and Palestine during the whole period, and

Matthew at least must have known an Aramaic version of the Prayer, and might have ventured to find a less rare word to substitute for ἐπιούσιον.

In the petition for forgiveness, Matthew uses an expression that is not found elsewhere in the New Testament (or in profane Greek), of forgiving 'debts' (ὀφειλήματα). In the Lukan version, the noun is replaced by ἁμαρτίας, 'sins', in keeping with a very widespread usage of LXX. In the second clause of the petition, Luke retains the cognate verb ὀφείλω—as we forgive everyone who is indebted (παντὶ τῷ ὀφείλοντι) to us (Lk.11:4). The verb ἀφίημι is commonly used of the remission of a debt, or of a fine or other penalty; but only occasionally of the forgiveness of a wrong, in classical Greek writings. In LXX, however, it occurs with great frequency in the sense of 'forgive'. Joseph's brothers, for instance, tell Joseph that with his dying breath their father Jacob gave them a message to Joseph, 'I ask you to forgive (ἄφες) the wrongdoing and sin done by your brothers' (Gen.50:16f.; their conduct is called ἀδικία and ἁμαρτία). Far more frequently it reports the grant of God's forgiveness, after a sacrifice of expiation, for violation of his commandments, whether ceremonial or moral. All through the book of Leviticus, especially, we find sentences of this type: 'The priest shall make expiation for him for his sin; and it shall be forgiven him' (ἀφεθήσεται αὐτῷ— Lev.4:26,31,35; 5:13, etc., LXX). There is no trace in LXX of the thought of sins as debts, but the figure occurs frequently in Targums and in rabbinical literature. This is perhaps occasioned by the fact that the Aramaic word *ḥoba* can be used in either sense. It may be that this was the word used in the original Aramaic of this Prayer. The figure of sins as debts is used by Matthew in the parable of the Unforgiving Slave (18:23–35), and it appears again in the double phrase of Colossians 2:13f., God has 'forgiven us all our trespasses, having cancelled the bond (χειρόγραφον) which stood against us, with its legal demands.'

The linking of God's forgiveness of our sins with our forgiveness of wrongs done to us is often found in Jewish writings, usually with the thought that God's forgiveness is *conditional* upon our readiness to forgive others. Those who are themselves merciful will receive God's mercy (so in the beatitude, 5:7). In the Psalms we find expressed the general thesis that God's attitude to us is based upon our attitude to him and to others, even to the extent that he shows himself 'perverse' with those who are crooked, as well as loyal to those that are loyal ('to the merciful . . . merciful,' *AV*; see the whole passage Ps.18:25f.). This is far removed from the conception of God set forth in 5:45. The phrasing of Matthew in this petition suggests that our forgiveness of others must be shown before we can ask his forgiveness for ourselves; we make the prayer confidently, when we can affirm that 'we have forgiven' those who have wronged us. This is precisely the attitude of Ben-Sirach:

> Forgive your neighbour the wrong he has done,
> and then your sins will be pardoned when you pray.
> . . .
> Does a person have no mercy towards a fellow man,
> and yet pray to be forgiven for his own sins? (Ecclus.28:2,4)

The distinctively Christian emphasis looks upon our forgiveness of others not as the condition but as the natural consequence of the free forgiveness which God has granted to us in Christ. 'Be kind to one another, tender-hearted, forgiving one another, as God in Christ forgave us' (Eph.4:32).

It will be remembered that in the parable of the Unforgiving Slave, the action of the king in remitting the whole of an enormous debt is done freely, without requiring a prior assurance that the slave has shown mercy to his fellows (18:27); the forgiveness is revoked only when the master finds that the man has exacted repayment from a fellow-slave (vv.32–34).

In Luke, the Matthaean perfect ἀφήκαμεν is replaced by the present ἐφίομεν—'as we forgive every one who is indebted to us'. Too much stress cannot be laid on the choice of tense, for the Aramaic verb system is totally different from the Greek, and it is likely that the same verb of the Aramaic original underlies both the Greek renderings. But the present gives a more satisfactory sense; it suggests that in asking God to forgive us, we pledge that we here and now forgive anyone who has wronged us, not that we have earned the right to expect forgiveness because we have already forgiven others.

Third Example: Fasting 6:16–18

[16] When you fast, do not put on gloomy looks, like the hypocrites, who disfigure their faces so that they may be noticed by people in this fasting. Truly I tell you, they have received their reward. [17] When you fast, anoint your head and wash your face, [18] so that your fasting may not be noted by other people, but only by your Father who is in the secret place; and your Father, who sees all in its secrecy, will reward you.

It is assumed that fasting is a religious exercise which has a place in the individual's worship of God. The communal fasts such as are prescribed for the Day of Atonement (in the Priestly Code, Lev.16: 29–31, etc.) are not envisaged, but only private fasts such as might be undertaken by individuals as an expression of grief, or of penitence, or of preparation for communion with God (Neh.1:4; Dan.9:3; 10:2f., etc.). Here it is indicated that individuals might undertake a fast as a work of merit, hoping that God will reward them for their piety. The 'hypocrites' no doubt entertained such hopes, but they also wanted to win the admiration of their neighbours. They therefore show obvious outward signs of their fasting; they look gloomy, and even 'cause their faces to disappear' (that is the literal meaning of ἀφανίζουσιν γὰρ τὰ πρόσωπα αὐτῶν), perhaps by smearing them with ashes? Whatever they hope from God, their primary desire is to win a reputation for exceptional piety. This is all the reward they will ever get; they are paid off in full by the gain in social prestige.

VERSE 17: It is assumed that the followers of Jesus will fast, and this is by no means forbidden, nor is the notion that this is a work of merit rejected. Only it must be done without parade, without concern for the regard of other people. The counsel 'to anoint your head and wash your face' suggests special attention to personal appearance, as if getting ready for a banquet. This verges on recommending another form of disguise, another mode of ostentation, equally designed to mislead the observer, though not to create an impression of superior piety. Prof. E. Schweizer suggests that this distorts the intention of the original saying; he thinks that similar distortions have affected the sayings dealing with almsgiving and prayer as well. He tries to distinguish three strata: 'a saying of Jesus that can no longer be determined in detail; a threefold admonition about true devotion, shaped by the community when it was still firmly rooted in Judaism; and the redaction by Matthew himself' (*The Good News According to Matthew*, p. 142). Granted the need to take account of the effects of community shaping, and also of Matthew's final work of redaction, is the approach of Schweizer too much determined by a prior *theological* objection to the whole idea that any human actions, however pure in intention, can be a work of merit which God will reward?

VERSE 18: Compare verses 4 and 6.

5   WARNINGS AGAINST TWO DANGERS 6:19–34

The first part of chapter 6 has a well defined unity; it is built around the three examples of pious action which illustrate the general injunction of verse 1. The second part has no such formal unity of structure. The materials are diverse and drawn from different sources, and it is probable that some of the sayings were originally spoken in a context which was not preserved in the oral tradition, so that each evangelist felt free to set them in a context of his own devising, in keeping with the interpretation which he himself had come to attach to them. Matthew seems to have brought the sayings of verses 19 to 34 together, and ordered them as he has, because he saw them as bearing upon two aspects of the spiritual danger involved in concern for the material things of life. This danger is experienced in one way by the rich, or more broadly by those who have more than enough for subsistence; they are tempted to accumulate wealth. It is experienced in a different way by the very poor, in that they are tempted to worry about where their next meal is to come from, or where they are to find the means of getting something to wear when the clothes now on their backs wear out. For both, the danger is that the great quest of life—the search for an entrance into the kingdom of heaven—may be subordinated to the urge to accumulate worldly wealth ('treasures on earth'), or to the worry over the means of subsistence—what we are to eat and what we are to wear. And to both the charge is given to hold with singleness of heart to the one supreme end of life. 'Seek first the kingdom (of God) and his righteousness'; with the assurance that all the material things which we need will be ours as well (v.33).

Against Acquisitiveness 6:19—24

THE FUNDAMENTAL CHARGE
[19] Do not lay up for yourselves treasures on earth, where moth and worm consume and where thieves break in and steal, [20] but lay up for yourselves treasures in heaven, where neither moth nor worm consumes and where thieves do not break in and steal.
Supplementary comment: [21] For where your treasure is, there will your heart be also.

THE PARABLE OF THE EYE
[22] The eye is the lamp of the body. So, if your eye is sound, your whole body will be full of light; [23a] but if your eye is evil, your whole body will be full of darkness.
Supplementary comment: [23b] If then the light in you is darkness, how great is the darkness!

THE PARABLE OF THE SLAVE

[24a] No man can serve two masters; for either he will hate the one and love the other, or he will be devoted to the one and despise the other.

Supplementary comment: [24b] You cannot serve God and mammon.

The kind of 'treasures on earth' which are envisaged in the basic charge are textiles, which may be destroyed by insects, and such things as gold, silver, and jewels, which may be carried off by robbers. 'Treasures in heaven' cannot be so precisely defined, but may be taken to refer to the 'reward' that the 'Father who sees in secret' will bestow upon those who give alms, pray, and fast, without show, with no thought of the 'reward' that they may receive by way of a reputation for piety. The treasures that can be accumulated on earth are not a secure possession; treasures laid up in heaven are beyond the reach of destruction or theft—they are ours forever.

The phrase that we have indicated as a 'supplementary comment' is given in the Greek in the second person singular, whereas the charge itself is in the plural. It is not only that the application is now made to the individual; there is also the introduction of a different consideration. The choice of indestructible over perishable treasures is presented basically as a matter of common sense; the supplementary comment lays the stress upon the thought that what is really involved is the 'heart' of man, his whole inward being. If he accumulates earthly treasures—chests of sumptuous clothing or of gold and jewels—his heart is bound to earth; if he seeks to accumulate treasures in heaven, his heart is fixed on heavenly things.

The parallel sayings in Luke are not included in his version of the Sermon, but are attached to the Parable of the Rich Fool (Lk.12: 16–21), who has no thought but that he should 'take (his) ease, eat, drink, and be merry'. Somewhat incongruously, Luke follows this immediately with the charge to have no anxieties about food and clothing (vv.22–31), which certainly cause no worry to the rich man of the parable; and only then does he introduce the sayings about the treasures that can never be lost. He gives them in a quite different form; they must have come to him in a source which was not used by Matthew. The Lukan passage runs as follows:

[Sell your possessions, and give alms]; provide yourselves with purses that do not grow old, with a treasure in the heavens that does not fail, where no thief approaches and no moth destroys. For where your treasure is, there will your heart be also. (Lk.12:33–34)

The 'treasure in the heavens', the thief and the moth as the means of loss, are here again, as in Matthew, but without the balanced contrast. In place of the charge not to lay up treasures on earth, we have the positive charge to give them away. The supplementary comment is there, but with no shift to the singular number. There is no word corresponding to 'worm'. In Matthew, the Greek word is βρῶσις, which means literally 'eating'. The more familiar rendering 'rust' goes back to Tyndale, and is used in all the classic English versions except the Geneva Bible (1562), which replaces it with 'canker'. But it never means 'rust' in LXX or elsewhere, and it is hard to imagine any kind of 'treasure' that would be liable to 'rust' (iron, for instance, is not stored up as treasure). The 'eating' creature could be the mouse; or we might take 'moth and eating' as a hendiadys for 'eating by moths'. Recent French and German translations generally give 'worm' (*ver*, *Wurm*), or (German) the more general *Frass* (used, like the verb *fressen*, of eating done by animals). In any case, the thought is of destruction by natural pests; with which is coupled the threat of loss by human malefactors. Thieves 'break through (and steal)'—literally 'dig through'—either by digging up a pot of coins that has been buried in the soil (a common way of safeguarding money; cf. Mt.13:44), or (more likely) by digging under the wall of the house. All this is cast in terms of the ways of the ancient world, where there were no safe deposit boxes and no police forces; everyone had to take his own precautions for protecting his goods. Often enough, all such precautions are vain; one way or another, the hoarded treasure is apt to disappear.

Are we to take these words of Jesus as flatly forbidding his followers to put by any kind of savings at all? If so, we should have to regard them as utterly impractical and even unwise. Without some accumulation of capital, no new venture could ever be undertaken, from the opening of a shop to the building of a factory. The words assume that the treasures are hoarded; they are prized for their own sake, not put to work to create jobs and produce goods.

The parable of the eye, in the Matthaean context, is to be understood as a further warning against the acquisitive spirit—it is an indication of spiritual blindness. It is not likely that the parable was originally framed with this intent; the connection with the warning against laying up treasures on earth is made by Matthew. In Luke it is worked into a series of sayings linked by the key words 'lamp' and 'light' (Lk.11:33–36); and this Lukan sequence is likewise a literary arrangement made by the evangelist, which gives us no help in determining how Jesus himself used the parable or what he meant it to teach. The whole context in Luke is quite different from that in Matthew; it is not included in the Lukan version of the Sermon, nor is it addressed to the disciples. It is spoken to crowds who have just been rebuked for their failure to perceive that something greater than Solomon or Jonah is present (vv.29–32). They lack spiritual insight, but their blindness is not connected with the urge to accumulate earthly treasures; it is shown by their inability to see what is in front of their eyes in the person of Jesus.

The figure itself seems to be a commonplace—if the eyes are bad, the whole person is blind. The eye is called the 'lamp' of the body in the sense that it is the organ by which one sees the path that he wants to follow. If it is 'sound' (ἁπλοῦς, 'simple'), you can see where you are going; if it is 'bad' (πονηρός, 'evil'), you grope about in the darkness and lose all sense of direction. The 'evil' eye is often used in Jewish writings as a figure of the grudging spirit, and this sense is probably to be given to the expression here. Anyone who is bent upon laying up treasures on earth is unwilling to share his possessions with others, and this grudging spirit makes him blind to the things that are of the first importance. The last sentence seems intended to suggest the spiritual application. It is bad enough to be physically blind, so that your body moves in darkness; but if you are spiritually blind, so that you cannot see that treasures in heaven are to be desired above all the treasures of earth, what a darkness that is! In Luke, this is given in the shape of a word of warning. 'Therefore be careful lest the light in you be darkness.'

The third illustration is taken from the institution of slavery. It was legally possible for a slave to be owned by two masters. The saying of Jesus points out what usually happens; the slave will generally be more attached to one of his masters than to the other. The slave, of course, would not be able to change his situation, for he could not reject the claims of either of the two who shared ownership of him. Jesus warns that anyone who tries to serve God while still giving half his allegiance to wealth puts himself into the impossible position of such a slave. God will not accept a half-obedience; we must choose which master we will serve and devote ourselves whole-heartedly to him. The man who is bent on laying up treasures on earth is a slave of 'mammon'; he cannot at the same time be a servant of God. 'Mammon' is a hebraized form of the Aramaic *mamona*, which means simply 'property'. In this saying it is personified, and this personification led to the error of taking it as the name of a god, as in Milton's

'Mammon, the least erected spirit that fell from heav'n.' (*Paradise Lost*, i.679f.)

Against Anxiety 6:25–34

[25] Therefore I tell you, do not be anxious about your life, what you shall eat or what you shall drink, nor about your body, what you shall put on. Is not life more than food, and the body more than clothing? [26] Look at the birds of the air: they neither sow nor reap nor gather into barns, and yet your heavenly Father feeds them. Are you not of more value than they? [27] And which of you by being anxious can add one cubit to his span of life? [28] And why are you anxious about clothing? Consider the lilies of the field, how they grow: they neither toil nor spin; [29] yet I tell you that Solomon in all his glory was not arrayed like one of these. [30] But if God so clothes the grass of the field, which today is alive and tomorrow is thrown into the oven, will he not much more clothe you, O men of little faith? [31] Therefore do not be anxious, saying, 'What shall we eat?' or 'What shall we drink?' or 'What shall we wear?' [32] For the Gentiles seek all these things; and your heavenly Father knows that you need them all. [33] But seek first his kingdom and his righteousness, and all these things shall be yours as well.

[34] Therefore do not be anxious about tomorrow, for tomorrow will bring anxieties of its own. The day's own trouble is enough for the day.

This section was drawn by Matthew from a source which was used also by Luke, though it is not included in his version of the Sermon. As we noted above, Luke has placed it immediately after the parable of the Rich Fool and before the saying about 'treasure in the heavens'. Luke has worked in some sayings which are not found in Matthew, and has not included some phrases which Matthew has inserted into his text. Each evangelist has expanded the source independently. But it will also appear upon close examination that the source itself gave an expanded version of a group of sayings which was somewhat briefer. The saying of verse 27 (Lk.12:25) is given in almost identical words in the two Gospels, and is set in exactly the same place within the passage, so that there can be no doubt that it was included in the source; yet it is clear that it does not fit in with the general thought. Worries about how soon one may die (or about one's height) are not at all like worries about where one is to find his next day's lunch; and while there is no possibility of adding to one's span of life, it is not always impossible to get some extra food or clothing. Other passages which stand in similar parallelism may be regarded as additions made in the source, on other grounds—chiefly in that they interrupt the rhythmic flow of the passage by prose phrases (*see* P. Gaechter, *Das Matthäusevangelium* (1963), p. 228). Among such verses 28 and 30 (Lk.12:28, 30). The additions which Matthew has introduced on his own initiative reveal themselves by the comparison with Luke, and also by their interruption of the basic rhythm; they would include the phrases 'and what you will drink' (vv.25,31), 'of the air', and 'of the field' (vv.26,28), 'they grow' (v.28), 'heavenly' (v.26), and perhaps 'first' (v.33). And it is agreed by virtually all commentators that verse 34 is a floating saying, which has been attracted into this place by the word association ('anxious', and 'morrow').

This group of sayings is not directed to people who can think of storing up treasures on earth, but to those who have barely enough to live upon. They deal with the despairing questions of those who live in destitution, the poorest of the poor. The charge 'do not be anxious' must seem a hard saying to people in such straits—advice that is easy to give but difficult to follow. How can any person fail to worry when there is no food in the house and no clothes fit to wear? Is it really any help to think of the birds and the wild flowers, or to recall that God enables the birds to find their food and clothes the wild flowers with a beauty beyond that of royal robes? In the Galilee of Jesus' time there were no welfare agencies, no mother's allowances, no unemployment insurance—no governmental relief programs to protect people from the worst effects of utter poverty. It is not that Jesus had no acquaintance with poverty—he must have encountered it every day, and in fact he and his followers were dependent upon the charity of some women whom he had healed, 'who provided for them out of their means' (Lk.8:2f.). How could he tell others, who had no such friends to help them, to have no anxiety about the bare necessities of life, to be as free of care as the birds of the sky or the lilies of the field?

The answer is surely to be found in the completeness of Jesus' trust in God, his sublime confidence that the heavenly Father will provide for the needs of his children. He has taught his followers to pray that God will give them today bread sufficient for their needs, and he has no doubt that God will answer their prayer. He seeks to evoke in those who surround him the same limitless faith in God's providence. Above all, he 'still insists that even for the destitute the first necessity is not the provision of food and clothing for the body, but care for the things of the spirit' (F.W. Beare, *The Earliest Records of Jesus* (1962), p. 65).

The accent is on *worry*. It is not only the destitute who are obsessed with anxiety about material things; there have been millionaires who lived in perpetual fear that they would lose all their money (by theft or fraud or a crash in the stock market) and would end up in poverty. More broadly, nearly all of us, whatever our circumstances, are tempted at times to worry about what the future will bring, even though we can be sure that we will not lack food and clothing. The charge of Jesus, 'Do not be anxious', is meant for us all.

When Jesus speaks of how God feeds the birds and clothes the wildflowers with beauty, he is not thinking of the fact that they get along very well without working, nor is he suggesting that we could count on God to supply us with food and clothing if we just sat back and did nothing to earn them. He offers no encouragement to laziness; he knows that from the beginning man has been under the law: 'In the sweat of your face you shall eat bread till you return to the ground' (Gen.3:19). If we are to have anything to eat, someone must sow and reap and gather into barns; if we are to have anything to wear, someone must do the spinning and weaving and tailoring; and Jesus is far from teaching that those who seek the kingdom of God and his righteousness should leave these mundane necessary tasks to those who take no interest in the things of God. The birds of the air and the lilies of the field are held before us as reminders that we need not worry, any more than they do—not, that we need not work. The God to whom we pray as our heavenly Father is the God of all nature. He cares for the littlest things; how can we fail to believe that he will care for his children? For though all in nature is God's and lives by his continual providence, nothing is as precious as man. 'Are you not of more value than they?' If he clothes the wildflowers with such glorious beauty, though they are to last but for a day, 'will he not much more clothe you' who are called to have part in his eternal Kingdom?

The appeal to 'look at the birds' and to 'consider the lilies of the field' draws a lesson from God's providence as shown in nature. Another saying, which is secondary in this passage, though it had already been used in the common source which Luke also employed (Lk.12:25), appeals to common sense—nothing whatever is accomplished by worrying about it. 'Which of you by being anxious can add one cubit to his span of life?' (or, 'to his stature'—v.27). There is no reference here to God, to his providence or to anything in his nature and his relationship to us. This is a floating saying, and probably owes its place in the passage solely to coincidence of wording, in the use of the verb μεριμνῶ, 'be anxious'. It has nothing in it that is in any way characteristic of Jesus. The wording is odd, to say the least. The cubit is a unit of length, not of time (it represents the length of the forearm, something like eighteen inches). What can be the meaning of adding eighteen inches to one's span of life? The suggestion has been made that it means 'you cannot, by worrying about it, add to your life time enough for a single short step.' The alternative rendering (KJV) of adding to the 'stature' is no better; no one would wish to be eighteen inches taller. In any case, the saying is clearly out of place, for in the whole passage Jesus is not seeking to show that worry is useless, but that it is at bottom a token of the lack of faith in God.

'Lilies of the field' may stand for all kinds of wildflowers which grow in the meadows of Galilee, but it has been suggested that Jesus thinks particularly of the purple anemone, which would evoke comparison with the royal purple of Solomon. Beautiful as they are, they wither and are cut along with the grass around them. In Palestine, wood is so scarce that the cut grass must be made into bundles and used to heat the oven for baking bread. 'Birds of the air' (literally, 'of the sky') are termed 'ravens' in Luke. This is perhaps the original wording, and would recall the words of a psalm:

Sing to the Lord with thanksgiving;
. . .
he makes grass grow upon the hills.
He gives to the beasts their food,
and to the young ravens which cry. (Ps.147:7–9)

The raven is classed among the unclean birds, an 'abomination among the birds' (Lev.11:13,15), and perhaps this has led Matthew to avoid mentioning them; yet even they look for their food to God,

Who provides for the raven its prey,
when its young ones croak for lack of food? (Job.38:41, *NEB*)

All these sayings reflect a conception of nature which is far removed from our current ways of thinking. Jesus does not think in terms of 'laws of nature', or of 'nature' and 'the natural world' as of a realm that may be observed and studied without any reference to the supernatural, to the continual activity of God. If the clouds gather and the rains fall, it is because God causes them to do so; fire and hail, snow and frost and stormy winds are fulfilling his word (Ps.148:8). This is not poetic fancy; it is the way in which the

Hebrew thinks of God and sees God's action in every thing that takes place in the world around us.

The mention of 'the Gentiles' in verse 32 (Lk.12:30—'all the nations of the world') is not disparaging; it is a reminder that something more is to be expected of those who know God as their heavenly Father than of those who do not know him at all. The quest for food and clothing is not wrong in itself; God is well aware that his children need these things, just as do Gentiles. There is perhaps an underlying suggestion that in pagan religions generally, the primary object of the rites is to ensure a good crop, and the increase of the flocks and of the family. For those who are privileged to know the one living and true God, the quest for material things, even for food and clothing, must take second place to the quest for his kingdom and righteousness. This is in keeping with the order of petitions in the Lord's Prayer: we pray for the hallowing of his name, for the coming of his kingdom, and for the doing of his will, before we ask for our bread. His kingdom and his righteousness are inseparable—the way of the Kingdom is the way of righteousness. We recall the initial warning that 'unless your righteousness exceeds that of the scribes and Pharisees, you will never enter the kingdom of heaven' (5:20). In pagan religions generally, there is no such association of ethics and religion; in the Greek world, it was above all the philosophers who became the ethical instructors, and they found religion an obstacle, not an aid, when they sought to lead men into the way of virtue.

The closing verse is a Matthaean addition, and owes its place here to the verbal link in the charge 'do not be anxious.' But it may be that Matthew sees something more than a mere verbal association. Perhaps he wants to remind us that Jesus does not offer any assurance that life will be better tomorrow than it is today. There is no resort to a facile optimism. We must face today's problems with no faint dream that they will disappear overnight; but there is no point in anticipating them. For tomorrow, as for today, we pray, 'Thy will be done.'

6 MISCELLANEOUS INSTRUCTIONS 7:1–12

On Finding Fault 7:1–5

[1] Do not judge, that you may not be judged. [2] For with the judgement which you make, you will be judged; and with the measure you give, repayment will be made to you. [3] Why do you keep looking at the splinter that is in your brother's eye and pay no heed to the

beam that is in your own eye? [4] Or how can you say to your brother, 'Come, let me get the splinter out of your eye,' when look!—the beam is in your own eye? [5] Hypocrite! first get the beam out of your own eye, and then you will see clearly enough to get the splinter out of your brother's eye.

In the Lukan parallel (Lk.6:37a,38c,41f.), this passage follows directly upon the charge to 'love your enemies', with its concluding words (as Luke gives them), 'Be merciful, as your Father is merciful.' This gives an admirable connection, which has been lost in Matthew's rearrangement by the insertion of his entire chapter 6.

It has been suggested that Matthew is arranging his materials in the latter part of the Sermon to present them as a development of the thought of the Lord's Prayer. The whole section on acquisitiveness and anxiety is seen as an extended comment on the first clauses of the Prayer. The name of our heavenly Father is sanctified when we devote ourselves to laying up treasures in heaven, and when we refuse to divide our allegiance between God and Mammon. The prayer for our daily bread frees us from anxiety about our material needs. Now the prayer for the forgiveness of our sins, coupled as it is with the pledge that we have forgiven (and will go on forgiving) wrongs done to us by others, is developed along the line that has already been indicated in the brief preliminary comment which follows immediately upon the prayer (6:14–15). Forgive others their trespasses, as you pray and believe that God will forgive you; there is a basic similarity to this in the (negatively expressed) charge: 'Do not judge, that you may not be judged.' For the clause 'that you may not be judged' means in effect 'that God may not judge you'. (This is another instance of the tendency, prevalent in Judaism, to avoid speaking directly of God.) And this in turn is in tune with the beatitude, 'Blessed are the merciful, for they shall obtain mercy' from God (5:7). All through, there is an insistence that our relationship with God is inseparably linked with our relationships with our fellows. If we look to him for mercy, we must ourselves show mercy to others; if we pray that he will forgive us, we must be ready to forgive those who have done us wrong; if we hope to escape condemnation in the day of his judgement, we must not sit in judgement on others.

It is evident that as Matthew understands the words, they do not mean that we may not judge the conduct and character of our neighbours at all, but that our judgements must not be harsh. That is at least implied in the next verse—'with the judgement which you make, you will be judged.' The passive is again used of the judgement of God; it is not that *others* will judge you as you judge others; but that God will judge you with severity or leniency to match the severity or leniency which you have used towards others. The figure of 'measure' is taken from the language of commercial transactions. In documents covering a loan of grain, it is regularly specified that the grain to be repaid will be measured with the same measure that was used in providing the grain to the borrower. In Luke, the image is further developed to the effect that if you give good measure it will be returned (by God) with still greater generosity. 'Give, and it will be given to you; good measure, pressed down, shaken together, running over, will be put into your lap' (Lk.6:38—the 'lap' is the garment held to make a container for the grain). In the same spirit, Paul encourages his Gentile congregations to give generously for the relief of their impoverished brethren in Judaea. He writes: 'He who sows sparingly will also reap sparingly, and he who sows bountifully will also reap bountifully . . . And God is able to provide you with every blessing in abundance, so that you may always have enough of everything and may provide in abundance for every good work' (2 Cor.9:6,8).

On Safeguarding Holy Things 7:6

[6] Do not give what is holy to the dogs, and do not throw your pearls down before swine—they will trample them under their feet and then turn upon you and tear you to pieces.

This strange saying has no parallel in the other Gospels (it is taken up in the Gospel of Thomas). Matthew may have understood it as a modification of the absolute prohibition of 'judging', as if to suggest that there is none the less some need for discrimination. It has sometimes been taken as a warning against misplaced zeal in proselytizing; and an early tradition connects it with the church's practice of restricting participation in the Eucharist to the baptized. None of these suggestions is at all convincing. The point of the figure is hard to determine, especially the meaning of 'dogs' and 'pigs'. We sometimes find these terms used by Jewish teachers in scornful reference to Gentiles, but this is not conceivable on the lips of Jesus. The 'dogs' and 'pigs' of the figure are clearly not the pets of the household or of the pigpen, but savage dogs and wild boars. In Jewish law, the pig was an unclean animal that could not be used for food or for sacrifice, and pigs were not raised by Jewish peasants. It is just as hard to determine the intended reference of 'the holy' and of the 'pearls', which are set in parallelism, as two ways of expressing the same thing. But what are these precious things which are holy? We can hardly suppose that they stand for the gospel and the sayings of Jesus, as if these were too precious to be communicated to Gentiles or to unbelievers (wild dogs and wild boars). At a pinch, we might interpret the fierce reception of the precious holy things as a warning that the gospel is not only rejected with scorn (trampled under foot) but with positive danger to the preachers ('They will turn upon you and tear you to pieces') but this is far from plausible. Is the fear of arousing a hostile reaction a reason for abstaining from preaching the gospel to those who most need it?

Perhaps we must fall back upon the comment of A.C. McNeile (*Matthew, ad loc.*) that 'as the original context is unknown, an exact interpretation is impossible.'

We are inclined to feel that such a saying has been introduced into the tradition before Matthew from some other source. The problem remains, what can it have meant to Matthew, who undoubtedly passed it along as an utterance of Jesus, and placed it at this point in his Gospel? As it cannot possibly be looked upon as an introduction to the Golden Rule (v.12), we must suppose that he linked it in some sense with the little section on Judging which precedes (vv.1–5).

Assurances that God Answers our Prayers 7:7–11

⁷ Ask and it will be given to you; seek, and you will find; knock, and it will be opened to you. ⁸ For everyone who asks receives, everyone who seeks finds, and to everyone who knocks it will be opened. ⁹ Who is there among you who would give his son a stone when he asks for bread? ¹⁰ Or give him a serpent when he asks for a fish? ¹¹ Then, if you who are wicked know how to give good gifts to your children, how much more will your heavenly Father give good things to those who ask him?

VERSES 7–8: These are not general truths. They do not apply to human requests of one another, and they do not apply to all our prayers to God. Other people do not always give us what we ask, and all of us have known the disappointment, sometimes the bitterness, of unanswered prayer. If we recall that the theme of the whole Sermon is the kingdom of heaven, and the way of winning admission to it, we may apply the words specifically to petitions for entrance. Of this primarily we have the assurance that everyone who asks receives, that everyone who seeks finds, and that everyone who knocks at the gate is admitted. It is God who grants the most precious of all gifts, who is found by all who seek, and who opens to all who knock at the gates of his mercy.

In the Matthaean version of these sayings, we have the broader suggestion of 'good things' as that for which we ask and which our heavenly Father will give, even more surely than an earthly father will give his son the bread or the fish for which he asks. In Luke, it is 'the Holy Spirit' which is given to those who ask (Lk.11:13). For Luke, the Kingdom is signalized by the coming of the Spirit (Lk.24: 49; Acts 1:5,8; 2:1—4,14—18,38f.); all the evangelists agree that the bestowing of the Spirit is the gift of the ascended Christ (John 7:39; 14:16f.,26; 15:26; 16:7; 20:19—23). For Matthew, all other 'good things' are given with the Kingdom: 'Seek first his kingdom and his righteousness, and all these things shall be yours as well' (Mt.6:33).

VERSE 10: Where Matthew speaks of 'bread—stone' and 'fish—serpent', Luke uses 'fish—serpent' and 'egg—scorpion' for the contrast.

VERSE 11: In both versions, 'wicked' is used of human character —not perhaps absolutely, but in comparison with the goodness of God. If we, despite the wickedness of our hearts, can none the less be counted on to be kind to our children and not to mock their requests to us for everyday food, how much more can God, in whom there is no trace of evil, be counted on to fill all our needs, temporal and also spiritual?

The Golden Rule 7:12

[12] Whatever you desire that others should do for you, do so for them; for this is the law and the prophets.

This saying is found in a negative form, in a reply of the great Hillel (*c.* 60 BC—AD 20) to a questioner who demanded of him that he should state the substance of the Law while standing on one foot. 'What is hateful to you, do not do to anyone else: this is the whole Law and the rest is commentary.' Without the second clause, it appears already in the book of Tobit (4:15): 'What you hate, do not do to anyone', and in the *Letter of Aristeas* (*c.* 100 BC). Thus it was a familiar sentiment in Judaism. But it is not peculiarly Jewish. It was given by Confucius, and is found also in the literatures of Buddhism and of Islam, and of the wisdom of Greece and Rome (Herodotus, Seneca).

It is not in itself an all-sufficient guide for daily living. It is not evident that what we would desire others to do for us is invariably for our good. It is God, not other people, who is to be the model for our conduct; nothing less is worthy of those who call him 'Father'. No great significance is to be attached to the fact that the negative formulation is invariable in all the non-Christian writings, including the Jewish. Jewish interpreters actually regard the negative form as superior, and with some justice. In early Christian literature, it is cited indifferently in the negative and in the positive form.

The phrase picks up the words of 5:17: 'Do not think that I have come to destroy the law and the prophets: I have not come to destroy but to fulfil.' Matthew again makes use of the rhetorical device of inclusion, to mark off the body of the Sermon. In spite of the apparent insistence on every iota and stroke in the Law, this saying indicates that the Law is fulfilled in substance when we make the Golden Rule the guiding principle of life. With this we may compare the teaching of Paul: 'The commandments . . . are summed up in this sentence, "You shall love your neighbour as yourself." Love does no wrong to a neighbour; therefore love is the fulfilling of the law' (Rom.13:9f.).

7   FINALE: EXHORTATIONS, WARNINGS AND CLOSING PARABLE 7:13–27

The main body of the Sermon is marked off by the sentences about the Law and the Prophets (5:17; 7:12). The Beatitudes and the sayings which follow them (5:3–16) are a prelude, and this group of exhortations and warnings are a finale. The parable of the Two Houses form a general conclusion to the whole structure. At the beginning, Jesus 'opened his mouth and taught them' (5:2); at the end, he impresses on them the vital importance of doing the things that he has taught (7:24–27).

The Two Ways 7:13–14

[13] Go in through the narrow gate. The gate that leads to destruction is wide and the highway is broad, and many take it; [14] but the gate that opens the way to life is narrow and the road toilsome, and few find it.

The figure of the Two Ways is widely used by Greek and Roman moralists (Hesiod, Seneca, and many others), and in Hebrew and

Jewish literature. Hesiod warns his brother Perses that 'Wickedness is easy to choose and plentiful; the way is smooth and near to hand. But the immortal gods have decreed that we must sweat to win virtue; the path is long and steep and rough to begin with, but when the summit is reached it becomes easy, difficult though it had been' (*Works and Days* 286–292). The sophist Prodicus illustrates this figure by the story of Heracles at the crossroads (of life), where he finds himself obliged to choose between the two forks. The road to the left is level and pleasant-looking, but it leads to a precipice. The road to the right is rocky and difficult to tread and confronts the traveller with toils and struggles, but it leads to serene heights and to well-deserved repose. Among the Pythagoreans it is developed in the form of the 'Pythagorean Y', which applies it to the choice which the individual must make when he reaches the age of moral responsibility.

In the literature of Israel, there appears to be no suggestion that the way of evil is easy and the way of virtue hard and toilsome. On the contrary, it is the way of the transgressor that is hard, while 'the path of the just is a level highway' (Prov.13:15; 15:19).

In the text before us, the figure of the Two Ways is combined with that of Two Gates. It is not clear how the two are connected, or even what kind of 'way' is conceived as accessible through a 'gate', or why a wide Gate is appropriate to a wide Way, or a narrow Gate to a hard Way—the width of the gate seems to be irrelevant to the wideness or narrowness of the way upon which it opens. There appears to be a combination of two independent figures—in the one, the kingdom of heaven is 'life' attained by one momentous decision, by choosing the right Gate; in the other, the Kingdom lies at the end of a toilsome journey.

It is of course possible to expound to the effect that two things are necessary—first, to make the difficult initial decision, to enter by the narrow gate; secondly, to continue along the toilsome road to which the narrow gate has given access.

In Luke the saying is introduced by a question put to Jesus (not in the Sermon). Some one said to him, 'Will those who are saved be few?' The answer is, 'Strive to enter by the narrow door; for many, I tell you, will strive to enter and will not be able' (13:23f.). There is no mention of the Two Ways; the door admits to a house, not to a road or path and the difficulty of gaining admission is not that the door is narrow but that the seeker has arrived too late and found it shut. 'Once the master of the house has risen and shut the door, and you begin to stand outside and knock at the door, saying, "Lord, open to us," he will answer you, "I do not know where you come from . . . depart from me" ' (vv.25–27). The initial question is never answered—it is not affirmed that few will be saved. The whole emphasis is laid on the need for acting without delay. 'Now is the accepted time; now is the day of salvation' (2 Cor.6:2).

False Prophets 7:15–20

[15] Beware of the false prophets who come to you in the garb of sheep, but inwardly are predatory wolves. [16] You will recognize them by their fruits. Do we gather grapes from thorn bushes, or figs from thistles? [17] Thus every good tree produces good fruit and every poor tree produces poor fruit. [18] A good tree cannot bear poor fruit nor a poor tree good fruit, [19] and any tree that does not produce good fruit is cut down and thrown on a fire. [20] So you will recognize them by their fruits.

Jesus may have warned his hearers against being inveigled by false prophets, but for Matthew the words are meant as a warning to the church of his own time against being led astray by some who profess to be Christian prophets, and are outwardly indistinguishable from true prophets of Christ. In the 'Synoptic Apocalypse' (Mk.13 and parallels) the church of the last days is warned that 'false Christs [i.e., Messianic pretenders] and false prophets will rise up and will show signs and wonders that would lead astray the elect, if that were possible' (Mk.13:21f.; Mt.24:24). The prophesying itself, and the 'signs and wonders' that might seem to support their claims are but the 'garb of sheep' which conceal the wolf-life character. But in this passage of Matthew, the reference is not to a danger that will appear in the end-time, but to a phenomenon present in the life of the early church. The gift of prophecy was highly honoured in the early church as one of the gifts of the Spirit. 'God has appointed in the church first apostles, second prophets, third teachers . . .' (1 Cor.12: 28), yet Paul has already been obliged to warn the Corinthians that not all charismatic speakers are to be accepted, for 'no one speaking by the Spirit of God ever says "Jesus be accursed" ' (12:3). A genera-tion later another apostolic writer charges his people in similar terms: 'Beloved, do not believe every spirit, but test the spirits to see whether they are of God; for many false prophets have gone out into the world' (1 Jn.4:1).

This was not a problem in the Judaism of the time of Jesus. The function of prophecy was indeed honoured in ancient Israel. There were guilds or schools of prophets all through Hebrew history, right

down to the fall of Jerusalem to the Babylonians in 586 BC. Many
of the great classical prophets appear to have been solitaries (Elijah,
Amos), but many were attended by bands of disciples (Elisha, 2 Ki.
6:1–4; Isaiah, Isa.8:16). There were official prophets, attached to
the court, who were consulted by the king to foretell the prospects
of success in a projected campaign (I Ki.20:13ff.; 22:5–28; etc.).
But too often the court prophets gave the kind of response that the
king desired, and were challenged by recalcitrant individual prophets,
like Micaiah or Jeremiah. On the eve of the siege of Jerusalem, the
official prophets advised resistance and prophesied that it would be
successful, but Jeremiah proclaims to Zedekiah the king, 'Do not
listen to the words of the prophets who are saying to you, "you shall
not serve the king of Babylon", for it is a lie which they are
prophesying to you. I have not sent them, says the Lord, but they
are prophesying falsely in my name' (Jer.27:14f.; cf. chap.28). After
the disaster which followed, the function of prophecy fell into
disrepute. As early as the eighth century, the prophet Micah had
declared, 'The sun shall go down upon the prophets, and the day
shall be black upon them,' and accused them of divining for money
(Mic.3:6,11). And a later prophet couples 'the prophets and the
unclean spirit' and declares that they will be purged out of the land
along with the idols, in the day that the Lord cleanses his people
from sin and uncleanness (Zech.13:1f., perhaps as late as the third
century BC). He goes on to say that 'if any one again appears as a
prophet, his father and mother that bore him will say to him, "You
shall not live, for you speak lies in the name of the Lord"' (v.3).

There was a generally accepted belief in contemporary Judaism
that prophecy had long ceased. All revelation was given in the Law,
and the need was above all for scholars who could pass on the
tradition of its interpretation, the 'scribes', of whom Ezra was
regarded as the first. 'Moses received the Law from God on Mount
Sinai; he passed it on to Joshua, Joshua to the Prophets, and the
Prophets to Ezra and the men of the Great Synagogue' (Mishnah,
Tractate *Pirke Aboth*, 1:1). Once Judaism developed into a religion
of the Book, any new 'prophet' was bound to be regarded with
suspicion. In such a community, there was no need for a warning
against 'false prophets'.

In the earliest Christian communities, on the other hand, one of
the most marked features was the revival of prophecy. The Spirit
was poured forth, and the promise was fulfilled that 'your sons and
your daughters shall prophesy' (Joel 2:28; Acts 2:17). In the church
at Antioch, which sent Barnabas and Paul on their first great

missionary journey to Cyprus and southern Asia (Minor), 'there were prophets and teachers' (Acts 13:1). Paul gives a vivid description of the somewhat disorderly scenes in the church at Corinth, when several prophets would try to speak at once, and the apostle is obliged to lay down the rule: 'Let two or three prophets speak, and let the others weigh what is spoken. If a revelation is made to another sitting by, let the first be silent. For you can all prophesy one by one, so that all may learn and all be encouraged' (1 Cor. 14:29—31). But as in Israel, the church found its prophets often enough self-seeking and in one way and another 'false' and devised ways to test them, primarily by their 'fruits'. The *Didache*, or *Teaching of the Twelve Apostles* (early second century), warns that 'not everyone who speaks in a spirit is a prophet, except he have the behaviour of the Lord. From his behaviour, then, the false prophet and the true prophet shall be known' (7:8). If he asks gifts for himself, in his ecstatic utterance, he is a humbug. The practice became disreputable and soon died away, though it had a temporary revival in Asia Minor late in the second century in the Montanist movement.

The warning against false prophets in Matthew belongs, like the Didache, to the church of the early second century, not to the Judaism of the time of Jesus nor to the Christianity of the apostolic age. False prophets are a danger, but the true prophet is still recognized as a minister of Christ, sent by him, and sometimes dying the martyr's death (Mt.23:34).

The warning against false prophets is followed by a catena of sayings about trees and their fruits which Matthew has put together from different contexts. There is a partial parallel in Luke's version of the sermon (Lk.6:43f.), where it follows immediately upon the prohibition of judging and leads on to an application to good and evil utterance, which Matthew uses in a different context (Lk.6:45; Mt.12:35). Luke does not associate it with false prophets. Verse 19 is transferred from the tradition of sayings of John the Baptist (Mt.3:10).

False Professions 7:21—23

21 Not everyone who addresses me as 'Lord, Lord,' shall enter the kingdom of heaven, but only the one who does the will of my Father who is in heaven. 22 On that day, many will say to me, 'Lord, Lord did we not prophesy in your name, and cast out demons in your name, and in your name do many miracles?' 23 Then I will

tell them openly, 'I have never known you. Depart from me, you evildoers!'

VERSE 21: The phrase 'to do the will of God' occurs frequently in rabbinical writings, and even 'to do the will of (the) Father who is in heaven'. Among the *Pirke Aboth* ('Sayings of the Fathers') there is included a saying attributed to Rabbi Jehudah ben Thema (mid second century): 'Be bold as a leopard, swift as an eagle, fleet as a hart, and strong as a lion to do the will of your Father who is in heaven' (*Aboth* 5:22). Jesus alone speaks of '*My* Father who is in heaven.'

Kyrie, 'Lord', is a common form of respectful address, no more meaningful in itself than our 'Sir'. In the present context, however, it clearly supposes the use as a title of worship, in accordance with later Christian practice. Those who use it suppose that it is enough to assure their admission to the kingdom of heaven. T.W. Manson (*Sayings*, p.176) suggested that Matthew consciously shaped the saying to make it a rebuttal of the Pauline doctrine that 'everyone who calls upon the name of the Lord will be saved' (Rom.10:13, cited from Joel 2:32 LXX). As the following verses show, these are people who give Jesus the title without obeying him. This is clearly brought out in the Lukan parallel: 'Why do you call me 'Lord, Lord,' and yet do not do what I bid you?' (Lk.6:46; also in the Sermon but without the Matthaean continuation.)

'Jesus is not addressed as 'Lord' in this religious sense during his lifetime; it becomes the cult title after his resurrection, when he is known as Lord of the church that confesses him' (McNeile, *Matthew, ad loc.*).

VERSE 22: Prophesying, exorcism of demons, and even the working of miracles are not the 'fruits' by which the true prophet is to be known from the false. The one thing that matters is obedience to the will of God.

'On that day'—i.e., on the day of judgement. It is presupposed that Jesus is the judge who gives sentence of exclusion from the kingdom of heaven. So Paul speaks of 'that day when, according to my gospel, God will judge the secrets of human hearts by Christ Jesus' (Rom.2:16).

VERSE 23: The second clause of the judgement is drawn from Psalm 6:8.

The Parable of the Two Houses 7:24—27

24 In conclusion, whoever hears these words of mine and acts upon

them is to be likened to a prudent man who built his house upon the bedrock. [25] When rain poured down, the streams rose and the winds blew and beat upon that house, but it did not fall, for it had been founded on the bedrock. [26] Whoever hears these words of mine and does not act upon them is to be likened to a foolish man who built his house on the sand. [27] When rain poured down, the streams rose and the winds blew and beat upon that house, and it fell, and was completely ruined.

The sermon as it appears in Luke concludes with what is basically the same parable, but some of the details are greatly changed. If, as is generally agreed, the two evangelists were drawing upon the same source, with an opening section of beatitudes and with a parable of two builders as its conclusion, it is surprising that there should be such great changes both in the beginning and in the ending. Either the source itself lay before them in two independent versions, or else one of them has adapted the common source with astounding freedom. (It is of course possible that both of them have revised freely, but independently. The one thing that does not seem possible is that Luke has been using Matthew, treating him with this freedom.)

In Luke, the second man has built his house with no foundation at all; and the work of the first is described with much more detail, emphasizing the depth as well as the solidity of the foundation. 'He dug deep and laid the foundation upon the bedrock,' while the other 'built his house on the ground, without a foundation' (Lk.6: 48,49). Luke makes no mention of wind and rain, but mentions only the flooding caused by the rise of a river (singular, not plural as in Matthew). There are some other changes of wording of less moment, such as the substitution of 'it [the river in flood] was not able to shake it', for Matthew's 'it [the house] did not fall.'

These differences could reflect differing climatic conditions as known to the two evangelists. Luke may come from a region in which danger comes chiefly from a river overflowing its channels, which could be caused by heavy rains far upstream, while Matthew may be more familiar with localities in which storms of wind and rain are accompanied with flooding as the streams rise. It may be remarked that sand is not always an unstable foundation for a house; in some regions it is excellent.

The parable makes extraordinary claims for the teaching of Jesus; it is certainly implied that he speaks with more than human authority. 'These words of mine' will refer to all the teaching of the sermon, which constitute the laws of the kingdom of heaven, based upon the law given through Moses, and now reinterpreted by Jesus. The life that is built upon the observance of these laws is secure against all assaults; the life that fails to observe them is fated to utter ruin.

The main emphasis is laid upon the fact that it is not enough to know these laws; they must be carried into action. 'If you know these things, blessed are you if you do them' (Jn.13:17).

CONCLUDING RUBRIC: REACTION OF THE CROWDS 7:28–29

[28] When Jesus had finished these sayings, the crowds were astonished at his teaching; [29] for he gave his teaching to them as one with authority, and not as their scribes.

VERSE 28: We encounter here for the first time, the formula employed as a kind of rubric by Matthew at the close of each of his five major discourses. The construction καὶ ἐγένετο (ὅτε) is frequently employed in LXX, as a literal rendering of the Hebrew *way'hi*, made familiar to us by the *AV* 'and it came to pass', introducing a clause of time, as here. It is often adopted by Luke—one of his deliberate imitations of the Septuagint; but is never used by Matthew except in these rubrics, and in 9:10 (Moulton, *Grammar*, Vol. I, 'Prolegomena', p. 16).

The astonishment of the crowds is taken over from Mark 1:22, where Jesus has been teaching in a synagogue at Capernaum. Nothing is reported by Mark of the subject of the teaching—not even its theme; but after witnessing an exorcism, the people exclaim, 'What is this? A new teaching! With authority he gives orders to the unclean spirits and they obey him!' (1:23–27). This exorcism is not reported by Matthew.

VERSE 29: The contrast is striking. Such authority as the scribes exercised rested upon their knowledge of the law of Moses, and especially on the traditional interpretations of its provisions given by their predecessors, which constituted the 'oral law'. They did not venture to make deliverances on their own authority.

The authority of Jesus is greatly stressed by Matthew. The crowds recognize the note of authority in his teaching. He has 'authority on earth to forgive sins' (9:6). He can confer authority on his disciples to exorcise demons and to heal diseases (10:1). Finally, the risen Jesus reveals to his disciples that all authority in heaven and on earth has been given to him (28:18).

'Their scribes'—the possessive is added by Matthew (it is found in some of the later, inferior manuscripts of Mark, by assimilation to the text of Matthew). Matthew knows of Christian scribes, and wants to make a distinction between them and the scribes of the synagogue.

II   A SEQUENCE OF MIRACLE STORIES
Mt. 8:1–9:35

In the three chapters of the Sermon on the Mount, Matthew has gathered and arranged a representative selection of sayings of Jesus which serve to set forth his teachings on the moral requirements of life in the kingdom of heaven. He now offers a collection of miracle stories to show how the powers of the coming Kingdom were manifested in the healing ministry of Jesus. Again he makes a formal arrangement of his materials, which are drawn from different sources —some from Mark, some from Q (those which he shares with Luke), and some from sources otherwise unknown, which only he has employed. They are arranged in three groups of three miracles each (one includes within it the story of another healing, so that the total number is sometimes reckoned as ten). The groups are separated by brief passages of non-miraculous anecdote and controversy, and some of the stories are accompanied by sayings of Jesus which were not originally attached to them. The whole passage may be analysed as follows:

1 First Group of Miracle Stories 8:1–17
   The Cleansing of a Leper 8:1–4 (Markan)
   The Healing of a Centurion's Boy 8:5–13 (Q)
   The Healing of Peter's Mother-in-law 8:14–15 (Markan)
   First Supplement: Exorcisms at Evening 8:16 (Markan)
   Second Supplement: Fulfilment of Prophecy 8:17 (Markan)
2 Interlude: Responses to Candidates for Discipleship 8:18–22 (Q)
3 Second Group of Miracle Stories 8:23–9:8
   Jesus Stills a Storm 8:23–27 (Markan)
   Jesus Exorcises Demons 8:28–9:1 (Markan)
   Jesus Heals a Paralytic 9:2–8 (Markan)
4 Interlude: Jesus in Controversy 9:9–17 (Markan)
   The Call of Matthew: Controversy with the Pharisees 9:9–13 (Markan)
   Controversy with Disciples of John: the Practice of Fasting 9:14–15 (Markan)
   Supplement: Sayings about the Old and the New 9:16–17 (Markan)

5 Third Group of Miracle Stories 9:18–34
    Jesus Raises a Dead Girl to Life; He Heals a Woman with a
    Haemorrhage 9:18–26 (Markan)
    Jesus Restores Sight to Two Blind Men 9:27–31 (doublet of
    a Markan story)
    Jesus Restores Speech to a Dumb Man 9:32–33 [34]
    Conclusion: Jesus Resumes his Tour of Galilee 9:35

This arrangement in tripled triplicate is purely formal. There is no trace of chronological sequence—Matthew is not attempting to offer a consecutive narrative of events. Most of the materials are taken from Mark—all but three of the miracle stories, all the controversies, and also the story of the call of the tax collector. But the Markan order is drastically altered, and much intervening Markan narrative is held back for use at a later point. The section Mark 2:1–22 is kept intact but is made to follow upon another intact section (Mk.4:35–5:20) which Mark holds till after his account of the teaching in parables (this is not introduced by Matthew until his thirteenth chapter); and the passage which directly follows this in Mark is held back by Matthew to be used as the first story of his third group. The second story of this third group appears to be a doublet of the Markan story of Bar-Timaeus (Mk.10:46–52), which Mark lays at Jericho, as Jesus is leaving the town for Jerusalem on his last journey (the same story is told again by Matthew at that point).

But Matthew's changes are not confined to these matters of order. We must also take note of the way he reduces each story to its bare essentials. The words of Jesus are seldom altered, but the narrative element is shortened by the removal of much of the detail, in a way which usually robs the story of much of its colour. The compensation for this lack of colour is given in the greater concentration on the figure of Jesus, as the clusters of others—disciples, mediating 'elders of the Jews' (Lk.7:3–6), messengers, or throngs—are left out of the picture; the light is focused wholly upon Jesus and the person to be healed. In some instances, the initiative of Jesus is heightened; he does not wait to be asked but volunteers his help (8:7,15); the disciples do not 'take him, as he was, in the boat' (Mk.4:36)—he goes aboard and they follow (Mt.8:23). Besides all this, there is a greater emphasis on the *word* of Jesus as the one means of healing (Mt.8:13; 9:22).

It should also be noted that Matthew gives a much lesser proportion of his book to stories of miracle than does his principal source, the Gospel of Mark. More than half of the miracle stories related by Matthew are included in this one collection; the others—eight in all —are scattered through the next twelve chapters, and in most of these the primary interest is not in the miracle as such, but in its symbolical significance. The number of stories is approximately the same as in Mark, but they are always given in a drastically reduced form, and the teaching material is vastly increased. The result is that, while Mark devotes about twenty per cent of his Gospel to miracle stories, up to the beginning of the Passion story, we find that in Matthew this has shrunk to less than thirteen per cent. This cannot be taken to indicate anything like a distaste for miracle, such as a modern reader is apt to feel. Matthew actually heightens the miraculous in some ways, even though he reduces the space that he allots to it in his book. Where Mark will say that Jesus healed *many* that were sick, Matthew will tell us that he healed them *all* (Mk.1:34; Mt.8:16). In the stories of the miraculous feedings of the multitudes, Mark is content to put the numbers at five thousand (Mk.6:44) and four thousand (Mk.8:9); in both places, Matthew adds the phrase 'besides women and children' (Mt.14:21; 15:38). In the story of the cursing of the fig tree, as Mark tells it, the tree shows no effect until the next day, when it is seen to have withered away; but in Matthew's version, it withers instantaneously (Mk.11:12–14,20; Mt.21:19). Again, where Matthew omits a Markan story (Mk.7:32–36), he gives us instead a comprehensive description of a general healing in the most extravagant terms: 'Great crowds came to him bringing with them the lame, the maimed, the blind, the dumb, and many others, and laid them at his feet, and he healed them, so that the throng were amazed, when they saw the dumb speaking, the maimed made whole, the lame walking, and the blind seeing; and they glorified the God of Israel' (Mt.15:30f.). It is quite evident that Matthew is by no means averse to miracle, but we cannot fail to see that he keeps it in proportion. For him, the teaching ministry of Jesus is the primary thing, and the working of miracles is more or less incidental.

1   FIRST GROUP OF MIRACLE STORIES *8:1–17*

The Cleansing of a Leper 8:1–4

¹ When he came down from the mountain, great crowds followed him.

² A leper now approached him and knelt before him, saying, 'Sir, if you will, you can make me clean.' ³ And he streched out his hand

and touched him, saying, 'I will, be cleansed.' And his leprosy was cleansed immediately. ⁴And Jesus said to him, 'Tell no one, but go show yourself to the priest and offer the gift that Moses commanded, for a testimony to them.'

VERSE 1: This introductory sentence is not found in the Markan parallel (Mk.1:14ff.). It has no bearing on the story, and it is not clear that these 'great crowds' are the same as those who have formed the audience for the sermon and have been 'astonished at his teaching' (7:28). If crowds were watching the cleansing of the leper, there would seem to be no point in the injunction to him to tell nobody about it (v.4).

VERSE 2: The words 'leper' and 'leprosy' (λεπρός, λέπρα) here and elsewhere in the Gospels are used of a skin disease which may be psoriasis or vitiligo or ringworm, or any kind of eczema, but is almost certainly not to be understood as what we now call leprosy (Hansen's disease, or elephantiasis), for that was extremely rare in Palestine at this period. In the ancient law, it is assumed to be curable, and regulations are laid down for the priest to establish the cure as well as to make the diagnosis (Lev.13 and 14; the law also deals with 'leprosy' in a garment or in a house).¹

The story in Mark is very brief, but even so Matthew succeeds in paring it even more. Mark appears to regard it as an exorcism, as if the leprosy were caused by the presence of a demon. Jesus shows anger (ὀργισθείς, 'angered', must be preferred to the more frequently attested reading σπλαγχνισθείς, 'moved with pity'); and it is also said that Jesus 'shouted at him and cast him out' (ἐμβριμησάμενος αὐτῷ εὐθὺς ἐξέβαλον αὐτόν—a difficult sentence; see the note of V. Taylor, *Mark, ad loc.*). Both these expressions are removed by Matthew (and also by Luke); there can be no doubt that they are meant to indicate anger at the demon of leprosy, not at the afflicted man.

The vocative of Kyrios (κύριος) is generally used as a respectful form of salutation, adequately rendered by 'Sir'. It is not used in the Markan story (Mark seldom used *Kyrios* of Jesus in any form, and only once in the vocative (7:28; significantly, on the lips of an alien). It is frequently used by Matthew, Luke, and John, not only in the vocative but also in the other cases; this reflects the confession of Jesus as 'Lord' in the worship of his church.

¹ See the article, 'Leprosy' by G.R. Driver *et al.* in *Hastings Dictionary of the Bible* (rev.edn., 1963, ed. F.G. Grant and H.H. Rowley), pp. 575–78.

'Approached'—another instance of Matthew's characteristic use of this verb (προσέρχομαι) to heighten the impression of majesty in Jesus (see on 4:11).

The use of the verb 'cleanse, make clean' (καθαρίζω) reflects the fact that 'leprosy' rendered the sufferer ritually 'unclean' (Lev.13: 45f.). In LXX it is used in the sense 'pronounce clean' (Lev.13:37).

VERSE 3: The stretching out of the hand and the touch are characteristics of the miracle worker. In the iconography of the miracle stories, Jesus is often depicted with the wand of the thaumaturge. There is a relic here of the primitive notion that power is transmitted through the touch; this is ritually formalized in the laying on of hands. Matthew tends to avoid manipulations, such as the use of spittle (Mk.8:23; Jn.9:6) or putting fingers into the ears and touching the tongue (Mk.7:33, of a deaf-mute); but he finds the touch of the healer's hand acceptable.

VERSE 4: Jesus instructs the man to comply with the law; 'the gift that Moses commanded' (Matthew omits the Markan phrase 'for your cleansing' (Mk.1:44), retained by Luke). The 'gift' was substantial— two male lambs, one ewe lamb, and offerings of cereal and of olive oil (Lev.14:10); the quantities are reduced for anyone who cannot afford so much (vv.21–32).

If Matthew has chosen to place this story in the forefront of his collection, it is probably because he sees in it an illustration of the principle that Jesus did not come to abolish the law, but to fulfil it (Mt.5:17). He sends the leper to the priest, to show himself and to make the offering prescribed in the Law of Moses, 'for a testimony to them'—that is, as evidence that Jesus keeps the Law and teaches others to keep it (5:19).

Strangely enough, to our minds, the rites of cleansing prescribed in the law begin with a procedure of primitive magic. The priest takes two living birds, commands one of them to be killed in an earthen vessel over running water, and then dips the living bird, together with a bundle of cedar, scarlet cloth, and hyssop, in the blood of the slain bird, and uses this to sprinkle the blood over the man who is to be cleansed. The sprinkling is done seven times, the priest pronounces the man clean, and lets the living bird fly away (Lev.14:4–7). After this the leper must wash his body and his garments; the lambs are sacrificed, the oil and cereal are presented, and the priest now puts some of the blood on the tip of the man's right ear, on the thumb of his right hand, and on the great toe of his right foot; he repeats this procedure with a little of the oil. We are evidently given to understand that Jesus accepted the Law so completely as to regard even this ritual as a divine ordinance which must be obeyed.

Matthew does not tell us what the cleansed leper actually did; he proceeds at once to speak of Jesus' entrance into Capernaum and his encounter with a Roman centurion. In Mark, however, the leper 'went out and began to talk freely about it' (disobeying the command of Jesus to 'say nothing to anyone'), and the consequence was that 'Jesus could no longer enter a town, but was out in the country' (Mk.1:45). Probably Matthew was reluctant to report such direct disobedience to a command of Jesus, or to say that he 'could not' do anything that he planned. In Mark, Jesus does indeed return to Capernaum, but 'after some days'; and his next act is the healing of a paralytic, but not the paralytic of the story which Matthew now relates. (The Markan story is deferred by Matthew to be used in his second group, and Jesus has gone back and forth across the lake in the meanwhile.)

The Healing of a Centurion's Boy 8:5–13

⁵ When he came into Capernaum a centurion made an approach to him, and asked for help. ⁶ 'Sir,' he said, 'my boy is lying at home paralysed, in great pain.' ⁷ Jesus said to him, 'I will go and heal him.' ⁸ But the centurion answered, 'I am not worthy to have you come under my roof; but if only you speak the word, my boy will be healed. ⁹ For I too am a man under authority, with soldiers at my command. I say to one, "Go", and he goes; to another I say, "Come", and he comes; and I say to my slave, "Do this", and he does it." ¹⁰ As Jesus heard this he was astonished; and he said to his followers, 'I tell you truly, I have not found such faith with anyone in Israel. ¹¹ I tell you, many will come from east and west and will feast with Abraham and Isaac and Jacob in the kingdom of heaven, while the sons of the kingdom will be thrown out into the darkness outside; there they will wail and gnash their teeth.' ¹³ And Jesus said to the centurion, 'Go; let it be done for you as you have believed.' And the boy was healed at that very moment.

Although this is undoubtedly a miracle story, its emphasis is less on the miracle than on the faith of the centurion—a faith which goes beyond anything that Jesus has encountered in Israel. For the centurion is a Gentile, and in his faith Jesus foresees a sign of the future response to the gospel among the Gentiles and the future rejection of Israel.

VERSE 5: The centurion is given a Roman title, but he is probably the officer commanding the garrison posted at Capernaum, which would be a detachment of the army of Herod Antipas. Its task would be not to defend the frontier, but to hold the restless native population of northern Galilee under control.

VERSE 6: The centurion's 'boy' ($\pi\alpha\hat{\iota}\varsigma$) is probably understood by Matthew to be a servant; in the parallel story in Luke he is called a slave ($\delta o\hat{\nu}\lambda o\varsigma$ Lk.7:2,10—in v.7 Luke too uses the word $\pi\alpha\hat{\iota}\varsigma$). The two words are alternative renderings of the one Aramaic word *talya*. But $\pi\alpha\hat{\iota}\varsigma$ can also mean 'son', and in a similar Johannine story the boy is called the son ($\upsilon\iota\delta\varsigma$) of the officer (Jn.4:46–53). In the Lukan parallel, the slave is not said to be 'paralysed', but to be 'sick and at the point of death' (in the Johannine story too he is 'at the point of death' (4:47) and is suffering from a fever (v.52). It is possible that Matthew has introduced the notion of paralysis from a recollection of the Markan story which in Mark follows upon the healing of the leper.

VERSE 7: Many commentators take the words of Jesus as a question, as if Jesus were surprised that the centurion should invite a Jew to enter a Gentile house and so incur defilement. The reply of the centurion (vv.8f.) would then be intended to show that no such breach of Jewish custom would be necessary. This seems over-subtle. It is more in keeping with the Matthaean approach that Jesus should take the initiative and set his own course. In the preceding story, he has committed a far greater breach of ritual obligation by touching a leper. In the Lukan version of the story, the centurion does not appear in person, but through intermediaries—first a group of Jewish elders and then some friends (7:3,6f.). The Jewish elders themselves urge Jesus 'to come and heal the slave'; Luke cannot mean to suggest that they are instigating him to incur defilement. In any case, the words of Jesus do not emphasize his 'coming', which is expressed by a participle subordinated to the main verb, 'heal' ($\dot{\epsilon}\lambda\vartheta\grave{\omega}\nu \vartheta\epsilon\rho\alpha\pi\epsilon\acute{\nu}\sigma\omega$).

VERSE 8: The centurion's humble confession that he is 'unworthy' to receive Jesus as a visitor in his house is not to be understood as an acceptance of the Jewish attitude towards Gentiles (Acts 10:28—'He [Peter] said to them, "You know how unlawful it is for a Jew to associate with or to visit any one of another nation"'). It is a recognition of the personal greatness of Jesus. In Luke, the recognition of the centurion's inferiority is carried further by his use of intermediaries and his explanation—'I did not count myself worthy to come to you in person' (Lk.7:7).

VERSE 9: The centurion's confidence that Jesus has only to give the word and the boy will be healed is based on his own knowledge of the army. He sees the position of Jesus as analogous to his own. He is 'under authority', and therefore exercises authority over subordinates, and when he speaks they will do what he bids. If the analogy can be pressed so far, this may mean that he recognizes Jesus as the bearer of an authority given to him by God, and as having subordinates at his disposal to carry out such duties as he lays upon them. This could not mean human agents, but only angels, or supernatural beings of some kind. But this is probably going beyond what is justified. The basic thought seems to be that as in the military sphere the commander can accomplish what he wills by simply giving the word of command, so Jesus can have things accomplished in his ministry of healing by simply giving the word.

VERSE 10: This saying of Jesus is the heart of the story. A number of important witnesses give it in a form which is more like that of Luke: 'Not even in Israel have I found such faith.' The sense is not substantially different.

The saying presupposes that Jesus has been at work in Israel for a fairly long time, and has been less than satisfied with the response to his preaching. This is not at all the impression that we have received from what we have read in Matthew up to this point. He has given us nothing but a concise report of a mission in Galilee (4:23ff.), which brought rapid acclaim to Jesus and attracted crowds of followers. (The Lukan story is placed at a later stage of the ministry, and is preceded with a number of miracle stories, controversies, and the appointment of the Twelve, as well as the Lukan version of the great Sermon; but even so we are left with the impression of wonderful success.) This makes it all the more likely that the saying, which implies disappointment, is authentic.

VERSES 11–12: This saying is not attached to the miracle story in the Lukan version, and it is probable that Matthew introduced it here because he felt that it was an appropriate comment on the remarkable faith of this Gentile—many will respond to Jesus with the same faith and will receive the same reward.

'shall sit at table' (ἀνακλιθήσονται—literally, 'shall recline'). The word is appropriate to the imagery of the banquet, which is often used as a symbol of blessedness both in Judaism and in many Hellenistic mystery cults, most conspicuously in those of Dionysus. Tombstones of the period frequently picture the deceased person as participating in a banquet, which is often spread in the Elysian Fields. Since the patriarchs are mentioned as hosts (or as the guests of honour), the thought must bear upon the life to come. But the figure is not developed here. The central thought is that the inheritance promised to Israel will be enjoyed by many Gentiles, while 'the sons of the kingdom'—that is, Israelites, descendents of the patriarchs, the natural heirs of the Kingdom—find themselves excluded.

In Luke, this saying is not attached to the story of the believing centurion, but to warnings of the consequences of failure to enter the house before the master shuts the door (Lk.13:23—30).

'Weeping and gnashing of teeth'—the same phrase is found also in the Lukan parallel, where it is attached to a parable of the last judgement. There it suggests remorse over lost opportunities, on the part of those who have failed to enter while the door was open, as they see people 'come from east and west, and from north and south, and sit at table in the kingdom of God,' to enjoy the blessings that might have been theirs (Lk.13:29). 'The outer darkness' is a phrase peculiar to Matthew. It keeps up the figure of the Kingdom as a banquet, picturing it as held in a palace full of light, in contrast with the darkness out of doors. For Matthew, both phrases undoubtedly represent the fate of the damned in hell (cf. Mt.22:13; 25:30; in 13:42,50 the 'weeping and gnashing of teeth' is linked with the fate of the wicked who are to be 'cast into the furnace of fire').

VERSE 13: Jesus effects the healing at a distance; the same feature marks the Lukan parallel (Lk.7:10), and is retained, with greater stress, in the Johannine version (Jn.4:50—54). The only other story in the Gospels which exhibits this is that of the Canaanite (Mk. 'Greek, Syro-Phoenician by race'—7:24—30) woman. The fact that Luke omits this story may be an indication that he (like a number of modern scholars) regards it as a doublet of the story of the centurion. In both stories, the centre of interest is not so much the miracle as the faith of a Gentile. Possibly the healing at a distance is to be understood as reflecting the consistent restriction of the ministry of Jesus to Israel (this enters explicitly into the story of the Canaanite woman); we may think of it as symbolizing by a spatial metaphor the historical fact that Gentile participation in the blessings of the gospel is separated in time from the period of the earthly ministry of Jesus. It is scarcely to be taken as a matter-of-fact record of an actual occurrence.

The Healing of Peter's Mother-in-law 8:14—15

14 When Jesus entered Peter's house, he saw his mother-in-law lying in

bed with a fever. [15] He touched her hand, the fever left her, and she
got up and served him.

The Markan story is itself very brief, but Matthew still manages to
abbreviate it. In Mark, it follows the scene in the synagogue (Mk.1:
21–28), which Matthew omits, and it opens with the words, 'He left
the synagogue and entered the house of Simon and Andrew, with
James and John.' Matthew drops all mention of the four fishermen,
and makes no real connection with his preceding paragraph. In Mark,
the others tell him about the woman's illness; here he sees her for
himself and acts to heal her on his own initiative, with no prompting.
In Mark, Jesus takes the sick woman by the hand and lifts her up;
in Matthew, he touches her and she rises without assistance. In both,
the healing is so complete that she is able to 'serve' him—that is, to
give him his supper—at once. In Mark, she serves a meal for them all.
Matthew concerns himself entirely with Jesus and the woman to be
healed; the four disciples have no part to play and he leaves them
completely out of the picture. The fact that the woman is the
mother-in-law of Peter is immaterial to the miracle; it may be an
indication that the story had at some point been incorporated in a
cycle of Peter stories. It is out of keeping with all that we can discern
about the transmission of the tradition to imagine, as many critics
do, that we have here an almost verbatim transcript, in the third
person, of a story that was originally told by Peter in the first person
(so V. Taylor, *Mark*, p. 178). Even so astute a critic as E. Haenchen is
carried away by this romanticism, to the point of suggesting that this
was 'perhaps the first healing that Jesus achieved, and perhaps it was
this that first made him aware of the healing powers which God had
bestowed upon him' (*Der Weg Jesu* (1966), p. 89).
  Jesus accomplishes this healing by a touch (as in the cleansing of
the leper), but without a word. This silence is exceptional in such
stories. In Luke, no actual words are given, but we are told that Jesus
'stood over her and rebuked the fever, and it left her' (Lk.4:39). This
indicates that Luke interpreted the story as an exorcism—the fever
is a demon. The same notion may be reflected in the Markan-
Matthaean expression, 'the fever left her.'
  Nothing is said of Peter's wife; she is mentioned elsewhere in the
New Testament only in an incidental remark of Paul (1 Cor.9:5—
if the Cephas of this passage is to be identified as Peter). According
to John, Bethsaida was 'the city of Andrew and Peter' (John 1:44);
this has led to the conjecture that the brothers moved to Capernaum
at the time of Peter's marriage and lived with the parents of the

bride, perhaps even became partners in the fishing enterprise of the father-in-law. These attempts at harmonization lead nowhere.

First Supplement: Exorcisms at Evening 8:16

[16] That evening they brought to him many who were possessed with demons; and he cast out the demons with a word, and healed all who were sick.

'That evening'. In the setting of Mark, the healing in Peter's house takes place on a sabbath. As the sabbath ends at sundown, the people wait until then to bring their sick to Jesus. Matthew omits the vivid Markan touch: 'the whole city was gathered together around the door' (Mk.1:33). Mark speaks of people 'who were sick or possessed with demons' (v.32); Matthew mentions only 'many who were possessed with demons'. If he afterwards tells us that Jesus 'healed all who were sick', this may be simply a carry-over from Mark, or it may indicate that he attributes sickness to demon possession. Matthew omits the injunction of silence (Mk.1:34b), which pertains to Mark's distinctive doctrine of the 'Messianic secret' (the demons recognize the divine nature of Jesus, but Jesus wills to keep this hidden until the time comes for it to be revealed).

Second Supplement: Fulfilment of Prophecy 8:17

[17] This was to fulfil what was spoken by the prophet Isaiah, 'He took our infirmities and bore our diseases.'

In this fulfilment citation, as in the others, Matthew does not give the text of LXX, but an independent Greek rendering of the Hebrew text. This may well be of his own making, for it carries an interpretation that fits Matthew's context. In the original prophecy (Isa.53:4), the words are part of an oracle which proclaims that the sufferings of Israel, the 'servant of the Lord', are vicarious and redemptive. The 'servant' suffers for the sins of others, and it is these others who confess,

> Surely he has borne our sicknesses
> and carried our pains;
> yet we esteemed him stricken,
> smitten by God, and afflicted.
> But he was wounded for our transgressions,
> he was bruised for our iniquities. (Isa.53:4f.)

In Matthew's application, there is no trace of this thought of vicarious suffering; Jesus does not 'take' or 'bear' the diseases of the people whom he cures by suffering from them in his own person—he takes them away, or bears them off, by his word of power.

2   INTERLUDE: RESPONSES TO CANDIDATES FOR DISCIPLESHIP
8:18–22

[18] Seeing a crowd around him, Jesus gave orders to cross to the other side. [19] A scribe approached, and said to him, 'Teacher, I will follow you wherever you go.' [20] Jesus said to him, 'The foxes have lairs and the birds of the air have nests, but the Son of man has nowhere to lay his head.' [21] Another of his disciples said to him, 'Lord, permit me first to go and bury my father.' [22] Jesus said to him, 'Follow me, and let the dead bury their dead.'

There is no real connection with the preceding scene—the mass healings in the evening. In the Markan narrative, these mass healings at Capernaum are described as taking place at the close of the first day of Jesus' public activity (Mk.1:32–34), and Jesus does not leave until the next morning; when he does, it is not to cross the sea, but to begin a tour of Galilee (v.39). The crossing of the sea, and the miracle of the stilling of the storm which accompanies it, are not found in Mark until much later (Mk.4:35–41). Matthew has not prepared us for a crossing of the sea, and does not trouble to satisfy curiosity about whether the scene of the healings was at the shore or, if not, how they all moved down to the lake. In Mark, the readers had been told well before this that Jesus had arranged to have a boat available 'because of the crowd, lest they should crush him' (Mk.3:9), and he had used the bows of the boat as a pulpit for his teaching in parables (Mk.4:1f.; taken over in Mt.13:2). But up to this point we have heard nothing of a boat in Matthew's story—he simply assumes that the means of crossing the lake are ready. The story which will follow presupposes a vessel large enough to carry Jesus and his disciples, and sturdy enough to weather a bad storm.

VERSE 18: Matthew does not ask why Jesus now wishes to escape from the crowd around him. Is there some thought that he does not welcome an easy popularity (cf. Mk.1:37f.)?

He 'gave orders'—Matthew emphasizes the authority of Jesus. He commands, and his disciples obey.

The 'other side' of the lake will take him out of Galilee, and if they were making for territories of Gadara from Capernaum, they would have to row the entire length of the lake (about twelve miles). Matthew implies that Jesus is moving away from Capernaum and its environs, not simply starting out for an evening sail. The two questioners do not want to lose the chance of association with him. (In the event, the inhabitants of the region where he lands ask him to leave, and he returns to Capernaum—8:34–9:1.)

The verses which follow have their parallel in Luke, but at a much later stage of the narrative (Lk.9:57–60; Luke introduces a third applicant in v.61); it falls after the Transfiguration, and is laid on the road which will take Jesus to Jerusalem.

VERSE 19: In Matthew, the first applicant is a scribe (not so in Luke), and it is striking that the first scribe to appear on the scene is not a critic, but one who proposes to follow Jesus wherever he goes, that is, to become one of his permanent disciples (cf. Davies, *Setting*, Appendix X, 'Rabbis and their Pupils', pp. 455f.). Matthew himself may well have been a converted scribe.

VERSE 20: The response of Jesus may well have been originally a proverb contrasting the miserable condition of man with the birds and the beasts, 'presumably an old proverb which tradition has turned into a saying of Jesus' (Bultmann, *HST*, p. 28). The phrase 'the son of man' ($\dot{o}$ $\upsilon\dot{\iota}\dot{o}\varsigma$ $\tau o\hat{\upsilon}$ $\dot{\alpha}\nu\vartheta\rho\dot{\omega}\pi o\upsilon$) represents the Aramaic *bar-nasha*, and this is not a title but a way of saying 'man'. In the Gospels, however, it has been transformed into a title of Jesus, developed out of the apocalyptic figure of 'one like a son of man' which appears first in the book of Daniel (7:13; interpreted in v.27 as a symbol of 'the people of the saints of the Most High'). Here it is used by Matthew as a reference of Jesus to himself, and the saying becomes a warning that those who would follow Jesus in the hope of sharing his Kingdom must be prepared to endure the hardship which is his lot on earth. The saying is not very appropriate as a picture of the present circumstances of Jesus; the settlement at Capernaum implies that he has at least some kind of roof over his head, and the narrative mentions 'the house'.

VERSE 21: In Luke, the second questioner is not said to be one of the disciples; and his request is a response to the call of Jesus, 'Follow me' (Lk.9:59). Without this introductory call, the man's request is brought in rather abruptly. It presupposes, like the proposal of the scribe, that Jesus is leaving on a journey that will take him away from the neighbourhood. Luke also includes in the response of Jesus a sentence that is not found in Matthew: 'As for you, go and proclaim the kingdom of God' (v.60). This gives a compelling motive for rejecting the man's appeal that he may wait to bury his father before leaving home to follow Jesus. The task of preparing Israel for the coming of the Kingdom is so urgent—the Kingdom is so close at hand—that it must take precedence over the most stringent of filial duties. It is not clear just how the situation of the man is envisaged. Has the father just died, or is he at the point of death, so that the man is asking for only a few hours to attend to the burial? Or is he asking for a longer time—to stay with his father until he dies, however long that may be—and so to postpone his commitment to Jesus indefinitely, until he has no family obligations to hold him back? The third response in the Lukan version would speak rather for the former, for there the questioner asks only for time enough to say farewell to his family (Lk.9:61). The summons to follow Jesus admits of no delay, not even the slightest. It is not suggested, nor even implied, that either of the candidates was deterred by the response which he received from Jesus.

In the ancient world, the duty of burying the dead was taken as a most weighty responsibility in all societies. It is at the heart of the tragedy of Sophocles' *Antigone*; it is reflected in the *Iliad*, when the wraith of Patroclus appears to Achilles, and reproaches him for his delay in burying his slain companion (*Iliad* 23.65–92); in Virgil's *Aeneid*, again, the spectre of the helmsman, who has been swept overboard in a storm, appears to Aeneas and implores him to deliver him from his distress by giving him what could only be a token burial (*Aeneid* 6.337–83). Among the Jews, it was counted among the high virtues that a man should bury the dead body of an unknown fellow-Israelite (Tob.1:17f.). A sanction greater than custom or any superstition pertained to the burial of parents. It was taught that this was among the requirements imposed by the fifth commandment of the Decalogue. The words of Jesus do not imply that he treats this duty lightly; on the contrary, the more weight is attached to it, the more is the urgency of the call enhanced.

VERSE 22: 'Let the dead bury their dead' is a strange saying, and has provoked some extravagent interpretations—as, for instance, that the first 'dead' means the spiritually dead, and only the second refers to literal corpses. But it probably means no more than 'let that matter take care of itself.'

3 SECOND GROUP OF MIRACLE STORIES *8:23–9:8*

Jesus Stills a Storm 8:23–27

[23] When Jesus had gone aboard the boat, his disciples followed him.

²⁴ A great storm arose on the lake, so great that the boat was being covered by the waves; but Jesus himself went on sleeping. ²⁵ They made their approach and woke him, saying, 'Save, Lord, we are perishing.' ²⁶ He said to them, 'Why are you afraid, you men of little faith?' Then he rose and rebuked the winds and the lake, and there was a dead calm. ²⁷ And the men were astonished, and said, 'What manner of man is this, that even the winds and the waves obey him?'

VERSE 23: Matthew avoids the Markan wording, which speaks of the disciples 'taking' Jesus with them; for him, Jesus embarks first and his disciples 'follow'—the true role of the disciple.

VERSE 24: Storm—Matthew uses the word σεισμός, literally 'earthquake'. In Mark (and Luke) the term is λαῖλαψ [ἀνέμου], which is generally used of a hurricane, but would appear here to mean a squall. The picture of the boat being 'covered' by the waves is the impression of one looking on from the shore; in a heavy storm, even a large boat will seem to disappear for the moment, only to emerge on the crest of the next wave.

Jesus was sleeping—Matthew omits the vivid detail of Mark, who tells us that 'he was sleeping in the stern, on the cushion' (Mk.4:38).

VERSE 25: Even in this emergency, the disciples 'approach' Jesus with a certain formality. The participle προσελθόντες is a Matthaean addition to the Markan wording. Matthew further enhances the respectful attitude of the disciples in the changed wording of their plea. In Mark, there is an element of reproach, even of irritation: 'Teacher, don't you care? We are perishing!' (4:38). In Matthew, they address their teacher as 'Lord', and make no accusation of any lack of care; they simply cry out their plea for rescue: 'Save!' (In Greek there is no object.) The prayer κύριε, σῶσον may have been a ritual form in Matthew's church, like the later *Kyrie eleison*, 'Lord, have mercy.'

VERSE 26: In Mark, Jesus stills the storm before he rebukes the disciples; in Matthew, he chides the disciples first, and the rebuke is cast in milder language—'men of little faith' in place of the accusation that they have no faith. This is characteristic of Matthew; the disciples are treated more gently than in Mark. Partly this is due to the increased reverence for the apostles which came with time; even more, it reflects Matthew's tendency to see 'the disciples' not merely as the immediate companions of Jesus, but also as the representatives, or symbols, of the Christian believers of his own (and future) time. Their faith is less strong than it should be, but it is alive in them and he seeks to strengthen it. He could not feel that Jesus would say to them, 'Have you no faith?' (Mk.4:40.)

In Mark, Jesus rebukes the wind, and says to the lake, 'Peace, be still!' Matthew seldom omits words of Jesus which he finds in his source, but he does so here, as does Luke also (Lk.8:24). But the strange (to us) notion of 'rebuking' the elements is retained. This may indicate that the storm is regarded as a demon; but perhaps we should compare it with expressions in the Old Testament in which God commands the forces of nature (Job 38:11; Ps.78:23; Ps.107:25, etc.). But the words given to Jesus in Mark strongly suggest an address to a demon ($\phi\iota\mu\acuteo\omega$ means strictly 'muzzle'; cf. Mk.1:25).

In the natural order, after a great storm the waters take a long time to quiet down, even if the wind falls quickly. Here the 'dead calm' follows immediately, just as in healing-miracles the person healed is restored to full health on the instant (cf. 8:15 above; 9:7, etc.).

For Matthew, as for the other evangelists, this is a miracle story, and no purpose is served by attempts to imagine a credible event which might have given rise to it. But the significance of the story is not confined to the external miracle. From the earliest times, the boat on the stormy sea has been seen as a figure of the church in the world, buffeted by persecutions and beset by doubts, but protected by a power that can save it from all its dangers. The disciples of Matthew's times are taught that when storms come in their own lives, they are not to fear, but to call upon Jesus for help: 'Lord, save!' and to have faith that he will deliver them.

The Gentile centurion has given a lesson in faith; nature gives another, in the obedience of winds and waves to the command of Jesus.

Jesus Exorcises Demons 8:28—9:1

28 When he got to the other side, to the land of the Gadarenes, two demoniacs met him, coming out of the tombs; they were so very fierce that no one could pass by, along that road. 29 They shouted, 'What have you to do with us, Son of God? Have you come here to torment us before the time?' 30 Now there was a herd of many swine feeding, a long way from them. 31 The demons begged him, 'If you cast us out, send us into the herd of swine.' 32 He said to them, 'Go.' And they went out [of the men] and went into the pigs, and the whole herd rushed over the cliff into the lake and perished in the waters. 33 The herdsmen ran; they went back to the town and told

the whole story, the affair of the demoniacs. [34] And the whole town came out to encounter Jesus, and as soon as they saw him they begged him to leave their neighbourhood. 9:1 Getting into a boat, he crossed over and came to his own city.

Matthew makes great changes in the Markan story (Mk.5:1–20). In Mark, we hear of one demoniac, who professes that he is possessed not by a single demon, but by an entire legion (vv.9,15; the Roman legion at full strength numbered 6,000 infantry). Matthew makes no mention of such a host of demons, but speaks of two demoniacs in place of Mark's one. He reduces the dialogue between Jesus and the demons, leaving only the first protest against Jesus' coming, and the one word of command, 'Go!' The description of maniacal behaviour is left out entirely (Mk.5:2f.). But his most surprising omission is the description of the changed condition of the demoniac. In Mark we are told that when the people came out to see what had happened, they found the man 'sitting there, clothed and in his right mind— the man who had had the legion' (Mk.5:15). Matthew shows no interest in the men, once the demons have been cast out—he tells only of the disaster that comes upon the herd of swine. And he does not take up the Markan sequel—the man's request to go with Jesus, the refusal, and the missionary activity of the erstwhile maniac, who 'went away and proclaimed in the Decapolis how much Jesus had done for him' (vv.18–20).

VERSE 28: 'Gadarenes'. In all three Synoptic versions, the manuscripts vary among Gadarenes, Gerasenes, and Gergesenes. Gerasa and Gadara are cities of the Decapolis ('Ten Towns'), a federation of Greek cities in central Palestine, some of them east of the lake of Galilee and the Jordan Valley, some of them to the west. Gerasa (Jerash) must have been 'among the most magnificent of ancient cities' (*IDB*, article 'Gerasa', p. 383), but it is located more than thirty miles southeast of the lake of Galilee. Gadara was a much less important place, not so far from the lake of Galilee, yet still five miles to the southeast—the boat from Capernaum would have to sail the whole length of the lake from north to south, at least thirteen miles, and it would still not land in 'the country of the Gadarenes', much less of the Gerasenes. Gergesa is first mentioned in literature by Origen (early third century), and he professes to have heard about it as the scene of the miracle from local people. It is somewhat uncertainly identified with an ancient site on a cliff overlooking the lake—a place that would provide the 'steep bank' for the fatal rush of the pigs, and the 'tombs' (caverns used for burials) for the dwellings of the maniacs. It is quite impossible to tell where the boat may have landed, or where Mark and the other evangelists imagine the miracle to have taken place. At all events, they all think of the eastern shore of the lake, where the Gentile inhabitants might keep pigs—unthinkable in Jewish territory.

'Two demoniacs'—it is hard to tell why Matthew doubles the one demoniac of Mark (and Luke); we shall see that he does the same with the blind man of Jericho (Mk.10:46ff.; Mt.20:29f., with a doublet in Mt.9:27ff.).

'No one could pass by, along that road.' An added touch—Mark says that 'he had often been bound with fetters and chains', without explaining why. Insanity is attributed to possession by demons.

VERSE 29: Jesus is never addressed as 'Son of God', except by demons, in any of the Gospels. They, it is assumed, have supernatural knowledge of his true nature, which is not revealed to men, even to his disciples. In Mark, the demon calls Jesus 'Son of the Most High God', and even invokes the name of God to deter him from exercising his power to punish him. 'I adjure you by God, do not torment me.' Matthew's change is interpretative. He will not have a demon invoking the name of God, and he takes the 'torment' to mean the inflicting of everlasting punishment which is in store for the devil and all his hosts (Rev.20:10 speaks of 'the lake of fire and brimstone,' where 'they will be tormented day and night for ever and ever'). The demons know that they cannot escape this final destiny, but they accuse Jesus of advancing the time. 'Have you come to torment us before the time?'

Jesus has not yet spoken a word to them (in Matthew's version), but the demons realize that he is about to drive them out of the men, and they beg him to send them into the nearby swine. In Mark, they have first asked him not to send them out of the country. In this unclean land of Gentiles and herds of swine, they are at home. The Jewish abhorrence of swine as unclean beasts is reflected in the notion that these evil (in Mark, unclean) spirits are quite ready to take up their abode in pigs, if they are compelled to abandon their human habitation.

VERSE 30: 'Many swine'—Mark gives the number as 'about two thousand'; this is related to the 'legion' of demons whom they must host.

VERSE 31: 'Demons'—this is the only place in the New Testament where the Greek word *daimon* ($\delta\alpha\iota\mu\omega\nu$) is found. It occurs once (in some manuscripts, not in Vaticanus or Alexandrinus) in LXX (Isa. 65:11), where it renders the Hebrew *Gad* (the Gad is the tutelary divinity of the Syrian town, the Greek *Tyche*, τυχή). The demons are so completely identified with the human beings whom they possess that the words can be attributed indifferently to them or to their victims. (Elsewhere in the New Testament the usual word is δαιμόνιον.)

VERSE 32: There is no formula of exorcism. The command 'Go!' is given in response to the request that Jesus will send them into the swine.

'Perished in the waters'—the thought is probably that the demons perish with the swine, or perhaps that they vanish into 'the abyss' (Lk.8:31). The granting of their request leads to their complete undoing.

For a Jewish story teller, and a Jewish audience, the destruction of a herd of swine would be no calamity, but rather a cause for merriment. Not surprisingly, the reaction of the owners is not the same.

VERSES 8:34—9:1: Does Matthew mean to suggest that Jesus had intended to extend his mission into Gentile lands, and returns to Capernaum only because the inhabitants have rejected him? This is not very plausible, for Matthew consistently lays stress on the conviction of Jesus that his ministry is restricted to Israel (15:24; cf. 10:5,23). The decision to cross the lake was not motivated by anything but a desire to get away from the crowds (8:18), and it may be that the return is merely hastened by the hostility of the inhabitants of the town on the other shore. Yet, as we have seen, the words of the candidates for discipleship (vv.19,21) appear to imply that Jesus was not expected to return soon.

All the stories of miracle are difficult for the modern reader, and this one is perhaps the most difficult of all. We no longer regard insanity as caused by demon possession, and we do not expect our psychiatrists to be exorcists. We must recognize that this story was shaped by people who did believe that demons entered into the bodies of human beings—and why not into the bodies of pigs?—and caused all manner of diseases and abnormal behaviour. The story of the pigs was probably, in its origins, nothing more than a local recollection of a panic which seized a herd and resulted in its destruction; our word 'panic' echoes the Greek notion that the mass fright which could affect herds—or armies!—was caused by the god Pan (or by Dionysus—Euripides, *Bacchae*, 302–305).

It is unprofitable to attempt to explain such a story in terms that will make it intelligible to ourselves. There is no reason to doubt that Jesus restored to a sound mind people who were mentally ill, in a way that he as well as they looked upon as the exorcism of evil spirits. Plenty of examples of the same kind of thing can be found in the experiences of Christian missionaries in India and Africa, even when the missionaries themselves no more believe in the reality of demon possession than we do. But for us the main interest in such stories as this does not lie in asking what may have actually happened that could give rise to so strange a tale, but in discovering what it meant to Matthew and his readers. For them it was an integral part of their faith that Jesus was mightier than the demons. As he had cast them out during his earthly ministry, he was still able to cast them out. The church did not think of these stories as wonder-tales of a bygone time, but as illustrations of a power that was still at work in their midst. In this story, there is perhaps the further point, that the power of Jesus is not limited to the land of Israel. He is as strong to save in the pagan regions of the Decapolis as in Galilee or Judaea.

Jesus Heals a Paralytic 9:2—8

[2] Now they brought to him a paralytic, lying on a bed. When Jesus saw their faith, he said to the paralytic, 'Courage! child. Your sins are forgiven.' [3] Some of the scribes said to themselves, 'This man is blaspheming.' [4] Knowing their thoughts, Jesus said, 'Why do you harbour evil thoughts in your hearts? [5] Which is easier, to say, "Your sins are forgiven", or to say, "Get up and walk"? [6] But to let you know that the Son of man has authority on earth to forgive sins'—with that he said to the paralytic—'Get up, pick up your bed and go home.' [7] And he got up and went home. [8] When the crowds saw it they were filled with awe, and glorified God for granting such authority to men.

This story has been told by Mark, but at a much earlier stage of his narrative. In Mark the scene is laid in Capernaum, but it does not follow a crossing of the lake. Jesus has just returned from a mission tour of Galilee; the last act of which we have been told is the cleansing of the leper (Mk.1:40—44). In the Markan story, the bearers of the paralytic—there are four of them—have given proof of their faith not merely by bringing their friend to Jesus, but by making an opening in the roof of his house and letting down their stretcher, since the crowds were so great that they could not carry him in through the door (Mk.2:2—4). This whole picture is discarded by Matthew, and there remains only the words—left with no particular motivation—'when Jesus saw their faith'. Mark has also a much fuller account of the thoughts of the scribes; he has them indicate why they look upon Jesus' words of forgiveness as blasphemous by the question, 'Who can forgive sins but God alone?' (v.7). Matthew cuts this away and makes further abbreviations in the remainder of the story, but his most significant change comes in the way he tells of the reaction of the crowds. In Mark, they say, 'We never saw anything like this'; and Luke expresses the same thought in other words, 'We have seen strange things today' (Mk.2:12; Lk.5:26). Plainly, in these two versions, the people are thinking of the healing. In Matthew, they glorify God 'who gave such authority to men'. This echoes the claim of Jesus that he, the Son of man, has authority on earth to forgive sins; and Matthew suggests that the crowds have seen in the miracle demonstrative proof that the claim is valid; the authority to forgive sins is stressed more than the miracle.

VERSE 2: Matthew has omitted the Markan description of the crowds that gather as soon as they hear that Jesus has come home— in his version, they are introduced abruptly at the end, with a note of their reaction (v.8). 'They brought'—the phrase is indefinite, the subject not expressed ($\pi\rho o\sigma\acute{e}\phi\epsilon\rho o\nu$), and no further reference is made to the bearers except that 'Jesus saw their faith'—a faith which is shown only in the fact of bringing the invalid to Jesus, with no suggestion that they had any difficulty in getting near him. As Matthew does not even hint that Jesus is in a house, and says nothing of any press of people, there was no particular difficulty to overcome.

Nothing is said about the faith of the paralytic; the faith of his friends is sufficient to enable Jesus to act. In the same way, the faith of the centurion sufficed to procure healing for his boy (8:13). The faith is the confidence that Jesus is able to heal.

The phrase 'he said to the paralytic' is repeated in verse 6, with words that are more directly appropriate to the situation: 'Get up, pick up your bed and go home.' If all that comes in between were omitted—the pronouncement of forgiveness, the hostile reaction of the scribes, and the retort of Jesus (vv.2c—6a)—it would not occur to anyone to suppose that anything was missing. It is generally taken, then, that this section is a secondary addition to the original account of the healing. The controversy over the authority to forgive sins is, however, not conceivable as ever having existed independently of its present context. It will hardly be seen as a Markan addition, but rather as a supplement introduced into the miracle story at some earlier stage of the tradition, though it is precisely this aspect of controversy that has led Mark to place it here; in his construction, it is the first in a series of controversy passages, perhaps formed into a collection before his time, which occupies the remainder of the chapter and includes the first episode of chapter 3 (on the question of sabbath observance). The purpose of the addition is not in doubt; it is to claim the precedent of Jesus for the church's exercise of the ministry of absolution. This comes out most clearly in the distinctive Matthaean conclusion.

Vincent Taylor recognizes that the controversy section is not an integral part of the miracle story, but he suggests that we may have here a fusion of a miracle story (the healing of the paralytic) with a pronouncement story or apothegm (Bultmann's term) 'from which the beginning and the ending are missing'. He thinks that 'the sequel must have been a cure, but related more briefly than in the existing story'; and suggests that 'the original beginning and end of the Pronouncement-story were cut away and replaced by the fuller details of the Miracle-story' (*Formation of the Gospel Tradition* (1935), pp.66–68. He holds to the same explanation in his commentary on Mark).

The association of the forgiveness of sins with the healing of paralysis (or other illness) is of course not to be explained as an anticipation of modern psychosomatic diagnosis and treatment, though many commentators are tempted to make play with such ideas. 'Jesus could not fail to observe how closely mental, spiritual, and physical conditions are connected, in this respect anticipating the conclusions of modern psychotherapy regarding hysterical forms of paralysis' (V. Taylor, *St. Mark*, p.195; somewhat more cautiously P. Bonnard, *Matthieu, ad loc.*: 'ces conceptions sont peut-être moins contraire à la psychiatrie aujourd'hui qu'il y a 50 ou 60 ans'). It is not necessary to look farther than the Psalms, where the Lord is blessed as the one 'who forgives all your iniquity, who heals all your diseases' (Ps.103:3). It is not implied that the man's paralysis is the result of his sins, any more than that it is a physical consequence of his sense of guilt (note that the verb σώξω means both 'save' and 'heal').

It is remarkable that nowhere else in the Gospels, with the exception of Luke 7:48, is Jesus represented as pronouncing the forgiveness of sins.

VERSE 3: The appearance of scribes is unexpected—less perhaps in Matthew, where the scene appears to be laid in the open, than in Mark, where it is inside a crowded house. But the interlude of the controversy over forgiveness is not at all conditioned by the circumstances of the healing.

'Said to themselves'—for Mark's 'reasoned in their hearts'. They do not utter their criticisms aloud; Jesus perceives what they are thinking (Mark adds, 'in his spirit'). The thought is not that he sees them scowling, and divines what must be going through their minds; for the evangelist, Jesus has a supernatural knowledge of their inward thoughts. This is made explicit in the Gospel of John (see esp. Jn.2:24f.).

VERSE 6: Jesus again refers to himself as 'the Son of man'; here the phrase is not generic, as in the original sense of the proverb in 8:20 ('man'), but personal—virtually a substitute for the pronoun 'I', with an overtone of 'I, as man' (a man commissioned by God). Jesus would not challenge the scribal belief that only God can forgive sins, but he is claiming that God has authorized him, 'on earth', to exercise this 'authority'. This sense comes out clearly in verse 8.

'Pick up your bed.' The 'bed' would be a light mattress or pallet, perhaps with a wooden frame which would enable it to be used as a litter.

VERSE 7: The man's action gives proof that the cure is effective. The narrator takes no further interest in him or his friends; there is no attempt to suggest joy or gratitude. In Luke's version, it is added that he went to his house 'glorifying God' (Lk.5:25), but there is nothing corresponding to this in Mark or in Matthew.

VERSE 8: In the typical miracle story, there is a well-defined form. Vincent Taylor describes it as 'a popular narrative form with special features of its own' (*Formation*, p.121). Such stories basically exhibit four elements: a description of the patient's condition, an account of the healing, evidence of its reality, and an acclamation of the witnesses (M. Dibelius, *Formgeschichte*, 3rd edn. 1959, p. 67). In Mark, and also in the Lukan version, this acclamation is quite in accordance with the usual kind of reaction that is noted. 'They were all astounded (ἐξίστασθαι) and glorified God, saying, "we never saw anything like this"' (Mark); 'Amazement (ἔκστασις) seized them all and they glorified God and were filled with awe, saying, "we have seen unbelievable things (παράδοξα) today"' (Luke). In Matthew there is a significant departure from this chorus of amazement and acclamation. 'The crowds' (not previously mentioned in Matthew's version) 'were filled with awe' (not amazement), and are impressed above all by the demonstration of 'authority' to forgive sins, which God has given to 'men'. This remarkable shift to the plural 'men' does not indicate at all that Matthew thinks of this as a general authority which God has granted to all men. The thought is that the authority of Jesus to pronounce the forgiveness of sins is now exercised by the ministers of his church. The practice of absolution in the church of Matthew's time causes offence to the 'scribes'— the leaders of the Jewish community (the rabbis, as they were coming to be called). They do not themselves venture to confer absolution, and they regard it as blasphemy on the part of the ministers of the church that they do so. The church defends its practice by appealing to the example of Jesus, and to the effectiveness of its own ministry of healing. The authority of Jesus, as 'the Son of man', exercised upon earth, is transmitted to 'men' who have received his commission, to continue his ministry 'upon earth'.

It is not always realized that the ministry of absolution in the church is not a part of its inheritance from Judaism, neither is it in any way the adoption of a pagan practice. It is a distinctively Christian rite, and the church could not fail to ascribe its origin and its ultimate authority to Jesus. This authority is conferred explicitly in the insufflation story of the Gospel of John: 'If you forgive the sins of any, they are forgiven; if you retain the sins of any, they are retained' (Jn.20:22f.; cf. Mt.16:19; 18:18).

4   INTERLUDE: JESUS IN CONTROVERSY *9:9—17*

The Call of Matthew: Controversy with the Pharisees 9:9—13

⁹ As Jesus passed along from there, he saw a man by the name of Matthew seated at the tax office and said to him, 'Follow me'; and he rose and followed him. ¹⁰ And as he sat at the table in the house, many tax collectors and sinners came and dined with Jesus and his disciples. ¹¹ When the Pharisees saw this, they said to his disciples, 'Why does your teacher eat with tax collectors and sinners?' ¹² But when Jesus heard of this, he said, 'Those who are well have no need of a physician, but those who are sick. Go and learn what this means, "I desire mercy, and not sacrifice." ¹³ For I came not to call righteous men, but sinners.'

In this interlude, Matthew is able to hold to the order of Mark, who had included these sections in his sequence of controversy stories (Mk.1:2—3:6). He abandons the Markan introduction, which separates the story of the call of the tax collector from that of the paralytic by a picture of Jesus at the lakeshore, teaching crowds of people (Mk.2:13). More striking is his substitution of the name of Matthew for 'Levi the son of Alpheus'. The story as Mark gives it is so like in form to the stories of the call of the first disciples (Mk.1:

16–20; Mt.4:18–22) as to suggest that Levi too is called to become one of the inner circle; this impression is heightened by Luke, who adds the clause: 'he left everything' (Lk.5:28; as Peter and Andrew, James and John left their nets and their boats). But the name of Levi is not included in any of the lists of the Twelve that are given in the New Testament, and it would appear that Matthew has chosen a name at random from his own list, and put it in the place of the otherwise unknown Levi, who is never mentioned again. Once it was assumed that the publican was called to become a member of the group that was to be closely associated with Jesus in his work, it was natural enough that efforts should be made to identify him with one of the Twelve. The writer of our Gospel picked upon the name of Matthew; there is no need to imagine that he had any special knowledge to draw upon, much less to suppose that he introduced his own name! There are indications that he was himself a trained scribe, and none whatever that he had ever earned his living as a tax collector.

Certain important witnesses (including the great bilingual D, the Caesarean Theta, and many manuscripts of the Old Latin) reflect an effort to overcome the problem of identification in the text of Mark in a different way. Noting that the lists of apostles all contain a certain 'James, son of Alpheus' (the 'St. James the Less' of our liturgies, of whom nothing whatever is known), the scribes substituted his name for that of 'Levi, son of Alpheus'.

But in the context, the name of the man is of no consequence. The story may well have circulated independently in the oral tradition at some time, simply as an example of the power of Jesus to draw men into his service, with an appeal to the hearers to respond as he had responded to the Master's call. Here it serves mainly as an introduction to the controversy story which follows, which reveals the difference between the attitude of Jesus to such outcasts as tax collectors and that of the religious leaders and moral guides of Judaism.

VERSE 9: The 'tax office' might be a booth, or merely a table on the street. The man seated there would not be himself a *publicanus*, the wealthy man who contracted to collect the taxes and remit them to the government, but a minor employee, stationed at Capernaum. The taxes would be collected for Antipas, the tetrarch of Galilee and Peraea, and they would be levied upon practically all the goods carried by the caravans that passed along the road from Damascus to the sea. None the less, it is assumed that this man was well off, since he is able to provide a banquet for a large number of his associates (described as 'many tax collectors and sinners'—v.10), along with Jesus and his disciples.

VERSES 10–11: Matthew omits the observation of Mark that 'there were many [tax collectors and sinners] who followed him.' Without these words, we are left with the impression that these guests were not already followers of Jesus, but business associates invited by the host to let them meet the teacher whom he had decided to follow. The scene is in some degree artificially contrived. The accusation against Jesus that he kept company with the wrong kind of people recurs in a still vaguer setting in Luke 15:1f., where it serves as an occasion for the parable of the Lost Sheep (and the accompanying parables of the Lost Coin and the Prodigal Son). In both cases, the evangelist wishes to create a setting for the response of Jesus. It is not clear how we are intended to understand the circumstances. The Pharisees are hardly to be imagined as guests at the same banquet, and there is no attempt to indicate when and where they encounter the disciples to offer their criticisms of Jesus. In any case, we are puzzled to account for these Pharisees. In Mark, they are called 'the scribes of the Pharisees'—an expression that is found nowhere else—and in Luke this is altered to the more conventional 'the Pharisees and their scribes'. In all these variations, the story does not speak of 'some' (Pharisees, or scribes) but of '*the*' (Pharisees, etc.). That is, it treats them as stock figures, who are there simply to voice a standing objection of the religious and moral leaders of Judaism to the Christian principle of openness. The reproach that was addressed against Jesus is still laid to the account of his church, and the church defends itself by appealing to the example of its Master, and to his conception of his mission on earth, which it has inherited. It does not look upon itself as a community of 'righteous' people—so healthy that they have no need of a physician—but as 'sinners' whom Jesus has called into fellowship with himself, as 'sick' people whom he has healed; and who welcome into their fellowship all those whom Jesus calls, however they may fail to meet the standards of legal purity which were set by the Pharisees and the scribes.

VERSES 12–13: In Mark (and Luke), the reply of Jesus begins with a proverb or maxim of general significance, and then applies it to his own understanding of his mission. The figure of the physician, whose whole profession is to care for the sick, not the healthy, is found also in Greek anecdotes of Cynic teachers. When Antisthenes was criticized for keeping company with evil men, he replied: 'Physicians too are commonly found associating with the

sick, but they do not catch the fever' (Diog. Laert., *Lives* VI.1.1).
Sinners are the first concern of Jesus, as the sick are the concern of
the physician.

'I came'—the words can hardly be taken in any sense but that of
'I came into the world', or, 'I came down from heaven.' That is to
say, they convey a consciousness not merely of prophetic mission
or of Messianic dignity, but of heavenly origin. It is doubtful whether
Jesus thought or spoke of himself in terms like these; it seems more
likely that his words have been cast into this form as an expression
of the church's faith in him as the Son of God. Such a phrase 'serves
to gather up the significance of the appearance of Jesus as a whole';
and there is a clear tendency in the tradition to create other
christological phrases in the same form (see R. Bultmann, *HST*, p.
156, with note 2, and the supplement, p. 409).

Between the proverb and its application to the mission of Jesus,
Matthew has introduced a citation from Scripture (Hos.6:6), with a
formula frequently used by rabbinic teachers: 'Go and learn' (from
a passage which will throw light on the matter); as 'Go and learn
from the commandment, . . . from Moses, . . . from Abimelech,' etc.
They are taken from the LXX (text of Codex A, etc.), and are an
almost literal rendering of the Hebrew. The Hebrew idiom does not
convey a flat repudiation of the sacrificial system, but affirms that
it is meaningless without the faithful love of the worshipper. The
Greek word ἔλεος was used by the LXX translator to render the
Hebrew *ḥeṣed*, which in *AV* is often rendered 'loving kindness', and
in *RSV* (not very felicitously) 'steadfast love'. It is one of the richest
words of the Hebrew moral and religious vocabulary, and our word
'mercy', though it corresponds well enough to the Greek word ἔλεος,
is inadequate to bring out the thought of the Hebrew; for *ḥeṣed* is
at once the love of God for his people, which holds him faithful to
the covenant by which He graciously vouchsafed to be their God,
and their reciprocating love which alone could fulfil their pledge to
be his people. Hosea has protested that the offering of the sacrifices
prescribed by the Law is no substitute for the response of the heart
in fidelity to God. The words of Hosea are now applied to a different
situation. For the confidence of ancient Israel in the sufficiency of
the sacrificial system, the Pharisees are confident in the sufficiency
of faithful, even meticulous, observance of the provisions of the Law;
and among these they lay stress on the laws of purity. They were
careful to keep themselves unspotted by association with 'sinners'.
They are invited to 'go and learn' all that is involved in the oracle of
Hosea. There is more here than a direct and literal application of the

words—the whole story has nothing to do with the acceptability of sacrifices—but they reveal a basic understanding of the will of God for his people that goes far beyond the mere fulfilment of legal requirements and regulations. The 'mercy' (or 'faithful love') desired by God calls for the welcome of the sinner, and his restoration to fellowship. The critics are left to work out the meaning of the oracle for themselves.

As far as the structure of the story goes, in Matthew, the words of Jesus are taken to be addressed to 'the Pharisees', but it is difficult to see how the evangelist imagines such an encounter to have taken place. It can hardly have been in the tax collector's dining hall, which would be shunned by Pharisees. It is quite impossible to reconstruct the picture, and we can only regard it as an artificial construction, made to frame the words of Jesus.

Controversy with Disciples of John: the Practice of Fasting
9:14–15

[14] The disciples of John now made their approach to him. They asked: 'Why is it that we and the Pharisees are fasting, yet you and your disciples are not?' [15] Jesus answered: 'Can the wedding guests fast while the bridegroom is with them? Days will come when the bridegroom is taken away from them—then they will fast.'

It is a question whether the followers of John assert that Jesus and his disciples do not practise fasting at all, or only that they are not observing a special season of fasting at this time. The temptation story suggests that on occasion Jesus himself fasted (4:2); and the teaching on fasting in chapter 6 does not forbid or even find fault with the practice of fasting as a religious exercise, but only with doing it to attract attention and win good opinions—looking dismal and disfiguring their faces, 'in order that their fasting may be noticed' (6:16). On the other hand, the answer of Jesus seems to assume that during his lifetime he and his disciples did not fast at all, but that the disciples would practise fasting after his death.

VERSE 14: The combination of the disciples of John with the Pharisees is surprising. Usually, the Gospels speak of the two sects as having nothing in common (Mt.3:7; Lk.7:29f.). It is possible, of course, that they were alike in fasting more frequently than normal Jewish piety required. This is the interpretation of Luke, who reshapes both the introduction and the question. The disciples of John are not now the questioners. Certain unidentified people ('they') remark that the disciples of John observe frequent fasts and make (frequent?) prayers, and so do the disciples of the Pharisees, 'but your people eat and drink' (or perhaps, 'go on eating and drinking'—Lk.5:33). In any case, it is clear that Jesus and his disciples are not austere enough to satisfy the questioners' notion of how religiously minded people ought to behave. The comparison is meant to be unfavourable to Jesus and his followers; they do not match the level of moral rigour of their rivals.

VERSE 15: The figure of the wedding feast is a well-known symbol of the joys of 'the age to come', or the kingdom of God. The reply of Jesus implies that in that festive time, Jesus plays the role of the bridegroom; thus it makes the highest christological claim imaginable. The figure is taken up in various ways in the New Testament writings, generally with the followers of Jesus pictured not as guests at the mystic marriage, but as (collectively) the bride (Rev.21:9f.; 2 Cor.11:2; less obviously, but magnificently, Eph.5:25–27). The figure has Old Testament roots, especially in Hosea, with the conception that Yahweh is the husband of Israel (Hos.2:16,19f.; cf. Isa.54:5).

In Matthew's version of the parable of the great banquet (22:2–10; cf.Lk.14:16–24, quite differently conceived), it becomes a marriage feast given by a king for his son; but all attention is fixed upon the king and the guests—the son plays no part in the action.

The thought is perfectly clear, so far as the first part of the answer is concerned. It implies not only that Jesus is the bridegroom at the wedding feast seen as the inauguration of the kingdom of God, but that the feast is already going on, and the disciples of Jesus are there as guests, or even as 'best men'—'sons of the bride-chamber'. This is 'realized eschatology' if it is to be found anywhere! (Dodd, *Parables*, 88f.)

But there is a difficulty in the second part of the saying, which speaks of days that will come when the bridegroom will be taken away from them, and they too will fast. With this, we have a departure from the normal figure of the wedding feast, for the words certainly do not refer to the bridegroom's departure on a honeymoon! This is a departure that gives cause for fasting (mourning), and is of course a reference to the coming death of Christ. The words justify the church in adopting a discipline of fasting, even though Jesus and his disciples had not fasted during his lifetime. There are two differences of practice involved here—the difference between the more rigorous practice of the disciples of John and the Pharisees on the one hand, and the laxer attitude of the disciples of Jesus; and then the difference between the practice of Jesus himself and of his disciples during his life, and that of his church after his death. There is an intermingling here of the past and the present that leaves a good deal of confusion.

It is not suggested, in the challenge of these disciples of John, that the disciples of Jesus are failing to observe a fast that is kept by everyone else in the Jewish community. The question implies that the disciples of John and the Pharisees practise a discipline of fasting which goes beyond the common custom and is a proof of superior piety—they impose upon themselves a rule of life that goes beyond what the Law requires of every Israelite. What the specific rule of fasting was for these two groups is not known. In the well-known Lukan parable, the Pharisee claims, among other things that mark him out from other men, that he fasts twice a week (Lk.18:12), but it is by no means certain that all Pharisees did so, and nothing is known of the practice of the disciples of John. In general, the question implies that the disciples of Jesus are not distinguished for any exceptional piety, and that in this matter of fasting they fall below the standards of the Pharisees, while the disciples of John live up to this superior level.

The immediate point of the answer in its second part would seem to be that there is a noticeable difference between the practice of Jesus and of his disciples during his lifetime on earth with respect to fasting, and the practice of the contemporary church. Early documents give evidence that the church practised fasting as a regular discipline quite as assiduously as the members of the Jewish community. In the *Didache* (second century), the only difference mentioned is that Christians are to fast on Wednesdays and Fridays, while 'the hypocrites' fast on Mondays and Thursdays (*Didache* 8.1; The Apostolic Fathers, Vol.I, Loeb Library, ed. K. Lake (1912), p. 321). But the practice was not uniform in early times, any more than it is today. Some groups of Christians even rejected it outright; in the *Gospel of Thomas*, for instance, a saying attributed to Jesus runs: 'If you fast you will beget sin for yourselves!' True, no one would regard this as an authentic saying of Jesus, any more than the two which accompany it: 'If you pray you will be condemned, and if you give alms you will do evil to your spirits' (Saying 14, cf. Saying 6).

In the New Testament fasting is not described as a general practice, and Paul never counsels his converts to fast—he cannot have regarded it as necessary for those whom he 'exhorted and encouraged and charged to lead a life worthy of God' (1 Thess.2:

11f.). But there is abundant evidence that by the second century the pre-Easter (Lenten) fast was widely observed in the churches, and in perhaps lesser degree a pre-baptismal fast (so far as they did not coincide; baptism was regularly administered at Easter).

In the Markan arrangement, this is the third in a series of controversy stories, which are linked by nothing but the element of controversy. There is no real connection of time or place with the dispute over the acceptance of 'tax collectors and sinners'; Matthew's τότε ('then') carries no weight at all in this respect. Matthew has simplified and organized his Markan material, to bring forward the criticisms of three distinct groups—first, 'some of the scribes' (v.3), then 'the Pharisees' (v.11), and now 'the disciples of John'. We are not to take this as evidence that Capernaum had suddenly become a rallying point for these three groups of the nation, and that they took it in turn to assail Jesus, or the conduct of his disciples, from different angles. 'The disciples of John', like 'the Pharisees', are not holding a general convention; the phrases are formal, and their words summarize the kind of objections which were laid against the conduct of Christians within the Jewish community of the apostolic age. The fact that it is the disciples of Jesus, and not Jesus himself, that are criticized for failure to conform to the rule of fasting which is kept by the disciples of John betrays the reality of the situation, that the controversy belongs to the post-Easter period.

Supplement: Sayings about the Old and the New 9:16—17

[16] No one puts a patch of unbleached cloth on an old cloak; for (if he does) the patch pulls away from the cloak and the tear is made worse than ever. [17] And no one pours new wine into old wineskins; for if he does, the skins break—the wine runs out, and the wineskins are ruined. But we put new wine into new wineskins and both are kept in good condition.

These two sayings have no particular connection with the question of fasting. There is no means of discerning in what connection they were actually spoken, and thus it is not possible to tell how they were meant to be applied. In themselves, they are matter-of-fact observations about the danger of mixing the old and the new; they do not even hint whether they give superiority to the old or to the new. Unfamiliar as the thought may be, given the usual Christian interpretation of the two sayings, Luke actually seems to take them as giving the preference to the old; for he adds a third saying, 'No one after drinking old wine wants new wine; for he says, "The old is good" ' (5:39). True, but does it give the sense in which the first two are to be understood? All we can say is that Luke evidently thought so. He may, of course, have taken it to suggest that the conservatism of religious people is a barrier to new ideas (T.W. Manson, *Sayings*, p. 255).

I find it difficult to share the raptures of some distinguished commentators over these verses (Swete, Rawlinson, more recently V. Taylor), who are sure that Jesus is giving powerful expression to a radical, even revolutionary, understanding of his gospel in relation to Judaism. Did Jesus really think that Judaism was a torn old cloak that could not be repaired without total ruin both of it and the gospel? Or as an old container incapable of retaining the life-giving teaching which he now brought? This is surely untenable as a general interpretation of the attitude of Jesus to his ancestral religion.

It appears more likely that in them we hear echoes of debates in the early church, and that they give metaphorical expression to the views of those who have come to hold that the gospel of Christ could not be imposed upon, or fitted into, the framework of Judaism. But in themselves, they could equally well be understood as expressing the view of those who were reluctant to give Christian teaching a place in the synagogue, holding that their inherited faith would not be improved by the infiltration of these new ideas, but only brought to ruin. Or, in the contrary sense, that the truth and power of the gospel could only be lost by trying to force it into an uneasy alliance with traditional Judaism. 'If justification were through the law, then Christ died to no purpose'; 'if you receive circumcision, Christ will do you no good at all'; 'for freedom Christ has made us free; stand fast, and do not put your neck again into the yoke of slavery!' (Gal.2:21; 5:2,1.) This is the sense in which it must have been understood by Mark and, perhaps less clearly, by Matthew.

5   THIRD GROUP OF MIRACLE STORIES *9:18–34*

Jesus Raises a Dead Girl to Life: He Heals a Woman with a Haemorrhage 9:18–26

[18] While he was still saying these things to them, a ruler made his approach, knelt down before him, and said, 'My daughter has just died; come, pray, and lay your hand upon her, and she will return to life.' [19] Jesus rose and followed him, along with his disciples.

[20] Now a woman who had been suffering from a haemorrhage for twelve years, touched the hem of his cloak from behind him,

²¹ for she kept saying to herself, 'If only I may touch his cloak, I shall be healed.' ²² Jesus turned, looked at her, and said, 'Courage, daughter! Your faith has delivered you.' And the woman was healed from that moment.

²³ Jesus went into the ruler's house. He saw the flute players and the throng of mourners ²⁴ and said, 'Go away. The girl is not dead but asleep.' They laughed loudly at him. ²⁵ But when the throng had been sent out, he went in and grasped her hand, and the girl rose. ²⁶ This story was reported throughout all that region.

The strange intermingling of two miracle stories which we have here was probably devised by Mark, who often uses this 'device of "sand-wiched" narratives' (C.H. Dodd, *Historical Tradition*, p.23). There is no intrinsic connection between them; the only apparent link is verbal—the girl is twelve years old (not in Matthew), and the woman has been suffering for twelve years.

Matthew systematically abbreviates the Markan narratives, but here he outdoes himself, with the result that his version is only one third the length of Mark's. No such shortening takes place in Luke. In the process, the situation is totally changed. Here the 'ruler' appears while Jesus is still talking to the critics of his attitude towards fasting; in Mark, the action begins on the lakeshore, where the usual 'great crowd' has gathered about him after his return from across the lake (Mk.5:21), and the crowd presses around him as he goes with Jairus to his house. In Matthew there is no crowd, and this in itself affects the telling of the woman's approach. Again, in Matthew, the ruler tells Jesus at once that his daughter is dead, and this eliminates the Markan interlude of messengers coming to tell Jairus that his daughter has passed away, and there is no point in troubling Jesus any further—in Mark, he had said that his daughter was at the point of death. Both stories lose most of their vividness.

VERSE 18: The name Jairus, given in Mark and retained by Luke, is excised by Matthew. Almost always, these stories were trans-mitted without names. There was a tendency for names to be attached to them much later (*see* B. Metzger, 'Names for the Nameless'). Apart from the Passion narrative, names are not given except to John the Baptist and (sometimes) to the disciples, with the sole exception of the Bar-Timaeus of Mark 10:46, and this name is not retained by Matthew or by Luke.

Again, Matthew calls him simply 'a ruler' (ἄρχων), while in Mark he is 'one of the synagogue rulers' (ἀρχισυναγωγός), and in Luke 'a ruler of the synagogue' (ἄρχων τῆς συναγωγῆς). An 'archon' could be a municipal official. Like others who come to Jesus for help, the ruler 'makes his approach' (προσελθών); the effect is enhanced by the use of the verb προσεκύνει, 'worship' (fall prostrate in the act of proskynesis), in place of Mark's 'fell at his feet'.

The most radical change, however, is that in Matthew the girl is said to be already dead, and the ruler beseeches Jesus to lay his hand on her so that she may be brought back to life. In Mark, she is not dead, but near death, and the prayer is that Jesus may lay his hands upon her 'in order that she may be saved and go on living' (Mk.5:23).

VERSES 20–21: Again Matthew uses his favourite verb προσελθοῦσα (on this occasion, also used by Luke (8:44), in place of the simple ἐλθοῦσα of Mark. He omits the long account of her medical history (Mk.5:26; Lk.8:43).

'The hem [more exactly, tassel] of his cloak'—for Mark's 'his cloak'.

'I shall be healed'—the Greek verb σώζω has the double sense of 'heal' and 'save'. This is not peculiar to the New Testament; it is well established in classical usage.

VERSE 22: Much of the Markan detail is cut away by Matthew. In particular, he eliminates the naive notion that the woman is healed as soon as she touches Jesus' cloak (Mk.5:29), and the continuance in the same vein with the indication that Jesus was at once aware that 'power had gone forth from him' (v.30). In Matthew, Jesus is aware only of a tug at his cloak; and the woman is not healed by the magic of the touch but by the word of Jesus, spoken in response to her faith. With this simplification, there is no longer any place for the question of Jesus, 'Who touched me?', the surprised remonstrance of the disciples (vv.30b–32), and the moving description of the woman's embarrassed confession (v.33).

VERSE 23: The flute players would be professionals, engaged to lead in the mourning for the dead girl. The quickness of their appearance on the scene is surprising to us, but not at all out of keeping with the ways of the time. Burial followed death by a few hours, and always on the same day, and mourners would be readily available on the spur of the moment. Mark does not mention fluteplaying, but only a 'crowd weeping and keening' (Mk.5:38).

VERSE 24: 'Not dead, but asleep'—not meant to suggest that she is not really dead; the story describes a miracle of resurrection, just as definitely as the Lazarus story (Jn.11:11–14). The language reflects Christian usage; for the Christian, death is not the end, but is like a sleep from which we awaken to new life. So Paul speaks with the utmost simplicity of 'the dead in Christ' as 'those who have fallen asleep' (1 Thess.4:13–17; cf. 1 Cor.15:6–51). The verb is already used in this sense in classical writers (Homer, Sophocles, etc.), though without any thought of an awakening from that 'sacred sleep' (Callimachus); it is even called 'the eternal sleep' (*IG* 14:929, in an epitaph). And in LXX, the death of a king is often expressed in the phrase, 'he slept with his fathers' (1 Ki.2:10, etc.), with no more thought of a future restoration to life than in the Greek writers.

VERSE 25: The awakening of the girl is described with the utmost simplicity. No one accompanies Jesus to the bedside; in Mark, he takes along her parents and three of his disciples—Peter, James, and John (Mk.5:37,40). Matthew also omits the use of the words of power (kept by Mark in the Aramaic *Talitha koum*; cf. Mk.7:34), which may have savoured too much of the technique of the magician. The use of foreign words occurs frequently in contemporary (pagan) miracle stories (Bultmann, *HST*, pp.222f.).

'She rose'—the verb ἠγέρθη replaces the ἀνέστη 'stood up' of Mark (retained by Luke). It is probably intended to suggest the specific notion of resurrection, as in the predictions of the Passion, etc. But ἀνίστημι, is also used of resurrection, and the cognate noun ἀνάστασις is the regular term for 'resurrection'.

Matthew has omitted entirely the Markan elaboration of what followed upon the restoration of life. In Mark, the reality of her condition is demonstrated in that she not only stands up but walks, and Jesus orders them to give her something to eat (Mk.5:42f.). Matthew also cuts away any mention of the ecstatic astonishment of the witnesses, and the injunction not to tell anyone about the miracle.

VERSE 26 is the Matthaean conclusion; it will be repeated in verse 31.

Jesus Restores Sight to Two Blind Men 9:27–31

27 As Jesus was on his way from there, two blind men followed him crying out, 'Have mercy upon us, Son of David!' 28 When he had entered the house, the blind men made their approach to him and Jesus said to them, 'Do you believe that I am able to do this?' They replied, 'Yes, Sir.' 29 Thereupon Jesus touched their eyes, saying, 'According to your faith, let it be done for you,' 30 and their eyes were opened. Jesus said to them fiercely, 'See to it that no one knows about this'; 31 but they went forth and published his fame throughout all that region.

The story of the blind men is clearly a doublet of the miracle at Jericho, though Matthew has included it at that point also. The coincidences of vocabulary are unmistakeable evidence of the relationship. In both instances, Matthew has transformed the one blind beggar of Mark into two. The appeal of Jesus as 'son of David' is used in all three versions of the story. There are substantial modifications here, in that the healing takes place in the house, not in the open road; the question about their faith is a new feature. In both his versions of the story, Matthew introduces the theme of the 'touch' of Jesus—'he touched their eyes.' Verse 30 is a considerable enlargement on the simple statement that 'they received their sight.'

The verb ἐμβριμάομαι is rare in classical usage, but is used of the 'snorting' of horses—hardly a possible sense in this context. It must suggest agitation of spirit and even anger. Vincent Taylor discusses it at length in relation to the healing of the leper (*Mark, ad* 1.43). Is it perhaps an unconscious retention from a form in which the blindness was looked upon as due to demon possession? If there is harshness involved, and a certain fierceness of expression, this could not conceivably be directed against the men, but only against the demon who caused their condition.

Both this prohibition to spread the story and its sequel are found only in this Matthaean version. In the Jericho story, the blind men follow Jesus, presumably to Jerusalem.

Jesus Restores Speech to a Dumb Man 9:32–33 [34]

[32] As they were going out, people brought into his presence a dumb man, possessed by a demon, [33] and when the demon was cast out, the dumb man recovered his speech. The crowds were struck with amazement and said, 'Nothing like this was ever seen in Israel'; [34] but the Pharisees said, 'It is by the prince of demons that he casts out the demons.'

The dumb man of this story is directly said to be possessed by a demon. It too is a doublet of a story retold by Matthew elsewhere (12:22–24), with the additional particular that the man is deaf as well as dumb. There is no Markan parallel. Verse 33 has a Lukan parallel, minus the words of the amazed crowd (Lk.11:14).

CONCLUSION: JESUS RESUMES HIS TOUR OF GALILEE *9:35*

[35] Jesus went about all the cities and villages, teaching in their

synagogues and preaching the gospel of the kingdom, and healing every kind of disease and infirmity.

The brief conclusion of verse 35 repeats almost *verbatim* the words of 4:23, making a change only from 'all Galilee' to 'all the cities and villages'. This 'inclusio' binds together the two great intervening sections—the Sermon on the Mount, and the catena of miracle stories. It must be recalled that in ancient manuscripts there were nothing akin to our 'chapters' or other divisions (or even to mark the end of a word or of a sentence). If a writer wanted to indicate to the reader how he intended his material to be organized, he had no other means than the incorporation of such signals into his text. In Matthew, this appears most strikingly in the rubrics with which he marks the end of each of his five great collections of sayings. The 'inclusio' technique has already been noted in the parallel phrasing of 5:3 and 5:10, and of 5:17 and 7:12.

III   THE SECOND MAJOR DISCOURSE: THE MISSION CHARGE
9:36–11:1

Introduction: The Need and the Opportunity 9:36–38

1 The Commissioning of the Twelve 10:1–4
2 Directions for the Conduct of the Missioners 10:5–15
3 Warnings of Dangers to be Encountered 10:16–23
4 Encouragement to Face Dangers Fearlessly 10:24–33
5 Predictions of Divisions and Conflicts 10:34–39
6 Promises of Reward 10:40–42
   The Closing Rubric 11:1

INTRODUCTION: THE NEED AND THE OPPORTUNITY *9:36–38*

36 As he looked upon the crowds, Jesus felt deep concern for them because they were harassed and helpless, like sheep without a shepherd. 37 He said to his disciples, 'The harvest is plentiful, but the reapers are few; 38 so pray to the Lord of the harvest to send reapers into his harvest field.'

VERSE 36: 'The crowds'—apparently a reminiscence of the crowds which gathered about Jesus in the course of his first preaching tour

(4:25), though nothing has been said here of such a following. The first crowds provided the audience for the great Sermon (5:1—7:29). The crowds now around him provide the occasion for enlisting the disciples for participation in the mission of preaching and healing.

The words 'like sheep without a shepherd' are transferred by Matthew from Mark's introduction to the miracle of the loaves (Mk.6:34); they derive ultimately from Micaiah's vision of the armies of Ahab thrown into disarray by the death of the king (1 Ki.22:17).

VERSE 37: In this need of the nation, Jesus sees an opportunity. The harvest, in Jewish symbolism, stands for the judgement and the final separation of good from evil (so in the parables of chap. 13, explicitly in vv.39—43). The harassed and helpless condition of Israel makes it ready to respond to the gospel of the Kingdom. The divine judgement is seen primarily under the aspect of redemption, but it has its reverse side—those who refuse to hear the message of salvation will bring upon themselves a fate worse than that of Sodom and Gomorrah (10:15).

Jesus invites his disciples to pray that God, 'the Lord of the harvest', will send reapers to bring the harvest in. But the fact that he encourages them to pray that God will take the action needed does not lead him to sit back with folded hands to await the outcome. He himself now takes measures to fulfil the task of harvesting. The prayer to God is not an excuse for inaction, but a challenge to dedicated enterprise for him.

1   THE COMMISSIONING OF THE TWELVE *10:1—4*

¹ Summoning his twelve disciples, Jesus gave them authority to exorcise evil spirits and to heal every kind of disease and infirmity.
² These are the names of the twelve apostles: first Simon who is called Peter, and his brother Andrew; James the son of Zebedee and his brother John; ³ Philip and Bartholomew, Thomas and Matthew the tax collector, James the son of Alpheus, and Thaddaeus, ⁴ Simon the Cananaean, and Judas Iscariot who was to betray him.

VERSE 1: It is assumed that Jesus has already chosen a group of twelve, though Matthew has not followed Mark in telling when or how they came to be selected (Mk.3:13—19). In Luke the choice of the Twelve is set immediately before his version of the great Sermon, and it is addressed primarily to them (Lk.6:12—16,20).

VERSES 2—4: For the first and only time in Matthew, the Twelve are called 'apostles'. It is probable that he does not think of the word as a fixed title, but takes it as appropriate to the immediate task to which they are 'sent'. It is cognate with the verb ἀποστέλλω, 'I send', of verse 16 (in the aorist, v.5).

The list of names shows some variation in all four times that it is given in the New Testament (Mk.3:16–19; Lk.6:14–16; Acts 1:13, which of course does not include Judas Iscariot). The name of Peter always stands at the head of the list and that of Judas at the end; even in the list of Acts the name of Judas is placed at the end of the list, though it is now 'Judas son of James', who is not mentioned at all in the lists of Mark and Matthew. Only in this Gospel is Matthew called 'the tax collector'. A second Simon appears in all the lists. In Matthew as in Mark he is called 'the Cananaean', but in Luke he is called 'the Zealot', which may be his understanding of the unusual term 'Cananaean'. Jerome, however, takes it to mean 'from Cana'. The older English versions rendered it 'Canaanite', but this is almost certainly wrong. If Luke is right in interpreting it to mean 'Zealot', it is almost as strange to find that Jesus called a terrorist into the inner circle as that he should bring in a tax collector. It would be as absurd to imagine that he would continue with his revolutionary activities as to suppose that the tax collector continued to carry on his old occupation after he became a disciple. It is even more ridiculous to allege that the presence of a Zealot in the chosen group of twelve indicates that Jesus himself had, or sympathized with, the revolutionary intentions of the Zealot movement.

Of most of these twelve, we know remarkably little as individuals, though they soon came to be revered in the church, and legends about them multiplied without end. Several of them are given occasional parts to play in the Gospel of John (Andrew, Philip, Thomas, and a second Judas besides the traitor). Thomas acquired a special place in the legends of the Syrian churches; he gave his name to two apocryphal Gospels; and it was believed that he eventually travelled to India and founded there a Christian church which still exists in the southern part of the country. Peter alone can be said to be known to history in any serious way. He encountered Paul at Antioch, and was known to travel with his wife (Gal.2:11–14; 1 Cor.9:5); one of the factions at Corinth professed a particular allegiance to him (1 Cor.1:12). It is now generally agreed that he went to Rome, and suffered martyrdom in the Neronian persecution, and even that he was buried on the Vatican hill under the present cathedral which is dedicated to him.

It is evident, too, that the apostles never functioned as a college, though some expressions in Acts might leave the impression that they did. When Paul went up to Jerusalem after his conversion, he went to visit Peter, and he saw no other apostles except James the brother of Jesus (who was not one of the twelve). On his next visit, he found that the 'pillars' of the church there were a kind of triumvirate of James (the brother of Jesus), John, and Peter-Cephas (Gal.2:9), and it was James (according to the narrative of Acts) who presided over the Christian community and framed the decree which was adopted and sent out to Antioch and the churches of Syria and Cilicia (Acts 15:13–29).

In modern study, the historicity of the apostolate has been called in question by a number of competent scholars. It is, of course, not denied that Paul knew of apostles as pre-eminent among those whom God gave to the church and equipped with particular spiritual gifts (1 Cor.12:28), but the title does not denote a stated office, but a charismatic function, and is by no means limited to the Twelve who had been disciples of Jesus. Paul can speak of the risen Jesus as appearing to the Twelve, and 'then to all the apostles' (1 Cor.15:5,7). As early as 1911, Wellhausen had taken the position that Jesus did not select any company of twelve to accompany him (*Einleitung in die drei ersten Evangelien*, pp.138ff.). R. Bultmann holds that the notion of an inner circle of twelve is not historical, but dogmatic, and that the Twelve are at first looked upon 'not as apostles but as the eschatological regents' of the church while it still regarded itself primarily as the eschatological congregation (*Theology* I, p.37). Still more radical approaches are taken by G. Klein (*Die zwölf Apostel*, 1961), and now by W. Schmithals in his stimulating work *The Office of Apostle in the Early Church* (ET, 1969).

The question is reviewed, and the historicity of the apostolate defended, by R.P. Meye in a dissertation presented to the University of Basel and published in an expanded form as *Jesus and the Twelve: Discipleship and Revelation in Mark's Gospel* (1968); he discusses Klein's argument, but is not acquainted with the weighty treatise of Schmithals. He arrives at the hazardous conclusion that 'the New Testament, and Markan, picture of the Twelve as the company of Jesus is not at all open to doubt.' But doubts are in fact justified; the arguments of Klein and Schmithals are not to be so lightly dismissed. As Schmithals rightly puts it, 'today less than ever can one speak of assured results of the investigation of the Christian apostolate' (p.20,n.4).

2 DIRECTIONS FOR THE CONDUCT OF THE MISSIONERS *10:5–15*

[5] These twelve Jesus sent out on mission, giving them this charge:

'Do not take the road to Gentiles; do not enter any city of the Samaritans. [6] Go rather to the lost sheep of Israel. [7] Preach the message as you go, proclaiming that the kingdom of heaven is at hand. [8] Heal the sick, raise the dead, cleanse lepers, cast out demons. You have received freely, give freely. [9] Procure no gold or silver or bronze for your money-belts; [10] take no wallet, no change of clothing, no sandals, no staff; for the labourer is worthy of his food.

[11] Whatever city or village you enter, ask to be directed to a worthy man, and remain with him until you leave. [12] When you enter his house, give it your greeting, saying, "Peace be upon this house!" [13] And if the house be worthy, let your peace remain upon it; if it be unworthy, let your peace return upon you. [14] Wherever they do not receive you, shake off the dust of your feet as you leave that house or that city. [15] Truly I tell you, it will be more tolerable for Sodom and Gomorrah in the day of judgement than for that city.'

With this begins the second of the major collections in which Matthew has arranged scattered sayings of Jesus in the form of a discourse. It is easy to see that this, like the others, is a composite structure, and that great parts of it are not at all compatible with the situation which Matthew has devised for its delivery. Most of the sayings, indeed, reflect conditions which did not exist in the lifetime of Jesus for his followers, and must be seen rather as bearing upon the mission of those early years of the church, when it was still limiting its approach to Jews; some elements even reflect a later period when the movement is carried into Gentile territories, where the missionaries are liable to be put on trial before 'kings and governors' (vv.17f.). One section is transferred outright from the apocalyptic discourse of Mark 13, although most of that discourse is given by Matthew in its Markan context, immediately before the commencement of the passion narrative (chap.24).

Within the general structure, it comes at the end of an account of all but unbroken success, as great crowds from all over the Holy Land and beyond come to Jesus as he moves through the villages of Galilee, to hear him preach and teach, and to wonder at his miraculous powers of healing (4:23–9:35). He sees in them a flock 'harassed and helpless, like sheep without a shepherd', but also as a field of opportunity—a bountiful harvest ripe for the reaping (9:36–38). In this discourse, he commissions the Twelve to become his co-workers in the reaping.

VERSES 5–6: With these opening verses we are faced at once with a prohibition which could have no relevance to the actual situation of the disciples. It is impossible to suppose that they would have any urge to carry the gospel to Gentiles or to Samaritans now, seeing that when they began the work of evangelization after the death and resurrection of Jesus, they were so slow to carry the word beyond the ranks of Israel. Even then, the first preaching to Gentiles was not done by any of the Twelve, but by unknown men of the Hellenist group who were driven from Jerusalem by the persecution which broke out with the martyr death of Stephen (Acts 8:1,4; 11:19–21). Even after the Gentile mission had been carried on for some time with resounding success, the leaders of the Jerusalem church still restricted their mission to the Jewish people, even in agreeing to sanction the continued activity of Paul and Barnabas among Gentiles (Gal.2:9). Can we imagine that Jesus ever found it necessary, or advisable, to forbid them to go to Gentiles and Samaritans? The conclusion can hardly be avoided, that words like these emanated from those circles of the early church which were opposed to such an extension of the mission. They may have originated as a deliverance of a Christian prophet, given as a word of the risen Lord.

'Lost sheep'—not merely the disinherited, but the whole nation, seen as 'sheep without a shepherd' (9:36).

For Matthew, the prohibition was superseded by the command of the risen Christ to 'make disciples of all the nations' (28:19).

VERSES 7–8: These two verses, like the preceding two, are peculiar to Matthew, though there is a partial parallel to verse 7 in Luke 9:2; there it is not part of the charge but is worked into the introduction. The message which they are to deliver is the same as that of Jesus (4:17), without mention of the summons to repent. The miracles which they are to perform are likewise those of Jesus. The list is surprising in that it mentions the cleansing of lepers and the raising of the dead as well as healings and exorcisms. The accomplishments of the apostles in Acts do not include the cleansing of lepers; but we hear of two miracles of raising dead persons—one ascribed to Peter (Acts 9:36–41), and one to Paul (20:9–12). It is doubtful whether Luke intends the latter story as a miraculous restoration, since Paul affirms that 'the life is still in him,' after his fall from a third-story window. Perhaps the language is meant to be taken metaphorically, as of the cleansing of the heart from the infection of sin, and the gift of life to those who have 'been dead in trespasses and sins' (Eph.2:1; 5:14; Rom.6:13).

'Freely'—as a gift. It is strange that this fine saying has not been preserved elsewhere in the tradition. Paul reminds the Corinthians that he preached the gospel of God to them freely, without exacting payment (2 Cor.11:7); and to the Romans he writes that we are 'all justified freely by God's grace, through the redemption that is in Christ Jesus' (Rom.3:24).

VERSES 9–10: No supplies are to be carried; the missioners are to travel with no luggage and no money. The prohibited list differs in detail from those of Mark and Luke. Mark permits them to wear sandals and to carrry a staff; Luke forbids the staff, but has nothing to say about the wearing of sandals; according to Matthew, they are to travel barefoot. Matthew mentions different types of coins— gold, silver, bronze; Mark speaks only of bronze, and Luke only of silver—either of these terms could be used colloquially to mean simply cash (like 'brass' in England or 'dough' in America). It seems unlikely that gold coins would be available to the company of disciples—men who have abandoned their gainful occupations to follow Jesus around the countryside. No doubt they would have been at the disposal of Matthew's church, and it is their condition that is present to his mind. Matthew adds the maxim: 'every workman deserves his food.' They are to trust that they will be given hospitality along the way, although they cannot pay for it, Luke includes this saying in his second charge (10:7) where it reads 'pay' ($\mu\iota\sigma\theta\acute{o}\varsigma$), for Matthew's 'food' ($\tau\rho o\phi\acute{\eta}$). If this is a proverb transferred to spiritual from material meaning, 'pay' is more likely to be original —then as now, workmen feel that they deserve something more than their food for their labours. For the general sense, compare Rom. 15:27. Paul knows of the saying in some form—perhaps as an injunction of the risen Christ, for he affirms that 'the Lord has commanded that those who proclaim the gospel should get their living by the gospel', though he himself will not take advantage of this privilege (1 Cor.9:14–18).

VERSES 11–14: The brief Markan charge speaks only of remaining at the one house which first receives them, and of shaking the dust from beneath their feet as they leave a place where they are refused a hearing (6:10f.). Luke follows Matthew at this point, but in his second charge he incorporates much of the more comprehensive Matthaean instructions (10:4–12), with the addition of two unusual provisions: they are to 'greet no one on the road' (v.4), and to 'eat and drink what is provided by them' (v.7)—perhaps envisaging a Gentile house, which might offer food forbidden by Jewish law, but possibly a mere counsel not to be choosy.

Matthew's 'shake off the dust of your feet' would suggest shaking off the dust raised by your feet which has clung to your robes. It is the cloak that is shaken, not the feet, as symbol of disavowal of responsibility for the fate that awaits them (cf. Neh.5:13; and see the comment of Schlatter, *Matthäus, ad loc.*). Probably Matthew has corrected the Markan mistake (repeated by Luke), which speaks of 'the dust that is on your feet'.

VERSE 15: The unresponsive towns of Israel will be more terribly punished than Sodom and Gomorrah, in the day of judgement, because their opportunities have been greater (cf. Amos 3:2, 'You only have I known of all the families of the earth; therefore I will punish you for all your iniquities'). Or in the words of Jesus: 'To whom much is given, of them shall much be required' (Lk.12:48).

This saying is not included in the Markan charge, nor is it used by Luke at this point; Luke gives it in a slightly different wording in his charge to the seventy-two (10:12).

3　WARNINGS OF DANGERS TO BE ENCOUNTERED *10:16–23*

[16] I am sending you out like sheep in the midst of wolves, so you must be as wise as serpents and as innocent as doves. [17] Be on guard against people, for they will hale you before sanhedrins and will have you flogged in their synagogues; [18] and for my sake you will be brought before governors and kings, to give your testimony to them and to the Gentiles. [19] But when they hale you off to trial, do not be worried over how or what you are to speak, for what you are to say will be given to you in that moment. [20] It will not be you that speak, but the Spirit of your Father speaking through you.

[21] Brother will deliver up brother to death, and a father his child; children will rebel against parents and put them to death. [22] You will be hated by all for the sake of my name. But everyone who endures to the end will be saved.

[23] When they persecute you in this city, flee to the next, for I tell you, you will not have gone through all the cities of Israel before the Son of man comes.

VERSE 16: This verse sets the keynote for the remainder of the discourse (except for the final paragraph, vv.40–42). It looks far beyond the immediate mission of the Twelve to envisage the future task of the evangelization of the world. 'Now the subject is no longer what is required of the disciples for their mission in the villages of Galilee, but what will be applicable to the whole of apostolic activity until the Parousia' (Schlatter, *Matthäus, ad loc.*). The disciples were sent out as reapers to gather in a ripe harvest, and a generally friendly reception is anticipated. Now they are sent out 'like sheep in the midst of wolves,' in a world where they move in constant danger, without power to withstand the attacks of their enemies. They must learn to suffer and to die, like their Master. The wiliness of the serpent and the innocence of the dove will not, of course, protect them from arrest, floggings, and death by execution, but they must guard their integrity. The exhortation of 1 Peter 3:13–18 might almost be a commentary on the words. If they are put on trial for their faith, they must make their defence 'with gentleness and respect, keeping [their] consciences clear . . . for it is better to suffer for doing right, if that should be God's will, than for doing wrong,' always remembering that Christ did not answer reviling by reviling, or brutal treatment by threats (1 Peter 2:23).

VERSE 17 warns of maltreatment by Jewish authorities (councils and synagogues); verse 18 of trials in Gentile courts (before governors and kings); their sufferings will be a testimony to Jews and Gentiles alike.

These two verses (17, 18) and the next four (19–22) are transferred almost word for word from Mark's apocalyptic discourse (Mk.13:9–13; cf. Lk.21:12–19—greatly revised in wording, possibly drawn from a separate source but set in the same context).

VERSE 19: Perhaps the wording here has been modified by Christian ideas of the Spirit. The wording given in Luke looks like an earlier form: 'I will give you a mouth and wisdom' (21:15).

VERSE 21: The kind of acute conflict within the family that is envisaged here cannot be imagined as arising in Jesus' lifetime, but it certainly came in the next generation, and continued long afterwards. According to Jerome (late fourth century): 'We often see this come to pass in the persecutions.' Compare the words of verses 35f.

VERSE 23: This verse returns to the notion of a mission confined to Israel. It may well reflect one type of argument brought forward by Jewish Christians to justify opposition to any mission to Gentiles; it is quite in the spirit of verse 5. The coming of the Son of man can only mean the Parousia, the return of Jesus in glory at the end of the age (Mt.24:3,30, etc.), and it echoes the early conviction that there was little time remaining. There is no reason to suppose that Jesus himself imagined that the great event would come about in the next few weeks—before the disciples had run out of Israelite towns for preaching or for a refuge from persecution, or that he expected spectacular results from this mission (if, indeed, he ever organized it).

4 ENCOURAGEMENT TO FACE DANGERS FEARLESSLY *10:24–33*

²⁴ A disciple is not above his teacher nor a slave above his master.

²⁵ It is enough for the disciple if he is treated like his teacher, or for the slave to be treated like his master. If they called the master of the house Beelzebul, what worse name will they find for the people of his household staff!

²⁶ So have no fear of them; for there is nothing covered that will not be revealed, nothing hidden that will not be made known. ²⁷ What I tell you in the dark you are to speak in the light; what you hear whispered in your ear you are to proclaim upon the house-tops.

²⁸ Have no fear of those that kill the body but have no power to kill the soul. Fear him, rather, who is able to destroy both soul and body in hell.

²⁹ Are not two sparrows sold for a penny? Yet not one of them will fall to the ground without your Father's will; ³⁰ but for you, the very hairs of your head are all numbered. ³¹ So have no fear; you are of more value than countless sparrows.

³² Everyone who acknowledges me before men I will acknowledge before my Father in heaven; ³³ but everyone who denies me before men I will deny before my Father in heaven.

VERSES 24–25: These verses are general reflections on the likelihood that the disciple or the slave will not receive any better treatment than the master. They may count themselves fortunate if they are not handled more roughly still. They have no special pertinence to the projected mission, but suggest what kind of treatment the followers of a master who was put to death on the cross may expect in the same world to which he came.

The (partial) parallels in the other Gospels are not incorporated into a mission charge at all. One is used by Luke in his version of the great Sermon, where it is applied to blind men trying to lead other blind men, and so to the injunction against finding faults in other people while your own faults remain uncorrected (Lk.6:40–42). In John it is brought into the farewell discourse of Jesus at the Last Supper, in relation to the command that the disciples should follow Jesus' own example of the lowliest service. If Jesus, the Lord and Master, washes their feet, they must not think that they are too exalted to do the same (Jn.13:14–16). It is taken up again in the same discourse in a sense more akin to that of our passage. 'If the world hates you, you know that it has hated me before it hated you. . . . Remember the word that I said to you, "A slave is no greater than his master." If they persecuted me, they will persecute you; if they kept my word, they will also keep yours' (Jn.15:18,20). This is the sense in which it is applied here in Matthew.

VERSE 25 gives verbal abuse as an example of maltreatment to be expected. It echoes the accusation of 9:34. Name calling is of course the lightest form of persecution, though it can be cutting enough. It is hardly comparable to the savage floggings in the synagogues (v.17), or to the threat of death (v.28).

Beelzebul is a transliteration from Aramaic of one of the many names given·to the devil in Jewish usage; it anticipates the Beelzebul controversy which Matthew will report in chapter 12 (vv.24ff.), where he is called 'the prince of demons' as in 9:34.

VERSES 26–33: This section, made up of a number of sayings once used separately and in different contexts, constitutes a challenge to confess the name of Jesus openly, without fear of the consequences to themselves.

VERSE 26: The saying about the public revelation of secret communications is here used with *imperative* force—they must proclaim publicly what Jesus has taught them privately; the sense is made clear in verse 27. In Luke, an altered form of the saying is predictive, and is apparently taken to be a warning against saying privately what they do not want to be repeated in public—the truth is sure to come out, no matter what efforts are made to hide it. It follows upon a warning against Pharisaism (Lk.12:1–3). Luke does not incorporate it into either of his mission charges (chaps.9,10). It is followed, however, by the Lukan version of vv.28–33. Evidently in the common source (Q), these verses were already grouped together, and not in the context of a mission charge. The change of context is quite inexplicable, if Luke was drawing directly upon Matthew and not on a common source (as is held by those who think of 'dispensing with Q' [A.M. Farrer]. The Markan parallel is used in association with the saying about setting a lamp on a stand, not under a bushel or under a bed (Mk.4:21f.), following the interpretation of the parable of the sower as if it meant that the understanding of parables (and of the 'mystery of the kingdom of God'—v.11) is not to be limited forever to the disciples.

VERSE 28: In the Lukan version, this saying takes the form (12:4): 'Fear not those who kill the body and after that have no more that they can do.' Luke avoids the strange expression 'kill (or destroy) the soul'. Among the Greeks, the common belief was that the soul was dissolved upon the death of the body. Glaucon is astonished, even incredulous, at the suggestion that 'the soul is immortal and never perishes' (Plato, *Republic* X, 9D); and Cebes is sure that many will find it incredible that the soul should subsist in any form after death, for they are 'under the apprehension that when the soul is separated from the body it no longer exists anywhere, but is destroyed and perishes on the very day on which a man dies' (*Phaedo* 70a). Both Greek and Roman epitaphs bear evidence that this was the general belief. In Hebrew thought, man consists indeed of soul and body, but nowhere do we find the notion that the soul has an independent existence; what survives in Sheol is not called a 'soul' and has but a shadowy existence in the underworld, like the 'souls' of Homer. When ideas of a future life finally begin to be entertained in Israel they are cast in the form of a resurrection—'many of the sleepers in the dust of the earth shall awake' (Dan.12:2). The idea of God destroying the soul is anomalous. Apart from that, it is doubtful if anyone was given courage to face death, rather than disavow his faith, by the threat that he would meet a far worse fate at the hands of God if he shrank from the death of the body.

VERSES 29–31: With these verses, they are encouraged to face whatever may come, in the confidence that they will never be left without God. Nothing is of less value than a sparrow—the thought is of birds sold in the market for food—yet even these trifling creatures are under the Father's care, and not one of them falls to the ground apart from his will. He does not protect them from falling, and he will not save the disciples from execution; but that does not mean that he has ceased to concern himself with them. 'Of more value than many sparrows' seems like a weak assurance, when the value of sparrows has been set so low! The thought is, of course, that they are of incomparable value in God's sight.

VERSES 32–33: In these verses, courage is to be sustained in the face of danger and death by the assurance that steadfastness will be rewarded and apostasy punished when they appear before the throne of God in heaven for judgement. Jesus will acknowledge them as his, if they have acknowledged him before human tribunals.

In the Lukan parallel (12:8f.), 'the Son of man' takes the place of the 'I' of this passage in the first verse, and in both verses, 'before the angels of God' replaces Matthew's 'before my Father who is in heaven'. For both Luke and Matthew, 'the Son of man' on the lips of Jesus can be used as a surrogate for the personal pronoun (which Luke uses in v. 9). If 'Son of man' is the earlier form, there would appear to be a distinction between Jesus and the Son of man; the thought will be that the judgement of the Son of man, to be given in heaven, will correspond to the attitudes taken to Jesus during earthly trials. ('Before the angels of God' is simply a surrogate for 'in God's own presence', another way of avoiding direct mention of God; cf. Lk.15:10.)

5 PREDICTIONS OF DIVISIONS AND CONFLICTS *10:34–39*

[34] Do not imagine that I came to bring peace upon the earth; I have come to bring not peace, but a sword. [35] For I came to set a son against his father and a daughter-in-law against her mother-in-law; [36] a person's enemies will be those of his own household. [37] Anyone who loves father or mother more than me is not worthy of me, and anyone who loves son or daughter more than me is not worthy of me. [38] Anyone who does not accept his cross and follow me is not worthy of me. [39] Whoever finds his life will lose it, and whoever loses his life for my sake will find it.

Jesus now warns them that the gospel will bring bitter domestic strife, but that the risk of alienating members of one's own family must not be weighed against alienation from him.

VERSE 34: The 'sword' is used metaphorically. It is the instrument that divides families. The *effects* produced by the preaching are given as the *purpose* for which Christ came. This is in accord with a Semitic manner of speaking, and indeed thinking, about God. 'Does evil befall a city unless the Lord has done it?' (Amos 3:6.) Whatever comes to pass is seen as the fulfilment of the divine purpose. The ultimate effect of the coming of Christ is reconciliation to God and enduring peace; but the immediate effect of the preaching of peace is often strife.

VERSES 35–36: These divisive effects are expressed in the words of an oracle of the book of Micah, where it is the climax of a lament over the total breakdown of moral life in Israel, in domestic as in public relationships (Mic.7:1–6). The same passage lies behind verse 21 also. When the son or daughter of a devout family became a Christian while the father and mother did not (or vice versa), it caused the bitterest hostility within the family. This came about in Gentile families perhaps even more acutely than in Jewish; for all the members of the family had a part to play in the domestic cult which was carried on every day, as well as in the ceremonies of the public cults. A son or a daughter converted to Christianity could not so much as pour a libation to the household gods, or walk in procession to the temple, or to Eleusis, say. Such an attitude could not fail to infuriate the parents. It could also happen that the children would rebel when the parents were converted. For many, this alienation would be harder to bear than the danger of arrest, or flogging, or death.

VERSE 37: If such a situation arises, the duty to Christ must be set above the unity of the family. In Luke, this saying takes the stronger form: 'If anyone comes to me and does not hate his father and mother and children and brothers and sisters, and more than that, his own life too, he cannot be my disciple' (Lk.14:26). This is the more Semitic manner of speaking—Luke's words are the literal translation of an Aramaic original; but the verb 'hate' does not carry its full sense. It means no more than 'love less', and Matthew has turned this into the positive—not that they must love the immediate family less than Jesus, but that they must love him more. Loyalty to the Master must override even the closest family ties.

Undoubtedly, the bitter choice often had to be made, and in many parts of the world still has to be made. Even a change of denomination, as from Baptist to Anglican—still more from Protestant to Roman Catholic—can cause alienation from friend and family; how much more the change from the worship of Zeus and Apollo and Artemis to the worship of the one living and true God.

VERSE 38: In Luke also this verse, with slight changes in wording, follows the demand to set loyalty to Christ above family ties. To 'accept' (Matthew) or 'carry' (Luke) the cross means to accept the sentence of death in themselves (cf. 2 Cor.4:10f.); as if they were already condemned to death by crucifixion and carrying the cross to the place of execution.

It has been questioned whether this figurative use of the cross would be made before Jesus himself had been crucified.

VERSE 39: This saying is found in association with the demand for carrying the cross in 16:24f. where Matthew is following Mark (8:34f.). It is not found in the Lukan parallel in either of these places, but is given in a totally different context in Luke 17:33. It is an independent saying, not essentially connected with the demand to bear the cross. 'Life' is used in two different senses; in the first clause it means the physical life, in the second it is the true life, the life of the spirit.

It has become more and more clear that the discourse has moved far beyond the instruction for a mission to be carried on in the villages during the life time of Jesus. At Jewish hands, they might face flogging in the synagogue, or stoning by an angry mob, but not crucifixion; and there is nothing to indicate that sharp conflicts within the family were occasioned in those days.

6 PROMISES OF REWARD *10:40–42*

[40] Whoever welcomes you welcomes me, and whoever welcomes me

welcomes him who sent me. [41] Whoever welcomes a prophet as a prophet will receive the reward of a prophet, and whoever receives a righteous man as a righteous man will receive the reward of a righteous man. [42] And whoever gives a cup of cold water to one of these little ones simply because he is a disciple, I tell you truly, he will not fail to receive his reward.

The literary relationship between Mark and Matthew in these three verses is exceptionally hard to analyse. Verse 41 has no Markan parallel at all. For any kind of parallel we have to turn to Mark 9:37 and 41, which run as follows: 'Whoever gives you a cup of water to drink because you are Christ's, truly I tell you that he will not fail to receive his reward' (v.41); and, 'Whoever receives one such child in my name receives me, and whoever receives me, receives not me but him who sent me' (v.37). Verse 37 is used in part by Matthew in chapter 18 (v.5), in a context corresponding to that of the Markan passage; the second part of it is used by Matthew in the opening sentence of this group (v.40). Mark 9:41 is clearly the main basis of Matthew's closing verse here (v.42), but the phrasing is influenced by the 'child' of Mark 9:41, which in chapter 18 of Matthew is followed by a word about 'these little ones', in keeping with a Matthaean tendency to interpret references to 'children' or 'little ones' as meaning disciples. T.W. Manson remarks that 'the early Church was more interested in the original disciples than in children; and we should expect the tendency of the tradition to be to transfer sayings concerning "children" or "little ones" to disciples' (*Sayings*, p.138). He attempts to disentangle the confusion that has thus been occasioned in this and similar passages, but admits reluctantly that 'any results attained cannot be more than probable conjectures.'

The general declaration of verse 40 is developed into a recurring theme in the Gospel of John (see, for instance, Jn.5:32; 12:44f.; 13:20).

The three phrases of Matthew, all introduced by εἰς ὄνομα, 'in name' ('because') speak of the rewards to be received by those who show kindness to 'a prophet', 'a righteous man', 'one of these little ones' — different ways of referring to the disciples (the 'you' of verse 40). The rewards of discipleship are not for the disciples alone but for all who welcome them because they are Christ's.

Nothing is said of the nature of the 'reward'. It is sufficient that God will bestow it, and what it may turn out to be will be beyond all that we can ask or think.

A strange feature of Matthew's account of this charge is that, although we have been told that Jesus sent out the Twelve, we are never told that they went or that they came back, let alone where they went or how they were actually received. Both Mark and Luke give brief accounts of the mission and of the return of the disciples to report to Jesus (Mk.6:12f.; Lk.9:6; cf. Lk.10:17). There is nothing whatever in the texts to give grounds for the conjecture that the mission was of great importance, less still for the notion that its importance lies in its failure (V. Taylor, *The Life and Ministry of Jesus* (1955), chaps. 24,25). It must be said that if it had all that importance, Matthew entirely failed to realize it; and as for its supposed failure, Mark and Luke both report that it was entirely successful.

But Matthew as usual is not much interested in the matter as a one-time occurrence in the life of Jesus. Once again, 'the disciples' are stylized images of the Christian believers of his own time, and the mission charge is a code of directions for the missionary activity of his own church, around the turn of the century. Like the 'pillars' of the Jerusalem church, it regarded itself as called to direct its missionary activities to Jews (Gal.2:9), even though it knows that the risen Lord has given commission for the evangelization of all the nations (28:19). When the disciples are called 'apostles', this is not a title of office reserved for the original group, but a description of their work of mission; in his view, all Christians are meant to be apostles, and every believer is 'sent out' by Jesus to preach the gospel of the Kingdom. Nothing is said of that particular mission or of any return from it, because it is still in progress and will continue until the coming of the Son of man and the end of the age. The directions, the warnings, and the promises of reward are addressed to the church of Matthew's time, and are far more appropriate to its situation than to the conditions that faced the Twelve seventy years before. The gospel is to be preached in all the world for a testimony to all the nations before the coming of the end (24:14), but the mission of the Gentiles is for others, even though it was extended by the risen Christ. Not for Matthew is the restless ambition of Paul to preach the gospel where Christ had not been named (Rom.15:20f.). Like James and the church of Jerusalem, he will give the right hand of fellowship to those who go to the Gentiles, but his heart is set upon the redemption of Israel despite the apostasy that has brought disaster.

See the excellent study of the mission in the article of Fr. Schuyler Brown, 'The Mission to Israel in Matthew's Central Section (Mt.9:35–11:1)', *ZNTW* 69 (1978), pp. 73–90.

THE CLOSING RUBRIC *11:1*

[1] When Jesus had finished giving directions to his twelve disciples, he went away from there to teach and preach in their towns.

The whole interest in the mission disappears. After an appropriate form of the rubric which Matthew uses to mark the close of each of the major discourses, he concerns himself only with the renewed missionary activity of Jesus. The disciples make no appearance until they are brought on the scene abruptly at the beginning of chapter 12, and there is no further mention of the mission.

There is reason to doubt whether any such mission of the disciples took place during the lifetime of Jesus. Even Vincent Taylor admits that 'the Markan narrative appears to have been put together by the Evangelist himself; it is little more than a framework for the Mission Charge to the Twelve' (*Mark*, p.302). The admission would seem of itself to demolish his argument that it has some kind of historical kernel. It seems to be generally agreed that the sayings of the charge are prior to the narrative; that is to say, what little account of it we have was created to make a framework for sayings which were transmitted as instructions given by Jesus for the conduct of a mission by his disciples, but the tradition gave no setting for them. It is then argued that the existence of such sayings is evidence enough that Jesus actually organized a mission of some kind. But the more reasonable conclusion to draw is that the sayings were first uttered by a prophet as direction given by the risen Lord to his church not very long after the resurrection. As Bultmann put it, 'originally it was the risen (or ascended) Lord who spoke . . . i.e., we have a Church product here' (*HST*, p.145). This applies particularly to the twelve verses of Matthew's version of the charge which are all that really bear upon the conduct of the mission (vv.5–16); the remainder of his compilation consists of more general warnings, exhortations, and promises.

See the discussion in my article, 'The Mission of the Disciples and the Mission Charge: Matthew 10 and Parallels', in *JBL* 89, Vol.70, Pt.I (1970), pp.1–13.

C

Doubts, Criticisms, and Overt Hostility

Mt. 11:2–13:58

The organization of the mission appears as a high water mark in the ministry of Jesus as Matthew has been describing it. Up to that point the dominant note has been one of rapid and widespread success, extending far beyond the villages of Galilee through which he has been moving (4:23–25). 'Great crowds' follow him, listen with astonishment to his teaching, and recognize in it a note of authority which is not to be found in their scribes (7:28f.), and marvel at his miracles of healing (9:33). The crowds become so great and their needs so manifest that Jesus gives authority to his twelve disciples to exercise a ministry like his own. He sees a bountiful harvest ripe for the reaping, and he enlists helpers for the task.

In the chapters which follow, the atmosphere changes. It is no longer a story of resounding success and increasing popular appeal. Jesus begins to face doubts and questionings and even open hostility. There have been occasional notes of opposition in the earlier chapters, but these have been all but submerged in the waves of acclaim. Jesus has found no faith in Israel to compare with that of the Gentile centurion (8:10); the Gadarene people have begged him to leave their neighbourhood (8:34). Scribes have accused him of blasphemy (9:3), and Pharisees have questioned his disciples about his practice of associating with tax collectors and sinners (9:11), and followers of John the Baptist have suggested that he was less demanding than they and the Pharisees in the discipline of fasting (9:14).

So far, these have been no more than rumblings in the background which scarcely disturbed the swelling notes of enthusiasm and admiration. But from this point on it is made evident that the opposition has been much more serious and the response less gratifying than has been indicated before. John the Baptist has come to doubt the validity of Jesus' ministry (11:2f.). The very people who criticized John for his asceticism are now criticizing Jesus for his lack of it—they are calling him 'glutton and drunkard, a friend of tax collectors and sinners' (11:15–19). Towns which witnessed his miracles have not responded to his call for repentance (11:20ff.); even Capernaum, where he has chosen to establish headquarters, has brought upon itself a harsher condemnation than that of Sodom. His truth has made no impression on 'wise and prudent people', but has been received only by 'babes' (11:25). Jesus acknowledges that this has come about by God's good pleasure, and gives thanks.

The voices of criticism are heard more loudly. Jesus is challenged over his laxness—or the laxness of his disciples—in sabbath observance (12:1–8); and when he works a miracle of healing on the sabbath, the Pharisees form a conspiracy to destroy him (12:9–15). When he gives speech and healing to a man who had been dumb and blind, by exorcising the demon that possessed him, the charge is made that his power over demons is given to him by the prince of demons (12:22–24). Finally he must break with his own family: those who do the will of God will hereafter be his brother and sister and mother (12:46–50).

This is the background against which Matthew will introduce the parable discourse of chapter 13. It marks lines of division among his hearers, between those who do the will of his Father in heaven, to whom it is given to know 'the secrets of the kingdom of heaven' (13:11), and those who see without seeing, and hear without hearing or understanding (13:13).

The division is thus:

I Criticism Mounts 11:2–12:50
II The Third Major Discourse: A Collection of Parables 13:1–52
Finale: Jesus Rejected in his own Village 13:53–58

I CRITICISM MOUNTS
Mt. 11:2–12:50

This section of the Gospel may be outlined as follows:

1 Jesus and John the Baptist 11:2–19
 The Questionings of John and the Response of Jesus 11:2–6
 Jesus Pays Tribute to John 11:7–15
 The Parable of Children in the Market Places 11:16–19
2 The Verdict of Jesus on the Cities of Galilee 11:20–24
3 Thanksgiving, Proclamation, and Invitation 11:25–30
 The Prayer of Thanksgiving 11:25–26
 Jesus Proclaims his Unique Relationship to the Father 11:27
 The Great Invitation 11:28–30

1 JESUS AND JOHN THE BAPTIST *11:2–19*

The Questionings of John and the Response of Jesus 11:2–6

² When John in his prison heard about the activities of the Christ, he sent disciples of his ³ to ask him, 'Are you the Coming One, or are we to await someone else?' ⁴ Jesus answered them: 'Go take word to John of what you hear and see:

⁵ The blind receive their sight, and the lame walk;
Lepers are made clean, and deaf people receive their hearing;
The dead are raised to life, and the poor have the gospel preached to them.

⁶ And blessed are those who do not find me a stumbling-block.'

The scene rests upon the recognition that the ministry of Jesus does not correspond to the picture that John had drawn of the mightier one to follow him, who would be the agent of divine judgement on Israel—exercising his power in a manner that John could describe as a baptism with wind and fire, a purging of the threshing floor, a hewing down of the tree to the roots (3:10–12). John had warned his hearers to flee from the wrath to come, and he looked to his greater successor to appear as the minister of that wrath. What he has heard about Jesus makes him wonder whether he was mistaken in his initial conviction that Jesus was the one to fulfil this task (3:14). The reply of Jesus affirms that he has a totally different conception of the mission which he has received from God—he has come not to punish but to heal.

VERSE 2: There has been no word of John since he was cast into prison just before Jesus opened his ministry in Galilee (4:12). From other sources we learn that he was held in the dungeons of the fortress Machaerus, on the east shore of the Dead Sea. Little is known of the conditions of his imprisonment, but it is assumed here that he was able to keep in communication with his disciples and to hear about what Jesus has been doing in Galilee.

'The Christ'—used here with the full significance of the title. The question is whether Jesus can be hailed as the promised Messiah, or whether the nature of his activities rules out any claim to fulfil the role.

VERSE 3: 'The Coming One', that is the Messiah, with a particular undertone of reference to what John has said of the mightier one who is to come after him (3:11).

VERSE 4: 'What you hear and see'. Matthew gives no report of anything done or said in the hearing of these messengers. Luke, working with the same source, supplies a picture of Jesus performing miracles on the spot (7:21), to prepare the way for the response of Jesus.

VERSE 5: The reply is cast substantially in phrases from the book of Isaiah, such as

Behold, your God will come . . .
    He will come and save you.
Then the eyes of the blind shall be opened,
    and the ears of the deaf unstopped;
Then shall the lame man leap as a hart,
    and the tongue of the dumb shall sing. (Isa. 35:4–6)

The preaching of the gospel to the poor recalls the Spirit-gifted figure of Isaiah 61:1. The healing of lepers and the raising of the dead are not among the promises held out in Isaiah.

The words of Jesus are cast in a poetical structure, and may have originated as a Christian hymn of praise for the wonders of the Messianic age. The setting in a mission of disciples of John is secondary; 'it belongs to those passages in which the Baptist is called as a witness to the Messiahship of Jesus' (Bultmann, *HST*, p.23; and see the long discussion by A. Fridrichsen in his *Problem of Miracle*, pp.97–99).

The activities (ἔργα) of Jesus are not limited to miracles. The response to the questionings of John is indeed given by an appeal to miraculous deeds, but the real significance of them is in the appeal to prophecy. The argument is that in his healings and exorcisms, as truly as in his preaching to the poor, Jesus demonstrates that he is indeed the one of whom the prophets have spoken. As Fridrichsen has pointed out, miracles in themselves were too commonly performed by charlatans of every kind in that age to be of much evidential value; they were as much an embarrassment as an aid to Christianity. But there was unquestionably a powerful appeal in the argument from prophecy. There are remarkably few references to the miracles of Jesus in the New Testament apart from the Gospels; and even in them they are relatively few in number. The evangelists recognize that they do not awaken a true faith in Jesus. They strike people with amazement and attract crowds; but we will be told shortly that Jesus is not deceived into supposing that this means very much. The very cities where most of his 'mighty works' had been done are upbraided because they did not repent (11:20f.; cf. Jn.2:23–25). His opponents are not convinced by miracles; they still ask him to show them 'a sign from heaven' (12:38; 16:1–4, etc.).

VERSE 6: The beatitude is an independent saying, with only the loosest relationship to the response to John. It reflects the fact that the career of Jesus was not Messianic in any sense that would correspond to Jewish expectations of the Messiah. The cross proved to be the ultimate 'stumbling-block' to Jews (1 Cor.1:23); a crucified Messiah was unthinkable.

Jesus Pays Tribute to John 11:7–15

[7] As they were leaving, Jesus began to speak about John to the crowds:

Why did you go out into the wilderness?
  Was it to see a reed shaken by the wind?
[8] Why then did you go out?
  Was it to see a man dressed in soft clothes?
As you know, those who wear soft clothes are
  in the residences of the kings.
[9] But why then did you go out?
  Was it to see a prophet?
Yes, I tell you, and more than a prophet.
[10] This is the man of whom it is written:
  'See, I am sending my messenger before your face,
    who will prepare your way before you.'

[11] 'I tell you truly, among men born of women there has never been any one greater than John the Baptist; yet one who is least in the kingdom of heaven is greater than John.

[12] 'From the days of John the Baptist until now, the kingdom of heaven is subjected to violence, and violent people ravage it. [13] All the prophets and also the law prophesied until John, [14] and if you are willing to accept it, he is the Elijah who is to come. [15] Whoever has ears, let him hear!'

The passage is a compilation of sayings which was available also to Luke for the most part. Matthew makes some additions, and two of the verses are employed by Luke in a different context (vv.12f.; Lk.16:16). Verse 14 may be a Matthaean addition, or it may have been in the common source Q and omitted by Luke because he rejects the identification of John with the expected Elijah. Verse 15 is one of those tags which can be attached to any group of sayings (cf. Mt.13:9,43; and the endings of the letters to the seven churches of Asia, Rev. chaps. 2 and 3).

VERSE 7: The crowds are the stock audience of the declaration about John. They are introduced artificially and have no real part to play. They may be taken to represent the amorphous groups in Syria to whom Matthew wants to appeal, who are hesitating between the rival claims of the Christians and the followers of John, who in some areas continued to exist as a sect which regarded him (John) as the Messiah. It is of course possible that Jesus at times spoke highly of John, but in this tribute his words are not to be distinguished from utterances of Christian teachers who are eager to win members of the continuing Baptist sect to membership in the church (cf. Acts 19:1–12). The attitude of the church was friendly to them; it was probably felt that like Apollos they only needed to have the way of God expounded more accurately (Acts 18:24–26).

VERSE 8: The 'soft clothing' has a suggestion of effeminacy (cf. the use of μαλακοί in 1 Cor.6:9, specifically of effeminates). There are overtones of scorn for the courtiers who frequented the palaces of Herod.

VERSE 9: 'More than a prophet'—that is, the last and greatest of all, and even more, the precursor of Jesus the Messiah.

VERSE 10: 'My messenger' is the translation of the word *malachi*, which has come to be treated as the name of the prophet to whom the book is ascribed. The citation is taken from Malachi 3:1, but it does not correspond exactly either to the Hebrew text or to LXX. In Mark 1:2, it is fused with a phrase from Isaiah 40:3, and the whole quotation ascribed to Isaiah. In Mark it is not given as a saying of Jesus; it is worked into the introduction to the report of the mission of John.

VERSE 11: This saying seems to combine a remarkable tribute to John with a still more remarkable note of depreciation. He may be hailed as the greatest man who ever lived, but the humblest Christian believer is greater still. The 'greatness' of the Christian believer does not lie in his personality or his accomplishments, but solely in his high privilege of admission to the kingdom of heaven. Jesus does not estimate greatness by human standards; among his followers, the greatest is as unassuming as a little child (18:4), and must make himself the servant, even the slave, of all (20:25–27). The saying may have been framed to help persuade followers of John that for all the greatness of their master something far greater is open to them if they will come into 'the kingdom of heaven', by transferring their allegiance to Christ and becoming members of his church.

VERSE 12: The point of this saying is in doubt. Is the 'violence' praised or condemned? In the view of Lagrange, it is the 'holy energy' of those who storm their way into the Kingdom in spite of all hindrance and discouragement. It is difficult, however, to understand the verb ἁρπάζουσιν as conveying anything other than hostile action; the 'violent people' (βιασταί), attack the Kingdom to plunder it (cf. ἁρπάσαι, διαρπάσει, 'plunder', in 12:29).

The Lukan parallel to vv.12f. appears in a different context, and in reverse order (16:16); it is linked with Luke's version of the saying which Matthew has given in the Sermon on the Mount about the inviolability of the Law (Mt.5:18). The noun βιασταί and the verb ἁρπάζουσιν do not appear; but the verb βιάζεται represents the same thought. The Lukan passage runs: 'The law and the prophets [continued] until John; from then the kingdom of God is preached and everyone forces a way (βιάζεται) into it.' This Lukan form of the saying raises its own problems, and does not help us to determine what the words meant to Matthew, let alone what Jesus may have intended to convey. In both versions, there is implied a basic unity between the Johannine movement and that of Jesus. Both are directed towards the kingdom of heaven and both are attacked by 'violent people', who will bring about the death of John and not long afterwards the crucifixion of Jesus.

VERSE 13: 'The prophets and the law'—the usual order is inverted, probably because Matthew thinks of the whole body of scripture primarily in terms of prophecy; the law also 'prophesies'. It was a commonplace of Christian hermeneutics that Moses was a prophet who wrote of Christ (Jn.1:45; 5:46f.; cf. Lk.16:29–31). John evidently is viewed as belonging to the old dispensation, of prophecy; the turn of the ages has come with Jesus, the time of fulfilment (cf. Mt.13:16f., etc.).

Jesus specifically identifies Elijah—the Elijah whose return was prophesied (Mal.4:5)—with John the Baptist. The identification is made again in the dialogue set in the descent from the mountain of the transfiguration (17:10–13, taken from Mk.9:11–13) where it is related to the scribal doctrine that 'Elijah must first come.' In the middle of the second century, we still find the distinguished rabbi Trypho (Tarphon of Ephesus) rejecting Justin's teaching that Jesus is the Messiah on the ground that Elijah has not yet made his appearance. Luke silently rejects the identification, and in the Fourth Gospel John himself denied outright that he is Elijah (Jn.1: 21). The saying belongs to the controversy of later times over the Messianic claims made for Jesus by his disciples, and the continued refusal by the Jews to acknowledge them.

It is difficult, if not impossible, to establish the historical relationship between John and Jesus, but one thing is clear—that John did not at any time become a disciple of Jesus. Even in the Fourth Gospel, where John is depicted as pointing out Jesus to his own disciples as 'the Lamb of God who takes away the sins of the world' (Jn.1:29,35f.), he does not himself become a follower of his.

It is all the more remarkable that he should have come to be recognized by the church as one of its saints, and given a place of honour higher than all others but the Virgin Mary. This is reflected in the iconography, especially of the Orthodox churches, where he and the Virgin stand on either side of Christ in the Deesis panel upon the Royal Door of the sanctuary; and in the *Confiteor*, which begins, 'I confess to Almighty God, to the blessed Virgin Mary, to blessed Michael the Archangel, to St. John the Baptist, to the holy apostles Peter and Paul, and to all the saints, . . .'

The Parable of Children in the Market Places 11:16–19

16 'To what am I to compare this generation? It is like children sitting in the market places and crying to the others:

17 We played the flute for you, and you did not dance;
we mourned, and you did not beat your breasts.

18 For John came neither eating nor drinking, and they say, "He is possessed"; the Son of man came eating and drinking, and they say, "Look at him—a glutton and a drunkard, a friend of tax collectors and sinners."

19 Wisdom is justified by her works.'

The general point of the parable is clear. The same people who criticize John for his austere manner of life are now criticizing Jesus for his lack of austerity. The further jibe that he is 'a friend of tax collectors and sinners', is an echo of words ascribed to the Pharisees in Matthew 9:11 (cf. Lk.15:1f.). 'Eating and drinking' of course bears upon *what* is eaten and drunk; John lived meagrely (on 'locusts and wild honey', according to 3:4), and he probably abstained from wine, as Jesus clearly did not. Elsewhere the followers of Jesus are contrasted unfavourably with the disciples of John in that they do not fast (9:14f.). There was evidently a conspicuous difference between John's way of life and that of Jesus. The public reaction has been equally hostile to both, for the message is unpalatable and those who bear it will not please their hearers, no matter how they frame their lives.

VERSE 17: In the form given to it by Matthew, the parable seems to suggest two groups of children, one which would like to play games of some kind—whether Marriage or Funeral—and complains that 'the others' will not join in. In Luke (7:31–35), the two groups complain 'to one another'—the one group plays airs for a wedding on the flute, and the other will not dance; the second group chants a dirge, and the other will not play up to this lead by acting as mourners (beating breasts). The games of the children reflect the marriage and funeral customs of the time (flutes and dancing at the wedding; dirging and beating of breasts at the funeral; for both, professionals were often engaged).

VERSE 18: 'The Son of man' is merely a surrogate for the personal pronoun 'I' (as often).

VERSE 19: The final sentence appears to be a proverb of some kind. Its meaning is uncertain and it has no clear connection with the parable. In Luke it is given the form, 'Wisdom is justified by all her children' (7:35). In the context, 'justified' probably means 'recognized for what it is'—perhaps, in the Matthaean phrasing, 'by its results' (words); or in the more plausible Lukan form, 'by those who have true insight' (who may be described as 'children of wisdom'—a Semitic idiom, meaning those who are wise themselves).

2   THE VERDICT OF JESUS ON THE CITIES OF GALILEE *11:20–24*

²⁰ He then denounced the cities in which most of his miracles had been done, because they had not repented.

²¹ 'Woe to you, Chorazin! Woe to you, Bethsaida! For if the miracles which were done in you had been done in Tyre and Sidon, they would long ago have repented in sackcloth and ashes. ²² Let me tell you, it shall be more tolerable for Tyre and Sidon in the day of judgement than for you.

²³ And you, Capernaum!

Will you be exalted to heaven?
You will be brought down to Hades.

For if the miracles which were done in you had been done in Sodom, it would have remained standing till this day. ²⁴ Let me tell you, it will be more tolerable for Sodom in the day of judgement than for you.'

The placing of this section in Matthew is hard to understand. It clearly presupposes that Jesus has concluded his work in Galilee and around the lake, and recognizes that it has had no real effect in leading people to repentance. Yet in the Matthaean framework, he pronounces these words to a general audience in the course of a mission tour of 'their cities' (11:1); while his disciples are sent on missions of their own, because the task is so great that many helpers are needed (9:35–38; 10:1–8, and ff.); and the mission is continuing in Galilee over the next seven chapters (with excursions to the north). Jesus does not leave Galilee until he begins his final journey to Jerusalem by way of the Peraea (19:1). Luke gives the denunciation in a shorter version as part of the second mission charge to the disciples (Lk.10:13–15), where it is equally out of place, though in Luke's story Jesus has now left Galilee (from 9:51).

VERSE 20: Did Jesus himself think that a display of miraculous powers should incline the hearts of people to repentance? In the eyes of Matthew, the miracles demonstrated that Jesus acted as he spoke, with Messianic authority; for him, as for the early Christians generally, the miracles ought to have accredited the miracle worker as an authoritative moral teacher, but the reader today sees no logical connection.

The main point is that it is recognized in the tradition that Jesus did not find the response which he expected to his call for repentance, however great the crowds which gathered to see and benefit by his miraculous powers. Fame, popularity, even the inclination of the masses to 'hear him gladly' (Mk.12:37), did not issue in any serious change of heart and life.

VERSE 21: Chorazin is not mentioned anywhere else in the Bible, and only once (doubtfully) in the Talmud. This casual reference to it as one of the towns which had seen many mighty works of Jesus is a striking indication of how great are the gaps in our information about the career of Jesus. Bethsaida is said in the Fourth Gospel to have been the native town of Peter and Andrew, and of Philip (Jn.1:44), but it is not mentioned elsewhere in Matthew and only twice in Mark. Apart from this denunciation, we should have nothing to suggest to us that it was a major centre of Jesus' public ministry. It is on the east bank of the Lake, not far from Capernaum, in the region known as Gaulinitis (but the location is in doubt, and in John 12:21 it is called 'Bethsaida of Galilee').

'Tyre and Sidon', the great ports of Phoenicia, are regarded by the Hebrew prophets as conspicuous centres of wealth and power, and of arrogance, which are to feel the weight of the Lord's displeasure. It is chiefly Tyre that is lashed by the prophetic oracles, for Sidon had declined in importance after its destruction by the Assyrians under Esar-Haddon in 677 BC, and even more after it was burned to the ground by the Persians under Artaxerxes Ochus in 351. Tyre flourished until it was taken by Alexander the Great in 333–332 after a siege of seven months, when thirty thousand of its people were sold in the slave markets. They were both far greater than the insignificant fishing villages (unduly dignified as 'cities') of the lake of Galilee. Yet these little places are warned that they have earned a worse fate than that of Tyre and Sidon, by reason of the greater evidence of the power of God that they have witnessed in the miracles of Jesus. 'To whom much is given, much shall be required.'

It is hardly to be supposed that these cities, or villages, are to be dealt with *en masse* on 'the day of judgement'.

VERSE 23: The address to Capernaum is made in terms taken directly from a taunt song addressed to the king of Babylon (as the poem is edited):

> You said in your heart,
>   'I will ascend to heaven;
> above the stars of God
>   I will set my throne on high;
> . . . .
> But now you shall be brought down to Hades (Sheol),
>   to the depths of the Pit.' (Isa.14:13–15)

This is spoken of the little town which Jesus had chosen as his headquarters (Mt.4:13). It suggests that he had been disdainfully treated there, and had found the people unduly vain about the place, but there is no trace elsewhere of such a tradition. Capernaum was no Babylon; it had not far to fall, whatever its pretensions.

'Sodom'—according to Israelite legend, Sodom was destroyed by 'brimstone and fire from the Lord out of heaven' (Gen.19:24). The sins of Capernaum will be judged even more sternly, because they have had such incomparable blessings.

The Lukan parallel does not contain the reference to Sodom.

The passage is probably a true reflection of the disappointment of Jesus in the results of his work in Galilee, seeing that it stands in such glaring contrast to the popular acclaim which the Gospel story pictures. But it is also possible that it originates as the prophetic response to the failure of an apostolic mission in northern Galilee.

Matthew probably intends it to convey a warning to the Jews of his own time that if they do not repent and believe in Jesus, they must expect a worse fate than that of Tyre and Sidon, or of Sodom.

3 THANKSGIVING, PROCLAMATION, AND INVITATION *11:25–30*

The passage consists of three parts, each essentially independent of the other two. The first two parts had already been linked in the source Q, as is shown by their presence in Luke, though in a totally different context, and with minor changes of wording (Lk.10:21f., following the return of the Seventy from their mission). The third part is peculiar to Matthew. The linking of the first two was perhaps occasioned by the use of the verb ἀποκαλύπτω, 'reveal' in both of them (vv.25,27), along with the repeated occurrence of πατήρ, 'Father'. The third part (vv.28–30), found only in Matthew, has not even a *Stichwort* to connect it with the others.

The Prayer of Thanksgiving 11:25–26

²⁵ At that time Jesus spoke these words:
  'I thank you, Father, Lord of heaven and earth, that you have hidden these things from wise and prudent people and have revealed them to babes. ²⁶ Yes, Father, for such was your good pleasure.'

Jesus accepts the failure of his work in Galilee as the will of God the Father, and he will not repine. This would appear to be the connection of thought made by Matthew; but in fact the prayer introduces a contrast between two types of hearers which has nothing to do with the failure of the inhabitants of certain Galilean villages to repent. The people of Bethsaida and Capernaum are scarcely to be counted among the 'wise and prudent' from whom the revelation is hidden; nor does the denunciation of the towns carry any reference to 'babes' among them to whom the truth has been made known.

  The contrast 'wise and prudent' as against 'babes' can only mean the contrast between the schooled and the unschooled. The rabbis liked to call themselves 'disciples of the wise': it is especially the scribes, the masters of sacred learning, who have not been able to recognize the truth of God in Jesus. 'Babes' will apply specifically to the immediate disciples of Jesus, men of the people with no training in letters and in the scribal interpretations of the Law. There is a parallel thought in Paul's words to the Corinthians (1 Cor.

1:20,26–29). 'Where is the wise man? Where is the scribe? . . . Has not God made foolish the wisdom of the world? . . . But God chose what is foolish in the world to shame the wise . . . so that no human being might boast in the presence of God.'

Jesus Proclaims his Unique Relationship to the Father 11:27

[27] All things have been delivered to me by my Father; and no one knows the Son except the Father, and no one knows the Father except the Son and those to whom the Son wills to reveal him.

In the Lukan version, there is the significant change of 'knows the Son' to 'knows who the Son is', and 'knows the Father' to 'knows who the Father is'.

The passage has nothing comparable to it elsewhere in the Synoptic Gospels. It is much more akin to the lofty hieratic self-proclamation of the Gospel of John. This 'meteorite from the Johannine heaven' (von Hase) is undoubtedly a theological (Christological) composition from the hand of an unknown mystic of the early church. It teaches that the knowledge of God is a mystery which cannot be attained except by revelation, and the revelation is mediated only through the Son (Jesus). Not only that, but the knowledge of Jesus himself is a mystery which is reserved for the Father alone.

This stress on 'knowing', and on its attainment by revelation through the aid of a mediator, suggests that we have here a fragment of an incipient Gnosticism, or a trace of the tendencies which we find in the Gnostic and Hermetic literature. The knowledge of God is indeed a frequent theme of Hebrew prophets, but it is not treated by them as a mystery hidden from all but those who have received a special revelation. If Israel does not 'know' God, it is because she has been persistently rebellious and disobedient, not because the true knowledge has been hidden to her. God has made himself known in Israel, but to know him means to live in accordance with his will. So Jeremiah can say of King Josiah to his unworthy son Jehoiakim:

> Did not your father eat and drink
>   and do justice and righteousness?
> Then it was well with him.
> He judged the cause of the poor and needy;
>   then it was well.
> Is not this to know me?
>   says the Lord. (Jer.22:15f.)

This is not the same notion of 'knowledge' that underlies our passage.

Elsewhere in the Synoptic tradition, Jesus does not speak of himself absolutely as 'the Son' (with the doubtful exception of Mt.24:36; Mk.13:32, where any special knowledge is denied).

The entire passage should be regarded as a later construction of Christological speculation, not as an utterance of Jesus himself.

The Great Invitation 11:28–30

28 Come to me, all you that toil and bear burdens,
   and I will give you rest.
29 Take my yoke upon you and learn of me,
   for I am gentle and humble in heart,
   and you will find rest for your souls.
30 For my yoke is easy, and my burden is light.

This invitation is not addressed to a particular audience, but to all. It may have originated as an utterance of the personified Wisdom of God, such as we find in the book of Proverbs (chap. 8, for instance). The language is clearly related to the words of Ben-Sirach, who speaks of how his devotion to the study of the law has brought him 'much rest' ($\pi o\lambda\lambda\grave{\eta}v$ $\grave{\alpha}v\acute{\alpha}\pi\alpha\upsilon\sigma\iota v$). The law to him is Wisdom, and he invites his readers to 'acquire Wisdom for yourselves without money. Bring your necks under her yoke, and let your souls receive instruction; it is to be found close by. See with your eyes that I have laboured little, and found for myself much rest' (Ecclus.51:25–27).

If the verses do not actually come from some similar book of Wisdom, it is clear that they stand in that tradition, and that Jesus speaks as the incarnate Wisdom (as again in 23:34), and the 'yoke' is the yoke of instruction in the Law as it has been interpreted by him. But it is a question whether the teaching of Jesus, if we take it as a kind of Law, is any less of a burden than that imposed by the scribes through their tradition (23:4). As T.W. Manson remarked on this saying: 'easy and light are not the epithets that one would spontaneously apply to the teaching, particularly to its moral demands' (*Sayings*, p. 35; he argues for a different understanding of the purport of the teaching).

There are several indications in the New Testament that the Law was felt as an intolerable burden—a yoke which could hardly be borne. Peter, in remonstrating with those who sought to require Gentile converts to keep the Law of Moses, cries to them: 'Why do you make trial of God by putting a yoke upon the neck of the Gentiles which neither our fathers nor we have been able to bear?' (Acts 15:10). Paul himself, brought up under the strict discipline of Pharisaism, came to feel that in his own experience the Law, though holy and just and good, left him in captivity to an inward law which impelled him to sin, till he found in Christ deliverance 'from this body of death' (Rom.7:12,24f.). In the light of these passages, we may take the toilers to be those who strive earnestly to keep the Law, and the burdens will be the burdens which the scribal traditions impose as requirements of God. The thought, then, is not of physical toil and burdens of anxiety or grief, but of the unremitting struggles of Israelites of whom Paul testifies that 'they have a zeal of God, but it is not enlightened, for . . . seeking to establish their own righteousness, they did not submit to the righteousness of God' (Rom.10:2f.). In this sense, the saying may be taken as akin in essence to Paul's doctrine of justification by faith, without the works of the Law.

4 CONTROVERSY OVER SABBATH OBSERVANCE *12:1–21*

The controversy over sabbath observance falls into three parts: the dispute over plucking grain on the sabbath (vv.1–8); the dispute over healing on the sabbath (vv.9–14); and a citation of scripture which is applied to the activity of Jesus (vv.15–21).

The Dispute over Plucking Grain on the Sabbath 12:1–8

[1] At that time Jesus went through the grainfields on the sabbath. His disciples became hungry, and plucked heads of the grain and ate them. [2] When the Pharisees noticed this, they said to him, 'Look, your disciples are doing what it is forbidden to do on the sabbath. [3] But he said to them, 'Have you not read what David did, when he and those with him were hungry—[4] how he went into the house of God and ate the loaves consecrated to God, which it was not lawful for him and his companions to eat but only for the priests? [5] Or have you not read in the law that the priests in the temple violate the law on the sabbath without incurring guilt? [6] Let me tell you, something greater than the temple is here. [7] If you knew what the words mean, "I desire mercy and not sacrifice," you would not have condemned the guiltless. [8] For the Son of man is lord of the sabbath.'

The passage is drawn from Mark (2:23–28), where it is the fourth in a sequence of controversy stories (Mk.2:1–3:6) which Mark had probably found already collected in an earlier source. Mark has used the sequence as a foil to the picture of swift and spectacular success, or at least of popular reputation, which Jesus won in the first days of his ministry (Mk.1:21–45). Matthew has broken up the Markan sequence and rearranged it into two groups. The first three have been woven into the collection of miracle stories which follow the Sermon on the Mount (9:2–17); the first of them becomes the third in Matthew's second group of miracles stories, and the second and third are kept in the same sequence as a non-miraculous interlude. Matthew now brings the last two of the Markan collection into a controversy sequence of his own. Luke retains the Markan sequence in its unity (Lk.5:17–6:11), and places it immediately after the healing of the leper, as in Mark.

The controversy presupposes not only the law of the sabbath rest as laid down in the Ten Commandments, but also the body of regulations which had been developed by the scribes. The Mishnah recognizes that the written law was far less comprehensive than the traditional rules of application. 'The rules about the sabbath . . . are like mountains hanging on a hair, for Scripture is scanty and the rules many' (Tractate *Hagigah* I.8). The commandment forbids the Israelite to do any manner of work on the sabbath; the rules treated the plucking of a little grain as reaping, and rubbing them out in the hands as threshing, and thus brought the action of the disciples under the category of 'work', involving a violation of the commandment. Under other circumstances it was not against the law to pluck a little grain from another man's field in passing; the law actually enjoined that the harvesters should leave a little to be gleaned by the poor and the sojourner (Lev.19:9f.; Deut.24:19–22; cf. Ruth 2:1–16). The point at issue was whether the slightest gleaning might be done on the sabbath.

The situation described is an artificial framework devised by Mark (or by a predecessor) for the sayings of Jesus. There is no reason to doubt that there were frequent debates between Christian and non-Christian Jews over questions of sabbath observance as long as the relations with the synagogues were a matter of concern to Christians, and it is probable that the disputes began during the ministry of Jesus. Some occasion of debate over the sabbath may have provided the original occasion for the sayings, but the fact that it is the disciples who are criticized, not Jesus himself, indicates that this pericope was framed in the apostolic church after the death of Jesus (Bultmann, *HST*, p.16).

VERSE 1: 'at that time'—a characteristic formula of connection, with no chronological significance; Mark reads only 'on the sabbath'.

The remark about the hunger of the disciples is transferred by Matthew from the Markan phrase about David and his men (Mk.2:25).

The disciples appear on the scene for the first time since the delivery of the mission charge (chap. 10), with no indication of where they have been in the meanwhile.

VERSE 2: 'the Pharisees'—one might expect rather 'certain Pharisees': no specific group is meant. 'The Pharisees' are simply stock characters, introduced to voice Pharisaic criticism of what they regarded as Christian laxity in sabbath observance. If we were dealing with an actual occurrence, it would be strange that Pharisees should just happen to be taking a sabbath stroll in the neighbourhood at the time.

VERSE 3: The story of David's eating the sacred bread is told in 1 Sam.21:1–6. It is given by the priest only after David has assured him that 'the vessels of the young men are holy'—that is, they have not engaged in sexual intercourse in their flight, and are in a fit spiritual condition to eat the bread ordinarily reserved for the priests. Nothing is made of this condition in the pericope.

'The loaves consecrated to God'—literally, 'bread of the setting forth' ($\tau\hat{\eta}\varsigma$ $\pi\rho o\theta\acute{e}\sigma\epsilon\omega\varsigma$); these were the twelve loaves placed every sabbath on a golden table, along with frankincense, 'set in order before the Lord continually on behalf of the people of Israel' (Lev.24:5–9). In LXX they are usually called $\check{\alpha}\rho\tau o\iota$ $\tau o\hat{\upsilon}$ $\tau\rho o\sigma\acute{\omega}\pi o\upsilon$, or $\tau\hat{\eta}\varsigma$ $\pi\rho o\sigma\phi o\rho\hat{\alpha}\varsigma$, 'loaves of the Face' or 'of the offering', for the Hebrew *lehem hapanim*, 'bread of the Face'. Primitive notions of the danger in the holy survive in the notion that the dedicated bread might be eaten only by the priests; to touch anything holy with profane hands is to incur danger.

There is no clear connection between this incident and the question of the sabbath commandment. The grain eaten by the disciples was not consecrated food, and it is not said that David and his men came to Nob on a sabbath. In both cases it might be argued that there was a breach of the Law. Would Jesus then hold that since King David many centuries earlier broke one law, his disciples were free now to break another? How far could such a principle be carried? Or that anyone who is hungry is free to break any law? It is not suggested that in fact the plucking of a few ears of grain cannot reasonably be defined as 'work' in terms of the command to keep the sabbath holy.

Matthew has removed Mark's erroneous references to Abiathar as the high priest. In the old story, the priest of Nob was called

Ahimelech; Abiathar was his son, and after the slaughter of the priests of Nob he escaped and took refuge with David (1 Sam.22: 20–23).

VERSES 5–7—interpolated by Matthew into the Markan story. Jesus finds another justification for his disciples in the necessary violation of the command to do no work by the priests, who must perform duties in the temple every sabbath day, without incurring guilt; where he is present, there is 'something greater than the temple'. To crown the argument, a passage of scripture is cited, and turned against the carping criticism of the Pharisees.

Again, the connection of thought is very loose, and the argument has not much force. The plucking of grain is not seriously comparable with the duties of the priests in the temple. Is there any sense in which it can be said that in plucking grain as they walk through the fields the disciples are performing services which must be done on the sabbath? It seems to be granted that the action of the disciples is indeed a breach of the commandment, but it is argued that the breach is justified by the high service—greater than that of the temple—to which they are appointed in the company of Jesus. It is not suggested that their hunger is a sufficient defence.

The phrase 'greater than the temple' probably does not apply to Jesus but to the Kingdom which he proclaims, or (?) to the deeper interpretation of the law which he teaches (E. Schweizer, *The Good News according to Matthew*, p.278).

On true rabbinical principles, Matthew does not consider that a principle of casuistry has been established unless it can be supported by a passage of scripture. The passage cited by Matthew (Hos.6:6) is given in the rendering of LXX (A Q*, Rahlfs), which chooses the Greek word ἔλεος ('pity, mercy, compassion') to render the Hebrew ḥeṣed. This is an exceptionally rich word, but difficult to translate into another language, whether Greek or English; it is 'a characteristically Hebraic term for which we have no complete English equivalent' (Dodd, *The Bible and the Greeks*, p.59; and, see his discussion, pp.59–65). In the Hosea passage it is rendered 'loyalty' in *NEB*, and 'steadfast love' in *RSV*; it is basically the loving response to the love of God which belongs to the covenant relationship. All these senses are appropriate to the citation of the words here. The criticism made by the Pharisees marks a failure in love, shown in the lack of a merciful spirit.

The same utterance was used movingly by one of the great rabbis after the destruction of the temple. As a colleague was lamenting at the sight of the ruined edifice, crying, 'Woe unto us! that this, the

place where the iniquities of Israel were atoned for, is laid waste!'
Rabbi Johanan ben Zakkai answered him: 'My son, be not grieved;
we have another atonement as effective as this. And what is it? It is
acts of loving kindness, for it is said, "For I desire mercy and not
sacrifice" ' (Davies, *Setting*, p.306).

'Guiltless'—not because they have not violated a commandment
but because the breach was justified, in the light of the act of David
and the regular practice of the priests.

Jesus may well have quoted these words of Hosea on some
occasion, but they are not really relevant either here or in 9:13, and
it is not very profitable to conjecture the situation which may have
prompted him to use them (see the notes of McNeile on both
passages; cf. Manson, *Sayings*, pp.187f.).

The claim that Jesus (as Son of man, Messiah) is master of the
sabbath is not an argument to convince Pharisees, or anyone who is
not already prepared to grant that Jesus is the divine Lord (*Kyrios*,
master) of all. Within the context of a Jewish disputation about
sabbath observance it would carry no weight at all. This confirms our
previous observation that the whole pericope belongs to the
Christian-Jewish controversies of the first age of the church, not to
the lifetime of Jesus.

The Dispute over Healing on the Sabbath 12:9–14

⁹ Leaving that place, he went into one of their synagogues. ¹⁰ A man
with a withered hand was there, and they put the question to him:
'Is it lawful to heal on the sabbath?' wanting to find ground for
laying a charge against him. ¹¹ He said to them: 'Who among you, if
he has a sheep that falls into a pit on the sabbath, will not take hold
of it and lift it out? ¹² How much more is a human being worth than
a sheep! So it is lawful to do good on the sabbath.' ¹³ With that he
said to the man, 'Stretch out your hand.' ¹⁴ He stretched it out, and
it was restored, sound as the other.

¹⁴ The Pharisees went out and plotted together to destroy him.

The dispute here moves along quite different lines. The strict legalist
might feel himself bound not to pluck grain on the sabbath, but it is
taken for granted that no one—not even the most scrupulous
Pharisee, would leave a sheep in a pit until the sabbath was over. It is
assumed also that the critics of Jesus will agree that a human being is
worth far more than a sheep. How then can it be wrong to help a

person out of his trouble on the sabbath, if you would not hesitate to help a mere sheep?

It appears that the scribes would not have granted the force of the argument. They would have held that unless the man's life was in danger, he could perfectly well wait a day until the sabbath was over. This is the attitude of the ruler of the synagogue in a Lukan story of how Jesus healed a crippled woman on the sabbath. This ruler said to the people, 'There are six days on which work ought to be done; come on those days and be healed, and not on the sabbath day' (Lk.13:14). (There too Jesus appeals to the common care for animals —every one of them will lead an ox or an ass to water on the sabbath day; what justification is there for delaying help to a human being?) The rabbis of a later date were still divided over the question of what it was permissible to do on the sabbath for an animal in a pit; some held that food might be brought to it and some that mats and cushions could be let down to it, so that it could get out by its own efforts. It is hard for us to look with any sympathy on this kind of discussion.

Matthew, according to his custom, has drastically abbreviated the Markan story (Mk.3:1—6). He has omitted the statement that Jesus 'said to the man who had the withered hand, "Come here"' (v.3). More surprisingly, he has cut the challenging words: 'Is it lawful on the sabbath to do good or to do harm, to save life or to kill' (v.4), and with them the note that 'they were silent', and that 'Jesus looked around at them with anger, grieved at their hardness of heart' (vv.4f.). He also omits Mark's mention of 'the Herodians' as allied with the Pharisees in the plot to bring about the death of Jesus. On the other hand, the question of Jesus about the sheep in the pit is a Matthaean addition to Mark; this saying has a parallel in Luke, but it is brought into another story, clearly a doublet of this one (Lk.14: 1—6).

VERSE 14: The growing hostility of the Pharisees is brought to a new pitch by the freedom with which he approaches the question of sabbath observance. They form a plot to bring him to his death. This may seem like an exaggerated reaction to a trifling difference of opinion. But sabbath observance was no trifle to the Jews, and in any case this was no more than the last straw; the Pharisees had already found more weighty reasons for their hatred. They now began to realize that the basic Pharisaic conception of true religion was at stake. The Gospel of John also connects the sabbath question with the murderous hostility to Jesus, but sets with it a more serious offence. 'This was why the Jews sought all the more to kill him, because he not only kept breaking the sabbath [by healings], but also called God his own Father, making himself equal with God' (Jn. 5:18).

But sabbatarianism has shown itself capable of strange fanaticism in Christian circles also.

INTERLUDE: JESUS AS 'THE SERVANT' OF PROPHETIC EXPECTATION *12:15–21*

[15] Knowing of this plot, Jesus withdrew from that locality. Crowds followed him in great numbers, and he healed them all; [16] he charged them sternly not to make him known, [17] in order that the word spoken through the prophet Isaiah might be fulfilled:

[18] Behold! here is my servant whom I have chosen,
>   my beloved, in whom I am well pleased.
> I will put my Spirit upon him,
>   and he will proclaim justice to the nations.
> [19] He will not wrangle nor shout,
>   and none will hear his voice raised in the streets.
> [20] The crushed reed he will not break,
>   and the smouldering wick he will not snuff out,
>   till he brings justice forth to victory.
> [21] The nations will set their hopes on his name.

Mark has followed his sequence of controversy stories with a generalizing summary of the activities and practices of Jesus (Mk.3: 7–12). In Matthew the summary is used again to follow the fifth and last story of the Markan sequence, but it is greatly reduced, and serves now chiefly to provide a narrative introduction for an oracle of Isaiah, which seems to him to have described the character and attitudes of Jesus beforehand.

VERSE 15: 'He healed them all'—an exaggeration of Mark's 'he healed many'. (Does Matthew intend to suggest that all in the crowds that followed Jesus were sick?)

VERSE 16: The injunction to silence is in Mark laid not upon the sick, but upon the demons who have been expelled. It rests upon his well-known theory of the 'Messianic secret' that Jesus walked the world incognito, but was recognized by the demons, who are presumed to have supernatural insight. Traces of the theory are seen here and there in Matthew, but as a half-unconscious inheritance from Mark. He is more concerned to bring out the notion that the prohibition was evidence that Jesus—unlike the general run of thaumaturges—sought no publicity, but avoided it; and that this was in accordance with Messianic prophecy.

VERSES 17–21: The oracle is cited by Matthew in a form which differs from the Hebrew, but also from the text of the LXX and the freer Aramaic of the Targum. In the course of a thorough analysis, K. Stendahl finds a 'unique interweaving of traditions of interpretation supported on different sides,' along with certain 'completely original readings. . . . It can only have a satisfactory understanding as a targumized text which is the fruit of reflexion and acquaintance with the interpretation of the Scriptures' (*School*, p.115). The Septuagint identifies the 'servant' specifically with 'Jacob', and the 'beloved' (LXX, 'elect') with Israel. Matthew clearly identifies him with Jesus.

It may be observed that the servant concept is applied to Jesus, but not in a context of suffering. Matthew seems to think primarily of the emphasis on the quietness of the servant as reflected in Jesus' withdrawal from the scene of disputation, and of the care for the weak—the 'crushed reed' and the 'smouldering wick'. The note of justice and hope for the nations (Gentiles), not for Israel alone, goes beyond the immediate context and anticipates the destined extension of the gospel in later days (cf. Mt.24:14 and esp. 28:19f.).

5   THE DISPUTE OVER THE SOURCE OF JESUS' POWERS *12:22–37*

22 A man blind and dumb was brought to him—possessed by a demon; Jesus healed him, so that the dumb man spoke and could see. 23 The crowds were all astounded, and they began to say, 'Can this be the son of David?' 24 But the Pharisees overheard this, and they said, 'This fellow casts out demons only by the help of Beelzebul, the prince of demons.' 25 Knowing what was in their minds, he said to them, 'Every kingdom divided against itself is ruined, and any city or house that is divided against itself will break down. 26 If Satan is casting out Satan, he is divided against himself. How then will his kingdom stand? 27 And if I am casting out the demons by the help of Beelzebul, who is aiding your own people to cast them out? For that, they themselves will be your judges! 28 But if it is by the aid of the Spirit of God that I am casting out the demons, then clearly the kingdom of God has already come upon you. 29 How can anyone get into the house of the strong man and take his goods as plunder, unless he first has tied up the strong man? Only then will he plunder his house.

³⁰ Anyone who is not with me is against me, and anyone who does not gather with me scatters.

³¹ And now let me tell you this: Every sin or blasphemy will be forgiven, but blasphemy against the Spirit will not be forgiven. ³² Whoever says a word against the Son of man will be forgiven, but whoever speaks against the Holy Spirit will never be forgiven, either in this age or in the age to come.

³³ You must grow a good tree if you would have good fruit; if the tree you grow is bad, its fruit will be bad. The tree is known by its fruit. ³⁴ You spawn of vipers! How can you speak good words when you are evil? For the mouth speaks only what overflows from the heart. ³⁵ The good man from his good treasure brings out good utterances, and the bad man out of his bad treasure brings out bad utterances. ³⁶ Let me tell you, you will be called to a reckoning on the day of judgement for every idle word you speak; ³⁷ by your words you will be justified, and by your words you will be condemned.'

We have here again a sequence created by Matthew out of a number of sayings which the tradition, and his sources, had transmitted in scattered fashion. He has framed for them a more or less artificial introduction (vv.22—24). A miracle of healing, viewed as an exorcism, provokes a double reaction. On the part of the crowds, it makes them wonder if Jesus may be the Messiah ('the Son of David'); on the part of the Pharisees, it brings the accusation that this power to cast out demons is given to Jesus by the ruler of the kingdom of demons. Jesus has left the scene of his former encounters with the Pharisees (v.15), but they still dog his footsteps. Both they and the crowds are necessary elements in the stage setting for the group of sayings. Though the speculation that he may be the Messiah is not itself developed, it is the immediate occasion of the Pharisaic attack —the powers which astound the crowds are not Messianic, conferred by God, but demonic. This exorcist is nothing but an instrument of the arch-demon.

The introductory story (vv.22—24), not found in Mark, is a doublet of the last miracle story of chapter 9 (vv.32—34), where the restoration of speech to a dumb demoniac is followed by the double reaction of the amazement of the crowds and the hostile criticism of the Pharisees. In Mark the accusation of demon possession is preceded by a story of an attempt of his family to take charge of him, fearing that he is out of his mind (Mk.3:21—ἐξέστη; equivalent to saying that he is possessed by a demon).

The Matthaean discourse on demon possession is constructed by him as an expansion of a brief group of sayings of Jesus in Mark, in which he rebuts a charge brought by 'scribes who came down from Jerusalem' (Mk.3:22). With these Markan sentences, Matthew combines other sayings on the same theme which are drawn from Q (vv. 27f.,30 / / Lk.11:19f.,23). This is followed by further sayings of different origins which were not originally related to the theme of demon possession at all (vv.33–36). Some of them are used by Luke in his version of the great Sermon (Lk.6:43–45), and paralleled in a different wording by Matthew in his Sermon on the Mount (7:16–20); in totally different contexts. Verse 34 echoes the violent language attribute to John the Baptist (3:7). The final three verses are peculiar to Matthew (v.35–37).

Both story and discourse belong to a universe of thought which is so totally foreign to us as to be all but unintelligible. They reflect the notion, accepted by the crowd and the Pharisees and presumably also by Jesus, that blindness and dumbness are caused by demon possession. In Luke's version, it is the demon who is said to be dumb (blindness is not mentioned—Lk.11:14). For those who do not attribute blindness and dumbness to demon possession, but to physical deficiencies, the whole discussion, so far as it concerns the action of demons and the powers of a 'prince of demons', lacks any basis in reality. It was, of course, vital in terms of the notions of the time.

VERSE 22: The miracle of healing is told with unusual brevity, as is its parallel in 9:33f. The interest of the evangelist is not in the miracle as such, but in the reactions of the crowds and the Pharisees.

VERSE 23: The question is cast in a form which expects the answer, 'no'. Possibly the pronoun 'this' ($o\tilde{v}\tau o\varsigma$) is used with a certain degree of contempt. 'Can this fellow be the Messiah?'—he corresponds so little to what is expected of our Messiah. But 'the crowds' in Matthew are usually friendly, and it is more likely that the word is neutral in the question of the crowd, and is taken up with the note of contempt in the accusation of the Pharisees.

'Son of David' is a favourite term of Matthew. He uses it eight times as a title of Jesus, against only two occurrences each in Mark and Luke, and none at all in the rest of the New Testament. John, however, mentions divergent views of Jesus among the people of Jerusalem, some of them holding that he is the Messiah, others objecting that he does not fit the description given in the scriptures (Jn.7:40–44; cf.vv.12, 25–27).

VERSE 24: The 'Prince ($\dot{\alpha}\rho\chi\dot{\omega}\nu$) of the demons' is given many names in the Judaism of the period. The commonest is perhaps 'Satan', but we also find 'Beliar', or 'Belial', 'Asmodeus', and others. Διάβολος, 'devil', is cognate with the verb διαβάλλω, 'accuse', and is a Greek translation of the Hebrew *satan*, which means generally 'the opponent' or 'obstructor'—not of God, but of human beings. In Job, for instance, 'the satan' comes before God questioning Job's integrity, and it is by God's permission that he brings disaster upon the godly man. Nowhere in the Old Testament is he conceived as a spiritual power standing at the head of a realm of darkness with hosts of demons as his agents. This later view, which is that of the New Testament writers generally, developed in and after the Persian period (from the late fifth century BC), when the powerful counter-deity of Zoroastrianism, Angra Mainyu, was introduced into Hebrew thought by way of a new understanding of the originally unimportant denizen of the court of Yahweh, the satan.

Beelzebul—the name is spelled in different ways in the manuscripts. In the great fourth-century codices Aleph and B, it is given as βεεζεβουλ, and this was printed in the text by Westcott and Hort, and again in the BFBS edition of 1956, but nearly all modern editors prefer βεελζεβουλ. The familiar Beelzebub (*AV*, etc.) is taken over from the latin Vulgate; it is also supported by the Syriac Peshitta and Curetonian; but is not read by any Greek witnesses. In that form it appears to be adapted to an Aramaic form of the Hebrew Baal-zebub, the god of Ekron (mentioned in 2 Ki.1:2f., 6,16) which would mean literally 'Lord of flies'. This form is usually taken to be a corruption of Baal-zebul, 'Lord of the House'; and the spelling used in our text would represent a transliteration of the Aramaic form of this title. The god of Ekron is the only baal mentioned in the Old Testament who is given an epithet like this; the baals generally were distinguished only by a toponymic (Baal of Bosrah, Baal of Tyre, etc.), though the name Hadad occurs (in inscriptions) for some of the great baals of Syria. It is strange that this one title of a local baal should have survived in popular usage among the Jews, and given to the 'prince of demons'.

VERSES 25–26: In Mark, Jesus begins his rebuttal by the question, 'How can Satan cast out Satan?' which answers his critics by a *reductio ad absurdum*.

VERSES 27–28: This passage, found also in Luke, but not in Mark, actually destroys the argument. If the validity of Jewish exorcisms is recognized, there would be no reason for excitement over the exorcisms of Jesus. It is assumed that exorcisms are regularly practised by people whom the Pharisees themselves recognized as faithful Jews ('your own people'—literally, 'your sons'). In fact, Jewish exorcists were well known, not only in Palestine but in the Diaspora (cf. Acts 19:13ff.), and apparently some of them even ventured to invoke the name of Jesus against the demons (Mk.9:38–40; Lk.9:49–50).

But if the work of Jewish exorcists is valid, and gives rise neither to conjectures that the exorcist is the Messiah nor to the accusation that he is an agent empowered by the prince of demons, why should the exorcisms of Jesus lead to either conclusion about him? On the other hand, if his exorcisms are worked 'by the Spirit of God', and this is an indication that the kingdom of God has already arrived in power, why should not the successful exorcisms of other Jewish exorcists be equally good evidence of the arrival of the Kingdom? In sum, the argument of these verses is wholly lacking in logic.

For Matthew's 'by the Spirit of God', Luke has the phrase 'by the finger of God' (Lk.11:20). This is a reminiscence of the comment of the magicians of Egypt on the miracles of Aaron (Ex.8:19). The unusual 'finger of God' may be the earlier, and altered by Matthew to give it a definitely Christian tinge.

Much has been made of the use of the Greek verb $\phi\theta\alpha\nu\omega$ here (in the aorist $\epsilon\phi\theta\alpha\sigma\epsilon\nu$). This verb properly means to 'anticipate', or 'to be beforehand' (in this sense it is usually completed by a participle). It has sometimes been suggested that its use here carries the suggestion that the Kingdom is already present, before the conditions of its realization are established; it is not merely 'at hand' ($\eta\gamma\gamma\iota\kappa\epsilon\nu$) as in the proclamation of John the Baptist (3:2), taken up by Jesus (4:17), and committed to the Twelve (10:7), but actively manifesting its powers in anticipation of 'the age to come'. This probably imports a nuance of classical usage into the vocabulary of a period which had lost its feeling for such things. In later Greek, $\phi\theta\alpha\nu\omega$ means simply 'arrive', with no touch of arriving beforehand, or anticipation.

VERSE 29: Satan is now pictured as a 'strong man' (in Luke, he is 'fully armed' and 'guards his palace' and the 'stronger one' (Jesus) 'strips him of the armour in which he trusted'—Lk.11:21f.). A strange figure; it implies that Jesus has already worsted Satan in a conflict (supramundane, or is there a reference to the Temptation story?), and therefore can act as he will in Satan's domain ('plunder his house'). The 'house' probably means rather his 'household'—his whole army of demons. (The Greek $o\iota\kappa\iota\alpha$ has the double meaning of 'house' and 'household'.)

This saying also is out of tune with the appeal to the exorcisms operated by the recognized Jewish exorcists; it is not suggested that *they* have broken the power of 'the strong man' before driving out his subordinate demons!

VERSE 30: A vagrant saying, which had become attached to the saying about the 'strong man' in the earlier tradition (cf. Lk.11:23). The metaphor of 'gather' and 'scatter' might refer to sheep without a shepherd, the sheep are scattered (cf. 9:36); the mission of Jesus is to 'gather into one the children of God that are scattered abroad' (Jn.11:52). Those who rally to his cause help in his work of gathering; those who oppose him promote the scattering of God's people, the work of the devil. The preceding verses speak of the conflict in terms of a duel between the strong Satan and the stronger Christ; this verse shifts to the thought of a general continuing struggle in which there is no neutrality. Every human being is faced with the decision to act with Christ, or to oppose him.

VERSES 31–32: Matthew has recast the Markan passage (Mk.3: 28–30), omitting the closing phrases (vv.29b–30), and probably altering the wording of the remainder under the influence of a parallel in Q (cf. Lk.12:10). The more or less technical term 'blasphemy' should perhaps be avoided; the Greek βλασφημέω, βλασφημία has the more general sense of 'speak injuriously, slander, abuse', but where the object of abuse is divine, as here ('the Holy Spirit'), it comes close to blasphemy in its usual connotation.

The 'unforgivable sin'—often misunderstood, and because of the misunderstanding a weight on many consciences, is nothing else than the attribution to the devil and his agents of good deeds accomplished through the power of the Spirit of God. It is the ultimate form of spiritual perversity such as is denounced by the prophet Isaiah:

> Woe to those who call evil good and good evil,
>> who put darkness for light
>>> and light for darkness,
>> who put bitter for sweet
>>> and sweet for bitter! (Isa.5:20)

VERSES 33–37: The attack on the Pharisees continues in vv.33–37, but again it is Matthew who has woven the sayings into this context. The connection is scarcely more than verbal. It is suggested by the slanderous *word* which is now declared to be the inevitable issue of an evil heart. T.W. Manson remarks that 'the statement of v.36 is now a commonplace of psychology. The whole technique of psychoanalysis is built upon the principle that the "idle" word reveals character more truly and completely than the deliberate, considered statement' (*Sayings*, p.191). But the accusation made by the Pharisees is hardly an 'idle word'. The saying belongs to a broader field than the dispute over the source of Jesus' powers.

6 THE DEMAND FOR A SIGN *12:38–42*

[38] Some of the scribes and Pharisees replied to his rebuke with the challenge: 'Teacher, we want to see a sign from you.' [39] He responded, 'An evil and adulterous generation demands a sign; no sign will be given to it but the sign of the prophet Jonah. [40] For as Jonah was in the belly of the whale for three days and three nights, so will the Son of man be in the bowels of the earth for three days and three nights.

[41] The men of Nineveh will rise up with this generation at the Judgement, and will condemn it; for they repented at the preaching of Jonah, and mark you, something greater than Jonah is here. [42] The Queen of the South will be raised up at the Judgement with this generation and will condemn it; for she came from the ends of the earth to hear Solomon in his wisdom, and mark you, something greater than Solomon is here.'

This passage is probably not to be taken as based upon the parallel Markan section (Mk.8:11f.), which is much briefer and differs in almost every word; moreover, Matthew includes a parallel to the Markan section in another context (16:1–4; see below), and this would itself indicate that he had two versions of the dispute before him and used them both. The version given here is paralleled in Luke 11:[16],29–32, but Luke places it in the context of the Markan version and in fact conflates the two. The Q version, which we have here, looks like a compilation which began with something like the Markan version and elaborated it. In Mark, Jesus says bluntly: 'Why does this generation want a sign? No sign will be given to this generation' (8:12). The phrase 'but the sign of the prophet Jonah' is the primary addition (which really weakens the force of the flat denial of any sign whatsoever), and the editor has then felt obliged to offer a supplemental explanation of what 'the sign of Jonah' might mean. In Luke (and probably in the common source), this takes the relatively simple form, 'As Jonah was a sign to the Ninevites, so will the Son of man be [a sign] to this generation' (Lk.11:30). We may then attribute to Matthew the elaboration of v.40, making the experience of Jonah a symbol of the death and resurrection of Jesus; it is not related to the words about the appearance of the men of Nineveh at the Judgement, any more than to the appearance of the Queen of the South. We might even venture to suggest that the two examples (the Ninevites and the Queen) came into being as a double structure, independent of the refusal of a sign; cf. the similar double construction with reference to the Judgement in the condemnation of the cities of Galilee (Mt.11:22,24).

VERSE 38: The introduction is framed by Matthew. In Luke, the questioners are vaguely described as 'others'. The Pharisees are taken from the Markan version, and Matthew brings in the scribes of his own motion.

'A sign' ($\sigma\eta\mu\epsilon\hat{\iota}o\nu$) is regularly used in the Fourth Gospel to signify 'miracle', which in the Synoptics is usually called $\delta\acute{\upsilon}\nu\alpha\mu\iota\varsigma$, 'a mighty work'. Paul also tells us that 'Jews ask for signs' (1 Cor.1:22). What kind of 'sign' they had in mind is not clear, in either case. In the Pauline context, it is related to 'the word of the cross', the preaching of 'Christ crucified', which is a 'stumbling-block' to Jews as something totally at variance with what was expected of the Messiah. Here the offence of the cross does not enter into the matter, but it is still the claim that Jesus is the Messiah that is at issue. The 'sign' demanded is something spectacular, and inexplicable as a natural phenomenon. Since Jesus did not make Messianic claims for himself, the demand for a 'sign' to prove them can have been made only in the controversies between Christians and Jews in the apostolic age. Luke calls it 'a sign from heaven'.

The kind of 'sign' would be something akin to the three signs which Moses was to perform before the people of Israel to convince them that he was God's authorized spokesman (Ex.4:7–10).

VERSE 39: 'Adulterous'—not in the sense that is normally given to adultery, but in the figurative sense that derives from the Old Testament, equating unfaithfulness to God with marital infidelity. God is the 'husband' of Israel, and when she goes astray after other gods, she becomes an 'adulteress' (Hos.2:2–13; Ezek.16:15–34; 23:1–21, etc.). The scribes and Pharisees could not be accused of worshipping other gods; the term 'adulterous' here means more generally 'disloyal'.

VERSE 40: There is no way of reckoning the period between the crucifixion of Jesus and the resurrection appearances as continuing for three days and three nights. All our accounts set the crucifixion on a Friday and the first resurrection appearances on the Sunday. As in the phrase 'after three days' (which is another way of saying 'on the third day'), it is possible to speak of three days, but not of three nights. The 'three days and three nights' is a direct transfer of the phrase in the Jonah story (Jonah 1:17) in disregard for the Christian tradition.

'Whale'—Matthew adopts the word of the Septuagint; the Hebrew text speaks of 'a great fish'.

7 THE RETURN OF THE DEMON *12:43–45*

[43] When an unclean spirit goes out from a person, it roams through waterless regions looking for a place to rest without finding it. [44] Then it says, 'I shall return to the house from which I came out'; and when it comes, it finds the house unoccupied, swept, and made tidy. [45] With that, it goes off and fetches seven other spirits more wicked than itself and they go in and settle there, and the last state of that person is worse than ever. So shall it be with this wicked generation.

The passage has no parallel in Mark. It is given by Luke in almost the same words, but without the last sentence (11:24–26). In Luke, it follows upon the saying, 'Anyone who is not with me is against me', etc. (Lk.11:23 // Mt.12:30). Its placing in Matthew is occasioned by the recurrence of words ('evil generation', v.39) and its relation to the general theme of exorcism (from v.22). But it is hard to say what its point is, or was in the tradition. It is not particularly appropriate here. Basically, it would suggest that often enough exorcisms had no more than a temporary effect, and this may well have been the common observation. In the stories of exorcisms, there is seldom any indication of the future behaviour of the sufferer—perhaps only in the case of the demoniac of Gerasa (Mk.5:18–20 // Lk.8:38f.), and this touch is omitted in Matthew.

But does the story intend to speak of an exorcism which has a passing success? It is taken for granted by all interpreters that the demon 'goes out' only because he is *driven* out by an exorcist. But the verb itself does not ordinarily convey any notion of action under compulsion. The sketch speaks of a demon, but not of an exorcist; and as it stands, it could suggest that the demon acts on a mere whim in leaving his victim for a time to spend a while in the natural habitat of demons—the waterless desert. It is undoubtedly of his own motion that he returns and brings a company with him.

But even taking it as implying that he makes his exit under compulsion, there is no hint of how his human habitation has been 'swept and garnished', like a house made ready for a new occupant. The word 'unoccupied', or 'vacant' (σχολάζοντα), is a Matthaean addition, and perhaps indicates that he wishes to give a warning that there must be a *positive* response to the action of Jesus. Once the house is vacated by the unclean spirit, a welcome must be offered to the divine Spirit to take up his dwelling there; or more broadly, a response of repentance is futile if it is not accompanied by amendment of life. But the closing sentence, which is also a Matthaean addition, suggests that he applies the story as a parable to the spiritual fate of Israel. The ephemeral response of the people to the preaching of Jesus, now showing signs of turning to indifference and even hostility, issues in a worsening of their condition. The demons that have been overcome and cast out by the power of Jesus will return with greater force than ever. This line of interpretation, it must be confessed, is more than a little forced. The most natural interpretation would see in the story a scoffing comment on the efficacy of exorcisms by one who had observed how often the demoniac suffered a relapse and was more disturbed in mind than ever.

8   JESUS REPUDIATES HIS FAMILY *12:46–50*

[46] While he was still speaking to the crowds, his mother and his brothers came and stood outside, wanting to speak to him. [48] Jesus responded to the man who told him about them by saying, 'Who is my mother? Who are my brothers?' [49] And stretching out his hand towards his disciples, he said, 'Here are my mother and my brothers. [50] For whoever does the will of my Father in heaven is my brother and my sister and my mother.'

Some good manuscripts, with support from the Latin versions, include as verse 47 (so *AV*) the sentence: [47] Some one told him, 'Your mother and your brothers are standing outside, wanting to speak to you.'

Despite good attestation, it is probable that this reading is a gloss, introduced by assimilation to the parallels in Mark and Luke. It is not found in the great codices Aleph and B, and is not represented in the older Syriac versions or in the Sahidic. It is Matthew's habit to cut away repetitive phrases such as this.

VERSE 46: 'While he was still speaking to the crowds'—an introduction framed by Matthew, making an artificial connection with the discourse which precedes. It creates a certain incoherence; if Jesus is still addressing crowds, it must be in the open air; but if his family are standing 'outside', this would imply that he was in a house.

Joseph does not appear along with the mother of Jesus and his brothers; he is in fact never mentioned after the infancy narratives, and it is assumed that he died before Jesus began his public ministry. His brothers and sisters are still living with their mother in Nazareth (Mk.6:3—four brothers are named; / / Mt.13:55). In the Gospel of John, it is said that 'his brothers did not believe in him' (Jn.7:3–5). The oldest brother, James, is listed among the first witnesses to the resurrection (1 Cor.15:7), and he became the leader of the church in Jerusalem not long afterwards, and remained its head until his death (Acts 15:13ff.; 21:18; Josephus and Hegesippus tell of his death in the sixties).

This pericope reflects a tradition that the immediate family of Jesus, including even his mother, had no sympathy with his mission. In Mark we are even told that at one point they were ready to put him under restraint, supposing him to be out of his mind (Mk.3:21; omitted by Matthew and Luke). In an earlier source, this Markan pericope may have been the prelude to this scene of repudiation of the ties of family. For Matthew, the emphasis is not so much on the disavowal of the family as on the privilege of an acknowledged relationship with Jesus which is now extended to his disciples, to all who do the will of his Father in heaven.

VERSE 49: 'The disciples' again represent the Christian believers of Matthew's time (and of all time) as well as the immediate followers of Jesus. The words are introduced by Matthew in place of Mark's 'those who were seated around him' (Mk.3:34).

VERSE 50: It is striking to find that Jesus introduces 'my sister' here, although the story mentions only his mother and brothers. Such a recognition of the equal place of women in the community is not part of the inheritance from Judaism, nor does it become a feature of early Christianity in general. Women are indeed described as 'co-heirs of the grace of life' (1 Pet.3:7), and Paul can speak of certain women who have been valued fellow-workers in the gospel (Phil.4:3); but it cannot be claimed that the church made any significant advance over Judaism in the matter of the status of women. Paul, for all his openness, seems to think that there is a prescriptive obligation on Christian women to accept the subordinate role which was established for them in the synagogue (1 Cor.14:34–36).[1]

---

[1] On the Corinthians passage, see the remarks of Jean Héring in his commentary (*CNT* VII, p.130): 'It goes without saying that the reason for imposing this

II THE THIRD MAJOR DISCOURSE: A COLLECTION
OF PARABLES
Mt.13:1–52

The parables of this chapter are not shaped into a sustained discourse, like the Sermon on the Mount and the Mission Charge. There are changes of scene and of auditors. At the beginning, the scene is laid on the lakeshore, with Jesus seated in the prow of a fishing vessel, and 'great crowds' standing on the beach. Jesus is approached by his disciples, and to them alone he gives the key to the meaning of the parable (the Sower). He seems to remain on the boat, and the crowds are still there when he resumes teaching with three more parables. But with that there is an explicit change of scene: Jesus 'went into the house, and his disciples came to him' (v.36), and the remainder of the discourse is given in the house.

After an introductory section on the structure of the collection, the discussion of the parables is arranged as follows:

(partial) silence on the woman must be sought uniquely in the concern not to violate the rules of good behaviour generally accepted at the time. We are moving, then, in the realm of the relative, as Calvin clearly perceived. In our contemporary civilization, where women, in enjoyment of all rights, do not shock anybody by taking the floor to speak in public, we are permitted to suppose that the restriction envisaged by the apostle has no longer any reason to be maintained.'

Mark has supplied Matthew with only two of his seven parables (the Sower and the Mustard Seed); of the five others, the parable of the Leaven is given also by Luke, coupled with that of the Mustard Seed but in a different context; and the remaining four are peculiar to Matthew. Two of these are provided with allegorical interpretations, which are almost certainly composed by Matthew himself. In Luke, the scene by the lakeshore is not indicated, and the entire sequence is reduced to the one parable of the Sower (with its allegorical interpretation (as in Mark); Jesus is surrounded by 'a great crowd', but he delivers the parable in the course of a tour 'through cities and villages', presumably somewhere in Galilee (Lk.8:1–15).

In Matthew, the collection of parables is spoken against the background of doubts and criticisms which have been gathering head since Jesus sent out the Twelve to share his mission. The disciples are now seen as a privileged group, who have been granted insights to which the nation as a whole is blind. They are the 'babes' who are open to the divine revelation which remains 'hidden . . . from wise and prudent people' (11:25); and to them it is given 'to know the secrets of the kingdom of heaven' (13:11). In part, the parables are given to assure them that, even though much labour seems to be wasted, there will be an abundant harvest. The mustard seed will grow to a great shrub; the leaven will make its power felt through the whole mass of dough. There will be those who become aware of the treasure that is there for the taking, who can appreciate at its true value the pearl of the highest worth, and will give up all that is dear to them to win the great prize.

But even more insistently, the parables sound the note of warning. The community which is forming about Jesus—the church that is to be—will not be wholly good, without alloy of evil. There will be weeds among the wheat, and they may not be rooted out until the time of harvest, the end of the age. All kinds of fish will be taken up in the net, both good and bad, and the separation will be made on the day of judgement. There is a mingling of motives, but it is evident that the pastoral anxiety of Matthew leads him to lay stress chiefly on the dreadful day of judgement that the members of the church must face, for all their privilege. Membership of the church is no more an assurance of entrance into the kingdom of heaven than was descent from Abraham; it remains true for the church as for Israel, that 'every tree that does not bear good fruit is cut down and thrown into the fire' (3:10b; cf. 13:41f.,49f.). Even the counsel of patience, the charge to judge nothing before the time (13:30), is passed over in the detailed allegorical interpretation of the parable of the Tares, in order that attention may be riveted on the certainty of the judgement, when 'the Son of man will send his angels, and they will gather out of his kingdom all causes of sin and all evil-doers, and will throw them into the furnace of fire' (13:41; cf. v.49).

Like all the other elements of the tradition concerning Jesus, the parables passed through a relatively long period of oral transmission before finding the form in which they have come down to us in the written Gospels. During that period they were adapted in various ways to serve the needs of the churches, whether in preaching to the unconverted, or in controversy with opponents, or in the instruction of converts. They were handled with considerable freedom by individual teachers and preachers, as they came to be used in circumstances quite different from those of the ministry of Jesus, and in the context of new problems which arose in the course of the mission. In general, the bearers of the tradition were not greatly concerned to preserve the immediate historical setting in which these words of Jesus were first spoken, or even to take note of the kind of audience which first listened to them. The setting in which we find them in our Gospels—often enough varying from one Gospel to another—cannot be taken to give a reliable indication of the situation in the life of Jesus which gave him occasion to frame them in the first place, and it is seldom (if ever) possible to recover with any degree of sureness the nature of that situation. It is generally recognized that in many cases the evangelist, or the tradition before him, has taken parables (and other types of sayings of Jesus) which were originally spoken to opponents, and reported them as given to the disciples of Jesus. Or again, as the church came to think of the promised coming of the kingdom of God in terms of a return of Jesus in heavenly glory, the understanding of many parables which were intended to awaken the hearers to the urgency of repentance were shaped to encourage vigilance in the members of the Christian churches. Many other factors have entered into the transforming of the parables in their use by the churches (Jeremias lists ten 'principles of transformation', *Parables*, p.23). And over and above all the variety of particular influences, we have to take account of the fact that the parables, like the tradition as a whole, have been transposed from reports of what Jesus once said on earth to Galileans and Judaeans, to opponents and to disciples, to crowds and to guests at dinner parties, into words which Jesus the risen Lord speaks to the Christian readers of the Gospels to meet the needs of the churches in the contemporary situation.

It may be taken for granted that each evangelist attached some meaning to every parable for which he found a place in his Gospel, but we cannot assume that this was the meaning which Jesus intended when he gave it to other hearers in an earlier generation and under circumstances and conditions which no longer faced the Gospel writer. Nor can we suppose that the evangelist is concerned to retain the emphasis which the parable had received at some intermediate point of the tradition, in the handling of some unknown teacher or preacher at some equally unknown place. The form of a parable, as of any other unit of the tradition, may indeed reflect traces of the use made of it at an earlier stage, but we have as little hope of reconstructing such later circumstances of its transmission as of determining with any assurance the particular context in which it was spoken by Jesus and the point of teaching which he was seeking to clarify. What we do have at our disposal is the finished work of the evangelist, and from that we may hope to discover what the parable meant to him. In the exercise of his literary freedom (and his theological responsibility) he has given each parable a particular place in the structure of his Gospel. The meaning which he attaches to it will be indicated in large degree by the context in which he has placed it, by his account of the events which precede and follow it, and sometimes by phrases of introduction or of conclusion which he has included. Our primary task, accordingly, is to seek first for the meaning of the parable in the mind of the evangelist, and to see it in relation to the whole fabric of his Gospel. We renounce, at least for the time being, any attempt to form conjectures about what it may possibly have meant when it was first spoken, or what sense may have been given to it in some quarter of the so-called 'primitive' church.

1   THE PARABLE OF THE SOWER AND ITS INTERPRETATION *13:1–23*

The Parable Proper 13:1–9

[1] On that day Jesus went out of the house and sat down by the lake. [2] Great crowds gathered about him, so he went aboard a fishing vessel and sat in the prow, and the whole crowd stood along the shore. [3] He now said many things to them in parables, beginning with the words: 'A man went out to sow. [4] In the sowing, some grains fell on the pathway and the birds came and ate them up. [5] Some fell on rocky ground where there was not much soil. It came up quickly, just because the soil was so shallow, [6] but when the sun rose high the shoots were scorched, and as they had put down no roots they withered away. [7] Other grains fell among the thorns, and the thorns

grew up and choked them. ⁸ But some fell on the good soil and produced a crop, a hundred, or sixty, or thirty times what was sown. ⁹ If you have ears, hear this.'

VERSES 1–2: The picture is taken over from Mark 4:1f. Mark had told his readers how Jesus had made preparations for such use of a boat well in advance (Mk.3:9; not included in Matthew). However, the local setting has no bearing upon the understanding of the parable, and Luke sees no need to retain it (Lk.8:4). 'On that day'— not a precise chronological indication, but merely a stock Matthaean phrase of introduction. Mark does not suggest that the parable was spoken on the same day as the visit of Jesus' mother and brothers, and in Luke the two pericopes are widely separated.

'He went out of the house'—another Matthaean touch; Mark makes no mention of a house, and in Luke the parable is spoken in the course of a journey back and forth through city and village (8:1). Probably Matthew is thinking of the house in Capernaum where Jesus has settled, where he can go in and out as he wishes; in verse 36, he goes into the house. There has been no mention of this house since the end of chapter 9 (v.28). The activities of the last three chapters have been set in an itinerant mission (9:35; 11:1), with no mention of locations and no indication of a return to Capernaum.

VERSE 3: 'A man'—literally, 'the sower' (ὁ σπείρων). The participle with the article is an Aramaism; it does not refer to one particular sower. He is 'the sower' only for the time being, he would have other things to do on the farm. The whole picture is a faithful representation of the Palestinian farming practice—the sowing was done *before* the field was ploughed. The sower would stride back and forth, tossing the seed without trying to avoid bad patches which would be hard to distinguish amid the unploughed stubble.

VERSE 4: 'On the pathway'—the preposition παρά commonly means 'alongside', but here the sense 'on' is required. Seed sown alongside the road, or path, would be no more exposed to birds than if it were in the middle of the field. The pathway—τὴν ὁδόν—means not 'the road', but the path which villagers have made through the stubble; if the seed were ploughed in quickly enough, it would be made safe from the birds.

VERSE 5: εὐθύς can hardly mean 'immediately' in this context; no seed springs up without some days of germination. A quick early growth is suggested, which cannot be sustained because there is not enough soil to enable the seed to form roots.

VERSE 8: 'A hundredfold' would be an enormous return, even with modern methods of fertilization and in the richest soil. There is a good deal of exaggeration even in the thirtyfold. This does not mean that we should read into it a symbol of 'the eschatological overflowing of the divine fulness, surpassing all human measure' (Jeremias, *Parables*, p.150); there is no need to see in it anything other than typical oriental hyperbole.

VERSE 9: The injunction to 'listen' is undoubtedly meant to make the hearer realize that there is more in the parable than appears on the surface. Matthew takes the sentence over from his source (Mark); it is by no means certain that it was originally attached to the parable. But what deeper meaning was the hearer of Jesus, or the reader of the Gospel, supposed to find in it?

The reader of the Gospel will have an explanation provided for him. He will be told that this parable is an allegory of the results which follow upon the preaching of the Gospel. The seed that is sown is 'the word of the kingdom' (v.19), the path, the rocky ground, the thistles, and the good soil are different types of hearers. The birds that devour the seed sown on the path are 'the evil one' (v.19); the rocky ground is the hearer who shows some early promise, but soon falls away when trouble comes upon him 'on account of the word' (vv.20–21); the thorns are 'the anxieties of the times and the lure of wealth'; and the good soil is the understanding hearer in whom the word brings a rich return. Only the sower is left without an identification.

It is safe to say that none of this is inherent in the parable, and that no hearer could ever have arrived at such an interpretation without the key. It was not transparent to the disciples, although they have been granted insight into 'the secrets of the kingdom of heaven', any more than to the crowds, representatives of the people of Israel, who have eyes that do not see and ears that do not hear, and have no understanding. In this case, understanding is not dependent on spiritual enlightenment—the knowledge of the secrets of the kingdom of heaven—but on possession of the key to the allegory; and the failure to make anything of it is not due to any hardness of heart or spiritual blindness, but to the lack of the key. Is it at all conceivable that Jesus delivered such a parable to crowds by the seashore, and then left them to make of it what they could, reserving the indispensable key for the private instruction of his disciples? It cannot be doubted that if Jesus ever pronounced this parable, it was under other circumstances and in connection with instruction to which the parable bore some obvious relationship. As none of the evangelists has given us any notion of the substance of such instruction, it is impossible for us to discover the point which it was originally designed to bring home to the hearers. On the other hand, once the attendant circumstances had been forgotten, such a parable would not be transmitted without *some* key to its meaning, and the allegorical explanation which is found first in Mark and, following him, in Matthew and in Luke, must have been attached to it long before the earliest Gospel was written. Some unknown teacher of the early church composed this allegorical exposition to meet the needs of his hearers, probably to impress upon them how much depended upon the kind of response which they made to the gospel as it was preached to them. It might be taken as an illustration of the experience of the generation which left Egypt in the wilderness, which the writer of Hebrews uses in much the same way. 'For good news came to us just as it did to them; but the message which they heard did not profit them, because it did not meet with faith in the hearers' (Heb.4:2). But this is a totally artificial way of interpreting the parable, and it cannot be ascribed to Jesus. For that matter, what is there in this 'interpretation' which could not be given openly to the crowds? There is nothing esoteric about it.

Jesus Explains Why he Speaks in Parables 13:10–15

[10] The disciples made their approach. They said to him; 'Why do you speak to them in parables?' [11] He answered, 'To you it is given to know the mysteries of the kingdom of heaven, but it is not given to them. [12] For to those who have, more will be given and they will have an abundance; but even what [little] they have will be taken away from those who have nothing. [13] It is for this reason that I speak to them in parables, because they see without seeing and hear without hearing or understanding. [14] In them is fulfilled the oracle of Isaiah which runs:

> You will hear and hear
>   and never understand,
> and you will look and look
>   and never see.
> [15] For the hearts of this people have been dulled,
>   they have stuffed their ears
>   and have closed their eyes,
> lest they might see with their eyes
>   and hear with their ears
> and understand with their hearts
>   and should be converted,
>   and I should heal them.'

VERSE 10: Matthew has changed the question and the setting. In Mark, the scene shifts from the lakeshore with its listening crowds to a more private place; the questioners wait until Jesus is alone. And the Matthaean questioners are 'the disciples' (that is, in Matthew's stylized representation, the spokesmen of the Christians of Matthew's own church), whereas in Mark, it is 'those who were about him with the twelve'—probably meaning to suggest a wider circle of adherents. Their question is not put into words; they ask him vaguely 'about the parables' (Mk.4:10). It is not clear what they wanted to learn 'about the parables'. Luke takes it to mean that they asked him 'what this parable meant' (Lk.8:9); but Matthew turns it into a question about his purpose in using parables—'Why do you speak to them in parables?' This adapts the words better to the reply, which will deal with precisely that problem; but as the use of parables was a common practice of Jewish teachers, it is hardly natural that the disciples of Jesus should ask why their master adopted the same method.

VERSE 11: The answer of Jesus implies that teaching is given in parables because it is meant only for the initiated, the few to whom 'it is given to know the secrets of the kingdom of heaven.' He omits the Markan clause 'but to those outside everything is in parables' (Mk.4:11); for this he substitutes the simplified 'to them it is not given' (to know these secrets).

VERSE 12: This appears to be originally a pessimistic, even cynical bit of folk-wisdom, to the effect of 'the rich get richer and the poor get poorer.' In its use here, it is spiritualized, to give the sense that the first attainments lead on to further progress. The greater advances cannot be made without the elementary steps, and what little one has gained may be lost if it is not built upon. The saying is given in Mark, but not at this point; it is reserved for a different chain of sayings which follow the interpretation (4:21–25). It occurs again in an appendix to the parable of the Talents (Pounds [Minas] in Luke), where it appears to be more apposite (Mt.25:29; Lk.19: 26); God gives wider responsibilities to those who have made good use of the lesser opportunities that he has put in their way. (The passives, 'shall be given . . . shall be taken', are 'circumlocutions for the divine name' [Jeremias, *Parables*, p.62,n.58]—"God will give more . . . God will take away.") In placing the saying here, Matthew probably intends to draw from the parable a warning of the necessity which is laid upon the hearer to foster the growth of the word which has been sown in his heart.

VERSE 13 would in itself suggest that Jesus uses parables because the people have difficulty in understanding his more direct teaching. But the citation which follows attributes this lack of understanding to a stubborn *refusal* to respond. Even so, there is a noticeable softening of Mark's staggering assertion, that 'for those outside everything is in parables *in order that* (ἵνα) they may indeed see . . . and hear . . . and not understand, lest (μήποτε) they might repent and be forgiven' (Mk.4:11f.). It may indeed be, as has been argued, that Mark's ἵνα ('in order that') and Matthew's ὅτι ('because') are alternative renderings of the Aramaic particle *dᵉ*; the Targum of Jonathan, in this passage, actually reads *dᵉ*, but uses it in the sense of the relative 'who'. Mark's form of the citation has certainly been influenced by a tradition which later found place in the Targum, for his closing phrase, 'lest (they should repent, and) it should be forgiven to them' (μήποτε [ἐπιστρέφωσιν καὶ] ἀφεθῇ αὐτοῖς); this translates no Greek variant reading but is 'a characteristic Targumic paraphrase of Hebrew *rapha'*, peculiar to the Targum of Isaiah' (Black, *Aramaic Approach*, p.215). The LXX text reads (strangely) 'lest they should see . . . and should repent, and I shall heal them' (καὶ ἰάσομαι αὐτούς), in place of the Hebrew 'lest . . . they repent and be healed.' But if Matthew had Mark's words before him, and changed ἵνα to ὅτι, he is not choosing a different rendering of the one Aramaic particle, but is deliberately altering the Greek of Mark; and this can only be because he shrinks from the baldness of Mark's assertion that Jesus spoke parables *in order that* his hearers might not understand—and ultimately, in order that they might not repent and be forgiven. Matthew agrees that the parables generally were not understood by the hearers, but he affirms that this failure to understand was caused by their culpable hardness of heart and self-willed blindness, not by any intention of Jesus to leave them in their plight.

Matthew gives the whole text of Isaiah 6:9—10, of which Mark had used only two lines. He cites the passage in the Greek version (LXX), which differs widely from the Hebrew. This enables him to treat the words as a prediction of a future situation, which he identifies as the ministry of Jesus—they find their fulfilment in the crowds who now see and hear without comprehending anything. In the Hebrew, the verbs are not futures, as in the Greek translation. They are imperatives and jussives, and would be rendered literally much as they are in *RSV*, as follows:

(Go, and say to this people:)
'Hear and hear, but do not understand:
See and see, but do not perceive.'
Make the heart of this people fat [insensitive],

and their ears heavy,
and shut [smear over] their eyes,
lest they see with their eyes
. . . . . .
and convert [turn, or repent], and be healed.

'The imperative is used here idiomatically to express a future certainty' (R.B.Y. Scott, *IB, ad loc.*), and the LXX translator has thus interpreted correctly in using his futures; but the prophet was actually speaking of the unreceptive attitude of his own hearers, not of a time centuries in the future. In the latter part of the oracle, however, the translator has rendered the imperatives by a series of indicatives:

their hearts have become impervious,
and they have heard with dull ears,
and they have closed their eyes.

This change stresses more directly the moral guilt of the people of Israel. They have stuffed their ears and shut their eyes and hardened their hearts, '*lest* they should hear . . . and see . . . and repent and be healed.' If they do not respond to the appeal of the prophet, it is because they do not want to repent; and as long as they continue in that attitude, they cannot be healed.

Matthew is not concerned with the Israel of the eighth century before Christ, but with the Israel of his own time. If the hearers of a former age turned deaf ears and blind eyes to the prophet Isaiah by reason of a settled unwillingness to repent, this is of interest to the evangelist chiefly because he sees in it the pattern of what happened in the ministry of Jesus, and is still going on in his own days.

Jesus Blesses the Disciples 13:16–17

16 'But blessed are your eyes, for they see, and your ears, for they hear. 17 Truly I tell you, many prophets and righteous men have longed to see what you see, and did not see it; they have longed to hear what you hear, and did not hear it.'

These two verses are found also in Luke, with a few differences of wording, and set in a different context. Luke brings them in immediately after the declaration of Jesus that the Father alone knows who he is, and that no one knows who the Father is except Jesus and those to whom Jesus the Son reveals him (Lk.10:21–24).

The main difference is in verse 16, where the Lukan parallel reads,

'Blessed are the eyes which see the things that you see' (v.23). Matthew's wording picks up the phrasing of the oracle cited above (v.15), and makes a pointed contrast between the crowds who neither see nor hear and the disciples who both see and hear. This is another way of expressing the contrast of verse 11 between those to whom it has been granted to know the secrets of the kingdom of heaven, and the others to whom it is not given to have such insight.

VERSE 17: 'righteous men' (δίκαιοι) perhaps is Matthew's substitution of one of his key terms for an earlier 'kings' (Luke). The thought remains the same; what could only be anticipated with longing by the worthiest heroes of faith in earlier times is now enjoyed by the followers of Jesus: the dreams and visions have become reality. The theme is developed in several of the epistles, especially Hebrews. 'For the law, since it has but a shadow of the good things to come (τῶν μελλόντων ἀγαθῶν) . . . can never make perfect' (Heb.10:1); and again, 'these all, though well attested by their faith, did not receive what was promised, since God had foreseen something better for us, that apart from us they should not be made perfect' (11:39f.). In Ephesians, again, the author (writing in the character of Paul) speaks of 'my insight into the mystery of Christ which was not made known to mankind in other generations as it has now been revealed to his holy apostles and prophets by the Spirit' (Eph.3:4f.).

An Allegorical Interpretation of the Parable 13:18—23

[18] 'You then shall hear what is signified by the parable of the sower. [19] When people hear the word of the Kingdom and do not apprehend it, the evil one comes and snatches away what was sown in their hearts. This is what was sown on the pathway. [20] What was sown on rocky ground represents those who hear the word and receive it at once, with joy; [21] but the seed puts down no roots in them, and when affliction or persecution comes upon them on account of the word they at once fall away. [22] What was sown among the thorns represents those who hear the word, but the worldly anxiety and the lure of riches choke the seed and it produces nothing. [23] But what was sown on the good ground represents those who hear and understand the word, and it yields a bountiful harvest—a hundred, or sixty, or thirty times over.'

The parable as it stands is unintelligible, at least as anything more than a description of a farmer's difficulties in raising a crop. The setting by the lake (as in Mark and Matthew) and the vaguer setting given in Luke 8:4, are not of any help to us in our attempts to see what problem Jesus had in mind or what his hearers could find in it apart from an account of things which were quite familiar to every peasant. In Matthew, as in Mark before him, the parable follows a section in which Jesus is meeting with increasing doubts and even with open hostility, and we may assume that these evangelists take it to be in some sense a comment on the mixed reception that the message is receiving. Whether it was so intended by Jesus is another question. To this day there is nothing like a general agreement on what it was originally meant to teach, and good scholars offer surprisingly different interpretations.

The passage before us is the earliest in the long chain of interpretations, and is attributed to Jesus himself. It is given privately to the disciples, not to the crowds who heard it on the lakeshore— though it contains nothing that calls for secrecy. It is now generally agreed that it does not in fact preserve the interpretation given by Jesus, but is the work of a Christian expositor of the apostolic age. Such attempts as are still made from time to time to defend its authenticity are based on the claim that none of the explanations offered by modern scholars are any more plausible; but this observation would rather lead to the conclusion that, if parable and interpretation belong together as the product of one mind, then the parable itself is not an authentic utterance of Jesus.

But we shall see that the interpretation does not fit the parable. It treats this picture of a grower's difficulties with natural hazards as an analysis of the causes in human dispositions for the frequent failure of the Christian evangelist to win hearers who will remain steadfast. The allegorist makes nothing of the abundance of the harvest which more than rewards the grower for all his wasted effort; his attention is devoted to the exploration of why some of the sowing goes for nothing. The natural hazards of agriculture are made to serve as illustrations of the various ways in which people who hear the gospel fail to become lasting and fruitful Christians.

Matthew takes over the allegorical exposition from Mark, but Mark himself received it from earlier tradition. (Jeremias, *Parables*, pp.77ff.). Once the original meaning of the parable was forgotten, it would soon have ceased to be transmitted at all if some key to its meaning had not been supplied.

VERSE 18: Matthew is obliged to drop the reproach with which Jesus introduces the interpretation in Mark, 'Do you not understand this parable? How then will you understand all the parables?' (Mk. 4:13). Such words could not be addressed to the very men who had just been blessed because of their ability to see and hear. (Matthew regularly tones down criticisms of the disciples.) None the less, they do not understand this parable any better than the crowds to whom the knowledge of the secrets of the Kingdom was not given. What was needed was not spiritual insight, but a clue to the significance of birds, thistles, rocky ledges, and so forth.

VERSE 19: The seed is 'the word of the Kingdom' (in Mark, simply 'the word'); but the allegorist does not offer any clue to the meaning of the sower. He may take him to mean any preacher of the gospel; the tendency to identify him as Jesus is not derived from either the parable or from this interpretation, but is borrowed from the interpretation of the parable of the Wheat and the Tares (v.37— 'he who sows . . . is the Son of man').

It has also been proposed (see the Excursus below) to understand the sower as God.

The birds of the parable that snatch away the seed before it can be ploughed under are a natural hazard; the allegorist takes them to be a figure of the devil.

VERSE 20: The 'rocky ground' is not any great slab of rock, but a place where the underlying limestone is covered with a light layer of soil that makes it impossible for the sower to see it. It is the shallow soil that suggests the comparison with the shallow-minded hearer.

VERSE 22: The thorns will be unperceived amid the stubble; they would be cut down when the field was harvested, but would come again to vigorous life as the season advanced.

VERSE 23: The good soil probably made up by far the greater part of the field; the abundant crop which it produces is more than enough to compensate for the few handfuls of seed that goes to waste on patches of thorns, outcroppings of rock, or the path beaten through the stubble.

In this interpretation, nothing is made of the character of the sower or the quality of the seed. The ground is interpreted in terms of the human recipients of the gospel message, and the allegorist is interested primarily in the way in which different types of hearer respond. This suggests the attempt of an experienced evangelist who has seen all the different reactions of people. The parable itself gives no indication that the teller is analysing the varieties of character; and it is hard to imagine that Jesus meant to teach that the gospel could only take root in a heart that was already fit to receive it. On the contrary, he summons precisely those who are not fit—who are called first of all to repent.

Excursus: On Current Interpretations of the Parable

Until late in the nineteenth century, Christian interpreters accepted this allegorical treatment as an exposition given by Jesus himself to his disciples. Sometimes more extravagant extensions of the allegory were offered. The different kinds of soils (hearers) were interpreted as bearing upon the different vocations of Christians—laity, clergy, virgins, martyrs, monks. Jülicher tells of a nineteenth-century scholar who proposed to take the four types of hearers as stubborn Judaizers, free-thinking liberals, radical Gentile Christians, and the genuine followers of Paul. Bernhard Weiss was perhaps the first of the great modern critics to recognize that the allegorical interpretation is a product of the early church; it is wrong from the start when it tells us that 'the sower sows the word' (so Mark; in Matthew, 'the word of the kingdom'), for the theme of the parable is not the fate of the Kingdom but the results of the Kingdom-founding activities of Jesus (see Jülicher, *Gleichnisreden* II. p.533). But Weiss falls into the same trap of allegorical fancy.

Jülicher's great work on the parables (*Die Gleichnisreden Jesu* (1899; 2nd edn.,1910) broke the spell. He firmly rejected every trace of allegory in interpretation. He is sometimes criticized for carrying the rejection through too radically, and ending up with nothing but a set of moral generalities (Jeremias, *Parables*, p.19; Dodd, *Parables*, p.13). Dodd finds that the general effect of Jülicher's method is 'rather flattening' and asks, 'Was all this wealth of loving observation and imaginative rendering of nature and of common life used merely to adorn moral generalities? Was the Jesus of the Gospels just an eminently sound and practical teacher who patiently led simple minds to appreciate the great enduring commonplaces of morals and religion? This is not the impression created by the Gospels as a whole.' We shall return to the interpretations offered by him and by Jeremias later in this excursus.

Rudolf Bultmann is not at all sure how the parable of the sower is to be understood. He has made the general statement that 'in the transmission of the tradition, the original meaning of many parables has become obscure,' and goes on:

For instance, the parable of the Sower (Mk.4:3—9). Is it meant to comfort the person whose work is unsuccessful? Is it in this sense at the same time a half-resigned, half-thankful monologue of Jesus? Is it an exhortation addressed to the hearers of the word of God? of Jesus' preaching, or of the church's proclamation? Or is there in the original parable no concern with the word in the first place, and should it be understood somewhat in the sense of 4 Esd. 8:41: 'For as a peasant sows many seeds and plants many plants, yet not all he sows survives and not all his plants take root, so likewise not all those who are sown in the world will be saved.' (*HST*, p.216; independently translated.)

Most interpreters still take the sower of the parable to be Jesus himself, or else a figure of the preacher of the gospel, and the sowing is taken to be a figure of preaching. This is not self-evident, and one wonders if it would occur to anyone to interpret in this way if he were not prompted to it by the allegorical interpretation given in the Gospel. The allegorist himself does not give a clue to the sower or to the sowing—only to the seed. C.H. Dodd parts company with his colleagues. He points out that Jesus thinks of his work and that of his disciples not as sowing but as harvesting; the crop is ready for the sickle. 'The harvest is plentiful but the labourers are few' (Mt.9:37); he thinks especially of the saying in John 4:35b, 'lift up your eyes and see that the fields are already white for harvest.' He takes the sower for a figure of God, and the sowing for his work with Israel in the past centuries. The loss of seed in various ways represents the unresponsiveness, the apostasies, the captivities that came on Israel. Despite them all, the sowing of God has resulted in a bountiful harvest and needs only harvesters to reap it. This is the task in which Jesus is engaged, and which his disciples are called to share. We must remark that there is a good deal of allegorizing here, too, and also that his words are in strong contrast with his proposed interpretation of the parable of the leaven, that in 'the ministry of Jesus . . . the power of God's kingdom worked from within, mightily permeating the dead lump of religious Judaism in his time' (*Parables*, p.155). Can contemporary Israel be likened both to a field golden with a bountiful harvest and to an inert mass of dough, by the same teacher?

This interpretation grows out of Dodd's general theory of 'realized eschatology'. 'Jesus intended to proclaim the kingdom of God not as something to come in the near future, but as a matter of present experience' (*ibid.*,p.31). All the parables are therefore to be understood as related to 'a brief and tremendous crisis in which He is the principal figure, and which indeed His appearance brought about; . . . we should expect the parables to bear upon the actual and critical situation in which Jesus and his hearers stood' (p.13).

Jeremias likewise tries to conjure up a situation in the life of Jesus

—totally different from the situation envisaged by the evangelist—to which a parable might reasonably have been addressed. He attempts, therefore, to remove parables (and other sayings) from their setting in the life and thought of the primitive church 'in the attempt to recover their original setting in the life of Jesus, if we are to hear once again the original tones of Jesus' (*Parables*, p.22). This parable, then, he imagines to have been called forth by doubts arising out of the failure of Jesus to win over many of his hearers, and even of some desertions among the ranks of those who have been disciples (for this, he is obliged to resort to the statement of John 6:66: 'After this many of his disciples drew back and no longer went about with him'). 'Did not all this contradict the claims of his mission? Consider the husbandman, says Jesus; he might well despair in view of the many adverse factors which destroy and threaten his seed. Nevertheless he remains unshaken in his confidence that a rich harvest will reward his labours' (pp.150f.). So Jesus is full of confidence, and encourages his disciples to have faith that God will bring forth an abundant harvest, even though they are painfully aware of repeated failures. This presupposes that Jesus is not instructing the crowds by the shore who hear the parable, but means only to hearten his disciples in the face of a situation which seems less promising than in the halcyon days of the first mission in Galilee.

In more recent interpretation, this whole approach is renounced. The question is no longer put of what the parable may have meant to Jesus, but what it meant to the evangelist as indicated by the setting in which he placed it in his Gospel. Professor Bonnard, for example, sees it as no part of his task as commentator to attempt a return to Jesus from the primitive church. Instead, he seeks to discern the significance which Matthew attached to the parables of this chapter in grouping them at this particular place. Granted that this may not be the significance that Jesus intended them to have, he recognizes that Dodd and Jeremias have made useful contributions in their attempts to go behind Matthew and the tradition as it came to Matthew; he holds (quite rightly) that their results remain in the field of conjecture. 'Our first task is not to understand hypothetical parables as they may have been pronounced by Jesus in such or such a circumstance of his career, but to gather the sense which Matthew gave to them in his own circumstances, at the point in which we see them today in this Gospel' (*Matthieu*, p.189).

Bonnard examines the parable in relation to the other parables of this chapter and to the state of Jesus' fortunes as Matthew pictures them. He rejects the view that the parable of the Sower is principally concerned not with the failures, but with the harvest that is gathered in spite of them. Four of the six verses describe the ways in which seed fails to produce grain, and in each case the loss is caused by external agents—birds, the heat of the sun, thorns (vv.4–7). He admits that in Palestinian conditions any peasant would be happy with the overall results of his sowing, but he denies that the losses are negligible (so also C.F.D. Moule, *The Birth of the New Testament* (1962), p.150). If Jesus is the sower, 'do not these repeated failures contradict his claim to be invested with Messianic authority? *Can one combine the notion of failure with the notion of Messianic authority?*' (*Matthieu*, p. 191; his italics). He is sure that the crowds around Jesus could not fail to ask themselves this question, and no more serious question about him could be raised. This leads him to conclude that the central lesson is that 'the kingdom of God inaugurated by Jesus will not be established without many serious failures' (p. 192).

This interpretation is not entirely satisfying in itself. There is no reason to suppose that Jesus made claims to Messianic authority, and certainly Matthew does not hold that the crowds around him understood him to make such a claim. But it may serve to indicate the contemporary tendency to ask what the parable as given meant to the evangelist in his circumstances, and to avoid the question as put by Dodd and Jeremias of what it may have meant to Jesus in the circumstances of his mission so many years before.

2   THE PARABLE OF THE WHEAT AND THE TARES *13:24–30*

[24] He put another parable before them in these words: 'The kingdom of heaven is to be compared to a man who sowed good seed in his field, [25] but when everyone was sleeping, an enemy of his came along and sowed tares among the wheat, and went off. [26] When the grain sprouted and began to form ears, the tares made their appearance also. [27] The proprietor's slaves came to him and said, 'Sir, you sowed good seed in your field, did you not? Where have the tares come from?' [28] He replied, 'Some enemy of mine has done this.' The slaves then asked, 'Do you want us to go and pull them up?' [29] 'No!' he said, 'for in pulling them up you may root out the wheat along with them. [30] Let them both grow together until the harvest; at the time of reaping I will tell the reapers, "First pull up the tares and tie them in bundles for burning; and gather the wheat into my granary."'

This parable is found only in Matthew. In his sequence it takes the place of Mark's parable of the Seed Growing Secretly (Mk.4:26–29), and for all its differences it may be a radical reshaping of that strange parable, partly to accommodate it to the allegorical interpretation which will be given later (vv.36–43; see T.W. Manson, *Sayings*, p.193). The interpretation is undoubtedly a creation of Matthew, though he ascribes it to Jesus, and in some particulars it casts its shadow before and disturbs the coherence of the parable. But it seems likely that Matthew received the parable itself from an earlier source and reshaped it, for the interpretation takes no account whatever of that which is given the central emphasis in the parable, that is, the injunction to avoid any premature attempt to dispose of the tares. If Matthew had composed the parable for the sake of the allegorical interpretation which he gives, he would hardly have allowed the weight to rest upon the feature which is totally disregarded in his allegorical key. Any influence of the Markan parable which is displaced can be detected only in a word or two (the verb καθεύδειν, 'sleep'?). The presence of weeds and the problem of removing them are totally foreign to the parable of the Seed Growing Secretly. It is probable that Matthew has elaborated a parable which was given to him in the tradition, but that it was not the Markan parable.

As it stands, the Matthaean parable compares the kingdom of heaven, under one aspect, to the situation of a landed proprietor who finds that his wheat field is full of noxious weeds, and decides that no attempt shall be made to clean them out before the harvest. The general picture corresponds accurately enough to the agriculture of Palestine—a large estate, operated by slave labour; grain fields marked by considerable quantities of weeds; the use of weeds for fuel. It is supposed that in this case the weeds are particularly abundant and that they cannot easily be distinguished from wheat until the growth is well advanced. It is asserted by commentators that the weeds in question (ζιζάνια) are the noxious darnel (*Lolium tumulentum*) which is poisonous.

Problems arise in connection with a number of details. The slaves play no role as farm labourers. They appear on the scene only when the growth is far advanced, but only to ask their master whether he wants them to pull up the weeds. They did not sow the seed—that was done by the owner; and they are not to do the harvesting; the owner will tell 'the reapers' how he wants the job done. The slaves are introduced only to elicit the master's response. Again, we are told that it was in fact the practice in Palestine to root out darnel while the crop was still growing (Jeremias, *Parables*, p. 225), and even to do it more than once. The landowner's directions are therefore a departure from current practice. Possibly it was one of the points made in the original parable that in the kingdom of heaven the procedures of everyday life are *not* followed; but then the kingdom of heaven could no longer be said to be like what happens in the given situation, but to be quite unlike it. The dialogue between master and slaves reads very oddly. If the slaves are farm workers, they will know that fields commonly produce weeds, no matter how clean the seed that was sown; and it would be a peculiar landowner who would jump to the conclusion that if there were weeds in his field, some viciously disposed neighbour must have planted them on a dark night. In terms of the parable itself, moreover, the origin of the weeds is irrelevant, as is their character. They would have to be separated from the wheat in any case, and the only question that matters is whether the separation is to be undertaken at once or left until harvest time. The whole dialogue, with the 'enemy' and the 'slaves', is artificially created to prepare for the interpretation which will attribute the presence of bad people among the good *in the church* to the activity of the devil; it is already anticipated that the sower of the good seed is Jesus ('the Son of man'—v.37), and that his 'enemy', the devil, works his own adherents ('sons of the evil one'—v.38) in among the true followers of Jesus (the 'sons of the kingdom'—*ibid.*). But this in turn presupposes the emergence of the church as a community owing allegiance to Jesus, and so brings us into a circle of ideas which do not belong to the circumstances of Jesus' life. There could be no question of *purging* the quite unorganized and perpetually fluctuating groups which crowded around him wherever he happened to appear.

Once this dialogue is removed, we have a simple and coherent picture. If it is meant to illustrate some aspect of the kingdom of heaven, however, it is doubtful whether it can be given a plausible application as an utterance of Jesus. In any case, we could do no more than conjecture how Jesus may have applied it in his teaching. There is nothing to suggest where or when he uttered such a parable, and it is impossible to say to whom it was addressed. What would it have meant to the crowds lining the lakeshore (v.2, *supra*)? Are we to imagine that they were dreaming of conducting a purge of Israel? What could it mean to his own disciples, to whom he had just explained (?) the parable of the sower? They are certainly not in a position to undertake any purging of the Kingdom; they themselves were drawn from the classes that the more stringent Pharisees would have been inclined to purge! Even in the most simplified form, this parable appears to find a place only in relation to a constituted church, which thinks of itself as the present form of the kingdom of heaven and is already faced with problems of discipline—in particular, of whether it should expel from its ranks those whose lives are in some way evil.

As the church developed and faced such problems, some teacher may have created a parable like this to illustrate Paul's injunction to 'judge nothing before the time, before the Lord comes' (1 Cor.4:5). Its essential thought is given in the instruction to 'let both grow together until the harvest', and in the warning that an intemperate zeal to get rid of 'unworthy' members may have the unhappy consequence of driving out some of the worthiest. (Experience has shown that this is the usual consequence of heresy hunts.) This is not unrelated to the much more sweeping command, 'Judge not!' (Mt.7:1); and is in keeping with the principle of unlimited forgiveness which is laid down in Matthew 18. Consistently, indeed, the function of the church is seen in terms of conversion and restoration of the sinful, in keeping with the mission of its Lord who 'came not to call righteous people, but sinners' (Mt.9:13).

VERSE 24: The introduction ('The kingdom of God may be compared to . . .') is a filling out of a formula that occurs frequently in rabbinic parables (spoken, like those of Jesus, in Aramaic). The rabbinic formula is very brief indeed, consisting simply of the announcement, 'A parable. [It is] like . . . [a king, etc.].' The Aramaic particle *l*^{e}, meaning 'like', is a syncopated manner of saying, 'It may be compared with such an occurrence as this. . . .' The comparison is not with the king, or (as here) with the man whose experience will be described, but with what he experiences or does. Clearly, the parable does not give a description of the kingdom of heaven, but uses the experience of the farmer with his crop of wheat to illustrate an aspect of the Kingdom (as church), and of its administration.

'Good seed'—the quality of the seed is emphasized only to pave the way for the allegorical development, leading on to the contrast with the production of tares. If tares are found growing among the wheat, it is not to be attributed to the farmer, for the seed which he sowed was good. (In the parable of the sower, there was no need to mention that *good* seed was sown; nor is it really relevant here apart from the intrusion of the mythical theme of the 'enemy'.)

VERSES 25—26: For the basic parable, all that was needed was the bare observation that 'when the seed sprouted and began to form ears, the tares made their appearance also.' The fantastic picture of an 'enemy' who sows the tares during the night lays the ground for the myth which will be expounded in the allegorical explanation.

VERSES 27–29: Again, the basic parable requires only the question of the slaves, 'Do you want us to go and pull out the tares?' The rest is mere window-dressing.

VERSE 30: The reapers would cut the crop with sickles. Wheat and tares would be cut together, and the reaper would then have to separate them as they lay on the ground. The tares are tied in bundles for burning, not for mere destruction but for use as fuel; this belongs to the Palestinian environment where wood is scarce, and dried grasses and cakes of dung must be used for the stove. The parable does not go into detail about the handling of the wheat, which would have to be threshed and winnowed before being stored. The farmer's granary, $ἀποϑήκη$, is not likely to be a barn, or even a bin in a barn; in Palestine grain was generally stored in underground pits, sometimes lined with brick, or in large pottery jars.

3 THE PARABLE OF THE MUSTARD SEED *13:31–32*

[31] He gave them another parable, in these words: 'The kingdom of heaven is like a grain of mustard, which a man sowed in his field. [32] It is the tiniest of all seeds, but when it has made its growth it is the largest of herbs and becomes a tree, such that the birds of the sky come and nest in its branches.'

Again, the parable is given without its setting, so that we do not know anything about the people to whom Jesus was speaking, or what point he was trying to drive home. In itself, it amounts to no more than the commonplace that 'great oaks from little acorns grow.'

The parable is a Matthaean revision of Mark, with reduction of Mark's verbosity and other changes which are not improvements. In verse 31, he substitutes the laboured phrase 'which a man took and sowed in his field' for Mark's simpler (and better) 'when it is sown in the earth'. And in verse 32, he has the 'largest of herbs' turn into a tree, where Mark had said only that 'it puts out branches.' Mark's 'branches' are reserved by Matthew for the last clause, where the birds are said to make nests 'in the branches' instead of 'under its shade' (Mark). As there are some points of correspondence between Matthew and Luke in the wording of this parable, it is possible that some of the changes are due to a partial use of the source 'Q', by conflation.

The mention of the birds nesting in or under the tree is meant to emphasize the size of the shrub and so to heighten the contrast with its minute beginnings; but the wording in both versions is reminiscent of the figure which compares the Pharaoh of Egypt with an immense cedar tree (Ez.31:1–9); note especially v. 6:

> All the birds of the air
>   made their nests in its boughs;
> under its branches all the beasts of the field
>   brought forth their young;
> and under its shadow
>   dwelt all great nations.

It is probable that the reminiscence of the Ezekiel passage has led Matthew and Luke (or their source Q) to speak of the mustard plant as growing into a *tree*; but the largest mustard plant is far removed from the grandeur of a gigantic cedar of Lebanon! We find it hard to agree with interpreters (Dodd, Jeremias) who find great significance in the image of the birds nesting in the branches, and suggest that the parable portrays (Dodd) or foreshadows (Jeremias) the flocking of the Gentiles into the kingdom. 'Out of the most insignificant beginnings, invisible to the human eye, God creates his mighty Kingdom, which embraces all the peoples of the world' (Jeremias, *Parables*, p. 149). 'Jesus is asserting that the time has come when the blessings of the Reign of God are available to all men. . . . The Kingdom of God is here; the birds are flocking to find shelter in the shade of the tree' (Dodd, *Parables*, p.154). It must be said that this is imposing upon the parable the critic's own general interpretation of the message of Jesus. It is another way of allegorizing a detail which in itself does no more than stress the great difference between the size of the seed and the magnitude of the plant.

4 THE PARABLE OF THE LEAVEN *13:33*

[33] He gave them another parable. 'The kingdom of heaven is like leaven which a woman took and hid in three measures of flour until the dough finished rising.'

This is not a Markan parable. It is given also in Luke, again in immediate succession to the parable of the mustard seed, and with no change except in the introductory formula (in Luke, it becomes the more or less standard, 'To what shall I liken the kingdom of God?'—13:20f.). Since we are not given the context in which it was spoken, it is not possible to determine what it meant. The 'three measures' are a vast quantity for a housewife's baking; the 'measure' (σάτον, equivalent to the Hebrew *seah*) held about twelve quarts, so that the 'three measures' of this mammoth baking would amount to thirty-six quarts (or about forty litres). This would make enough bread to feed a crowd, something close to a hundred large loaves. Nothing is said of the other necessary ingredients (liquid, salt, shortening); and the interest is limited to the rising of the dough, with no mention of kneading or of the subsequent baking. We are left with the contrast between the vast quantity of dough swollen by the action of the leaven, and the small amount of leaven which produces so great a result (though there is no mention of the *littleness* of the leaven, as in the saying, 'a little leaven ferments the whole lump of dough'—1 Cor.5:6; Gal.5:9). As in the parable of the mustard seed, we are invited to contemplate the great result that can follow upon a seemingly trifling cause.

Traditionally, this parable has been interpreted as an optimistic view of the future of the Kingdom: 'Like leaven, this [the doctrine of "the Kingdom"] will spread rapidly until it has accomplished the purpose for which it was taught' (Allen, *Matthew* (ICC, 1907), p.152); 'the leaven represents God's kingdom or the preaching of the kingdom' (Creed, *Luke* (1930), p.21). Dodd remarks that 'the working of leaven in dough is not a slow, imperceptible process...; soon the whole mass swells and bubbles, as fermentation rapidly advances. The ministry of Jesus was like that. There was in it no element of external coercion, but in it the power of God's Kingdom worked from within, mightily permeating the dead lump of religious Judaism in his time' (*Parables*, p.155). Disregarding the unjustified denigration of 'religious Judaism', we must ask whether *Judaism* was actually so 'permeated' by the work of Jesus. Jeremias tries to conjure up a situation in the life of Jesus which might call forth this parable (and that of the mustard seed). He imagines that some doubt was expressed about the notion that these nondescript groups of fishermen and peasants could possibly be the nucleus of the redeemed community of the Messianic Age. Jesus replies that from this insignificant beginning such great results can and indeed must flow, as the tiny mustard seed gives rise to the huge shrub, and as the leaven irresistibly penetrates the whole mass of dough; so surely 'will God's miraculous power cause my small band to swell into the mighty host of the people of God in the Messianic Age, embracing the Gentiles' (*Parables*, p.149). It is hard to imagine the kind of objectors who would draw such a lesson from these two parables.

All these commentators take note that in the rest of the New Testament, and in rabbinical teachings, the leaven is a symbol of the dangerous, corrupting effects of *evil*. Jesus himself warns his disciples against 'the leaven of the Pharisees and Sadducees' (Mt. 16:6, 11f.; in Mark it is 'the leaven of the Pharisees and the leaven of Herod'—8:15). This causes them no problem; they simply allege that Jesus now employs the symbol in the opposite sense. Lohmeyer alone makes an effort to take the evil symbolism into account. In Israel, in preparation for Passover and the festival of Unleavened Bread, each household carefully got rid of every trace of leaven (dough normally kept over from the previous baking and left to ferment for use in the next bread-making). Leavened bread was totally forbidden in connection with the sacrifices (Ex.34:18); according to Josephus, the loaves of 'the Bread of the Presence' (*AV* 'shewbread') were unleavened. In general, leaven was a symbol of ceremonial impurity and so was commonly used as a symbol of moral impurity; Paul is entirely in keeping with Jewish thinking when he contrasts 'the leaven of malice and wickedness' with 'the unleavened bread of sincerity and truth'. Lohmeyer ventures to ask if Jesus is trying to say that the 'tax collectors and sinners', the 'people of the land' (*Am-ha-Arez*) who make up his followers, are 'unclean' in terms of Jewish ritual requirements and in the judgement of the Pharisees, but that they will none the less turn out to be the initiators of the redeemed community. Lohmeyer suggests that the choice of this figure is related to 'the struggle and the victory over temple and cult which Jesus carried on in word and work until his death on the cross' (*Matthäus*, pp.220ff.). But this does not appear to reflect the leaven's effects on the mass in which it is working!

It is by no means impossible, seeing that we have no means of recovering the context in which the parable was created, that it was originally a warning against the dangerous contagion of evil. It could be understood as an illustration of the warning against 'the leaven of the Pharisees'.

At any rate, it is doubtful that Jesus thought either of his message or of his disciples as a hidden but powerful influence working irresistibly to change Israel or the world at large.

5 SUMMARY: JESUS' TEACHING IN PARABLES FULFILS THE SCRIPTURES *13:34–35*

[34] Jesus said all these things to the crowds in parables, and he never

spoke to them without a parable, [35] in order that what was spoken through the prophet might be fulfilled: to wit,

I shall open my mouth in parables,
I shall proclaim things hidden since the foundation of the world

Matthew has revised Mark radically here. In the first verse of the passage he has omitted Mark's words, 'as they were able to hear', which would suggest that Jesus used parables to make his thoughts more easily understood by people of limited capacity. In the second verse, he omits Mark's statement that Jesus 'explained everything privately to his own disciples' (Mk.4:33f.). More than that, he brings in the citation from the Old Testament (Ps.78:2); he looks upon the psalms as words of prophecy, so that he can think of these lines as 'spoken through the prophet'. Codex Sinaiticus and a few Caesarean manuscripts add the name Isaiah, which is obviously wrong, and Jerome tells us that 'all the old codices' gave the name of the prophet as Asaph, to whom the psalm is attributed in the Hebrew Psalter.

The first line of the citation follows LXX word for word (Hebrew uses the singular, 'a proverb'), but the second line is quite different from LXX and from all other Greek versions known to us. It is probably to be taken as an independent rendering of the Hebrew; literal in its choice of the main verb ('I shall belch out'; usually rendered in LXX by a verb meaning 'roar', or 'bellow'), but freely interpretative in the remaining words. The psalm does not in fact go on with parables or with things long hidden, but recites well-known events of Israel's history (experiences of the Exodus from Egypt, the fall of the ancient sanctuary at Shiloh, and the accession of David to the throne). The verse cited has certainly no bearing upon the ministry of Jesus or even upon the Messianic Age in general; and the translation as given in Matthew is not framed to be faithful to the Old Testament text, but to serve the evangelist's purpose— however arbitrarily from our point of view—of supporting his belief that the whole career and character of Jesus is portrayed prophetically in the sacred scriptures of Israel. It also expresses his conception of Jesus as the Revealer of secret truths which are inherent in the creation but have hitherto been hidden from human knowledge; 'the mystery of Christ, which was not made known to mankind in other generations as it has now been revealed to his holy apostles and prophets by the Spirit' (Eph.3:4f.). In Christ, all things were made new, but evangelist and apostle were persuaded that it was all in keeping with the eternal purpose of God.

The passage in Mark comes naturally as a conclusion to the whole section on parables; but Matthew proceeds at once with a considerable additional section of parabolic discourse, beginning with an allegorical exposition of the parable of the tares, and continuing with three more parables, all peculiar to his Gospel.

6 THE PARABLE OF THE TARES EXPOUNDED *13:36–43*

[36] With that, Jesus dismissed the crowds and went into the house. His disciples presented themselves before him and said, 'Explain for us the parable of the tares of the field.' [37] He answered as follows: 'He who sows the good seed is the Son of man; [38] the field is the world; the good seed stands for the sons of the kingdom, and the tares for the sons of the evil one; [39] the enemy who sowed them is the devil; the harvest is the end of the age; and the reapers are angels. [40] Just as the tares are gathered and burned in the fire, so shall it be at the end of the age. [41] The Son of man shall send out his angels and they shall gather out of his kingdom all things, that cause trouble and all who live lawlessly, [42] and shall throw them into the fiery furnace; weeping will be heard there, and gnashing of teeth. [43] Then the righteous shall shine out like the sun in the kingdom of their Father. If you have ears, hear this.'

There can be little doubt that this 'interpretation' is the work of Matthew; it 'exhibits a simply unique collection of the linguistic characteristics of the Evangelist Matthew' (Jeremias, *Parables*, p.82 —he goes on to list no less than thirty-seven examples). Further, it is not the work of the composer of the original parable, for with all its details it misses the central lesson of patience, that tares and wheat must be allowed to grow together for the time being. At most, the framer of the allegorical exposition (Matthew) may have introduced extraneous elements into the basic parable to make the allegory fuller.

VERSE 36: The scene is formally changed from the lakeshore to 'the house'—presumably the house where Jesus had taken up residence in Capernaum (4:13; 13:1); and the audience is now limited to the disciples. Their question implies that the parable is obscure; this is in line with Matthew's general theory of parables, that they are essentially enigmatic and cannot be understood without a key. 'Explain' or 'expound' (διασάφησον) means literally 'make clear'.

VERSES 37–39: The answer of Jesus provides the necessary key. The parable, thus interpreted, has nothing to do with agriculture; it is a cryptic picture of the nature and destiny of the human race, seen as consisting of two quantities, distinguished as 'sons of the kingdom' and 'sons of the evil one'—that is, of the devil. The members of these two groups come into the world in the character imparted to them by their origin. There is no suggestion of a choice open to individuals between the service of God and the service of the devil; in this frame of things, there is no room for repentance. Their appointed destiny is fixed at their entrance into the world.

The sower is identified as Jesus himself—the Son of man; perhaps this title is chosen to indicate that he is to act in his role of Judge (cf. 25:31ff.; 16:27). The seed which he sows is not the gospel message, 'the word', as in the interpretation of the parable of the Sower (Mk.4:14; Lk.8:11—'the seed is the word of God'; cf. Mt.13: 19 above), but human beings, who are already 'sons of the kingdom'. There is no place for the thought of a seed that will grow in different ways, or will be in some part wasted on hardpan or rocks or thistles. The devil, as the enemy of the Son of man, makes a counter-sowing; he brings into the world human beings who derive their nature from him—they are his 'sons'. This picture is pure myth—human beings are not seen as individuals with personal characters, capable of progress or of degeneration, but as belonging to one of two classes, according to their origin in the Son of man or in the devil. This is surely a conception of man which is quite alien to Jesus and to the Bible generally. Can it be that Matthew himself really thinks of mankind in these terms, or has he borrowed some alien myth without realizing its implications?

If 'the field is the world', the parable must be understood as bearing upon the state of the human race in its entirety. It would be more in accord with Matthew's general outlook, to see it as reflecting the state of the Christian church, with its mixture of good and bad. This is in fact the way in which the parable is generally interpreted. Matthew is profoundly aware that by no means all who profess and call themselves disciples of Christ are true to him. His work abounds in warnings of Jesus that 'not every one who says to me, "Lord, Lord," shall enter the kingdom of heaven, but he who does the will of my Father in heaven' (7:21). It may be that he intends to convey by his interpretation of this parable a solemn warning to professing Christians who cause others to fall away and who themselves live evil lives that they will not be protected in the day of judgement by their claim to be followers of Jesus, but will be visited with fearful punishment.

VERSES 40—42: After the multiple clues to the parable have been

set out in order, concluding with the point that 'the harvest is the
end of the age, and the reapers are angels', the interpretation turns
into an apocalyptic picture of the last things. The emphasis is clearly
on the fate of those who are figured by the tares, and their fate is to
be burned. There is something grotesque in his turning the perfectly
appropriate account of the use of the bundled weeds for fuel into a
figure of the burning of human beings; and of the reapers who
separate the tares from the wheat and bind them in bundles for
burning into agents not only of the separation of the evil from the
good, but of the infliction of punishment on the evil. In the classical
iconography of the Last Judgement, it is the demons who toss the
souls of the damned into hell; in Matthew's interpretation, the
'angels' act strangely like demons. 'Weeping and gnashing of teeth' is
a good figure for remorse, but remarkably weak for the reaction of
people who are feeling the torments of fire; screams of anguish
would seem more appropriate.

VERSE 43: The verse is reminiscent of the words of the great
Hebrew apocalypse: 'Those who are wise shall shine like the brightness of the firmament; and those who turn many to righteousness
like the stars for ever and ever' (Dan.12:3). The 'fiery furnace' of
course comes from the same book, though there it is not prepared
for the wicked but for the faithful servants of the God of Israel
(Dan.3:6,16f., etc.). As McNeile remarks, 'the apocalyptic expectations are of a popular and conventional character, and are expressed,
to a large extent, in stereotyped formulas' (*Matthew*, p.203).

The interpretation appears to make a distinction between a
'kingdom of the Son of man' ('his kingdom'—v.41), from which the
angels will expel everything evil; and 'the kingdom of the Father'
('their Father'—v.43), which must mean the creation now fully
redeemed ('delivered from its bondage to corruption into the
glorious freedom of the sons of God' (Rom.8:21). This would
correspond to the apocalyptic programme sketched by Paul, when he
speaks of an interim reign of Christ, which continues 'until he has
put all his enemies under his feet' (1 Cor.15:25). This is not the final
state, for 'then comes the end, when he delivers the kingdom to God
the Father . . . then the Son himself will also be subjected to him
who put all things under him, that God may be all in all' (vv.24,28).
The same range of thought is pictured in the Apocalypse of John, in
the notion that Jesus, with the martyrs restored to life, reigns for a
thousand years (Rev.20:4–6); and it is only after that preliminary
reign that the final triumph of God is brought to pass (Rev.20:7–
15;21:1–22:5).

7   THE PARABLE OF THE BURIED TREASURE *13:44*

[44] 'The Kingdom of heaven is like a treasure hidden in a field which a man found and buried again, while he went off joyfully, sold all he owned, and bought that field.'

Again the parable is given without any indication of the context, apart from the fact that Matthew represents it as spoken only to the disciples of Jesus. There is nothing in it of an esoteric nature, and it could perfectly well have been given to a general audience.

It was not uncommon for people to safeguard their money and other valuables by burying them in the earth (on their own property, of course. The 'treasure' would probably consist of coins, or perhaps also of jewels. Such a hoard might remain untouched for years, or indeed for centuries; archaeologists still turn up pots of ancient coins in the course of their excavations. The parable is not concerned with the laws of 'treasure trove' (in British law, such finds are the property of the Crown). The farm labourer would not think twice about the rights of ownership. The field is not his; he is there to work it—perhaps to plough it—for the owner; and when the hoarded gold is turned up by his plough he covers it again without saying anything to the owner, till he can raise enough money to buy the field for himself. To raise the money he has to sell all that he owns, but he does not think of that as a sacrifice of cherished possessions. He is full of joy at the unexpected chance to enrich himself beyond all his hopes.

The point of the parable is clear. One who discovers the kingdom of heaven, and realizes that it is worth more than all else in life, gladly makes it his own, whatever the cost. 'Surprised by Joy', he will suffer the loss of all things, and count them as refuse, that he may gain Christ and be found in him (Phil.3:8f.).

8   THE PARABLE OF THE PRICELESS PEARL *13:45–46*

[45] 'Again, the kingdom of heaven is like a trader in quest of fine pearls, [46] who when he found a pearl of high value went off and sold all that he had, and bought it.'

This parable forms a pair with the parable of the Buried Treasure. There is no great significance in the fact that this trader is searching for fine pearls, whereas the labourer came upon his treasure by sheer chance while he was occupied with his daily work in the field. In both parables, the point is made that the kingdom of heaven surpasses all earthly goods, and once its true worth is perceived, the finder will give all that he possesses to win it. This is the sense in which we are to understand the seemingly severe demand: 'Any of you that does not take leave of all his possessions cannot be my disciple' (Lk.14:33). Anyone who counts the cost of discipleship has completely failed to grasp the greatness of the reward.

9   THE PARABLE OF THE FISHNET *13:47–50*

[47] 'Again, the kingdom of heaven is like a dragnet which is let down into the sea and brings in fish of every kind; [48] when it is full, they haul it to the shore, sit down, and pack the good fish in baskets while they throw away the bad. [49] So shall it be at the end of the age. The angels will come forth and will separate the wicked from among the righteous [50] and will throw them into the fiery furnace; weeping will be heard there, and the gnashing of teeth.'

There is an obvious kinship between this parable and that of the Tares, at least as it is understood by Matthew. The kingdom is compared not to the fishing but to the judgement. The interpretation does not entirely fit the picture given in the parable. In the parable, the fish are sorted as soon as the catch is landed, and by the fishermen themselves; in the interpretation, the sorting is quite incongruously deferred until 'the end of the age', and is not done by the fishermen, but by the angels. The notion that the wicked are thrown into a fiery furnace is evidently transferred from the interpretation of the parable of the Tares, altogether inappropriately. Bundles of weeds could be used for burning, but whatever the fishermen might do with the fish which they discarded, they would not burn them. If they did not throw them back into the water, they would bury them, perhaps for the purpose of fertilizing. In any case, they could not be left around for any length of time. The interpretation is obviously secondary, not only to the parable of the dragnet, but also to the Matthaean allegorical interpretation of the parable of the Tares. Matthew must have composed it himself, though he does not give any list of correspondences; the good and bad fish represent the wicked and the righteous, but the fishermen who catch the fish are not figures of the angels who separate the wicked from the good; and no clue is given to what is meant by the net, by the sea, or by the baskets in which the good fish are packed. Indeed, the parable does not lend itself to full-blown allegorization.

It is generally held that the fishing is a figure for the preaching of the gospel. This is based on the phrase 'I will make you fishers of men', in the call of the first disciples (Mt.4:19). If that is the true sense, it is hard to see the point of the second action of the fishermen, of sorting the fish that they have just caught, not by species (as by putting carp in one box and trout in another), but by their marketability. The distinction between 'good' and 'bad' is not based upon the actual sorting of fish, but is an anticipation of the separation of wicked from righteous in the Last Judgement. 'Bad' in this context cannot have its basic meaning of 'rotten'—for all the fish are fresh, just out of the water; it can only mean that they are unsaleable, either because they are of kinds forbidden by Jewish law (Lev.11:10–12—'everything that has not fins and scales' is not to be eaten, because 'it is an abomination to you'), or because they are not good eating. But if the netting of the fish 'of every kind' is a figure of evangelizing—which is precisely directed not to the gathering in of the righteous, but to the calling of sinners—the evangelists are surely not meant to sort out their converts at once, and to get rid of 'the bad'!

These considerations have led a number of commentators to suggest that the original parable consisted only of the initial verse: 'the kingdom of heaven is like a dragnet which is let down into the sea and gathers in fish of every kind.' There is no suggestion here that 'of every kind' means 'good and bad'; but only that there are several species (the lake of Galilee is said to have contained at least twenty-four different species of fish). The thought would then be simply that the appeal of the Gospel makes no discrimination of rank or class, wealth or poverty, trade or profession. The grace of God is offered freely to all. (See esp. T.W. Manson, *Sayings*, pp.197f.) The sorting of the fish, as well as the allegorical application to the Last Judgement, is 'Matthaean embroidery' (Manson).

There is no indication of the fate of the good, comparable to the close of the interpretation of the Parable of the Tares (they will 'shine forth like the sun in the kingdom of their Father'). Matthew is obsessed by the dreadful punishment reserved for the wicked; he is less concerned with the anticipated bliss of the righteous.

CONCLUSION: THE DISCIPLE AS TRAINED SCRIBE *13:51–52*

[51] 'Have you understood all these things?' They answered, 'Yes.' [52] He said to them, 'Therefore, every scribe who has been made a

disciple for the service of the kingdom of heaven is like a householder who brings out of his stores things new and old.'

This is Matthew's conclusion to the whole parable collection. From
the beginning he has avoided the Markan phrases which accuse the
disciples of Jesus of *failure* to understand (Mk.4:13; cf.v.34 —
'privately to his own disciples he explained everything'). In Matthew,
the disciples are pronounced blessed because they see and hear (13:
16). Now they profess to have a true understanding of all that he
has been teaching. 'Therefore' (διά τοῦτο) comes in rather strangely;
it seems to provide a loose connection with the parable of the Scribe
which follows, and which may have been framed in a different
context. The disciple who understands, it is implied, is a well-trained
scribe, who can pass on what he himself has learned and develop new
thoughts out of it.

It is often suggested that Matthew gives in these words a kind of
self-portrait, or at least an indication of how he conceives his
function as evangelist. The comparison with a householder
(οἰκοδεσπότης —'master of the house') suggests that he holds a
position of authority; but his office is to distribute to other members
of the household. He has at his disposal a 'treasure' (θησαυρός)—the
word means the storehouse, rather than the contents. 'Things old and
new'—in the household, these would be articles of clothing and
adornment (which could be old or new), and food. Figuratively
these represent the stores of learning which the scribe has
accumulated. The 'old' and the 'new' could mean the ancient Law of
Israel, written and oral, on the one hand; and the interpretation and
application given to it by Jesus, on the other. But we are tempted to
feel that for the evangelist it means the tradition of the teaching
given by Jesus and the interpretation and application which is now
supplied by the evangelist. He has been 'made a disciple' to Jesus,
and has learned from him 'the mystery of the kingdom of heaven',
especially as it is set forth in these parables. The business of the
Jewish scribe was to master the Law itself, as written in the books of
Moses, and also the tradition of its interpretation, which was
conceived to do no more than make explicit what was implicitly set
forth already in the written Law. The experienced scribe would make
his own contribution to the growth of this tradition, as he was asked
to show how it applied to a variety of emergent situations. But he
would still think of himself not as making new law, or as innovating
in any way, but as bringing out what was contained albeit somewhat
cryptically in the Law as given. So he thinks of the Christian scribe

as versed in the Law of Moses and also in the Law of Christ, itself
the fulfilment, not the abolition, of the ancient Law (5:17f.). The
teaching of Christ has itself begun to have a built-up tradition of
interpretation, and there is a developing Christian scribal tradition.
The evangelist feels himself to stand in this tradition, as its guardian
and dispenser.

There was undoubtedly a danger here, from which the later church
has never wholly escaped. Matthew has not understood as deeply as
did Paul that 'Christ is the end of the law for righteousness for
everyone who has faith' (Rom.10:4). There is an incipient legalism
here, which in a Tertullian will take 'old' and 'new' in the sense of
'old law' and 'new law' (*antiqua lex, nova lex*). The conflict between
Jesus and the scribes went deeper than dispute over traditional
interpretations of the written law, or the validity of the oral law; it
involves the infinite difference between life under law and life under
grace.

T.W. Manson therefore remarked that 'this saying represents
perfectly the Jewish Christian ideal: it may well be doubted whether
it represents the convictions of Jesus Himself' (*Sayings*, p.190).

In the book of Ecclesiasticus (Wisdom of Jesus Ben-Sirach), the
work of the scribe is praised as follows:

> He who devotes himself
> to the study of the law of the Most High
> will seek out the wisdom of all the ancients
> and will be concerned with prophecies;
> . . . .
> he will seek out the hidden meaning of proverbs
> and be at home with the obscurities of parables. (Ecclus.39:1,3)

It is quite possible that Matthew was himself a professional scribe,
and that he held this office in the church in which he worked. It is
evident at least that he thinks of the church as led by scribes, or that
it includes scribes among its leaders. Where Paul speaks of 'first
apostles, second prophets, third teachers . . .' (1 Cor.12:28; cf. Eph.
4:11), the Christ of Matthew will say, 'I will send you prophets and
wise men and scribes' (23:34).

FINALE: JESUS REJECTED IN HIS OWN VILLAGE
Mt.13:53—58

[53] When Jesus had finished delivering these parables, he went away
from that place. [54] He made his way to his own village; and there he

taught the people in their synagogue in such manner that they were astounded. They asked, 'Where did this wisdom and these mighty works come from? [55] Is this man not the carpenter's son? Is not his mother called Mary? and his brothers James and Joseph and Simon and Judas? [56] And his sisters—are they not with us, all of them? Where then does he get all these gifts?' [57] They turned their backs on him; and Jesus said to them, 'A prophet is not left unhonoured except in his ñative place and in his own household.' [58] And he did not do many miracles there, because of their unbelief.

The formula of verse 53 marks at once the end of the third Matthaean collection of sayings, and the transition to another phase of activity. The account of the Rejection in Nazareth is drawn from Mark, with small but significant revisions. In Matthew, it follows directly upon the parable discourse; but in Mark a long section comprising three extended miracle stories (4:35—5:43) intervenes between the parables and the incident at Nazareth.

VERSE 54: 'his own village'—Matthew keeps the peculiar Markan phrase εἰς τὴν πατρίδα αὐτοῦ, without naming Nazareth (Nazareth is never mentioned in Mark except in the story of the baptism—1:9). The word πατρίς properly means 'fatherland, homeland', but it had long since come to be used in the sense of 'native place'. It is probably used here in anticipation of the proverb that Jesus will cite; a similar observation is attributed to a number of Greek philosophers (see Bauer, *ad voc.*). 'Their' synagogue—reflects Matthew's sense of the alienation between synagogue and church; probably among Jewish Christians their own local meeting-place was also called a synagogue (cf. Jas.2:2). In Mark, Jesus is accompanied by his disciples; Matthew sets Jesus by himself, in the face of a hostile audience. The comments of the hearers are abbreviated, after Matthew's custom, but he retains the reference to miracles, though Jesus has not done any in this village (cf. Lk.4:23).

VERSES 55—56: 'Carpenter's son'—in Mark, he is called 'the carpenter, the son of Mary'. In the east, this would be a deliberately offensive way of referring to him, implying that he is illegitimate. Even if Joseph were dead, which is probable, Jesus would still be known as 'son of Joseph' (cf. Jn.1:45; Salome may be named as 'the mother' of James and John, but they are 'the sons of Zebedee' (Mt.20:20).

The same names are given in Mark, except that Mark has Joses in place of Joseph. The absence of any mention of Joseph the father suggests that he is dead by this time. The telling out of all the brothers by name, and the mention of 'all his sisters' (v.56) stresses the fact that the whole family is well known in the village, and is of no particular distinction; it is not a family which would be expected to produce such a prodigy as Jesus. There is nothing in the canonical Gospels to intimate that these brothers and sisters are not children of Mary; the notion that they were all older than Jesus, children of Joseph by a former wife (and so half-brothers and half-sisters to Jesus) belongs to early legend, and is probably related to the later doctrine of the *perpetual* virginity of Mary.

VERSE 57: 'turned their backs on him'. This is a free rendering of the verb ἐσκανδαλίζοντο (from σκάνδαλον, 'stumbling-block'). It conveys something close to the idea of apostasy, the renunciation of faith (cf. 24:10).

The words of Jesus are probably not of his own coining, but a proverbial saying. 'In his household', οἰκία—Mark uses the fuller phrase, 'among his relatives and in his household'. Either Matthew felt that this was redundancy, or else he shrank from saying openly that Jesus was disowned by his own family. However, Mark has already indicated that this was the case (3:21; cf. 3:31—35); and John declares flatly that 'his brothers did not believe in him' (Jn. 7:5). However, his brother James became one of the three 'pillars' of the early church in Jerusalem, and indeed its presiding officer (Gal.1:19; 2:9; Acts 15:13; 21:18ff.).

VERSE 58: Matthew modifies the Markan wording, probably because he declines to believe that Jesus '*could* do no mighty work there'. Even Mark modifies his own statement by adding, 'except that he laid his hands on a few sick people and healed them' (6:5). Matthew prefers to say that Jesus 'did not do many mighty works there'. He retains the Markan phrase 'because of their unbelief', but with his rewording he conveys that the (comparative) lack of miracles is a consequence, even a kind of punishment, of the unbelief. Jesus did not lack the power to work his miracles, but refused to exercise it in the face of unbelief. In Mark, the phrase 'because of their unbelief' is not given as the cause of Jesus' inability to work miracles there; he says only that Jesus 'was astounded because of their unbelief' (6:6). In Matthew, it is 'the people', 'the crowds', 'the disciples' and even Pilate that are astounded; Jesus is amazed only once, and then it is not at unbelief, but at faith (8:10—the faith of a Gentile, surpassing anything that he has found in Israel).

D

Sharpening of the Conflict: Emergence of a New Israel

Mt. 14:1–25:46

The rejection of Jesus at Nazareth marks the end of a long section of the Gospel in which the popular enthusiasm of the early days begins to be overclouded by doubts, criticisms, and hostility. Now the sky grows darker. The death of John the Baptist at the hands of Herod foreshadows the fate that is in store for Jesus, and Jesus challenges openly the kind of guidance that is being given by the leaders of Israel. On the other side, the first signs appear that the followers of Jesus will emerge as a distinct community of faith which will become the Christian church. This may well be called a New Israel. It depends on Jesus for the food which he abundantly supplies; it looks to him for salvation from the perils of the stormy seas that must be travelled. The disciples confess him as Messiah and Son of the Living God, and he designates Peter as the one who will hold authority in the church that he will be founding. To a chosen few, he reveals his divine glory in a transfiguration. His next step is to lay down the principles on which the new community is to conduct itself—care for the weak, restoration of the erring, and unlimited forgiveness. With that, he starts on his journey to Jerusalem (19:1). The way is marked by renewed controversy with the Pharisees, but even more by anecdotes and parables that bear upon the principles of the new community; and the whole is overshadowed by the warnings that this journey will bring Jesus into the power of his enemies, who will put him to death.

With his arrival in Jerusalem (21:1), the conflict becomes acute. Jesus is acclaimed by the crowds as Son of David, and acts with authority in the temple. He is challenged by the chief priests and the elders of the people, and throws back their challenge so boldly that they are bent on arresting him. He foils the attempts of Pharisees and Sadducees to entangle him in his talk, and reduces them to silence. Thereupon he denounces the scribes and Pharisees as consummate hypocrites and warns them that they will soon be called to account for their crimes, and he abandons the temple once for all.

From that point until the beginning of the Passion Narrative (in 25:1) he addresses his words only to his own disciples, chiefly to prepare them for what the future has in store, and to urge upon them the need for vigilance and faithfulness. And this final address reaches its climax in a dramatic scenario of the Last Judgement.

Part D is arranged for discussion as follows:

I   RENEWED ACTIVITIES IN GALILEE AND THE NORTH
Mt.14:1–18:35

This section consists of:

1   THE DEATH OF JOHN THE BAPTIST *14:1–12*

[1] At that time Herod the tetrarch heard of the reputation of Jesus, [2] and he said to his attendants, 'This is John the Baptist; he has been raised from the dead, and that is why such powers are at work in him.'

³ For Herod had arrested John, put him in chains, and thrown him into prison over the affair of Herodias, the wife of his brother Philip; ⁴ John had warned him, 'It is not lawful for you to have her to wife.' ⁵ Herod was inclined to execute him, but he was afraid of the masses, for they looked on John as a prophet. ⁶ But when they were celebrating Herod's birthday, the daughter of Herodias danced before the company and so delighted Herod ⁷ that he promised her on his oath to give her whatever she might ask him for. ⁸ Prompted to it by her mother, she said, 'Give me here on a platter the head of John the Baptist.' ⁹ Herod was distressed, but because of his oath and the presence of his guests he gave orders for her request to be granted— ¹⁰ he sent a message and had John beheaded in the prison, ¹¹ and his head was brought to the hall on a platter and given to the girl; and she gave it to her mother. ¹² John's disciples came and removed his body and buried it; and they went to Jesus and told him about it.

As usual, Matthew has abbreviated the Markan story, and as a result has left some incoherences. The lines of introduction (vv. 1f.) are more suitably placed in Mark, where they follow the report of the successful mission of the disciples in the course of which 'they cast out many demons, and anounted many sick people with oil and healed them' (Mk.6:13). Matthew has spoken of this mission at an earlier point (chap.10), but without reporting its results. Now Herod makes his comments immediately after we have heard of the rejection of Jesus in Nazareth, which would not be likely to cause Herod to think of him as a John *redivivus*. In Mark, also, the superstitious notion of Herod is followed by a report of ideas about Jesus current among the people (6:15f.); Matthew omits this, because these popular judgements will be reported by the disciples in the scene at Caesarea Philippi (16:14; cf. Mk.8:28), and he sees no need to give the report twice.

The alterations in the story of the execution are more serious. In Mark, it is Herodias who is angry at John and wants to have him executed (6:19), whereas Herod is moved by a certain awe and admiration for John, recognizes that he is a saint ('a just and holy man'), and listens to him with pleasure, though it all put him in a difficulty (ἠπόρει). This conveys the impression of a prince who realizes that the arrest of John has left him in an uncomfortable situation, but one which he has no thought of terminating by executing his prisoner. In Matthew, there is no hint that Herod takes any pleasure in hearing John, on the contrary, he is only restrained from having him executed out of hand by his fear of the public reaction. After this, we are surprised to hear that the tetrarch 'was distressed' by the girl's request. Matthew takes this over from Mark without noticing that it is not in keeping with what he has said of Herod's readiness to put the prophet to death.

The dancing girl is called 'the daughter of Herodias'. If this is correct, she must have been the child of a former marriage, for Herodias had been married to Herod for less than three years. In Mark, according to some of the best witnesses, she is called the daughter of Herod, and her name is given as Herodias (Mk.6:22; the text is uncertain, but it is probably αὐτοῦ that is the true reading; see the discussion in Metzger's *Textual Commentary*, pp.89f.). The familiar name Salome is not mentioned in any of the Gospels; it is given by Josephus as the name of a daughter of Herodias. But that Salome—not her mother—was the wife of Herod's brother Philip; the Herodias of our story had formerly been the wife of another brother of Philip, who lived in Rome. To clear the way for his marriage with Herodias, Herod had first to get a divorce from his wife who was a daughter of the king of the Nabataeans; some years later her father went to war against Herod and defeated him (AD 36). Both Mark and Matthew have got the complex marital relationships of the Herod brothers mixed up, as well they might.

But there are more difficulties about the story. For one thing it is all but inconceivable that a princess of the Herodian house—however dissolute the court may have been—should dance before strange men at a banquet. As Wellhausen long ago suggested, the κοράσιον (v.11) would more likely be a slave-girl. Again, Herod was not in a position to offer 'the half of his kingdom' (Mk.6:23; Matthew omits this extravagant offer!). Herod ruled by permission of the Romans, and was certainly not free to dispose of his lands as he pleased. It is of course possible that he was drunk enough to offer anything (so Lagrange, Rawlinson, and others); but it is much more likely that the story has been shaped with a recollection of the banquet of Ahasuerus (Esther 5:3—'What is your request? It shall be given you, even to the half of my kingdom').

But above all, the motive for the execution of John is given by Josephus (much more plausibly), not as the fury of a woman rebuked, but as the concern of Herod over the possible danger represented by John's popularity; he was afraid 'lest the degree to which he had gained the confidence of the people might lead him to some rebellion . . . he thought it much better to anticipate any mischief he might cause, by putting him to death.' Josephus also tells us that John was imprisoned and executed in the fortress of

Machaerus, on the east bank of the Dead Sea; this is a long way from the nearest parts of Galilee, and yet the guests mentioned in the Markan account included 'the leading men of Galilee' (6:21). If we had only the Gospel story, we would be left with the impression that the banquet was held in Tiberias or some other Galilean residence of the tetrarch, and that John was imprisoned there.

In sum, it is hard to see in this story anything more than popular legend, shaped in its literary handling by reminiscences of the banquet of Ahasuerus and by the story of the relations between the prophet Elijah and the rulers of Samaria—Ahab and Jezebel. In the framework of the Gospel narrative, it foreshadows the coming death of Jesus.

VERSE 12: Mark ends his story about the execution of John the Baptist by telling us only that 'his disciples came and took away his body and laid it in a tomb.' He continues by an account of how 'the apostles' returned to Jesus from their mission and 'reported to him all that they had done and taught' (6:30). Of this Matthew retains only the one word ἀπήγγειλαν—'they reported'; but now it is the disciples of John who do the reporting, and what they report is not the success of any mission, but the killing of their master John.

2 THE FEEDING OF THE FIVE THOUSAND *14:13–21*

[13] When Jesus heard of this he went away from there by boat to an uninhabited place, privately. The crowds got word of his departure and followed him on foot from the towns. [14] When he landed, he saw a great crowd and took pity on them and healed their sick. [15] When it grew late the disciples made their approach to him and said, 'The place is deserted and the day is nearly over. Dismiss the crowds, so that they may go off to the villages and buy food for themselves.' [16] Jesus replied, 'There is no need for them to go off; give them food yourselves.' [17] They protested, 'We have nothing here but five loaves and two fish.' [18] 'Bring them here to me,' said Jesus. [19] He told the crowds to sit down on the grass; then he took the five loaves of bread and the two fish, and after looking up to heaven and giving thanks, he broke the loaves and gave them to his disciples, and the disciples passed them to the crowds. [20] They all ate their fill; and they picked up the fragments which were left over—twelve baskets full. [21] The crowd that shared in this food numbered about five thousand men, and women and children besides.

Matthew's introduction is not entirely clear. In Mark, the reason for travelling by boat to a quiet place is that the apostles may be given a rest after their mission. People are coming and going in such numbers that Jesus and his disciples can hardly find time to eat (Mk.6:31). In Matthew, there is no mention of the return from the mission; Jesus goes away after hearing of the execution of John, as if he were seeking refuge from a dangerous neighbourhood. But if his move was prompted by the menace of Herod, he would not get out of reach of the tetrarch by travelling to a spot only a few miles away on the shores of the same lake. In fact, we are not told where he was when he went aboard the boat. The last time any mention of place was given, he was at Nazareth, which is nine or ten miles from the lake; now it is assumed that he is somewhere on the shore where a boat is available. The disciples are not mentioned until verse 15, but presumably they were with him during the trip on the lake. Since crowds of people are able to go after them on foot, and to reach the 'uninhabited place' before them, they cannot have had far to row. The crowds are said to come 'from all the towns' (or 'cities'—πόλεων), but there are no towns of any size along the west shore, if we are thinking of the area around Capernaum.

VERSES 13—14: At the arrival, just as at the departure, only Jesus is mentioned, as 'leaving in a boat' and as 'seeing the great crowd' when he got out. Jesus takes pity on them, as in Mark, but not 'because they were like sheep without a shepherd' (Mk.6:34; Matthew has transferred this phrase to his introduction to the mission charge—9:36). Mark states that 'he taught them many things'; Matthew substitutes, 'he healed their sick.'

VERSES 15—16: The dialogue follows the Markan wording closely at the beginning; the clause, 'there is no need for them to go away', is a Matthaean addition. But after that, Matthew omits the further dialogue (Mk.6:37b,38), with the half-insolent question of the disciples, 'Are we to go and buy loaves for two hundred denarii, to give them food to eat?' along with the question of Jesus and the reply of the disciples. In Matthew's version, the disciples volunteer the information about the meagre amount of food available to them.

A story like this is difficult for a modern reader to understand. It is of course preposterous, if it be taken literally, as an account of an actual event. But if we are not capable of believing that several thousand people were fed with five loaves of bread and two fish, is it even worth looking for any kind of significance in the story at all?

It must at least be said that the Gospel writers themselves, even if they took it to be literally true (as they probably did), saw something more in it than a miracle of the satisfying of hunger. This is made explicit in the Gospel of John, where the story is used as an introduction to a discourse of Jesus on the bread of life; it is taken as a symbol of the Christian Eucharist. Something of this is latent in the Synoptic accounts also, and from the earliest times the bread and fish have been depicted on the table in symbolic representations of the Eucharist.

On the quite needless assumption that such a story must have grown (however wildly) out of some actual incident in the career of Jesus, various rationalizing explanations have been offered. Perhaps the most popular is that given by H.E.G. Paulus in 1828, that when Jesus and his followers began to share their small store of food with others, the rest of the crowd brought out the food which they had in their wallets, and so there was enough and to spare for all. The fact of a picnic on the grass, to which all brought something, is turned in the telling into a miracle story. This has been rightly characterized as banal and inept, but it has found many to accept it as a reasonable explanation, even among the ranks of scholars (Johannes Weiss!). Equally ridiculous is the suggestion of Ernest Renan, that Jesus withdrew to the desert and was followed by many; by the exercise of extreme frugality, the group managed to survive on almost nothing; this was looked upon as a miracle. The view of Albert Schweitzer also gets rid of the miraculous element by the simple device of removing the statement that 'they ate their fill' (and its amplification in the notion that they picked up twelve basketfuls of fragments that were left over). We are then left, he thinks, with a token 'meal' in which each person received a minute portion of bread as a sign of the promised participation in the Messianic banquet; the feeding of the multitudes was an 'eschatological sacrament'. Jesus, as the coming Messiah, consecrates the participants through the portion of bread which he distributes by the hands of his apostles, as partakers in the coming Messianic meal. This can hardly be classed among the *rationalizing* interpretations; but it must be said that there is nothing to show that the story ever existed except as a miracle story.

Among those who recognize it as intrinsically the story of a miracle, there are some who look upon it as a kind of midrash on the much less extravagant story of Elisha (2 Ki.4:42–44) which is certainly narrated as a miracle wrought by the prophet. A man brings to Elisha twenty barley loaves (and fresh ears of grain). Elisha bids his servant to give them to 'the men' (whoever they are) 'that they may eat'. The servant remonstrates, 'How am I to set this before a hundred men?' But Elisha repeats his command, with the assurance that the LORD has said, 'They shall eat and have some left'. And so it came to pass; 'they ate and had some left, according to the word of the LORD.' Naturally, if such a story were to be transferred to Jesus, the Christian narrator would take it for granted that Jesus would do something much more marvellous than Elisha. If we are to admit conjectures along such lines as these, it will be agreed that the numbers would tend to be multiplied in the popular imagination. The five thousand men of the Markan story has been enhanced by Matthew to the extent of an indefinite number of women and children; at some earlier stage the numbers may have been much smaller (perhaps five hundred?). In a different version (Mk.8:1–9 = Mt.15:32–38) the numbers are put at about four thousand in Mark, and Matthew again enhances this by the addition of women and children. John and Luke retain the five thousand of the first Markan/ Matthaean version (Jn.6:1–14; Lk.9:10–17). There is, it must be said, no evidence that the story ever was told in a form that suggested a significantly smaller number of participants (hundreds in place of thousands). In any event, the story was probably from the beginning intended to manifest Jesus as endued with miraculous powers.

There is, however, a departure from the usual pattern of the miracle story in that nothing is said of the reaction of the onlookers (amazement, fear, faith, etc.). Neither the disciples nor the crowds say anything to suggest that they have witnessed something out of the ordinary. (John alone repairs the omission; the people are convinced that Jesus is 'the prophet who is to come into the world,' and they plan to 'take him by force to make him king'—Jn.6:14f.) It is not even suggested that the event leads to the spread of his fame (as, for instance, in 9:31). People who have heard of the healing powers of Jesus come from great distances to have him heal their sick (4:24), but we are never told that they came to ask for a multiplication of their food supplies.

3 JESUS WALKS ON THE LAKE *14:22–33*

[22] Jesus immediately compelled the disciples to board the boat and go on before him to the other side, while he dismissed the crowds. [23] Once he had dismissed them, he went up on the mountain by himself to pray, and late in the night he was there alone. [24] The boat was by this time well out on the lake, and was being battered by the waves, for the wind was against them. [25] In the fourth watch of the night, Jesus came to them, walking over the lake, [26] and the disciples,

when they saw him walking on the lake, were terrified, saying to themselves, 'It is a ghost!' and they cried out for fear. [27] But Jesus spoke to them at once, to say, 'Take heart, it is I; do not be frightened.'

[28] Peter replied, 'Lord, if it is you, command me to come to you over the waters.' [29] Jesus said, 'Come!' and Peter, getting out of the boat, walked on the waters and came to Jesus, [30] but when he became aware of the wind he was frightened. As he began to sink he cried out, 'Lord, save me!' [31] Jesus at once reached out his hand and grasped him, saying to him, 'O man of little faith! Why did you doubt?'

[32] When they got into the boat the wind fell; [33] and the men in the boat fell on their knees before him, saying, 'Truly you are the Son of God.'

The basic story is again taken from Mark, with the usual abbreviations. In particular, Matthew omits the phrase 'to Bethsaida', leaving us with no indication of where the marvel was supposed to have taken place. He omits the Markan phrase 'seeing them labouring in their rowing', either because he thought it superfluous, or possibly, because he realized that Jesus on the mountain would not be able to see a boat halfway across the lake (this, however, seems more like a modern criticism than one that would occur to Matthew). At the same time, he speaks of the boat labouring against the waves (not of the men labouring at the oars—the same verb is retained). He omits the puzzling words, 'He wished to pass by them' (Mk.6:48), which afford no reasonable explanation. The most significant change comes at the very end, where he omits Mark's critical reflection that the disciples 'did not understand the matter of the loaves, but their hearts were hardened'. In general, Matthew (and Luke also) tones down the harshness of Mark's criticisms of the disciples; but here he reverses the comment completely; he tells us that they understood so well that they confessed Jesus as the Son of God! This anticipates the confession of faith which Mark will reserve for the episode of Caesarea Philippi (Mk.8:27ff.; Mt.16:13–16). According to Mark, 'they were utterly astounded', but the astonishment did not lead to understanding, much less to faith—'their hearts were hardened.'

But the most notable change by far is not to be seen in these revisions, but in the insertion into the Markan story of a new episode, in which Peter attempts to duplicate his Master's marvellous feat, with a temporary success. This is hardly to be seen as a variant that has arisen in oral transmission. Certainly it is not an independent fragment, which Matthew has simply conflated with the Markan story, for it can never have existed except as a supplement to that. We may hold, then, that it is a literary creation of Matthew himself, a midrashic expansion of the story which he found in Mark. This would mean that he had no thought of it as an actual occurrence, but that he created it, a pure fiction, as a vehicle of Christian teaching. Our task is not to search for some kind of action that may have given rise to such a story, but to ask what kind of lesson Matthew meant to teach.

We may suggest, then, that Matthew is depicting the Christian— represented by Peter, not as a leader of the community but as a venturesome disciple—afloat and wave-tossed, beset by fears, yet sustained by a measure of faith. He becomes aware that Jesus is at hand, though the vision is dim and uncertain. At the command of the half-seen, half-unseen Jesus, he ventures courageously to leave the boat and to walk upon the waves as his Master has done; but once he becomes awake to the danger, his courage evaporates and he begins to sink. Yet as soon as he cries to Jesus for help, he is saved. So the Christian who attempts some great thing is apt to falter, to lose his courage and to weaken in his faith, if he allows himself to take thought for the immediate risks of his situation; there is no security for him except in the Lord, who is present to help in time of need.

The basic story is equally a vehicle of instruction, not in any degree an account of an actual occurrence. We need take no heed of attempts to find a simple core of fact beneath it. It has been suggested, in an attempt at rationalization, that Jesus was actually walking in the surf near the shore when those in the boat first caught sight of him; and in the misty darkness just before the dawn they imagined that they were seeing a phantom walking upon the water of the lake. But would the account of such a momentary hallucination be passed on in any form? Why would the disciples tell others of how they had taken Jesus for a ghost striding over the waves when it turned out that he was there in flesh and blood, wading through the surf close to shore? Would the story be worth telling, and worth repeating, except as a wonder-tale of Jesus?

The basic story has overtones of the Christian experience of the risen Jesus. As in the story of the stilling of the storm, the boat is a figure of the church, and the waters of the lake, where the rowers must labour against contrary winds and high waves, are a figure of the hostile world. Jesus on the mountain communing with the Father in prayer will represent the ascended Jesus. His followers are conscious of his absence ('for we walk by faith, not by sight. We are of good courage, and we would rather be away from the body and at home with the Lord'—2 Cor.5:7f.). Yet he is able to come to them, however great the danger and the turmoil, and to dispel all their fears. As Matthew invented the story of Peter's venture, so some Christian teacher before him invented the basic story of Jesus walking on the sea, and attached it to the story of the feeding of the multitudes. His imagination had no need to be provided with a trifling story of hallucination and fear of a ghost.

VERSE 22: The strange commencement, taken over from Mark, offers no explanation of why Jesus should 'compel' his disciples to leave without him, or why it should be necessary for him to 'dismiss' the crowds. Would they not disperse of their own accord if he simply got into the boat with his disciples and left them? Would they accept dismissal more easily if the disciples went away and Jesus alone remained? We are inclined to feel that this is no more than an artificial setting for the marvel that is to follow, which requires that the disciples should be out on the lake without Jesus.

VERSES 23–24: The location is left vague. There are no mountains above the shore of the lake of Galilee in the neighbourhood of Capernaum; the hills above the lake on the west bank rise no higher than 500 feet above sea level (about 1200 feet above the lake of Galilee, which is 700 feet below sea level). 'The mountain' is not a geographical height; it is a symbol of the place where Jesus communes with the Father. With two exceptions (11:25ff.;26:39,42), there is no indication of the content of any prayer of Jesus in the Synoptic Gospels. Like Mark, Matthew seldom so much as mentions Jesus praying; he has no parallel to Mark 1:35. Luke, on the other hand, makes several references to Jesus praying on the occasion of a significant action (6:12, of night-long prayer before the appointment of the Twelve; 9:28, before the Transfiguration; cf.11:1). [Besides the 'High-Priestly' prayer of chap. 17, John reports prayers of Jesus in 11:41f.; 12:27f.] Jesus encourages his disciples to pray, gives them a prayer for their own use, and promises them that their prayers will be answered; but he never leads them in prayer, nor joins with them in their prayers.

'late in the night'—ὀψίας δὲ γενομένης, exactly the same phrase as was used in v. 15, where it must mean 'late in the afternoon'. In the meanwhile, the bread and fish have been distributed to a crowd of more than five thousand people, with only twelve serving at the meal; the fragments have been gathered into baskets and, after all that, the disciples have rowed a considerable distance against the wind.

VERSE 25: The time is given according to the Roman reckoning; the fourth watch would be roughly from 3 to 6 a.m. The Jews divided the night into three watches.

VERSE 27: 'It is I'—ἐγώ εἰμι, literally, 'I am.' This mode of speech is frequently attributed to Jesus in the Gospels. In LXX, it is generally a self-proclamation of God.

VERSE 28: Peter is not speaking for all the disciples—there is no trace of a notion that they should all get out of the boat and walk over the waters!

'if it is you'—Is it suggested that Peter is not quite sure?

It is hard to imagine that a fisherman should seriously propose to get out of his boat while it was tossing in heavy waves; and it is if anything still less credible that Jesus should bid him to do so. It would not be easy for them to clamber into the boat while it was still tossing; but according to the story it is only after they have climbed or been pulled over the gunwale that the wind dies down.

Loisy suggests that the Petrine supplement foreshadows (that is, is based on) the immediate failure and subsequent recovery of Peter at the time of the crucifixion; it 'figures his denial after a sincere protestation of fidelity; and the intervention of Jesus [figures] the appearance of Christ which restores to him the conscience and the courage of an apostle, the chief of the apostles' (*Evangiles Synoptiques*, p.943).

For Matthew, it probably is an assurance to his readers that Jesus will rescue them from any situation into which they may fall through excess of zeal and 'little faith'. Like the great apostle, their courage may fail when they allow themselves to think of the surrounding danger, but they will find Jesus ready and able to save.

There may be echoes here of a number of Old Testament themes. Those who 'went down to the sea in ships . . . saw the deeds of the Lord . . . their courage melted away . . . then they cried unto the Lord in their trouble, and he delivered them from their distress; he made the storm be still and the waves of the sea were hushed' (Ps.107:23–29). The God of Israel 'trampled the waves of the sea' (Job 9:8); he 'makes a way in the sea, a path in the mighty waters' (Isa.43:16; cf. Ps.77:19).

4   HEALINGS AT GENNESARET *14:34–36*

[34] When they had completed the crossing, they went ashore at Gennesaret. [35] As soon as the men of that place recognized him, they sent word to all the neighbourhood and brought to him all that were

sick. [36] They begged him to let them touch only the hem of his cloak; and all who touched it were completely healed.

This passage is an abbreviated version of a Markan paragraph. Matthew omits details which are of no great consequence, as that 'they let down the anchor' (Mk.6:53), that the sick were brought to Jesus 'on beds' (v.55), that Jesus moves from the shore through the countryside, and that wherever he went, 'into villages or towns or open fields, they laid the sick in the market places' (vv.55c,56a).

In the reports of the healing ministry of Jesus, we hear generally of individual sufferers, and of some dialogue between Jesus and the sick person (or some representative—as the centurion of Capernaum [8:5–13]; the father of the epileptic boy [17:14ff.]). Mass healings are the exception; but they are mentioned also in 8:16 and 15:29–31. Healing by a touch of the hem of Jesus' cloak is mentioned also in the story of the woman with a haemorrhage (9:20–22—though in that case, Jesus declares that her faith has healed her). In the book of Acts, Luke tells of how people hoped that Peter's shadow might suffice to heal those on whom it fell, as he passed along the street (Acts 5:12–15); and how 'handkerchiefs or aprons' which had come from Paul's body were carried to the sick, 'and diseases left them and the evil spirits came out of them' (Acts 19:12). Stories like these reflect a primitive notion of Power as something mysterious which passes by contact—it may be by a touch of the hand, or even by contact with the clothing of the bearer of Power. There is nothing moral about it, any more than about an electrical current; and it is not essentially associated with belief in a personal divinity. What we have in these stories, whether of Jesus or of his apostles (or of the king who heals 'the king's evil' [scrofula] by his touch), belongs to the realm of magic. That such stories are found in the New Testament is evidence of the survival within the earliest Christian communities of elements of primitive conceptions of man and his world.

[An interesting example from the Old Testament is seen in the story of Elisha and the restoration of life to the child of the Shunamite woman (2 Ki.4:18–37). When he hears that the child is dead, Elisha first sends his servant Gehazi ahead, giving him his staff and instructing him to lay the staff on the face of the child. Clearly, he expects that the staff will be the channel of the prophet's power. Gehazi did as he had been instructed, and 'laid the staff upon the face of the child, but there was no sound or sign of life' (v.31). Elisha must make the contact in person: 'he went up and lay upon the child, putting his mouth upon his mouth, his eyes upon his eyes, and his hands upon his hands; and as he stretched himself upon him, the flesh of the child became warm' (v.34); and after the procedure is repeated, 'the child sneezed seven times, and the child opened his eyes' (v.35). A similar story is told of Elijah, without the use of the staff, and with a greater emphasis on prayer (2 Ki.17:17—24). And in another story, the bones of Elisha suffice to bring a dead man to life, when he is thrown into Elisha's grave (2 Ki.13:21).]

VERSE 34: Gennesaret is a small but fertile valley to the west of the lake of Galilee, a few miles south of Capernaum; the lake of Galilee is sometimes called the lake of Gennesaret (Lk.5:1; cf. 1 Macc. 11:67). According to Mark, Jesus had told them to cross to Bethsaida, which is on the east shore of the lake. But the topographical notices are confused, and it is impossible to tell how the evangelists thought of the movements of the boat and the company.

5   THE LAWS OF PURITY *15:1—20*

[1] Pharisees and scribes from Jerusalem now made approach to Jesus, with the question: [2] 'Why do your disciples transgress the tradition of the elders? They do not wash their hands when they eat food.' [3] He retorted, 'Why do you transgress the commandment of God, for the sake of your tradition? [4] God said, "Honour your father and your mother" and "Anyone who curses father or mother must be put to death." [5] But you say, "If anyone tells his father or his mother, 'What you might have received from me is a gift (set aside for God),' then he must not honour his father." [6] With that you nullify the word of God for the sake of your tradition. [7] You hypocrites! Isaiah spoke to the point when he prophesied about you:

[8] This people honours me with lip-service
   but their hearts are far from me.
[9] They offer me worship in vain,
   for they teach as doctrines the commandments of men.'

[10] He summoned the crowd to him and said to them, 'Hear and understand! [11] It is not what goes into the mouth that defiles a person, but what comes out of the mouth—it is this that defiles.'

[12] The disciples thereupon made approach to him to say, 'Do you know that the Pharisees were revolted when they heard that saying?' [13] He answered, 'Every plant that my heavenly Father has not planted will be rooted up. [14] Let them be. They are blind guides of blind followers, and if one blind person leads another they will both fall into a pit.'

¹⁵ Peter went on to ask: 'Explain the saying to us', ¹⁶ and Jesus
said, 'Are you still without understanding? ¹⁷ Do you not see that
whatever goes into the mouth passes into the stomach and is
evacuated? ¹⁸ But what comes out of the mouth proceeds from the
heart, and it is this that defiles a person. ¹⁹ For evil thoughts come
out of the heart—murder, adultery, fornication, theft, false witness,
slander. ²⁰ These are the things that defile, but to eat with hands
unwashed does not defile anyone.'

The 'washing of hands' which is the subject of controversy in this
passage has nothing to do with ordinary cleanliness or common
practice. It is a ritual washing, intended to remove a ceremonial
'uncleanness' in terms of the Levitical Law. Many animals are
'unclean', such as camels, badgers, hares, and hogs, and anyone who
touches one of them is rendered 'unclean' (Lev.11:4–8,24ff.; see the
article 'Clean and Unclean', by L.E. Toombs, in *IDB*). The washing
of hands is not a rite prescribed in the written Law, but was
introduced at some later time by scribal authority and so made part
of 'the tradition of the elders'. By the time of Jesus, a vast body of
such traditional lore had grown up, and was looked upon as 'oral
Law' and as possessing equal authority with the written Law. This, at
least, was the position of the scribes, the learned expositors of the
Law, and also of the powerful party of the Pharisees; but it was not
accepted by the Sadducees or by the priesthood, and the mass of
practices prescribed by the scribal tradition was largely ignored by
the 'people of the land' (*'am-ha-'arez*), for whom much of it was
altogether impractical. Much of the 'oral Law' was an accumulation of
opinions given by scribes in connection with situations which were
not explicitly envisaged by the written Law—an ancient code could
not be expected to deal with everything that might arise in the
historical and social conditions of a later period. But since the Law
was regarded not as a collection of man-made ordinances but as a
system of divine pronouncements, it could not be amended to meet
new circumstances as they arose. It was the task of the scribes, then,
to expound and apply the Law to cases for which it did not provide.
Over a period of time, their expositions and applications
accumulated and were transmitted by word of mouth from generation to generation. Each scribe looked upon it as a prime duty to
'raise up many disciples' (Mishnah, *Aboth* 1:1), and to teach them
what he had learned from his own teacher. Basically, this was done
by requiring the disciple to recite his teacher's words and to commit
them to memory exactly: 'the teacher's instruction, the pupil's

learning—in fact all study and maintenance of knowledge within this discipline—rests on the principle of oral repetition' (B. Gerhardsson, *Memory and Manuscript*, p.28). But they did not think of this body of traditional lore as an accumulation of scribal opinions, but as a part of the Law which was given to Moses on Mount Sinai, and communicated to 'the elders' orally, and by them transmitted to succeeding generations; and the chain of transmission was supposedly guaranteed.

In this passage, the rite of the washing of hands is no more than a peg to raise the far wider question of the essential meaning of defilement and purity, and within that, the validity of the oral Law *in toto*. It is evident, however, that the sayings of Jesus go beyond a challenge to the validity of the *oral* Law, and in effect undermine the *written* Law of purity as well. As Mark clearly sees (Mk.7:19, omitted by Matthew), they amount to a declaration that all foods are clean. The question became important in the church as soon as it admitted Gentiles; the Jewish food laws, still observed by the orthodox Jews to-day, could not be allowed to be a barrier to full communion between Jews and Gentiles in the church of Christ. It was of fundamental importance that Paul could say, 'I know and am persuaded in the Lord Jesus that nothing is unclean in itself' (Rom.14:14), even though he is ready to make concessions to the prejudices of others in the matter (1 Cor.8:4–13).

VERSE 1: 'Pharisees and scribes'—the usual order of reference in Matthew, 'scribes and Pharisees', is disturbed under the influence of the Markan passage, which speaks of 'the Pharisees, and some of the scribes coming from Jerusalem' (Mk.7:1).

VERSE 2: The ritual washing of hands, which is the particular topic in dispute here, has nothing to do with habits of personal cleanliness. It moves in the area of primitive notions of the pure and the impure, strange and unreal to us. The Mishnah deals with the ritual requirements in detail in the tractate *Yadaim* ('Hands'). It discusses such matters as the quantity of water that is needed—an egg cup would hold enough for one person, a volume equivalent to that of six eggs would suffice for five or for ten or for a hundred. Water that is unfit for cattle to drink may be used provided it is taken directly from the earth, but not if it has been put into vessels; and so forth.

This is another of those incidents in which it is the conduct of the disciples that is attacked, not that of Jesus himself. This is usually an indication that we are dealing with a reflection of a controversy between Jews and Christian believers in the early church. The setting is obviously contrived; we can hardly suppose that scribes have come from Jerusalem to Galilee to question Jesus about the behaviour of his disciples.

VERSE 3: The defence of Jesus is a counter-attack. The people who are criticizing the disciples for violating rules introduced by human teachers are themselves guilty of the far greater offence of nullifying the word of God himself, and using their 'tradition' to justify the violation.

VERSES 4–6: δῶρον, 'gift,' is a Greek rendering of the Hebrew term *qorban*, used in sacrificial terminology of an offering or oblation. The presupposition is that the gift has not been offered yet, but has been vowed; and it is argued that once the vow is made, the property cannot be used for other purposes, even to relieve the needs of parents. From the second century we have a certain amount of Jewish evidence bearing upon the question of whether and on what conditions such a vow might be annulled; generally it may be said that the rabbis agree with Jesus; one rabbi actually declares that a way of annulment may be opened 'by reason of the honour due to father and mother', and it is said that 'the Sages agree with Rabbi Eliezer that in a matter between a man and his father and mother, the way may be opened for him by reason of the honour due to his father and mother' (Tractate *Nedarim*, ix.1).

It is evident that the scribes and rabbis were not all of one opinion on the matter. The situation presupposed in this pericope may rest upon an actual case, possibly known to Jesus but more likely to the early Christian teacher who framed the story, of someone who repudiated responsibility to aid his needy parents and found some scribe to support him by a rigid insistence that a vow once spoken, even in a rash moment, could not under any circumstances be revoked. M. Black cites a passage bearing on the same theme from the Talmud: 'If anyone expressly lays such a Korban on his relatives, then they are bound by it and cannot receive anything from him that is covered by the Korban' (*Aramaic Approach*, p.139). To Jesus, this amounts to allowing a man-made tradition to nullify the sixth commandment; the command 'you shall honour' is applied to mean 'you must not honour' your parents, if you have bound yourself by a vow to give them nothing in their time of need.

VERSES 8–9: The reproach which Isaiah addressed to all Israel in the eighth century BC is applied to the scribes and Pharisees of the time of Jesus and the church. The citation (Isa.29:13) is made from LXX, with one slight change in the last line, not from the Hebrew text. Isaiah, however, was not speaking of evading duties imposed by

a commandment by interpreters who resorted to man-made
tradition, but of people whose worship of God is no more than an
outward show. The last line of the Hebrew text says nothing about
teaching doctrines, but of the mechanical use in worship of words
put into their mouths by seers and prophets (29:10).

VERSE 10: The original questioners now disappear: Jesus
summons the crowd, and makes a cryptic pronouncement (v.11),
after which they too disappear and the remainder of the scene is
played between Jesus and Peter (as spokesman for the disciples).

VERSE 11: Matthew changes the wording of the saying by introducing the phrases 'into the mouth' and 'out of the mouth'; in Mark,
it is not so restricted to food, but reads broadly, 'there is nothing
outside a person which by going into him can defile him; but the
things which come out of a person are what defile him' (Mk.7:15).
Matthew's change makes the reversion to the original question more
clear, and serves well enough for the first clause; but it makes
difficulty for him when he comes to the explanation of the second
clause, for there the things that come out of the person are not
words but thoughts and deeds, and these are not said to come out of
the mouth but out of the heart. He is then obliged to make the
rather awkward connection by inserting verse 18: 'What comes out
of the mouth proceeds from the heart.' This recalls his insistence on
the guilt incurred by words, even careless words (12:34–37).

The saying is called a 'parable' (v.15), in the sense (often attached
to the Hebrew *mashal*) of a riddle. Taken as a word addressed to
crowds who hear it pronounced as it were in the void, it has indeed a
riddling character, at least in its Markan formulation. Not limited to
the question of the food laws, it annuls in principle the whole mass
of laws of ritual purity which are laid down in the books of Leviticus
and Numbers, and makes nonsense of much of the traditional
religious practice of the Jewish people. If nothing external to a
person can cause defilement, there can be no unclean foods, and
besides that, no defilement can be caused by a corpse, or by
menstruation or childbirth, or by emission of semen, or by a skin
disease, or by the ashes of a red heifer (Lev.12–15; Num.19; etc.).

VERSE 12: Nothing is said about the reaction of the crowds, but
the evangelists probably assume that they did not understand. The
comment of the disciples tells us that the Pharisees were 'revolted'
(ἐσκανδαλίσθησαν)—the verb may mean 'shocked', or 'offended',
but has often the force of 'led into sin' (cf. 13:21; 24:10). There is a
touch of that here—the saying causes the Pharisees to sin in that
they reject Jesus. Probably we are intended to gather that they have

left the scene in anger. Nothing is said of the scribes of verse 1, yet this is basically a question of scribal debate.

VERSES 13–14: The remark of the disciples and the response of Jesus which follows are not taken from Mark. Matthew's insertion is partly of his own composition, but the saying about the blind leading the blind is found as a separate 'parable' in Luke, in the form of a question (Lk.6:39), in a totally different context. It is used by him in his Sermon on the Plain, and is linked with the warning against judging, when you have faults of your own that you should first remove (Lk.6:39–42 // Mt.7:1–5). In that context, it is not the Pharisees who are 'blind guides', but anyone who seeks to remove a speck from a brother's eye without seeing the log that is in his own eye. The saying of verse 13 is peculiar to Matthew, and it is unlikely that it was originally directed against Pharisaism as a 'plant that my heavenly Father has not planted'. We can hardly hope to recover the original context. Matthew has come upon it as a vagrant saying and after his fashion has worked it along with other material into a context which he thought suitable.

VERSE 15: The theme of the saying is resumed by the request of Peter (in Mark, of the disciples) to have the 'parable' explained. As in chapter 13, the disciples no more understand the saying than does the crowd; they do not understand the 'mysteries of the kingdom of heaven' by any personal illumination. Again we have the theme that the parables are given to conceal the truth from the many, and are explained privately to the disciples (cf. Mk.4:34). In the Markan version, the disciples ask him about the parable after he has 'entered the house and left the crowd' (Mk.7:17).

Matthew brings the figure of Peter into greater prominence than any of the other evangelists. In this instance, he is not given any real pre-eminence; he is as lacking in understanding as the rest of them, and merely acts as spokesman for the group. The reply of Jesus is addressed to them all.

VERSE 19: In the Markan version, we have a double catalogue of sins—seven in the plural, six in the singular (Mk.7:21f.). This is certainly a formal construction made by a trained scribe. Matthew abbreviates it and creates his own catalogue of vices, seven in number, all in the plural.

6 JESUS AND THE CANAANITE WOMAN *15:21–28*

²¹ When Jesus left there, he went into the territories of Tyre and Sidon. ²² A Canaanite woman of those parts came out and cried,

'Have mercy on me, O Lord, Son of David! My daughter is badly afflicted by a demon.' [23] He gave her no answer; and now his disciples made their approach to him with the request, 'Send her off, for she keeps shouting after us.' [24] He replied, 'I am sent only to the lost sheep of the house of Israel.' [25] But she came and knelt at his feet, with the plea, 'Lord, help me!' [26] He answered, 'It is not right to take the children's bread and toss it to the dogs.' [27] But she said, 'Yes, Lord, yet even the dogs eat of the crumbs that are dropped from their masters' table.' [28] Jesus now answered, 'Woman, you have great faith. Let it be done as you wish.' And her daughter was healed from that moment.

The Matthaean version of this story differs from that of Mark to a surprising degree—so much so that it has made some commentators inclined to suppose that Matthew has made use of a second form of the tradition and has conflated it with Mark. In Mark, Jesus is alone when he comes to the Phoenician coast; in Matthew, he is accompanied by his disciples. In Mark, he goes into a house, wishing nothing to be known of his presence; in Matthew, he walks in the open street with his disciples. In Mark, the woman is called 'a Greek, Syro-Phoenician by race', and her daugher 'had an unclean spirit'. Despite his attempt to remain incognito, she hears of his arrival at once, goes into the house, and begs him to drive the demon out of her child, kneeling at his feet; and the whole scene unfolds indoors. In Matthew, she is called a Canaanite; she 'comes out' and shouts after him in the street, so that his disciples and all can hear, and the whole scene unrolls out of doors. She herself tells him of her daughter's trouble, addressing him as 'Lord ($\kappa \acute{\nu} \rho \iota \epsilon$), Son of David.' The two verses which follow (vv.23,24) are not represented in Mark at all. In them we are told that Jesus at first gave the woman no answer; then that the disciples—who are now mentioned for the first time—intervened to ask him to send the woman away, to put an end to her importunities; and it is only now that the woman kneels before Jesus with her plea for help. From that point, Matthew reverts to the Markan pattern. The disciples disappear for good, and Jesus administers the violent rebuff: 'It is not right to take the children's bread and toss it to the dogs', omitting Mark's first clause ('Let the children be fed first'). The reply of the woman is the same in substance as in Mark: she accepts the disgraceful epithet of 'dogs' for her people—for herself and her daughter—and asks only to be treated as the dogs are treated, by being given the crumbs. This sounds like grovelling humility, but Jesus takes it as an expression of great faith. In this, Matthew again departs from the Markan text, and his conclusion is completely reshaped after the manner of the story of the centurion's child (8:13), with the same emphasis on faith, and on the instantaneous healing.

VERSE 22: 'a Canaanite woman'—Matthew's term is a simplification of the peculiar Markan phrase, 'a Greek woman, Syro-Phoenician by race.' Perhaps Mark uses 'Greek' in the broad sense of 'Gentile' (as Paul sometimes does—Rom.1:16, etc.); the prefix 'Syro' will distinguish her from the Phoenicians of their settlements abroad (in Libya, Carthage, etc.). Matthew's word has overtones of the derogatory use of the term in the Old Testament, linking the woman with the older inhabitants of the land of Israel who were dispossessed by the Hebrew invaders; according to the book of Judges, they ought to have been exterminated (Judges 2:1–5), and there was to be no fraternization with them.

'Came out'—not out of her country, as if Jesus had remained within the northern boundary of Israel; but out of her house. Matthew revises Mark's picture, perhaps because he would not have Jesus violate Jewish custom by entering a house in a heathen city.

'Lord, Son of David'—the title is out of place on the lips of a 'Canaanite'. What could the Davidic monarchy or the Israelite Messianic hopes attached to that dynasty mean to her? Jesus was not generally recognized as Messiah in Israel, or even among his own disciples (they acknowledge him for the first time in the confession made by Peter at Caesarea Philippi, Mt.16:16; and then he forbids them to tell others of his Messiahship, v.20); how then would a woman in a foreign land call him by this title? Is Matthew perhaps introducing a familiar liturgical phrase used in Jewish-Christian circles: 'Have mercy, Lord, Son of David'? *Kyrie*, 'Lord', would by itself mean no more than 'Sir'—a respectful form of address; and it is so used in Mark; but here it clearly has the force of a cult title. Such a usage is not established for the lifetime of Jesus; it is a development of the apostolic church.

VERSES 23–24: These two verses are interpolated by Matthew into the Markan story. The silence of Jesus implies a refusal to grant the woman's request. The disciples, not hitherto mentioned, find the woman a nuisance; they show no trace of compassion for her. As they will rebuke the people who bring children to Jesus to receive his blessing (19:13), they want merely to be rid of her with her importunate cries. Their intervention has no point except to provide a setting for a saying of Jesus, a declaration that his mission is confined to Israel (not found in Mark). It is in the spirit of the opening instructions given to the disciples in the mission charge (10:6), which itself reflects the exclusiveness of the earliest Christian missionary preaching in Palestine.

VERSE 25: 'knelt'—in Mark, she is kneeling throughout the scene. She makes her plea now in the pathetic words, 'Lord, help me!'

VERSE 26: Matthew now reverts to the Markan story. Jesus replies to the woman even more brutally than in Mark, for the omitted phrase, 'Let the children first be fed', at least holds out some hope that a time will come when the blessing will be made available to the Gentiles. In Matthew, the offensive words are unrelieved by even this slight hint of better things to come: 'It is not right to take the children's bread and toss it to the dogs.' These words exhibit the worst kind of chauvinism. Only Jews are entitled to be treated as 'children' of God; the Gentiles are 'dogs'. It is simply absurd to suppose that the brutality is alleviated by the fact that the 'dogs' are not street curs, but pets of the children that frisk around the table (Lagrange), 'little dogs' (κυνάρια); the diminutive had lost its force in Hellenistic Greek (Taylor, *Mark*, p.350). No more attractive is the notion that by this violent rebuff Jesus is 'trying her faith' (McNeile and many others, including Luther!). And it is altogether too subtle to suppose that Jesus is really rolling the matter over in his own mind before deciding (J. Weiss, V. Taylor, *et al.*), and that the words are an expression of his own misgivings rather than a response to her plea. These suggestions are so many tokens of the embarrassment of commentators in their desperate attempts to get away from the incredible insolence of the saying.

VERSE 27: It is not inconceivable that a woman made desperate by the condition of her daughter should so humble herself as to accept the insult and plead that even the dogs are given some small share of the children's food; but are we to imagine that Jesus of all people would wish to evoke such an acceptance? Yet serious commentators invite us to believe this (e.g., Schlatter, *Matthäus*, pp.489f.).

The story is best understood as a retrojection into the life of Jesus of the controversy over the propriety of extending the Christian mission beyond Israel, with echoes of the bitterness of the struggle within the early church. The evangelists know that Jesus did not initiate the Gentile mission himself; his own practice accords with the conviction voiced in the words: 'I was sent only to the lost sheep of the house of Israel.' The whole of Israel is envisaged, not alone the despised and dispossessed; he sees the nation in its entirety as 'harassed and helpless, like sheep without a shepherd' (9:36; cf.

1 Ki.22:17). Jesus offers the leadership that can alone restore unity and order in the peace of the covenant. It is an exception to his general practice that he enters Gentile territory (only here and in the story of the demoniacs of Gadara, 8:28–34), or that he heals a Gentile (only here, in the case of the Gadarene demoniacs, and in the story of the centurion's child, or servant, 8:5–13).

This limitation is tacitly recognized in the Fourth Gospel also, where the Gentile centurion of Matthew and Luke is transformed into a 'royal official' (βασιλικός); though he is still resident in Capernaum, he has a sick child for whom he pleads, believes the word spoken by Jesus, and finds that his son was healed instantaneously, and at a distance (Jn.4:46–53). There is not the slightest intimation here that he was a Gentile; John takes him to be a civil servant in the employ of Herod Antipas. Still more clearly, when certain Greeks come up to Philip and express the wish to see Jesus, they are not brought into his presence. Jesus sees in their approach a sign of his coming 'glorification'; only when he has been 'lifted up' [on the cross] will he 'draw all people' to himself (12:20–32). Paul recognizes the facts when he writes that 'Christ became a servant to the circumcised for the sake of God's truthfulness, to confirm the promises made to the patriarchs' (Rom.15:8; cf. his repeated 'to the Jew first, and also to the Greek', as in Rom.1:16; 2:9,10). Even in the epistle to the Ephesians, with its strong insistence that the one household of faith embraces Jews and Gentiles on equal terms, it is none the less held that this unity was made possible only through the death of Christ. The 'wall of partition' was not broken down until Christ had abolished the legal system of Judaism, 'in order that he might create one new man in place of the two, so making peace; and might reconcile us both to God in one body through the cross, thereby bringing the hostility to an end . . .' (Eph.2:14–18). Until that sacrifice of reconciliation was accomplished, the Gentiles were 'separated from Christ, alienated from the commonwealth of Israel, and strangers to the covenants of promise, having no hope' (2:12).

The attitude attributed to Jesus in the atrocious saying of verse 26 is completely out of keeping with everything else that is reported of him. But it may be taken to reflect not unfairly the attitude of some zealous members of the Jewish Christian community of the apostolic age. For some years they kept to the practice of Jesus (and also to his precept, if we accept as authentic the opening instruction of the mission charge, 10:5f.). Those who were driven out of Jerusalem by persecution preached as they journeyed, but only to Jews (Acts 11:19). At the city of Antioch, in Syria, they made the revolutionary departure—perhaps the most significant innovation in Christian history—they 'spoke to the Greeks also, preaching the Lord Jesus . . . and a great number that believed turned to the Lord . . . and in Antioch the disciples were for the first time called "Christians" ' (vv.20–26). The story of Peter's preaching to the household of the Roman centurion Cornelius at Caesarea (Acts 10:1–11:18) reveals not only the initial restriction of the Christian mission to Jews, but the derogatory attitude of the first Christian leaders towards Gentiles. Peter himself—and we can hardly look upon him as more particularist than the other apostles—had to learn that he must not call any person 'common or unclean' (10:28; 'common' is here used in the technical sense of 'defiling', as in Mk.7:2). The context shows clearly that until his vision at Joppa (10:9–16) he had regarded all Gentiles as 'unclean', and any contact with them as defiling. A community that shared such attitudes would be quite capable of imagining that Jesus could refuse help to a Gentile woman, and to rebuff her with the brutal words which this story puts into his mouth.

We suggest, then, that the saying was first coined, and attributed to Jesus, by a prophet who shared these chauvinistic views, and that the story of Jesus' inexplicable side trip into Phoenicia was created to provide a framework for it. But in the handling of the evangelists it is taken up not to establish it as a guideline for the church, but to denature it by diverting attention to the significant outcome—that Jesus actually granted the request of the woman and healed her daughter. To both Mark and Matthew, though they are not bold enough to deny the authenticity of the saying, the emphasis is not laid upon it but upon the fact of the healing; and in Matthew, by his intimation that faith gives access to the healing powers of Christ, for the Gentile as well as for the Jew.

See the brilliant studies of this pericope by T.A. Burkill, in his *New Light on the Earliest Gospel* (1972), chaps.3,4, and 5, especially chapter 5, 'The Life History of Mark 7:24–31.'

7 THE SECOND MIRACLE OF THE LOAVES AND FISHES *15:29–39*

[29] After leaving there, Jesus went to the lake of Galilee; he went up on the mountain and seated himself there. [30] Crowds upon crowds made approach to him, bringing with them lame people, and some that were maimed or blind or dumb, and many others; they laid them at the feet of Jesus, and he healed them, [31] so that the crowds were amazed, when they heard the dumb speaking, and saw the

maimed made whole, the lame walking, and the blind given their sight; and they glorified the God of Israel.

³² Then Jesus called his disciples to him and said, 'I am concerned for the crowd, for they have been with me now for three days and they have nothing to eat. I do not want to send them away unfed, lest they faint from hunger on their journey.' ³³ The disciples answered him, 'Where are we to find bread enough here in the wilderness to satisfy so great a crowd?' ³⁴ Jesus asked, 'How many loaves have you?' and they replied, 'Seven; and there are a few small fish.' ³⁵ Commanding the crowd to sit down on the ground, ³⁶ he took the seven loaves and the fishes; and after giving thanks he broke them and gave them to the disciples, and the disciples distributed them to the crowds. ³⁷ They all ate and were satisfied, and the fragments left over were gathered up, seven baskets full. ³⁸ Four thousand men ate this meal, besides women and children.

³⁹ After he had dismissed the crowds, Jesus got into the boat and went to the region of Magadan.

In the Markan parallel, we have two separate pericopes. In the first (Mk.7:31–37) Jesus returns to the lake of Galilee by a strangely circuitous route—north from Tyre to Sidon, then apparently by a wide sweep to the east to pass through the Decapolis. Jesus heals a deaf-mute, taking him apart from the crowd, and making use of strange manipulations and groans and a word of power, which is preserved in Aramaic (Ephphatha, 'be opened')—this may have savoured too much of magical techniques to appeal to Matthew. Jesus gives the familiar charge to the onlookers to tell no one about it, but he is not obeyed; and the scene ends with the acclamation: 'He has done all things well; he even makes the deaf hear and the dumb speak.'

In the second pericope (Mk.8:1–10), there is a change of time (given in the vague indication 'in those days'), and a change of audience ('again a great crowd had gathered'); Jesus feeds four thousand with seven loaves and a few small fish, and there is enough left over to fill seven baskets. After the crowd is dismissed, Jesus and his disciples get aboard their boat and go over the water to 'the region of Dalmanoutha'.

Matthew has discarded the first part of the Markan passage (vv.31–37), retaining from it only a brief mention of the return to the lake. In place of Mark's story of the deaf-mute, Matthew gives a picture of mass healings. Jesus goes up on 'the mountain', and seats himself, as if to begin a formal discourse (cf.5:1). Crowds gather and bring with them numbers of disabled people, and Jesus heals them. (It seems strange that he should first ascend a mountain, with all the needless difficulty this imposed on all the disabled who came seeking his aid.) No dumb or mute person is singled out; dumbness is mentioned as one of a variety of afflictions for which Jesus provides the remedy (vv.30f.); and in their acclamations they do not express their wonder at the powers of Jesus in anything resembling the words given in Mark; it is said only that 'they glorified the God of Israel' (v.31).

VERSE 29: Matthew takes no interest in the route by which Jesus travelled back from the coast around Tyre and Sidon, and he gives no inkling of where the journey ended except the vague indication that it was somewhere on the lake of Galilee. 'The mountain' is conventional, and has no geographical significance.

VERSE 30: The 'great crowds' of Matthew take the place of a vague 'they' in Mark; and only one sufferer is brought to Jesus; it is only incidentally that a crowd is mentioned, and then only to say that Jesus took the man away from them to work his cure in privacy.

VERSE 31: 'they glorified the God of Israel.' In the Markan story, it is Jesus who is acclaimed—'he has done all things well; he makes the deaf hear and the dumb speak.' This is the only place in Matthew where we find the phrase 'the God of Israel'; and it occurs only once more in the New Testament (Lk.1:68). It is often used in the Old Testament, usually attached to the name Yahweh. Perhaps Matthew means to suggest that the crowds are made up of Gentiles (McNeile, Gaechter, Schmid, *et al.*). He would then be following up the story of the Canaanite woman's daughter, with the apparent hesitation of Jesus to use his healing powers for the benefit of a Gentile, with this account of multiple healings of Gentiles, and the conversion of Gentile multitudes to the worship of the God of Israel. Once the barrier of racial privilege is broken at one point, the mission of Jesus no longer is restricted to Israel; among the Gentiles also he heals the disabled—gives hearing to the deaf, speech to the dumb, and sight to the blind; and in the next episode he will feed the Gentiles with the bread of life as he has previously fed the thousands of Israel.

VERSE 32: Matthew has rewritten the Markan introduction to remove the indication of a change of scene; the story of the feeding of the four thousand is thus made a continuation of the account of the multiple healings. The crowd for whom Jesus feels compassion is the same as that which brought its cripples, its blind, and its deaf and dumb to Jesus and witnessed the healings.

We learn incidentally that they have been with Jesus for three days; it is possible that this mention of so long a time has prompted Matthew to elaborate the single healing of Mark into the mass healings of the remodelled introduction. The Markan wording is followed closely, even to the retention of the hanging nominative ἡμέραι τρεῖς, to express duration of time. Matthew omits the clause 'and some of them came from far away'. It is obvious that we have before us a variant version of the story of the feeding of the five thousand (14:14–22); it is not used by either Luke or John. In this doublet the story is told more concisely. It is only through the question of the disciples that we learn that the place is 'in the wilderness' (v.33); there are no nearby villages in which they might find food (as in 14:15), and no suggestion of how much the bread to feed the crowd might cost. There are variants of no real significance in the numbers of loaves, of baskets, and of people, and in the word for 'baskets'. Whatever word is used, the thought is evidently of small hampers for provisions, seeing that no large carriers would be brought into a wilderness by people journeying on foot. But it is probably unwise to think in terms of the size of things in a miracle story; the σπυρίς is big enough to hold Paul when he is let down through an opening in the wall of Damascus (Acts 9:25). It is hard to take seriously the attempt of Austin Farrer to develop a 'Markan arithmetic of loaves and thousands (which) finds its place in the Matthaean history of the Three' (*St. Matthew and St. Mark*, pp.118f.).

The same considerations apply to the interpretation as to that of the first miracle of the loaves. The one further question that now arises is that of the reason of the two evangelists for offering two versions of what is essentially a single legend, or cult-myth. It is not enough to say that Mark has found the two versions in different sources and has copied them both down without recognizing their original identity; and that Matthew has followed more or less mechanically. They have both restricted themselves to a comparatively small number of incidents for use in their narrative (for we must suppose that many more stories about Jesus were current in the oral traditions available to them). In this one case, they have introduced for the second time not this one story alone, but a more extensive cycle (see McNeile's 'Additional Note on xiv.13–xvi.12', where he marks out six elements in the double cycle, commencing with the multiplication of the loaves; he suggests that the 'two parts, xiv.13– xv.31 and xv.32–xvi.12 . . . are probably not consecutive, but parallel'). The whole of the second cycle is omitted by Luke.

It is evident that even in Mark, the second version of the miraculous feeding is more finished than the first, and shows indications of having been shaped by a writer (prior to Mark) as part of a wider account, of which traces remain, especially in the 'three days' of Mk.8:2: there is nothing in the present context to indicate how Jesus has occupied himself with the crowd for so long a time. Matthew has tidied the story up a little further, but even in Mark it does not convey the feeling of a transcript from oral tradition, largely untouched, which we observe in the first version of the story. The 'three days' tempt us to think of a Resurrection setting. At the end, Jesus goes over the lake to 'the regions of Magadan'. 'Magadan' replaces the 'Dalmanoutha' of Mark, but seeing that neither place has ever been identified, it is futile to ask where the party landed or why Matthew made the change.

8   JESUS REFUSES TO GIVE A SIGN *16:1–4*

[1] The Pharisees and Sadducees made approach to Jesus to test him by asking him to show them a sign from heaven. [2] He replied by saying: [4] 'An evil and adulterous generation demands a sign, and no sign shall be given it except the sign of Jonah.' With that, he left them and went away.

Many manuscripts and early versions include after verse 2 above, the words: [2b] 'In the evening you say, "It will be fair weather, for the sky is red", [3] and in the morning you say, "Today it will be stormy, for the sky is red and threatening." You know how to interpret the appearance of the sky, but you cannot see the signs of the times.' A similar remark is attributed to Jesus in Luke 12:54f., but it is addressed to the crowds and mentions not the colour of the sky but the rising of a cloud and the blowing of a wind from the south. The Lukan text is solidly attested; the Matthaean words are without the support of the two great fourth-century uncials Aleph and B and some important cursives, and are missing from the Old Syriac (Curetonian and Sinaiticus), and from much of the Coptic evidence.

VERSE 1: At this point in Mark, only the Pharisees are mentioned (8:11). Matthew is anticipating the form which he will give to the sayings of verses 6 and 11. A combined delegation of Pharisees and Sadducees is unlikely in itself, still more its timely appearance in 'the regions of Magadan' so soon after Jesus has returned from a trip to Phoenicia.

VERSE 4: On the 'sign of Jonah', see the notes on Mt.12:49. In Mark, the refusal of a sign is not qualified by any exception: 'no sign shall be given.' Matthew draws upon the previous refusal (not paralleled in Mark) of 12:39.

'Evil and adulterous' does not imply sexual laxity; it involves an extension of the figure used by Old Testament prophets which spoke of infidelity to the God of Israel as 'adultery' (Hos.2:2ff.; 9:1; Ezek.16, etc.). This accusation replaces the question of the Markan passage: 'Why does this generation seek a sign?' (Mk.8:12).

9   THE LEAVEN OF THE PHARISEES AND SADDUCEES *16:5–12*

[5] When the disciples reached the other side, it turned out that they had forgotten to bring bread. [6] Jesus said to them, 'Take heed, beware of the leaven of the Pharisees and Sadducees.' [7] And they discussed it among themselves, saying, 'We brought no bread.' [8] But Jesus, aware of their thinking, said, 'Why do you debate like this among yourselves, you men of little faith, saying that you have no bread? [9] Do you not yet perceive? Do you not remember the five loaves which fed the five thousand, and how many baskets you took up? [10] Or the seven loaves which fed the four thousand, and how many baskets you took up? [11] How can you fail to perceive that I was not talking about bread when I warned you to take heed of the leaven of the Pharisees and Sadducees?' [12] Then they realized that he had not told them to beware of the leaven of bread, but of the teaching of the Pharisees and Sadducees.

In Mark, this conversation appears to take place in the boat, when they have again taken off from their landing-place (Mk.8:13). There is no mention of this recrossing of the lake in Matthew, nor of the arrival at Bethsaida (Mk.8:22ff.—Matthew omits the entire incident of the healing of a blind man at Bethsaida). As a consequence, the discussion about 'leaven' is left hanging in the air. Jesus has left his questioners and gone away (v.4, above), but where has he gone with the disciples?

VERSE 6: The warning in Mark does not mention the Sadducees but speaks of 'the leaven of the Pharisees and of Herod'. By the time Matthew wrote, there was no more question of any Herod ruling in Judaea or anywhere else; and indeed even in Mark, the mention of Herod is a carry-over from an earlier time (cf. Mk.3:6, where the passage speaks of a league between the Pharisees and 'the Herodians' to bring Jesus to his death). Of course, if Matthew has come to take 'leaven' as a figure for 'teaching', the mention of Herod would be absurd, for whatever 'the leaven of Herod' might mean (and this is hard to say) it would certainly not mean 'teaching'—Herod was not a rabbi!

VERSE 7: The saying puzzles the disciples, but their notion that the words of Jesus have any kind of reference to their lack of bread is incredibly obtuse. Matthew has softened the rebuke which Jesus administers; they do not understand because of their 'little faith' (ὀλιγόπιστοι and ὀλιγοπιστία—rare words of Matthew's coining). In Mark, Jesus asks 'Do you not yet perceive or understand? Are your hearts hardened? Having eyes do you not see, and having ears do you not hear? Do you not remember?' (Mk.8:17f.).

But the entire episode is highly artificial. It appears to have been framed by Mark as a setting for the incomprehensible saying, 'Beware of the leaven of the Pharisees and the leaven of Herod.' He himself offers no interpretation, and we cannot tell what it may have meant to him. In Luke it is given (in a different context) in the form, 'Beware of the leaven of the Pharisees', with no mention of either Herod or the Sadducees, and it is interpreted as 'hypocrisy' (Lk.12:1). We might speculate that, if it is an authentic word of Jesus, it may have been a warning against the temptation of 'seeking to establish their own righteousness', with a zeal of God that is not enlightened (Rom.10:3,2). But the Gospels do not give us any real indication of the situation in which such a word was actually spoken, and without knowledge of the original context it is impossible to determine the meaning with any degree of certainty.

VERSES 9—11: It is often noted that the attitude of the disciples, when they face the problem of providing food for the four thousand, is incomprehensible on the part of men who have already witnessed the feeding of the five thousand. Mark and Matthew have accepted this degree of obtuseness readily enough, but they are staggered by the fact that after *two* such miracles, the disciples can still imagine that Jesus is concerned about a shortage of bread for him and his small company.

VERSE 12: Matthew makes an effort to interpret the saying about 'leaven'. We can at least say that this interpretation cannot go back to Jesus, since it would be quite inapplicable to the saying as given in Matthew's source (Mark). There is the further difficulty that it would be hard to imagine any 'teaching' which could be ascribed to the Pharisees and Sadducees in common, apart from that which was common to all Judaism. Generally, they are distinguished by radically different doctrines (of Torah, of resurrection, of angels, etc.).

10   PETER'S CONFESSION *16:13—20*

¹³ When Jesus came into the district of Caesarea Philippi, he asked his

disciples, 'Who do people say that the Son of man is?' ¹⁴ They said, 'Some say John the Baptist, some say Elijah, and others say Jeremiah or one of the prophets.' ¹⁵ He said to them, 'And who do you say that I am?' ¹⁶ Simon Peter answered, 'You are the Christ, the Son of the living God.'

¹⁷ Jesus responded, 'Blessed are you, Simon, son of Jonas! For flesh and blood has not revealed this to you, but my Father who is in heaven. ¹⁸ And now I tell you, you are Peter, and on this rock I will build my church; and the gates of Hades will have no power against it. ¹⁹ I shall give you the keys of the kingdom of heaven, and whatever you bind upon earth shall be bound in heaven, and whatever you loose upon earth shall be loosed in heaven.'

²⁰ Then he strictly forbade them to say to anyone that he was the Christ.

This strange episode (vv.13–16) is taken over from Mark, but Matthew enlarges it with a supplement (vv.17–19) which interprets it in application to the future role of Peter in the church. In this form it has given rise to centuries of controversy, especially in the Western Church, where it came to be invoked in support of the claims made by and for the Roman Papacy.

In Mark, Jesus does not confirm or approve the Messianic confession; we are told only that he forbade them to speak of him in such terms to others. Nor does Peter use the phrase, 'the Son of the living God'—this is a Matthaean addition. The Markan passage gives no indication of what Messiahship means to Peter at this time, but it is unlikely that Mark imagined that it could ever have meant something different from what it had come to mean to the church.

VERSE 13: Caesarea Philippi was a town on the southwest slopes of Mount Hermon, over twenty miles north of the lake of Galilee near the sources of the river Jordan. It was included at this time in the territories given to Philip, the third son of Herod the Great. Beginning as a settlement by a sacred spring where a Canaanite baal had long been worshipped, the Greeks made it a shrine of Pan and the Nymphs, and called it Paneas. It was built up as a city by Philip, and named Caesarea in honour of the emperor Tiberius; as 'Philip's' Caesarea it is distinguished from the coastal Caesarea (Caesarea Maritima) which was built, or rather rebuilt, by Herod the Great and named in honour of Augustus (between 22 and 10 BC). The population of the area was largely Gentile, partly Greek and partly Syrian.

The motive of a journey of Jesus into this area is unknown; it is often conjectured that all through this time Jesus was avoiding the territories of Herod Antipas, as if he feared that he might meet the same fate as John the Baptist. (Luke, however, reports that when Jesus was warned about the hostility of Herod, he replied with a flat refusal to go away until the appointed time—Lk.13:31—33.) Not much confidence can be placed in any of the scanty indications that are given of the movements of Jesus. It is unlikely that Mark picked upon the name of Caesarea Philippi at random, but it would be vain to speculate on how or why it became attached to the pericope. Luke omits any mention of the locality; in his Gospel it follows immediately upon the miracle of the loaves (the five thousand, he omits the entire section which follows in Mark, 6:45— 8:26) with no suggestion of a journey to the north.

'The Son of man' here is substituted for the 'I' of Mark. The question is artificial in itself; Jesus is not asking for information about the views of the general populace. But in this form it is made still more peculiar, for it assumes that the disciples will recognize that Jesus is speaking of himself, when he says 'the Son of man', but does not assume that this is a Messianic designation. If they know him as 'Son of man', what point is there in asking them who he is taken to be by them?

VERSE 14: 'Jeremiah' is a Matthaean addition. We have already been told that Herod took Jesus for a John returned to life (14:2); and in Mark, this was given as one of the various notions current among the people (Mk.6:14ff.), along with identifications with Elijah, or a prophet. It is striking that nothing is said of any Jews entertaining the possibility that he is the Messiah (as in Jn.7:40f.— 'Can this be the Son of David?').

VERSE 16: In Mark, there has been no earlier hint that the disciples thought of Jesus as more than a teacher and healer; but in Matthew they have already hailed him as 'Son of God' (14:33). The addition of the name 'Simon' to Mark's 'Peter' (alone), paves the way for the blessing which Jesus will pronounce on the 'prince of the apostles' (v.17).

'The Son of the living God' is a Christological confession cast in the language of the early church. The 'living' God carries with it the Jewish conviction that all the gods of the nations are mere semblances ('idols') or vanities; for Gentiles, conversion to the Christian faith means a turning 'to God from idols to serve a living and true God' (1 Thess.1:9). But in this context there is not the remotest suggestion that any other god could be envisaged than the God of Israel. Cullmann (*Peter*, p.172) suggests that the expansion reflects Matthew's 'slight (?) tendency to edifying liturgical paraphrase'. In Jewish thought, the Messiah is uniformly a *human* figure; if he is called God's 'son', it is only in the sense that this can be said of every king of Israel. The phrase defines what 'Messiah' has come to mean to Christians in the light of the resurrection of Jesus from the dead (Rom.1:3f.: 'descended from David according to the flesh, but designated Son of God in power according to the Spirit of holiness by his resurrection from the dead').

VERSES 17–19: In Mark, Jesus neither welcomes nor rejects the confession of his Messiahship; he merely enjoins secrecy. Matthew retains the same injunction (v.20), but he first inserts a section in which he proclaims that Peter's confession is evidence that he has received a divine revelation; and that he is to hold a place of unique authority in the church that is to be. This insertion has given rise to endless discussion and debate, both as to its genuineness and as to its meaning.

The question of authenticity does not arise at all once we reject the notion that Jesus himself professed to be the promised 'Messiah'. But even for those who hold that he did think of himself in Messianic terms (though totally different from the current conceptions in Judaism), this group of sayings does not commend itself as a genuine utterance of Jesus. The grounds for rejection are found partly in the mention of the founding of a 'church', even of 'my' church; and again in the fact that in the early church the evidence all indicates that Peter never enjoyed anything resembling the kind of authority which is here attributed to him.

Nowhere else in the Gospels does Jesus speak of founding a church. The very word ἐκκλησία, 'church', does not occur anywhere else in the Gospels, except for Matthew 18:17, which is itself suspect, and actually uses the word in a different sense (see the notes *ad loc.*). The absence of the word would not in itself be decisive; but we must recognize that 'the thing which the word denotes' is not to be found either (*contra* Cullmann, *Peter*, pp.187f.). Cullman argues that the very notion of a Messiah requires as its complement the notion of a Messianic community (*Peter*, p.189; cf. K.L. Schmidt, 'Die Kirche des Urchristentums' in the Deissmann Festschrift (1927)). But this very argument leads into the untenable position that Jesus set out to form a sect of his own, within but separated from Israel, the people of God. 'My' church could only mean a sect, like the Qumran community; and nothing is gained by invoking Isaiah's notion of a 'remnant' of Israel that alone should be saved. The only church that Jesus could envisage is 'the church of God'; and in fact, the New

Testament writers invariably speak of 'the church of God', not 'the church of Christ', when they mean to refer to the entire Christian community. Paul will indeed speak of 'the churches of Christ', in the plural, to refer to local gatherings of Christian believers; but in their totality they form 'the church of God'.

Even more formidable is the objection that Peter never in fact enjoyed any such primacy in the administration of the early church as is here assigned to him. Paul feels no inhibition about rebuking him at Antioch (Gal.2:1ff.), and a significant party in the Jerusalem community openly challenges his actions in preaching to the household of the Gentile Cornelius (Acts 11:2). In the gathering of 'apostles and elders' at Jerusalem which met to consider the propriety of the Gentile mission conducted by Paul and Barnabas at Antioch, it is James and not Peter who is pictured as presiding and even as framing the decision which was to be embodied in a formal decree (Acts 15:1—29). Whatever the critical questions raised by this report of Acts, Paul himself mentions the name of James first, when he speaks of the three 'pillars' (Gal.2:9), without the slightest suggestion that Peter holds supreme authority.

But criticism is now less concerned with questions of authenticity than it was a generation ago. As Bonnard puts it, 'We shall not allow ourselves to be distracted from our study by the somewhat wearisome question of authenticity' (*Comm., ad loc.*). The primary task is not to determine what actually took place (if anything did) at Caesarea Philippi, but what this pericope meant to the evangelists, and in particular to the evangelist Matthew.

The language of these verses (17—19) is entirely Semitic in tone; it cannot be doubted that it has been drawn by Matthew from an Aramaic source, and that it originated in some debate within the Palestinian community.

VERSE 17 takes the form of a beatitude. Peter is blessed because he has received a divine revelation. With this, the whole character of his confession is altered in retrospect; it is no longer a confession of the whole group of disciples for whom Peter acts as spokesman (as in Mark), but the expression of a private conviction with no suggestion that it is shared by the other disciples. They have all been through the same experience of life in the company of Jesus, hearing his teachings and witnessing his mighty deeds, but only to Peter has the revelation been vouchsafed.

'Son of Jonas' Βαριωνα is a transliteration of the Aramaic *Bar-Iona*; it corresponds in form to his confession of Jesus as 'Son of the living God'. 'Flesh and blood' is a literal rendering into Greek of a

Semitic phrase often used by the rabbis to refer to human beings in their weakness, in contrast to God.

It has been suggested that we have a reflection here of the language of Paul in Galatians 1:12,16: 'I did not receive [my gospel] from man, nor was I taught it, but it came through a revelation of Jesus Christ. . . . I did not confer with flesh and blood.' Partly on this basis, T.W. Manson made the conjecture that 'the challenge implied in the claim was directed against Paul himself' (*Sayings*, p.204). W.D. Davies, on the other hand, denies that there is any polemic against Paul here, and appears to entertain favorably the notion that the challenge is directed against James of Jerusalem (*Setting of the Sermon on the Mount*, pp.338–39). In any case, it can scarcely be doubted that the saying arises out of some controversy in the Palestinian church, and is intended to justify the exaltation of Peter in the face of attempts to give an equal or even a higher status to some other Christian leader.

VERSE 18: The play on words—'Peter', this 'rock'—requires a change in Greek from πέτρος (properly, 'stone') to πέτρα. In Aramaic, the two words would be identical—*Kepha* the name given to Peter, transliterated into Greek as Kephas (Gal.2:9), and *kepha*, 'rock'. The symbol itself is Hebraic: Abraham is the 'rock' from which Israel was hewn, and in a rabbinic midrash, God finds in him a rock on which he can base and build the world (Billerbeck, *Komm.* I, p.73).

In this and the following verse, we have a series of verbs in the future tense. Jesus speaks not of his present activity but of the shape of things to come.

'The gates of Hades'—in Greek mythology, the whole underworld, the abode of the dead, is 'the house of Hades'; like the Hebrew *Sheol*, it is neither a heaven nor a hell, but a dark and joyless realm which receives all the dead—not to an abundant life, but to a shadowy existence without strength or understanding. The phrase here means simply 'death'. The church which Jesus will found will be immune from death.

VERSE 19: The figure of the kingdom of heaven as a great house, or palace, with 'keys', does not appear to be a familiar image in Judaism. The 'keys' are probably not to be understood as entrance keys, as if to suggest that Peter is authorized to admit or to refuse admission, but rather to the bundle of keys carried by the chief steward, for the opening of rooms and storechambers within the house—symbols of responsibilities to be exercised within the house of God (cf. Mt.24:45, etc.). 'Bind' and 'loose' are technical terms of the rabbinic vocabulary, denoting the authoritative declaration that an action or course of conduct is permitted or forbidden by the Law of Moses. It has nothing to do with the power of absolution, though it may carry with it the authority to expel an offender from the synagogue or to readmit him. This appears to be the sense given to the parallel saying in Mt.18:18, where the power of discipline is assigned to the assembled church (the local congregation), not to Peter personally or to any individual. The saying attributed to Jesus in John 20:23 appears to be an interpretation of this saying precisely in the sense of conferring the power of absolution.

'In heaven' (literally, in accordance with the Semitic idiom, 'in the heavens')—that is, in the presence of God. God himself will ratify in heaven the decisions that Peter pronounces on earth. In the corresponding saying in Matthew 18, the ratification in heaven is not automatic; it is granted in answer to prayer.

With verse 20, we have the return to the Markan passage, and Jesus addresses his injunction no longer to Peter individually, but to the disciples generally. They are not to tell anyone that he is the Messiah.

11 JESUS FORETELLS HIS DEATH AND RESURRECTION: THE REACTION OF PETER *16:21–23*

[21] From that time on, Jesus began to make known to his disciples that it was necessary for him to go to Jerusalem, to suffer many things at the hands of the elders, the chief priests, and the scribes, to be put to death, and on the third day to be raised from the dead. [22] At this, Peter took him and began to remonstrate with him, saying: 'God be gracious to you, Lord! This will not happen to you.' [23] But Jesus turned on his heel and said to Peter, 'You devil! Get behind me! You are a stumbling block to me, for you are set on human ambitions, not on the things of God.'

VERSE 21: ἀπό τότε, 'from that time'—a Matthaean addition to the Markan text, to emphasize that this is a turning point in the story (cf. 4:17, when 'Jesus began to preach'). The main theme now becomes the preparation of the disciples for the approaching ordeal at Jerusalem, and for their own share in suffering.

'Elders, chief priests, scribes'—the three groups which made up the great Sanhedrin of Jerusalem, the supreme court and council of the nation. 'Chief priests' have not been mentioned before, for the simple reason that Jesus has not been in Jerusalem, where they exercised their functions. 'Elders' have not been encountered previously; where the word is used, it refers to the scribes of an earlier generation who transmitted the oral law (15:2), not to active members of the governing council. Scribes have appeared on the scene frequently, as opponents of Jesus. The Sanhedrin possessed great authority among Jews everywhere, not only in the Holy Land; though it possessed no forces (apart from the temple police), its edicts were willingly obeyed. The prediction does not include 'the Pharisees' among those at whose hands Jesus will suffer, though they have been his most determined opponents throughout his ministry. This is in keeping with the fact that they play no part in the passion narrative. Some elders, a number of scribes, and possibly a few priests would be attached to the sect of the Pharisees; the higher ranks of the priesthood were generally Sadducean.

In this first form of the prediction of the passion, the details of Jesus' sufferings are not mentioned. The second is even more concise (17:22f.); but in the third, Jesus speaks specifically of the passing of the death sentence, the transfer to Roman (Gentile) authorities, and then to mocking, scourging, and crucifixion (20:18f.); Matthew introduces a fourth form of the prediction (26:2), given in a very succinct phrasing.

'Necessary'—the necessity does not lie in the nature of things, but in 'the definite plan and foreknowledge of God' (Acts 2:23), as made known through the prophecies. The New Testament writers do not share the Greek notions of $\dot{\alpha}\nu\dot{\alpha}\gamma\kappa\eta$, an inexorable Necessity to which mankind is subject. The will of God is not arbitrary, but 'good and acceptable and perfect' (Rom.12:2).

'On the third day' replaces Mark's 'after three days'. It is the more usual phrase, reflecting the words of Hosea 6:2, 'on the third day he will raise us up.' So Paul writes, 'he is risen on the third day according to the scriptures' (1 Cor.15:4). Vincent Taylor (*Mark*, p.378) brings together evidence to show that 'in the LXX and in late Greek writers the two phrases were identical in meaning.'

VERSE 22: The participle $\pi\rho\sigma\sigma\lambda\alpha\beta\dot{\sigma}\mu\epsilon\nu\sigma\varsigma$, 'took', may be intended to suggest that Peter took Jesus aside, or that he took him by the arm. The verb $\dot{\epsilon}\pi\iota\tau\iota\mu\dot{\alpha}\omega$, 'remonstrate', has the strong sense of 'rebuke' in the very next clause, in the Markan version (Mk.8:32,33): Peter 'began to rebuke Jesus', and 'Jesus . . . rebuked Peter.' But in verse 20, the same verb appears to mean simply 'charged', with no suggestion of censure.

The words of Peter's rebuke, or remonstrance, are not given in Mark; they are probably a midrashic supplement composed by Matthew. $\ddot{\iota}\lambda\epsilon\omega\varsigma$, 'gracious', or 'merciful', expresses the shocked conviction that God will not let such terrible things be done to Jesus. As is usual in the reaction of the disciples to the predictions of the passion, the assurance that Jesus will be raised from the dead is disregarded; Peter's mind is wholly occupied with the thought of the predicted sufferings and death (cf. 17:22, where they all were 'greatly distressed').

VERSE 23: The address to Peter as 'You devil!' (literally, 'Satan') comes all the more forcibly after the words of blessing and promise of verses 17–19. It re-emphasizes Matthew's insistent warnings that there is no absolute within the community of faith. Not everyone who calls Jesus 'Lord' will enter the kingdom of heaven; many that can boast of 'mighty deeds' which they have done in his name will hear him deny all knowledge of them (7:21–23). Even the one to whom the keys of the Kingdom have been promised can become an instrument of the devil.

The whole story of remonstrance and rebuke is omitted in Luke. In John it is transmuted into a totally different episode, in which Peter holds firm while many are falling away, and it is not he but Judas who is called 'a devil' (Jn.6:66–71).

'You are a stumbling block to me'—another Matthaean supplement to Mark. Peter's refusal to face the necessity of the death of Christ is of the nature of a temptation for Jesus to shrink from drinking the cup that is decreed for him.

The verb $\phi\rho o\nu\acute{e}\omega$ ($\phi\rho o\nu e\hat{\iota}\tau e$, 'you are set on') is used of the inward disposition, the whole cast of mind and feeling—a 'visceral' rather than a mental attitude. We may compare the phrasing here with Paul's contrast between those who are set on ($\phi\rho o\nu o\hat{\upsilon}\sigma\iota\nu$) the things of the flesh and those who are set on the things of the Spirit (Rom. 8:5); notice the like use of the cognate noun $\phi\rho\acute{o}\nu\eta\mu a$ in verses 6 and 7. It is not the mind as the seat of conscious thought that is intended, but the heart and will. The accusation is not that Peter has some wrong ideas, but that his outlook is governed by ambitions and desires which belong to the realm of Satan, not by whole-hearted acceptance of the will of God.

12   THE WAY OF THE CROSS *16:24–28*

[24] Then Jesus said to his disciples, 'If anyone is resolved to come after me, let him deny himself and take up his cross and follow me. [25] For whoever is bent on saving his life will lose it, and whoever loses his life for my sake will save it. [26] What good will it do any person if he

gains the whole world and pays for it with the loss of his life? Or what will anyone give in exchange for his life?

[27] The Son of man will come in his Father's glory, with his angels attending him, and then he will repay everyone in accordance with his conduct. [28] Truly I tell you, there are some among those standing here who will not taste death before they see the Son of man coming in his kingly power.'

VERSE 24: Matthew omits the Markan mention of the summoning of 'the crowd' (Mk.8:34), with good reason; he cannot suppose that in the neighbourhood of Caesarea Philippi a crowd was at hand to be summoned, as in the villages of Galilee where Jesus was now well known. The message which is now to be delivered is not for the general public but for such as choose to become disciples—to 'come after' Jesus. For Matthew, this means not only his immediate followers, but the Christian believers of the evangelist's own time (and of all times).

'Deny himself'—not simply to give up some small comforts, but to renounce all earthly ambitions and desires, to accept the hazard of losing life itself. This is explained in another way in the challenge to 'take up his cross'; (a figurative expression, based on the fact that a man condemned to execution was obliged to carry his own cross to the place of crucifixion). Such a figure must anticipate the crucifixion of Jesus. As the manner of his death could not yet be known, the use of such a figure must be proleptic—it would not have meaning until the cross had ceased to be a symbol of shame, and had become the central symbol of salvation. The disciple of Jesus is called to accept for himself the death that Jesus was to endure for his sake.

It has been suggested that Jesus already realizes that he will come into conflict with Roman power and may therefore expect to be crucified (crucifixion was a Roman, not a Jewish, mode of execution); but in fact there has been no preparation for such a thought in the Gospel. John the Baptist has been executed by Herod, by decapitation; and Jesus himself has just spoken of sufferings at the hands of the Jewish authorities ('elders, high priests, and scribes').

VERSES 25–26: 'Life' ($\psi v \chi \acute{\eta}$) is used in two senses—that of mere physical existence and that of the true and essential self, the "soul". Anyone who preserves his mortal life (for a few years, at best) at the cost of his true life (in Platonic terms, his immortal soul) is making a bad bargain. 'Gaining the whole world' hardly comes into question— the immediate disciples of Jesus and the humble people who made up his church in the time of Matthew and Mark were not dreaming of wealth and power. This saying looks like a proverb of profane wisdom—what is the point of making millions if you kill yourself in the effort?

VERSE 27: The transition to this verse is mediated in Mark by a verse which Matthew has omitted (Mk.8:38). Anyone who is 'ashamed' of Jesus—that is, denies faith in him in an earthly court, for fear of death—will find that Jesus will be 'ashamed' of him— that is, will refuse to recognize him as his own—when he comes as 'Son of man' (in judgement). Matthew recasts this, focusing attention entirely upon the coming of Jesus as Son of man, to judge the world.

VERSE 28: Matthew again recasts the Markan saying (Mk.9:1); for the arrival of the kingdom of God, he substitutes the coming of Jesus as Son of man, in his Kingdom.

In these verses, Jesus is not explicitly identified with 'the Son of man'; and this has been taken to indicate that Jesus did not identify himself with the Son of man of apocalyptic expectation, but spoke of the Son of man as a heavenly figure who is related to him only in that he will base his judgements of individuals on the manner of response which each has made to Jesus. It is far from certain that Jesus made use of the Son of man imagery in any sense (see esp. P. Vielhauer, 'Gottesreich und Menschensohn' in the *Festschrift für Günther Dehn* (1957), pp.51–79). But in any case, it cannot be disputed that the evangelists make the identification. Jesus, for them, has appeared as 'Son of man' in his earthly ministry, in lowliness and suffering; and he will appear again in heavenly glory to establish the kingdom of God on earth and to judge the world. Matthew can therefore equate the coming of the Son of man in his Kingdom with the coming of the kingdom of God. But only Matthew speaks of the Kingdom as 'his' (the Son's) Kingdom (cf. 13:41).

The saying certainly anticipates that the great event will take place within the life time of people then living; cf. 24:34—'this generation will not pass away till all these things take place.'

13 THE TRANSFIGURATION *17:1–8*

[1] Six days later, Jesus took along with him Peter and James and John the brother of James and led them up on a high mountain, by themselves. [2] There he was transformed before their eyes—his face shone like the sun and his clothes became white as light. [3] And now Moses and Elijah appeared to them, conversing with him. [4] Peter spoke up to say, 'Lord, it is good that we are here. If you will, I shall make

three booths here, one for you, one for Moses, and one for Elijah.'
[5] While he was still speaking, a luminous cloud overshadowed them,
and a voice was heard from the cloud, saying, 'This is my beloved
Son, in whom I am well pleased; listen to him.' [6] The disciples were
terrified when they heard this, and fell on their faces; [7] but Jesus
approached, touched them, and said, 'Stand up; do not be afraid.'
[8] And when they looked up they saw no one but Jesus, alone.

Speculations about the location of the 'high mountain' are futile and
misguided. The scene is so obviously a creation of mythopoetic
imagination that attempts to give it a topographical locality totally
mistake its meaning. The traditional 'Mount of the Transfiguration'
is Mount Tabor in the valley of Jezreel, far away from the neighbourhood of Caesarea Philippi (where the preceding scene is laid). Still
toying with the notion that there was a literal mountain, Vincent
Taylor remarks that Mount Tabor is not very high (1843 feet), and
that Mount Hermon (9100 feet) is preferred by 'most modern
commentators' (*Mark, ad loc.*). It might be hard to determine just
what height above sea level would be required for a theophany
(Christophany)!

The story as we have it is unquestionably a literary creation, not
a fragment of tradition shaped by the processes of oral transmission.
There is not the slightest hope of recovering any element of historical
fact that might conceivably lie behind it. It cannot be flatly denied
that these disciples may have at some time felt that they saw their
Master's face made radiant as by a mystic sense of communion with
God. Vincent Taylor reminds us that in studies of Christian
mysticism we read of a 'luminous glory which transfigures the faces
of the saints in ecstatic prayer' (*Mark*, p.387). But the story before
us does not indicate a moment of spiritual exaltation which brings a
glow to the face of Jesus, but a transformation of his entire person
which even extends to his clothing. What is described is a metamor-
phosis ($\mu\epsilon\tau\epsilon\mu\rho\rho\phi\omega\vartheta\eta$, v.2) in which he is revealed in his essential
divine glory, no longer veiled by the trappings of human form and
appearance. It is like the transformation of Demeter, when she
stands in her divine majesty before the royal family of Eleusis. She
had come to them in the guise of an old woman, past the age of
child-bearing, and was engaged as nurse for the royal infant. But at
the last she 'changed her stature and her looks, . . . beauty spread
round about her and a lovely fragrance was wafted from her sweet-
smelling robes, and from the divine body of the goddess a light shone
afar . . . , so that the strong house was filled with brightness as of

lightning.' (*Homeric Hymns*, ed. and trans. A.G. Evelyn-White, Loeb Library, II.275–80.)

There is no real justification for taking this metamorphosis as a misplaced resurrection story, or an anticipation of the future coming of Jesus in glory as the Son of man. We shall be nearer to the thought of the evangelists if we see it as 'a dramatic demonstration of the glory of Jesus' messianic status. . . . [it] does not disclose a status which Jesus is to enjoy on a future occasion, whether it be at his resurrection or at his parousia.' (T.A. Burkill, *Mysterious Revelation* (1963), pp.158,160.) That is to say, it is not a vision of what is to be, but a revelation of what actually is, of the unchanging glory which has been concealed beneath the lowliness of a human life.

In this sense, it confirms the truth and deepens the meaning of the confession voiced by Peter at Caesarea Philippi. The manifestation is indeed temporary, but the reality which here becomes manifest is eternal and unchanging. Jesus appears in the glory which he had with the Father before the world was. He is seen in the 'body of glory' (Phil.3:21), in which he will indeed be manifested at the resurrection and at his parousia; to that extent there is an anticipation of the glory that 'every eye shall see' (Rev.1:7); but primarily it is an unveiling of the essential glory which remains his throughout his earthly life.

VERSE 1: 'Six days'—such precise notes of time are hardly ever found in the story, and it is probable that here we should not see a surprising outburst of interest in the chronology, but a symbol derived from Jewish legend and ritual. It is after Moses has spent six days on Mount Sinai that the voice of the Lord speaks to him out of an overshadowing cloud (Ex.24:16). Six days of fasting preceded the great feasts of the Jewish calendar, and the High Priest spent six days in the Temple before making the great sacrifice of the Day of Atonement (*Mishnah*, Tractate 'Yoma', I.1). Austin Farrer, having persuaded himself that the key to Mark (and to Matthew) is to be found in the use of numbers, suggested that the six days fitted well 'into St Mark's simple harmony of numbers'. It is twice three (!), and

It is curious how the interval 'after three days' has scarcely been introduced, when it is doubled: 'after three days' Messiah will rise, 'after six days' from the announcement of it his glory is manifested on the Mountain. . . . After six days the three go up the mountain and, by miracle, find themselves involved in a drama for six persons—there are the unearthly three—Moses, Elias, and Jesus supernaturalised by glory—and there are the earthly three. (*St Matthew and St Mark* (1954), pp.111f.)

The 'high mountain' is likewise a symbol of the place of revelation. Traditionally, it has been identified as Mount Tabor (at least since the time of Jerome), but it is no more a geographical locality than the mount of the Sermon or the mountain to which Jesus was carried by the devil, from which he could see all the kingdoms of the world.

VERSE 2: 'He was transformed'—the familiar term 'transfigured' came into our English versions through the Vulgate, *transfiguratus est*. Paul uses the same verb of the continuing transformation of the Christian through his vision of the glory of the Lord (2 Cor.3:18), and exhorts us to 'be transformed by the renewing of the mind' (Rom.12:2—μεταμορφοῦσθε). Here, of course, the thought is not of an inward change or of a renewing of the mind of Jesus. It is the visible form that is changed to become the manifestation of the invisible essence.

'His face shone like the sun': Through Moses' communion with God on Mount Sinai, 'the sight of the skin of his face was glorified' (δεδόξασται, LXX, Ex.34:29–35). The verb of the LXX is not taken up here; it is perhaps echoed in the Lukan version, where we are told that the disciples 'saw his glory' (Lk.9:32). In the Hebrew of Exodus, the text reads: 'The skin of his face shone.' The Markan story does not mention the face of Jesus, but only the whiteness of his clothes.

'White as the light'—white clothing is the apparel of angels (as, e.g., in the resurrection story, Mt.28:3) and of the glorified saints (Rev.3:4; 7:9,13f.). In Mark's description, his clothes are 'gleaming' (στίλβοντα), 'very white, as no fuller on earth could bleach them' (Mk.9:3); in Luke, they are 'white, gleaming like lightning' (ἐξαστράπτων—Lk.9:29). Christian believers are thankful that God has 'qualified [them] to share in the inheritance of the saints in the light' (Col.1:12). Broadly, 'light' is a symbol of the divine glory made manifest; and 'the light of the glory of the knowledge of God' is given above all 'in the face of Christ' (2 Cor.4:6).

VERSE 3: 'Moses and Elijah' (in Mark, 'Elijah and Moses') are here as representatives of 'the Law' and 'the prophets', who have testified of Christ. Their presence confirms the unity of the revelation of God in Christ with the revelation made through Moses and all the prophets, and prepares for the divine assurance that the revelation in the Son supersedes all that has gone before. 'God, who at many times and in many ways spoke to our fathers by the prophets has in these last days spoken to us by a Son . . . who is the effulgence of his glory' (Heb.1:1–3).

'Conversing with Jesus': Matthew, like Mark, does not suggest the subject of conversation; Luke takes it that they 'spoke of his exodus, which he was to accomplish in Jerusalem' (Lk.9:31).

VERSE 4: The 'booths' which Peter proposes to build are the kind of temporary shelters which were made for the feast of Booths (*sukkoth*) or of Ingathering, which was the third and latest of the three harvest festivals of the Hebrew calendar. It took its name from the fact that every worshipper was required to construct a 'booth' for himself, in which he slept and ate his meals for the seven days which the festival lasted. Such booths were probably constructed at first from vine branches; but later 'branches of palm trees, and boughs of leafy trees, and willows of the brook' are mentioned (Lev.23:39—43). It was the most important festival of the year; Jews from abroad chose this above all times to go on pilgrimage to Jerusalem, and it is foretold that in the end-time, when Yahweh has made himself King over all the earth, all people everywhere 'shall go up year after year to worship the King, the Lord of Hosts, and to keep the feast of booths' (Zech.14:9,16). Some notion of the establishment of the kingdom of God perhaps lies in the background of the strange proposal, but Mark suggests that it was prompted by sheer fright ('he did not know what to say, for they were exceedingly afraid', Mk.9:6; cf. Lk.9:34). Matthew omits this; the disciples feel no fear until they hear the heavenly voice (v.6).

'If you will'—a Matthaean modification; Peter will do nothing unless Jesus wills it.

VERSE 5: 'Luminous' ($\phi\omega\tau\epsilon\iota\nu\dot{\eta}$) is another Matthaean addition; the scene is so charged with light that even the cloud cannot be dark.

'Overshadowed'—a rare verb in Greek, recalling the language of the Exodus theophany: 'Moses could not enter the tent of testimony, for the cloud overshadowed ($\dot{\epsilon}\pi\epsilon\sigma\kappa\dot{\iota}\alpha\sigma\epsilon\nu$) it, and the tent was filled with the glory of the Lord' (Ex.40:35, LXX).

The voice which speaks from the cloud, like the 'voice from heaven' of the baptism story (3:17) is the voice of God. The phrasing reflects the Jewish inclination to avoid anthropomorphic expressions by resorting to paraphrase, when referring to God.

It is not clear whether the evangelist thinks of the cloud as enveloping the three heavenly beings, so that they are hidden from the sight of the disciples, or whether it hovers above the whole scene; in Luke, the three disciples also 'entered the cloud'. In any case, the words are addressed to the disciples, confirming the truth of the confession that Jesus is 'the Son of the living God'.

'Hear him'—in part, rejecting any thought that Moses and Elijah are to be heard as speaking with the same authority as Jesus; but primarily, demanding obedience to his commands.

It is striking up to this point, the part of Jesus has been wholly passive; he is seen in his glory, but he neither speaks nor acts.

VERSE 6: The entire verse is a Matthaean addition to the Markan story. The revelation of God's presence overwhelms them with fear, and silences them; the vision of the transfigured Jesus in itself had no such effect.

VERSE 7 is a further Matthaean addition. Jesus now speaks and acts for the first time in this episode.

'Approached'—this is the first time that Jesus is said to 'approach' others. It has always been the others who 'approach' Jesus, and apart from this verse, Jesus is said to 'approach' only in the final scene of the book (28:18), when he reveals himself as the Lord to whom all authority in heaven and on earth has been committed. That is, in both instances, Jesus 'approaches' his disciples, and approaches as from a heavenly state. In all the other instances, Jesus is approached —by supernatural beings (Satan, angels—4:3,11), by the sick (8:2, and in many miracle stories), by questioners or petitioners, by both friends and foes. It must be emphasized that this usage is peculiar to Matthew, and it appears to be designed to enhance the majesty of Jesus. He must be approached with a certain formality, with the respect due to his dignity, not with casual ease (cf. B. Rigaux, *Témoignage de l'évangile de Matthieu* (1967), pp.253f.). When he himself 'approaches', it is a descent from realms of glory. (See note on 4:3 above.)

VERSE 8: No attempt is made to describe the vanishing of the luminous cloud and of the celestial visitants. Jesus, and Jesus alone, is present to them as he was before.

14 SUPPLEMENT: ABOUT THE COMING OF ELIJAH *17:9–13*

[9] As they were going down the mountain Jesus charged them: 'Do not tell anyone about the vision until the Son of man is raised from the dead.'
[10] The disciples asked him, 'Why do the scribes say that Elijah must first come?' [11] He answered, 'Elijah is coming and will re-establish all things—[12] but I tell you, Elijah has already come and they did not recognize him, but did to him whatever they wished. So too the Son of man is going to suffer at their hands.' [13] Then the disciples understood that he had spoken to them of John the Baptist.

VERSE 9 indicates that the myth of the transfiguration was not introduced into the tradition about Jesus until after the resurrection. It has often been held that it is in its origin a story of an appearance of Jesus in glorious form, after his resurrection. Professor Dodd has shown, however, that it is wholly unlike any of the other resurrection narratives. 'If the theory of a displaced post-resurrection appearance is to be evoked for the understanding of this difficult pericope, it must be without any support from form-criticism, and indeed in the teeth of the presumption which formal analysis establishes' (*Studies in the Gospels*, p.25).

Matthew omits the statement of Mark that 'they kept the matter to themselves, debating what the "rising from the dead" might mean' (Mk.9:10). Matthew might well find this incomprehensible, seeing that the doctrine of resurrection was well established in Judaism, and the resurrection of Jesus had been foretold by him already.

VERSES 10–13 are a simplifying revision of the basic Markan passage (9:11–13). They are not pertinent to the story of the transfiguration, but make a natural sequel to the sayings which precede it (Mt.16:27f.//Mk.8:38, 9:1), especially the words: 'There are some of those standing here who will not taste of death until they see the Son of man coming in his kingdom' (Matthew); 'until they see the kingdom of God come in power' (Mark). It is this coming of the Kingdom, or of the Son of man, which was to be preceded by the return of Elijah. This was not a notion invented by the scribes; it rests on the accepted interpretation of a well-known prophecy (Mal.4:5), which declares: 'Behold, I will send you Elijah the prophet before the great and terrible day of the Lord comes.' In the *Dialogue with Trypho* of Justin Martyr, the great rabbi (probably to be identified with the historical Tarphon of Lydda) argues that Jesus cannot have been the Messiah because Elijah has not yet put in his appearance.

Jesus seems to grant this understanding of the oracle, but holds that it has been fulfilled in the coming of John the Baptist. The enemies of Elijah sought his life, but he escaped by fleeing to Mount Horeb, and lived to resume his prophetic ministry (1 Ki.19; 21:1–27; 2 Ki., chaps.1,2). But the enemies of John brought him to his death: 'they did with him what they wished.' In this Jesus sees a prefiguring of his own destiny—'the Son of man too will suffer at their hands.'

The passage is a fragment of early Christian apologetic, developed to meet the scribal objection, couched in much the same terms as 'Trypho' will employ in a later generation.

The progression of thought is still not entirely clear, but Matthew has done what he could with the obscurities of Mark. He omits the remark that the disciples were puzzled over 'what the rising from the dead meant' (Mk.9:10), and he replaces the question of Jesus (Mk. 9:12) with the prediction: 'So the Son of man also will be treated by them' (v.12b). He makes explicit the identification of the expected Elijah with John the Baptist, which Mark leaves to be inferred; and he omits the Markan phrase, 'as it is written of him' (Mk.9:13). See the discussion of this paragraph by Austin Farrer in his *St. Matthew and St. Mark*, pp.4–7.

15 JESUS HEALS AN EPILEPTIC BOY *17:14–20 [21]*

¹⁴ When they came to the crowd, a man made his approach to Jesus, knelt down and said to him, ¹⁵ 'Lord, have mercy upon my son, for he suffers from epilepsy: often he falls into the fire and often into the water. ¹⁶ I brought him to your disciples and they were unable to heal him.' ¹⁷ Jesus replied, 'O unbelieving and perverse generation! How long shall I be with you? How long shall I bear with you? Bring him here to me.' ¹⁸ Jesus rebuked him, and the demon came out of him, and from that hour the boy was healed.

¹⁹ Afterwards the disciples made their approach to Jesus in private, and asked him, 'Why were we unable to cast out the demon?' ²⁰ He answered them, 'Because of your little faith. For truly I tell you, if you have faith like a grain of mustard seed, you will say to this mountain, "Move from here to there", and it will move. Nothing will be impossible to you.'

[Verse 21, though found in the majority of witnesses, is clearly an intrusion due to scribal assimilation to the text of Mark (9:29). It runs: 'This kind does not go out except by prayer and fasting.']

The Matthaean version of this incident is not only much shorter than the Markan account (Mk.9:14–29), but also introduces different themes. The introduction is radically recast; the description of the illness mentions only the tendency to fall into fire or into water; the entire description of the seizure which takes place in the presence of Jesus (Mk.9:20), and the dialogue between Jesus and the father (vv.21–24) are omitted; the actual healing is recounted in its bare essentials without the words spoken by Jesus to the demon, the account of a last convulsion, or the action of Jesus in taking the boy by the hand and lifting him to his feet (vv.25–27). The most striking difference, however, comes in the sequel where the reason for the failure of the disciples is given as their 'little faith', while in Mark it is said that the secret of success lies in prayer.

VERSE 14: The appearance of 'the crowd' in the vicinity of Caesarea Philippi is really inexplicable, and indicates that the story was originally laid somewhere in Galilee, where Jesus had acquired a large following. It is, of course, carried over from Mark (9:14). The Markan story starts as if it were about to describe a controversy with scribes (the presence of scribes would also be most unusual in the pagan region of the foothills of Mount Hermon); the crowd has gathered to enjoy a dispute between the scribes and the disciples of Jesus, and Jesus asks what the dispute is about; but then this theme is abruptly abandoned and the scribes play no part in the story as it unfolds, nor are we ever told what the subject of dispute may have been. It can hardly be supposed that such an introduction was framed in the first instance to lead into a miracle story, and it is natural enough that both Matthew and Luke agree in eliminating any reference to a dispute, or to the presence of scribes, who serve no purpose in the story once the dispute is forgotten.

The broader question remains of why Mark, and Matthew and Luke after him, have linked this miracle story with the transfiguration.

'Kneeling' is a Matthaean touch; in Mark and Luke, the man calls to Jesus from the crowd.

VERSE 15: 'Lord' (Κύριε) replaces the 'teacher' (διδάσκαλε) of Mark (and Luke).

The verb 'have mercy' ἐλέησον—is perhaps a liturgical touch in Matthew; at this point in Mark, the father makes no request, but simply describes his son's condition.

'Epileptic': Matthew uses the verb σεληνιάζω (from σελήνη, 'moon'), literally 'be moonstruck'; hence *AV*, 'lunatic'. It is used technically of epilepsy, probably from some notion that the epileptic was liable to a seizure at certain phases of the moon.

The symptoms of the illness are graphically described in Mark: the boy's trouble is attributed to a demon, said to be 'dumb'—indicating that the boy himself is dumb—who 'dashes him down', so that 'he foams and grinds his teeth and becomes rigid.' In a fuller description, the father says that the demon 'has often cast him into the fire and into the water, to destroy him' (Mk.9:18,22). Demonic possession is not mentioned in Matthew at this point, though in verse 18 the healing is described in terms of an exorcism.

VERSE 16: The inability of the disciples to help the boy is a key thought in all three forms of the story. The authority to cast out demons has been granted to them (Mt.10:1,8; cf. Mk.6:7), and has actually been exercised by them, according to Mark and Luke (Mk.6:13; Lk.10:17). Does this note reflect the experience of Matthew's church (and of others) that exorcisms were not always effective?

VERSE 17: The exclamation of Jesus (found in all three Synoptics) is without parallel in the Gospels. It implies that Jesus is a visitant from a higher realm who feels that his presence among human beings is an ordeal. The words do not form a reply to the father; they are not addressed to him, nor to the crowd, still less to the disciples, but to that whole 'generation'. Are we then to think of Jesus as impatient with the whole human race?

'Faithless and perverse' fills out the Markan phrasing ('faithless') in reminiscence of the words of Moses about Israel: 'they are a perverse and crooked generation' (Deut.32:5; cf. Phil.2:15).

v.18. 'Jesus rebuked him'—not the boy, but the demon, who 'came out of him'. In Mark, it is more explicit: 'he rebuked the unclean spirit' (9:25).

The cure is instantaneous, but nothing is said of how it was known. The mere statement replaces a vivid Markan picture, in which the boy undergoes a dreadful seizure and is left on the ground as if dead; he remains helpless until 'Jesus took him by the hand and lifted him up.' Matthew probably could not imagine that more than the word of Jesus was needed, or that the demon could throw the boy into a convulsion after Jesus had commanded him to 'come out of him, and never enter him again' (Mark).

16   A SECOND PROPHECY OF THE PASSION *17:22–23*

²² As they were gathering in Galilee, Jesus said to them, 'The Son of man is going to be delivered into the hands of men. ²³ and they will kill him, and on the third day he will be raised.' They were deeply grieved.

The prediction of the passion is given here in a much less circumstantial form than before (Mt.16:21). The doctrine of *necessity* ($\delta\epsilon\hat{\iota}$) does not appear, and there is no mention of 'elders, chief priests, and scribes' as the agents of the death of Jesus. (In the third prediction, on the other hand [Mt.20:18f.], the details are multiplied.)

VERSE 22: The setting of the saying is vague. There has been no mention of a return from the north into Galilee, nor of any scattering of the disciples, yet they are said to be gathering in Galilee, without any suggestion of the purpose. This vagueness is the more surprising in that Mark has spoken of them leaving the region of the healing, and has indicated that they are journeying as it were secretly, through Galilee, so that Jesus may teach his disciples privately (Mk.9:31). In Luke there is no change of scene; Jesus speaks to his disciples in the presence of all those who 'were filled with amazement at all that he was doing' (Lk.9:43b—44).

'The verb *deliver* (παραδιδόναι), when applied to Jesus . . . belongs to the theological terminology of the Passion, from its most archaic formulations on' (Bonnard, *Matthieu*, p.263). It is God who 'delivers' Jesus into the hands of his enemies (here, it is the human enemies immediately responsible for his death). Cf. Paul's moving words of assurance: 'If God be for us, who can be against us? He who did not spare his own Son, but freely delivered him up (παρέδωκεν αὐτόν) for us all, will he not also freely give us all things with him?' (Rom. 8:31f.) If 'men' are permitted to work their evil will upon Jesus, even to the point of putting him to death, this does not mean that God has lost control of events. It is just in this that God most signally manifests his love for mankind, in that he makes the sacrifice of his own Son. 'God so loved the world that he gave his only Son' (Jn.3:16).

VERSE 23: The reaction of the disciples—'they were deeply grieved'—suggests that they take in only the prediction of death; they would not be *grieved* at the assurance of resurrection. Matthew substitutes this for the words of Mark (followed in substance by Luke) that 'they did not understand the saying, and they were afraid to ask him' (Mk.9:32; Lk.9:45).

17   THE QUESTION OF PAYING THE TEMPLE TAX *17:24—27*

[24] When they came to Capernaum, the collectors of the Didrachma approached them. They took hold of Peter and said, 'Does not your teacher pay the Didrachma?' [25] He said, 'Yes.' When he came into the house, Jesus anticipated his question by saying, 'What would you say, Simon? From whom do the kings of earth collect taxes or tribute? From their own sons, or from aliens?' [26] He answered, 'From aliens'; and Jesus said, 'Then the sons are exempt. [27] However, that we may not cause offence to them, go down to the lake and cast your line; take the first fish that comes to it, and when you open its mouth you will find a stater—give that to them for you and me.'

This curious little story is peculiar to Matthew. It is a kind of parallel to the question about the tribute money (Mt.22:15–22), which is found in Mark and Luke also; but the point of departure is not the tribute to be paid to the Emperor but the dues which were imposed by Jewish law for the upkeep of the Temple. Undoubtedly, the question soon arose of whether Christians (it would concern only Jewish Christians) should continue to pay these dues after their conversion to the faith of Christ, but such a problem would not exist during the lifetime of Jesus. The payment of these dues was required by the law of Moses. In Ex.30:11–16, the amount is set at 'half a shekel according to the shekel of the sanctuary'; in Neh.10:32ff., the people subscribe to a covenant 'to charge ourselves yearly with the third part of a shekel for the service of the house of our God.' At the New Testament period, the dues were set at two drachmas per person, and so the tax was commonly called 'the Didrachma'. The actual value of both the shekel and the drachma varied from one time to another, and the rate of exchange fluctuated, just as with the dollar and the pound in our own days. Refusal to pay the Didrachma would be equivalent to deliberate withdrawal from the religious community of Judaism.

VERSE 24: It is implied that the whole company is now back in Capernaum, but the collectors find Peter alone (or search him out), and question him in the absence of Jesus—not, however, about his own payment of the tax, but about the attitude of Jesus. The other disciples have no part in the scene.

VERSE 25: Jesus, although he has not been present, has super-natural knowledge of all that has been said; he does not wait for Peter to tell him about it. But by mentioning 'taxes' (τέλη) and 'tribute' (κῆνσον, from the Latin *census*) and introducing them as the payments required by earthly rulers, Jesus broadens the scope of the question. For the church of Matthew, which had broken with the synagogue, the question of paying dues for the support of the Temple at Jerusalem was no longer relevant; but there was evidently still some debate over whether Christians, as children of the heavenly King, should accept civil responsibilities; and specifically, whether they should pay taxes for the support of pagan governments (part of which would be used for the financing of the state religion and a number of cults).

The question which Jesus puts to Peter would not apply in the modern state, which taxes its own citizens and lets certain categories of foreigners go free (diplomats, visiting scholars, etc.) More than that, the ancient state also taxed its own citizens, and there were even certain taxes (in the Roman Empire) for which citizens alone were liable—notably, the tax for the armed forces. When Caracalla extended the privilege of Roman citizenship to all free inhabitants of the Empire, it was partly done in order to make a much greater number of people liable to such taxes.

VERSE 27: The Greek stater was worth four drachmas.

Additional notes:

(i) The suggestion of v.27, that Peter will find a stater in the mouth of the first fish that he catches, and this will be enough to pay the Didrachma for the two of them, is *not* the point of the pericope. This should be regarded as a bit of folk-tale, and should not be allowed to divert attention from the central thought.

(ii) The situation pictured in v.24 is artificial—simply a framework for the saying of Jesus.

(iii) All male Jews of twenty and upwards were obligated to pay an annual poll-tax of a didrachmon (so Josephus), or a half-shekel (Exodus) or a third of a shekel, for the upkeep of the sanctuary. The question of whether Christians were liable to this poll-tax would arise only for Jewish-Christians, and the question would not arise in any form for converted Gentiles, unless in circles which thought of Christianity as a sect of Judaism (such as those who held that Gentiles must be circumcised and taught to keep the law of Moses— cf. Acts 15:1). For Jews who now belonged to the church of Christ, but did not see in their faith in Christ a break with the community of Israel, the question arose only when they consciously ceased to take part in the temple worship, and came to regard it as superseded. This probably did not become acute until the Temple was destroyed in the year 70. Peter and John go up to the Temple to pray at the hour of prayer; Paul (according to Acts) takes part in rites of the Temple in the late 50s. Somewhere in the background of this pericope lies a debate within the church over whether Christian Jews should continue to contribute to the support of the Temple, and it was settled that they would agree to do so—not as a formal obligation, but to avoid giving offence to their fellow Jews who did not believe. Refusal to pay the tax would involve the open declaration that they no longer looked upon themselves as members of the Jewish community.

(iv) After AD 70, the situation changed, in that the tax was still collected, as a poll-tax on Jews, but the proceeds now went to the temple of Jupiter Capitolinus (the *fiscus Iudaicus*); this was collected through the reigns of the Flavian emperors (Vespasian, Titus,

Domitian), but was abolished by Nerva (97—98). For Christian Jews, this posed a real dilemma. Would they accept the obligation laid upon all other Jews of paying this tax for the cult of Jupiter? Apparently, this pericope indicates that they were still prepared to affirm solidarity with the Jewish community by paying. (Would Domitian have excused them from paying, on the ground that they were not in fact Jews?)

II THE FOURTH MAJOR DISCOURSE
Mt. 18:1—35

Matthew again organizes into a connected discourse a number of sayings of diverse origins. In this form he presents them as an address given by Jesus to his disciples, apparently at Capernaum (17:24), shortly before the journey to Jerusalem. This setting is devised by him, not given by the tradition as he received it. The formal setting is of no significance; in reality, it is the risen Christ who speaks to lay down rules and principles for his church. They deal with issues and problems which arise in the life of an organized community, in which he is to be present, not in the flesh, but in the spirit, wherever two or three are gathered in his name (18:20).

An important part of the collected materials is based upon the somewhat loose assortment of sayings already gathered by Mark at this point of his narrative (Mk.9:33—50). Along with these Matthew has incorporated sayings from Q (/ / Lk.15:3—7; 17:3f.), and has woven in with these some sayings found only in this Gospel— notably, the parable of the Unforgiving Slave, verses 23—35. (See the analysis and exposition of R. Schnackenburg in the Wikenhauser Festschrift *Synoptische Studien* (1953), pp.184—206; further discussion by W. Trilling, *Das Wahre Israel* (1959; 2nd edn., 1964), pp.106—23; and R. Pesch, 'Die sogenannte Gemeindeordnung Mt. 18', in *BZ* 7.2 (July 1963), pp.220—35.)

The discourse as constructed by Matthew falls into two parts, each ending with a parable, *viz.*:

1: verses 1—14, where the theme is the treatment of 'little ones', or 'children' ($\mu\iota\kappa\rho\sigma\iota$, $\pi\alpha\iota\delta\iota\alpha$); and

2: verses 1—14, where the theme is the relationship of members of the church (brothers, $\dot{\alpha}\delta\epsilon\lambda\phi\sigma\iota$) to one another, in forgiveness without limit, and forbearance in the exercise of discipline.

1 TREATMENT OF LITTLE ONES *18:1–14*

¹ In that hour the disciples made approach to Jesus to ask: 'Who is greatest in the kingdom of heaven?' ² He called a child over, had it stand before them, ³ and said, 'Truly I tell you, unless you turn about and become like the little children, you will not enter the kingdom of heaven. ⁴ Whoever humbles himself like this little child will be the greatest in the kingdom of heaven.

⁵ Whoever receives one such little child in my name receives me. ⁶ But anyone who causes one of these little ones who believe in me to get into trouble would be better off if a huge millstone were hung about his neck and he were drowned in the depths of the sea.

⁷ Woe to the world that such troubles come! The troubles must come, but woe to the one who is responsible for their coming. ⁸ If your hand or your foot is getting you into trouble, cut it off and throw it away from you; it is better for you to enter into life maimed or lame than to keep both hands and both feet and be cast into the eternal fire. ⁹ If your eye gets you into trouble, knock it out and throw it away from you; it is better for you to enter into life one-eyed than to keep both eyes and be thrown into the hell of fire.

¹⁰ Take heed! Do not despise one of these little ones; for I tell you, their angels in heaven have continual access to my heavenly Father.

¹² What do you think? If a man has a hundred sheep and one of them goes astray, will he not leave the ninety-nine others in the mountain pasture and go to hunt for the one that is straying? ¹³ And once he finds it, he takes more joy in it, I tell you, than in the ninety-nine that have not gone astray. ¹⁴ For it is not the will of my heavenly Father that a single one of these little ones should be lost.'

[Verse 11, found in Codex D and in the mass of Byzantine cursives and lectionaries, the later uncials, supported by the Latin versions and the Curetonian Syriac, is not read in the better Greek witnesses (B, Aleph, L, the main Caesarean manuscripts Theta and its allies, and some very good cursives) or in the Sinaitic Syriac or the Egyptian versions. It runs: 'For the Son of man came to save the lost.' It appears to be an interpolation based upon Luke 19:10, and is clearly out of place here.]

VERSE 1: 'Made approach'—another instance of Matthew's special use of προσέρχομαι.

'In that hour'—not to be taken literally, exact though it sounds. It is not to be supposed that the rest of the disciples come to Jesus in a group at the very moment of his conversation with Peter about the temple tax (17:24–27). Cf. 'in those days' (3:1), when the last occurrence mentioned was the settlement of the Holy Family at Nazareth soon after the death of Herod—some thirty years before.

'Who is greatest'—the comparative μείξων (in classical usage 'greater') is used for the superlative, as frequently in the colloquial Greek of the period. In Aramaic, there is no comparison of adjectives or adverbs; this contributes to the inexactness of usage in the Gospels (BDF § 244; N. Turner in the third volume of Moulton's *Grammar*, chap.3).

The question is not prompted by reaction to the high status conferred on Peter in 16:17ff. It is a generalizing of the question raised in the dispute over precedence (Mk.9:33–37), which is laid under contribution throughout this Matthaean introduction.

'The disciples' as so often means less the immediate followers of Jesus than the Christian believers of Matthew's time. Matthew intends the lesson in humility for them.

Note that in the Matthaean form it is not suggested that the disciples have been discussing among themselves which of them shall have the highest posts in the coming Kingdom (as in Mk.9:34). It raises the question in a general, almost an academic, form. Matthew deprecates *any* kind of insistence on rank and dignity in the church (cf. 23:8–12). It was not of course 'academic' in the sense that it was removed from the concrete realities of life; in Matthew's time, as today, there was danger of church leaders attempting to 'lord it over the flock' (cf. 1 Pet.5:3; etc.).

VERSE 2: The little child of the story is not necessarily a boy; it could just as well be a little girl. The Greek word παιδίον is neuter.

VERSE 3: 'Turn about'—reverse your whole direction. The Greek στραφῆτε is a literal rendering of the Aramaic-Hebrew *shub*, which retains its primary sense of 'turn back, return' but is often given the metaphorical meaning of 'repent', 'turn back to God' (from evil or from apostasy—Hos.6:1, and often). In LXX it is usually rendered by a compounded form (ἀνα or ἐπι-στ.), and in NT the usual term is μετανοέω (Mt.3:2, etc.). The very fact that the question is raised reveals a false notion of the nature of the kingdom of heaven. Anyone whose heart is set on high position will not even be granted admittance to the Kingdom.

VERSE 4: It is now explained that the child is an example of humility, 'not of innocence, nor of purity, nor of moral perfection' (Bonnard). In Paul, the child is a symbol of the lack of malice; he bids the Corinthians not be children in disposition (ταῖς φρεσίν), but to be infants (νηπιάξεσθε) in malice (1 Cor.14:20). Children are not as a rule particularly humble. The point is that they are not set on rank and title. In the ancient world, they were generally regarded as of no account; but those who are like them in their insignificance are counted greatest in the kingdom of heaven.

The thought is already shifting from that of small children to that of simple and unpretentious disciples—undistinguished members of the church. In the following verses, this sense emerges clearly, as they become 'these little ones who believe in me' (vv.6,10,14). Matthew applies the words of Jesus to the humblest believers, whatever their age. Jesus spoke of his followers as 'children', and may have addressed them as 'Children' (cf.Jn.21:5). This has led to a certain confusion in the tradition of his sayings about children. As T.W. Manson remarks: 'Now the early Church was more interested in the original disciples than in children; and we should expect the tendency of the tradition to be to transfer sayings concerning "children" or "little ones" to the disciples' (*Sayings*, p.138).

VERSES 5—6: The whole thought is now directed to how these 'little ones' are to be treated, not on the requirement to become like them. On verse 5, see 10:40—42, where 'these little children' are set in parallelism with 'you' (the disciples on mission), 'a prophet' and 'a righteous man'. The 'little ones' must be treated with kindness and respect. In verse 6, we have a warning of the unspeakable fate that is in store at the Judgement for anyone who causes trouble for them. The verb σκανδαλίζομαι, literally 'be a stumbling-block', verges on the meaning 'lead into apostasy'. It is probably, at least in the understanding of Matthew, aimed at false teachers who lead simple Christians into error or unbelief, rather than at vicious people who lead children into criminal conduct.

'Huge millstone'—μύλος ὀνικός, literally, a millstone worked by donkey power.

VERSES 7—9: The word σκάνδαλον (stumbling-block, offence, trouble—v.7) becomes a link-word which leads Matthew to add a series of sayings in which the verb σκανδαλίζομαι occurs, though they have nothing to do with the treatment of others, but with self-discipline. If something in your life is a source of spiritual ill to you, get rid of it, however great the cost—even if it is as hard as cutting off a foot or a hand or knocking out one of your eyes. Two of the same sayings have already been introduced by Matthew, more appropriately, in the Sermon on the Mount, in connection with warnings against adultery (5:29f.). Here the link is merely verbal; Matthew appears to be following Mark somewhat mechanically in this context (Mk.9:43—47).

VERSE 10: The concluding paragraph of this section is introduced by the solemn injunction not to despise a single one of 'these little ones', with the reminder that every one of them is under the care of an angel who has direct and continual access to the throne of God. This access is expressed in the Semitic idiom, they 'behold his face'. In this figure, God is pictured as an oriental monarch surrounded by such ceremony that not even his courtiers are permitted to see him except when they receive special permission (cf. Esther 4:11— even Queen Esther may not approach Ahasuerus unless by his grace and favour). The doctrine of angels was developed in Judaism after the exile, under Persian influences; it is scarcely adumbrated in the earlier books of the Old Testament, and comes into its own in the book of Daniel, the intertestament literature, and the Qumran documents. The general doctrine of the rabbinical schools was that God could not be seen even by angels; according to the great Rabbi Aqiba (early second century), 'even the angels 'who possess eternal life do not behold the Glory.' This makes it all the more striking that Jesus should speak of the angels who look after the welfare of the 'little ones' as always in God's presence.

Nothing in any of the Jewish literature suggests that any angels have special charge over children, or over the weak.

VERSES 12–14: This is the Matthaean version of the parable of the Lost Sheep, but it has remarkable differences from the Lukan version (Lk.15:4–7). As usual Matthew removes much colourful detail—the shepherd laying the sheep on his shoulders, his invitation to his friends and neighbours to rejoice with him over its recovery. More important, the parable is given an entirely different point. In Luke, it is offered by Jesus in defence of his practice of ministering to outcasts (Lk.15:2), and it is associated with two other parables (the Lost Coin, the Lost [Prodigal] Son), which likewise stress the joy in the recovery of that which was lost, and proclaim that this human joy is a true picture of the joy of God in the sinner who repents. In Matthew, there is no such emphasis on joy (though the shepherd rejoices over the recovered sheep 'more than over the ninety-nine that never went astray'). There is no suggestion that the actions of Jesus are like those of the shepherd, nor is his joy seen as a reflection of the joy of God. He is an example to Christian pastors. If they are to do the will of God, they must not take lightly the loss of a single one of the flock, however insignificant. And we recall the insistence throughout the Gospel that only those who do the will of the Father in heaven will be admitted to the kingdom of heaven (7:21–23). They and they only will be acknowledged by Jesus as his 'brother, and sister, and mother' (12:50).

2 CONCERN FOR THE ERRING: THE DOCTRINE OF UNLIMITED FORGIVENESS *18:15–35*

[15] 'If your brother commits an offence, go and tell him his fault, between you and him, alone. If he heeds you, you have won over your brother. [16] If he will not heed, take one or two others with you, that "in the evidence of two or three witnesses, every matter may be confirmed." [17] If he refuses to heed them, tell it to the church; and if he still refuses to heed the church, let him be as a Gentile or a tax collector to you. [18] Truly I tell you, whatever you bind upon earth shall be bound in heaven, and whatever you loose upon earth shall be loosed in heaven. [19] Again I tell you, if two of you agree upon earth about anything for which you ask, it shall be done for you by my Father in heaven. [20] For where two or three are gathered in my name, I am there among them.'

[21] Peter now made his approach and asked, 'How often am I to forgive my brother, Lord, when he commits an offence against me? As many as seven times?' [22] Jesus answered, 'I do not tell you to forgive him up to seven times, but up to seventy-seven times.

[23] 'For the kingdom of heaven may be compared with this story of a king who decided to inspect the accounts of his slaves. [24] Once he began to examine the books, one of them was brought before him who was in default in the amount of ten thousand talents. [25] As he had no means of repaying this, his master [the king] gave orders for him and his wife and children to be sold, and the debt repaid. [26] The slave fell on his knees before him and pleaded with him, "Have patience with me, and I will repay it all." [27] The slave's master was moved with pity for him, released him, and remitted the debt. [28] But that slave went out and found one of his fellow slaves who owed him a hundred dinars; he took him by the throat and demanded, "Pay what you owe!" [29] His fellow slave fell on his knees before him, pleading, "Have patience with me, and I will pay it back it you." [30] But he refused; he went off and had him thrown into jail, until he should pay what he owed. [31] When his fellow slaves saw what had been done, they were very much upset and went and told their master the whole story. [32] The master summoned him, and said to him, "You wicked slave! I remitted that entire debt of yours when you pleaded with me. [33] Were you not bound to have pity on your fellow slave as I took pity on you?" [34] In his fury, the master handed him over to the torturers, till he should repay the whole debt. [35] That is how my heavenly Father will deal with you, if you do not, every one of you, forgive your brethren with all your hearts.'

The 'children' or 'little ones' of the first part of the discourse are now included among the 'brothers'; and the trouble that may come upon them is not apostasy or error, but an offence that violates the bond of brotherhood. The main line of teaching is that the community is kept united by the free exercise of forgiveness—forgiveness without limit. As God has freely forgiven every one of them, they must always be ready and willing to forgive one another.

This teaching is strongly emphasized by Paul in many of his letters. 'Brethren, if a man is overtaken in any trespass, you who are spiritual should restore him in a spirit of gentleness' (Gal.6:1). 'We that are strong ought to bear with the failings of the weak, and not to please ourselves' (Rom.15:1). He calls on them to exercise 'compassion, kindness, . . . and patience, forbearing one another and, if one has a complaint against another, forgiving each other; as the Lord has forgiven you, so you also must forgive' (Col.3:12f.). It is beautifully expressed in the letter to the Ephesians. To lead a life worthy of their high calling, they must always be 'forbearing one another in love, eager to maintain the unity of the Spirit in the bond of peace' (4:1–3); they are to 'be kind to one another, tender-hearted, forgiving one another, as God in Christ forgave you' (4:32).

VERSES 15–16: An offence committed by a brother is to be dealt with privately, if it be at all possible. It is taken for granted that the community life is affected by any ill-treatment of one member by another; but the first step is for the offended brother to seek reconciliation privately; if that fails, he is not to bring it at once to the attention of the whole community, but to make an attempt to straighten things out with his brother by invoking the help of one or two others.

The citation of the regulation governing evidence is not really pertinent here. The reference is to a passage in Deuteronomy, which runs: 'A single witness shall not prevail against a man for any crime or for any wrong. . . . Only on the evidence of two witnesses, or of three, shall a charge be sustained' (19:15). In the Gospel teaching; the others are brought along not to confirm the evidence that an offence has been committed, but to make it unnecessary to bring a charge at all.

VERSE 17: 'The church'—not as in 16:18, of the church which Jesus will build with Peter as the foundation stone ('rock'), but of the local group of believers. It is to function as a court for the discipline of its members (as in 1 Cor. chaps.3,4,5; cf. 2 Cor.2:5–8).

These two passages are the only places in the Gospels which introduce the word ἐκκλησία, 'church'. As in Paul, so also in

Matthew, it can mean either the whole body of believers everywhere, or the local group which is a unit in the larger whole.

'As a Gentile and a tax collector': There is not the least likelihood that Jesus himself ever spoke with such disparagement of Gentiles or tax collectors. These are quite evidently the words of a Jewish-Christian group which still thinks of Gentiles as 'common' (unholy) or 'unclean' (Acts 10:14,28; 11:8f.). It is well known that Jesus did not share the general Jewish disdain for tax collectors and defended himself against criticism for friendliness to them (Mt.9:10—13)—he even commends their conduct towards John the Baptist, in contrast to that of the chief priests and elders(21:31f.). The words here amount to a sentence of excommunication.

It is striking that the action is to be taken by the local community, with no hint of a council of elders, let alone an authoritative officer, like a bishop. Matthew insists on the equality of all members: no one is to exercise authority over the others, as in Gentile kingdoms (20:25ff.), and no one is to be called 'Rabbi' or 'Master', for 'you have one teacher, and you are all brethren, and you have one master, the Christ' (23:8,10).

VERSE 18: The authority of 'binding' and 'loosing', given to Peter in 16:18, is now conferred on the church, even on the local congregation when it meets as a court. Its sentence, whatever it may be, will be ratified 'in heaven', that is by God himself. Here 'binding' and 'loosing' clearly bear upon the power of absolution; in John 20:23 it is expressed in terms of retaining or forgiving sins. In both cases, it is the risen Christ who speaks.

VERSE 19: This may be taken as a widening of the grace bestowed, but it is probable that in the context Matthew intends it to be understood simply as indicating that the number present on a given occasion does not limit the authority of the Christian church.

VERSE 20: Again, the thought is probably (in Matthew's understanding) that the Christian group in session as a court of discipline, is assured that Christ is present to preside over its decisions, however few the numbers. In itself, of course, it would carry the wider meaning—in every Christian gathering, no matter how small, Christ promises to be present. It may have originated in a quite different context.

There is a similar rabbinic saying which affirms that the Glory of God (the Shekinah) rests upon every group of ten that comes into the synagogue, or even if there be only three who are judging, or two, or one (Schlatter, *Matthaeus*, 558). Similarly, with a magnifying of the Torah: 'Where two are sitting together, and studying words of the Torah, the Shekinah rests upon them' (Mishnah, *Aboth* 3.3). For Christians, Jesus is the embodiment of Torah, and 'the effulgence of the glory' of God (Heb.1:3).

VERSES 21–22: The question of Peter already goes beyond the limits permitted by the rabbis. A Tosephta runs: 'If a man sins once, twice, or three times, they forgive him; if he sins a fourth time, they do not forgive him' (*Joma* 5.13). When he suggests seven times as the limit, 'Peter thinks he has taken a long step towards his Master' (Bonnard). But the answer of Jesus effectively removes all limits. It turns the revenge of Lamech (Gen.4:24), to be exacted seventy-seven times, into the injunction that forgiveness is to be granted seventy-seven times. This means, of course, that there is no question of keeping count: the spirit of forgiveness is not subject to formal or legal regulation.

The grammarians agreed that the Greek phrase ἑβδομηκοντάκις ἑπτα means 'seventy-seven times', not seventy times seven. It reproduces exactly the LXX of the Lamech passage; the Hebrew is quite unambiguous (Gen.4:24). The ancient versions generally take it to mean 'seventy times seven' (e.g., Vulg. *septuagies septies*).

VERSES 23–35: The whole chapter presses home the insistence of Jesus on forgiveness and reconciliation. The Christian community is a community of those whose sins have been forgiven by God; it shows itself unworthy of the divine forgiveness if its members are unwilling to forgive the comparatively trifling offences of a brother. The concluding parable illustrates this doctrine by a horrible example of refusal to forgive an equal by one who has received from his king forgiveness of something infinitely greater.

In rabbinic parables, the king is often used as a figure for God. To some extent, this symbolism hovers in the background, but the behaviour of this king, shifting from his initial decision to sell the defaulting official into slavery along with his wife and children, then the generous impulse to remit the whole of his vast debt, to the final order to hand him over to the torturers—this hardly belongs to any Christian (or Jewish) conception of God, let alone to that of a 'Father in heaven'. It is a shock to us all when we read Matthew's threatening words, actually reported by him as words of Jesus, that 'my heavenly Father will deal with you like that, if you do not forgive with all your hearts' (v.35). The parable itself simply uses the illustration from an oriental despotism to bring out sharply the absurdity of a Christian who has been forgiven by God refusing to forgive his brother for an infinitely lighter injury to himself.

VERSE 24: The incredible figure of ten thousand talents would represent the total revenue of a wealthy province. According to Josephus, the taxes paid in a year by Judaea, Idumaea, Samaria, Galilee, and Peraea amounted to only 800 talents. It cannot be thought of as a loan, a debt which the 'slave' has incurred. We must think rather of him as the satrap of a great province of the Persian Empire, let us say, who has diverted to his own use vast sums that should have been sent on to the imperial treasury. The figure need not be taken literally, indeed, but there is no way that it could be taken as the amount of a personal loan.

VERSE 25: The sale of a slave along with his wife and children and all his property would of course not begin to pay back so vast a sum. But there is considerable incongruity in the sentence, if it is taken as a form of punishment. If the defaulting official is a slave already, how can he be punished by being sold to a different master? Of course, if he is conceived as a high provincial governor, a kind of viceroy, he may be called a 'slave' only by way of convention: all the subjects of an oriental despot may be regarded as his slaves.

VERSE 26: Given the magnitude of the sum, there is no way that the defaulter could be helped by an extension of time. Unless he were left in a position to continue his defalcations, he could not hope to cover the losses to the treasury, no matter how much time he was granted. The appeal simply prepares the way for the similar plea to be made by his own debtor.

VERSE 27: The sudden and unexpected generosity is not out of touch with the realities of the imagined situation. A Sultan, or a Caliph, or an Indian prince would be capable of as much extravagance in grace as in cruelty.

VERSES 28–29: The debt owed by the fellow slave is trifling—a matter of a few months' wages for a labourer. If time were allowed, he could certainly manage to repay it.

VERSE 30: The story is not spelled out in detail. Presumably the man's imprisonment would follow upon legal proceedings. It is presupposed that imprisonment for debt was permitted by law, as it still was in Britain and America in the last century. Who can forget Dickens' grim pictures of life in the Fleet (Pickwick Papers, etc.)?

VERSE 31: The indignation of the other slaves is natural, and a legitimate part of the parable. It need not be taken to picture the indignation of Christians when they see one of their number behaving heartlessly to a brother.

VERSES 32–34: The grant of full forgiveness is retracted as soon as the master learns of the meanness of the one to whom he had been so kind. The punishment—not merely imprisonment but torture—belongs to the furniture of the story. Torture was forbidden in Jewish law, but even so it was employed by Herod the Great and probably also by his sons, as by most governments of the time. In the Eastern monarchies it was regularly employed against defaulting or unjust governors. Of course no amount of torture would make it possible for him to repay the immense sum which he owed.

VERSE 35: The closing tag is no part of the parable, but an addition made by Matthew, most incongruously. He cannot believe that God keeps a corps of torturers. In some translations, the brutality of the saying is disguised by the euphemistic rendering 'jailers' (*RSV*). It may be said that the expression is no worse than the hell of fire that Matthew pictures as the abode of the damned. Certainly the thought goes beyond the figure of the parable to the thought of the Last Judgement. In subsequent Christian interpretation, the 'torturers' are allegorized as 'the avenging angels' (Origen, *et al.*).

It may be observed that the master is not called a king except in the opening; in the rest of the parable, we have a story of slaves and their master, not of a king and his ministers of state. Perhaps it is Matthew who is responsible for introducing the figure of the king, just as in the parable of the Great Feast he has turned the man with one slave of Luke's version into a king with numerous slaves. In that case, he has probably transmuted the modest debt of the original parable into the enormous ten thousand talents which are mentioned here. This would be comparable to his heightening of the money entrusted (25:14ff.) from the single mina of Luke (19:13) to five, two, and one talents. (Even the one talent is equivalent to 500 minas.)

It is at least open to question whether this parable goes back to Jesus in any form. Certainly in the form given to it by Matthew, it shows evidence of working-over in the course of transmission and (or) in the editorial treatment of the evangelist. Without any parallel in other Gospels to aid us, it would be vain to conjecture what form it may have had originally. The general theme, of course, goes back to Jesus: he expects God's free forgiveness to be reflected in our readiness to forgive others.

The relationship of these regulations to the rules of community discipline at Qumran is discussed by W.D. Davies (*Setting*, pp.221ff.).

III   THE JOURNEY TO JERUSALEM
Mt. 19:1—20:34

In Matthew as in Mark, this is the only visit made by Jesus to Jerusalem during his life. Luke also mentions only this visit during his public career, but he introduces two earlier visits, in infancy and childhood—once for the Presentation in the Temple (Lk.2:22—38), and another at the Passover of his twelfth year, with the incidental remark that his parents went up to Jerusalem every year at the Passover festival, presumably taking Jesus with them (Lk.2:41ff.). In John, on the other hand, this pattern is completely shattered. Jesus begins his public ministry in Judaea (Jn.1:35—51), and after an interlude in Galilee (2:1—12), he returns to Jerusalem for Passover, and throughout the remainder of his career he is pictured as almost continually active in Jerusalem and Judaea, with only occasional appearances in Galilee and Samaria. The Galileans know of him mainly through what they have seen of his activities in Jerusalem (Jn.4:45). John never makes any mention of the tours in Galilee of which the three Synoptic evangelists tell, when 'he went throughout all Galilee, preaching in their synagogues and casting out demons' (Mk.1:39; Mt.4:23; Lk.4:14f., etc.). It is impossible to tell much about the actual movements of Jesus, but it is probable that the greater part of his public ministry was spent in Galilee, as the Synoptic Gospels all suggest; and that even at the end he was known to the people of Jerusalem as 'Jesus the prophet from Nazareth in Galilee' (Mt.21:11). On the other hand, it is not at all likely that he never went into the southern regions of the land of Israel after the opening of his work in Galilee (Mk.1:14f. and parallels) until the time of the journey that issued in his crucifixion.

In Mark, the events laid in the course of this last journey to Jerusalem are recounted in a single chapter (chap. 10). In Matthew, the same events are given, and in the same order (with a number of variations and small but important additions); but with the insertion of the parable of the Labourers in the Vineyard (20:1—16—peculiar to Matthew), the narrative occupies two chapters. In Luke, the journey is given far greater prominence; it occupies almost ten chapters (Lk.9:51—18:43), and includes large amounts of material which is found only in that Gospel. Luke, moreover, represents it explicitly as a journey undertaken with the deliberate purpose of ending his work on earth. 'When the days drew near for him to be received up, he set his face to go to Jerusalem' (Lk.9:51; cf.13:33).

In John, with its repeated movements from Galilee to Jerusalem and back, there could be no place for such a section.

On the east bank of the Jordan, Jesus is still in the territories ruled by Herod Antipas; he does not enter Judaea until he crosses the river again, presumably at Jericho.

The pattern of Matthew's narrative then is:

Introduction: Departure from Galilee 19:1–2
1 Questions about Marriage and Divorce 19:3–12
    About the Law of Divorce 19:3–9
    About Celibacy 19:10–12
2 Jesus Blesses the Children 19:13–15
3 The Call to Renunciation 19:16–30
    The Call Refused 19:16–22
    Supplement: The Dangers of Wealth 19:23–26
    The Call Accepted 19:27–30
4 The Parable of the Eccentric Employer 20:1–16
5 The Third Prediction of the Passion 20:17–19
6 Greatness in the Christian Community 20:20–28
7 Jesus Restores Sight to Blind Men 20:29–34

INTRODUCTION: DEPARTURE FROM GALILEE *19:1–2*

[1] When Jesus had finished these sayings, he went away from Galilee and entered the regions of Judaea beyond the Jordan. [2] Great crowds followed him, and he healed them there.

'Judaea' here appears to be used in the broad sense, to include the lands which at this time were known as the Peraea—the area east of the Jordan and the Dead Sea, bordering on Samaria in the northern part and on Judah in the southern part. This territory was not part of the 'Judaea' which came under Roman rule following the banishment of Archelaus (AD 6) and was now administered by Pontius Pilate as prefect. The Peraea was under the rule of Herod Antipas, along with Galilee and Samaria. The route taken by Jesus is not indicated; we are not even told whether he crossed the Jordan north of the lake of Galilee or at one of the fords south of the lake; and no places along the route are mentioned. The topography has no relevance to the story in any case. The same 'crowds' attend Jesus, he carries on the same ministry of teaching and healing, is accompanied by the same disciples as before, and encounters the same opponents.

'He healed them there'—for Mark's 'he taught them, as his custom was' (Mk.10:1).

In the opening clause we find a variant of the rubric which Matthew sets at the end of each of his five major discourses.

1 QUESTIONS ABOUT MARRIAGE AND DIVORCE *19:3–12*

About the Law of Divorce *19:3–9*

[3] Pharisees now made approach to him and tested him with the question, 'Is it lawful for a man to divorce his wife for any cause?' [4] He answered, 'Have you not read that he who created them from the beginning "made them male and female", [5] and said, "For this reason a man shall leave his father and his mother and shall be joined to his wife, and the two shall be one flesh"? [6] So they are no longer two, but "one flesh". What God, then, has joined together, let not man put asunder.'

[7] They said to him, 'Why then did Moses enact the law that one should give her a certificate of divorce, and send her off?' [8] He said to them, 'Moses permitted you to divorce your wives by reason of the hardness of your hearts; but from the beginning it was not so. [9] I tell you, anyone who divorces his wife except for unchastity, and marries another, commits adultery.'

The attitude of Jesus towards divorce has already been stated in relation to his interpretation of the seventh commandment (Mt.5: [27f.] 31f.). Here Matthew is making use of a Markan section (Mk.10:2–12), but he makes some remarkable revisions, and adds a supplement which is if anything more remarkable still. To begin with, the question is reframed by the addition of the phrase 'for any cause', so that it is no longer a question of whether divorce is to be allowed at all (as in Mark), but of the *terms* on which it may be permitted. This brings it into the atmosphere of rabbinic casuistry. No Jewish teacher could argue that divorce was prohibited by the Law of Moses. In the discussions of the rabbis, it is taken for granted that divorce is permitted, and the only question to be raised is that of the ground which is to be regarded as adequate. It is presupposed, in Jewish law, that a man may divorce his wife, at least under certain conditions, but there is no provision at all for the wife to divorce the husband, whatever cause of complaint he may give her. The only relevant passage of the sacred Law is found in Deuteronomy 24:1–4, which deals with a situation in which the wife 'finds no favour' in the eyes of her husband, 'because he has found some indecency [literally, "nakedness of a thing"] in her'. The problem for the rabbis was to determine the application of the term translated 'indecency'. The more rigorous school of Shammai held that it meant adultery, and that divorce was not permitted for any lesser offence. The rival school of Hillel interpreted it to mean that a man had sufficient grounds for divorce if his wife burned his food. Somewhat later (early second century) Rabbi Aqiba holds that he is permitted to divorce her if he finds another woman more beautiful than she! (Aqiba also teaches that a wife may seek a divorce, if her husband falls into a sickness or enters a profession that puts her into an intolerable situation that she could not have foreseen.)

VERSE 3: 'Tested'—πειράζοντες. They are not simply asking him to state his position on a question that was answered in different ways by scribes, but are trying to make him declare publicly that he rejects the teaching of the law of Moses.

VERSES 4–6: Both Jesus and the Pharisees who are questioning him agree that the great Lawgiver sanctioned divorce. In the Markan account, Jesus first elicits from them a citation of the Mosaic law of divorce (Mk.10:3f.), and then interprets this as a concession to human hardheartedness, and declares that the priority belongs to the creation story, which teaches that the union of man and woman in marriage is indissoluble. In Matthew, Jesus first makes appeal to the creation story, and only then do the Pharisees bring up the Mosaic provision for divorce.

But if we read the entire section in Deuteronomy, it will be clear that the Law code is not dealing with the conditions under which divorce is permitted. It takes for granted the actual situation in Israel in the sixth century—not in the time of Moses. Divorce does take place, and a certificate of divorce is given by the husband to the wife. The Law deals only with a situation which may arise subsequently, if the woman has remarried and lost her second husband either by death or by his divorcing her. It ordains that under these circumstances the first man may not remarry the wife, now set free from her second husband (by death or divorce), 'for that is an abomination before the Lord' (Deut.24:4). The only Law that is promulgated is that 'the former husband, who sent her away, may not take her again to be his wife.' It is assumed, not ordained, that, if he 'writes her a certificate of divorce and puts it in her hand and sends her out of his house', it will be because 'she finds no favour in his eyes because he has found some indecency in her.' This is not itself a matter of legislation, but a statement of the circumstances which call for legislative regulation.

The passage which Jesus cites (vv.4—6a) is taken from the two creation stories of Genesis. The phrase 'male and female he created them' (Gen.1:27) comes from the first story (Gen.1:1—2:4a), which is part of the 'priestly' strand of the Pentateuch (composed in the fifth or sixth century BC). It makes no mention of marriage, and it places the creation of man, male and female, after the making of the animals. The phrase of verse 5, 'For this reason a man shall leave his father and his mother and be joined to his wife, and the two shall become one flesh', is taken from the much earlier, much less sophisticated strand which is usually known as 'J' (by reason of its use of the divine name Jahweh [Yahweh]); it is dated with some probability as early as the tenth century BC. The passage cited is not connected with the twofold creation of man in the ancient text; the link is made by Jesus, or probably by a Christian scribe of pre-Markan days. It is cited from the Greek version (LXX), to which is owed the use of the future ('shall leave' etc.). The Hebrew text is more accurately rendered (as in *RSV*; cf. also *NEB*): 'Therefore [*NEB*: "That is why"] a man leaves his father and mother and cleaves to his wife, and they become one flesh.' The word 'therefore' does not refer back to Gen.1:26f. (the dual creation of male and female), but to the crude legend that 'the Lord God caused a deep sleep to come upon the man, and while he slept took one of his ribs . . . and made it into a woman and brought her to the man' (Gen.2:21f.). It is the man who then said joyfully, 'This at last is bone of my bone and flesh of my flesh . . .' (Gen.2:23). The writer then comments that this is why 'a man leaves his father and his mother and cleaves to his wife, and they become one flesh.' This is not given as an ordinance of God, but as an explanation of why man and wife in marriage enter into an intimate relationship, independent of the previous family—'they become one flesh.'

From this Jesus draws the inference that such a union, being the consequence of God's creative action, is not to be broken by any human decision.

All this is far removed from any range of thinking that is possible for ourselves. We cannot imagine that any social institution (such as marriage) could be validated by the language of a myth, whatever value the myth may have in other respects. This does not mean that it is impossible that Jesus may have thought and argued in this fashion. It is in keeping with the manner in which words and phrases from the ancient scriptures were seized upon and linked together by the Jewish scribes to determine personal conduct.

VERSE 8: Moses (or the Deuteronomic legislation attributed to him) could be said to have 'permitted' men to divorce their wives only in the sense that he did not forbid the continuance of the existing practice. The Law does not deal with divorce in itself, but only with a situation that might arise if ever the husband wished to remarry the wife after she had married and lost a second husband.

VERSE 9: Matthew adds to this a saying of Jesus which is akin to one used in a different context in the Sermon on the Mount, where it is attached to his reinterpretation of the law against adultery (Mt.5:31f.). The Markan passage which he is following here does not contain the proviso, 'except for adultery', and it adds a second pronouncement which bears upon the case of a woman who divorces her husband (Mk.10:12). In Jewish Law, there was no provision for a woman to divorce her husband; it was natural enough for Matthew to cut this saying out of the passage. (It would of course be impossible for Jesus to speak of a situation which would never arise among his people.) Mark or one of his sources has framed the words in relation to a non-Jewish environment, in which divorce was permitted to the wife.

In the sayings about divorce in the Sermon on the Mount, Jesus declares that 'everyone who divorces his wife, except for unchastity, makes her an adulteress,' and adds that 'whoever marries a divorced woman commits adultery.' Now it is the divorcing husband, not the divorced wife, who is declared to be an adulterer; and the Markan saying which pronounces the divorced wife to be an adulteress if she remarries is omitted—nothing is here said about the situation of the woman.

About Celibacy 19:10–12

¹⁰ The disciples said to him, 'If such is the case of a man with his wife, it is not expedient to marry.' ¹¹ He said to them, 'Not all persons can accept this saying, but only those to whom the gift is given. ¹² For there are eunuchs who have been such from their mother's womb, and some who were made eunuchs by men, and there are some who have made themselves eunuchs for the sake of the kingdom of heaven. Let anyone who can accept this, accept it.'

This supplement, which has no parallel elsewhere in the Gospels, offers many difficulties of interpretation. Some editors feel themselves embarrassed in their attempts at interpretation. Allen (*ICC*) thinks that the whole passage (vv.3–13) 'suffers from inconsistency of thought due to literary revision and compilation'. McNeile holds that 'It is probable that vv.10–12 originally stood in another context, following some utterance on self-denial for the sake of the Kingdom of Heaven, which might include the renunciation of marriage'; he even raises the possibility that 'for Jesus Himself also dedication to his Father's business may have involved a conscious act of abnegation.' W.D. Davies remarks that 'the addition of xix.10–12 to xix.3–9 is confused and confusing' (*Setting*, p.395).

VERSE 10: The comment is decidedly strange, if taken as a suggestion actually made by followers of Jesus. At least one of the disciples (Peter) was himself married; can we suppose that all the others seriously thought it would be better not to marry at all if it were not permissible to dissolve the bond except when the wife was unfaithful?

It may be that here, as in other instances, 'the disciples' represent the Christian believers of Matthew's own church. The whole supplement would then be regarded as a fragment of debate *within the apostolic church* over the application of Jesus' drastic teaching on the indissolubility of marriage. Such teaching was by no means general in Judaism, and was unknown in the Gentile societies around. A hint that problems did arise, and were debated, in the apostolic church is given in Paul's first letter to the Corinthians; they became especially acute when one partner to the marriage became a Christian while the other remained attached to the ancestral religion (1 Cor. 7:10–16). Paul certainly modifies the absoluteness of Jesus' teaching in his desire to meet the circumstances of the Corinthian community with which he has to deal. Does Matthew here read back into the time of Jesus a discussion among Christian scribes concerning the problems raised by the same teaching of Jesus? W.D. Davies speaks of 'the attempt made in Matthew to come to terms with the actualities of marriage: the material from M in xix.10–12 reflects the same kind of concern, to make the ethic of Jesus practicable, as we find in Paul. Radicalism is tempered to the generality.' (*Setting*, p.395; see his careful discussion, pp.393–95.)

VERSE 11: Is the reply of Jesus intended as a comment on the remark of the disciples, or as a recognition of the fact that his radical teaching will not be acceptable to everyone? Is he implicitly granting that his own teaching, which he has just given in such drastic terms, is not capable of general application, and is meant only for those who are able to accept it, 'those to whom it is given'? The alternative, that it is simply a dry comment to the effect that not everyone will accept their notion that it would be better not to marry if no divorce was possible, seems quite banal.

VERSE 12 seems to suggest that it will be better for followers of

Jesus not to marry; there is at least the implication that voluntary celibacy is desirable for one who would devote himself to the kingdom of heaven—for anyone who can receive (χωρεῖν) it. This in turn would suggest that Matthew understands the saying of Jesus in verse 11 as a response to the comment of 'the disciples' in verse 10. 'The renunciation of marriage is indeed desirable, but not for everyone—only for those to whom it is given (οἱς δέδοτει); not to evade the obligations of matrimony, but to leave oneself free for unhampered service to the work of the Kingdom.'

'Eunuchs from their mother's womb'—born without the normal development of the organs of sex.

'Made eunuchs by men'—either forcibly emasculated, or voluntarily submitting to emasculation. The latter happens often enough today, usually by vasectomy, but it may be doubted whether it was likely to occur in the ancient world.

'Made themselves eunuchs'—the primary meaning of the words would refer to self-emasculation. This was well known in the Mediterranean world, particularly in the cult of the Asian mother-goddess (Cybele is one of her many names). Her priests were *galli*, and they dedicated themselves to her service in a wild ecstasy by slashing off their testicles. No Christian writer would think of this as done 'for the sake of the kingdom of God'. Origen of Alexandria is the most famous example of a Christian who was moved by these words to emasculate himself, thinking that it was 'for the sake of the kingdom of God'. But it is probable that in a document as early as the Gospel of Matthew the words are rightly interpreted (as in the whole tradition) of the acceptance of voluntary celibacy for the sake of greater freedom in the service of the gospel. Paul is the example that at once comes to mind (1 Cor.9:5). He affirms that he has every right to take a wife, 'like the other apostles and the brothers of the Lord and Cephas'. Yet he clearly feels that his own choice of celibacy is wiser, seeing that 'the unmarried man is anxious about the affairs of the Lord, how to please the Lord; but the married man is anxious about worldly affairs, how to please his wife, and his interests are divided' (1 Cor.7:32ff.). He has already expressed the wish that 'all were as I myself am' (1 Cor.7:7); but in the same breath he admits that 'each has his own special gift from God, one of one kind and one of another'. This is in the spirit of the saying of Jesus: 'Not all men can receive this saying, but only those to whom it is given.'

P. Benoit (*Bible de Jerusalem*) tells us in one of his few notes that 'Jesus invites to perpetual continence those who are prepared to make this sacrifice to give them greater assurance of entrance into the kingdom of the heavens, and to serve it better.' It is not suggested in the text that a voluntary celibacy gives one any greater assurance of entrance into the kingdom of heaven. 'For the sake of' (διά) is more naturally taken to mean 'to serve'.

2   JESUS BLESSES THE CHILDREN *19:13–15*

¹³ Children were now brought before him for him to lay his hands on them and pray. The disciples rebuked them, ¹⁴ but Jesus said, 'Let the children alone, and do not prevent them from coming to me, for the kingdom of heaven belongs to such as these.' ¹⁵ He laid his hands on them and went away from there.

The thought of marriage leads naturally enough to the consideration of the place of children. Matthew makes some characteristic changes in the Markan story (10:13–16). In Mark, people bring their children in order that Jesus may touch them. Luke does not shun the expression, but Matthew may have felt that it suggested a magic in the touch of Jesus, and substituted the double phrase, 'that he might lay his hands on them and pray'. It is possible that he is indicating the way in which baptism was administered in his church. He omits the Markan remark that 'Jesus was indignant'; and also the gesture of affection, 'he put his arms around them'. He leaves out Mark's verse 15: 'truly I tell you, whoever does not receive the kingdom of God as a child shall not enter into it'—perhaps because he has used a somewhat similar phrase in the preceding chapter (18:3)— 'If you do not turn and become like the children, you will not enter into the kingdom of heaven.' Finally, he omits the verb κατευλόγει of Mark ('he blessed them') as redundant—the act of laying on his hands was itself a blessing.

VERSE 13: The laying on of hands is usually connected (in the Gospels) with the healings (so in Mt.9:18, the only other occurrence in Matthew). It was often used among the Jews as a gesture of blessing. In Acts, it is used in healing stories, but more often in the conveying of the gift of the Holy Spirit (8:17ff.; 9:17; 19:6).

No reason is given for the attitude of the disciples. Do they rebuke the parents ('those that brought them'—Mk.), or the children themselves?

VERSE 14: Matthew is not interested in the details of the story, in the minds of the disciples, or in the question of who brought the children. It is told for the sake of the saying of Jesus, which certainly requires a situation in which attempts have been made to keep children away from him. If any importance were attached to the timing of the incident, it would be strange that no attempt had been made to bring children to Jesus for his blessing until he crossed the Jordan into an area where he had never been before, or that his disciples had had no previous opportunity to learn how their Master felt about the matter.

'Such as these'—conveys in itself the thought that is made explicit in the additional saying found in Mark and Luke, which Matthew has omitted. Entrance into the Kingdom is not a matter of age but of disposition.

The story is not likely to owe its place in the Gospels simply to its human interest. It will have been retained because the early church was divided over the place of children in the community. But there is not enough information at our disposal to make it possible to discern the terms of the debate. This is still a matter of debate in the modern church. (Should infants be admitted to the church by baptism? Should small children be invited to partake of the eucharistic bread?) But we may not read the terms of our own controversies back into the first generation of the church.

3 THE CALL TO RENUNCIATION *19:16–30*

This consists of two sections corresponding to each other, the one representing the rejection of the summons to give up possessions, because of reluctance to part with earthly possessions for the sake of a heavenly goal; the other representing the acceptance of the summons and telling of the compensations. Verses 23–26 constitute a supplement to the first section.

The connection with the preceding incident (the blessing of the children) appears to be merely verbal. 'The kingdom of heaven belongs to such as these' leads on to the thought of the kind of person to whom the Kingdom does not belong—those who prize their possessions more highly than the Kingdom which they seek to enter—more than the eternal life which they hope to gain. This in turn leads on to the thought of the compensation promised to those who sacrifice everything they possess for the sake of Jesus.

The Call Refused 19:16–22

[16] A man now made approach to him and said, 'Teacher, what good thing am I to do that I may gain eternal life?' [17] Jesus answered, 'Why

do you question me about the good? There is One who is the good.
But, if you wish to enter into that life, keep the commandments.'
¹⁸ The man said, 'Which commandments?' And Jesus said, ' "Do not
murder, do not commit adultery, do not steal, do not bear false
witness, ¹⁹ honour your father and your mother", and "love your
neighbour as yourself." ' ²⁰ The young man said to him, 'All these
I have kept. What is still lacking?' ²¹ Jesus said to him, 'If you desire
to be perfect, go sell your possessions and give to the poor, and you
will have treasure in heaven; and come, follow me.' ²² But when the
young man heard this, he went away sad, for he was a man of great
wealth.

VERSES 16–17: As usual, Matthew cuts away the picturesque
details of the Markan narrative, which he finds not essential to the
story. In Mark, the man 'ran up and fell on his knees before him'; in
Matthew he makes a ceremonial approach ($\pi\rho\sigma\epsilon\lambda\theta\acute{\omega}\nu$).

The most striking change made by Matthew, however, is in the
wording of the man's request, along with a corresponding change in
the reply of Jesus. In Mark, the man addresses Jesus as 'Good
master'; and Jesus takes this up with the response, 'Why do you call
me good? No one is good but God alone.' Matthew transfers the
word 'good' to the man's question: 'What good thing am I do do?'
With that the Markan form of the reply of Jesus would be inappro-
riate, since the man has not called him 'good'; and Matthew alters
the response to the wholly artificial, 'Why do you ask me about the
good?'—as if the man were seeking a definition of the idea of goodness. Yet he retains the substance of the following saying, omitting
only $\vartheta\epsilon\acute{o}\varsigma$, 'God' (which may not have been in his Markan text—it
is lacking in the Latin texts of Mark and in the Curetonian Syriac and
some mss. of the Bohairic version; but this may be no more than a
case of assimilation to the Matthaean text). But the saying, 'There is
One who is the good' really presupposes the refusal of Jesus to
accept the title 'good' for himself. It is obvious that Matthew has
been driven to desperate straits to remove any suggestion that Jesus
disclaims goodness for himself; perhaps also he would find it incompatible with his Christology to imply any lack in Jesus of the
goodness of God.

Another change is the substitution of the verb $\sigma\chi\acute{\omega}$, 'gain', for
Mark's $\kappa\lambda\eta\rho\sigma\nu\sigma\mu\acute{\eta}\sigma\omega$, 'inherit'.

VERSE 18: Matthew also changes the citation of the commandments from the Markan form. He introduces a brief dialogue, lacking
in Mark, in which Jesus at first gives the general direction: 'Keep the

commandments', and mentions specific commandments only when the man asks him to be specific: 'Which (commandments)?' He then omits the Markan 'do not defraud' (μὴ ἀποστερήσῃς), probably because he could not find it among the Ten Commandments (this probably accounts for the omission of the words in B W Delta Psi *et al.* in Mark also). In keeping with his own emphasis on the priority of love, he adds, 'you shall love your neighbour as yourself.'

VERSE 20: 'Young man'—this is the only mention of the man's age in any of the Synoptics. It may be an inference from the words of the Markan version, 'All these I have kept from my youth', though this would suggest rather that he is now an older man. It has been suggested that Matthew is drawing upon the phrasing of Psalm 118 (LXX 119 Heb.): 9f. (There is little in the LXX rendering to support this conjecture; even the 'young man' is νεώτερος in LXX, not νεανίσκος as here.)

'All these I have kept'—there was in Judaism no general acceptance of the view that no person can keep the commandments perfectly; even Paul could say that in his Pharisaic days he was 'blameless as to righteousness under the law' (Phil.3:6)—though he was showing his zeal in persecuting the church! He will also recognize that sin had terrible power over him, and that the commandment tended to provoke, not to extinguish, desire (Rom.7:7–23). The rich man is not so conscious of a war within—'another law at war with the law of my mind and making me captive to the law of sin which dwells in my members' (v.23). Yet with all his moral self-assurance, he is not wholly at ease. He is impelled to ask, 'What is still lacking? How do I still come short of what is required to assure me of life eternal?'

VERSE 21: Matthew again cuts away as unessential the Markan reference to the feelings of Jesus ('Jesus looking upon him loved him'—Mk.10:21).

Profound effects have resulted from the Matthaean change in Jesus' reply. In place of taking up the man's own words, as in Mark —'there is one thing lacking'—Matthew introduces the fateful phrase, 'If you wish to be perfect'. This led to the widespread notion of two levels of moral demand laid upon the Christian—one for the rank and file believer, and a more stringent one for those who would be 'perfect'. Inevitably, this came to be applied to the distinction between clergy and laity, and especially to the monastic vocation with its requirements of poverty, celibacy (supported also by appeal to Mt.19:12), and obedience. No attempt was ever made to impose poverty upon all Christian believers, let alone celibacy; but it was widely held that anything short of the monastic discipline lacked the fullness of moral achievement (to be 'perfect'). But in Matthew's view—and presumably in that of Jesus—there was no thought of anything short of 'perfection' in the demand laid upon all. In the Sermon on the Mount, as we have seen, Jesus charges all who hear to 'be perfect as your Father in heaven is perfect' (Mt.5:48). (The word τέλειος is not used at all in the other Gospels.)

The summons to dispose of all possessions is not a general command, nor could it well be—possessions could not be sold unless it was permitted to others to buy them. It is linked here with the further challenge, 'Come, follow me!' The evangelist evidently thinks that Jesus is calling this man, as he called the four fishermen (Mt.4: 18–22), to join him as one of the group, for all of whom it meant the abandonment of their former livelihood (cf. v.27 below).

VERSE 22: The man's possessions mean more to him than the attainment of the eternal life for which he professes to be seeking.

Supplement: The Dangers of Wealth 19:23–26

[23] Jesus said to his disciples, 'Truly I tell you, a rich person will find it hard to enter into the kingdom of heaven. [24] Let me tell you again, it is easier for a camel to pass through the eye of a needle than for a rich person to enter into the kingdom of God.' [25] At this the disciples were much amazed and said, 'Who then can be saved?' [26] Jesus looked at them and said, 'With mankind this is impossible, but with God all things are possible.'

The story of the encounter of Jesus with the rich man is complete in itself. It is now followed by some general pronouncement on the danger of wealth, for one who is seeking spiritual ends. This one man is not exceptional. Matthew again abbreviates the Markan passage, omitting the whole of Mark's verse 24.

VERSE 24: Jesus uses another of his tremendous hyperboles. 'It is easier for a camel to go through the eye of a needle than for a rich man to enter into the kingdom of God.' A few manuscripts and some versions read κάμιλος, 'rope, cable, hawser,' in place of κάμηλος, 'camel'. In itself, this is tempting—the notion of attempting to put a hawser through the eye of a needle in place of a thread makes a more harmonious figure without diminishing the degree of impossibility! It is, however, dismissed by the grammarians as a 'Byzantine invention', belonging only to 'the museum of exegetical curiosities'

(Moulton-Howard, Vol.II, p.72; cf. Blass-Debrunner, § 24—'rationalisierende Künstelei'; they can find no trace of it in Greek usage before Suidas [tenth cent.])

VERSE 25: The great astonishment of the disciples, and especially the form of their questioning: 'Who then can be saved?' are surprising. Has Jesus ever said anything to make them think that wealth is a prerequisite for entrance into the Kingdom? Have they forgotten his pronouncement, 'Blessed are you poor, for yours is the kingdom of heaven' (Lk.6:20; Mt.5:3)? The words are surely nothing but a reflection of the reluctance of people to believe that wealth is not a passport to everything, even to heaven.

VERSE 26: The pronouncement of Jesus is not really appropriate in this context, implying as it does that the salvation of a rich man is a conspicious example of divine omnipotence. The salvation of *any* person, rich or poor, is 'impossible with men'. The power of God is shown in the redemption of sinners, and the matter of wealth is irrelevant.

Luke has tried to relieve the difficulty of imagining such a question on the lips of disciples by attributing it to bystanders ('those who heard'—Lk.18:26). (Such a query is more likely to have been put by a wealthy person than by disciples who were themselves poor people.)

'To be saved' is here used as equivalent in meaning to the phrases, 'gain life eternal' (v.16), 'enter into the life' (v.17), and 'enter into the kingdom of heaven [of God]' (vv.23,24).

The Call Accepted 19:27–30

²⁷ Upon this, Peter said to him, 'Look, we have given up everything and followed you. What will there be for us?' ²⁸ And Jesus assured them, 'In the regenerated world, when the Son of man is seated on his glorious throne, you who have followed me will also be seated on twelve thrones, governing the twelve tribes of Israel. ²⁹ And every one who has given up houses, or brothers, sisters, father, mother, children, or lands, for the sake of my name, will be recompensed a hundredfold, and will inherit life eternal. ³⁰ But many that are first will be last, and the last first.'

VERSE 27: Peter acts as spokesman for the disciples. The wealthy man has refused to part with his great possessions; the disciples have given up all they owned, to follow Jesus. Matthew makes explicit the thought that lies beneath the words, 'What will there be for us?'

Perhaps the 'treasure in heaven' which was promised to the rich man (v.21)? Some special reward is expected.

VERSE 28: In Matthew, such a special reward is promised in most surprising terms. A high destiny is reserved for the Twelve—a place of honour in the Kingdom that no others can share. In the imagery of an apocalyptic scenario, Jesus speaks of a παλιγγενεσία, a 'regeneration', in the form of a judgement scene, with the Son of man seated on his glorious throne (cf. Mt.25:31) and the Twelve seated in company with him, each on a throne of his own, 'judging the twelve tribes of Israel'.

'The time of the regeneration'—clearly has the general sense of 'when the kingdom of heaven is established'. The word *palingenesia* is not found elsewhere in this sense. It was apparently first developed by the Stoics to mean the commencement of the next cycle of the universe, following the cosmic conflagration (ἐκπύρωσις) in which the universe would be totally consumed. But in Stoic theory, this *palingenesia* was periodic, and the new cycle could not but be an exact replica of the one that preceded it, for the universe as it is, is the best of all possible worlds, and everything comes to pass in accord with perfect reason and common law (which may be personified as the will of Zeus, but is basically impersonal—see my article 'Stoics' in *IDB*, with bibliography). Christian thinkers of course were far from holding that the universe as it is has no blemishes; and for them the 'regeneration', whatever they might call it, was not periodic, nor was it the commencement of a cycle essentially the same as the old. It was final, once for all, and it meant an order of things in which all the evils of this present age will be done away.

Again, the Christian notion which finds expression here is linked with the enthronement of the Son of man—the glorified Jesus; and the new order which is inaugurated by his coming in power and glory is an order of righteousness. Thus in 2 Peter 3:10–13, Stoic language is linked with 'the day of the Lord'. There will be an *ekpurōsis*, a cosmic conflagration, in which 'the heavens will be kindled and dissolved, and the elements will melt with fire.' What follows after that is not a repetition of the same cycle. 'According to his promise we wait for new heavens and a new earth in which righteousness dwells.' So also the seer of the Apocalypse foresees the glorious future as something wholly new (Apoc.21:1–22:3). 'I saw a new heaven and a new earth; for the first heaven and the first earth had passed away' (21:1); the 'twelve apostles of the Lamb' are exalted, not as seated on thrones, but as having their names inscribed on the twelve gates of the holy city (21:14); Christ (the Lamb) is enthroned with God (22:1,3); there is no more suffering or death (21:4); and there will be nothing unclean (21:27) or accursed (22:3).

In this regeneration, the central figure is to be the Son of man. With this, the language reverts to purely Jewish imagery of apocalyptic. The figure of Daniel's vision, described as 'one like a son of man' (7:13) (which is interpreted as representing 'the people of the saints of the Most High'—v.27) is individualized, and treated as a vision of Jesus. To this figure 'like a human being ("son of man")' is given 'dominion and glory and kingdom' (v.14). So Jesus is pictured as seated upon a glorious throne, as Judge and Ruler of the regenerated universe which is to be established. The promise that the Twelve will share his kingly rule is depicted in similar terms—they will 'sit on twelve thrones'. This also has its parallels in Jewish literature; in some of the later literature, 'the elders of Israel' or 'the great ones of Israel' are to be seated on thrones set up for them by the angels, and 'they are seated and God is seated as Father of judgement with them, and they judge the nations of the world' (see Schlatter, ad loc.). The same thought lies behind the words of Paul: 'Do you not know that the saints shall judge the world?' (1 Cor.6:2—though here it is not the apostles alone, but the whole body of Christian believers that shares the judging). Again, in the Apocalypse, the promise is made to all who have part in the first resurrection that 'they shall be priests of God and of Christ and they shall reign with him a thousand years' (20:6); and all the citizens of the holy city 'shall reign for ever and ever' (22:5).

'Judging'—probably to be taken in the wider sense of the Hebrew *shaphat*. The Hebrew 'judge', such as Gideon or Samuel, is the divinely gifted deliverer and counsellor of Israel; in the times before the monarchy he is virtually the ruler of the nation; as G.F. Moore puts it, 'The judges were the succession of rulers and defenders of Israel before the hereditary monarchy, as the kings were afterwards' (*Judges*, ICC (1895), p.xii). It was Israel's hope that in the age to come, God would 'restore our judges as at the first' (*Shemoneh Esreh*, 11). Here Jesus promises that the Twelve will reign as 'judges' in the restored Israel.

'The twelve tribes of Israel': The tribal system of Israel had been permanently shattered by the deportations of Sargon towards the end of the eighth century BC, when the ten tribes of the northern kingdom ceased to exist as tribes. It had indeed lost most of its significance with the emergence of the monarchy more than two centuries earlier. The surviving kingdom consisted solely of the tribes of Judah and Benjamin, and was known collectively by the name of

Judah alone. But the notion survived in memory and imagination, and prophets continued to deliver oracles of promise which foretold the restoration of Israel in terms of a reunion of the twelve tribes, and the partition of the land among them, tribe by tribe (Ezek.47: 13ff.). Josephus can even inform his readers that the ten tribes were still to be found 'beyond the Euphrates, to this day, countless myriads, in numbers beyond reckoning' (*Antiq.* XI.133). All this is romantic fancy.

As the notion of the 'twelve tribes' remained alive in Israel as a symbol of the people of God redeemed and restored to wholeness, it was carried over into Christian imagery as a symbol of the Christian church. The epistle of James is addressed 'to the twelve tribes of the Diaspora', and 1 Peter 'to the elect sojourners of the Diaspora'. The churches scattered all about the Mediterranean world, and in lands to the east, are conscious that they belong to a single community of faith, and that they have a common homeland—not in the land of Israel, but in an 'inheritance incorruptible . . . kept in the heavens' for them; cf. the words of Paul, 'Our commonwealth is in heaven' (Phil.3:20).

It is not conceivable that Jesus himself could ever have spoken these words. They come from a Palestinian Christianity dominated by vivid apocalyptic expectations couched in traditional Jewish imagery. But they do not come from the very earliest times. The kind of exaltation of the apostles, the notion of them as a collegiate body governing the church, belongs to the second generation (or later). Indeed, this promise of exaltation for the Twelve is at stark variance with the warnings against the desire for pre-eminence (Mt. 20:20–28), and with the affirmation that 'to sit at my right hand and at my left is not mine to grant' (v.23).

A very different form of the promise is given in Luke, but in a totally different context. It is spoken at the Last Supper, after the institution of the Eucharist. It runs: 'You are those who have continued with me in my trials; and I assign to you, as my Father has assigned to me, a kingdom, that you may eat and drink at my table in my kingdom, and sit on thrones judging the twelve tribes of Israel' (Lk.22:28–30). This looks like a secondary form of the saying, combining somewhat incongruously the imagery of the Messianic feast with that of the thrones of shared rule. 'To dine at a king's table is not a sign of sharing his authority' (J.M. Creed, *Gospel according to St. Luke* (1930), *ad loc.*).

VERSES 29–30: Only now does Matthew come to his version of the answer of Jesus given in Mark. No special privilege is to be the reward of the apostles. Everyone who, like them, has given up what he most cherished in order to cast in his lot with Jesus will receive the same reward. The Markan saying is recast; but the same list of renunciations is given and in the same order—houses ('house' in Mark), brothers, sisters, father, mother, children, fields—a strange mixture of properties (houses and fields, with no mention of other possessions such as gold or jewels) with personal kinsfolk. For all such sacrifices there will be a hundredfold compensation (Mark adds 'now in this time'). The thought is probably that rich new bonds of relationship will be formed; at least this is the sense implied in the Markan addition which defines the hundredfold compensation strangely in the same terms as the list of things sacrificed—house, family, fields—adding 'with persecutions' (Mk.10:30). Matthew could not accept the apparent notion that the hundredfold compensation should be taken so literally, as if it would mean a hundred times as many houses and fields, a hundred wives, fathers and mothers, a hundred times as many brothers, sisters, and children! (The recompense of Job was ample—Job 42:10–13; cf.1:2f.—the Lord gave him twice as much as he had before, in the matter of material possessions, but only the same number of sons and daughters.) But as Jesus has acknowledged as his brothers and sisters and mother all who do the will of his Father in heaven (Mt.12:50), so he assures his disciples that they will find a far wider circle of spiritual kin in the immense community of his followers.

4 THE PARABLE OF THE ECCENTRIC EMPLOYER *20:1–16*

[1] For the kingdom of heaven is like a householder who went out early in the morning to hire labourers to work in his vineyard. [2] He made an arrangement with the labourers to pay them a denarius a day, and sent them off to the vineyard. [3] Going out again about nine in the morning, he saw some others standing idle in the market place, [4] and said to them, 'You go to work in the vineyard too, and I will pay you whatever is right.' [5] They went off to the work and the master came back again about noon, and again in mid-afternoon, and did the same thing. [6] An hour or so before sundown he went out again and found others standing there, and said to them, 'Why are you standing about here idle for the whole day?' [7] They replied to him, 'Because no one has hired us.' So he said, 'You go to work in the vineyard too.' [8] When evening came, the master of the vineyard said to his steward, 'Call the workers and pay them their wages, beginning with the last and on to the first.' [9] And when those that

had been hired an hour before sundown came up, they received a denarius each. ¹⁰ When the men of the first group came up, they thought that they would get more, but they too received a denarius apiece. ¹¹ On receiving this, they grumbled against the master, ¹² complaining, 'These latecomers have only worked for an hour, and you have put them on the same footing with us who have carried the burden of the whole day and the heat.' ¹³ But he replied to one of them, 'Friend, I am not cheating you. Did you not agree to work for me for a denarius? ¹⁴ Take your wages and be off. I have made up my mind to pay these latecomers the same as you; ¹⁵ am I not free to do what I choose with my own money? Or are you jealous over my generosity to others?'

[¹⁶ So the last will be first and the first last.]

The parable reflects the life of the Galilean countryside in the time of Jesus. The vineyard will be a large property, so that when the grapes are ready to be gathered, the owner needs to hire additional workers to get the task completed quickly, while the fruit is in prime condition. He has no difficulty in securing casual labour; he can go into town at any hour of the day and find unemployed men standing around in the market area. There is nothing out of the way about his repeated visits—not all the unemployed are eager enough to be up with the dawn, looking for a full day's work. Some do not show up until noon or mid-afternoon—some come around only when the day is almost over. The unusual element in the picture lies in the owner's treatment of the workers. It was certainly not common practice for a Palestinian landowner to pay a full day's wage for an hour's work, or even for a half day or a few hours. It is precisely here that we find the point of the parable, and it is reinforced by the not unnatural grumbling of those who have received no more for working from dawn till sunset than was given to those who put in only an hour in the cool of evening.

VERSE 1: 'Early in the morning'—the working day began with the dawn.

VERSE 2: A denarius a day was the usual wage for ordinary labour. There was no minimum; the employer was free to make a bargain on any terms he could get the workers to accept.

VERSES 3–5: 'Nine in the morning', 'noon', 'mid-afternoon', 'an hour or so before sundown'—literally, 'at the third, the sixth, the ninth, the eleventh hour'—the day was divided into twelve hours of more or less equal length, for the period between sunrise and sunset.

VERSES 6–7: The little dialogue has no particular significance, except as emphasizing that it was late in the day for men to be looking for work. They would not have been there all day—evidently the master hired all the workers that he could find on each occasion. (Nor would they be 'standing', literally; the Oriental with nothing to occupy him would very soon sit or crouch on the ground.) If the master comes looking for workers so late in the day, it can only be that there is great urgency about getting in the harvest, even before nightfall.

VERSE 8: Nothing is said about their pay; it is assumed that he will give them what is fair, as was promised to the group hired at the third hour. The rate of a denarius a day was mentioned specifically only for the first group.

The instruction that the steward is to 'begin with the last' is required by the story. If those who were first hired were paid first, they would not be around to observe that the last were given pay for the full day, like themselves. It has nothing to do with the general principle that in the judgement of God, there will be a reversal of human judgements, so that 'the last will be first and the first last' (v.16).

VERSE 9: Nothing is said to explain why the master gives a full day's pay for an hour's work—as, for instance, that he realizes that the latecomers, even though they were too lazy to get up early and work all day, *need* the denarius as much as the others.

The creator of the parable does not feel it necessary to say that the groups who had come in the course of the day all received the same pay. The point is made sufficiently by the contrast between the first and the last.

VERSES 10–12: It would be quite untrue to life to suppose that the first comers would not feel aggrieved when they found that they were to get no more than those who had done so much less work. The parable still keeps to a true representation of how people actually react in such a situation.

It is not necessary to suppose (as Jeremias does) that the dissatisfied labourers have to go off to the owner's house to do their grumbling, forcing the others to go along with them. The owner is pictured as standing by, while his overseer pays off the workers.

VERSES 13–15: The answer of the owner is quite in keeping with the situation. A landowner would not take kindly to the suggestion that if he is generous to some of his workers, paying them more than they have earned, he puts himself under an obligation to revise his entire wage scale!

VERSE 14: 'Take what is yours, and go'—It is sheer allegorizing to interpret it as meaning that the Pharisees (Jeremias), and all who resent God's goodness to the undeserving, are sent away in disgrace. They are simply told that they have received the wage which they had agreed to take and have no need to stay around any longer.

VERSE 15: 'With my own money'—perhaps, 'on my own estate'. Still true to life—the typical reaction of a landowner. In ancient times, an employer's right to do what he wished with his own money would not be challenged as it is today.

'Are you jealous over my generosity to others?' Literally, 'Is your eye evil, because I am good?' The 'evil eye' is probably the attitude that grudges the good fortune of others. The thought is close to our 'Is your nose out of joint because of my generosity?'

Here we may discern the point of the parable, at least as it was understood by Matthew. He thinks of those who are shocked at Jesus' readiness to welcome the outcast. They 'grumble' or 'murmur', as the Israelites 'murmured' against Moses (and against God) in the wilderness (Ex.16:3—8, etc.). There is probably behind this the general doctrine that the rewards of God are not measured out according to the length of time that we have served him; perhaps also that the Gentiles, who are only now entering the service of God, will not fare less well than Israel, which has come through centuries of hardship.

5   THE THIRD PREDICTION OF THE PASSION *20:17—19*

[17] As Jesus was going up to Jerusalem, he took the twelve disciples aside, by themselves, and said to them on the way, [18] 'See, we are going up to Jerusalem; and the Son of man will be delivered to the chief priests and scribes and they will sentence him to death; [19] and they will hand him over to the Gentiles that they may mock him and scourge him and crucify him; and on the third day he will be raised.'

Matthew abbreviates the Markan introduction to this prediction (Mk.10:32) by cutting away the description of the wonderment of the disciples and the fear of the other followers of Jesus. In the prediction itself, he rewrites the wording of the latter part (Mk.10: 34), by changing the future indicatives to aorist participles, by omitting the verb 'spit' (ἐμπτύουσιν), and by substituting the verb 'crucify' for the more general 'put to death' of Mark. As always, he uses the phrase 'on the third day' for Mark's peculiar 'after three days', and the future passive of ἐγείρω ('he will be raised') for the future middle of ἀνίστημι ('he will rise'). There is evident here a tendency to make the prediction more specific, in keeping with what was actually to happen; this is the first and only time that death by crucifixion is introduced into the prediction (and then only by Matthew).

6 GREATNESS IN THE CHRISTIAN COMMUNITY *20:20–28*

²⁰ The mother of the sons of Zebedee made approach to Jesus with her sons, kneeling before him and asking a boon. ²¹ He said to her, 'What is it you wish?' She answered, 'Command that these two sons of mine shall sit one at your right hand and one at your left, in your kingdom.' ²² But Jesus answered, 'You do not know for what you are asking. Can you drink the cup that I am to drink?' They said, 'We can.' ²³ He said to them, 'My cup you will drink; but to sit on my right hand and on my left is not mine to grant: it is for those for whom it has been prepared by my Father.'
²⁴ Overhearing this, the other ten were angry at the brothers. ²⁵ But Jesus called them up to him and said, 'You know that the rulers of the Gentiles lord it over them, and their great men exercise authority over them. ²⁶ It is not to be so among you. Whoever aspires to greatness among you shall be your servant, ²⁷ and whoever wants to be first among you shall be your slave; ²⁸ just as the Son of man did not come to be served but to serve, and to give his life as a ransom for many.'

In the Markan version of this passage, it is 'James and John the [two] sons of Zebedee' who approach Jesus directly, with the request that he will do for them whatever they ask (!). Matthew puts the request in the mouth of their mother, in the more modest terms, that he will grant her 'something' (τι). The dialogue is modified accordingly in the verse following (v.21). But from that point on, the clearly artificial intervention of the mother is forgotten, and Jesus speaks directly to the two brothers and is answered by them; and Matthew follows Mark almost word for word, except that he omits Mark's phrase about the 'baptism' (Mk.10:38f.).

VERSE 20: προσῆλθεν—again Matthew uses the formal term; in Mark, the brothers simply 'come up', προσπορεύονται. 'Kneeling' is a further addition to Mark.

The mother of the sons of Zebedee is mentioned again as one of the women present at the cross (27:56); in Mark, the third woman is called Salome, but is not identified as anyone's mother (Mk.15:40).

Except for Simon Peter, the disciples of Jesus are seldom mentioned in the Gospels individually. James and John appear in company with Peter at the transfiguration (Mt.17:1—only Peter speaks—v.4) and at the raising of Jairus' daughter (Mk.5:37—omitted in Matthew). James and John together propose that they should invoke destruction upon a Samaritan village that refuses hospitality, and Jesus rebukes them (Lk.9:54f.—peculiar to Luke). Their call is linked with that of Peter and Andrew (Mt.4:18–22; cf. the independent version of Lk.5:1–11, where Andrew is not mentioned and the two brothers are introduced—in an obviously secondary intrusion—as 'partners with Simon', v.10). Last of all, Mark groups them with Peter and Andrew as a limited audience for the eschatological discourse which Jesus delivers on the Mount of Olives (Mk.13:3ff.); but in Matthew there is no such limitation—the words are addressed to 'the disciples' (Mt.24:3ff.; cf. Lk.17:22ff.).

In the Fourth Gospel, despite the tradition that John was its author, neither of the brothers is mentioned until the resurrection scene (John 21:1–14), which is an editorial addendum to the book (so Bultmann, Dodd, Barrett, Bernard, Lightfoot).

It is clear, then, that the disciples of Jesus individually left very little mark upon the tradition, apart from Peter and Judas Iscariot. Even Peter is better known to legend than to history. There is a measure of uncertainty about the names of some of them—the lists are not identical (Mt.10:2f.; Mk.3:14–19; Lk.6:13–16; Acts 1:13). John brings others by name into some anecdotes (Andrew, Philip, Thomas), and legends are built around them all in the succeeding centuries. But in the Synoptic Gospels—and that means, in the earliest tradition—there was little interest in them as individuals. The stories often portray them in a bad light, as here, though there is a tendency in Matthew and Luke to tone down whatever might seem discreditable in words or deeds ascribed to them.

The question therefore arises, why the sons of Zebedee should be named specifically here. Are we to suppose that there is an actual reminiscence that James and John had showed themselves eager for pre-eminence in the glorious kingdom of Jesus, and that the others had no personal ambitions? Or may we conjecture that we have a reflection here of some rivalry among the leaders in the early church? If at Corinth there were some who professed a particular allegiance to Peter, while others made claims for Apollos, and some for Paul (1 Cor.1:12), is it impossible or even unlikely that in early times there was something of the same kind of thing in the Jerusalem church? As James was executed by Herod Agrippa (Acts 12:2) who

died in AD 44, any rivalry in which he was concerned would have
to be seen as occurring within little more than a decade after the
crucifixion. That Peter for a time exercised an unchallenged leadership would seem to be indicated by the exceptional place which he
holds in the Gospels and in the early chapters of Acts; but it would
be almost inescapable that claims would be made by—or for—
others, before many years went by. When Paul first visits Jerusalem
as a Christian, he finds a triad of leaders. James the brother of Jesus,
and John share the leadership with Peter, and it is actually James
who has become, and remains, the principal figure (Gal.1:18f.; 2:9;
Acts 15:13ff.; 21:18). Possibly the brothers James and John made
up an earlier triad along with Peter, until James was executed and the
brother of Jesus replaced him. Such speculations are perhaps fruit-
less, but some development of this kind would help to explain why
James and John appear here as the aspirants to high place in the
Kingdom, and also why we have stories in which they and they alone
are privileged along with Peter, above all in the transfiguration, when
these three receive a revelation which must not be made known to
the others until after the resurrection (Mt.17:9).

VERSES 21–22: The request presupposes a 'kingdom' for Jesus,
resembling an earthly kingdom in which the ruler will be seated on a
throne with his chief favourites or principal advisers seated on either
side of him. The mother asks that this privilege may be accorded to
her two sons, apparently as a matter of favouritism, for there is no
suggestion that they have merits which would entitle them to such
preferment. (In Mark the mother is not mentioned; James and John
make the petition on their own behalf.) The answer of Jesus seems
to accept this notion of his kingdom, and he refuses the plea only on
the ground that the disposition of places in his kingdom is not made
at his pleasure, but is already determined by his Father. There is no
suggestion that the highest places are reserved for others, nor is
there any touch of rebuke for the presumption of making such a
request. Under the response there lies a doctrine of absolute divine
predestination—the places 'are prepared' for those whom the Father
has willed to occupy them; and there is also a doctrine of the subordination of Jesus to the Father (this is elaborated in the Fourth
Gospel—Jn.5:19–27; 12:44–50; etc.).

'The cup'—a familiar Jewish figure for an ordeal, though it may
also be an experience of joy—'the cup of salvation' (Ps.116:13),
'the cup of consolation' (Jer.16:7); more frequently it is a figure of
disaster or of punishment—'the cup of the wine of wrath' (Jer.25:
15–29), 'a cup of horror and desolation' (Ezek.23:33). Jesus uses

the same figure in the Gethsemane scene: 'If it be possible, let this cup pass from me' (Mt.26:39). There is no allusion here to the cup of the Last Supper (Mt.26:27); yet in Christian interpretation that cup becomes at once the symbol of Christ's death—'This is my blood of the covenant which is poured out for many for the forgiveness of sins' (Mt.26:28), and 'the cup of blessing which we bless' (1 Cor.10:16). Here it is plainly the cup of death. Mark follows with a second figure, 'be baptized with the baptism with which I am baptized' (Mk.10:38).

VERSE 23: 'My cup you will drink'—most critics take this to be a *vaticinium post eventum*, and draw from it the conclusion that James and John suffered martyrdom together at the hands of Herod Agrippa, though only James is mentioned (Acts 12:2). The tradition of the church came to tell that John lived to extreme old age, and became the author of an entire corpus of books—the Gospel to which his name is attached, the three epistles included in the canon, and the book of Revelation. Possibly this tradition was established early enough to lead to the loss of the name of John from the story of the martyrdom of James. In any case, the words foretell a martyr's death for the two brothers—not explicitly that they will suffer at the same time.

VERSE 25: If commonplace notions of the future kingdom are accepted in the petition of the mother and in the response of Jesus, the thought of any comparison with earthly kingdoms is now rejected. Domination over others and the exercise of authority are the way of the kingdoms of the nations (Gentiles), but this is not the way of Christ's kingdom. Insensibly, the terms of reference have shifted from the future Kingdom of Christ in his transcendental glory to the community of his followers on earth—that is, to the church. It is not to be a power structure, and all desire for precedence and privilege is excluded. The only greatness to which the disciple of Christ may aspire is the greatness of his service to others.

VERSE 28: Jesus himself gives the pattern. The use of the title 'Son of man' emphasizes the inherent loftiness of the person who nonetheless serves—a heavenly being who 'came' into this world not to assume dominion, but to serve humanity.

Matthew follows Mark in continuing with another clause—'and to give his life a ransom for many'. This no longer bears upon the *pattern* (of service) which is offered to the followers of Jesus, but introduces the theme of the redemptive significance of Jesus' death. The disciples are not summoned to give their lives 'as a ransom for many'. In the Lukan version of the dispute over precedence (not attached to a request of the sons of Zebedee), this element is omitted; the saying of Jesus is recast to run: 'Which is the greater, one who sits at table or one who serves? Is it not the one who sits at table? But I am among you as one who serves' (Lk.22:27—set incongruously in the talk around the table at the Last Supper). This is perhaps an indication that the second part of the saying is misplaced—that is, that Mark has attached a floating saying which was not given any definite setting in his source to the declaration that the Son of man came to serve.

The word 'ransom' (λύτρον) is not found anywhere else in the New Testament. There is a secondary form of the saying in 1 Timothy 2:6—(Christ Jesus who) 'gave himself as a ransom for all' (ἀντίλυτρον ὑπὲρ πάντων). The cognate verb λυτρόω is found a few times, always of the work of Christ. (Lk.24:21—here the hope of redemption is thought to have been crushed by his death; Titus 2:14—'who gave himself for us that he might redeem us from all iniquity'; and above all, 1 Peter 1:18—'you were ransomed . . . not with perishable things such as silver and gold, but with the precious blood of Christ'.)

λύτρον (in earlier Greek almost always in the plural (λύτρα) means basically money or other compensation paid to secure the release of a prisoner, the emancipation of a slave, or (in Hebrew law) the recovery of property claimed for God (Lev.25:24–55; chap. 27, etc. LXX) or dedicated to him, especially the firstborn of man or beast. But the verb (in LXX) comes to be used figuratively in the more general sense of *rescue*. God 'ransoms' or 'redeems' Israel from captivity, not by any kind of payment to her overlords, but by his great power. There is no question of a ransom to be paid to anyone. So here it is wrong to ask to whom Christ pays his life as a ransom. Undoubtedly the thought that the life is offered in sacrifice is present, and a sacrifice can only be offered to God (it is staggering to think that Christian theologians should ever have seriously imagined that in offering up his life, Christ paid a ransom to the devil!). But in the context created for the saying by Mark, and adopted without change by Matthew, the 'ransom'—the giving of the life—is the final and complete act of service.

7 JESUS RESTORES SIGHT TO BLIND MEN *20:29–34*

²⁹ As they were going out from Jericho a great crowd followed him. ³⁰ Two blind men were sitting by the road; and when they heard that

Jesus was passing they clamoured, 'Have mercy, Lord, Son of David!' [31] The crowd rebuked them, bidding them to be quiet; but they clamoured all the more, shouting, 'Have mercy upon us, Lord, Son of David!' [32] Jesus stood still, called them, and said, 'What do you wish me to do for you?' [33] They said, 'Lord, that our eyes may be opened.' [34] And Jesus, filled with compassion, touched their eyes; and immediately they could see, and they followed him.

Matthew has given the same story in a different version in 9:27–31, where it forms part of his great collection of miracle stories (8:1–9: 34). There are enough coincidences of vocabulary to indicate that the Markan story of Bartimaeus (Mk.10:46–52) is the basis of both Matthaean versions. In his characteristic fashion, Matthew has cut away much of the colourful detail of the Markan version—the vivid picture of the blind man throwing off his cloak and leaping up to come to Jesus (Mk.10:50), and the circumstantial account of the dialogue between him and the bystanders (v.49). He does not even mention that the man is a beggar, nor does he give him a name (Bartimaeus is found only in Mark). For the words of Jesus, 'Go, your faith has healed you' (Mk.10:52), he substitutes, 'according to your faith let it be done for you.' In both Matthaean versions, the one blind man of Mark has become two.

VERSE 29: At Jericho, Jesus is back on the west bank of the Jordan, but there is no mention of the crossing. Matthew's search for brevity leads him to omit even the phrase of Mark, 'they came to Jericho' (Mk.10:46)—they are leaving before we have so much as heard that they had come to the town. (In Luke, the incident is laid 'as they were approaching Jericho'—Lk.18:35.)

VERSE 30: It could be taken for granted that blind men sitting by the roadside would be there to beg.

'Passing by' (παράγει), for Mark's 'it is' (Jesus). This verb seldom occurs in the Gospels (three times in Matthew, three times in Mark, and once in John); in three occurrences in the epistles it is used with the sense of 'passing away' (of this world). It is all the more remarkable that the one occurrence in the Fourth Gospel is in the Johannine story of the healing of the man born blind (Jn.9:1).

'Jesus'—Mark adds 'the Nazarene' (followed by Luke). Its omission heightens the emphasis on the designation of Jesus as 'Son of David' and 'Lord'.

There are some textual variants in the wording of the cry (word order, omission of κύριε, 'Lord', in some good witnesses), but the striking thing is the use of the appellation, 'Son of David'. This title never occurs anywhere else in Mark or Luke, and never in any other New Testament writing. But Matthew uses it seven times. For him it is a highly significant title of Messiahship.

VERSE 32: 'Jesus . . . called them'—in Mark, he bids the people around him to call him, and they pass the word to him, 'Take heart; get up, he is calling you.'

VERSE 34: 'Full of compassion', σπλαγχνισθείς—it is exceptional for Matthew to add such a note of the emotional response of Jesus. He is much more apt to excise such elements from his Markan version.

'Followed him'—as in Mark, the conclusion of the story points on to the entry into Jerusalem, where Jesus will be welcomed as 'Son of David' (21:9). In Luke, there is a break in the connection of this episode and the journey on to Jerusalem. Luke interposes the Zacchaeus episode and the long parable of the minas (19:1—27).

IV   ACTIVITIES IN JERUSALEM
Mt. 21:1—22:46

The dramatic events of Jesus' visit to Jerusalem are organized in Matthew's account as follows:
1 The Entry into Jerusalem 21:1—11
2 Jesus in the Temple 21:12—17
3 Jesus Curses a Fig Tree 21:18—22
4 Jesus in Controversy: Challenge and Counter-Challenge 21:23—22:14
    Jesus is Challenged to Show his Credentials 21:23—27
    The Parable of the Two Sons 21:28—32
    The Parable of the Wicked Tenant-Farmers 21:33—46
    The Parable of the Rejected Invitation 22:1—14
5 Four Questions 22:15—46
    First Question 22:15—22
    Second Question 22:23—33
    Third Question 22:34—40
    Fourth Question 22:41—46

1   THE ENTRY OF JESUS INTO JERUSALEM *21:1—11*

²¹ When they had nearly reached Jerusalem, and had come to Bethphage by the Mount of Olives, Jesus sent off two of his disciples ² with the instructions: 'Go into the village over against us and you will at once see an ass tied there, and a colt with her. Untie them and

bring them to me. ³ If anyone says anything to you, you will say, "The Lord needs them and will send them back forthwith." ' ⁴ This took place in fulfilment of what was spoken through the prophet:

⁵ Tell the daughter of Zion,
'Behold, your king is coming to you,
mounted humbly upon an ass [and]
upon a colt, the foal of an ass.'

⁶ The disciples went and did as Jesus had instructed them. ⁷ They fetched the ass and the colt and laid their cloaks upon them, and Jesus mounted them. ⁸ The huge crowd spread their cloaks upon the roadway, and some brought branches from the trees and spread them on the way. ⁹ The crowds that went before him and those that followed him kept shouting, 'Hosanna to the Son of David! Blessed is he who comes in the name of the Lord! Hosanna in the Highest!' ¹⁰ As he entered Jerusalem, the whole city was thrown into a turmoil, asking, 'Who is this?' ¹¹ And the crowds told them, 'This is the prophet Jesus, from Nazareth in Galilee.'

The road from Jericho to Jerusalem carries us for some fifteen miles up a dry and stony wadi, with barren hills on either side where no sign of life is seen except for the occasional Bedouin with a few goats. Jericho, at the western edge of the Jordan valley, just five miles from the outlet of the river into the Dead Sea, is 400 metres below sea level (this is the lowest area on the surface of the earth). The summit of the hill on which Jerusalem is built is about 800 metres above sea level, so that the pilgrim throngs faced a steep ascent.

VERSE 1: Bethphage is a trifling hamlet close to the walls of Jerusalem. Mark mentions along with it Bethany, which is just off the route and may be the 'village opposite' of the following verse.

VERSE 2: 'An ass and a colt'—Mark mentions only 'a colt', and adds, 'on which no one has ever sat' (Mk.11:2; cf. Lk.19:30).

VERSES 4–5; Matthew introduces one of his formula quotations. It takes its introductory words from Isaiah 62:11 ('Tell the daughter of Zion'), but continues with a fragment of an oracle found in Zechariah 9:9. This oracle may have been composed in relation to the entry of Alexander the Great into Jerusalem in 332 BC (R.C. Dentan, *IB* VI, p.1090, and *ad loc.*). Unlike the Macedonian conqueror on his magnificent war horse, the Messianic king enters the city in the humblest guise, riding on an ass; and he comes to bring salvation and peace.

The verse runs as follows (LXX):

Rejoice greatly, daughter of Zion!
  Make proclamation, daughter of Jerusalem!
  Behold, your king is coming to you.
  He is righteous and brings salvation (δίκαιος καὶ σώζων),
    gentle (πραΰς) and mounted upon an ass and a young colt.

Matthew has substituted the phrase from Isaiah for the summons to Jerusalem; more remarkably, he has omitted the fourth line altogether, though 'those words would be more appropriate to Matthew's picture of Jesus as the Messiah, indeed, would constitute the very epitome of Matthew's Christology.' (Stendahl, *School of St. Matthew*, p.119.) In the closing words, he resorts to a literal rendering of the Hebrew. But it may well be that a recollection of the Greek text, which certainly suggests two animals, and even a rider mounted on two animals, has led Matthew to say that Jesus 'mounted on *them*', ludicrous though the picture is.

The same oracle is quoted in the Johannine version of the entry (Jn.12:15), but the conclusion is given in the abbreviated form, 'upon the colt of an ass'. This correctly renders the Hebrew parallelism, which mentions only one animal—an ass, the offspring of an ass. Matthew was certainly familiar with this form of expression, and his interpretation of it as meaning two animals simply 'gives evidence of his acquaintance with the hermeneutic methods of the rabbis'. (Stendahl, *School*, p.119.)

VERSES 6–7: Mark gives a circumstantial description of the taking of the colt. It is 'tied at the door, out in the open street'; some bystanders (in Luke, 'the owners') remonstrate, 'What are you doing, untying the colt?' but let it go when the disciples answer as Jesus had instructed them to do (Mk.11:4–6).

VERSE 7: The disciples make saddles of their cloaks (ἱμάτια).

VERSE 8: 'the very great crowd'—πλεῖστος here is certainly elative (BDF, 60). According to the story, Jesus has been attended by crowds all the way (Mt.19:2), and Matthew seems to suggest that still more joined them as they left Jericho (20:29). Pilgrims going up to Jerusalem for the festival were apt to join forces and make up a kind of procession.

The spreading of garments and branches on the road is a token of honour to Jesus; he is given 'red carpet treatment' in the only way that the means of the pilgrims allow. It is only in the Johannine version that we hear of palm branches (Jn.12:13); these are, however, brought out from Jerusalem by pilgrims who are already in the city. They could not be cut from trees at the gates of Jerusalem; the nearest palms would be found in the Jordan valley around Jericho.

VERSE 9: The acclamation 'hosanna!' is a Greek transliteration of the Hebrew cry *hosia'na*, 'Save us', as in Psalm 118:25, the last of the Hallel psalms which were sung in procession and in the home at the great festivals. Here it is used as a shout of praise, without thought of its original meaning.

The sentence 'Blessed is he who comes in the name of the Lord' is taken from the next verse of the same Psalm. Luke adds 'the king' (cf. Jn.12:13—'the King of Israel'), and interprets the final clause, 'Hosanna in the highest', as 'Peace in heaven and glory in the highest!' (Lk.19:38). Matthew and Luke seem to have revised Mark independently (Mark's expression 'the coming kingdom of our father David' is anomalous).

The Zechariah oracle is not cited by Mark (or by Luke), but it certainly underlies the Markan story and may even have led to its composition. John adds the comment that the disciples did not at the time attach any great significance to the manner of Jesus' entry into the city, and that it was only 'when Jesus was glorified' that they recognized its Messianic character. It was not at all uncommon for anyone to ride into the city on an ass, and the event may well have been quite unspectacular in its actual occurrence.

There is no reason to think that Jesus deliberately stage-managed his entry into the city with the intention of presenting himself in the guise of the lowly king of the oracle. For that matter, the procurement of the ass cannot be taken to show that Jesus had a friend in Bethany and knew that he always kept an ass (according to Mark, an unbroken colt!) tethered at his door. In Mark's own story, Jesus had never been near Jerusalem before. He has the supernatural knowledge of a prophet. The same feature is seen in the story of Saul and Samuel, when the prophet is able to tell the future king all about what will happen to him after he leaves—he will meet two men by Rachel's tomb; then three men will meet him by the oak of Tabor; and finally, he will meet a band of prophets and will prophesy with them (1 Sam.10:2–6). The story of the entry is composed with the same freedom of fancy.

VERSES 10–11: In Mark, the story ends with a quiet visit to the temple. Matthew alone tells of the tumultuous reaction within the city. It is somewhat incongruous that the crowds which have been acclaiming Jesus as 'the son of David', now identify him simply as 'the prophet Jesus from Nazareth of Galilee'. Luke, like Mark, makes no mention of any great stir in the city over Jesus' arrival. He tells of a remonstrance made by some Pharisees in the crowd; and then, before Jesus actually reaches the city, he laments over it, anticipating its failure to welcome its appointed deliverer, and foretelling the calamities that are to come upon it in the siege and capture of Jerusalem by the Romans (Lk.19:39f., 41–44).

ἐσείσθη (v.10), 'thrown into a turmoil' as if by an earthquake (σεισμός, 'earthquake'). At the news of the birth of Jesus, Jersualem was 'shaken' (ἐταράχθη) sharing the dismay of King Herod (2:3).

On Mt.21:1–11, see the article of W. Bauer, 'The "Colt" of Palm Sunday (Der Palmesel)', in *JBL* 72 (1973), pp.220–29.

2 JESUS IN THE TEMPLE *21:12–17*

[12] Jesus went into the temple and drove out all who were selling and buying in the temple, and overturned the tables of the money-changers and the seats of the dove sellers, [13] saying to them, 'It is written, "My house shall be called a house of prayer," but you are making it "a cave of bandits".'

[14] People who were blind and lame made approach to him in the temple, and he healed them. [15] But when the chief priests and the scribes saw the wonderful things that he had done, and when they heard the children raising the cry, 'Hosanna to the Son of David', in the temple, they were furious, [16] and they said to him, 'Do you hear what these children are saying?' Jesus answered, 'Yes! Have you never read "Out of the mouths of babes and sucklings you have brought forth praise"?' [17] With that he left them and went out of the city as far as Bethany, and camped there.

As Matthew has shaped the story, Jesus has entered Jerusalem in the morning, early enough to give him time to clear the traffickers out of the temple, to carry on a ministry of healing, and to meet a challenge from the authorities. In Mark, he arrives late in the day and has time only to 'look around' (περιβλεψάμενος) the temple like any other visitor before going back to Bethany with his disciples (Mk.11:11). The dramatic scene of the cleansing of the temple is put off until the next day. The encounter with the authorities comes later still (Mk.11:27ff.; in Matthew, this is given as a second challenge).

The buying and selling went on in the outer court of the temple, which was open to the public (Gentiles as well as Jews). It was necessary to the maintenance of the cult, so that animals meeting ritual requirements might be available for worshippers who came to offer sacrifices—oxen, sheep, goats, and pigeons must all be 'without blemish' (Lev. chaps.1–3; etc.); together with such accompaniments as incense, wine, salt, and oil. Similarly, the services of money-changers were needed, for the dues of the priests had to be paid in the local coinage ('reckoning by the shekel of the sanctuary'— Num.3:47, etc.) Apart from the fluctuations of 'foreign exchange' (with which we in our day are all too familiar), many of the coins in everyday use carried pagan symbols, such as the owl of Athena or the rattle of Isis; and many were cast with the head of the reigning emperor; and these were naturally not acceptable for sacred purposes among the Jews. Such a general expulsion of merchants and money-changers as is attributed here to Jesus would have made the continuance of sacrificial worship in the temple impossible.

Accordingly, it is inconceivable that this story should be taken as literal, historical truth. Origen suggested that the incident should be interpreted symbolically; Jerome thought that it was more marvellous than any of the other signs that Jesus did. The modern reader hardly realizes how great a disturbance would be involved. The animals for sacrifice would number in the thousands, and there would be even more pigeons. Naturally, these would require very large numbers of attendants, to feed and water them, apart from the merchants who sold them. Most of the pilgrims had come there precisely to offer sacrifices—are we to imagine that they would all, or any great number of them, be gratified to see Jesus remove the means necessary for the fulfilment of their pious intentions? Nothing is said of what happened to the flocks of oxen, sheep, and goats—are we to suppose that they were left to wander out into the alleys and streets around the temple, to fend for themselves? Commentators seldom make any attempt to give their readers any idea of the magnitude of the operation which would be required; they waste their energies in debating whether the incident took place at the beginning of the ministry, as in John, or at the end, as in the Synoptics. But no one man, however masterful his personality, could possibly carry out such a 'cleansing', even with the aid of his handful of disciples. It would need the application of force on a grand scale, if the merchants offered any opposition at all. Even then, we would have to suppose that the temple police were too scared to intervene, and that no one would think of calling in the Roman troops from the citadel of the Antonia close at hand. All this is not merely implausible; it is utterly incredible.

VERSE 12: 'Selling and buying'—the sellers would be the merchants who had been granted concessions by the temple authorities; but the buyers would be the pilgrims (or local worshippers) who were procuring animals to be sacrificed.

VERSE 13: The first citation, drawn from Isaiah 56:7, is far from contrasting the temple as 'a house of prayer' with the temple as a place of sacrifice. It is basically an assurance that Gentiles who are converted to the faith of Israel will find that 'their burnt offerings and sacrifices will be accepted' on the altar of God. That is why the temple will be called 'a house of prayer for all people'—it will be open to Gentiles (if they 'join themselves to the Lord . . . to love the name of the Lord'). The emphasis is really on the phrase 'for all people', which Matthew omits, though he had it before him in Mark. It has been suggested that Matthew was moved to make the omission because, by the time he wrote, the temple had been destroyed and could no longer be a house of prayer for anyone.

The second citation takes a phrase from the book of Jeremiah, where the temple is compared to 'a cave of bandits', not because of the buying and selling in its precincts, but because the worshippers 'steal, murder, commit adultery, swear falsely, burn incense to Baal' and then come to stand before God, as if the temple were no better than a bandits' cave (Jer.7:9–11). There may well have been grounds for holding that the prices charged for the materials of sacrifice were exorbitant, and that the money-changers cheated on the rates of exchange for foreign currency; at any rate, pilgrims probably thought so; but that is not what Jeremiah had in mind. For him, the 'bandits' were the people who came to worship, not the business men who operated the concessions.

Mark at this point tells us that 'the chief priests and the scribes heard it and sought a way to destroy him'; but were restrained from taking action for fear of the public reaction, 'because all the multitude was astonished at his teaching' (Mk.11:18). But Matthew does not even hint that the authorities paid any attention to what was going on, or even heard about it.

VERSE 14: Matthew is alone in reporting miracles of healing in the temple.

VERSE 15: The indignation of the chief priests and scribes is aroused not so much by the miracles, as by the acclamations of the children. Again, it is utterly incongruous that they should complain about the behaviour of the children while showing no sign of concern about the violent actions of Jesus!

We might notice also that Matthew has transferred the acclamations, 'Hosanna to the Son of David!' to the interior of the temple from the road outside the gates (v.9), and from the crowds to 'the children'. This paves the way for his introduction of the citation, 'out of the mouths of babes' etc. (text of Ps.8:3 LXX, quite different from the Hebrew), though children old enough to be shouting acclamations in the temple would not be precisely 'babes and sucklings'! The response of Jesus in the Lukan parallel to this is clearly far more appropriate: 'I tell you, if these were silent, the very stones would cry out.' (Lk.19:40—Jesus has still not reached the city.)

The 'chief priests' here make their first appearance in Matthew. The peculiar combination 'chief priests and scribes' takes the place of Matthew's frequent coupling of 'scribes and Pharisees'.

The Johannine version of the incident (Jn.2:13–17) shows little or no trace of dependence upon the Synoptic account and is evidently based upon an independent source. It is laid at the beginning of the ministry, not at the end. It mentions oxen and sheep as well as pigeons, and it tells us that Jesus made a whip of small cords to drive the merchants out—a slight enough hint of the violence of the action; one man with one whip would hardly suffice for such a task. (There is no suggestion in John, any more than in the Synoptics, that the disciples or the hordes of worshippers so much as lifted a finger to support Jesus.) The words of Jesus are addressed to the sellers of doves alone, and make no reference to the temple as 'a house of prayer' or 'a cave of bandits'; Jesus says: 'Take these things away; do not make my Father's house a shopping centre!' It is more than hinted that the action contributed in the end to his death; his disciples recall the words of the Psalm: 'Zeal for your house will devour me.' (Ps.69:9 LXX; the Hebrew text reads 'has devoured me'; cf. the *NEB* rendering, 'bitter enemies of thy temple tear me in pieces'.) And this is followed by a clash with 'the Jews', and the affirmation of Jesus: 'Destroy this temple, and in three days I will raise it up.' On this the evangelist comments that 'he spoke of the temple of his body.'

It is evident that John—though he no doubt thinks that the incident actually took place—is focusing attention on its ultimate (symbolic) significance. The symbolism is not made explicit in Matthew or in the Synoptics generally. But if we are justified in denying any historical factuality to the story, we must realize that it would never have been composed except as a Christian challenge to the continuing validity of the temple worship; and under it there lies implicit the belief that the true temple is the church, in which are offered the 'spiritual sacrifices acceptable to God through Jesus Christ' (1 Pet.2:5).

3   JESUS CURSES A FIG TREE *21:18–22*

[18] As he was returning into the city in the morning, he felt hungry, [19] and when he saw a fig tree by the roadside he went up to it and found on it nothing but leaves; and he said to it, 'Let no fruit come from you ever again', and the fig tree withered instantly. [20] His disciples, when they saw this, were astounded and said, 'How did the fig tree instantly wither?' [21] Jesus replied, 'If you have faith and do not doubt, you will not only do this thing of the fig tree, but even if you say to this mountain, "Be taken up and cast into the sea", it shall come to pass. [22] And whatever you ask in prayer you will receive, if you believe.'

This is the only cursing miracle in the Gospels. It will not be supposed that it is a report of an actual incident. The strange thing is that it should have found a place in the Gospels of Mark and Matthew—it is so out of keeping with everything else in their portrait of Jesus. Many have supposed that it is a transmutation of the parable of the fig tree given only in the Gospel of Luke (13:6–9), even though the parable speaks of the deferment of destruction of the tree, and the miracle tells of its instantaneous withering. (This would not be greater than the change of significance that can be seen in certain parables in the versions of the different evangelists—Jeremias, *Parables*, p. 48 and elsewhere.) But if conjectures are of any use in such a matter, it might be better to see the miracle story as originating in a passing remark of Jesus to the effect that the Israel with which he had to do was like a fig tree that made a good showing of leaves in the spring but never produced any fruit.

At all events, the story in its setting (linked with the purging of the temple) is surely taken by the evangelists as a sign of the coming destruction of Israel. In a different figure, John the Baptist spoke of imminent destruction in the words: 'Even now the axe is laid to the root of the trees; every tree therefore that does not bear good fruit is cut down and thrown into the fire' (Mt.3:10).

The disciples seem to be particularly struck by the swiftness with which the curse took effect. This is a Matthaean touch. In Mark, the story is divided, with the purging of the temple being recounted between the cursing of the tree and the discovery the next morning that it had withered away 'to its roots' (Mk.11:12–14:20). Mark also notes that 'it was not the season for figs', leaving the reader to wonder why then Jesus would hope to find figs on it and curse it when he found (as was to be expected) that there were none. Taken literally, what would this be but sheer spite?

In Matthew (as in Mark) the miracle story becomes the introduction to a saying, or rather a group of sayings, about the power of faith. These sayings appear to have been transmitted in the tradition independently of such an introduction. The first of them is the most striking—it speaks of the power of faith to move mountains. In some form it was known to Paul, who writes in a famous passage: 'Though I have all faith so as to move mountains, and have not love, I am nothing' (1 Cor.13:2). Matthew has already introduced it in a different context, following the story of the healing of the epileptic boy (17:20). There it is again a response to the disciples, who ask why they were unable to cast out the demon of epilepsy. Jesus replies, 'Because of your little faith. For truly I tell you, if you have faith as a grain of mustard seed, you will say to this mountain, "Move from here to there", and it will move; and nothing will be impossible to you.' In a still different context (in a response to the plea of the apostles, 'Lord, increase our faith'), Luke gives substantially the same saying in a strangely different version: 'If you had faith as a grain of mustard seed, you could say to this sycamine tree, "Be rooted up, and be planted in the sea", and it would obey you' (Lk.17:6).

In any of these forms, it evidently transmits a tradition that Jesus encouraged his disciples to attempt great things for God, undaunted by seeming impossibilities. We may assume that he was not expecting his words to be taken literally, as if he were training them to perform stupendous feats of magic. As T.W. Manson has put it: 'The word of Jesus does not invite Christians to become conjurers and magicians, but heroes like those whose exploits are celebrated in the eleventh chapter of Hebrews.' (*Sayings*, p.141.)

The saying itself is probably an application of a profane maxim which bore upon the fact that with resolution and self-confidence men can accomplish—and have accomplished—things that seemed as impossible as casting a mountain into the sea. But there is a change of measureless significance when the accent is shifted from self-confidence to confidence in God. In Mark, the changed emphasis is even more strongly accentuated when the saying is prefaced by the injunction, 'Have faith in God' (Mk.11:22). In this spirit William Carey preached a famous sermon on the theme: 'Attempt great things for God; expect great things from God.'

Verse 22 generalizes the thought: the prayer of faith, whatever its petition, will receive that for which it asks.

[Mark notes, as Matthew does not, that 'it was not the season for figs.' But is he not himself responsible for placing the story in the

Passover period? It has no intrinsic relationship to this particular visit of Jesus to Jerusalem, or indeed to the road between Bethany and Jerusalem. It is possible, even likely, that it was at first transmitted without any indication of time or place; and would be more appropriately shaped if it thought of Jesus coming up to a fig tree in full leaf at a time when figs were in season—in June or later in the summer.]

4   JESUS IN CONTROVERSY: CHALLENGE AND COUNTER-CHALLENGE *21:23–22:14*

In this sequence, Jesus is depicted in controversy with the Jewish authorities—'the chief priests and the elders of the people' (v.23); 'the chief priests and the Pharisees' (v.45). When he is challenged to show who gave him authority to act as he has been doing, he refuses to answer except by the counter-challenge to his opponents to declare themselves on whether they accept the mission of John the Baptist as God-given. From that he turns to the attack, in a sequence of three parables. In the first, he compares the religious leaders unfavourably with the people whom they despise, the tax collectors and the harlots, on the basis of their responses to the preaching of John the Baptist. In the second, he compares them with tenants who refuse to give the owner his due, and warns them that the trust which they have abused will be put into the hands of others. With this, the projected punishment bears implicitly upon the whole people ($\lambda\alpha\acute{o}s$); the vineyard of God will be given to a 'nation' ($\check{\epsilon}\theta\nu o s$) which will fulfil its duty to God. In the third parable, the final refusal of the gospel by Israel is foreshadowed, and consequent upon it the gathering in of Gentiles to take the place of those who have rejected the proffered blessing. To this Matthew attaches what may have been originally an independent parable (22:11–14), as a warning that the newly invited guests must also meet the host's test of fitness.

This arrangement of the materials is the editorial work of Matthew. The three parables given by Matthew are represented in Mark and Luke by only the one parable of the Tenants. Neither of the others appears at all in Mark; Luke gives a version of the parable of the Rejected Invitation in another context, and depicts the banquet as a feast given by a private citizen, not as a marriage feast for a king's son (Lk.14:15–24). He has Jesus tell it at the dinner table of a Pharisee, somewhere on the journey from the north

(14:1ff.). The change of setting carries with it a change in interpretation and application.

Jesus is Challenged to Show his Credentials 21:23–27

²³ After he entered the temple, the chief priests and the elders of the people made an approach to him as he was teaching. They said, 'By what authority are you doing these things? Who gave you this authority?' ²⁴ Jesus answered them, 'I too will ask you one thing. If you give me the answer. I also will tell you by what authority I do these things. ²⁵ The baptism of John—whence did it come? From heaven, or from men?' They thought it over, saying to themselves, 'If we say, "from heaven", he will ask us, "then why did you not believe him?" ²⁶ But if we say, "from men", we are afraid of the masses, for they all look upon John as a prophet.' ²⁷ So they gave Jesus the answer, 'We do not know.' And he said to them, 'Neither do I tell you by what authority I am doing these things.'

It is hard to see in this anything like a real dialogue, or even the fragments of a real dialogue. Why would the chief priests and elders —presumably representing the Great Sanhedrin of Jerusalem—feel any obligation to answer a question about their own attitude to John the Baptist before requiring Jesus to give an account of himself and to show what authority he claimed to possess? For that matter, why should Jesus decline to say directly that he was commissioned by God? The question, of course, is a challenge. They are not asking for information about him; they know that he has no authority (in their sense of the word) to act as he has been doing. The temple was under the jurisdiction of the Sanhedrin, which they represented; the merchants and the money-changers exercised their trades under concessions granted by the Sanhedrin. They knew without asking that no authority had been granted to Jesus to interfere with the existing arrangements. At the end, there is no attempt to describe their reaction. Would chief priests and elders, acting in their own precincts, be so easily silenced by an agitator from Galilee (as they would regard him)? Or would Jesus look upon his own mission and that of John the Baptist as so similar that the recognition of the one must carry with it the recognition of the other?

VERSE 23: No reference is made to the events of the previous day, but the question presupposes that things have not returned to normal. 'These things' that Jesus is doing must include more than is specifically mentioned (in Matthew, teaching; in Mark, walking around; in Luke, teaching the people and preaching the gospel). The evangelists will hardly have supposed that the merchants had come back to ply their trade as usual, and that Jesus now permitted what he had so forcibly assailed the day before. Would the chief priests and elders even stop to ask him to justify his actions? Would they not at long last direct the temple police, and if necessary call in the Roman garrison, to put a stop to it all?

For the Christians who told the story, of course, the authority of Jesus did not rest upon the Sanhedrin or any earthly power. He acted as the King-Messiah, and his authorization came from God.

VERSE 25: 'Heaven' here is a paraphrase for 'God', in conformity with Jewish reluctance to use the word 'God' directly.

The representatives of the Sanhedrin do not step aside to hold a conference; the thoughts that come into their minds are known to the teller of the story (and in his mind, presumably, to Jesus). The assumption is that Jesus knew in advance that his question would put them into this very dilemma.

VERSE 26: The theme of the fear of mass reaction is taken up again in v.46, and in the story of the plot to arrest Jesus and put him to death (26:3—5).

The Parable of the Two Sons 21:28—32

28 'What do you think of this? A man had two sons. He came to the first and said, "Son, go work in the vineyard today". 29 He answered "I will not", but afterwards he changed his mind and went. 30 The father went to his other son and said the same thing to him; and he answered, "Yes, sir", but he did not go. 31 Which of the two did the will of the father?' They said, 'The first.' Jesus said to them, 'Truly I tell you, the tax collectors and the harlots go before you into the kingdom of heaven. 32 For John came to you in the way of righteousness and you did not believe him, but the tax collectors and the harlots believed him; and you, even when you saw this, did not afterwards repent and believe him.'

Verse 32 is not an integral part of the parable, but a Matthaean supplement, designed to follow up the mention of John in the preceding section.

The parable proper (vv.28—31) uses the figure of the two sons to represent two kinds of people: the religious leaders, who make formal professions of piety but fail to do what God requires and, in contrast, the tax collectors and the harlots, who followed a way of life far from anything prescribed by the law of God, but repented in response to the preaching and were now keeping the commandments. The requirement for entering the kingdom of heaven has been defined by Jesus as 'to do the will of my Father who is in heaven' (7:21); it is not met by professions of obedience which are not matched by actions.

There are difficulties in the parable in this context. The chief priests and elders would be astonished to have it suggested that they were not working in the vineyard of God as they had promised. It is hardly likely that the chief priests and elders of the people, *en masse*, were accused of failing to carry out their duties to God. There is no indication of how they were failing in obedience; they were administering the temple, seeing to the sacrifices, judging cases brought before the Sanhedrin, and so forth. They were certainly performing the public duties which were appointed for them. And there is nothing to indicate that either John or Jesus managed to effect a mass conversion of harlots and tax collectors. The taxes were still collected, and no doubt there was no great scarcity of harlots in Jerusalem and through the country as a result of the mission of John.

The Greek text of this parable presents some very strange variations, even in manuscripts of the first quality. The text here translated is that of Codex Sinaiticus, with strong versional and good patristic support. It was printed by Tischendorf, and is now adopted in the UBS text and in the latest edition of Nestle. The text of Codex Vaticanus gives the same sense, in substance, but inverts the order of appearance of the two sons—it is the first who says 'Yes' and does not go, and the second who says 'I will not' and afterwards repents and goes. The answer, corresponding to this change of order, is 'the latter' (ὁ ὕστερος [B]; ὁ ἔσχατος [Theta]). This was chosen for their text by Westcott and Hort. It is supported by a few Greek manuscripts and has some slight patristic support. The third major variation shows a more radical change. The two sons are introduced in the order of our text (the first goes, after an initial refusal; the second says 'Yes' but does not go), and the answer given is 'the last' (ὁ ἔσχατος—Codex Bezae; many Old Latin manuscripts and the Sinaitic Syriac). The priests and elders give their vote for the son who says 'Yes' and does not go! This is obvious nonsense, though Jerome (and others after him) tried to defend it as showing the sheer perversity of the Jewish leaders, who give the wrong answer in order to spoil the point.

See the discussion of these readings in B. Metzger's *Textual Commentary on the Greek New Testament* (1971), pp.55f.

The Parable of the Wicked Tenant-Farmers 21:33–46

³³ 'Hear another parable. There was a landowner who planted a vine-yard, grew a hedge around it, dug a wine press in it, and built a tower. He let it out to tenant-farmers, and went abroad. ³⁴ When the time of vintage arrived, he sent his slaves to the tenants to collect his [share of the] fruit. ³⁵ The tenants now seized his slaves; one they lashed, one they killed, and one they stoned. ³⁶ Again he sent other slaves, more numerous than the first, and they gave the same treatment to them. ³⁷ Last of all he sent his son to them, saying to himself, "They will respect my son." ³⁸ But when the tenants saw the son, they said to one another, "This is the heir; come, let us kill him and get his inheritance." ³⁹ So they seized him, pulled him out of the vineyard, and killed him. ⁴⁰ Now then, when the owner of the vineyard comes, what will he do to those tenants?' ⁴¹ They replied to him, 'He will bring those wretches to a wretched end, and let the vineyard to other tenants, who will turn over to him his share of the fruit at the vintage times.'

⁴² Jesus said to them, 'Have you never read in the scriptures,

The stone which the builders rejected—
This has been made the cornerstone.
This is from the Lord,
and it is marvellous in our eyes.

⁴³ Therefore I tell you, the kingdom of God will be taken away from you and given to a nation producing the fruits proper to it.' ⁴⁵ When the chief priests and the Pharisees heard his parables, they realized that he was speaking about them; ⁴⁶ they wanted to take him into custody, but they were afraid of the masses, for they looked upon Jesus as a prophet.

Our best witnesses include a verse 44, which runs: 'Whoever falls over this stone will be smashed in pieces; and it will crush anyone on whom it falls.' The textual evidence in favour of this reading is over-whelming. It is found in both Aleph and B, as well as many other uncials and cursives; and in the Latin Vulgate, the Syriac versions (Peshitta, Curetonian, Harclean), and in the writings of several Fathers. Only one great uncial omits it (Codex D), and one important cursive (33); along with some manuscripts of the Old Latin, the Sinaitic Syriac, and the Greek Christian writers Irenaeus, Origen, and Eusebius.

Modern editors of the Greek text indicate their suspicions of the reading by enclosing it in brackets, though their respect for the textual evidence forbids them to reject it outright. They suspect it as an early assimilation to Luke 20:18. In *RSV* and *NEB* it is relegated to the margin. It is certainly misplaced in the Matthaean text; it would come in more appropriately before verse 43 than after it.

There is a curious incongruity in the double notion of the 'stone'; if it is solidly in place in the building, it cannot be lying around for any to fall over and hurt himself, or loose enough to fall and hurt a passerby. But a similar double use of the 'stone' occurs in 1 Peter, where the stone has been made the keystone (or copestone) of the edifice, yet remains 'a stone to trip over' and 'a rock to cause damage' (1 Pet.2:7f.; the second quotation is taken from Isa.8:14). See my notes on the passage in *The First Epistle of Peter* (1970), p.125.

The parable begins with words that recall, and are in part taken directly from, Isaiah's 'Song of the Vineyard' (Isa.5:1—7). In this poem, the owner describes his care of the vineyard in his own words: 'I made a hedge around it ($\phi\rho\alpha\gamma\mu\grave{o}\nu$ $\pi\epsilon\rho\iota\acute{e}\vartheta\eta\kappa\alpha$) . . . I planted a vineyard ($\dot{\epsilon}\phi\acute{v}\tau\epsilon\upsilon\sigma\alpha$ $\dot{\alpha}\mu\pi\acute{\epsilon}\lambda\omega\nu\alpha$) . . . I built a watchtower ($\mathring{\omega}\kappa o\delta\acute{o}\mu\eta\sigma\alpha$ $\pi\acute{v}\rho\gamma o\nu$) . . . and dug a winepress ($\pi\rho o\lambda\acute{\eta}\nu\iota o\nu$ $\mathring{\omega}\rho\upsilon\xi\alpha$).' All these phrases (from LXX) are taken up in the parable (except that $\pi\rho o\lambda\acute{\eta}\nu\iota o\nu$ is replaced by $\lambda\acute{\eta}\nu\iota o\nu$). At the end, the significance of the figure is explained:

> For the vineyard of the Lord of hosts
>   is the house of Israel,
> And the men of Judah
>   are his pleasant planting.

But that is as far as the borrowing goes. The complaint in Isaiah is not that Israel has not given God his share of the grape harvest, but that the grapes themselves were worthless:

> I looked for it to yield grapes,
>   but it yielded wild grapes. (v. 2b)

The point of this figure is made clear at the end:

> He looked for justice,
>   but behold! bloodshed;
>   for righteousness,
>   but behold! a cry! (of despair and anguish of the wronged). (v.7b)

The 'men of Judah' and the 'house of Israel' are not tenants (as in the parable); they are the vineyard itself; and the punishment for their wrongdoing is not that the 'vineyard' is let out to others, but that it is utterly destroyed (vv.5,6).

Other features of the parable (not of the Song) reflect conditions of life in rural Galilee. There are lands owned by absentee landlords, and worked by local peasants on a system of share-cropping; the rental is paid in kind, as a fixed amount of produce, or as a percentage of the whole crop. It is not unlikely that there were instances of violent assaults upon agents who came to collect the rent. The verisimilitude disappears, however, when we hear that the owner's only reaction to the brutality with which his first emissaries are treated is to send out others; and it becomes still less credible when he follows up the second catastrophe by sending his own son. In all this, allegory has taken over. The slaves now figure the succession of prophets whom God had sent age after age to Israel, only to see them treated with disdain and often enough with violence; and the son is a figure of Jesus himself. Even the detail of his being dragged out of the vineyard to be murdered (not found in Mark) reflects the fact that Jesus was taken out of Jerusalem to be crucified.

This parable has come down to us in four versions. Besides those of the three Synoptics, there is a generally simpler version in the Gospel of Thomas (Saying 65). A comparison of these makes it possible for us to trace out something, though not all, of the complicated history that lies behind the several versions. In Luke and in Thomas there is nothing of the language of Isaiah's 'Song of the Vineyard'; the parable speaks only of the relations between the owner and his tenants, with first his slaves and finally his son as intermediaries. 'A man planted a vineyard and let it out to peasants and went abroad for a considerable time' (Lk.20:9); 'A good ($\chi\rho\eta\sigma\tau\delta\varsigma$) man had a vineyard. He gave it to peasants so that they might work it and that he might receive its fruit from them' (Thomas). It would appear, then, that Mark (or his source) has been led by the use of the word 'vineyard' to fuse this parable of an absentee landlord and peasant share-croppers with the 'Song' of Isaiah. Further, in the earlier form, it seems probable that only three messengers were involved. (The customary pattern of three, familiar to us not only from sacred literature—three temptations, three slaves in the parable of the talents, three withdrawals and returns of Jesus in Gethsemane, etc.—but also from profane story—Goldilocks and the Three Bears, etc. See M. Dibelius, *Formgeschichte*, pp.251f. n.2: 'Die epischen Gesetze der Volkspoesie lassen sich . . . beobachten. Ich erwähne die Gesetze der Wiederholung . . . , der Dreizahl.') So we can perceive a series rising to a climax—the first slave is flogged, the second has his head cracked, the third is killed outright (Mk.12:3–5). In Luke, the third is wounded and thrown out. In Thomas, the third becomes the son, who is killed. This already gives a consistent picture, sufficient in itself to lead up to the decision of the owner to get rid of those tenants (indeed, to bring the death penalty upon them, as in Matthew and Luke). But the simple pattern is already spoiled in Mark, when to the first three servants he adds a succession of others ('and so with many others, some they beat and some they killed'—12:5b). Matthew has complicated things still more by multiplying the one slave of each coming into larger and larger numbers; and as in Thomas, the third message is carried by the owner's son. He also ruins the climactic effect by bringing murder into the treatment of the first slaves (beaten, killed, stoned). Luke alone retains the three slaves, sent one at a time, but does not have the third killed (as in Mark), as he wants to hold this climactic offence for the treatment of the son.

In one way or another, in all four versions the narrative of the parable ends with the sending of the son. This is undoubtedly a secondary feature. It reflects the interpretation of the death of Christ in relation to Israel's whole history as set forth in the speech of Stephen before the Sanhedrin (Acts 7), summed up in his final outburst: 'You stiff-necked people . . . you always resist the Holy Spirit. As your fathers did, so do you. Which of the prophets did your fathers not persecute? They killed those who announced beforehand the coming of the Righteous One, and you have now betrayed and murdered him' (vv.51f.).

The parable, then, does not (as it lies before us) look forward to the death of Jesus, but looks back to it, and sees it (from the perspective of the early church in its continuing conflict with Judaism) as the climactic event of a long history of rejection of God's prophets. It was bad enough to kill his servants (slaves), the prophets; but infinitely more dreadful was the offence of killing his Son. In any such form, it is a creation of the early church; and it is hazardous to conjecture that in some simpler, non-allegorical form it may go back to Jesus. In any case, it is for us to interpret the parable as Matthew has put it before us, not some different parable that Jesus may conceivably have created.

VERSE 33: The particulars of how the vineyard was prepared are essential to Isaiah's Song, for the owner can ask the inhabitants of Jerusalem and men of Judah to judge for themselves: 'What more was there to do for my vineyard that I have not done in it? When I looked for it to yield grapes, why did it yield wild grapes?' (Isa.5:

3f.) In the parable, on the contrary, these details are of no significance. The vineyard has brought forth the fruit expected of it; the fault lies in the refusal of the peasants to remit the owner's share to him.

VERSE 34: The slaves who are sent to collect the rent are also a feature that does not belong to the Song, which makes no mention of rental.

VERSE 35: The climactic effect of the Markan story is already lost. 'Flogged'—the literal meaning of $\delta\acute{\epsilon}\rho\omega$ is 'flay'; but it is already used in the weakened sense in classical authors (Aristophanes, Xenophon, etc.). But the sequence 'flogged, killed, stoned' is hardly climactic.

VERSE 36: There is no reason, in terms of the narrative, for sending a larger band of slaves; they are not being sent on a punitive expedition, to overpower the tenants by weight of numbers. Matthew thinks of the slaves as the prophets of Israel, and suggests that God shows his patience and good will by increasing his efforts to win Israel to obedience by sending more and more prophets to turn the people from their evil way.

VERSE 37: The sending of the son, in the same perspective, is the supreme manifestation of the desire of God that Israel should be saved. It reflects the Christology of Matthew (and of the church). Jesus is not just another in the succession of prophets, but God's own Son.

VERSE 38: It is said that in case of an intestacy, a piece of property belongs to whoever is actually in occupation—first come, first served (Jeremias, *Parables*, 75f.). This obliges us to make a host of suppositions—that the tenants think the father must be dead and his son has inherited the property, and that he has no children or other relatives who might have a claim. These peasants are not versed in the law of inheritance, or even concerned with legal rights and wrongs. They have gathered the grapes and they intend to keep them, though they know very well that the owner is legally entitled to his share; and they are silly enough to suppose that if the son is killed, no one will challenge their right to the property. They still think of him as 'the heir', not the present owner.

VERSE 39: In Mark, they drag his body out of the vineyard after they have killed him; this adds, to the guilt of murder, the grave offence of refusing burial to the corpse. Matthew and Luke have them take him out of the vineyard before they kill him; this is an added touch of allegory, introduced by reason of the significance attached by Christians to the circumstance that Jesus was crucified outside the city (cf. Heb.13:11f.).

VERSES 40—41: In Mark, Jesus answers his own question: 'He will come and destroy the tenants and will give the vineyard to others.' (So also Luke.) But Matthew has his hearers—still the chief priests and elders (v.23) or the Pharisees (v.45)—give the answer which is in effect their own condemnation. This is not in keeping with the statement that 'they perceived that he was speaking about them' (v.45).

'Who will give him the fruits in their seasons'—an addition of Matthew's. Since for him, the 'others' to whom the vineyard will be entrusted are the Christians, the words are perhaps meant to convey a warning that the members of the church must take warning from the fate of Israel, and fulfil their duties to God.

VERSE 42: The citation is taken from Psalm 118:22f., in the LXX version. It became in the understanding of the church a prophecy of the death and exaltation of Christ and of his headship of the community of God's people (1 Pet.2:7; Acts 4:10—11). It makes an abrupt transition from the figure of the vineyard to that of a building. It is not an appropriate application of the parable—how should the hearers equate the murdered son with the stone at first rejected but afterwards elevated to the key position? The connection depends not only upon the Christian interpretation of the parable as an allegory of the death of Christ, but also upon the Christian application of the Psalm as a prophecy of Christ's death and subsequent exaltation. All this is the fruit of early Christian hermeneutic. The citation supplies what was missing in the allegory of the parable—a reference to the resurrection and exaltation of the murdered Son.

VERSE 43: Matthew applies the saying of verse 42 directly to the hearers. 'The kingdom of God'—here certainly not 'God's kingly rule', but the *sphere* of his rule; not a future hope, but a present reality; not a spiritual ideal, but a concrete community.

'From you'—apparently the religious *leaders* of Israel, who now take the parable as directed against them. They will be identified as 'the chief priests and the Pharisees' (v.45; in v.23, the hearers are 'the chief priests and the elders of the people'). The wicked tenants no longer figure the people of Israel generally, but only those who have the responsibilities of administration. But the saying is much milder than the parable. The hearers themselves have declared that such wicked people as these tenants are sure to be put to a terrible death; but this saying threatens them only with cancellation of the lease.

But this limited application is at variance with the parable itself and with the Song of the Vineyard. In the parable, all the tenants are involved in the same guilt, not merely their overseers. It is really 'the inhabitants of Jerusalem and the men of Judah' that are guilty of all these offences, culminating in the murder of the Son. In terms of this saying, it appears that only a limited group (priests, elders, Pharisees) have been at fault; and that God will remove them from posts of authority and entrust Israel to other, more faithful leaders. This thought too has its base in the Old Testament, usually under the figure of unfaithful shepherds who will be replaced by good shepherds (Jer.23:1–4); or God himself will become their shepherd, or commission his servant David to assume the task (Ezek.34:1–24). But this is not a natural application of the parable, and the introduction of ἔθνει, 'to a nation', in place of the vague 'others' of verse 41 would indicate that Matthew is thinking of a church of Gentiles (ἔθνη) being granted 'the kingdom of God' in place of Israel, not a replacement of leaders. The emergence of the Gentile church as the people of God is at least adumbrated.

VERSES 45–46: The masses (οἱ ὄχλοι, 'the crowds') look upon Jesus as a prophet. They also looked upon John as a prophet; Matthew accentuates the parallelism by using the same words as in verse 26. For Matthew this means that they still do not know him for what he is in truth—the Messiah, the Son of God. For the moment, their respect for Jesus as a prophet is so great that the authorities do not dare to offend them by seizing Jesus forthwith; a few days later, they will be ready to shout, 'Let him be crucified' (27:22f.).

The Parable of the Rejected Invitation 22:1–14

[1] Jesus spoke to them again in parables, saying, [2] 'The kingdom of heaven may be compared to a king who arranged a marriage feast for his son. [3] He sent out his slaves to summon the guests whom he had invited, but they refused to come. [4] He again sent other slaves, bidding them say to the invited guests, "See, I have got my food all prepared; my oxen and my grain-fed beasts have been sacrificed. Everything is ready; come to the marriage feast." [5] But they still took no heed of it and went off, one to his field, another to his merchandizing; [6] while the rest of them seized his slaves, treated them with scorn, and even killed them. [7] The king flew into a fury and sent out his troops to destroy the murderers and burn down their city. [8] Then he said to his slaves, "The marriage feast is ready, but the guests who were invited were not fit for it. [9] So you must go

into the streets and invite everyone you find to the marriage feast."
¹⁰ Those slaves went out into the roadways, and gathered all the
people they found, bad as well as good; and the marriage hall was
filled with banqueters.

¹¹ When the king came in to look over the banqueters, he saw a
man who was not wearing a wedding robe, ¹² and said to him, "My
man, how is it that you came in here without a wedding robe?"
He could not utter a word. ¹³ The king then gave orders to the
servingmen, "Bind his hands and feet and throw him into the darkness outside, to wail and gnash his teeth." ¹⁴ For many are invited,
but few are chosen.'

We have now three versions of this parable; it is preserved in Luke as
well as in Matthew, and also in the Gospel of Thomas. The differences
are very great and show how much the parable has been altered, even
mangled, in transmission. If it actually goes back to Jesus, it is no
longer possible to tell in what form it was first uttered, or in what
context.

In its Matthaean form, it is a full-blown allegory. The king, as
often in rabbinic parables, is a figure of God; the marriage feast is a
symbol of the Messianic age with its plenty and its joy; the slaves
sent out to urge the guests to come are the prophets of Israel—as
in the parable of the wicked tenants, they are sent in two groups;
but there is nothing corresponding to the final sending of the son—it
would be grotesque to have him pleading with the guests to share the
festivities at his own wedding. The armies sent by the king are a
figure of the Roman armies which besieged and captured Jerusalem
in AD 70, killing and enslaving many, demolishing the temple, and
burning great areas of the city. The extension of the invitation to the
ragtag and bobtail of the city streets represents the carrying of the
gospel to the Gentiles, after Christ has been rejected by the Jews.
The inspection of the guests by the host-king must then figure the
last judgement, when God will judge the secrets of all hearts.

In this form, the parable is full of incongruities. Even though it
was the custom to let the invited guests know when to come, when
the dinner to which they had been invited was actually ready to be
served, it is hardly conceivable that a king would conform to such a
custom; still less, that he would send out a second group of slaves to
plead with his guests to show up for the feast. Again, it might be
barely conceivable that a royal invitation would be bluntly refused
while his guests went about their usual business; but it is more than
unlikely that some of them would not only refuse to come for all the

pleading, but would mishandle and even murder the king's messengers. To magnify the absurdities, the king punishes the murderers by killing them and burning down their city—which is, we must presume, his city too. While this military punitive expedition is being organized and completed, the banquet, roast oxen and all, is sitting around getting cold, for other guests to enjoy when they have been brought in from the streets, where they are still to be found amid the ruins of the burning city! And after all that, the king is offended when he sees that one of these people picked up in the streets by his slaves has come without the formal dress required for a wedding, and has him thrown out into the dark—even with his hands and feet bound.

In its Lukan version, we have a genuine parable, not an allegory. The context is entirely different. Jesus is not in the temple, not even in Jerusalem, but in the house of a wealthy Pharisee (Lk.14:1), in the course of his journey to the holy city (13:22). He is there to dine, along with other guests (14:7), and Luke makes this the occasion for a series of sayings of Jesus about the general theme of dinners—the conduct of guests, the duty of inviting those who will never be able to return your hospitality, and finally this parable, introduced by the remark of a pious guest, 'Happy is he who will eat bread in the kingdom of God!' (v.15). The parable is given as a comment on this, and its general theme is that such pious sentiments are all very well, but what is actually happening is that people are turning down the invitation of Jesus to 'eat bread in the kingdom of God', while they are occupied with their own earthly affairs. In Luke's version of the parable, the host is not a king, nor is the dinner a wedding feast for his son or for anyone else. The man sends only one slave with the last-moment word that the feast is ready. There is no mention of the guests assaulting the slave; they offer excuses for not coming, and Luke expands on the succinct words of Matthew—'one to his field, and one to his business'. One claims that he has bought a field and must go to inspect it; another has bought oxen—five yoke of them—and he must look them over; the third (again we have the familiar pattern of three) pleads as his excuse that he has just married a wife. All the excuses are paltry, and not such as could be offered to a king. They certainly involve discourtesy to the host, but they are at least conceivable. The host then sends his slave into the streets and lanes with instruction to bring in the poor and the crippled. Luke now introduces another note, with the idea of a second sending of the slave—this time into the countryside 'the highways and hedges'—v.23). This double sending is probably meant to figure first the mission to the poor with the gospel invitation which the respectable and pious people had rejected; and then, the extension of the gospel invitation to the Gentiles of the world outside. The parable concludes with the warning—in itself unnecessary—that 'none of those men who were invited shall taste my banquet' (v.24). They have already excluded themselves from participation by declining the invitation. Any allegorical element here is not conspicuous.

It might be remarked that we can hardly imagine that Luke has found this parable in Matthew and has pared it down in this fashion. Either the two evangelists have drawn it from a common source (Q), which Matthew has greatly elaborated; or it has come to them through independent channels of transmission.

The version of the Gospel of Thomas is much like that of Luke, of which it appears to be a revised edition. The host is a man in modest circumstances, not a king; he has only one servant to carry his messages. The three guests of the Lukan version have become four; the fourth pleads as his excuse that he has some rents to collect. At the end, there is a simplification—the servant is sent out only once to invite guests from the streets. And there is an independent conclusion or application: 'Tradesmen and merchants shall not enter the places of my Father.'

VERSE 1: 'In parables', though only one parable follows. This cannot be taken as related to the conjecture that Matthew has conflated two, or even three, parables in this one. If it has any significance, it may be only that in Matthew's source this was the first in a series of parables.

VERSE 2: The phrasing (literally, 'a man, a king'—$\dot{a}\nu\theta\rho\dot{\omega}\pi\omega$ $\beta a\sigma\iota\lambda\epsilon\hat{\iota}$) is framed in parallelism with the opening of the preceding parable ('a man, a householder'—$\dot{a}\nu\theta\rho\omega\pi\sigma\varsigma$ . . . $\sigma\dot{\iota}\kappa\sigma\delta\epsilon\sigma\pi\dot{\sigma}\tau\eta\varsigma$). It is a common Aramaism, with no more force than $\tau\dot{\iota}\varsigma$ (see M. Black, *Aramaic Approach*, pp.106f.,300f.).

'Marriage feast'—the figure of the feast is widely used as a symbol of the blessed life to come (as, for instance, in the cult of Dionysus, where the *bacchoi* are often pictured as enjoying everlasting revels); but it has also a more direct background in the prophetic imagery, such as that of Isaiah 25:6:

> On this mountain the Lord of hosts will prepare
> a banquet of rich fare for all the peoples,
> a banquet of wines well matured and richest fare,
> well-matured wines strained clear. (*NEB*)

By making it a marriage feast, Matthew combines with this the theme of the mystic marriage; and by introducing the son, he gives it the particular form of the marriage of Christ and the church. As early as Hosea, Israel was made acquainted with the theme of the marriage of God and his people (Hos.2; cf. Isa.54:5ff.: 'your Maker is your husband, the Lord of Hosts is his name'); and Christian theologians soon learned to think of the church as the bride of Christ (2 Cor.11: 2: 'I betrothed you to Christ to present you as a pure bride to her one husband'; cf. Eph.5:25–32; etc.). But the son plays no further part in the parable, nor does the marriage itself, apart from the feast (until the supplement, vv.11–13).

VERSE 3: 'His slaves'—once the host has been transformed into a king, the story cannot do with a single slave.

VERSE 4: 'Other slaves'—if Matthew is anticipating the punitive expedition of verse 7, which certainly figures the Roman capture of Jerusalem, he will have introduced this second mission of 'other slaves' as a figure of the Christian apostles and prophets. The 'sacrifice' of the beasts for the feast will then figure the accomplished sacrifice of Christ; cf. 1 Corinthians 5:7f., 'Christ our paschal lamb has been sacrificed for us; therefore let us keep the feast.'

VERSE 6: 'the rest' (οἱ λοιποί) appear somewhat awkwardly. They figure the people of the generation after the crucifixion (cf. Mt.23: 34) who will suffer persecution even more than the prophets of Israel: 'some . . . you will kill and crucify, and some you will scourge in your synagogues and pursue from town to town.'

VERSE 7: T.W. Manson suggested that in this verse we have a fragment of another parable, which might have been called, 'the parable of the rebellious citizens' (*Sayings*, p.225). An attempt to reconstruct it might run something like this: 'A king sent slaves (emissaries) to a disaffected city of his realm to restore order; the citizens maltreated them, even killing some of them, and the king then lost all patience and sent out a punitive expedition to execute those responsible and to reduce the city.' We might recall the story of David's vengeance on the Ammonites when they insulted his friendly messengers (2 Sam.10:1–5;12:26–31).

Whatever be its origin, it is surely a reference to the fall of Jerusalem to the Romans under Titus in AD 70. The Roman armies can be regarded as armies sent by God in the same sense that Isaiah looked upon the Assyrians as the instrument of God's anger against Israel (Isa.10:5f.).

VERSE 8: 'Not fit' is a remarkably mild way of characterizing these violent people!

VERSE 9: 'Streets' (διεξόδους) should mean something like the 'outlets' of the city—where the main roads issue into the open country; but it is probably to be taken more generally. Luke uses the double phrase 'the squares and alleys' (πλατείας καί ῥύμας).

VERSE 10: 'Bad as well as good'—Matthew lays the groundwork for the story of the inspection to come (vv.11ff.). Jesus came to call sinners; of course the gospel invitation went to bad and good alike, and especially to the bad.

VERSES 11–13: These verses are a supplement to the parable. They may be the deposit of another parable, along the lines of one attributed to a great rabbi of Matthew's time, Johanan ben Zakkai (so Jeremias, *Parables*, p.188; or better, Manson, *Sayings*, p.226). In that parable, a king has invited his servants to a feast. Some of them were confident that there would be plenty of time to prepare themselves, on the ground that the preparations would take time. The wiser ones argued that a palace was always supplied with everything needed for a feast, and that it could be put on at any moment. When the summons came quite suddenly, the wise were dressed and ready, but the others had to come in the clothes which they were wearing. The king turned away those who were not properly dressed, and welcomed the others to the banquet. The moral (as drawn by another rabbi who passes on the parable) is that people must repent and amend their ways at once, so that at any moment they may be ready for the summons of the Great King. It must be said that only a faint echo of such a parable can be found here—the 'bad and good' gathered in from the streets have had no opportunity to make themselves ready.

More likely, Matthew has himself devised this supplement as a warning to the members of the church. They have heard the gospel invitation and have been admitted to the company of the redeemed. But if they have not amended their ways and their doings, they will still be rejected at the Last Judgement. For it is certainly the separation of the good from the bad at the Last Judgement which Matthew has in mind, as, for instance, in the parable of the wheat and the tares (13:24–30,36–43). The servants who bind the culprit's hands and feet correspond to the angels of the Son of man who 'gather out of his kingdom all causes of sin and all evil-doers and throw them into the furnace of fire' (vv.41f.; there is even the same phrase as here, about 'weeping and gnashing of teeth'). The darkness outside the festive hall, and the furnace of fire in the other parable, are both figures of Gehenna. Matthew's hell is a place of fiery torment and of darkness and despair.

VERSE 14: This line is a tag, inappropriately attached to this parable. The king's slaves have brought in everyone they could find, but only one is cast out.

5 FOUR QUESTIONS *22:15–46*

The discussion of this section is greatly indebted to Professor David Daube's essay, 'Four Types of Question', in his book *The New Testament and Rabbinic Judaism* (London, 1956), pp.158–69. He draws attention to the striking resemblances between this question-sequence and a pattern of questions which belongs to the 'Haggadah of the Seder', a Jewish family service held on the eve of Passover. On this occasion, the father was questioned by his children on the meaning of the rites (cf.Ex.12:26), and in the Haggadah this was extended to include deliverances later than the exodus from Egypt. Following a formal pattern, the father is asked questions by three of the 'sons' in succession (the company often included more than one family, and the part of the 'sons' in the questioning might be taken by any of the younger men). The first question raises a point of law; the second is made with a note of scoffing; the third is put by 'the *tam*, the son of plain piety'; and the fourth is put by the father of the family on his own initiative. Granted that Jesus and his questioners are nothing like a family, nor is the occasion a domestic gathering on the eve of Passover, it remains that the pattern of questions shows a remarkable parallelism. The first question, put by the Pharisees, raises a question of law: Is it lawful to pay tribute to Caesar? The second, raised by the Sadducees, is openly a scoff at the doctrine of resurrection. The third, at least in the Markan version, is put by a scribe who is 'not far from the kingdom of God' (Mk.12:34; omitted by Matthew, who says that the questioner is 'tempting him'—22:35, see below); in the earlier version he corresponds to the 'son of plain piety'. And the fourth question, which ends the sequence, is put by Jesus himself.

The First Question *22:15–22*

[15] The Pharisees now formed a plan to ensnare him by means of his own words. [16] They sent their partisans to him, along with men of the Herodian party, to say, 'Teacher, we know that you are forthright and that you teach the way of God truthfully, without regard for those in high position, for you take no account of rank. [17] Tell us, then, your decision on the matter: Is it permissible to pay head-

tax to Caesar, or is it not?' [18] But Jesus knew what evil they had in mind. He answered, 'You hypocrites, why are you tempting me? [19] Show me the coin for the tax.' They brought him a denarius, [20] and he said to them, 'Whose head is this and whose name is on the coin?' [21] They replied, 'Caesar's.' Then he said, 'Very well. Pay Caesar what belongs to him, and pay God what is his.' [22] They were astonished by his answer, and they left him and went away.

VERSE 15: 'Formed a plan'—we have here a Latinism. The Greek συμβούλιον ἔλαβον is used five times in Matthew (nowhere else in the New Testament), but it is strange in Greek. It looks like a borrowing of the Latin *consilium ceperunt*, used often (in different tenses) in the sense of 'form a plan' or 'make a decision'. Latinisms are much less frequent than Semitisms in the vocabulary of the New Testament writers. See the remarks of J.H. Moulton in his *Prolegomena* (*Grammar of the Greek New Testament*, Vol.I), pp.20f.

VERSE 16: 'Partisans'—literally 'disciples'; here it probably means simply members of the sect. Mark does not use the word here; he seems to hold the chief priests, the scribes, and the elders responsible for the plot to entrap Jesus (Mk.11:27, 12:13). They send a mixed group of 'Pharisees and Herodians' to put the crafty question.

'Herodians'—nothing is known of such a group apart from its use here (with its parallel in Mark) and in Mark 3:6 (dropped in the Matthaean parallel, Mt.12:14). A very few manuscripts substitute 'leaven of the Herodians' for 'leaven of Herod' in Mark 8:15; this is an obvious corruption. Presumably they were supporters of Herod Antipas (tetrarch of Galilee and the Peraea at this time), or of the Herodian house, all of whom were unpopular with the masses of the population. They would not be natural associates of the Pharisees, but hatred, like misery, 'acquaints a man with strange bedfellows' (*The Tempest*, Act II, Scene 2). Herod the Great found the Pharisees his most inveterate opponents, and there is nothing to suggest that they were any better disposed towards his sons.

'Forthright'—the Greek word ἀληθής, carried over from Mark, is not used elsewhere in the Synoptic Gospels, but is a key word in the Gospel of John. It is correlative with the ἀλήθεια of the following clause—'in truth, truthfully'. They are not professing that they hold his doctrine to be true, but flattering him with feigned confidence in his fearless readiness to speak his mind, no matter who may take offence. 'The way of God' would be the *halakha* which Jesus teaches—rules of conduct.

VERSE 17: The first clause is an addition to Mark. The phrase

'What is your judgement', literally, 'How does it seem to you', (τί σοι δοκεῖ) is a locution much favoured by Matthew. On the lips of the High Priest, it calls for a legal judgement, as here (Mt.26:66).

The head-tax (κῆνσος, transliterating the Latin *census*) was a tax payable into the imperial exchequer (*fiscus*), imposed on every inhabitant of the country from the time of puberty until the age of sixty-five. It was resented by Jews as a repeated reminder of the fact that they were subject to a foreign power in their own land.

The attitude to the payment of taxes remained a moot issue in the early church. Paul still finds it necessary, nearly thirty years later than this, to lay down the rule for Christians. The authority of the state is divinely ordained, and the payment of taxes is to be made 'for the sake of conscience'. 'Pay all of them their dues: taxes to whom taxes are due, revenue to whom revenue is due' (Rom.13:1–7).

VERSE 19: 'Show me the coin' (in Mark, 'bring me')—not in itself an indication that Jesus has no such coins in his purse, but rather that he makes his critics supply the evidence for the settlement of the question.

'A denarius'—a Roman silver coin, used for the payment of the poll-tax (and in general commerce). Roman currency was the only legal tender for the tax.

VERSES 20–21: The denarius struck in the reign of Tiberius carried his head, with the inscription *Ti Caesar Divi Aug F. Augustus* (*Tiberius Caesar, Divi Augusti Filius, Augustus*—'Tiberius Caesar, Son of the Deified Augustus, Augustus'). Jesus had no need to ask; everyone knew that the denarius carried the image and the name of the reigning Caesar.

The famous saying leaves untouched the fundamental problem: how are we to draw the line between the legitimate requirements of the society to which we owe allegiance, and the demands of loyalty to God? The problem does not first arise in the context of the Roman occupation of Palestine. It was involved in Elijah's determined opposition to the religious policy of Ahab and Jezebel, and again in the stories of the three young Hebrews and of the refusal of Daniel to submit to the edict of Darius (Dan., chaps. 3 and 6). In classical literature, it is the theme of the *Antigone*. It arises quickly in the early church (Acts 4:5–20; 5:27–29). The declaration of Peter: 'We must obey God rather than men' did not suffice to solve the difficulty for Christians of the Middle Ages, in the long strife between Emperor and Pope, between kings and archbishops. In different forms it arises with acuteness when Christians live under totalitarian states, and is not ended by the determined insistence on the separation of church and state in some democratic societies. No rule of thumb will serve; it remains necessary for individuals to weigh how far they may go in submitting to demands of the state in a specific situation.

The Second Question 22:23–33

[23] On that day Sadducees made approach to Jesus. (They assert that there is no resurrection.) They put the question to him, [24] 'Teacher, Moses told us: "If a man dies leaving no children, his brother shall marry his widow and raise up offspring for his brother." [25] Among us there were seven brothers. The first married, and died without issue, leaving his widow to his brother. [26] The same thing happened with the second brother, and with the third, and so it went with all seven. [27] Last of all, the woman died also. [28] In the resurrection, then, which of the seven will have her to wife; for they all had her.' [29] Jesus replied in these words, 'You are in error, for you know neither the scriptures nor the power of God. [30] For in the resurrection they neither marry nor are given in marriage, but are as angels in heaven. [31] But on the doctrine of the resurrection of the dead, have you not read what was said to you by God: [32] "I am the God of Abraham and the God of Isaac and the God of Jacob." He is not God of the dead, but of the living.'

[33] The crowds were astounded at his teaching, when they heard this.

VERSE 23: Matthew has already mentioned the Sadducees four times, always in association with the Pharisees, as linked with them in a common rejection of the gospel. In Mark and Luke they are never mentioned except in this episode (where everything hinges on their denial of the doctrine of resurrection). The denial of the resurrection is not a form of scepticism, but a mark of conservatism; for in the history of Israelite religion, the doctrine of resurrection was comparatively recent (G. Fohrer, *History of Israelite Religion* (ET, 1972), pp.387–90). From the Sadducean point of view, it was the Pharisees who were the innovators.

VERSE 24: 'Moses'—regarded as the giver of the law contained in the Pentateuch. The words attributed to him are not an exact citation, but a paraphrase of bits of the regulations concerning 'levirate' marriage given in Deuteronomy 25:5–10, with some influence of the story of Judah and Tamar in Genesis 38. The institution was known also among other Semitic peoples. It is doubtful whether it was still in effect among the Jews of our period (see the article 'Marriage' in *IDB*, Vol.3 (1962), by O.J. Baab; esp. § 1(g), p.282). In the Judah-Tamar story, Tamar is married successively to the oldest and the second sons of Judah, and when he shows some natural reluctance to give her his youngest son, she entraps Judah himself into getting her with child.

VERSES 25–28: The example given by the Sadducees may well be a stock argument of theirs against the notion of resurrection—it is certainly meant to expose the absurdity of such ideas.

VERSE 29: 'You are in error', πλανᾶσθε—literally 'you are wandering', 'straying' (like sheep, Mt.18:12; 1 Pet.2:25; cf. Isa.53:6).

'Not knowing the scriptures'—the only books which the Sadducees acknowledged as authoritative 'scriptures' were the five books of 'Moses'. Jesus will show them that even these books provide evidence against their denial.

'The power of God'—the power which 'calls into existence the things that do not exist' is able also to give life to the dead (cf. Rom. 4:17). In the Gospel of John, the power to raise the dead is given by the Father to the Son (Jn.5:19–21).

VERSE 30: Belief in the resurrection of the dead does not carry with it the notion that they are raised to a life at all comparable with human existence on earth. The comparison with angels is made only in respect to the absence of marriage. It is not clear what ideas Jesus and his contemporaries may have entertained about the nature of angels and the conditions of their existence.

VERSE 31: It is the voice of God himself that Moses hears from the burning bush. But the words do not concern the doctrine of the resurrection. The God who speaks to Moses is simply identifying himself as the God who was worshipped by the patriarchs in their time. As McNeile remarks, 'It is an argumentum *ad literam* . . . the doctrine of the resurrection is made to stand on the use of the genitives with *theos*.' He thinks that such an argument would appeal to the hearers, and that 'the possibility must be allowed that Jesus condescended to a rabbinic style of argument' (*Commentary, ad loc.*).

In any case, the argument has no bearing on *resurrection*; at the most, it could be taken to imply the continued existence of the patriarchs, in some kind of immortality—a doctrine which has no necessary connection with the conception of the life to come which is conveyed by the term 'resurrection'. The patriarchs were still in their graves; what is implied in the argument is a continued spiritual communion with God.

VERSE 33: 'The crowds' reappear somewhat unexpectedly. They are not mentioned in the parallels in Mark and Luke.

The Third Question 22:34—40

[34] When the Pharisees heard that he had silenced the Sadducees, they gathered together, [35] and one of them (a lawyer) put a question to him, by way of a trap: [36] 'Teacher, which is the greatest commandment in the law?'
[37] Jesus replied, ' "You shall love the Lord your God with all your heart and with all your soul and with all your mind." [38] This is the greatest, the first commandment; [39] and the second is like it, "You shall love your neighbour as yourself." [40] On these two commandments hang all the law and the prophets.'

VERSE 34: In Mark, the question is put by a scribe, and there is no group of Pharisees with him, nor is there any mention of gratification at the discomfiture of the Sadducees.

VERSE 35: 'Lawyer' ($\nu o\mu\iota\kappa\acute{o}\varsigma$) appears only here in Matthew. Elsewhere in the Gospels it is confined to the vocabulary of Luke, who often uses it as the equivalent of $\gamma\rho\alpha\mu\mu\alpha\tau\epsilon\acute{\upsilon}\varsigma$, 'scribe'. In regular Greek usage, it is almost always an adjective, with the meaning of 'legal', 'forensic' (so in NT in Titus 3:9—'legal battles'). Despite a massive preponderance of textual evidence favouring its retention, it is probable that the word should be omitted from Matthew's text as an assimilation to the parallel text in Luke.

VERSE 36: 'Greatest'—the positive of the adjective is used in Greek, but in the sense of the superlative, a Semitic locution (Turner, in Vol.III of J.H. Moulton's *Grammar of New Testament Greek*, p.31, § 6; BDF, 245). In the Semitic languages, there are no degrees of comparison for adjectives and adverbs. Matthew's $\mu\epsilon\gamma\acute{\alpha}\lambda\eta$, 'great', replaces Mark's $\pi\rho\acute{\omega}\tau\eta$, 'first' (Matthew couples the two words in v. 38).

VERSE 37: In answer, Jesus quotes the *Shema* (the word in Hebrew means 'hear'), a confession of faith which goes back at least to the time of Josiah. The basic form is found in Deuteronomy 6:4f., where it runs: 'Hear, O Israel! Yahweh [the Lord] is our God, Yahweh alone; and you shall love Yahweh your God with all your heart and with all your soul and with all your might.' (*RSV* offers three different renderings of the first sentence.) In LXX, the Hebrew *lēbab*, 'heart', is in most manuscripts rendered by $\delta\iota\acute{\alpha}\nu o\iota\alpha$, 'mind'; *nephesh*, 'soul', by $\psi\upsilon\chi\acute{\eta}$, 'soul'; and *m'od*, 'might', by $\delta\acute{\upsilon}\nu\alpha\mu\iota\varsigma$, 'might', 'power', 'strength', etc. The form of the citation varies in all three Synoptics, and none of them agrees with any form of LXX known to us. Mark alone cites it in full, beginning with the opening summons (Mk.12:29), which is omitted in both Matthew and Luke —not unnaturally, since it is not a commandment, but a credal affirmation. Mark keeps to LXX in using the preposition ἐξ, 'out of' for the Hebrew *b*, 'with'; Matthew changes throughout to ἐν, 'with'; and Luke retains ἐξ for the first phrase, and then shifts to ἐν for the others; he and Mark include a rendering of the phrase 'with all your might' which is not found in the LXX at all. The *Shema* was recited every day, morning and evening, and was used frequently in the liturgy; but evidently, as with the Lord's Prayer, frequency of repetition did not ensure uniformity in the wording.

VERSE 39: The second commandment cited by Jesus was not combined with the *Shema* in Jewish recital. It is taken from a different part of the Pentateuch (Lev.19:18; already introduced by Matthew in 19:19, as a supplement to clauses from the Ten Commandments). In Luke, it is a 'lawyer' (scribe) who makes the combination; and when Jesus approves it, the lawyer asks for further enlightenment: 'And who is my neighbour?' (in terms of this commandment). This calls forth from Jesus the parable of the Good Samaritan (Lk.10:25–37). The elucidation was needed, for in Leviticus, the 'neighbour' is obviously limited to the fellow Israelite: 'You shall not take vengeance or bear any grudge against *the sons of your own people*, but you shall love your neighbour as yourself.' In the Sermon on the Mount, Jesus indicates that as commonly understood 'you shall love your neighbour' has for its converse, 'and hate your enemy' (Mt.5:43); he then goes on to give his own instruction, 'Love your enemies.' It is in this interpretation and application of the 'second' commandment, rather than in the mere coupling of it with the 'greatest and first', that the distinctive teaching of Jesus is to be seen.

VERSE 40: This verse is found only in Matthew. He has used a similar phrase to indicate the significance of the Golden Rule (7:12). Mark gives the less comprehensive saying, 'There is no other commandment greater than these' (Mk.12:31). Paul expresses substantially the same thought in Romans 13:9f.: 'The commandments . . . are summed up in this sentence, "You shall love your neighbour as yourself." Love does no wrong to a neighbour; therefore love is the fulfilling of the law.'

Neither Matthew nor Luke takes any note of the reaction of the questioner to this reply. In Mark, the scribe (there is no suggestion that he is a Pharisee) commends what Jesus has said, and is in turn commended by Jesus who 'saw that he had answered wisely' and 'said to him, "You are not far from the kingdom of God."' Matthew could not believe that a Jewish scribe had ever received such a compliment from Jesus; his question was actually meant as a trap, like the question about the tribute (v.35—πειράζων αὐτόν).

The Fourth Question 22:41—46

[41] When the Pharisees were gathered, Jesus put a question to them: [42] 'What is your opinion about the Messiah? Whose son is He?' They replied, 'David's.' [43] He went on, 'How is it then that David, speaking in the Spirit, calls him Lord, [44] when he says:

> The Lord said to my Lord,
> "Sit at my right hand
>   until I put your enemies beneath your feet"?

[45] Now then, if David calls him "Lord", how can he be his son?' [46] Not one of them was able to make him any reply, nor from that day on did anyone ever venture to put a question to him.

VERSE 41: Jesus now, like that father of the family at the Passover seder, puts the final question himself. Here it is put to a gathering of Pharisees (cf.v.34); in Mark, no specific audience is mentioned.

VERSE 42: In Mark, Jesus first asks, 'How is it that the scribes say that the Messiah is the son of David?' This would seem to imply that no one but the scribes would say this. Matthew knows that this was the general belief in Israel; and for him, of course, as for the church at large, it was the truth.

VERSE 43: 'In the Spirit' means virtually 'in the scripture'—it reflects the Jewish and Christian doctrine that the Psalms, like the Law and the prophets, were divinely inspired. But 'in the Spirit' is a Christian mode of speaking. David is assumed to be the author of the Psalm—his authorship, rejected by modern critics, was not challenged in ancient times.

VERSE 44: In Hebrew, the first 'Lord' is Yahweh, the second is the title *Adonai*, which had long been substituted for Yahweh in reading, to avoid uttering the sacred name. (The familiar hybrid 'Jehovah' is a combination of the consonants of the personal name Yahweh, which was too holy to be pronounced, with the vowels of Adonai.) In LXX, the name Yahweh was never transliterated, but the title *Kyrios*, 'Lord', was used to render it; and *Adonai* was rendered in the same way, but with the addition of the article—Κύριος, ὁ Κύριος.

The citation follows the LXX of Psalm 110:1, except that for the last phrase, 'a footstool of your feet' (Heb. 'your footstool'), it substitutes a phrase from Psalm 8:6b. Both Psalms were given a Messianic interpretation in early Christianity, and were applied to Christ ('the Lord' in Ps.110; 'the son of man' in Ps.8).

VERSE 45: To many modern readers, including even learned commentators, this is taken to imply that the Davidic descent of the Messiah is challenged. But there is no evidence whatsoever to indicate that the Davidic descent of Jesus was ever denied in the church; or that it had to defend itself against Jewish objections that Jesus could not be the Messiah because he was not a 'Son of David'. On the contrary, we have an established form of rabbinic discussion, which puts side by side two apparently contradictory passages of scripture, not to show that one is right and the other wrong, but to prove that they can be so interpreted as to show a perfect harmony.

A Christian interpreter would have no difficulty in resolving the apparent contradiction here; Jesus was 'descended from David according to the flesh, but declared to be the Son of God with power . . . by the resurrection from the dead' (Rom.1:3f.). For Matthew, the inability of the Pharisees to find the answer is just another sign of their spiritual blindness. The denunciations of chapter 23 are the follow-up.

In the course of the story, Jesus is in fact questioned again—by disciples, by the High Priest, and by Pilate.

V   THE FIFTH MAJOR DISCOURSE OF JESUS
Mt.23:1—25:46

This is the last of the five major discourses in which Matthew has assembled and organized sayings of Jesus. Like the others, it is not to be seen as a sustained utterance, delivered at this time by Jesus, but as a compilation put into this form by the evangelist. It is derived in part from Mark, in part from sayings spoken by Jesus in different contexts and brought into this connection for the first time by Matthew, and in part of elements composed by the evangelist. When and where the individual sayings were actually uttered we can no longer determine; a good many of them were literary formulations from the start. The place in which the compilation stands in this Gospel is due to the influence of the Markan source, where the apocalypse (Mk.13, taken up in Mt.24:1—36) is set at the close of the story of the public ministry of Jesus, directly before the opening of the Passion narrative. This apocalypse forms the central section of the Matthaean construction. His first section (chap.23) is represented in Mark by nothing more than the brief warning against the scribes (Mk.12:38—40, taken up in Mt.23:5f.); much of the remainder of the chapter is paralleled in Luke. The third section is made up in great part of materials peculiar to Matthew, though some elements are found also in Luke, in different contexts.

In such a compilation, no purpose is served by attempting to distinguish between sayings that may be authentic utterances of Jesus and sayings which were produced in the early church after his death and resurrection. They are all, 'authentic' or not, intended by Matthew to be received as instruction delivered by Christ the risen Lord to Christian believers, not as historical records of words spoken by Jesus several decades before the Gospel was published. Matthew does not write as an historian or archivist; his concern is not to preserve an accurate documentation of the past, but to instruct the Christians of his own time.

The fifth discourse, like the third (chap.13), is broken by a change of scene and audience. The first section is represented as delivered in the temple to an audience of 'the crowds' along with his disciples; for the remainder, Jesus has moved to the Mount of Olives, where he is alone with the disciples. But there can be little doubt that Matthew 'wants chapters 23 to 25 to be understood as a great unity' (J. Schmid, *Matthäus*, p.333).

The theme from beginning to end is judgement. As Matthew has organized it, it falls into three parts, with a powerful finale in the scenario of the Last Judgement, when the Son of man returns in glorious majesty to pronounce the ultimate doom of all mankind:

1 Judgement on Israel: Denunciation of the Scribes and Pharisees, and Lament over Jerusalem 23:1—39
    General Criticism of the Scribes and Pharisees, and Warning 23:1—12
    The Seven Woes 23:13—33
    Prediction of Further Crimes and Speedy Punishment 23: 34—36
    Lament over Jerusalem 23:37—39
2 The Apocalypse 24:1—36
    Jesus Predicts the Destruction of the Temple 24:1—2
    The Question of When? 24:3
    The Beginning of the End 24:4—8
    Effects of Persecution 24:9—14
    The Desecration of the Temple 24:15—28

1 JUDGEMENT ON ISRAEL: DENUNCIATION OF THE SCRIBES AND PHARISEES, AND LAMENT OVER JERUSALEM *23:1—39*

This entire chapter consists of a number of sayings which have no internal unity and are linked only by the atmosphere of hostility towards the religious leaders of Judaism. They can scarcely be taken to reflect the mind of Jesus. There is a sustained note of fierceness which betrays rather the bitterness engendered by persecution and by the continuing controversy between the Jewish-Christian churches of the late first century and the scribal-Pharisaic leadership which was rebuilding Judaism on intolerant lines after the fall of Jerusalem in AD 70.

General Criticism of the Scribes and Pharisees, and Warning 23:1—12

¹ Jesus then addressed the crowds and his disciples. ² He said, 'The scribes and the Pharisees sit on Moses' seat. ³ You must therefore carry out in practice whatever they tell you, but you must not follow their example, for they do not act on their own instructions. ⁴ They tie heavy burdens and load them on people's shoulders, but they will not lift a finger to help carry them. ⁵ Everything they do is done to make an impression on people; they wear broad phylacteries and long tassels; ⁶ they love to have the best seats at banquets ⁷ and the places of honour in the synagogues, and to have people call them 'Rabbi'. ⁸ But you must not take the title of rabbi, for there is only one who is Rabbi to you—your teacher; and all of you are brothers. ⁹ And do not give the title of 'father' to anyone on earth, for there is only one who is Father to you—the heavenly Father. ¹⁰ Do not allow yourselves to be called 'master', for you have only one Master, the Christ.

¹¹ The greatest of you must be your servant.

¹² Whoever exalts himself will be humbled, and whoever humbles himself will be exalted.'

We have here a catena of sayings which once circulated separately. Although the crowds are mentioned, only the first few lines are meant for them; the injunctions are meant for the disciples. The scribes and Pharisees are brought forward as bad examples, not to be imitated by leaders of the Christian community. 'The disciples', as so often in Matthew, are figures of the Christians of Matthew's own time, and the scribes and Pharisees represent (in what can only be called caricature) the leaders of the Jewish communities of the later period. The crowds stand for the still uncommitted Jewish groups who are at least prepared to give a hearing to the Christian gospel.

VERSE 1: This opening verse is constructed by Matthew. It conveys the impression that Jesus, after he has reduced his questioners to silence (22:46), gives a public harangue in the temple to the crowds that have gathered while the debates were still going on.

VERSE 2: The verse is peculiar to Matthew, and is puzzling in him. It may have originated in certain Jewish-Christian elements of the Jerusalem church which recognized the authority of the scribes and accepted their deliverances as binding, such as are mentioned in Acts 15:5.

'Moses' seat'—the post of teaching authority. This is hardly to be taken as a reference to a special chair in the synagogue for the chief elder. It is simply a metaphor; the scribes and Pharisees are those responsible for declaring to the people what the law of Moses requires of them. In practice, it was the scribes, not the whole body of Pharisees, who were trained in the exposition and application of the Law, written and oral. The Pharisees did not generally possess the learning necessary for such a task, and could not properly be said to 'sit in Moses' seat'. They were meticulous in observing the requirements of the Law as interpreted by the scribes, but they claimed no teaching authority for themselves. Matthew links scribes and Pharisees indiscriminately as the leaders of the community after the destruction of the temple and the virtual elimination of the priesthood as an effective power in the national life.

VERSE 3: The injunction to follow their direction is at variance with the rejection of the authority of the oral Law in the dispute of chapter 15, where the scribes and Pharisees are accused of nullifying the word of God by their tradition, which Jesus called merely 'precepts of men' (15:6,9). The words are no more than a foil for the charge that they do not themselves practice what they preach. As a blanket indictment of 'the scribes and the Pharisees', the charge is grossly unjust. There would be sanctimonious hypocrites among them, but most of them were scrupulous in the observance of the Law. Matthew puts them in the worst possible light, with no suggestion that they have any good features.

VERSE 4: The requirements of the Law as laid down by the scribes are regarded as a burden which the people can hardly bear. Paul himself, zealous for the inherited traditions as a strict Pharisee (Gal.1:14; Phil.3:6f.), came to look upon the Jewish legal system as 'a yoke of slavery', from which Christ has set us free (Gal.5:1; cf. Rom.7:24f.). Peter also is reported as calling the law of Moses 'a yoke upon the neck . . . which neither we nor our fathers have been able to bear' (Acts 15:10). The faith of Christ brought a sense of freedom which many had not found in Judaism.

Yet it must be remembered that there were many, probably including most of the scribes and Pharisees, to whom the Law was not a burden but a joy, and who would sing with all their hearts, 'Oh, how I love your law! It is my meditation all the day' (Ps.119: 97).

An additional phrase, 'and hard to bear' (καὶ δυσβάστακτα), has strong textual support, but is to be regarded as an assimilation to the parallel verse in Luke, where the saying is shaped into a Woe, and addressed to the 'lawyers' (that is, the scribes) alone (Lk.11:46). See the note of B.M. Metzger in his *Textual Commentary*, p.60.

VERSE 5: The criticism of ostentation and the unworthy motive of winning a reputation for piety is developed more extensively in the Sermon on the Mount (6:1–18).

'Phylacteries' (φυλακτήρια, usually 'amulets') were worn in compliance with the Law as written, 'These words which I command you this day shall be upon your heart . . . and you shall bind them as a sign upon your hand, and they shall be as frontlets between your eyes' (Deut.6:6,8; 11:18). These instructions appear not to have been taken literally until after the time of the Babylonian Exile (they were probably meant to be taken symbolically, as a pictorial way of urging Israelites never to let the commandments fade from their minds). The literature of Judaism gives detailed prescriptions about them. They were small boxes made of leather, called in Hebrew *t'phillim* ('prayers'). According to the Mishnah (Tractate *Shebuoth*), every male from the age of thirteen was to put them on for the daily prayers, morning and evening, one on the head and one on the left arm. They contained short passages from Exodus and Deuteronomy. The charge here is that the scribes and Pharisees display their piety by making their phylacteries more conspicuous than necessary. The tassels (κράσπεδα) were to be attached to 'the four corners of your cloak with which you cover yourself' (Deut.22: 12). The cloak in question was taken to mean the rectangular prayer shawl; here again, the thought is that the tassels were made unduly long, to convey the impression that the wearer was especially devout.

The proper length of the tassels was a matter in dispute among scholars. The school of Shammai prescribed longer tassels than the school of Hillel.

VERSES 6–7: The kind of conduct which is criticized here is hardly a sign of vanity. It would be strange if a person who was much in the public eye did not enjoy being recognized in ways like this. It is not likely that scribes and Pharisees generally craved such little marks of distinction beyond measure. The title 'rabbi' would not be given to all the adherents of the sect of the Pharisees. In fact, in the time of Jesus, it was scarcely a title, as it became in later generations. The word itself is simply the Hebrew adjective *rab*, 'great', with a pronominal suffix—'my great one'—and as it was often given to respected teachers, it is frequently rendered into Greek by the word $\delta\iota\delta\alpha\sigma\kappa\alpha\lambda o\varsigma$, 'teacher', as in the very next verse. In the Gospels, Jesus is often addressed as 'Rabbi', or 'Teacher', but he certainly held no office in the synagogue.

VERSES 8–10: 'Rabbi', 'Father', 'Master' ($\kappa\alpha\theta\eta\gamma\eta\tau\eta\varsigma$) are clearly assumed to be honorific designations given to leaders of the community. These injunctions are not aimed at the crowds who are supposed to be listening (v.1), but only at the disciples, and would have meaning for them only as leaders of a society which has not yet come into being—the Christian church. Before the emergence of the church as a distinct community, there was no likelihood that disciples of Jesus would be honoured by any of these titles. Matthew is not thinking of any situation in the lifetime of Jesus, but of the church of his own time, and he is concerned over a tendency of Christian teachers and other leaders to assert authority and to insist of being treated with deference by the rank and file of members. He is warning against the danger of a distinction between clergy and laity, which was already growing, at least in some quarters. Ignatius, himself bishop of Antioch at this time or very little later, thinks of the bishops as monarchs, and never ceases urging church people to be submissive to them. 'When you are in subjection to the bishop as to Jesus Christ . . . you are living according to Jesus Christ who died for our sake . . . . Therefore it is necessary that you should do nothing without the bishop, but also that you should be subject to the presbytery (the elders of the congregation). . . . . Likewise let all respect the deacons as Jesus Christ, even as the bishop is also a type of the Father, and the presbyters as the council of God and as the band of apostles.' ('*To the Trallians*', II.1,2; III.1.) Such a conception of the church is utterly abhorrent to Matthew.

VERSES 11–12: These two verses are loosely attached to the injunctions against the use of titles. Each is an independent saying. The first picks up the thought of 20:26b,27, where it is needed in the context. The second is a general maxim, based on the thought that 'The Lord opposes the proud but gives grace to the humble' (Prov.3:34, LXX; cited in 1 Pet.5:5). The impersonal passives, 'will be humbled', 'will be exalted', are paraphrases for 'God will bring low', 'God will exalt', in keeping with the tendency to avoid speaking directly of God.

The Seven Woes 23:13–33

[i] 13 Woe to you, scribes and Pharisees, hypocrites! You shut the kingdom of heaven against people; you do not enter yourselves and you refuse entrance to those who are going in.

[A number of later manuscripts give an interpolation which appears as verse 14 in the *Textus Receptus* and in the Latin Vulgate; in a few witnesses, it is placed before verse 13. It is clearly an adaptation of the warning against the scribes in Mark 12:40 (taken up in Lk.20:46f.). It runs:

14 Woe to you, scribes and Pharisees, hypocrites! You devour the houses of widows, while for a pretence you make long prayers. For this you will come under all the greater condemnation.]

[ii] 15 Woe to you, scribes and Pharisees, hypocrites! You travel over land and sea to make a proselyte, and when he is won you make him a child of hell twice as bad as yourselves.

[iii] 16 Woe to you, scribes and Pharisees, hypocrites! You say, 'If one swears by the temple, it amounts to nothing, but if he swears by the gold of the temple, his oath is binding.' 17 Fools, and blind! Which is greater—the gold, or the temple that sanctifies the gold? 18 You say, again, 'If one swears by the altar, it is nothing; but if one swears by the gift that is laid upon it, his oath is binding.' 19 Blind that you are! Which is greater—the gift, or the altar that sanctifies the gift? 20 Accordingly, one who swears by the altar swears by it and by everything that is upon it; 21 anyone who swears by the temple swears by it and by him who dwells in it; 22 and one who swears by heaven swears by the throne of God and by him who sits upon it.

[iv] 23 Woe to you, scribes and Pharisees, hypocrites! You tithe

mint and dill and cummin, but you neglect the weightier requirements of the Law—justice, mercy, and faithfulness. These you ought
to observe, without neglecting the others. [24] You blind guides! You
strain out a gnat and swallow a camel.

[v] [25] Woe to you, scribes and Pharisees, hypocrites! You clean
the outside of the cup or the dish, and leave the inside filled with
extortion and self-indulgence. [26] Blind Pharisee! First cleanse the
inside of the cup; then the outside will be clean too.

[vi] [27] Woe to you, scribes and Pharisees, hypocrites! You are like
whitewashed tombs which look beautiful from outside, but inside
they are filled with the bones of the dead and all manner of
corruption. [28] So you give an outward appearance of righteousness,
but inwardly you are full of hypocrisy and self-indulgence.

[vii] [29] Woe to you, scribes and Pharisees, hypocrites! You build
the tombs of the prophets and decorate the memorials of the
righteous, [30] piously declaring, 'If we had lived in the times of our
fathers, we would have taken no part with them in the killing of the
prophets.' [31] In these very words you bear witness against yourselves,
admitting that you are the sons of those who killed the prophets.

[32] Fill up, then, the measure of your fathers' crimes. [33] You
serpents! You brood of vipers! How can you escape condemnation to
hell?

This is beyond question a masterpiece of vituperation. Over the
centuries, among Christians, it has stigmatized the Pharisees, and
with them the scribes, as consummate hypocrites, so that the very
term 'Pharisee' has become a byword. Among our Jewish friends, this
is not so. Among them the Pharisees are held in honour, as they were
in the time of Jesus and subsequently in the Judaism that survived
the fall of Jerusalem, the destruction of the temple, and the virtual
disappearance of the priesthood. In fact, it was the Pharisees, under
the leadership of the scribes, that gave hope and cohesion to the
Jewish community after the disaster of the war with Rome and
maintained it in vigorous being, even after the greater calamity of the
revolt under Hadrian and the drastic measures of punishment that
left the Jews for eighteen centuries without a homeland to call their
own. This was not the accomplishment of a company of hypocrites
of the type described in these 'Woes'.

Matthew links Pharisees and scribes together as if they formed a
monolithic block of whom no good could be said. This conveys a
misleading notion of their relationship. Not all scribes were members
of the sect of the Pharisees, or of any other sect; and not many

Pharisees were scribes. What was required of a scribe was advanced and dedicated scholarship in the Law of Moses, written and oral; if he became a member of a sect, that had no more to do with his professional qualifications than a doctor's membership in a fraternal order has to do with his practice of medicine in our time.

There is no such linking of scribes and Pharisees in a common condemnation ·elsewhere. In Mark there are only two Woes, but neither mentions scribes or Pharisees (Mk.13:17; 14:21). Luke includes a sequence of four Woes in his version of the Sermon, to set against his four Beatitudes (6:24–26, with 20–23), but they have no parallel in Matthew. In his parallel to the Woes of Matthew's indictment, we have in Luke a double sequence of Woes, three directed against the Pharisees and three against the scribes, 'lawyers', as he calls them (11:42–48,52). They are not delivered in public, in the temple or even in Jerusalem, but in the house of a Pharisee who entertains Jesus at dinner, while he is still on the way to the city. Despite some striking differences in wording, they are so like those in Matthew as to indicate that the evangelists have drawn them from a common source (Q), with characteristic modifications.

VERSE 13: This first Woe of Matthew's arrangement is the last of the second Lukan sequence, and it is there directed against the scribes, the 'lawyers'—νομικοί. It runs very differently: 'You have taken away the key of knowledge; you have not entered yourselves, and you have hindered those who were trying to enter' (Lk.11:52). The saying is not easy to interpret in either form, but it seems to have the general sense that they reject the gospel of Christ for themselves, and do what they can to prevent others from responding to the call. As Matthew words it, there would be the underlying thought that Christ, or the church, is the way of access to the kingdom of heaven. In the Lukan wording, it would be that the only true key to the understanding of the scriptures is that which Christ gives (cf. Lk. 24:27, 44ff.).

'Knowledge', for Luke, is the knowledge of God.

VERSE 15: This verse is without parallel of any kind in the Gospels. An excess of zeal in the making of converts has not been a general fault in Judaism. In this period, Gentiles in significant numbers were attracted to the synagogues of the Diaspora, but not many actually became proselytes to Judaism. Most of them were content to remain more or less loosely attached to the synagogues, where they learned to worship the God of Israel. They were known as 'the God-fearing' (θεοσεβεῖς, σεβόμενοι τὸν θεόν), and they provided an inestimably valuable channel of access to Christian missionaries when they carried the gospel of Christ abroad (Acts 13:43—49; 17:4). We have no evidence that there was any active propaganda among the Gentile populations of the cities; those who became adherents of the synagogues, or occasionally took the ultimate step of becoming proselytes, appear to have come on their own initiative, being attracted by Jewish monotheism and disenchanted with the ancestral religions.

At any rate, it is strange that an intemperate zeal in the making of proselytes should be stigmatized as a mark of 'hypocrisy'. This would only be justified if the scribes and the Pharisees did not themselves believe in the religion which they were propagating. Perhaps the saying is an outburst of Matthew's exasperation at the attempts of the leaders of the Jewish communities to win over those who had been converted to Christianity. The charge that their converts became even worse than those who converted them is normal— Catholics often find that converts from Protestantism are bent on showing themselves 'more Catholic than the Pope'.

VERSES 16—20: This third Woe is again without parallel in the other Gospels. It is related to the injunction against swearing which is the theme of the fourth Antithesis (5:33—37). It does not fit the charge of hypocrisy particularly well, though it might be a cover for deceit—to swear by something that you do not hold sacred while you know that your victim will take your pledge seriously. There were debates among the scribes (at least, among the rabbis of the next centuries) about the validity of oaths, but we know of nothing that bears upon the distinctions made here. The details here mentioned—the temple and its decorations, the altar and the sacrifices—have nothing but an antiquarian interest today; it is surprising that they meant anything to Matthew's contemporaries.

VERSES 21—22: These verses do not deal with further distinctions of detail, but seem to express the thought that whatever form of words is used, the one who swears is really swearing by God, and his oath is equally binding whatever the form. In the Antithesis, on the other hand, we have a flat prohibition of swearing.

VERSE 23: In the Lukan version, this Woe is directed against the Pharisees (11:42). The changes of wording are slight. In place of 'mint, dill, cummin', Luke has 'mint, rue, and every herb'; and in place of 'justice, mercy, and faithfulness', he writes 'justice and the love of God', omitting the phrase 'the weightier matters of the Law'.

Not all herbs were subject to tithe, according to the written Law, where only grain, wine, and oil are specifically mentioned (Deut.14: 23). There is, however, a general provision that 'you shall tithe all the yield of your sowing, which comes forth from the field year by year' (Deut.14:22), and this led the scribes to extend the list to include the produce of the vegetable garden. Dill and cummin are listed in the Mishnah as subject to tithe; nothing is said of mint. The thought may be that 'the scribes and Pharisees' are so particular about the keeping of the Law that they go beyond both what is written and what the oral tradition has formally prescribed. It is doubtful, however, whether anyone outside a handful of specialists could say exactly what was to be tithed and what was exempt, and this is irrelevant to the main charge—that with all this attention to detail in trifling matters like the tithing of herbs from the garden, they have not been serious about the things that really matter. The saying in its Matthaean form echoes the great oracle of Micah: 'What does the Lord require of you but to do justice, and to love mercy, and to walk humbly with your God?' (Mic.6:8).

The word πίστις, 'faithfulness', represents the Hebrew *'emeth*; and ἔλεος, 'mercy', the Hebrew *hesed*; the two are often linked in the Old Testament scriptures. Both words have wider and deeper significance in Hebrew than these Greek renderings can convey; on the other hand, the Greek words carry a range of meaning that goes beyond the range of the Hebrew. *Hesed* especially means much more than 'mercy'—it is really better represented by Luke's 'love of God' (Tyndale's felicitous rendering was 'lovingkindness', retained in AV).

'Weightier matters'—the rabbis were inclined to dismiss any such distinction, on the ground that any command that God has given demands total obedience. 'James' comes close to this when he declares, 'Whoever keeps the whole law but fails in one point is guilty of all of it' (Jas.2:10). Here we have the caution that even such a small thing as the tithing of herbs is not negligible: 'These [weightier matters] you ought to have done without neglecting the others.'

VERSE 24 has no parallel in the Lukan version. The figure is based on the practice of putting wine through a strainer before drinking it. A 'gnat'—a small insect of any kind—might be strained out, but the imagery breaks down with the introduction of the 'camel'. There would be nothing like a camel in the wine; and it could not be swallowed. This is hyperbolical indeed, like the thought of passing a camel through the eye of a needle, or the log in the eye of one who proposes to remove a splinter from the eye of another (19:24;7:3ff.). Under a legalistic system, it is inevitable that every detail should be scrutinized and defined—how much activity can be allowed on the sabbath without breaching the commandment to do no manner of work; if one leaves the house, how far may he go and still not break the sabbath? If washings are prescribed in the Law, how much water is required, must it be running water, can it be taken from a pool, perhaps a pool from which horses or cattle have drunk? Even in the Mishnah, which contains many excellent things, much attention is given to this kind of discussion. There can be no doubt that when things like this are made a matter of conscience, it will be easy to take strict compliance with them for virtue, and to be blind to the need for compassion, generosity, and even fairness. In our own experience, it is not unknown to find men and women who are personally austere but wholly lacking in social conscience, and more apt to be censorious about the morality of others than charitable to offenders against their code. They

> Compound for sins they are inclined to
> By damming those they have no mind to.
> (S. Butler, *Hudibras*, Pt.I, c.1, 1.213f.)

VERSES 25–26: The general thought of this fifth Woe is that they are like people who clean the outside of a vessel but leave the inside dirty. But the wording is absurd, as it stands; 'extortion and self-indulgence' are not contained in vessels, but in people. The figure is confused with its application. In the Lukan version, it is partly remedied by changing the wording to 'you are full' (11:39), but with that the figure of cup and bowl is left hanging. Similarly, the cleansing of the inside of a vessel does not in itself make the outside clean. Wherever it originated, this pair of sayings seems to be a somewhat awkward way of expressing the thought that is given better in the figure of the tree and its fruit (7:17f.;12:33,35). Goodness can come only out of a good heart, and outward purifications make no sense unless they begin with a purified heart.

The Lukan version, in place of verse 26, gives the strange phrasing: 'Give for alms those things which are within; and everything is clean for you.' (11:41; v.40, not represented in Matthew, runs: 'You fools! Did not he who made the outside make the inside also?') The puzzling 'give alms' here is almost certainly an error due to misreading the underlying Aramaic. In Luke, the words are not shaped into the form of a Woe; they are a reproach levelled against Pharisees alone. The Matthaean phrase, 'Blind Pharisee!' (sing.) seems to indicate that the source made no mention of the scribes in relation to this accusation.

VERSES 27–28: Tombs were whitewashed, not to make them look beautiful, but to warn the passerby against the possibility of incurring defilement by contact with a corpse. In Matthew's figure, however, the coat of whitewash is compared to an outward show of piety put on to conceal inward evil. In the Lukan version, the change of wording alters the point of the comparison: 'You are like graves which are unseen, and people walk over them without knowing it' (thus incurring ritual defilement). There is no thought of an outward show of piety, but of wickedness which is all the more dangerous for being unseen.

VERSES 29–33: This little section is composite. The Woe consists basically of the first three verses, and this is all that is represented in the Lukan parallel (11:47f.), which is addressed to the scribes alone and is more concisely phrased. Verse 32 is peculiar to Matthew; it may be his own (ironic) supplement to the indictment. Verse 33 picks up a saying ascribed to John the Baptist (Mt.3:7), directed at Pharisees and Sadducees.

The Old Testament does not indicate that it was a common thing for prophets to be put to death by those whom they rebuked. The wholesale slaughter of prophets of Yahweh in the time of Ahab (1 Ki.18:13; 19:14) is not done to punish them for rebuking wickedness, but in pursuit of Jezebel's policy of establishing the worship of the Baal of Tyre in Israel. It was revenged by Elijah's slaughter of the prophets of Baal on Mount Carmel (1 Ki.18:40), and Jezebel retaliated by threatening his life (19:2). But no such threat was made when he rebuked the royal couple for contriving the death of Naboth (1 Ki.21). Micaiah was imprisoned and put on a diet of bread and water by Ahab when he prophesied disaster in a conflict with Syria (1 Ki.22:1–28). But Samuel was not attacked or even threatened by Saul for all his boldness (1 Sam.13:13–15; 15:17–31). Jeremiah was saved from death by the princes and people, with the reminder that Hezekiah had taken no action against Micah for his prophecies of national destruction (Jer.26:20–23).

Later legend built up the picture, until it came to be believed that it was the common fate of prophets to be put to death by kings, sometimes in the most horrible forms (cf. Heb.11:35b–38). Thus Stephen is reported as challenging the Sanhedrin with the words: 'Which of the prophets did your fathers not persecute? They killed those who announced beforehand the coming of the Righteous One whom you have now betrayed and murdered' (Acts 7:52). There it is the crucifixion of Jesus that is seen as the culmination of a long series of similar deeds; here it is the persecution of Christian missionaries which will 'fill up the measure' of past iniquities.

VERSE 30 is omitted in Luke, but with his reshaping of the opening phrases it is not needed. The verse makes clear the point of the jibe that they admit themselves to be sons of those who killed the prophets in the very words with which they disavow assent to the murders. The argument of course does not hold. The Genevans who erected a memorial to declare their grief over the execution of Servetus in the time of Calvin were far from showing that they approved of that sixteenth-century piece of savagery.

VERSE 32: 'Fill up the measure'—the punishment is delayed until the measure of martyrdoms is complete (cf. Rev.6:9–11).

Prediction of Further Crimes and Speedy Punishment 23:34–36

³⁴ Let me tell you, therefore, that I am sending to you prophets and wise men and scribes. Some of them you will kill, some you will crucify, and some you will scourge in your synagogues and drive from city to city. ³⁵ So you will bring on yourselves the guilt of all the righteous blood that has been shed upon earth, from the blood of righteous Abel to the blood of Zechariah the son of Barachiah, whom you killed between the sanctuary and the altar. ³⁶ Truly I tell you, all this will be visited on this generation.

Perhaps the most striking thing about these verses is that they transfer to Jesus, as his own pronouncement, what was originally an oracle taken from a book of Wisdom, otherwise unknown. It is so reported in Luke (11:49), and we cannot imagine that Luke has attributed to 'the Wisdom of God' a saying which was given in his source as a saying of Jesus.

VERSE 34: For 'prophets and wise men and scribes', Luke has 'prophets and apostles'. This clearly identifies those who are to be sent as leaders of the Christian church; cf. Paul's words: 'God has appointed in the church first apostles, second prophets, third teachers . . .' (1 Cor.12:28). Matthew never uses the word 'apostles', except in the list of their names (10:2); he does not think of the apostolate as a standing office. He knows of prophets and thinks of the disciples of Jesus as successors to the Hebrew prophets ('the prophets who were before you'—5:12). He tells us that Jesus forbade them to be called 'teachers' (vv.8,10). He does not speak elsewhere of 'wise men' (σοφοί) except when Jesus speaks of the learned in Israel for whom his revelation remained hidden (11:25). He has already compared the disciple who is able to understand what Jesus was teaching to 'a scribe schooled for the kingdom of heaven' (13:52). His words indicate that in his church there are leaders who are known as prophets, as sages, or as scribes—they stand so close to Jewish usages that they continue to use the familiar Jewish terminology.

'Kill and crucify'—as crucifixion was not a Jewish but a Roman method of executing, recourse to Roman officials is implied. Luke reads 'kill and persecute', and omits the fuller Matthaean details of specifically Jewish actions against them. Paul tells us that he himself was flogged five times in synagogues, and Acts speaks of the pursuit of the apostles from one town to another (13:50;14:19;17:13). But it seems that the persecutions were not so continual or so terrible as Matthew anticipated. See the monograph of D.R.G. Hare on *The Theme of Jewish Persecutions in the Gospel according to St. Matthew* (Cambridge, 1967).

VERSE 35: Strange that the scribes and Pharisees should be held responsible, and liable to punishment, for 'all the righteous blood shed on earth' even from prehistoric times. The thought is that they have incurred the same guilt of murder, and that the time has now come when the long-delayed vengeance of God will be wreaked. Luke speaks of Abel, omitting 'the righteous', and of Zechariah, omitting 'the son of Barachiah'. 'Zechariah' probably means the man who was stoned to death 'in the court of the house of the Lord' at the command of King Joash (2 Chron.24:2—23). His father, according to the story, was the priest Jehoiada who had saved the life of Joash and brought him to the throne (2 Chron.23). In later Jewish writings, he is identified with the prophet Zechariah, who is called the son of Berechiah, and this traditional identification has probably led to Matthew's addition 'the son of Barachiah'. Christian legend, accepted by Origen, soon identified the Zechariah of this passage with the father of John the Baptist, and some apocryphal writings tell of how he was killed in the sanctuary, not by scribes and Pharisees, but by assassins sent by Herod (*Protevangelium of James*, sec.23). But it has been held by some that the prediction refers to another Zechariah, son of Bariskaeus (or Baris, or Baruch—manuscripts differ in the spelling of the name), who was murdered in the temple by two Zealots in AD 67, at the outbreak of the Jewish revolt. This identification was first made by Chrysostom (*c*.400), and in modern times was supported by H.J. Holtzmann, J. Wellhausen, and Eduard Meyer, all of whom take it as a *vaticinium ex eventu*. We would expect a reference to murders of prophets and righteous men which began with Abel to end with something more or less contemporary with Jesus; if the last such murder that can be mentioned dates back several centuries, it would hardly prove an unbroken tendency to kill men of God. But it is probable that the reference is purely literary, and that it begins and ends with the first and the last victims that are mentioned in the sacred history.

VERSE 36: In Luke, the concluding verse takes the form, 'Yes, I tell you, it will come upon this generation' (11:51). Matthew's 'all these things' anticipates the apocalyptic disasters to be described in the next chapter; in Luke there is no such follow-up. Both evangelists have in mind the capture of Jerusalem and the destruction of the temple by the armies of Titus (AD 70); Christians looked upon this as God's punishment of Israel for its treatment of his Son.

Lament over Jerusalem 23:37—39

[37] O Jerusalem, Jerusalem! City that kills the prophets and stones the messengers that God sends to you! How often would I have gathered your children together as a hen gathers her brood under her wings, and you would not. [38] Now, your house is left to you. [39] For I tell you, from now you will see me no more until you say, 'Blessed is he who comes in the name of the Lord.'

VERSE 37: The notion that Jerusalem was the scene of the murder of prophets appears again in a saying of Jesus reported by Luke: 'It cannot be that a prophet should perish away from Jerusalem.' (Lk.13:33; followed immediately by the same lament over Jerusalem, vv.34f.)

'The messengers that God sends'—literally, 'those who are sent'. The generalizing participle, in the passive, is used to avoid speaking directly of God. 'Stoning' perhaps reflects the stoning of the Zechariah of the Joash incident (2 Chron.24:20—22).

'How often'—strange enough here, stranger still in Luke, where it is spoken before Jesus has even reached Jerusalem (Lk.13:34). As the story is told in the Synoptic Gospels, Jesus has never once been in Jerusalem since his ministry began.

VERSE 38: The weight of manuscript authority would favour the inclusion of the adjective ἔρημος, 'desolate', at the end of this verse, and it is in fact included by nearly all modern editors except Westcott and Hort. For the omission, we have the weighty evidence of B with the support of L (Codex Regius, which gives an excellent text in this part of Matthew after offering a commonplace Byzantine text as far as the seventeenth chapter). It is not included in the Lukan parallel. The oracle of Jeremiah, foretelling the fall of Jerusalem to Nebuchadnezzar, is echoed throughout the passage (Jer.22:1—9).

'Your house'—the temple. It is no longer God's house, for when Jesus leaves it, it is forsaken by God.

VERSE 39: Luke has set this whole lament, with its conclusion, at a much earlier point; and he appears to think that the saying was fulfilled when Jesus was hailed just before he entered the city with the acclamation, 'Blessed be the King who comes in the name of the Lord.' As Matthew has placed it, it can only be an anticipation of his coming in power and glory. The city will then acclaim him whom they have time and again ('how often'!) rejected, and are now about to send to his death.

It should be clear that there is very little in this chapter that can be regarded as language ever used by Jesus, or at all in accordance with his spirit. It is manifestly impossible to imagine him as delivering such a scathing denunciation in the temple. Obviously, the scribes and the Pharisees are not standing quietly among the crowds to hear themselves denounced in these unmeasured terms, and no conceivable purpose could be served by damning them *in absentia* for the benefit of the crowds, or of Jesus' own disciples.

A Christian expositor is under no obligation to defend such a mass of vituperation, even if it may be excused in Matthew to some extent by the inflamed hostility of the persecuted. The best that can be said is that the words may be taken as a warning addressed to the church and its leaders against allowing the hypocritical attitudes here denounced to develop in their own ranks. Matthew has no illusions about the character of the church as he knows it (24:10–12), and he may be using the scribes and Pharisees, as he describes them, as examples of what Christians must avoid *in themselves.*

2 THE APOCALYPSE 24:1–36

Nearly everything in this apocalyptic section of Matthew is taken over from Mark, but is greatly reduced in importance. In Mark it occupies a surprisingly great place, for it is the last and by far the longest of the collections of sayings of Jesus in the Gospel, and it is set at the end of the story of the public ministry. In Matthew, on the other hand, it is not complete in itself but is made part of the long discourse on Judgement which occupies three whole chapters. Moreover, the Matthaean discourse is only one of five major collections of sayings and is much less important than the great Sermon, which is the first of the five. Even within the extended Matthaean discourse on the end of the age, the apocalypse is outweighed in significance by the series of parables which follow it and the powerful scenario of the Last Judgement which forms its conclusion. The apocalyptic materials which are derived from Mark are subordinated to other modes of eschatological instruction.

Jesus Predicts the Destruction of the Temple 24:1–2

¹ Jesus went out of the temple and was going on his way when his
disciples made approach to him to point out to him the buildings of
the temple. ² He responded by saying, 'You are looking at all these
things, are you not? I tell you truly, not a single stone will be left
here upon another that will not be broken down.'

These opening verses make the transition from the denunciations,
with warnings of imminent judgement upon Israel, to the depiction
of catastrophes which will come upon the whole world.

VERSE 1: Matthew again takes up the narrative of Mark, with
characteristic changes of wording. We observe his formal προσῆλθον,
'made approach', and the substitution of 'the disciples' for Mark's
'one of his disciples'. The vivid exclamations found in Mark are
flattened down—'to show him the buildings' replaces the admiring
Markan phrases, 'What huge stones! What immense buildings!' In
the opening phrase Matthew brings out the thought that Jesus is now
abandoning the temple; he is not content with 'as he was going out
of the temple' (Mk.), he writes ἐξελθὼν . . . ἐπορεύετο, 'having gone
out . . . he was proceeding on his way.' Jesus puts into effect the
sentence of judgement, 'Your house is left to you' (23:38). There is
perhaps a suggestion that the desire to show him the magnificent
buildings is a kind of remonstrance, as if the disciples could hardly
believe that all this could ever come down in ruin, or cease to have
its old significance as the house of God.

VERSE 2: The response of Jesus will then carry overtones of
rebuke. Their appreciation of the architecture is misplaced; the
temple is doomed to destruction.

There is no need to look upon this saying as a *vaticinium ex
eventu*. Jesus could just as well prophesy the destruction of the
temple as Jeremiah had foretold the ruin of Solomon's temple six
centuries earlier (Jer.7:8–15). On the contrary, a prophecy after the
event could hardly have failed to mention the burning of the temple,
which was actually the means of its destruction.

The apocalypse itself does not speak of the destruction of the
temple, but of its desecration. On this and other grounds, we must
hold that the prediction was transmitted independently of the
apocalypse. In John, another form of the prediction is brought into
the story of the cleansing of the temple (Jn.2:19), and at the trial of
Jesus before the Sanhedrin, it was alleged that he had said something
like what is reported of him in John: 'I am able to destroy the

temple of God, and to build it in three days' (Mt.26:61); and at Stephen's appearance before the Sanhedrin, witnesses (said to be false) testified against him to the effect that they had heard him say 'that Jesus of Nazareth will destroy this place' (Acts 6:14). It is not possible to determine exactly what words Jesus may have used; but even the garbled accusations made before the Sanhedrin confirm the fact that Jesus foretold the destruction of the temple.

The Question of When? 24:3

³ While he was sitting on the Mount of Olives, the disciples made approach to him privately to ask: 'Tell us, when shall these things be? What will be the sign of your Parousia, and of the end of the age?'

The setting is taken directly from Mark, with no reference to the walk from the temple to the Mount of Olives a few hundred yards away. He omits Mark's phrase 'opposite the temple', as a needless precision. Again he introduces his favoured προσῆλθον, 'made approach'; and he substitutes 'the disciples' for Mark's select group of four—Peter and Andrew, James and John; just as in verse 1 he had substituted 'his disciples' for 'one of his disciples'. The ridge known as the Mount of Olives is more than two miles long. As will be seen, the whole discourse (at least to v.31) is a chain of common-places of apocalyptic imagery and cannot be imagined to contain much that goes back to Jesus. The site given by Mark for its delivery is not based on some recollection that Jesus spoke such words there; it may have some vague relation to the mention of the Mount in the apocalyptic vision of the capture and sack of Jerusalem in Zechariah 14 (vv.1—5). Or it may be no more than a reflection of the tradition that Jesus spent the nights on the Mount of Olives during his ministry in Jerusalem (Lk.21:37; Jn.18:2).

The form of the question is reshaped to make it more exact. Mark speaks only of 'these things' (ταῦτα), or 'all these things.' In Matthew, 'the sign when all these things are about to come to pass' becomes 'the sign of your Parousia and of the end of the age'.

The word παρουσία is widely used in inscriptions and papyri of the arrival, or expected arrival, of a person of high rank, as of an emperor's visit to a province, or the coming of a governor or other high official to a city. It has also a place in cultic usage, of the manifested presence of a divinity. Paul uses it several times of the advent of Jesus the risen Lord, the sense it has here; but it is never used in any of the other Gospels, nor in Matthew apart from this chapter. It is undoubtedly an anticipation of the technical usage of the word in the apostolic church. There was nothing to lead the disciples to think of the 'end of the age' in terms of the Parousia of the Lord Jesus, while they could make nothing of his prediction of resurrection.

See the study of the word by G. Milligan in his commentary on the epistles to the Thessalonians (*ICC*, 1908, Appendix F, pp.145–48).

The Beginning of the End 24:4–8

⁴ Jesus made this response: 'Take care that no one leads you astray. ⁵ For many will come in my name, saying, "I am the Christ", and they will lead many astray. ⁶ You will be hearing of wars and tidings of wars; see that you are not alarmed, for these things must be, and it is not yet the end. ⁷ Nation will rise against nation, and kingdom against kingdom, and there will be famines and earthquakes in one place after another. ⁸ All this is but the beginning of the pangs of birth.'

These verses follow Mark with no more than trifling changes—a word or two added ('the Christ'—v.5; 'famines and'—v.7; 'all' v.8), and one or two minor transpositions (v.8). In the main, the words and the word order are identical in the two Gospels.

The question 'when?' is not answered except by the 'not yet' of verse 6. Jesus undertakes to make it clear that life on earth is to continue for some time, and that difficult and dangerous experiences are in store before history comes to an end.

VERSES 4–5: The general warning against falling victim to any deceiver is related in the first instance to claimants to Messiahship. To come 'in my name' might mean 'claiming to be sent by me'; but the assertion 'I am the Christ' indicates the rise of impostors posing as Messiah. Probably Matthew thinks in terms of the Christian community awaiting the coming of the risen Christ in his glorious majesty, and the warning is meant to put Christians on their guard against anyone who professes to be Jesus reincarnated. The warning is elaborated along such lines in verses 23–27 [28] below.

VERSES 6–7: The establishment of the *pax Romana* by Augustus had largely put an end to the incessant wars that had plagued all the lands of the Mediterranean from the late fourth century BC on. These sayings anticipate a return to the chaotic conditions of the

Hellenistic Age. Famine still threatened whenever there was a crop failure (Mark's text does not mention famines; Luke has the word play λιμοὶ καὶ λοιμοί, 'famines and pestilences'—21:11). Famine and pestilence are apt to be a consequence of war. Earthquakes, however, come as often in peace as in wartime; but the apocalyptic outlook tends to include natural disasters with social chaos as marks of the collapse of the old order; cf. verse 29 below. Luke adds a mention of celestial phenomena: 'there will be terrors and great signs from heaven' (21:11).

VERSE 8: 'Beginning of birthpangs' (ἀρχὴ ὠδίνων)—The convulsions in society and in nature, terrifying in themselves, are seen under a positive aspect; in the same vein, rabbinical writings sometimes speak of 'birthpangs of Messiah'. A similar thought is given in the Gospel of John. 'When a woman is in travail she has sorrow, because her hour has come; but when she is delivered of the child she no longer remembers the anguish for joy that a child is born into the world. So you have sorrow now, but I will see you again and your hearts will rejoice, and no one will take your joy from you' (Jn.16: 21f.).

Effects of Persecution 24:9–14

⁹ Then they will deliver you up to tribulation and will put you to death; you will be hated by all nations for my sake. ¹⁰ Many will renounce their faith, and betray one another, and hate one another. ¹¹ Many false prophets will arise, and will lead many astray. ¹² Lawlessness will increase more and more, and because of this, the love of most will grow cold; ¹³ but whoever endures to the end will be saved. ¹⁴ This gospel of the kingdom will be preached over all the world for a testimony to all the nations, and only then will come the end.

At this point in the Markan apocalypse (Mk.13:9–13) comes a section which Matthew has transferred to his Mission Charge (10: 17–22), with a few unimportant alterations. A phrase or two from that Markan section is repeated here; but most of it is material peculiar to Matthew, and possibly framed by him.

VERSE 9: The second part of the verse is taken from Mark, except that Matthew has expanded 'hated by all' to 'hated by all nations' clearly in anticipation of the Gentile mission.

VERSES 10–12 introduce a note of extreme gloom over the effects of persecution, as Matthew has observed them in his own experience. He is far from sharing the romantic notion that persecution is good for the church, and that it issues in a refinement of spiritual life. It must be expected that some will apostasize—this is already noted in the 'interpretation' of the parable of the Sower (13:21). Betrayal, hatred of one's former comrades in the faith of Christ—this too came about, out of a hope of saving one's own skin by denouncing one's Christian associates. Only those who have never been under the harrow will imagine that the church or any other society is improved by persecutions. They are sometimes met with extraordinary heroism—the 'acts' of the martyrs record them for our remembrance—but it is the few that stand firm, while the courage of many more fails them under the ordeal.

VERSE 13: From Mark; repeated here after its use in 10:22.

VERSE 14: From Mark 13:10, with interesting changes. 'This gospel of the kingdom' replaces Mark's 'the gospel' without definition of its content. 'All over the world' is another Matthaean addition, and the word 'first' is omitted. In Mark, the gospel 'must first be preached'; here it 'will be preached' (future indicative passive, retaining the same verb). Mark's 'to all the nations' is transferred to the prepositional phrase 'for a witness to all the nations'; and the last sentence is probably Matthew's substitution for Mark's 'first'.

This obviously reflects an attitude very different from the saying of the Mission Charge: 'You will not have gone through all the cities of Israel before the Son of man comes' (10:23). All through this apocalypse, the end is conceived in relation to the coming of the Son of man—the glorified Jesus; this will be itself the coming of the end. In the Mission Charge, it will take place before the mission to Israel has been completed; in this passage it will not occur until the whole world has been evangelized.

The Desecration of the Temple 24:15—28

15 So when you see the desolating sacrilege set up in the Holy Place (Daniel the prophet speaks of this; let the reader understand what it means), 16 those who live in Judaea must flee to the mountains. 17 Let no one who is on the roof come down to get the things in the house, 18 let no one who is in the field turn back to fetch his cloak. 19 Woe to women who are pregnant or nursing a suckling child in those days! 20 Pray that your flight may not be in winter, or on a sabbath. 21 For there will come tribulation greater than the world has ever seen from its creation until now, or will ever see. 22 If those days

had not been shortened, not a living soul would be saved alive; but for the sake of the elect those days will be shortened.

²³ If anyone then says to you, 'The Christ is here, or there!' do not believe it. ²⁴ For false Christs and false prophets will appear on the scene, and they will display great signs and wonders, enough to deceive the very elect, if that were possible. ²⁵ I have warned you in advance. ²⁶ If they say, 'He is in the wilderness', do not go out; if they say, 'in the inner chambers', do not believe it. ²⁷ For as the lightning comes out of the east and lights up the sky through to the west, the parousia of the Son of man will be like that.

²⁸ Wherever the carcass is, the vultures will gather.

Matthew reverts to his Markan source at this point, and follows it closely throughout the section.

VERSE 15: Matthew makes additions and changes to give greater definition to the picture. Mark does not mention Daniel as the source. Matthew corrects the grammar, by replacing the masculine ἑστηκότα of Mark (a sense-construction, perhaps chosen deliberately to indicate that he takes the 'abomination' to be a statue, representing a god) by the neuter ἑστός, in agreement with its antecedent noun. He also changes Mark's vague 'where he ought not to be', into the more precise ἐν τόπῳ ἁγίῳ, 'in [the] Holy Place'. Otherwise, he copies Mark word for word.

The 'desolating sacrilege'—τὸ βδέλυγμα τῆς ἐρημώσεως is a more or less literal rendering (LXX) of a Hebrew phrase of Daniel, *shiqūts shomēm*. The Hebrew phrase is itself a contemptuous play on the proper Semitic form *baʾal shamēm* (Aramaic; Hebrew *baʾal shamayim*), 'the Baʾal [i.e. Lord] of the heavens'. There were a multitude of Semitic baʾals—many of them distinguished only by the name of the place where they were worshipped (the baʾal of Beyrouth, of Tyre, of Damascus, or even of small hamlets); nearly all of them were identified by the Greeks with Zeus. The great baʾal of the heavens was called in Greek Zeus Ouranios. In early times the God of Israel was sometimes called Baʾal, and children of Yahwist worshippers were given names compounded with baʾal, as the great deliverer Gideon is called Jerubbaal (Judges 7:1; 8:29). As one consequence of the long conflict between the prophets of Yahweh and the prophets of Baʾal (especially violent in the time of Ahab, when his Tyrian wife Jezebel introduced and favoured the cult of the great Baʾal of Tyre—1 Ki., chaps. 17,18), the name baʾal came to be abhorred in Israel and was generally displaced by a mocking substitute, *bosheth*, 'shame', or *shiqūts*, 'abomination'. The name of the son and successor of King Saul, properly Ishbaal, is systematically changed in the historical literature to Ishbosheth (2 Sam. 2:8–10, etc.). In the combination used in the book of Daniel, *shiqūts*, 'abomination' is substituted for Ba'al, and *shōmēm*, 'appalling', or 'making desolate' (participle of the verb *shamēm* in the Po'el), for *shamem*, 'the heavens'.

It has a very specific historical reference; Daniel is speaking of the action of Antiochus IV Epiphanes, ruler of the Seleucid empire, in building an altar to Zeus Ouranios (Ba'al-shamayim) upon the great altar of the temple in Jerusalem (168 BC). The story is told in the First Book of Maccabees (1:54), which also affirms that orders were given to sacrifice swine and other unclean animals (1:47). But the modern understanding of Daniel as a pseudepigraphic writing of Maccabean times was of course unknown to Mark, or to Matthew who follows him. They took it for granted that Daniel was not writing of events of his own time, but of things that were to come long after his death, and that these predictions were still to be fulfilled. Daniel himself is told to 'hide the decrees and seal the book until the time of the end'—$\H{\epsilon}\omega\varsigma$ $\kappa\alpha\iota\rho\sigma\hat{\upsilon}$ $\sigma\upsilon\nu\tau\epsilon\lambda\epsilon\iota\alpha\varsigma$ (Dan.12.4, LXX, Theodotion; cf. $\sigma\upsilon\nu\tau\acute{\epsilon}\lambda\epsilon\iota\alpha$ $\tau\sigma\hat{\upsilon}$ $\alpha\iota\hat{\omega}\nu\sigma\varsigma$, v.3). The evangelists had some knowledge of the profanation of the temple by Antiochus Epiphanes, but they probably saw in it no more than a foreshadowing of an ordeal still to come, at 'the time of the end'. They were far from imagining that in Daniel's perspective the time of the end meant the age of the Maccabees. For them, the time of the end was marked by the coming of Jesus in power or, as Matthew puts it, by 'the Parousia of the Son of man' and the establishment of the kingdom of God.

They are working with a circle of ideas such as are reflected in 2 Thessalonians, where we hear of a 'man of lawlessness . . . , the son of perdition, who opposes and exalts himself against every so-called god or object or worship, so that he takes his seat in the temple of God, proclaiming himself to be God' (2:3f.; cf. vv.9f.). Something like this is imagined by Matthew (and Mark) as the meaning behind the cryptic 'desolating sacrilege' of the book of Daniel. Notions of an 'Antichrist' were widely current in early Christian circles. See the excursus of R.H. Charles, on 'The Antichrist, Beliar, and Neronic Myths, and their ultimate Fusion in early Christian Literature' (*Revelation, ICC*, 1920, Vol.II, pp.76–87).

It has often been suggested that in this part of the chapter, Mark made use of a 'little apocalypse' which was originally called forth by the threat of Caligula (Gaius Caesar), the short-lived successor of Tiberius, to have his statue erected in the Holy of Holies of the temple in Jerusalem; he actually sent orders to Petronius, the legate of Syria, to have this done (AD 40). This particular desecration was avoided for a time by the delaying tactics of Petronius, and the threat was eliminated when Caligula was murdered (early in 41).

VERSES 16–22: The headlong flight suggests a civilian population trying frantically to escape the onset of an invading army. Nothing is said of Jerusalem, to follow up the veiled reference to desecration of the temple in verse 15. It is sometimes held that all this may be related to an oracle given to the church in Jerusalem at the outbreak of the Jewish revolt against Rome in AD 66, which impelled it to abandon the city and to migrate to Pella, a city of the Decapolis, east of the Jordan. Apart from the fact that there is no longer any mention of Jerusalem, the words are far from suggesting the deliberate migration of a community from one city to another. They speak of rural Judaea and of people who leave their homes in helter-skelter flight. 'The mountains' were meant originally to apply not to the trans-Jordan ranges but to the hills of the Judaean countryside, which abound in caves and caverns. Echoes of the book of Daniel are heard throughout the passage; a tribulation worse than the world has ever seen or ever will see is adapted from the saying, 'There will be a time of trouble, such as never has been since there was a nation till that time' (Dan.12:1b); and the account of the harrying of the land under Antiochus is laid under contribution. But there are no direct quotations; what we have looks rather like a free composition made by an apocalyptist working in a living literary tradition. Nothing in the passage is specifically Christian, but Jewish and Christian apocalyptic operated with the same kind of imagery and are not readily to be distinguished the one from the other. There is nothing to indicate that any actual sayings of Jesus have entered into the composition.

But for Mark, and for Matthew after him, the words were in some way significant for the life of the contemporary church. 'Judaea', then, must have been regarded by them as a cypher, and the tribulation understood as persecution of Christians in any part of the Roman world. If Mark is a Roman Gospel, as is generally held, 'Judaea' will be a cypher for Rome (as Babylon undoubtedly is in the book of Revelation and perhaps in 1 Peter). Matthew has no connection with Rome, and he may be thinking of a wider application to the provinces of the Empire. Both the evangelists envisage a persecution that aims at forcing Christians to fall into apostasy. The urgent command to flee without delay justifies the Christians in seeking to escape the toils of the persecutors; they are enjoined to confess their faith no matter what pressure is used upon them, but they are not required to invite martyrdom.

The shortening of the time of tribulation reflects a notion that the schedule of events is foreordained by God, but he remains free to alter it. 'For the sake of the elect'—not so that they may not perish in the general massacre, but that the world may be spared the last and worst stages of tribulation; compare the story of the destruction of Sodom and Gomorrah, where God is ready to spare the cities for the sake of a handful of righteous men, if even ten good men can be found there (Gen.18:23–32).

VERSES 23–28: The apocalypse now presupposes a time when Christ is awaited in his Messianic glory. The passage may have originated in Jewish circles, without any identification of 'the Christ' as Jesus. It suggests the fluidity of Messianic expectations—before any public appearance, the Messiah may be 'in the wilderness', and people are encouraged to leave home to join him there; or he may be secretly organizing his supporters from a hidden headquarters 'in the inner chambers'. The readers are warned to disregard any such rumours of a Messiah who is already in the world, but hidden, for there will be no secrecy about the arrival of the Son of man. It will be as visible to all as lightning; unmistakeable as the flock of vultures around a corpse.

Matthew has fallen into error by trying to be too precise. The lightning does not in fact spread from east to west. The grisly image of the vultures is a proverb which is not particularly appropriate to the context. In Luke, it is introduced by the question, 'Where, Lord?' (Lk.17:37), and is separated from the saying about the lightning, which would make the question 'Where?' totally absurd. The word ἀετοί generally means 'eagles', but it is used here loosely in the sense of 'vultures'. Eagles do not flock about a corpse.

The Arrival of the Son of Man 24:29–31

[29] Immediately after the tribulation of those days, the sun will turn dark and the moon will not give her light; the stars will fall from the sky, and the Powers of the heavens will be shaken. [30] Then the sign of the Son of man will appear in the sky; all the tribes of the earth will make lamentation, and will see the Son of man coming upon the clouds of the sky with power and great glory. [31] He will send out his angels with a great blast of the trumphet, and they will gather his elect from the four winds, from end to end of the heavens.

VERSE 29, except for the opening clause, is a combination of sayings from different prophets, especially Isaiah and Joel. Isaiah sings of the fall of Babylon in apocalyptic terms, relating it to 'the day of the Lord' (13:1–13). There he tells of the celestial phenomena in much the same language that we find here: 'The stars of the heavens and their constellations will not give their light; the sun will be dark at its rising, and the moon will not shed her light' (v.10); and again, 'all the stars will fall as leaves from heaven, as leaves fall from a fig tree' (34:4, LXX; in Hebrew, 'the host of heaven . . . shall fall'). This is no mere shower of meteors. 'Powers' is probably to be taken in the sense of the astral divinities, regarded as inhabiting the stars, especially the planets, and dominating the life of earth and of every human soul—the 'elemental spirits' ($\sigma\tauo\iota\chi\epsilon\hat{\iota}a$) of the Pauline letters (Gal.4:3,9; Col.2:8,20) or the 'world rulers' ($\kappa o\sigma\mu o\kappa\rho\acute{a}\tauo\rho\epsilon\varsigma$, Eph. 6:12). The falling of the stars from the sky shows that the spirits which inhabit them have been overthrown.

VERSE 30: 'The sign of the Son of man' is introduced by Matthew. The genitive could be taken as appositive (BDF, 167)— the 'sign' *is* the Son of man. But more likely Matthew thinks of some unusual manifestation in the sky—a star, for instance, or a comet. In patristic exegesis, it was understood to mean the cross. In Christian apocrypha, and later in iconography, Jesus is pictured as rising from the dead, brandishing his cross.

The rest of the verse is drawn basically from the vision of Daniel (which appears to be the source of all the 'Son of man' imagery). 'There came with the clouds of heaven one like a son of man.' In Daniel, however, the scene unfolds entirely in heaven; the mysterious figure who bears the likeness of a human being does not come to earth, but to the throne of God, 'the Ancient of Days' (7:9–13). The attendant angels are not found in Daniel. In Matthew, they are sent to gather together the elect from all over the world; in chapter 13, they are sent by the Son of man to 'gather out of his kingdom all causes of sin and all lawless people and throw them into the fiery furnace' (13:41f.).

The trumpet ($\sigma\acute{a}\lambda\pi\iota\gamma\xi$, for the Hebrew *shophar*) was used in Israel for religious purposes and for war. It gives signals to announce regular or special ceremonies of the cult, or to order the movement of troops. Originally, it was a ram's horn. It could be blown by priests or Levites, or by commanders of troops in the field. In the imagery of apocalyptic it is blown by God or by angels, nearly always as a signal that 'the day of the Lord' has arrived (Zech.9:14; Zeph.1:14ff.). It is found in the tenth benediction of the *Shemoneh*

'*Esreh* in relation to the final gathering together of the tribes of Israel in God's eschatological redemption of his people: 'Sound the great trumpet to announce our freedom; set up a standard to collect our captives, and gather us together from the four corners of the earth. Blessed art thou, O Lord, who gatherest the dispersed of thy people Israel.' In early Christian apocalyptic, it is sounded to announce the arrival of Jesus in glory, and the resurrection of the dead (1 Thess. 4:16; 1 Cor.15:51f.); and the book of Revelation envisions the unfolding of the things that are to come to pass in the future, as seven trumpets are sounded one after another by seven angels (Rev. 8:2–9:21;11:15–19).

In this Christian adaptation, our saying assumes that by the time of the Parousia there will be Christians scattered over the whole earth.

The Parable of the Fig Tree 24:32–36

³² Learn to read a parable in the fig tree. When its branches become tender and are putting forth leaves, you know that the summer is near. ³³ In the same way, when you see all these things, you will know that he is near, that he is at the doors. ³⁴ Truly I tell you, this generation will not pass away before all these things come to pass. ³⁵ Heaven and earth will pass away, but my words will never pass away. ³⁶ But of that day and hour, no one knows—not even the angels in heaven, not even the Son; it is known to the Father alone.

The section is taken directly from Mark with hardly a word changed.

VERSE 32: The introduction is oddly phrased—literally, 'from the fig tree learn the parable.' In Luke it is given the simple form: 'He spoke a parable to them.'

In this context, 'these things' can only mean the fearful calamities which have just been described. The leafing of the fig tree, which during the winter loses all its leaves and has the appearance of being dead, is a symbol of the life that has long been concealed but is now promising speedy fruitfulness. It is like the first streak of dawn that promises the ending of night and the coming of the full light of day. It is doubtful if this is the context for which it was framed (J. Jeremias, *Parables*, p.120; V. Taylor, *Mark*, p.522; Dodd, *Parables*, p.107, n.1).

VERSE 33: Only now are we given an answer to the question of verse 3: 'When will these things be?' Even the vague 'before this generation passes away' had proved to be wrong by the time of

Matthew, and was raising problems for Christians. Attempts were made very early to apply the prediction to the fall of Jerusalem, and this interpretation still finds some support. 'The establishment of the Messianic kingdom by a Son of man coming on the clouds . . . was realized when God closed the old era by destroying Jerusalem and definitively substituting for it the Church.' (P. Benoit, *Matthieu*, p.149, n.*b*; cf. p.150, n.*b*: 'This affirmation concerns the ruin of Jerusalem and not the end of the world'. This interpretation is not tenable; it must be recognized that the entire apocalyptic framework of early Christian preaching is shattered beyond any hope of rescue.

VERSE 35: An independent saying, artificially linked with the preceding verse by the coincidence of wording ('pass away'— παρέρχομαι in three forms—παρελθῇ, παρελεύσονται, παρελθῶσιν). It appears to be applied particularly to the prediction that the events described in this chapter will all take place before the end of that generation, the very 'words' (whether words of Jesus or not) which have turned out to have no enduring significance whatever!

VERSE 36: The affirmation that the 'day and hour' are known to God the Father alone, and not to Jesus 'the Son', may be compared with the statement that the grant of an exalted place in the Kingdom is determined by the Father and cannot be bestowed by Jesus at his discretion (20:23). The subordination of Jesus to the Father is taken for granted throughout the New Testament. Even in the Gospel of John, which goes so far as to proclaim the equality of the Son with the Father, still asserts that 'the Son can do nothing of himself, but only what he sees the Father doing' (Jn.5:19). In Acts, the risen Jesus discourages speculations about the time of the establishment of the Kingdom with the words, 'It is not for you to know the times or the seasons, which the Father has fixed by his own authority' (Acts 1:7).

3 EXHORTATIONS TO VIGILANCE *24:37–25:30*

In the last paragraph of the apocalypse, Matthew has followed Mark with scarcely the change of a syllable (Mt.24:32–36 // Mk.13:28–32). Mark continues with a series of exhortations to watchfulness. The theme is stated in Mark 13:33, 'Watch therefore, for you do not know when the time will come.' Matthew also continues with exhortations on the same theme, stated in other words, 'Watch therefore, for you do not know on what day your Lord is coming' (24:42); but he no longer develops it by the use of materials drawn from Mark. One brief Markan section (13:33–35) has echoes in Matthew

(25:13–15), in the introduction to the parable of the talents, which Mark does not use at all. It has a companion-piece in the Lukan parable of the minas (Lk.19:11–27), which Luke uses to dispel the illusion that the kingdom of God might appear at any moment (v.11) —the exact opposite of the point stressed by Matthew! In Matthew the exhortations are driven home by means of five parables—the Flood, the Thief in the Night, the Slave-Supervisor, the Ten Virgins, and the Talents. In the fourth parable alone, the emphasis no longer lies on the unexpectedness of the day, but on the reckoning itself.

The Parable of the Flood 24:37–42

[37] For as it was in the days of Noah, so shall it be at the Parousia of the Son of man. [38] For as in the days before the flood, when they went on eating and drinking, marrying and giving in marriage, up to the day in which Noah went into the ark, [39] and they paid no heed until the flood came and swept them away, so will it be at the Parousia of the Son of man. [40] Two will be in the field—one is taken and one is left. [41] Two women will be grinding at the mill—one is taken and one is left. [42] Be vigilant, then, for you do not know at what hour your Lord is coming.

The comparison is not consistent at all points. At the flood, those who had taken no heed were *all* swept away; at the Parousia there is to be an element of discrimination (though we are not told on what grounds)—of the pairs, one is taken and one is left. In the Lukan parallel (Lk.17:34f.), the pair working in the field is omitted, and a pair sleeping in one bed is introduced.

VERSE 37: The Parousia of the Son of man is seen under the aspect of catastrophe.

VERSES 38–39: In the Genesis story, the extreme wickedness of the inhabitants of earth is stressed (Gen.6:5–7, 12f.). In Jewish literature there is much speculation about the generation that perished in the Flood, generally developing the theme of extreme wickedness. In our passage, there is no such insistence on the wickedness of those who were swept away in the flood, but only on the lack of preparedness, the absorption in the daily round of living. There is spiritual danger for Christians also, not alone in extreme wickedness, but in forgetfulness of the nearness of the end, and the inescapable judgement of God.

VERSES 40–41: 'Taken' and 'left'—the two verbs mean only that the two meet different fates; it is not clear which is the better destiny—to be 'taken' or to be 'left'. In any case, the theme of an all-encompassing destruction, as in the flood, is not sustained.

VERSE 42: Matthew understands the parable as pointing up the need for unremitting spiritual vigilance. Precisely because the hour is uncertain, we must be ready at every moment. There will be no last-minute warning.

The Parousia of the Son of man is now seen in terms of the coming of 'your Lord'—that is, of Jesus. For his followers, this is not catastrophe but salvation; however this further thought is not made explicit.

The Parable of the Thief in the Night 24:43–44

[43] Keep this in mind: if the householder knew at what time of night the thief would be coming, he would keep awake and would not let his house be burgled. [44] In the same way you also must keep ready, for the Son of man is coming at an hour when you are not expecting him.

Matthew has linked this parable with the passage about the Flood, and verse 42 could be taken as introducing it as well as serving as the conclusion to the preceding parable. But it is intrinsically independent. The burglar who breaks into the house by night has nothing to do with the universal catastrophe of the Flood. In Luke, the two parables are widely separated; he uses the parable of the thief in association with that of a man who wants to find his household slaves awake when he returns home in the middle of the night from a wedding feast (Lk.12: [35–38], 39f.). The connection is still artificial; the slaves are not sitting up to protect the house against burglars.

Again, the coming of the Son of man is viewed under the aspect of catastrophe. Paul makes use of the same figure but applies it to 'the day of the Lord', and goes on to speak of its double aspect, as at once catastrophe (for the world at large) and salvation for those who live with Christ. 'For you yourselves know well that the day of the Lord will come like a thief in the night. When people are talking of peace and security, then sudden destruction will come upon them . . . and there will be no escape. But you are not in darkness, brethren, that the day should take you by surprise like a thief [or, "like thieves"] . . . . For God has not destined us for wrath, but to obtain salvation through our Lord Jesus Christ' (1 Thess.5:2–9). Matthew perhaps takes this to be generally understood by his readers, but he is more immediately concerned with the Parousia as menace, and with the need for preparedness.

VERSE 43: 'Burgled'—literally 'dug through' (διορυχθῆναι). The 'house' of the figure is probably made of clay, like most houses in the Palestine of that period. The burglar is perhaps pictured as breaking in by tunnelling under a wall.

It is far-fetched to imagine Jesus as referring to a recent break-in (so Jeremias, *Parables*, p.49). Such events were not rare; and Jesus may well have used the figure—not, as the evangelists do, of his own return, but of the 'day of the Lord', the 'day of wrath' (Amos 5: 18–20; Zeph.1:14ff).

The Parable of the Slave-Supervisor 24:45–51

[45] What then of the faithful, the prudent slave, whom the master has set in charge of his household, to give them their food at the proper time? [46] Blessed is the slave whom the master finds doing just that when he comes. [47] Truly, I tell you, he will put him in charge of all his possessions. [48] But what if, turning out to be a villainous slave, he says in his heart, 'My master is away for a long time', [49] and begins to bully his fellow slaves, and eats and drinks with drunkards? [50] The master of that slave will come on a day when he did not expect him, at a moment when he did not know of it; [51] he will cut him in pieces and will make him share the fate of the hypocrites, to wail and gnash his teeth.

Luke also places this parable immediately after the parable of the burglar, which would indicate that the two parables were already put together in a common source; but Luke interposes a question of Peter, 'Lord, are you telling this parable for us or for all?' (Lk.12: 41). Even without that, it is evident that there is a change of focus. This parable is a warning to those who are entrusted with the responsibilities of leadership in the community, not to the members at large; and while the note of unexpected suddenness in the coming is still sounded (v.50), the emphasis is much more on the factor of *delay* (v.48), which gives the slave scope for bad behaviour. This will be the dominant factor in the parable of the Ten Virgins, which follows.

It is conceivable, but far from obvious, that we have here a recast version of a parable of Jesus which was originally addressed to the scribes (Jeremias, *Parables*, p.58). If we are to indulge in guess-work, why not to the priests, who in the time of Jesus were the recognized persons entrusted with the spiritual welfare of the people of God? (Dodd, *Parables*, p.127.) It is not until the destruction of the temple by Titus (AD 70) and the ensuing reconstruction of Judaism as a religion without an operative sacrificial system that the scribes won any official position, and the rabbinate acquired the responsibility of providing the people with their spiritual food. Even so, the factor of delay in the coming of the day of reckoning, which is essential to the parable as it stands, is not pertinent to the situation of either priests or scribes—it cannot be understood except as a reflection of the church's situation when it became evident that Jesus was not coming so soon as had been expected. If this parable existed in some form more appropriate to the situation of Judaism in the times of Jesus, it is not possible for us now to recover it. Our proper concern, then, is to discern what it meant to Matthew and the church for whom he wrote around the end of the first century.

VERSE 45: 'Slave'—the figure reflects the fact of slavery in the ancient world; the domestics in a great household, even the chief ones, would usually be slaves. But 'slave' is already used in the Old Testament for one who is dedicated to the service of God, even though he is a free man, so far as civil status is concerned. Paul, the great apostle of liberty, does not shrink from describing himself as 'slave of Christ Jesus' (Rom.1:1; Gal.1:10; etc.); nor from speaking of himself and his fellow apostles as 'ourselves your slaves for the sake of Jesus' (2 Cor.4:5). He will tell his converts, many of them actually slaves to human masters, that 'he who was called in the Lord as a slave is a freedman of the Lord; likewise he who was free when called is a slave of Christ' (1 Cor.7:22). The metaphor of slavery would not be so repulsive to Christians of that time as it has become to us (for little more than a hundred years!).

The parable, then, pictures the church as a great household with a staff of slaves, and concerns itself only with the head slave. Luke calls him 'the steward' ($οἰκονόμος$—Lk.12:42). Since the monarchical episcopate had not yet developed, it cannot be supposed that the parable presupposes that the church is ruled by a single head. If it does, we should have to think of it as applying specifically to Peter, or (conceivably) James, who soon became head of the Jerusalem church. But it is better to see him as a figure of every one who is in a position of responsibility in the church.

'To give them their food at the proper time'—the functions of the one who holds such a position is not to exercise authority over the others but to see that they are well fed. The 'food' will of course be spiritual food; they 'hunger and thirst for righteousness' (Mt.5:6)

The head slave would have other functions, such as the assignment of tasks, but these are not mentioned.

VERSE 46: It is already presupposed that the head slave carries out his duties in his master's absence. This is another element that would not be pertinent in a parable aimed at priests and scribes. God is never thought of as absent from his temple, where the priests officiate, or from the groups which study the Torah (cf. the rabbinical saying, 'If two sit together and words of the Law [are spoken] between them, the divine Presence rests between them'—Aboth 3:2). But the early Christians thought in terms of Christ's departure and return; in the interval, he is absent (though he can also be thought of as always with them). Paul speaks rather of our absence from the Lord than of his absence from us; but he also links this with the thought of the judgement that we must all face. 'We know that as long as we are at home in the body, we are absent from the Lord . . . so whether at home or away, we make it our aim to please him. For we must all appear before the judgement seat of Christ, so that each one may receive good or evil, according to what he has done in the body' (2 Cor.5:6,9f.).

VERSE 48: The slave who is described as 'faithful, and prudent' turns out to be villainous (κακός). He cannot be trusted to do his duty when his master is not there to keep an eye on him. Instead of feeding the remainder of the staff, he treats them brutally (literally, 'begins to beat them'), and indulges himself in drunken revelry.

The words seem to indicate that some of the church's leaders were behaving badly, 'lording it over [their] faith' (2 Cor.1:24), or 'tyrannizing over those allotted to [their] care' (1 Pet.5:3, *NEB*); and also spending their time in taverns with hard-drinking cronies. The danger of arrogance developing in religious leaders is not a mediaeval or modern phenomenon; it began to show itself in Christian leaders within the apostolic age. We would not have these warnings in the Gospels and the Epistles, if the writers had no knowledge of such behaviour to make the warnings necessary.

'My master is away for a long time'—χρονίζει, (as in 25:5). The master is so long away that the slave begins to act as if he would never come back at all. The words reflect the fading of early Christian hopes that Jesus would return quickly. The delay of the Parousia is not explained (as, for instance, in 2 Pet.3:3–9). The one concern is that the delay should not lead to self-indulgence and arrogance, for sooner or later the master will come and call the slave to account.

VERSE 50: Emphasis is again laid on the unexpectedness of the coming, and the impossibility of calculating the time (cf. vv.36,42, 44, and the echo in 25:13). The lesson, however, is not 'be vigilant' (γρηγορεῖτε) but 'be faithful'. However long the master is away, the slave is still responsible for seeing to the food of the household.

VERSE 51: 'Cut him in pieces'—there is no doubt about the meaning of the Greek verb, which is used also in Luke (διχοτομήσει —cf. our word 'dichotomy'). Such a punishment is not unknown for slaves, but it sounds so savage, in a parable that so clearly thinks of the absent master as Christ, that translators have yielded to the temptation to soften it ('punish', *RSV*). Benoit (*Bible de Jerusalem*, 'Matthieu', p.152) suggests that it is better understood metaphorically: 'he will separate him' (from the rest of his servants), and he claims that the corresponding Hebrew verb is used in Qumran's 'Manual of Discipline'; an especially striking passage couples the expulsion from the holy community with consignment to the fate of the 'accursed', as here the returning master will 'make him share the fate of the hypocrites' (in Luke, 'the unbelieving'). 'God will set him apart for evil, and he will be cut off from the midst of all the sons of light. . . . He will put his lot in the midst of the accursed for ever' (1 QS ii.16– 17; translation of M. Burrows, *The Dead Sea Scrolls* (1955), p.373). However, there is an equal savagery in the punishment inflicted on the unforgiving debtor in the parable: the king 'delivered him to the torturers, till he should pay all his debt' (18:34). As a general rule, we must refrain from applying an allegorical significance to all the details of a parable.

'The hypocrites'—for Matthew, it is the scribes and the Pharisees who are described as hypocrites; Luke's 'unbelievers' (or 'unfaithful' —ἄπιστοι) is probably closer to the original expression.

The 'weeping and gnashing of teeth' shows that Matthew is thinking of final exclusion from the Kingdom, indeed of sentencing to hell. The master of the parable is the Christ of the Last Judgement.

The Parable of the Ten Virgins 25:1–13

[1] In that day, the kingdom of heaven will be like (this story of) ten virgins. They took their lamps and went out to escort the bridegroom. [2] Five of them were foolish and five were wise. [3] The foolish ones, when they took their lamps, took no oil along with them; [4] but the prudent ones took oil in their flasks, with the lamps. [5] As the bridegroom was long in coming, they all fell asleep and went on sleeping. [6] At midnight the cry was raised: 'Ho! the bridegroom is here! Go out to meet him!' [7] At once all those virgins rose, and

trimmed their lamps. [8] The foolish ones said to their prudent companions, 'Give us some of your oil, for our lamps are going out.' [9] But the prudent ones replied, 'No! there will not be enough for us and for you as well. Better go to the dealers and buy some for yourselves.' [10] While they were on their way to buy it, the bridegroom arrived; and the virgins who were ready went in with him to the marriage feast—and the door was shut. [11] Later, the others came along and made their plea: 'Lord, Lord, open the door to us.' [12] But he replied, 'Truly I tell you, I do not know you.'

[13] Keep vigilant, therefore, for you do not know the day or the moment.

The greatest difficulty is occasioned for us in our attempts to interpret this parable by the lack of information about Jewish marriage customs at the time. First of all, it is strange that we have a story of a marriage in which the bride never appears. The virgins 'came out', but where would they be to begin with—at their own homes, or at the home of the bride (presumably they are her bridesmaids), or perhaps at the home of the bridegroom, to which the wedding party proceeds? The 'lamps' are evidently taken to be oil lamps, those small clay (or bronze) vessels in the shape of a covered saucer with a spout for the wick, of which we have countless specimens in our museums. For a nocturnal procession these would not be very suitable—torches would be the thing. Is the bridegroom coming home from his wedding, or arriving for the wedding (not merely for the feast)? There is no suggestion of what may have caused the delay (whether after or before the wedding); if all the bridesmaids dozed off to sleep, it must have been a surprisingly long delay. In a Palestinian village, would the shops be open after midnight for the sale of a pint or so of oil? Taken in all, the picture is confusing.

J. Schmid (*RNT, Matthäus*) has offered a conjectural reconstruction. The bridegroom, escorted by his friends, is on his way to the house of the bride (her parents' house), to fetch her for the wedding. As she cannot come out to meet him on the road, a group of her young friends are to meet him and to light his way to the door with lamps. After that, the whole party will proceed to the bridegroom's house, where the wedding will take place, followed by the feast. This obviously includes features that the parable does not touch upon, and does not account for the long wait outdoors of the girls with the lamps.

J. Jeremias (*Parables*, pp.172—75) stoutly denies that the parable describes a situation which is incompatible with the realities of life in first-century Palestine. He even ventures—rather extravagantly—to claim that it gives 'an artistic picture of a wedding corresponding in every detail to the reality' (p.174). His argument is based upon two points: (1) that the rabbinical materials contain only occasional allusions to marriage customs, that the references are scattered over a long period, and that they cannot be expected to provide a complete picture; and (2) that there are parallels in modern Palestinian village customs to such things as the reception of the bridegroom with lamps, the celebration of weddings at night, and even the late arrival of the bridegroom (perhaps because arguments over the marriage settlements were prolonged). It may be questioned whether Arab weddings in Palestinian villages in the twentieth century are worth much as evidence for Jewish wedding customs in the first century.

It seems that we must agree with T.W. Manson (*Sayings*, p.242) that 'this parable is a curiously involved mixture of ideas drawn from various sources.' As we have it, it is a composition of Matthew himself, possibly 'the working up of something much simpler' (p.244). Manson adds that 'what this original, and probably genuine, parable was like we have now no means of determining' (p.245).

VERSE 1: The opening formula—'the kingdom of heaven shall be compared to ten virgins'—actually compares just one aspect of the *arrival* of the kingdom of heaven to one feature of the story of the ten virgins: it will manifest itself suddenly, after an unexpectedly long delay. 'The kingdom of heaven' here is equated with the coming of the Son of man (or 'your Lord') in the preceding parables. As the coming of the bridegroom in the parable finds some of the attendants insufficiently prepared, the arrival of the Kingdom—with the Parousia of the Son of man—will find some professed Christians unready. If they have not made the necessary preparations while there was time, there will be no opportunity to make up for their slackness at the last moment.

'Ten virgins'—no significance is attached to the number ten. That they are 'virgins' is not essential for the interpretation of the parable, but it reflects the fact that certain religious rites and duties pertain to virgins. There may also be an echo of the thought of the church as a virgin espoused to Christ. (2 Cor.11:2—'I betrothed you to one husband, to present you as a chaste virgin to Christ'.)

'The bridegroom'—some witnesses add here 'and the bride'; but this is clearly introduced by scribes (fairly early, since it is found in many Old Latin manuscripts as well as the Vulgate, and in the oldest

Syriac versions, in Codex Bezae, and in a few other Greek manuscripts). It was natural for a scribe to suppose that a bride must have some part in a wedding, but in fact she is given no mention afterwards. It is the bridegroom who comes (v.10), and who refuses to open the door to the latecomers (v.12).

VERSE 2: Neither the numbers, nor the equal division of 'wise' and 'foolish' have any significance. Their wisdom and folly are to be seen only in the degree of their preparedness.

VERSE 3: The foolish are mentioned first, and the evidence of their folly, because this is the object of the parable—to warn Christians of the like folly.

VERSE 4: 'Flasks' (ἄγγεια) could be of leather or of metal (silver or bronze) or of clay, like the lamps.

VERSE 5: No blame is attached to them for sleeping—the wise and the foolish all went to sleep.

VERSE 6: Who raised the cry is of no importance to the story. 'Midnight' is not a critical hour in itself; it serves only to emphasize the lateness of the bridegroom's coming. In Mark, the master of the house may arrive 'late or at midnight or at cockcrow or in the early morning' (Mk.13:35).

VERSES 7—8: It is assumed that the lamps are allowed to go on burning while the virgins sleep; so that when they are awakened, the lamps are going out and must be refilled as well as have the wicks trimmed.

VERSE 9: The refusal to share the added provision is not harshness but common sense. If there is not enough oil for ten lamps, it is better to greet the bridegroom with five lamps burning than with no lights at all. The allegory is overpressed when it is taken to teach that in the day of judgement there is no place for the little courtesies of everyday life (so Bonnard).

VERSE 10: Nothing is said of the events that follow the arrival of the bridegroom; it is certainly not indicated that the bridesmaids escort him into the house, that he joins his bride there, and that the whole party—the groom and his friends, the bride and her attendants—go together to another house, the bridegroom's, for the wedding and the festivities. All these features are drawn by Jeremias from a description of a Jerusalem wedding of 1906 as described by his father (*Parables*, p.173), not from the parable itself. The emphasis is laid wholly on the shutting of the door, which paves the way for the refusal of admission to the five who have gone to get a supply of oil.

VERSES 11—12: Once the door has been shut, it is too late to seek admission. We hear echoes of the Lukan parable with which Jesus drives home his reply to a question about the number that are to be saved. 'Strive to enter by the narrow door; for many, I tell you, will seek to enter and will not be able. When once the master of the house has risen up and shut the door, you will begin to stand outside and to knock at the door, pleading, "Lord, open to us"; and he will answer, "I do not know where you come from . . . depart from me . . ."' (Lk.13:24f.).

[There is clearly some kind of literary relationship here. It is easily explicable on the two-source theory. Luke will have kept the Q wording fairly closely, while Matthew will have elaborated it into the full-blown allegory of the Ten Virgins. What is not conceivable is that Luke should be secondary to Matthew here—that his parable should be an abbreviated version of Matthew's. Here, as usual, it is hard to dispense with Q.]

'Lord, Lord' (*Kyrie, Kyrie*) within the strict terms of a description of a village wedding, should be rendered 'Sir, sir' (as in *NEB*). But for Matthew, the picture has already been swallowed up by the reality to which it points. It is Christ the Lord who refuses admission to the Kingdom to those who seek admission too late, and he is addressed as 'Lord' (cf. Mt.7:21ff. and Lk.13:25).

VERSE 13: 'Keep vigilant', literally, 'keep awake' ($\gamma\rho\eta\gamma o\rho\epsilon\tilde{\iota}\tau\epsilon$) as in 24:42,44. But this concluding injunction is not the natural moral to be drawn from the parable. Wise and foolish alike have gone to sleep, and no blame attaches to them for that. Those who are excluded pay this penalty for what they failed to do before they went to sleep. It 'is one of those hortatory additions which people were so inclined to add to the parables' (Jeremias, *Parables*, p.50; he includes these under the tenth of his 'laws of transformation', pp.110–14).

The imagery of a feast is well established in Hebrew literature as a symbol of the joys of the Kingdom (the Messianic age); as it is of the future life of the blessed (the initiates) in the mystery-cults of the Greek world, especially the mysteries of Dionysos (F. Cumont, *Lux Perpetua* (Paris, 1949), pp.237–58). The conception of it as a *marriage* feast is linked with the theme of the relationship of Yahweh and his people as a marriage (accompanied by the stigmatizing of the worship of other gods as 'adultery' or 'playing the harlot'— especially developed by Hosea and Ezekiel—Hos.2:1–20; Ezek. chaps. 16 and 23). On the other hand, the marriage imagery never seems to have been carried over into the Messianic expectation (Jeremias, *Parables*, p.52; see also his article $\nu\nu\mu\phi\dot{\eta}$, $\nu\dot{\nu}\mu\phi\iota o\varsigma$ in

Kittel, *Theologisches Wörterbuch zum Neuen Testament*, Vol.IV, esp. section B.1,pp.1094f.). It is in a purely Christian development that Christ is conceived as the bridegroom and his church as the bride, in parallelism with the Yahweh-Israel relationship. That is to say, the allegorical understanding of the bridegroom as the Messiah reflects the developed Christology of the early church. This in turn leads to a peculiar combination of functions—the bridegroom comes to marry the bride, but his one significant role in this parable is seen as judgement—the exclusion of those who were not ready for his coming from the festal life of the Kingdom.

If Christ is the bridegroom, one would expect the church to be the bride; but in fact, as we have seen, the bride is never mentioned and the church is evidently figured by the ten virgins. That five are wise and five foolish, five admitted and five excluded, reflects Matthew's consistent perception of the church as a mixed body. The field grows tares among the wheat; the net gathers in good fish and bad; the king's slaves bring in bad as well as good to the marriage feast which he has arranged for his son; and the separation is made at the judgement.

The coming of the bridegroom figures the Parousia of the Son of man, and his long delay is the unexpected failure of Christ to come from heaven even after that generation had passed away (cf.24:34).

The cry that awakens the sleepers is the counterpart of the trumpet in the imagery of Paul (1 Cor.15:52), or of 'shout of command, cry of an archangel, and trumpet of God' (1 Thess.4:16). Ancient exegesis interprets the arrival of the bridegroom in terms of the death of Christian believers, and this continues to appear in modern expositors (especially Roman Catholics). Christ comes for each at his or her death, and they go with him into the heavenly banquet of eternal felicity. But this does not consort with the imagery of the parable, when all who are ready are admitted to the festal halls together; the thought bears upon the corporate destiny of the church, in relation to the Parousia.

The shutting of the door is the decisive event of the story. With that, there is no longer opportunity for repentance. It is basically the thought that is developed over and over in the Epistle to the Hebrews—we must make the necessary preparation 'while it is called "Today"' (Heb.3:7–15; cf. 6:1–8 and 12:15–17). The very event which brings the faithful into the Kingdom of their longing puts an end to hope for those who have not made preparation in time.

Again, we have an emphasis which does not really hold to the general imagery. In ordinary practice, no ultimate importance attaches to the shutting of the door after the banqueting party has entered the hall. The hostess may be angry when guests arrive late for dinner, but she is not likely to send them away.

Again, if the virgins address their plea to the bridegroom and if he takes it upon himself to refuse admission to a group (presumably) of his bride's wedding attendants, it is because the imagery of the parable has given way to the realities to which it points. The bridegroom is swallowed up in the figure of the inexorable Judge.[1]

The Parable of the Talents 25:14–30

[14] Again, it is like a man who, as he was going abroad, summoned his slaves and entrusted to them his funds. [15] To one he entrusted five talents, to another two, to another only one—to each in accordance with his ability. With that, he left on his journey. [16] The one who received the five talents went off and traded with them, and made a profit of another five talents. [17] In the same manner, the one with the two talents made a profit of two more. [18] But the one who was given only one talent went off to dig a hole in the ground, and there he hid his master's money. [19] After a long time, the master of those slaves came and went over their accounts with them. [20] The one with the five talents appeared before him bringing five talents more, reporting, 'Master, you entrusted me with five talents; here are another five talents which I have gained.' [21] The master said to him, 'Well done, my good, faithful slave. You have been faithful in little matters; I will put you in charge of many things. Enter into the joy of your master.' [22] Next the one with two talents made his appearance and reported 'Master, you entrusted me with two talents; here are two talents more that I have gained.' [23] The master said to him, 'Well done, my good, faithful slave. You have been faithful in little matters; I will put you in charge of many things. Enter into the joy of your master.' [24] Finally the one who had received the one talent

---

[1] *Literature*: 'Die Tragweite des Gleichnisses von den zehn Jungfrauen', by Max Meinertz, in Wikenhauser Festschrift, *Synoptische Studien* (n.d. [1953], München), pp.94–106.

The exegesis and exposition of this parable by Archbishop R.C. Trench (*Notes on the Parables of our Lord* (11th edn., London, 1870), pp.245–66) afford an excellent example of classic, eminently sober treatment of the parables in the times before Jülicher. His footnotes offer ample citations from the interpretations of the Latin Fathers, especially Augustine and Jerome. They also indicate the kind of problems which occupied the attention of exegetes of his own day.

made his appearance and reported, 'Master, I knew you for a hard-fisted man. You reap where you did not sow, and gather in profits where you have made no investment. ²⁵ I was afraid [to take risks], so I went and hid your talent in the ground. There it is—you have what is yours.' ²⁶ His master came back at him with the reply, 'A villainous, lazy slave! You knew (as you say) that I reap where I did not sow, and gather in profits where I have made no investment. ²⁷ Then—you ought to have deposited my money with the bankers, and upon my return I would have recovered my money with interest. ²⁸ Take the talent away from him, and give it to the slave who has the ten talents. ²⁹ For to every one that has, [more] will be given and he will have more than ever; from every one who has not, even what he has will be taken away. ³⁰ Throw that good-for-nothing slave out, into the dark; there to weep and gnash his teeth.'

This is a tale of financial activities. A 'talent' ($\tau\dot{\alpha}\lambda\alpha\nu\tau o\nu$) is a large sum of money, not a natural or supernatural (charismatic) gift. The master is a capitalist, with great wealth at his disposal; not only can he put substantial amounts of cash at the disposal of his slaves while he takes a long journey, but he can speak of these as trifling sums, and promise a great deal more to those who have made good use of their initial capital (vv.21,23). He is described as a rapacious man, making profits out of ventures in which he takes no risks and others do the work—true to type, we might say, so long as we think of him as an Oriental financier of the time, but not if we try to find in him a figure of God or of Christ and to transfer these characteristics accordingly. As in several other parables, a person by no means admirable can serve as a point of comparison for the purposes of a lesson (the unjust judge, the dishonest steward—Lk.18:2ff.; 16:1–8). At two points, none the less, Matthew has broken out of the frame of his imagery to represent the capitalist as a figure of Christ the Judge of all, whose rewards are not alone wider responsibilities but a share in his own (heavenly) joy, and whose punishments are not alone rebukes for failure to make use of opportunities but condemnation to hell.

The Lukan parable of the minas (usually 'pounds' in our translations) is certainly a variant form of the same original story, even though the shape has been radically changed in transmission. In Luke's version, there are ten slaves, and each is given the same amount. The distribution is not made 'to each according to his ability', but with a view to testing their capacities. The master is a nobleman, and his journey abroad is undertaken in the hope of securing for himself a kingdom. The sums involved are much smaller —each slave is given one mina, a mere hundredth part of the talent which is the smallest sum mentioned in Matthew. On the other hand, the results of investment are still more spectacular. In Matthew, the two successful slaves double their capital; in Luke, one has multiplied it ten times and one five times. In Matthew, greater responsibilities are promised to those who have done well; in Luke, they are given cities to govern—ten to the first and five to the second. And in Luke the primary parable is entangled with another, which appears to reflect the historical facts surrounding the accession of Archelaus to power after the death of Herod the Great. He went to Rome to secure Roman consent to his succession, and a delegation of Jews was sent to tell Augustus and the Senate that they wanted no more of him—'We do not want this man to reign over us.' On his return, having been confirmed as ethnarch and ruler of Judaea, he took a bloody revenge on the opponents who had petitioned against him. So the nobleman of the parable orders his enemies to be brought before him and executed (Lk.19:12–27).

Despite all the differences in detail, it is essentially the same parable. Though ten slaves receive a mina apiece, the subsequent accounting deals with only three of them. The first two are commended in almost the same words: 'Well done! my good [faithful] slave, you have been faithful in a trifle'; the excuse of the one who failed to make good use of his mina is framed in virtually the same terms, and so also is the response of the master. And in both, we have a story of the profitable use of money.

It may reasonably be conjectured that Matthew and Luke have both, though in different ways, embellished the basic parable (it is impossible to say how much of the embellishment may have come about in transmission before it came into their hands). Matthew has increased the amount of money involved, and to no trifling degree— his five talents represent five hundred times the mina which Luke allots to each. Luke has increased the number of slaves from three to ten. 'The delight of the oriental story teller in large numbers has thus led to embellishments in both versions of the story' (Jeremias, *Parables*, p.28). Both have also given it an application to the Parousia, which must be secondary to whatever may have been its application in the mind of Jesus, and the allegorizing tendency has led both to introduce alien elements into the story. In Luke, these are influenced also by conflation with a parable based on the events accompanying the accession of Archelaus (T.W. Manson, *Sayings*, p.313; Jeremias, *Parables*, p.59). It will also be noted that Luke understands the parable as designed to remove the misapprehension 'that the kingdom of God was to appear immediately' (Lk.19:11). In keeping with this, he places it just before the arrival of Jesus in Jerusalem, not in the context of the address spoken to the disciples on the Mount of Olives. He must then feel that its primary emphasis lies in the thought that there will be a period of activity before the Parousia (he does not use the word), which the followers of Jesus will be expected to put to good use. In Matthew, though the interval is said to be long (v.19), the emphasis is on the inevitable accounting rather than on the fact of delay. The activities of the slaves are not in the slightest degree affected by the length of the master's absence.

VERSE 14: In the Greek text, the first clause is an anacolouthon (literally, it runs, 'For as a man going abroad summoned his slaves, and . . . went abroad'). It is necessary to supply something like the beginning of the previous parable—'The kingdom of heaven may be compared, in its establishment, to the story of a man going abroad.'

VERSE 15: The sums are large. It is difficult to state the value of a talent in monetary terms, but in purchasing power it was enough to pay for 10,000 days of work by a labourer—that is, to meet a payroll for a work force of 50 men for 200 days. The mina of the Lukan story is just one per cent of this (100 drachmas, or denarii, against 10,000), and no one is given more.

'According to his ability'—quite in keeping with the circumstances; but it has nothing comparable in the Lukan version, and it may not be too much to suggest that Matthew has introduced the phrase because his mind is already occupied with the application of the parable to the life of the church. He recognizes that, though all Christians participate in the gifts of the Spirit, all are not equally gifted (cf. 1 Cor.12:4–7, 27–31). Yet (as the parable will insist) the least gifted is responsible for using such gifts as he has for the glory of God and the benefit of all.

VERSE 16: 'Traded (ἠργάσατο, literally, 'worked') with them'— though the verb has a wide general meaning, it is used from classical times of trade and finance. Luke uses the more specifically commercial verb πραγματεύω but in the report of the first servant he reverts to (πρὸς) ἐργάζομαι (v.16), and there it is the mina, not the slave, that has gained the increase. It is not said what means he used to double his capital (in Luke he multiplies it ten times—another 'embellishment').

VERSE 17: The activities of the second servant are not described in detail; he did as the first had done, with corresponding success.

VERSE 18: Hiding treasure—coins or jewels—in the ground was

by no means uncommon in ancient times (it is still done when the necessity for hiding is urgent, as during an invasion by enemy troops). Most of the ancient coins in our collections have come from hoards that were buried under the ground, usually in pots; they are sometimes turned up by the chance spade of a peasant, as in the parable of the hidden treasure (Mt.13:44), and sometimes by the systematic probing of the archaeologist.

In Luke, the third slave simply tucks the money away in some corner, rolled up in a napkin (19:20). It is not necessary to hold that he 'behaved with an inexcusable irresponsibility' (Jeremias, *Parables*, p.61). A mina does not call for the precautions that were needed for the relatively huge sum of a talent (so Trench, *Parables*, p.274). The rabbinical laws governing liability for trust funds are of no relevance to the understanding of the parable; the slave will not be criticized for failing to hide the money with proper care, but for putting it into storage instead of using it to make a profit.

VERSE 19: 'After a long time'—with the enormous rates of interest exacted in the East, the 'long time' is not required for the doubling of the capital; a money-lender in Cairo told me without a blush that he regarded five per cent a month as quite reasonable for a loan to a fellah. Indeed, the American novelist William Faulkner writes of a small town banker (Snopes) who would lend a man a quarter, and as long as he was paid five cents every Saturday night, did not care whether the loan was ever paid back (twenty per cent per week!). The 'long time' in this parable, like the delay of the bridegroom and of the master (24:48;25:5), reflects the delay of the Parousia.

VERSES 20–23: The accounting with the first two servants proceeds along the same lines; each reports that he has doubled the money entrusted to him and is commended by his master in exactly the same words.

The reward of good service is the promise of wider opportunities. 'Good' (ἀγαθέ) does not mean 'successful' or 'competent'; it is defined substantially in the adjective 'faithful', and it prepares the way for the condemnation of the third servant as 'bad' (πονηρός).

'Enter into the joy of your master' could be given a meaning in keeping with the imagery of the parable; as, that the master invites these slaves to be guests at the banquet which will be given to celebrate his return from his long journey. But this is decidedly forced. The thought has moved suddenly into the allegorical representation of the master as a figure of the returning Christ, and the 'joy' is the blessedness of the Kingdom.

The contrast 'few things'—'many things' is more appropriate in connection with the really trifling sums of the Lukan version than with the 'talents' of Matthew. This affords an indication that the small amounts (minas) of the Lukan version represent better the original terms of the parable.

VERSES 24–25: The main interest of the parable lies in the figure of the third servant, and he receives much more extended treatment, at almost twice the length accorded to the interviews with the other two together.

The third slave seeks to defend himself, in the face of the success of the others, by an attack on the character of his master, which made him afraid to take any risks.

'Hard' or 'hard-fisted' ($\sigma\kappa\lambda\eta\rho\delta\varsigma$)—the word can be used of a stone, and so of a person who is merciless in his dealings. Luke prefers the milder word $\alpha\dot{\upsilon}\sigma\tau\eta\rho\delta\varsigma$ (our 'austere'), sometimes used of a government inspector of finances who is 'strict' in his examination of accounts.

The figures of 'reaping' and 'gathering' are drawn from the vocabulary of agriculture, not of finance. They refer to the way of the capitalist, who makes his profits out of the toil of others.

The slave pleads that he was so frightened at the possibility that he would have losses to report to such a master that he took no risks at all—he was only too glad that he could restore intact the whole amount that had been entrusted to him.

VERSE 26: The master will take no such excuse. Even if the slave had formed such an opinion of his master, this was all the more reason for him to try to make a profit for him. If he was afraid to trade on his own account, he could at least have deposited the money with bankers, who would have paid interest on it. What he called fear, the master calls laziness—he did not want to bestir himself in his master's interest. He is convicted by his own words, which the master quotes back at him—not necessarily accepting them as a true description. This is made explicit in the Lukan version: 'Out of your own mouth I will judge you' (Lk.19:22).

VERSE 28: As he has failed to make use of his one talent, it is taken away from him; he will not be given a second opportunity. This is still perfectly in keeping with the basic story. The transfer of the talent to the first of the successful slaves is not demanded by the story—it paves the way for the maxim of the next verse. The same feature appears also in the Lukan version, where the incongruity is so marked that the attendants protest, 'Master, he has ten minas.' (They do not remark that he has also been rewarded with the rule of ten cities, which would make an extra mina of no significance.)

VERSE 29: The saying is not integral to the parable. It is a common maxim, like our saying, 'the rich get richer and the poor get poorer'—a more or less cynical comment on the injustices of life. It does not really fit the circumstances described in the parable, for none of the slaves had anything to start with—the initial capital was given to them when they had nothing. The point is to be found in the analogy with the spiritual realm—spiritual gifts atrophy if they are not used, and increase as they are exercised actively.

VERSE 30: With this verse, the thought moves wholly into the allegorical interpretation, which in turn reveals Matthew's understanding of the entire parable. The sentence now passed on the slave is no part of the picture of financial reckonings. 'The darkness outside', as in the supplement to the parable of the marriage feast (Mt.22:13), is hell; and it is further indicated by the phrase, 'where there will be weeping and the gnashing of teeth' (Mt.8:12, and six times in all; once in Luke (13:28), where it is a symbol of chagrin; nowhere else in the New Testament).

The Gospel of the Nazarenes—a second-century Targum of the Gospel of Matthew, which survives only in fragmentary citations given by later writers, mostly in Latin but some few in Greek and one in Syriac—makes a change which is probably prompted by the extreme harshness of the punishment meted out to the third slave. It retains the three slaves; but only one multiplies the capital, one stores it, and one wastes it in dissipation: '[The master] had three servants: one who squandered his master's substance with harlots and flute-girls, one who multiplied the gain, and one who hid the talent; and accordingly one was accepted (with joy), another merely rebuked, and another cast into prison.' (From Eusebius, *Theophania*; as in E. Hennecke's *New Testament Apocrypha*, ed. W. Schneemelcher (1959), ET G. Ogg (1963), p.149.)

CONCLUSION: THE LAST JUDGEMENT 25:31–46

[31] When the Son of man shall come in his glory, with all the angels attending him, he will take his seat upon his glorious throne. [32] All the nations will be gathered before him, and he shall separate them one from another as a shepherd separates the sheep from the goats; [33] he will place the sheep at his right hand and the goats at his left. [34] Then the king will say to those at his right, 'Come, you that my Father has blessed; inherit the kingdom that has been prepared for

you ever since the creation of the universe. [35] For when I was hungry, you fed me; when I was thirsty, you gave me drink. When I came as a foreigner, you invited me into your homes. [36] I was naked, and you clothed me. You visited me when I fell sick, and when I was in jail you came to see me.' [37] The righteous will respond to this by saying, 'Lord, when did we see you hungry, and feed you, or thirsty, and give you drink? [38] Or when did we see you as a foreigner, and invite you home, or see you naked, and clothe you? [39] Or when did we see you sick or in jail, and come to visit you?' [40] And the king will answer by declaring to them, 'Truly I tell you, whenever you did a kindness to one of my brothers here, even the least of them, you did it to me.' [41] Then he will say to those on his left hand, 'Away with you from my presence! You are accursed, doomed to that eternal fire prepared for the devil and his angels. [42] For when I was hungry, you gave me nothing to eat; when I was thirsty, you gave me nothing to drink. [43] When I came as a foreigner, you had no welcome for me; and when I was naked, you did not clothe me. When I was sick and in jail, you never visited me.' [44] To this they will answer, 'Lord, when did we ever see you hungry or thirsty or a foreigner, or naked or sick or in jail, and failed to do you any service?' [45] His answer will be, 'Whenever you failed to do a kindness to one of the least of these, you failed to do it to me.' [46] And these will go away to eternal punishment, but the righteous will enter upon life eternal.

This passage is not a parable, but an apocalyptic vision of the Last Judgement, like the throne-scene in the Book of Revelation (20:11—15); there is a still more striking parallel in the book of Enoch. (S. Mowinckel, *He that Cometh*, E.T. by G.W. Anderson (N.D., c.1954), chap.10, esp. sec.12, 'The Epiphany of the Son of Man', pp.388ff.)

Matthew has been ringing the changes on the theme of the coming of the Son of man throughout these closing chapters. For him, it is the coming of Jesus ('your Parousia'—24:3); it will be as sudden and conspicuous as the lightning (24:27); he will be seen 'coming on the clouds of heaven with power and great glory; and he will send out his angels with a loud trumpet call, and they will gather his elect from the four winds' (24:30f.). The day and the hour are unknown, and the world will be taken by surprise (24:36—42); like the burglar who breaks in at night, it will be unforeseen (24:43); it will be a day of reckoning, and woe betide the unfaithful (24:45—51). It may be delayed (24:48;25:5,19), but it is none the less certain, and woe to those who are not ready. Now he pictures it as an enthronement scene, when the Son of man is revealed as King and Judge of all the nations of earth, and appoints to each person his eternal destiny.

VERSE 31: Previously, the angels have been sent out by the Son of man—to 'gather out of his kingdom all causes of sin and all evildoers', 'to separate the evil from the righteous' (13:41,49f.), or 'to gather his elect from the four winds' (24:31). Here they have no active part tò play; they simply accompany the Son of man as a heavenly escort of honour.

'His glorious throne' ('throne of his glory' is a literal rendering of the Semitic idiom) is God's throne. As the term 'Son of man' is not used again in the passage, but is replaced by 'king' (vv.34, 40), it is possible that the king figure was original, and 'Son of man' a Christian adaptation. In Jewish prayers, God is often addressed as King, and there are many 'king parables' in which the king represents God. But would God be conceived as present in the persons of the hungry, the naked, the sick, the prisoner, the foreigner; and would he call them his brothers, in an imagery of purely Jewish inspiration? Is this imagery possible without the incarnation?

VERSE 32: 'All the nations'—to many commentators, this phrase suggests that it is only the Gentiles (ἔθνη) that are gathered before the Judge. This is surely insisting too strongly on the usual meaning of ἔθνη in Jewish terminology. It is simply not conceivable that the evangelist should think of God (or his appointed representative, the Son of man) as judging the Gentiles by one standard and the Jews by another. He is picturing a judgement of all mankind, without racial discrimination. When the judge separates them one from another, he is separating them as individuals, not as national groupings.

VERSE 33: There is no suggestion that they are there to be tried; the judgement as to their guilt has already been made, and all that remains is to pass sentence.

There is perhaps some echo here of the imagery of Ezekiel 34. In verse 17 we read: 'As for you, my flock, thus says the Lord: Behold, I judge between sheep and sheep, rams and he-goats.' But this is not to provide a better thing for the sheep than for the goats; as it goes on, 'Behold, I, I myself, will judge between the fat sheep and the lean sheep . . . I will judge between sheep and sheep' (vv.20,22). The imagery of Ezekiel is not exploited. There is no reason to see in the phrasing of Matthew anything more than an observation of what a shepherd actually does; when he brings his mixed flock into the fold, he puts the sheep into one area and the goats into another. That the sheep are put on his right and the goats on his left is no part of the analogy; it is an indication of the sentence that the Judge is about to pass. The right is the side of good omen, the left the side of ill omen. In keeping with this widespread notion of the distinction between the right and the left, it is natural that the Greeks should conceive that souls destined for the Elysian Fields should take the road to the right, and the souls sentenced to the pains of Tartarus should take the road to the left (Plato, *Republic* X.614C).

VERSE 34: 'The king'—at his Parousia, the Son of man is revealed as king. He has taken his place upon his glorious throne. 'This means that his enthronement is not only something which is visible in heaven. It is the great change of the ages, inaugurating the judgement and the age to come. Therefore it is also a revelation to the whole world . . . a cosmic event.' (Mowinckel, *He that Cometh*, p.389.)

The King—Son of man is not identified with God; he is God's Son, and speaks of him as 'my Father'.

'Inherit'—again we have the figure of the kingdom as a blessing to be 'inherited'; it is a transfer to the spiritual realm of the Hebrew notion of the land of Israel as an 'inheritance', granted by God and passing on from generation to generation. The verb is used in the sense of 'take possession of' the kingdom which God has prepared for them. It has been ready ever since the creation of the universe, and was always intended for those whom God should bless.

VERSES 35—36: The blessed ones are praised for the simplest deeds of kindness to those in need. No great acts of heroism are recorded of them, no conquests, no sufferings, no triumphs of faith (as in the roll call of Hebrews 11).

'Foreigner' (ξενός)—or more broadly, 'stranger'. The Greek word can also mean either 'host' or 'guest'. Among the Greeks, the person of one who was received as a guest was sacrosanct, and the relationship was under the care of Zeus as Zeus Xenios, who would punish any violation, whether on the part of the host or the guest. But the thought here is of one who has no claim of right. It is not even suggested that the foreigner is a visiting missionary or prophet.

The prisoner in jail, however, probably would suggest a Christian who was jailed for his faith; for there seems to be no evidence that Christians (or Jews) were expected to visit common criminals.

It is worth noticing that the burial of the dead is not mentioned, though this was regarded as a prime duty of the pious Jew (Tob.1: 16ff.; cf. Mt.8:21f.).

VERSES 37—39: The blessed are not conscious of having done any service to the King (that is, to Jesus). They have done what they could for those who were in need, without any thought beyond that.

VERSE 40: In the Mission Discourse of chapter 10, Jesus has declared that any kind of service done to them will be rewarded as done to him, and indeed to God. 'He who receives you receives me, and he who receives me receives him who sent me. . . . And whoever gives a cup of cold water to one of these little ones because he is a disciple, I tell you, he shall not lose his reward' (vv.40,42). Here the thought is generalized. 'One of the least of these my brethren' cannot be taken as restricted to disciples of Jesus; the thought now is that Jesus looks upon every kindness done to a person in need, however lowly, as a kindness done to himself.

VERSE 41: 'Accursed'—the curse is not, like the blessing (v.34), said explicitly to be pronounced against them by God, but this is certainly the thought. The curse takes effect in the sentence of the King. It is not arbitrary—they have brought the doom upon themselves by their failure to respond to human need.

'Eternal fire'—the imagery of fire is used frequently by Matthew of the future punishment for sin. It has no background in ancient Hebrew thought, which thinks of all the dead passing into Sheol without differentiation between righteous and wicked. Elsewhere Matthew has spoken of 'the Gehenna of fire' (5:22; 18:9), and more frequently of Gehenna (alone). In ancient times the valley of Hinnom, a ravine south of Jerusalem, had been the scene of a savage cult where children were burned in sacrifice (2 Chron.28:3; 2 Ki. 23:10), and towards the first century BC its name came to be used as a symbol of a place of fiery torment for the punishment of the wicked. Like the doctrine of resurrection, this probably is an aspect of the Iranian influences which made themselves felt from the time of the rise of Persia (sixth century BC); but the notion of a fiery hell is developed above all in Greek religion.

'Prepared for the devil and his angels'—the kingdom was prepared for the blessed; but the eternal fire was not prepared for the accursed, nor is it said to be prepared from the creation of the universe. It would be of no profit to speculate on what ideas the evangelist may have entertained about the devil and his angels, and how they incurred the punishment of eternal fire to which they are consigned and which is to be shared by the wicked.

VERSES 42–44: The accursed, now sentenced to hell, are not accused of violent crimes, or of offences on any grand scale, any more than the blessed were praised for heroic virtues. Their fault is that they have failed to help those whom they found in need.

VERSE 45: As the blessed were not aware of having given aid to the King, so the accursed are not aware of ever having failed to aid him in his time of need. They are taught, like the others, that the King looks upon all who are in need as his brothers, and takes any failure to meet their need as failure to give him honour.

VERSE 46: The sentence fixes the destiny of the accursed and of the blessed for ever. There is no hint that the eternal fire may be a discipline of purification, nor yet that it means total destruction. It is now defined as 'eternal punishment'.

Apart from the book of Revelation, the Gospel according to Matthew makes far more of the doctrine of hell as a place of eternal torment than any other book of the New Testament. It is possible, of course, that Jesus himself shared popular conceptions of the fate of the wicked; if this were so, it would not make them binding upon us any more than the notion that sickness is caused by demon possession. But we have seen that many of the sayings which are attributed to Jesus in Matthew are unmistakeably drawn from other sources (Jewish, or early Christian), and that many bear marks of composition by Matthew himself. Again, if Jesus actually made use of the imagery of a 'Gehenna of fire', the treatment of Matthew does not afford us the means of determining what ultimate meaning he attached to such symbolism. It is not to be taken for granted that it meant to him anything like what it meant to Matthew. There is indeed a strong probability that the tradition, apart from Matthew as an individual teacher, would tend to take such words in a painfully literal sense. There is certainly a tendency for the terrors of hell to be painted in more and more lurid colours—not only in Christian interpretation, but equally so in paganism.

In this final judgement scene, there is surprisingly little that is specifically Christian. The thought that the King looks upon the needy as his brothers, and that he thinks of kindness done or not done for them in their need as done or not done to him, is hardly to be seen as arising out of a purely Jewish application of the doctrine of God's care for the poor and needy. We would look in vain for a Jewish document which would speak of the needy as God's 'brothers'—'sons' they may indeed be called. But in Christian thought, Christian believers are called brothers of Christ, 'the first-born among many brethren' (Rom.8:29; cf. Heb.2:11f.).

But apart from that, it is to be noted that in this whole passage there is no trace of a doctrine of the forgiveness of sins, or of the grace of God. The righteous are invited to enter into the Kingdom because they have shown themselves worthy by their kind deeds, not because their sins are forgiven. There is no trace of a saving *faith* —the righteous have done their good deeds without any thought that they were serving Christ (or God). There is no mercy shown to the accursed, and the blessed have no need of mercy. There is justice for all, but is justice without mercy Christian?

E

The Passion Narrative

Mt. 26:1-27:66

In all four Gospels, the narrative of the Passion is given a dispropor-
tionate amount of space. It covers only three days, yet it occupies
two chapters out of 15 in Mark, two out of 27 in Matthew, two out
of 23 in Luke, and seven out of 19 in John. (The resurrection stories
are not part of the passion narrative.) It will be seen that the
disproportion is less remarkable in Matthew and Luke than in Mark,
and is much greater in John. The expansion in John, however, is
caused not by an extension of the narrative as such, but by the
insertion into its framework of long discourses of Jesus, and his
'high-priestly' prayer. In Matthew and Luke the disproportion is
reduced not by an abbreviation of the narrative itself, but by the
insertion of masses of sayings material into the Markan story of the
public ministry and the addition of cycles of infancy narratives,
while their passion narratives contain only brief sayings of Jesus.
More significant is that the incidents of the narrative are basically
the same and are recounted in the same order. As Professor Dodd has
put it:

In the Passion narrative . . . the three Synoptic Gospels scarcely differ in the
order of incidents. . . . In all this the Fourth Gospel conforms to the same
general scheme as the Synoptics. . . . The distinction between the narrative of
the Passion, where all follow a common scheme, and the account of the
Ministry, where the arrangement is much more fluid, seems to be inherent in the
idea of a written Gospel. (*Historical Tradition in the Fourth Gospel*, pp.21f.)

He even suggests the possibility that this may not be due to the
influence of Mark, but to 'the constraint of an older tradition
followed by all gospel writers' (*ibid.*).

This preponderance of attention given to the Passion narrative is
undoubtedly due to the centrality of the Cross in the church's
proclamation from the beginning (1 Cor.1:23; 2:2; 15:1ff.).
Bultmann can even say that 'we have to reckon this Kerygma as the
earliest connected tradition of the Passion and Death of Jesus. But
close to it . . . was a short narrative of historical reminiscence about
the Arrest, Condemnation and Execution of Jesus' (*HST*, p.275).

For our purpose, it is necessary to consider only the relationship of Matthew to Mark, which is much closer than in the story of the public ministry. The pattern was fixed very early, though certain incidents were worked into it by Mark (retained by Matthew, but not by Luke and John). Efforts have naturally been made to distinguish earlier and later strands (Bultmann, *HST*, p.277; V. Taylor, *Mark*, Additional Note J, pp.651–64; F. C. Grant, *The Earliest Gospel*, Chap. VIII, pp.175–87). Dr. Etienne Trocmé of Strasbourg even makes the intriguing suggestion that the author of the earliest Gospel, not himself the John Mark of Acts, may have added to his account of the ministry a very early narrative of the Passion written and adopted for cultic use in the Jerusalem church some decades before the complete Gospel appeared; he even ventures to conjecture that Peter himself may have been the author or at least the sponsor of this primitive liturgical document, and that Mark may have translated it into Greek. The Petrine authority behind this document, and the name of Mark, may have been subsequently attributed at Rome to the complete Gospel (*La formation de l'évangile selon Marc* (1963, ET 1975). See the extensive critical review by T. A. Burkill in his *New Light on The Earliest Gospel* (1972), chap. 7, pp.180–264).

Matthew follows Mark even more closely in the Passion narrative than in the account of the public ministry. He no longer has discourses of Jesus to insert into it, and he has used virtually all the episodes given in Mark, and in precisely the same order. More remarkable still, he makes no additions that amount to anything more than legendary embroidery—The Death of Judas (27:3–8); The Dream of Pilate's Wife (27:19); Pilate's Washing of his Hands and the acceptance of guilt for the blood of Jesus by 'the whole people' (27:24f.); the Guard at the Tomb (27:62–66, in preparation for the sequel in 28:11–15). More significant is the insertion within Markan episodes of sayings of Jesus, especially in the narrative of the Institution (26:26–29).

He follows Mark in two remarkable features of the early Passion narrative, namely, the disappearance of the Pharisees who have been pictured as the inveterate opponents of Jesus all through the story of the ministry; and the persistent silence of Jesus. The action against Jesus is wholly in the hands of 'the chief priests and scribes' (Mk.14:1; 'chief priests and the elders of the people', Mt.26:3); 'chief priests and scribes and elders' (Mk.14:43; 'chief priests and elders' Mt.26:47; so also in Mk.14:53 // Mt.26:57); 'chief priests with the elders and scribes and the whole Sanhedrin' (Mk.15:1 // 'all the chief priests and the elders of the people', Mt.27:1). The High Priest takes the initiative in questioning him, and in demanding sentence (Mk.14: 60–64 // Mt.26:62–65); 'the chief priests' lay the charges before Pilate, and instigate the crowds to demand his life, not that of Barabbas (Mk.15:3, 11; Matthew again includes the elders, 27:12, 20). At his crucifixion, the chief priests join with the scribes in taunting him (Mk.15:31; 'with the scribes and elders', Mt.27:41). The Pharisees are not so much as mentioned in all these proceedings. If we give due weight to the fact that the Passion narrative took shape so much earlier than the connected story of the ministry, this is bound to raise the question of how greatly the Pharisees have been misrepresented and maligned in the preceding chapters. Have several episodes of the ministry been reshaped to make it appear that the Pharisees, the chief antagonists of the church for which the Gospels were written, were likewise the deadly enemies of Jesus? (Cf. P. Winter, *On the Trial of Jesus* (1961), pp.124f., 132ff.)

Incidentally, it must be remarked that the Passion narrative must have been very highly venerated, if it could not be treated with the same freedom.

Only slightly less striking is the sustained silence of Jesus in the Passion narrative. Apart from a few sentences spoken at the Last Supper, he has almost nothing to say. This is not the silence of resignation or of despair. Jesus is confident that everything is unrolling in accordance with what has been foretold by the prophets, and in this he sees the will of God. The so-called 'cry of dereliction' (Mk.15:34 // Mt.27:46) is in fact a supreme confession of faith (see M. Dibelius, *Formgeschichte*, p.194; and his comments on the Gethsemane scene, pp.212ff.). The silence is an enhancement of his majesty.

We must also remark that Matthew includes fifteen of the seventeen Old Testament citations of Mark, and adds five more. As Professor Dodd has commented: 'All in all, the Matthaean Passion narrative may be said to be supported by the same scaffolding as Mark's, and it implies the same understanding of the sufferings and death of Christ' (*Historical Tradition*, p.35). Not one of them is taken from Isaiah 53, a fact that tells strongly against the theory that Jesus himself understood Messiahship in terms of a unique combination of the Son of man of Danielic imagery and the Suffering Servant of Deutero-Isaiah (as advocated, for instance, by V. Taylor).

In this area also, Matthew keeps to his usual practice of abbreviating by cutting away picturesque details which are not essential to the story. He finds it unnecessary to say that the woman of the anointing scene 'broke the jar' of ointment before pouring it over the head of Jesus, that Simon of Cyrene was 'coming in from the country' when he was pressed into service to carry the cross, or that he was 'the father of Alexander and Rufus'. Only one incident is omitted entirely—the Markan story of the young man who slipped out of his garment and ran away naked, at the Arrest. In the account of the arrangements for the Passover meal, he removes Mark's tale of a man carrying a water pot, who serves as guide to the house of the host, and he sees no need to describe the room even to the point of saying that they found it furnished and ready.

But some of his retouches have a dogmatic significance. They make it explicit that Jesus is wholly in control of events, and that he acts consistently with the will of the Father as it has been made known through the prophetic scriptures of Israel. At the outset, Jesus *announces* to his disciples that his arrest and execution will take place after two days (26:2), and this before anything has been said of the plot of the Sanhedrin. When he sends his disciples to the house where he is to eat the Passover, it is not to ask where the guest chamber is, but to *tell* the host that Jesus is coming to dine at his house (26:18). At the Arrest, he forbids armed resistance, and affirms that he has only to ask, and his Father will send 'more than twelve legions of angels' (26:53)—but, 'How then should the scriptures be fulfilled, that so it must be?'

We must also take note, with grief and embarrassment, that Matthew has taken questionable measures, in his work of revision, to enhance the guilt of the Jews, not merely of the leaders but of 'the whole people' (πᾶς ὁ λαός, 27:25), and to minimize the responsibility of the Roman authorities. The process is carried still further by Luke, who tells us that Pilate three times declared Jesus innocent, but allowed himself to be overborne by 'the chief priests and the rulers and the people', until he 'gave sentence that their demand should be granted' (Lk.23:13–24). And John makes it still more explicit that Pilate yields under intense Jewish pressure (Jn.19:4–16).

No significance can be attached to the countless trifling alterations of wording that Matthew makes in almost every pericope. Mgr. A. Descamps has examined them meticulously and could not but come to the conclusion that 'Matthew makes it a point of honour not to recopy his model *tel quel* . . . one cannot escape from the impression that he wants change for the sake of change.' ('Rédaction et Théologie dans le récit matthéen de la Passion', in the Louvain symposium *L'Évangile selon Matthieu: Rédaction et Théologie*, ed. M. Didier (1972), pp.367–69.)

The narrative may be outlined as follows:

TRANSITION TO THE PASSION NARRATIVE 26:1—2

[1] When Jesus had finished all these sayings, he said to his disciples, [2] 'You know that the Passover begins after two days; the Son of man will be delivered up to be crucified.'

Matthew adapts the Markan introduction to the Passion narrative in several ways; first, by prefixing to it a form of the rubric with which he concludes all five of his major discourses; secondly, by transposing the reference to the nearness of the Passover into direct discourse of Jesus, and joining with it a prediction of the Passion; and (less significantly) by removing the erroneous Markan mention of the feast of Unleavened Bread. (Strictly speaking, the feast of

Unleavened Bread began on the 14th Nisan, and the Passover on the 15th.)

VERSE 1: 'All these sayings'—probably the sayings of the eschatological discourse (chaps. 23 to 25); but Matthew may intend the phrase to refer to all the teachings that Jesus has given in the entire Gospel. There are to be no further 'discourses'. Matthew will report some isolated sayings of Jesus, but will not create any other collection.

VERSE 2: 'After two days'—probably 'the day after tomorrow'; though it could mean 'tomorrow'. ('After three days' is taken to mean the same thing as 'on the third day'.)

Matthew represents Jesus as knowing in advance that the death which he has three times predicted (16:21;17:22f.;20:18f.) will be inflicted upon him at this very festival. Jesus will not be taken by surprise; his sufferings are ordained for him by God and freely accepted, and the time is appointed.

1   THE PLOT, THE ANOINTING, THE TREACHERY OF JUDAS *26:3–16*

The Plot of the Chief Priests and Elders 26:3–5

³ The chief priests and the elders of the people held a meeting in the palace of the high priest Caiaphas. ⁴ They planned to seize Jesus by trickery and put him to death, ⁵ but they said, 'Not during the festival, lest there be a tumult among the people.'

Matthew continues to follow Mark, again with variations. He introduces the name Caiaphas, who is never mentioned in Mark; and he speaks of a formal session of the Sanhedrin to plan for the arrest and execution of Jesus, whereas Mark's words would suggest rather that they had this end continually in mind.

VERSE 5: The words of the plotters would most naturally be taken to mean that they intend to postpone the arrest and execution until after the festival, when the crowds of pilgrims will have left the city and the danger of a popular disturbance will be diminished. As the story is told, however, Jesus is arrested late on the night of Passover, after he and his disciples have partaken of the meal, and he is crucified on the next afternoon. It is not clear, however, that this timing corresponds to the facts.

The Anointing of Jesus 26:6–13

⁶ When Jesus was at Bethany, in the house of Simon the leper, ⁷ a woman made her approach to him carrying an alabaster flask of very

costly ointment, and she poured it down over his head as he was sitting at table. [8] The disciples were vexed at seeing this and said, 'Why this waste? [9] This ointment could have been sold for a large sum, and the money given to the poor.' [10] Jesus heard this and said to them? 'Why are you making trouble for the woman? It is a beautiful thing that she has done for me. [11] You always have the poor with you, but you do not always have me. [12] In pouring this ointment on my body she has done it by way of preparation for my burial. [13] Truly I tell you, wherever this gospel is preached in the whole world, the story of what she has done will be told in memory of her.'

Matthew keeps closely to the Markan form of the story, making only minor changes of wording. In verse 7 he introduces his formal expression 'made an approach' ($\pi\rho\sigma\sigma\hat{\eta}\lambda\theta\epsilon\nu$) in place of Mark's simple $\mathring{\eta}\lambda\theta\epsilon\nu$, 'came'; and he reduces Mark's complex description of the ointment to the one word $\beta\alpha\rho\acute{\upsilon}\tau\iota\mu\sigma\varsigma$ in place of Mark's $\pi\sigma\lambda\upsilon\tau\epsilon\lambda\acute{\eta}\varsigma$ (omitting the unusual $\pi\iota\sigma\tau\iota\kappa\acute{\eta}$). He cuts away the vivid detail that 'she broke the alabaster vase'. He substitutes the participle $\dot{\alpha}\nu\alpha\kappa\epsilon\iota\mu\acute{\epsilon}\nu\sigma\upsilon$ for Mark's $\kappa\alpha\tau\alpha\kappa\epsilon\iota\mu\acute{\epsilon}\nu\sigma\upsilon$ ('seated at table'). He identifies the fault-finders as 'the disciples', in place of Mark's vague 'some' ($\tau\acute{\iota}\nu\epsilon\varsigma$); John in his turn will point to Judas as the complainant, and accuse him of being motivated by dishonesty (Jn.12:4–6). For Mark's estimate of the value of the ointment—'three hundred denarii'—he is content to write 'much'. Having identified the critics with the disciples, he finds it inappropriate to retain Mark's savage 'they snarled at her' ($\dot{\epsilon}\nu\epsilon\beta\rho\iota\mu\hat{\omega}\nu\tau\sigma$). At the end of verse 11, he omits Mark's doubtful phrase $\ddot{\sigma}$ $\ddot{\epsilon}\sigma\chi\epsilon\nu$ $\dot{\epsilon}\pi\sigma\acute{\iota}\eta\sigma\epsilon\nu$ ('she has done what she could'—?); and in verse 12, he has recast the saying of Mark 14:8 without changing the meaning.

VERSE 6: 'Simon the leper' is mentioned as if the name were familiar, but he has never been mentioned before, nor does he play any part in the story. In the Lukan version (Lk.7:36–40), the host is named Simon, and he is a Pharisee who has invited Jesus to dinner —there is no suggestion that he is a leper, and indeed a leper could not have social intercourse with others, whether as host or guest. In John, the anointing takes place at Bethany, but in the house of Lazarus, and the woman who anoints Jesus is identified as Mary, the sister of Lazarus (Jn.12:1–8). There is no trace of any Simon. In Luke and John, the story is not incorporated in the Passion narrative; in John, the thought is retained that the act is an anticipation of burial; in Luke, it is simply a manifestation of love (Lk.7:44–47).

In Luke and John the woman pours the ointment on the feet of Jesus, not on his head as in Matthew and Mark.

Whatever may be said of the setting in Luke or in John, the story is obviously misplaced in Mark and Matthew. Mark has inserted it between two parts of the story of the plot, with which it has nothing to do (unless by way of foil—the dedication of the woman is set against the background of hatred and treachery). Plainly enough, the treason of Judas is the necessary complement of the plot of the priests, and verses 14 to 16 in Matthew belong closely with verses 3–5. This 'sandwiching' of one narrative into another is a characteristic device of Mark (Dodd, *Historical Tradition*, p.23, n.1), and Matthew has retained it here, as in the story of Jairus' daughter with that of the woman with the haemorrhage (Mt.9:18–26).

VERSE 7: The woman is not named, even though Jesus will affirm that the story will be told 'in memory of her'. In the parallel Lukan story, she is taken to be a harlot ("sinner" ἁμαρτωλός—Lk.7:37); and the story becomes a contrast of the repentant woman of the streets with the censorious Pharisee who has neglected to show the ordinary courtesies to his guest (cf.Mt.21:31f.).

'Costly ointment'—Mark calls it 'ointment of "pistic" nard'. The meaning of πιστική is uncertain. The same phrase is used in the Johannine version (Jn.12:3). Mark sets the value of it at 'over three hundred denarii': in John, it is 300 denarii even, and the quantity is given as a *litra*—a Roman pound; in our measure, 324 grams, or about twelve ounces—a gross exaggeration, though the valuation is probably about right. The alabaster flask would not contain more than an ounce or so; it was certainly lavish to pour out the whole contents of the flask, as it would be today to empty an entire bottle of perfume—even a quarter of an ounce.

VERSE 8: 'The disciples', in Matthew, generally represent the Christians of Matthew's own time. If he mentions them in place of Mark's indefinite 'some', this may be taken as a reflection of debates within his own community over the relative merits of expenditures on the accessories of worship (church furnishings?—perhaps even incense?) and the relief of the poor. The answer is then much in the spirit of Wordsworth's sonnet on King's College Chapel:

> Tax not the royal saint with vain expense
> . . . .
> Give all thou canst! high heaven rejects the lore
> Of nicely calculated less or more.

VERSE 10: The beauty of uncalculating generosity is not to be measured by the yardstick of utility.

Jesus is quite as much concerned with the needs of the poor as any of his disciples; he has told the rich man: 'Go sell what you own, and give to the poor . . . and come, follow me' (Mt.19:21).

We often find people who are not themselves noted for generosity criticizing the way in which others spend their own money. Synods are all too ready to suggest diverting funds which have been given for a specific purpose to some other end which is more appealing to those who have not contributed the funds in question. It is not to be assumed that the giver is bound to bestow his goods in ways that others consider more seemly.

In Mark, Jesus adds to the remark that 'the poor you always have with you', the further observation (omitted by Matthew, probably as too obvious to need mentioning), 'and whenever you will, you can do them good' (Mk.14:7).

VERSE 12: It is not suggested that the woman has herself thought of her action as a preparation of Jesus for his burial. This is the interpretation which Jesus gives to her act. If we are to conjecture her own motive and intention—beyond the generous impulse of love—we might suppose that she thinks of her act as a prophetic symbolism of Jesus' installation as King (1 Sam.10:1; 16:3; and esp. 2 Ki.9:1–13). But in the mind of Jesus, the way to his throne is the way of death; when he is anointed as king, he is anointed for burial.

VERSE 13: Since Jesus did not look forward to a continuing history long enough to permit of a mission spanning the whole world, the saying in this form can hardly have been uttered by him. How it may have been originated we cannot say. 'This' gospel ('this' is a Matthaean addition) means the proclamation of Jesus as Saviour, not the message that 'the kingdom of heaven is at hand.'

The Treachery of Judas 26:14–16

[14] One of the Twelve, Judas Iscariot by name, now went to the chief priests [15] with the proposition, 'What will you give me if I deliver him over to you?' And they paid him thirty pieces of silver. [16] From that moment he kept watching for an opportunity to betray him.

Besides a number of minor alterations of wording, Matthew introduces into the Markan story the proposal of Judas that he should be paid for his treason, the amount of the bribe, and the assertion that it was paid to him forthwith. Mark, followed by Luke, says only that money was promised.

The 'thirty pieces of silver' (silver shekels) and the verb ἔστησαν 'they paid' (placed in the scale, weighed out) are taken from Zechariah 11:12; there, they are the wages paid to the prophet when he renounces his contract as shepherd (the historical interpretation of the passage is much disputed).

Judas has not been mentioned previously in Matthew, except in the list of the Twelve (10:4).

2   THE LAST SUPPER 26:17–29

Preparation of the Passover 26:17–20

[17] On the first day of (the festival of) Unleavened Bread, the disciples made their approach to Jesus to ask him, 'Where do you want us to make the preparations for you to eat the Passover?' [18] He answered, 'Go into the city to such and such, and say to him "the Teacher says, My time is at hand; I will keep the Passover at your house, with my disciples".' [19] The disciples did as Jesus had told them, and made the preparations for the Passover, [20] and in the evening he sat down to table with the Twelve.

Matthew has greatly abbreviated the Markan story, in his usual way, removing much of the colour. Mark gives a vivid demonstration of Jesus' supernatural knowledge of what is to come. Matthew tells simply enough of an instruction to the disciples to call upon a certain friend—it is assumed that they know his name and where he lives—and to tell him that Jesus and his disciples will celebrate the Passover at his house. In the Markan story, Jesus tells them that when they go into the city they will be met by a man carrying a water jar; they are to follow him till he enters a house, apparently without a word, and they will ask the owner of the house to show them the room where he is to eat the Passover with his disciples, and he will show them a large loft ready with its furnishings.

It would seem that the afternoon of Passover was somewhat late to make arrangements for the use of a room for the group. This leads many commentators to suggest that Jesus had made private arrangements well beforehand, without the knowledge of his disciples; and that he has now only to put them into operation. But this is not at all the spirit in which the story is narrated. The evangelists do not think in the least of the practical difficulties of securing a large room at the last moment in a city crowded with pilgrims for the great festival. There is no more notion of prearrangement here than in the story of Samuel and Saul (1 Sam.10:3–6). Samuel tells Saul that he will meet two men by Rachel's tomb, and three more at the oak of Tabor, and a band of dancing ecstatics ('prophets') with musical instruments in hand; but no reader imagines that Samuel has arranged in advance for these people to be there to meet Saul as he journeys. The prophet is gifted with 'second sight'—he describes the scenes that will occur as he sees them by his inspired vision.

Matthew has removed much of the superfluous detail (though he has not done so in the similar story of the colt at Bethany—Mk.11: 2–6; Mt.21:2f,6). He emphasizes all the more strongly the thought that Jesus is in full charge of all the proceedings. The disciples are not to ask where the room is located, but to inform the man that Jesus will be celebrating the Passover with his disciples in his house.

Jesus Foretells his Betrayal 26:21–25

[21] While they were eating, he said, 'Truly I tell you, one of you will betray me.' [22] Deeply grieved, they began to say to him, every one of them, 'Surely not I, Lord!' [23] He answered, 'The one who has dipped his hand in the bowl with me will betray me. [24] The Son of man goes as it is written of him, but woe to that man by whom the Son of man is betrayed! It would have been better for him if he had never been born.' [25] Judas his betrayer protested, 'Surely it is not I, Rabbi.' Jesus said to him, 'You have said so.'

Though there is no citation (apart from Mark's one phrase, 'he who is eating with me'—14:18), the whole scene reflects the picture of the unfaithful friend of Psalm 41:9: 'Even my bosom friend in whom I trusted, who ate of my bread, has lifted up his heel against me.'

VERSE 22: It is remarkable that every one of the disciples is represented as wondering whether he would be capable of such a betrayal.

VERSE 23: The bowl would contain a sauce, in which each person at the table would dip a piece of bread or of meat with his fingers.

VERSE 25: This is a Matthaean addition; it is probably intended to be taken as a whispered exchange, in which Jesus reveals to Judas that he knows of the intended treachery. The words of verse 24 would then be a final warning to Judas—a last attempt to dissuade him from his dreadful action. But over it all hangs the conviction that the betrayal is predestined; things *must* take the course that has been predicted. But even within the iron framework of an ineluctable predestination, the personal responsibility of the agent of evil is not removed or even diminished, and will receive its fearful retribution.

The Institution of the Eucharist 26:26–29

26 While they were eating, Jesus took a loaf of bread, and after blessing it he gave it to his disciples with the words, 'Take this and eat; this is my body.' 27 And taking a cup of wine, he gave thanks and gave it to them, with the words, 'Drink of it, all of you, 28 for this is my blood of the covenant, which is poured out for many, for the remission of sins. 29 I tell you, I shall not drink of the fruit of the vine from this time until that day when I drink it with you, new, in the kingdom of my Father.'

Matthew follows Mark almost word for word, with two significant changes. Where Mark, after the giving of the cup, notes only that 'they all drank of it', Matthew transposes this into a command, 'Drink of it, all of you.' This brings it into a closer parallelism with the account of the giving of the bread, which is accompanied by the command to partake (in Mark, 'Take'; in Matthew, 'Take, eat'); probably it is brought into conformity with the formulas in use in Matthew's church. Still more significant is the addition by Matthew of the words 'for the forgiveness of sins'. In Mark, this phrase was used of the baptism of John—it was a 'baptism of repentance for the forgiveness of sins'. Matthew omitted the phrase at that point, and inserted it here. Almost certainly, this was done with the conscious intention of teaching that the forgiveness of sins is not given in baptism, but is effected by Christ's offering of his life in sacrifice.

3   THE ARREST 26:30–56

Jesus Predicts Peter's Denial 26:30–35

30 When they had sung a hymn, they went out to the Mount of Olives.
31 Now Jesus said to them, 'All of you will desert me in the coming night, for it is written, "I will smite the shepherd, and the sheep of the flock will be scattered." 32 But after I am raised from the dead, I will go to Galilee before you.' 33 Peter responded to him, 'Though they all desert you, I will never desert.' 34 Jesus said to him, 'Truly I tell you that this very night, before the cock crows, you will deny me three times.' 35 Peter said to him, 'Even if it means that I must die with you, I will not deny you,' and so said all the disciples.

The initial theme is the desertion of all the disciples. This will be described immediately after the arrest (v.56). It is only when Peter protests that he at least will remain faithful that Jesus foretells that he will deny all knowledge of Jesus. It is this, far more than the flight of all, that then becomes the main focus of attention; and Peter's successive denials will be described in detail (26:69–75).

VERSE 30: The verse is perhaps better taken as the conclusion of the preceding pericope. At Passover, the rites of the meal concluded with the singing of the second part of a group of psalms known as the *Hallel* (Pss. 115 to 118; Pss. 113 and 114 were sung at an earlier stage). If this last meal of Jesus with his disciples was not in fact a passover meal, there is of course no means of knowing what was sung. In any case, the sentence probably is included as a reflection of Christian liturgical custom.

VERSE 31: The citation (from Zech.13:7) is not an exact reproduction of either the Hebrew or LXX. In the original prophecy, we have an oracle which calls upon 'the sword' to smite:

> Arise, O sword, against my shepherd
> ... says the Lord of hosts.
> Strike the shepherd, that the sheep may be scattered. ...

There are remarkable divergences in the manuscripts of LXX. Codex Alexandrinus comes closest to the form given in Matthew: 'Strike the shepherd and the sheep of the flock will be scattered'; but Codex Vaticanus reads, 'Strike the shepherds and draw away the sheep.' (Other LXX manuscripts give different variants, but always use 'strike' in the imperative, not in the future, as in Matthew and Mark.) The oracle itself appears to predict the ravaging of the people of God by war ('the sword'), following the execution of a divinely appointed leader, till two thirds of them are killed; but in our passage only the one line is cited, and it is interpreted as foretelling the effects of the passion of Jesus upon his followers; it anticipates the wholesale desertion of verse 56 ('all the disciples forsook him and fled').

VERSE 32: The verb προάγω means sometimes 'go before' and sometimes 'lead'. If the latter sense is intended, it would indicate that the risen Jesus will rejoin them (in or near Jerusalem?) and lead them back to Galilee. It would be hard to see why. As translated here, it would mean that after the scattering of the flock, they will make their way back to their home in Galilee, and will find that Jesus has reached there before them, to lead his flock again. This is clearly what is envisaged in the Resurrection narrative of Mark, and again in Matthew (Mk.16:7; Mt.28:7,16ff.).

According to Luke, they do not return to Galilee at all; they are forbidden to leave Jerusalem (Acts 1:4), and all the Resurrection appearances take place in the city or its environs (Lk.24:13–31; 33–35; 36–42; Acts 1:3–9).

VERSE 33: Peter does not speak for the group, but for himself. Even if all the others 'fall away', he will hold firm. The others are not mentioned until the end (vs.35b).

VERSES 34–35: Matthew omits the second crowing of the cock (Mk.14:30,72).

'Deny'—not only will he desert, like the rest, but will openly repudiate any attachment to Jesus. The language anticipates the more or less technical use of the term in relation to Christian martyrdoms. Those who were put on trial as Christians might hope to escape death by denying that they were believers. Roman judges would usually force them to give proof of the genuineness of their denial by putting incense on the altar before the image of the emperor.

The Agony in Gethsemane 26:36–46

36 Now Jesus came with them to a place called Gethsemane; and he said to his disciples, 'Sit here, while I go apart yonder and pray.' 37 Taking along Peter and the two sons of Zebedee, he was overwhelmed with grief and dismay. 38 He said to them, 'I am sunk in grief, heavy enough to die of it. Remain here, and keep vigil with me.' 39 He went forward a little way and fell on the ground in prayer, saying, 'My Father, if it be possible, let this cup pass from me. Nevertheless, let it be not as I will, but as you will.' 40 He came to the disciples and found them asleep. He said to Peter, 'Is it so? Could you not keep vigil with me for one hour? 41 Keep vigil, and pray, that you may not enter into temptation. The spirit is eager, but the flesh is weak.' 42 Again, a second time, he went apart and prayed, saying, 'My Father, if this may not pass without my drinking it, your will be done.' 43 Again he went back and found them asleep, for their eyes were heavy. 44 He left them again, went apart for the third time, and prayed, again in the same words. 45 Then he came to the disciples and said to them, 'Sleep on now and get your rest. See, the moment is at hand, and the Son of man is delivered into the hands of sinners. 46 Rise, let us go. Here at hand is the one who is betraying me.'

There is no step-by-step description of events in the preceding part of the Gospel that is comparable to this. We have first the order to the disciples to sit where they are while Jesus goes apart to pray. Then we learn that he takes three of them with him (v.37), only to bid them to remain where they are while he goes apart by himself to pray (v.38). The words of his prayer are given, first in verse 39, and again, with some change, in verse 42. Mark gives the words of prayer only in the first instance (14:36). Three times Jesus goes apart from the three, and comes back to find them asleep.

The entire scene is omitted in John, but there seems to be an echo of it, or at least of the theme, in the very different scene (the Approach of the Greeks) in John 12:20–36, (esp. in vv.27–33). In John there is no Agony, but a serene acceptance that in the death on the cross God is glorified. A genuine agony of spirit is presupposed in the Epistle to the Hebrews, in an exposition of the high-priestly function of Jesus who 'offered up prayers and supplications, with loud cries and tears, to him who was able to save him from death' (Heb.5:7–10). The 'loud cries and tears' even go beyond the inward anguish of the Gethsemane story, but the words indicate that there was a strong tradition that Jesus was torn with dismay at the prospect of the fearful death which faced him. In Luke, we have a much shorter version of the Markan story. The words of the prayer, given only once as in Mark, are in much the same words, but the scene as a whole appears to be drawn from an independent source. There is no separation of the disciples—Jesus withdraws 'about a stone's throw' from the whole group (22:41); and there is no mention of a threefold return to find them sleeping—Jesus withdraws once and returns once, and they are said to be sleeping 'from sorrow' (v.45), not simply because they cannot keep their eyes open. But the most striking difference is the more vivid depiction of the anguish, and the appearance of an angel from heaven to strengthen him (vv.43f.). This sounds a note very like that of the passage in Hebrews. But these two verses may be an interpolation (see below).

As the story is told, none of the disciples were in a position to overhear the words of the prayer, for even the three who came with him farther than the others fell asleep. There was no one to make a note of what Jesus said in prayer. It must be supposed that the prayers are freely composed, somewhere in the transmission of the tradition, and it is a question whether the story as a whole, despite its poignancy, is anything more than an early legend. In any case, we are left wondering why in this one instance the evangelists lay so much stress on the deep depression of Jesus, since in general they avoid expressions of emotional reaction; and the few that are found in Mark are usually toned down or eliminated by Matthew and (less consistently) by Luke. Yet here he 'began to be sorrowful and despondent' (v.37), and he gives vent to his distress in words that echo the lament of the Psalmist: 'Why are you cast down, O my soul? . . . My soul is cast down within me . . . Why are you cast down, O my soul?' (Ps.42:5,6,11; cf.43:5). These verses are not used in Luke, but his version of the incident depicts the distress of Jesus even more vividly. ('in agony . . . his sweat became as it were drops of blood falling on the ground'—22:44, omitted, along with v.43, in Codex B, in Papyrus 75, and apparently also in Papyrus 69, and in several other important uncials, as well as in some early versions; see Metzger's note in his *Textual Commentary*; if it be an interpolation, it must have been introduced very early, for it is strongly attested generally.)

If in this one place these evangelists dwell upon the extreme nervous reaction of Jesus, it is perhaps because they wish to remind the church of their own time that even the most resolute may quail for the moment, in the face of imminent martyrdom. If the Son of God himself had his hour of agony, it is not strange that Christian martyrs sometimes break or come close to breaking under the strain. It is hardly possible that the story simply records what actually happened, as if the anguish of Jesus so deeply impressed the *sleeping* disciples that they could never forget it. The Gospels do not give us anything like this kind of conscientious reporting of unwelcome facts. (See esp. the remarks of M. Dibelius, *FG*, 122–24.)

VERSE 36: Gethsemane ('oil vat'), a secluded place somewhere on the Mount of Olives. Luke and John do not mention this name; John alone speaks of it as a garden (Jn.18:1). All the old olive groves were destroyed during the siege of the city by Titus in AD 70, so that the actual site cannot be determined.

VERSE 37: The choice of the three to go with Jesus apart from the other disciples is not integral to the story. It resumes a theme that has been used in the Transfiguration story where the chosen three witness the epiphany, and in Mark's version of the Raising of Jairus' Daughter (Mk.5:37), where they witness the miracle; here they do nothing but sleep. And the separation is forgotten at the end of the episode, when no mention is made of a return to the group that has been left behind, yet they are all together again for the arrival of Judas. If they are set apart at all, it is probably because of their previous professions of confidence. James and John have assured him that they are able to drink the cup that he is to drink (Mt.20:22), and Peter has just a moment before declared that he will never fail in his loyalty. All three fail him in the hour of his agony.

'Grief'—the infinitive λυπεῖσθαι anticipates the adjective περίλυπος of the next verse. It also makes the phrase a little milder, compared with Mark's ἐκθαμβεῖσθαι, which suggests amazement and terror (*NEB*, 'horror and dismay came over him').

VERSE 38: The words of the Psalm are intensified by the added phrase, '[grieved] to the point of death.' This is taken over from Mark, but the phrase 'with me' is a Matthaean addition. The injunction to 'keep vigil and pray' has already occurred in other contexts as a saying of Jesus. Here Mark and Matthew interpret γρηγορεῖτε literally, 'keep awake', not in the spiritual sense which it has, for instance, in 24:42; 25:13, and in the New Testament generally (Acts 20:31; 1 Cor.16:13; 1 Peter 5:8; etc.). It became one of the key injunctions of Christian moral instruction (ascetic self-discipline).

VERSE 39: Matthew has eliminated the description of the prayer in indirect discourse in Mark (14:35) but carried forward the phrase, 'if it be possible' (εἰ δυνατόν ἐστιν), into the prayer itself, where Mark reads 'all things are possible to you'. He has omitted Mark's 'Abba' (the Aramaic word for 'Father') and used the vocative with the possessive ('My Father') for Mark's nominative. The double phrase, 'Abba, Father', as in Mark, is used also by Paul in Gal.4:6 and Rom.8:15; this suggests that the double (Aramaic-Greek) phrase was retained liturgically in church usage, but not in Matthew's churches. Jesus, of course, would use only the Aramaic address in private prayer.

'This cup'—a metaphor for suffering, as in 20:22 and frequently in OT (Pss.11:6;75:8; Jer.25:15—28; Isa.51:17; etc.; all of God's wrath). But it may also be a symbol of divine blessing as in Psalm 16:5, 'The Lord is my chosen portion and my cup', and especially Psalm 116:13, 'the cup of salvation' (cf. 1 Cor.10:16, 'the cup of blessing'). Probably there is an undertone of the second thought here; the Christian reader will realize that the sufferings of his Lord have become the source of eternal blessing.

The emphasis, however, is primarily on the thought of acceptance of the will of God as 'good and acceptable and perfect' (Rom.12:2), even when it brings suffering and death upon his devoted servant.

VERSES 40—41: Matthew retains from Mark the addressing of the reproach to Peter alone, but he changes the verbs into the plural throughout, while Mark shifts into the plural only with the second of the two verses. This suggests that Mark has conflated a reproach addressed only to Peter (from one source), with a pair of sayings of a more general character which were floating independently in the traditions available to him. The words, 'Keep vigil and pray that you may not enter into temptation', are not pertinent to these particular circumstances, when no 'temptation' is overhanging them that could be avoided by keeping awake; the injunction bears upon the whole of the moral life, not upon the immediate situation in Gethsemane. The last saying again is not an injunction, but a reflexion on the weakness of human nature, which cannot always live up to the high principles which the 'spirit' approves—the 'inmost self' which 'delights in the law of God', but finds itself powerless to overcome the impulses of the 'flesh' (cf. Rom.7:14–25).

VERSE 42: The second prayer, said in Mark to be substantially the same as the first, is significantly different in Matthew. Jesus no longer prays that he may be spared the ordeal, but only that God's will may be done. He uses the third petition of the Lord's Prayer, as it is given in 6:10 (not in the Lukan version). For Matthew, Jesus acts in accordance with the prayer which he had taught to his disciples. The Kingdom comes and God's name is sanctified when his will is done on earth as in heaven. The disciples by their sleep have lost the opportunity to associate themselves with him in this ultimate acceptance of the will of God for him.

VERSE 43: Their sleepiness is laid to sheer weariness—they cannot keep their eyes open. On this occasion there is no reproach; Jesus lets them sleep on undisturbed.

VERSE 44 is a Matthaean addition; in Mark, Jesus comes the third time, but Mark does not mention that he went off, or that he prayed. It is at this point that Matthew uses the Markan phrase, 'saying the same words'. The prayer that is repeated is not the initial petition for deliverance, but the second prayer, that God's will may be done.

VERSES 45–46: The words are puzzling; it may be that they are meant to be taken as a question, 'Are you still asleep, still taking your rest?' But this sounds rather satirical. Perhaps it is simply to state that the time for preparation for the ordeal that they too must face is now past. But it comes strangely before the following 'Rise!'

All this is unchanged from Mark, except for the double use of ἤγγικεν, 'is at hand', which Mark uses only in the second phrase; 'the hour' and 'the betrayer' come upon them together.

Betrayal and Arrest 26:47–50

⁴⁷While he was still speaking, Judas, one of the Twelve, arrived, and with him a great crowd armed with swords and clubs, sent by the chief priests and elders of the people. ⁴⁸The betrayer had given them

a sign: 'He whom I kiss is the one; arrest him.' ⁴⁹ He made his approach to Jesus at once, said, 'Greetings, Rabbi', and kissed him. ⁵⁰ Jesus said to him, 'Friend, [do] what you are here to do.' With that they made their approach, laid hands on Jesus, and took him into custody.

Matthew keeps closely to the Markan story, with brief omissions and one considerable addition. In verse 47, he adds the word '$\pi o\lambda \acute{v}\varsigma$', 'large', after 'crowd', and the phrase 'of the people' after 'elders'; and omits Mark's mention of 'the scribes'; in verse 48 he omits the clause 'lead him away securely'; in verse 49 he adds the word 'Rabbi'. The first sentence of verse 50 is a Matthaean addition (Jesus said '. . . to do'), and Matthew introduces his characteristic expression, 'making their approach' ($\pi \rho o\sigma\epsilon\lambda\vartheta\acute{o}\nu\tau\epsilon\varsigma$).

VERSE 47: The 'crowd armed with swords and clubs' suggests a mob, but is said to be 'from the chief priests and elders of the people'. The Sanhedrin would surely have the Temple police at its disposal to make such an arrest. Luke speaks of 'a crowd', but does not mention the weapons. John brings in a detachment of Roman troops (even a 'cohort'—which at full strength would number 600 men); yet he has Jesus taken to Annas, the father-in-law of Caiaphas, whereas Roman troops would certainly take their prisoner to a cell in the fortress on the Temple mount (the Antonia), to await the governor's pleasure.

VERSE 50: The address of Jesus to Judas is peculiar to Matthew. In Mark, Jesus does not speak to Judas at all. In Luke, he reproaches him: 'Judas, are you betraying the Son of man with a kiss?' The meaning of the words as given in Matthew is not clear, but there seems to be no justification for the rendering 'Why are you here?' for there is no interrogative (the pronoun $\ddot{o}$ is the relative). But the clause (literally, 'for what you are here') requires a governing verb of some kind, and it would be in keeping with Matthew's emphasis that Jesus should be represented as completely in charge of all the proceedings, even the betrayal. He commands Judas to get on with his vile deed (cf. Jn.13:27).

The participle $\pi \rho o\sigma\epsilon\lambda\vartheta\acute{o}\nu\tau\epsilon\varsigma$ is again introduced by Matthew. Judas and the arresting party in turn 'make an approach' to Jesus; even under these circumstances, they recognize involuntarily his royal majesty, and come near him with due ceremony.

In John, the legionaries draw back and fall on their faces when he identifies himself (18:6)—even though they bind him before leading him to Annas (v.12).

Armed Resistance: Repudiated by Jesus 26:51–56

⁵¹ And now one of those with Jesus put his hand to his sword, drew it, and struck the slave of the high priest, cutting off his ear. ⁵² Upon that, Jesus said to him, 'Put your sword back into its sheath, for all who take the sword shall perish by the sword. ⁵³ Do you suppose that I cannot pray to my Father, and he will send me more than twelve legions of angels? ⁵⁴ How then could the scriptures be fulfilled [which foretell] that so it must come to pass?'

⁵⁵ Thereupon Jesus said to the crowds, 'Have you come out with swords and clubs to capture me, as if I were a brigand? Day by day I have sat in the Temple teaching and you did not seize me. ⁵⁶ But all this has come to pass in order that the scriptures of the prophets might be fulfilled.'

With that the disciples all forsook him and ran away.

Most of this passage is taken directly from Mark, with a number of the seemingly pointless alterations of wording that abound in the Passion narrative. In verse 51 he uses the compound ἀποσπάω in place of the simple σπάω of Mark, changing it at the same time from the participle to the indicative mood; and introduces a new (redundant) participial phrase to modify it—'stretching out his hand'; in the second clause he uses the verb πατάσσω in place of its synonym παίω which he found in Mark, shifting this time from the indicative mood to the participle. These changes look deliberate and utterly pointless. The same may be said of his substitution of the diminutive ὠτίον (ear) for Mark's double diminutive ὠτάριον. Luke adopts the classical οὖς; indeed the diminutive is otiose (BDF 111,3). It is not intended to suggest that the ear cut off was a very little ear. With equal pointlessness, Matthew replaces Mark's 'I was' by 'I sat' (teaching)—καθεζόμην for ἤμην, and there are a few other equally trifling alterations.

There is a substantial addition—the whole of verses 52–54. Only the first clause has a parallel in any other Gospel, and that not in the Synoptics but in John (18:11). At the end, Matthew does not pick up the puzzling little Markan story of the young man who escaped from his captors naked, by slipping out of his one garment (14:51f.).

The passage as a whole has a double emphasis. In Mark it is primarily directed to the refusal of Jesus to allow the use of force on his behalf, on the ground that the scriptures must be fulfilled. Matthew expands this by the assurance that ample force was available, if Jesus were to ask his Father to send it, but to make such a request would frustrate the will of God as made known in the prophetic scriptures. Luke says nothing of the availability of supernatural armies, but reports that Jesus touched the slave's ear and healed him (22:51).

VERSE 51: The basis of the passage is probably a tradition that there was a scuffle at the arrest of Jesus. Even in Mark, the report that one of the group that arrested Jesus had his ear cut off was probably a legendary amplification, as the identification of the wounded man as a slave of the High Priest certainly is. Matthew adds a slight further detail—that it was one of those 'with Jesus' who struck the blow, not simply 'one of those standing by'. In Luke and John we can observe further effects of the legendary tendency to amplify. Both of them tell us that the ear lost was the right ear, and John adds that the slave's name was Malchus (18:10). John has the further detail that it was Simon Peter who struck the blow, and that the command to put the sword back into its sheath was addressed to him. (Neither Luke nor John makes any reference at this point to the fulfilment of prophecy.)

VERSE 52: The second clause, 'All that take the sword shall perish by the sword', peculiar to Matthew, is a general maxim without particular relevance to this incident. It was probably transmitted independently.

VERSE 53: The phrase 'twelve legions of angels' rests upon the imagery of Roman military organization, transferred to the realm of the supernatural. The vision of Elisha's servant (2 Ki.6:17) adopts the imagery of the armed forces of the ninth century BC to the hosts of heaven in the same way ('horses and chariots of fire round about Elisha'). Similarly, the iconography of St. Michael the Archangel as developed in the art of the Middle Ages pictures him as carrying the shield and sword, and wearing the armour of a knight in panoply. The Roman legion at full strength numbered (after the reforms of Augustus) 6,000 heavy-armed infantry and 120 cavalry. In the first century, three legions were normally stationed in the province of Syria, for the defence of Rome's eastern frontier against her most powerful foe, the Parthians.

4 JESUS ON TRIAL *26:57–27:26*

Jesus before the Sanhedrin 26:57–68

[57] Those who had arrested Jesus brought him before Caiaphas the High Priest, where the scribes and the elders had assembled. [58] Peter followed him at a distance as far as the courtyard of the High Priest's

residence; he went into it and sat down with the attendants to see the outcome. [59] The chief priests and the whole Sanhedrin were trying to get false evidence against Jesus, to bring him to his death; [60] but they found none—although many witnesses came forward—until at last two came forward [61] and testified, 'This man declared, "I can destroy the Temple of God and build it within three days."' [62] The High Priest rose to his feet and said to him, 'Do you make no answer? What is this accusation that these men are making against you?' [63] Jesus kept silent. The High Priest said to him, 'I adjure you by the living God, tell us if you are the Messiah, the Son of God.' [64] Jesus said to him, 'Is it as you say? Only, let me tell you, from now on you will see the Son of man seated at the right hand of the Power and coming upon the clouds of heaven.' [65] Upon that the High Priest tore his robes, crying, 'He has uttered blasphemy! What need have we now of witnesses? You have heard the blasphemy. [66] What is your judgement?' They answered, 'He is guilty; he is liable to the death penalty.' [67] Then they spat in his face and buffeted him, and some of them beat him, [68] jeering, 'Prophesy for us, Messiah! Who was it that struck you?'

As in Mark, Jesus is brought before the Sanhedrin: some time after midnight (here), and again at dawn (27:1). The account is confused, partly because it attempts to compress into a few sentences the proceedings of two sessions of the Sanhedrin, but more because the evangelists are not accurately informed about what actually took place and not really interested in the details of legal procedure. It is by no means certain that Jesus was brought before the Sanhedrin at all; the difficulties of reconstructing the course of events are all but insurmountable. There is the further problem of deciding how far Christian tradition has misconceived the situation in its obvious tendency to heighten the responsibility of the Jewish authorities in bringing about the execution of Jesus, and to exculpate Pilate and Rome, in the teeth of the undisputed fact that Jesus was put to death by crucifixion—a Roman, not a Jewish, method of execution.

VERSE 57: Caiaphas is again named by Matthew (not by Mark). The 'chief priests' are not mentioned, though they appear in Mark as part of the assemblage, and will be mentioned in verse 9. Once again we are struck by the absence of any reference to Pharisees, though there were certainly Pharisaic members of the Sanhedrin. It is supposed that they have been summoned in advance to this night session in the residence of the High Priest, as if the machinery had been well prepared for an instantaneous trial.

VERSE 58: The way is paved for the story of Peter's denial. As usual, Matthew reduces the Markan story to its bare essentials, omitting any mention of the fire in the courtyard at which Peter could warm himself. The last phrase—'to see the outcome'—is a Matthaean addition. The 'attendants' may be men of the Temple police (the word ὑπηρέται is used in that sense in Jn.7:32,45f.; 18:3, etc.), but in any case not of those who had arrested Jesus.

VERSE 59 resumes the account of the court in session. It is now alleged that 'the chief priests and the whole Sanhedrin' (emphasizing the total connivance of the authorities) had suborned witnesses to give perjured testimony against Jesus. It is hard to imagine that the supreme council of the Jewish people would unitedly support such a policy. It was, of course, not difficult to hire professional 'witnesses' to give any desired testimony for a fee (it still happens, and not only in the Levant). The verdict has been determined before the trial begins, and arrangements have been made to have informers on hand.

'In order that they might put him to death': it is directly contrary to all that we know of the rules of Sanhedrin procedure to hold a trial on a capital charge at night. Our evidence, it must be admitted, comes from the Mishnah (Tractate *Sanhedrin*), which was not put together until late in the second century, more than a hundred years after the trial of Jesus, when the Great Sanhedrin had long ceased to function as the supreme court of the Jewish people; but the tractate seems to be an honest attempt to put on record the rules that were in force when the Sanhedrin was a living institution. (The compilers were not innovators; they were bent on promoting continuity with Israel's past.)

VERSE 60: Matthew shortens and simplifies Mark again, cutting away the clause, 'their testimonies were not in agreement'. Naturally, if witnesses were suborned to give false testimony, they would have been rehearsed to ensure their agreement. It is enough for Matthew that the court did not accept the word of these informers—rather strangely, if 'they were seeking false testimony' (v.59).

The two who came forward at the last are not called 'false witnesses' in Matthew (as they are in Mark), probably because he believed that Jesus had in fact said something to this effect.

VERSE 61: The saying about the destruction and rebuilding of the Temple evidently circulated in several forms as a saying of Jesus. Matthew has already reported explicitly a prediction of the destruction of the Temple (24:2), with no mention of any kind of rebuilding.

Mark gives the saying in the form: 'I will destroy this Temple made with hands, and in the space of three days I will build another, made without hands' (14:58; that is, a spiritual temple; cf. the same contrast in Paul's teaching about the life to come, where it is applied to the habitation of the blessed: after the dissolution of 'this earthly tent we live in', it is replaced by a 'building from God'; our 'eternal house' is not the grave, as in the epitaphs of pagans, but 'a house not made with hands'—2 Cor.5:1; cf. the 'spiritual body' of 1 Cor.15: 44).

In John we are given a quite different version of the saying, where it is interpreted by the evangelist as a prediction of Jesus' resurrection. 'Destroy this temple, and in three days I will raise it' (2:19); 'But he spoke of the temple of his body, and when he was raised from the dead his disciples remembered that he had said this' (v.21f.).

We may suggest that a genuine saying of Jesus which foretold the destruction of the Temple was reshaped under the influence of an early development of Christian doctrine about the church as the 'body' of Christ (1 Cor.12:27; Col.1:18; Eph.1:22f., etc.), the growing realization that the Temple worship had been superseded by the worship 'in spirit and truth' (Jn.4:23), and then by the actual destruction of the Temple. Once the church was conceived as the 'living temple' and as the 'body of Christ', it was no long step to take his prophecy of the destruction of the Temple as a veiled reference to his own death, and then to supplement it with a prophecy (likewise veiled) of his resurrection. John remarks significantly that the disciples attached no such significance to the saying until after Jesus was raised from the dead. Implicitly, Matthew hints at this in his suppression of the accusation that the two witnesses who reported this saying were 'false witnesses' like the others.

VERSE 63: Like Mark, Matthew is content to record the impressive silence of Jesus. In Luke, where the whole interrogation takes place at the early morning session, Jesus answers, 'If I tell you, you will not believe me; and if I question you, you will not answer' (Lk.22:67f.).

Matthew reshapes the question of the High Priest into a challenge. In Mark, he asks only, 'Are you the Messiah, the Son of the Blessed One?' In Matthew, he first invokes the authority of 'the living God', and bids him say whether he is 'the Messiah, the Son of God'. In either form, the question seems to take for granted that a claim to Messiahship carries with it a claim to be God's 'son'—though Hebrew tradition always speaks of the Messiah as a *human* ruler, a 'son of David'. The High Priest is made to speak in language that belongs to the Christology of the Church, not to any Hebraic Messianology.

VERSE 64: The first words of Jesus are of doubtful meaning. Does he mean to accept as true what the High Priest wants him to admit, or should the words be taken as a counter-question: 'Is that the way that *you* would put it?' In Mark, there is no room for doubt. Jesus answers flatly, 'I am' (ἐγώ εἰμί)—in language that recalls the self-proclamation of Deity, as, for instance, in Exodus 3:14, in the Isis aretalogies, and in the *Hermetica* (cf. the many 'I am' proclamations of the Second Isaiah, and again of the Fourth Gospel).

There are a number of merely verbal changes in the wording of the pronouncement which follows. The opening clause is added by Matthew, and also the phrase 'from now on' (ἀπ' ἄρτι). The figure of the Son of man rests upon the imagery of the book of Daniel; but there the 'one like a son of man' is not seated on the right hand of God ('the Power'), but comes to him (pictured in Daniel as 'one that was ancient of days'); he comes 'with [in Mark, "upon"] the clouds of heaven'—not to earth, but to the enthroned 'Most High', after the overthrow of the four earthly monarchs (Dan.7:9–13,26f.). For the Christian reader, of course, it is clear that 'the Son of man' means Jesus, and his coming with, or upon, the clouds of heaven foretells the return of Jesus in glory and power to take up his Kingdom. But it is hard to imagine how the High Priest could interpret the words in such a sense. What would lead him to suppose that Jesus was speaking of himself, when he used these apocalyptic words about the coming of the Son of man? The words could have no point at all except for one who had been taught a 'son of man' Christology. It is highly improbable that Jesus ever spoke of himself in such terms as these; and if he had, no High Priest—no non-Christian Jew, for that matter—could have regarded them as anything but the meaningless ravings of a fanatic.

VERSE 65: The reaction of the High Priest, and his words, are equally incredible. The rending of garments is a well-known Jewish gesture to express outrage; but the cry: 'He has spoken blasphemy!' (not in Mark) is not justified by the words attributed to Jesus. The claim to be the Messiah would not be regarded as blasphemous, however false it might be; and a prophecy about the coming of a 'Son of man' has not a trace of blasphemy about it. By the same token, there could be no appeal to the members of the court to recognize that they had heard Jesus speaking blasphemy.

VERSE 66: 'What is your judgement?'—in place of Mark's 'What is your opinion?' (δοκεῖ in place of φαίνεται) indicates that the High Priest is asking the court to make a judicial decision; and the answer is meant to suggest that they condemned Jesus to death. But the rules as known to us from the Mishnah laid down that if the verdict were 'Guilty', the case must be carried over till the next day before sentence was pronounced.

VERSES 67–68: Matthew cuts away the clause, 'they threw a cloth over his face' (Mark, Luke), although it is really needed to prepare for the demand that he should demonstrate his powers as a prophet by telling who had struck him, even though his face was covered.

But there is something incongruous about the notion that a session of the supreme court of the nation would break up in this unruly fashion, with the members of the Sanhedrin assailing the prisoner who was before them for judgement. Luke, with more plausibility, transfers this bit of horse-play to the guards who were holding Jesus in custody before the Sanhedrin assembled (Lk.22: 63–65). John has nothing resembling it (unless 18:22 may be regarded as a faint echo of it).

As the story is given in Mark and Matthew, it appears to be nothing but a fabrication. If there is any core of fact underneath it all, it is probably to be seen in something more like the kind of preliminary enquiry which is described in John, who has Jesus brought before Annas (the father-in-law of Caiaphas) for a summary questioning before he is taken to Caiaphas (Jn.18:12f.,19–24). (Annas had been High Priest some years earlier, but was deposed in AD 15 by the Roman governor, and replaced perhaps three years later by Caiaphas, who was still in office.) In John's account there is no calling of witnesses, no assembling of the Sanhedrin, and no verdict.

Interlude: Denial and Remorse of Peter 26:69–75

[69] Peter remained sitting in the courtyard outside. A servant-girl came along and said, 'You also were with Jesus the Galilaean.' [70] But he denied it before them all, declaring, 'I do not know what you are talking about.' [71] After he had gone out to the portal, another servant-girl saw him and said to those around, 'This man was with Jesus the Nazarene.' [72] He again denied, on oath, 'I do not know the man.' [73] After a little while the bystanders came near and said to Peter, 'It is true that you are one of them; your accent gives you away.' [74] At that, he began to voice imprecations, and to take oath

that 'I do not know the man.' Immediately a cock crowed; [75] and Peter remembered the word that Jesus had spoken: 'Before the cock crows, you will deny me three times'; and he went out and broke into bitter weeping.

Matthew revises the Markan story, but again the changes are trifling. In Mark the crowing of the cock is heard twice, in keeping with Mark's form of the prediction (Mk.14:30). In Mark it is the one maid who makes the two accusations; in Matthew, the second is made by another. Matthew speaks of Jesus as 'the Galilean' in verse 69, in place of Mark's 'the Nazarene'; but he uses 'the Nazarene' in verse 71 (no equivalent in Mark). He cuts away the preposition $\pi\alpha\rho(\alpha)$ of the participial form in verse 73 (but keeps to the same verb); and he changes Mark's $\dot{\alpha}\nu\alpha$—to $\kappa\alpha\tau\alpha$—in verse 74, with no effect upon the meaning. In the last verse, he changes Mark's 'throwing himself down' ($\dot{\epsilon}\pi\iota\beta\alpha\lambda\dot{\omega}\nu$) to 'going outside' ($\dot{\epsilon}\xi\epsilon\lambda\theta\dot{\omega}\nu\ \dot{\epsilon}\xi\omega$). This is the same type of trifling, pointless alteration that we have observed so often throughout the Passion narrative. Obviously, it is done deliberately, systematically, with method. About all we can say is that it confirms the priority of Mark to Matthew; for the rough-hewn, unadorned prose style of Mark (hardly to be called 'style' at all) is not the product of a writer capable of this kind of attention to minutiae.

VERSE 69: Mark and John speak of Peter warming himself at a fire. Mark tells us that the servant-girl was in the employ of the High Priest; John calls her 'the portress'.

VERSE 71: 'The portal'—Matthew seems to picture a wide gateway with space enough to give standing room for a number of people; Mark calls it 'the forecourt' ($\pi\rho\sigma\alpha\dot{\nu}\lambda\iota\sigma\nu$).

VERSE 73: It is implied that the Jews of Galilee spoke with a recognizable accent, which was probably looked upon as uncouth by inhabitants of the capital. The accent would prove that he came from Galilee, but hardly that he was among the followers of Jesus.

VERSE 74: The 'imprecations' do not mean mere profane language, but the invoking of a curse on himself if he does not speak the truth.

VERSE 75: It may be that the substitution of $\dot{\epsilon}\xi\epsilon\lambda\theta\dot{\omega}\nu\ \dot{\epsilon}\xi\omega$ for Mark's $\dot{\epsilon}\pi\iota\beta\alpha\lambda\dot{\omega}\nu$ is due to the difficulty of understanding $\dot{\epsilon}\pi\iota\beta\alpha\lambda\dot{\omega}\nu$ in this context; it still causes trouble to commentators and grammarians (Taylor, *Mark*, p.576). Matthew's version takes Peter out of the danger zone. His bitter remorse does not lead him to admit openly that he is in fact a follower of Jesus.

Jesus before Pilate 27:1–14

¹ Early in the morning, all the chief priests and the elders of the people devised a plan for bringing Jesus to his death. ² They put him in bonds, led him off, and delivered him to Pilate the Roman governor.

INTERLUDE: REMORSE AND SUICIDE OF JUDAS

³ When Judas, who had betrayed him, saw that he was doomed, he repented; and he brought back the thirty pieces of silver to the chief priests and the elders, ⁴ saying, 'I have sinned in betraying innocent blood.' They said, 'What is that to us? See to it yourself.' ⁵ He threw down the pieces of silver in the sanctuary and left them; he went off and hanged himself. ⁶ The chief priests, taking the pieces of silver, said, 'It is not lawful to put them into the treasury, for this is blood money.' ⁷ After some discussion they used them to buy the potter's field, to be a burial place for foreigners; ⁸ therefore that field has been called 'the Field of Blood' to this day. ⁹ Then there was fulfilled the oracle that was delivered through Jeremiah the prophet, which runs,

'They took the thirty pieces of silver, the price at which some of the sons of Israel valued the Valued One, ¹⁰ and they gave them for the potter's field, as the Lord commanded me.'

THE STORY OF THE TRIAL CONTINUES

¹¹ Jesus stood in the presence of the governor, and the governor asked him, 'Are you the king of the Jews?' Jesus said, 'So you have said.' ¹² When he was accused by the chief priests and elders, he made no answer. ¹³ Pilate said to him, 'Do you not hear all the charges that they are bringing against you?' ¹⁴ But Jesus gave him no answer, not even to a single charge; so that the governor was utterly astounded.

The story of the death of Judas is awkwardly interpolated into the account of Jesus' presentation before Pilate. The chief priests and elders, we have just been told, are haling Jesus into the presence of Pilate (v.2), and will be making accusations in the hall of judgement (v.12); but here they are represented as gathered somewhere in the temple where Judas can find them to give back the money which they had paid him to betray Jesus. The whole story is obviously fictional. We may suppose that it originated as an explanation of the strange name of the cemetery set apart for the burial of foreigners in Jerusalem. A different form of the legend is given in the book of Acts (1:18–19); in this story, it is Judas who buys the field with the money which he had received ('the reward of his wickedness'); but he suffered a ghastly retribution, apparently on the very field which he had purchased, where he suddenly died of a strange seizure ('he fell flat on his face and all his bowels gushed out'); and it was this circumstance which caused the place to be called 'Field of Blood'. There is no suggestion that it was used as a cemetery. Matthew wanted to work in the 'thirty pieces of silver' of the Zechariah oracle, which he had already mentioned in his story of the deal made with Judas (26:15), and he now combines this with a passage from Jeremiah, as part of the proof that all had been foretold. The citation as he gives it (vv.9f.) comes only in small part from Jeremiah, and none of it corresponds exactly to any known text of either Jeremiah or Zechariah.

The whole passage is said to have been 'spoken through the prophet Jeremiah', but in fact it contains only two stray phrases from Jeremiah, *viz.*, 18:2, 'go down to the potter's house' and 32:9, 'I bought the field at Anathoth from Hanamel my cousin, and weighed out the money to him, seventeen shekels of silver' (39:9 LXX). This is completely irrelevant in the Matthaean context; there is nothing but the mention of a potter in the one passage, and of a field that is purchased with pieces of silver (shekels) in the other. The concluding phrase, 'as the Lord commanded me', may be a reminiscence of Zech.11:13, 'Then the Lord said to me', but it reproduces the language of Exodus 9:12 (LXX), 'as the Lord had commanded' ('ordained'—of the hardening of Pharaoh's heart). The substance of the citation comes from Zechariah 11:13, but it is so mangled as to be almost impossible for us to disentangle. In the Hebrew text, it is the prophet who speaks, not of what others did, but of his own action: 'The Lord said to me, "Cast it to the potter: the lordly price at which I was paid off by them." So I took the thirty pieces of silver and cast them to the potter in the house of the Lord.' But the text is clearly corrupt, and modern interpreters generally read 'treasury' in place of 'potter'; this is how the word is rendered in the Syriac translation. In Greek (LXX), it is rendered χωνευτήριον, 'smelting-furnace'. Matthew appears to have some acquaintance with the reading behind the Syriac, and the 'treasury' is transferred into the words of the chief priests, when they find that it would not be permissible to put the money into the treasury (κορβανᾶς—a transliteration of the Aramaic word), since it was blood money. This is surely the most extravagant example of Matthew's handling of scriptures as proof-texts. Perhaps it is to be understood along the lines of Allen's suggestion, that the translator (the evangelist himself) allows the facts on which he is commenting to creep into his translation, and that he 'seems to have the Hebrew text in mind, and to have quoted from memory'. However he arrived at what he wrote, it must be agreed that he has botched it badly.

VERSE 1: The proceedings are described with much vagueness. It is hard to make out how the evangelist intends us to relate this morning activity of the chief priests and elders of the people with the night deliberations (judicial or pseudo-judicial) in the presence of Caiaphas (26:57–68). Matthew again makes strange alterations in the wording of Mark, who speaks of 'the chief priests with the elders and scribes', to which he adds, 'and the whole Sanhedrin' (Mk.15:1); Matthew makes no mention of 'the scribes' or of 'the whole Sanhedrin'. Does he wish to avoid representing this as a meeting of the Sanhedrin? Luke, on the other hand, makes this the first and only meeting of the Sanhedrin—there is no trace of a previous night session (Lk.22:66ff.).

VERSE 11: No foundation has been laid for the question of Pilate, 'Are you the king of the Jews?' As in Mark, the governor asks the question on his own initiative, before he has heard the reason for bringing the prisoner before him. Luke evidently felt it desirable to pave the way, and has therefore supplied a series of accusations made by the men of the Sanhedrin: 'We found this man perverting our nation, forbidding us to give tribute to Caesar, and claiming that he himself is Messiah, that is, King' (Lk.23:2). We are then left with the impression (by Luke) that the Sanhedrin held its meeting for the sole purpose of formulating the charges that were to be laid against Jesus.

Jesus neither admits nor denies the title; the words οὐ εἶπας, '[So] you have said', are ambiguous. It is perhaps intended to suggest that Jesus is indeed King of Israel, but not in any sense that Pilate would understand. John makes this explicit: 'My kingdom is not of this world; if my kingdom were of this world, my servants would be fighting to keep me from being handed over to the Jews' (Jn.18:36).

VERSE 12: At last we hear of accusations made by 'the chief priests and elders', but without any indication of the specific charges.

VERSE 14: The emphasis is on the silence of Jesus. No reference is made to the silence of the Suffering Servant ('like a sheep that before its shearers is dumb, so he opened not his mouth' (Isa.53:7); but that passage may well have influenced the shaping of the story. From this point, in Mark and Matthew, Jesus never speaks except to utter the 'cry of dereliction' (v.46 // Mk.15:34; from Ps.22:1). There is no such silence in Luke, where Jesus addresses the weeping women

of Jerusalem (23:28—31), and the repentant thief (23:43); and
makes his final prayer for the forgiveness of his executioners (23:46).
In John, Jesus holds an extended conversation with Pilate (18:33—
38), and utters four sayings from the cross (19:26—30).

It is not clear why the silence of Jesus caused such great astonishment in the prefect, or rather, why Matthew (after Mark, with
enhanced emphasis [λίαν]) thinks it worth mentioning. Factually,
of course, no one but Pilate was in a position to say how he was
impressed by the silence of Jesus; it can hardly be claimed that Mark
had a sure 'tradition' that he was astonished. Perhaps it was Mark
who was astonished that Jesus made no answer to the Jewish accusations, and thought that Pilate must have been equally astonished.

The Question of Amnesty: Jesus or Barabbas? 27:15—23

[15] At the festival, the governor had a custom of releasing for the
masses a prisoner of their choice. [16] They were holding at that time
a notorious prisoner, Jesus Barabbas by name. [17] So when they had
assembled, Pilate said to them, 'Whom do you wish me to release for
you, Jesus Barabbas or Jesus who is called Christ?' [18] For he knew
that it was out of envy that they had delivered him up. [19] While he
was seated on the tribunal, his wife sent word to him, 'Take no
action in the matter of that righteous man, for I have been deeply
disturbed today in a dream about him.' [20] The chief priests and the
elders had persuaded the masses that they should ask for the release
of Barabbas, and bring Jesus to his death. [21] So when the governor
asked them, 'Which of the two do you wish me to release for you?'
they said, 'Barabbas!' [22] Pilate said to them, 'Then what shall I do
with Jesus who is called Christ?' They all said, 'Let him be crucified!'
[23] He said, 'Why? What harm has he done?' But they shouted all the
more loudly, 'Let him be crucified!'

VERSES 16—17: The evidence for the reading Jesus Barabbas is
strong, though peculiar. On the basis of our existing manuscripts, we
should have to opt for the omission of Jesus, for it is included only
in a small group of Caesarean witnesses, and in the Sinaitic Syriac,
the Palestinian Syriac (lectionary), the Armenian version, and one of
the Georgian versions. The evidence which leads us to favour the
retention of the name Jesus here is not that of these more or less
secondary witnesses, but the testimony of Origen, who remarks that
'in many copies it is not stated that Barabbas was also called Jesus',
and comments that this omission 'may be right'. This shows clearly

that most of the manuscripts known to him around the year 200 actually read 'Jesus Barabbas'. But he indicates that he does not like that reading, on the ground that 'in the whole range of the scriptures we know that no one who is a sinner is called Jesus.' There is also a comment in a number of manuscripts, in the margin, that the commentator (usually named either as Chrysostom or as Anastasius of Antioch or—once only—as Origen) affirms that 'in many ancient manuscripts . . . I found Barabbas himself likewise called "Jesus".'

It is not unnatural that scribes (and theologians) should be offended that the notorious bandit should also bear the name of 'Jesus'; and that this feeling should bring about the dropping of the name from most of our best existing witnesses. But it is really impossible that Christian scribes should ever have attached the name 'Jesus' to Barabbas, if it were not there to begin with. There is, therefore, a strong intrinsic probability that the original text of Matthew gave the double name. Barabbas is a patronymic, not a personal name, and as a rule it would be attached to a personal name rather than be used by itself. It would give further offense to Christian ears that Barabbas, in Aramaic, would mean 'son of Abba'—that is, of 'the father', or possibly 'of the teacher' (*bar-rabban*).

Apart from the Gospels (not including Luke) there is no evidence that Pilate or any other Roman governor made a custom of granting amnesty to a criminal on the occasion of Passover or any other festival. If the charge were brigandage or, even more, if it were guerilla activity, it seems unlikely that a Roman governor would grant amnesty, especially in the explosive atmosphere of first-century Palestine. It is at least doubtful that Pilate ever contemplated the release of such a notorious prisoner as this Barabbas. (Matthew does not say what his crimes may have been, but in Mark we are told that 'he had been imprisoned along with the revolutionaries who had committed murder in the insurrection'—Mk.15:7.) In John he is called 'a bandit' λῃστής, and in Luke it is said that he had been put in prison 'because of an insurrection that had taken place in the city, and for murder' (Lk.23:19).

Whether the story be entirely fictional or not, we may say that it is included in the Gospels because it pictures the essential elements of the conflict in the Palestine of the period.[1] The Jewish people

[1] A. Schlatter, (*Matthäus*, p.774): 'Für einen Palästiner, der die Jahre 30—60 miterlebte, hatte dieser Vorgang die grösste Bedeutung. Entweder Jesus—oder der gegen die römische Herrschaft anstürmende Bandit, vor diese Wahl war die Judenschaft bleibend gestellt. Sie wählte den λῃστής (Bandit) nicht einzig an jenem Tag.'

were faced with the choice between insurrection, represented by Barabbas, and peaceful submission to the ruling power, waiting confidently for God to establish his Kingdom as represented by Jesus. Not once, but consistently, they chose Barabbas.[1]

The story has no further interest in Barabbas himself. It is concerned only with the case against Judaism—that the masses, prompted by their religious leaders, clamour for the crucifixion of Jesus and for the freeing of a guerilla leader.

VERSE 18: The assertion that Pilate knew that the hostile priests were moved by envy comes from Mark. It is not clear that Mark (or any Christian tradition behind him) knew so well what was in Pilate's mind. Nor is it at all evident that the religious leaders of Judaism were 'envious' of Jesus. What would give rise to envy? Fear that he might cause trouble for the nation, even to the point of bringing it to disaster, is more plausible. (Cf. the attitude attributed to 'the chief priests and the Pharisees gathered in the Sanhedrin'— 'If we let him go on thus, every one will believe in him, and the Romans will come and destroy both our holy place and our nation'; and expressed again in the cold cynicism of Caiaphas—Jn.11:47—50.)

VERSE 19: The dream of Pilate's wife is our earliest trace of the legend that was eventually to make her into a Christian saint (in the Eastern churches) under the name of Procula (or Procla). Her date in the calendar is 27 October. The Copts go so far as to make Pilate also a saint and martyr; they celebrate a joint festival of Pilate and Procla on 25 June.

VERSE 20: Nothing is said of when and how 'the chief priests and elders' had induced 'the crowds' to demand the release of Barabbas and the crucifixion of Jesus. Here again, the interest of the story is to enhance the general guilt of priests and masses and to diminish the responsibility of the Roman authorities.

VERSE 23: Here Pilate merely asks for some reason for inflicting the death penalty; it is implied, but not stated, that he as yet has been shown no cause for such action. In Luke, the exculpation of the governor goes much further; three times he formally declares that the finds Jesus not guilty (Lk.23:4,14f.,22—in an ascending order of clarity: 'I find no crime in this man'; 'I did not find this man guilty of any of your charges against him . . . nothing deserving of death has been done by him'; 'I have found in him no crime deserving death'). In John, the governor declares three times, 'I find no crime in him' (Jn.18:38; 19:4,6). It scarcely needs to be said that this is Christian propaganda, not objective reporting.

Pilate Washes his Hands 27:24—26

²⁴ When Pilate saw that he was accomplishing nothing, but rather that a riot was threatening to break out, he took water and washed his hands in the face of the crowd, saying, 'I am innocent of this [righteous] man's blood; it is your responsibility.' ²⁵ And all the people answered, 'His blood be upon us and upon our children.' ²⁶ Then he released Barabbas for them; and he had Jesus flogged, and delivered him up to be crucified.

The procedure of washing the hands as a repudiation of responsibility for a crime might have meaning for Jews, but was unknown among the Romans. Even in the Jewish law, it is prescribed only in relation to 'any one who is found slain, lying in the open country, and it is not known who killed him' (Deut.21:1—9); it has nothing to do with a situation in which a judge who is to pass sentence on a living man wishes to shift the responsibility onto other shoulders. The whole story—peculiar to Matthew—is surely to be regarded as a further step in the Christian programme of laying the whole guilt on the Jews, and absolving the Romans, so far as that could be done. But nothing could remove the prime difficulty of this propaganda, namely, that crucifixion was a Roman method of execution, not in the least Jewish.

The cry of verse 25, whereby the Jews of the time invoke upon themselves and upon their children the whole guilt for the death of Jesus, is of course nothing but hostile invention. No such cry was ever uttered. It is to be noted that it is no longer 'the crowd' (ὄχλος) or 'the crowds' or 'masses' (ὄχλοι) that raise the cry, it is 'the whole nation' (of Israel)—πᾶς ὁ λαός—the chosen race in its entirety! It is appalling for a Christian to think of how much suffering has been inflicted upon Jews throughout the ages, partly as a result of this completely fictitious scene.

VERSE 26 (a recasting of Mark 15:15) is all that can be maintained as factual, and that only in respect to the action of Pilate in having Jesus flogged, and giving orders for him to be crucified. (The verb παραδίδωμι again sounds the theme that the divine plan is being carried out, though by many different instruments; the rulers of Jesus 'give him up' to Pilate; Pilate 'gives him up' to the executioners.)

5 CRUCIFIXION, DEATH, AND BURIAL 27:27—66

Prelude: Jesus Mocked by the Soldiery 27:27—31

²⁷ Then the soldiers of the governor, having taken charge of Jesus in

the praetorium, brought together the entire cohort against him.
28 They stripped him of his clothing, and put on him a scarlet cloak
(chlamys), 29 plaited a crown of thorns and set it on his head, and
placed a reed in his right hand. They knelt down before him and said,
in mockery, 'Hail, King of the Jews!' 30 They spat on him, and took
the reed and beat him about the head. 31 And when they had done
with their mocking, they took off the chlamys and put his own
clothes back on him, and led him off for crucifixion.

VERSE 27: The 'taking charge' by the soldiers corresponds to the
'delivering up' of Pilate ($\pi\alpha\rho\acute{\epsilon}\delta\omega\kappa\epsilon\nu$, $\pi\alpha\rho\alpha\lambda\alpha\beta\acute{o}\nu\tau\epsilon\varsigma$); these
correlated verbs are frequently used of passing on and receiving a
tradition (e.g., 1 Cor.11:23). The participle here is introduced by
Matthew (it is not in Mark). Mark uses the curious phrase, 'the
soldiers led him inside the palace, which is the praetorium' (15:16),
whereas Matthew seems to eliminate any change of scene (his $\epsilon\grave{\iota}\varsigma$
with the accusative exhibits the tendency for $\epsilon\grave{\iota}\varsigma$ to replace $\epsilon\nu$
[with the dative] in the Koiné—a tendency which has completely
triumphed in modern Greek).

'The whole cohort'—the company of some hundreds which
Pilate had brought up with him from Caesarea.

VERSE 28: Mark speaks of a 'purple cloak' $\pi\acute{o}\rho\phi\upsilon\rho\alpha$; Matthew
of the chlamys, a short cape originally worn by horsemen from
Thessaly, but at this time a part of the foot soldier's equipment. In
the mockery of the soldiers, it is intended to represent a royal
robe—Jesus is to be attired as a king, with a reed in his hand as his
sceptre and an acanthus wreath as his crown.

VERSE 29: The reed-sceptre is peculiar to Matthew; in Mark it is
said only that they beat him about the head with a reed. Neither
Luke nor John make any mention of a reed.

In Luke, the whole episode of the mockery is transferred to the
residence of Herod Antipas, as part of a tale of how Pilate sent
Jesus over to Herod, who happened to be in Jerusalem at the time
(Lk.23:6—11). The other Gospels know nothing of such an episode,
and indeed it is hard to imagine that there was time for such a
movement back and forth on that morning if Jesus was crucified
at 'the third hour' (Mk.15:25), roughly about nine o'clock. (In
John, Jesus has not yet been sentenced; 'it was about the sixth hour'
when Pilate 'handed him over to them to be crucified'—Jn.19:14,
16.) Apart from the time problem, it is highly unlikely that the
Roman governor would arrange for an accused person to be transferred to the tetrarch of Galilee.

(Luke has a second reference to concerted action of Herod and Pontius Pilate in a prayer of the church (Acts 4:27). It follows up a citation of Psalm 2 which speaks of 'kings of the earth' and 'rulers' acting together 'against the Lord and against his Messiah' (Anointed, in Greek, χριστός), and it is likely that his whole story is a midrash on that Psalm.)

The Crucifixion 27:32-44

[32] As they were going out, they found a man of Cyrene, Simon by name; this man they pressed into service, to carry his cross. [33] When they had reached a place called Golgotha (which means 'Place of a Skull'), [34] they gave him wine to drink, mixed with gall; when he had tasted it, he refused to drink. [35] When they had crucified him they divided his clothes among them, casting lots for them, [36] and they kept watch over him there, sitting on the ground. [37] Above his head, they nailed up the charge against him inscribed on a tablet reading, 'This is Jesus the king of the Jews.' [38] Along with him they crucified two bandits, one on his right and one his left. [39] The people passing by jeered at him, wagging their heads [40] and saying, 'You that talked of destroying the temple and rebuilding it in three days, save yourself, if you are God's son, come down from the cross.' [41] In the same way the chief priests, and the scribes and elders along with them, made sport of him, saying, [42] 'He saved others; he cannot save himself. King of Israel that he is, let him come down from the cross and we will believe in him. [43] He trusted in God; let God rescue him now, if he wants him; for, said he, "I am God's son."' [44] Even the bandits who were crucified along with him reviled him in the same fashion.

This is not so much a connected story as a series of graphic touches. Simon appears for a moment, but nothing is said of what became of him afterwards. (Matthew omits the statements of Mark that he was 'the father of Alexander and Rufus', and that he was 'coming from a field' ['from the country'—*RSV*] Mk.15:21.) They reach Golgotha, and we are told abruptly that they offered him a drink of wine 'mixed with gall' (in Mark 'with myrrh'), which he tasted but refused to drink (in Mark he does not even taste it). The action of putting him on the cross is mentioned only in a participial clause (after they had crucified him), with the main clause telling of the soldiers throwing dice for his clothes. Then we are told that they sat on the ground and kept watch over him. The next sentence mentions the *titulus*—the placard attached to the cross to give information of the offence with which he was charged. Only then do we have the brief note that two others were crucified at the same time, one on either side of him. With that we are told of the jeering, first of the passing throng, then of the chief priests and scribes, and finally of the bandits who hung on crosses beside him. This raillery is evidently the heart of the crucifixion scene; it draws upon the taunting of the 'righteous man' as described in Wisdom 2:12–20:

> Let us lie in wait for the righteous man,
>> because he is inconvenient to us and opposes our actions;
> he reproaches us for sins against the law,
>> and accuses us of sins against our training.
> He professes to have knowledge of God,
>> and calls himself a child [or 'servant'] of the Lord.
> . . . .
> Let us see if his words are true,
>> and let us test what will happen at the end of his life;
> for if the righteous man is God's son,
>> he will help him,
>> and will deliver him from the hand of his adversaries.
> Let us test him with insult and torture,
> that we may find out how gentle he is,
>> and make trial of his forbearance.
> Let us condemn him to a shameful death,
>> for, according to what he says, he will be protected.

In verse 43 (not taken from Mark) Matthew all but cites Psalm 21 (22) 7f.:

> All who see me mock at me,
>> they make mouths at me, they wag their heads;
> 'He committed his cause to the Lord; let him deliver him.
>> let him rescue him, for he delights in him.'

(Many verses of this psalm are quoted, or more loosely drawn upon, in the Passion narrative. From an early time—before Mark or Matthew—it was read and interpreted, not unnaturally, as a portrayal of the crucifixion.)

The Death of Jesus 27:45–56

[45] From the sixth hour until the ninth there was darkness over the whole earth. [46] About the ninth hour Jesus shouted with a loud voice, 'Èli, Èli lema sabachthani?' (which means, 'My God, my God, why have you forsaken me?') [47] Some of the bystanders, when they heard this, said, 'This man is calling upon Elijah.' [48] One of them ran to get a sponge, filled it with vinegar, and stuck it on a reed and gave

it to him to drink. [49] The rest said, 'Let us see if Elijah comes to save him.' [50] And Jesus again cried out in a loud voice, and breathed his last.

[51] With that, the curtain of the sanctuary was torn in two from top to bottom, there was an earthquake, and the rocks were shattered. [52] Now the tombs were opened, and many bodies of saints who had fallen asleep were raised; [53] they went out from the tombs after his resurrection, went into the holy city, and made appearances to many. [54] When the centurion and the troops with him who were keeping watch over Jesus saw the earthquake and the other happenings, they were greatly frightened, and they said, 'Truly this man was God's son.'

[55] Many women were there, looking on from a distance—women who had followed Jesus from Galilee, doing him service; [56] among them were Mary Magdalene, and Mary the mother of James and Joseph, and the mother of the sons of Zebedee.

VERSE 45: It is possible that the evangelists intend to say 'over the whole land' (i.e., the land of Israel) rather than 'over all the earth' ($\pi \hat{\alpha} \sigma \alpha \nu$ [Mt.; Mk. and Lk. $\ddot{o} \lambda \eta \nu$] $\tau \dot{\eta} \nu$ $\gamma \hat{\eta} \nu$ could be taken in either sense). But it seems likely that they think in terms of a *cosmic* event.

VERSE 46: In terms of physiology, we are told that after hanging on a cross for six hours, the sufferer would hardly have strength and energy enough to raise his voice above a gasp or whisper; a 'loud voice' would be physically impossible. Of course, it would not occur to the evangelists to take the physical possibilities into account; in any case, they would not think of Jesus as being subject to ordinary human limitations.

The cry of Jesus consists of the opening verse of Psalm 22. In Mark, it is given in Aramaic (UBS text; in WH it is 'a transliteration of a Hebraized Aramaic original'—Taylor, *Mark, ad loc.*). In Matthew, the text as printed in most of our modern editions substitutes the Hebrew *eli* for the Aramaic *eloi* (Westcott and Hort retained the Aramaic *eloi*, with Aleph, B, 33, etc.). In both Gospels, the text has multiple variants (Metzger, *Textual Commentary*, pp.70,119f.).

Two questions arise (supposing that the words are audible to the watching throng): first, how would Jewish bystanders, supposing that they failed to recognize the Psalm, ever take either the Hebrew *Ēli* or the Aramaic *Ēloi* for an appeal to Elijah? Secondly, does the evangelist intend to convey to us that the last words of Jesus were a cry of despair (as is generally assumed), or does he think of Jesus as having in mind the entire Psalm, which issues in the triumph of faith over a situation of despair? Dibelius remarks (*Formgeschichte*, pp.194f.) that any one who imagines that a Christian evangelist would represent the so-called 'cry of dereliction' as an utterance of ultimate despair is far off the track:

Man setzt dabei einen Berichterstatter voraus, der, nur an der Geschichte interessiert, auch das Peinliche und dem Christentum Abträgliche treulich auf die Nachwelt bringt. Diesen Berichterstatter hat es nicht gegeben; denn die ganze Leidensgeschichte ist zur Erbauung und nicht zur Beirrung der Christen geschrieben. . . .

Schon die literarische Art der Leidensgeschichte schliesst . . . eine solche Deutung aus. . . . Denn jenes letzte Wort Jesu ist der Anfang des 22. Psalms, des Psalms, der den Christen ganz wesentlich das Verständnis der Passion erschlossen hatte . . . . Wer diesen Ruf des jüdischen Beters in höchster Not nachspricht, drückt nicht unfrommes Widerstreben gegen Gott aus; ein Bibelwort auf den Lippen eines Sterbenden bedeutet dieser Bibelfrömmigkeit unter allen Umständen Einklang mit Gott. . . . in keinem Fall kommt in diesem Ruf verzweifelte Trostlosigkeit zum Ausdruck, immer ist biblisches Wort Zeugnis des Glaubens.

Luke has substituted for this last word of Jesus an unambiguous, unmistakeable expression of absolute faith: 'Father, into your hands I commit my spirit' (from Ps.31:5). This is still described as uttered in a loud voice (Lk.23:46).

In John there is no 'loud voice', and nothing akin to the Markan-Matthaean word is spoken. Jesus' last word is τετέλεσται, 'It is finished' (Jn.19:30).

The convulsions of nature and the resurrection of dead saints (vv.51b–53) are peculiar to Matthew. Only the ripping apart of the curtain over the sanctuary is taken over from Mark (even this is not mentioned in Luke or John). The curtain was not visible from outside the temple. Its rending is not to be taken as a factual report, but as a symbol of the thought that is made explicit in the Epistle to the Hebrews, that through the death of Jesus, the Holy of Holies is opened for all time (Heb.9,10, esp. 10:19: 'we have confidence to enter the sanctuary by the blood of Jesus'), after the writer has pointed out (9:7) that by divine ordinance no one ever went behind the curtain into the sanctuary ('the Holy of Holies') except the high priest, and even he only entered it once a year (on the Day of Atonement). He interprets this symbolism to mean that 'by this the Holy Spirit indicates that the way into the sanctuary is not yet opened as long as the outer tent is still standing' (9:8).

VERSE 54: In Mark it is only the centurion who acknowledges that Jesus is God's Son; and that, simply from seeing how he died.

VERSE 55: The women are mentioned here to prepare the way for their visit to the sepulchre (28:1). The names are taken from Mark, with some variations. 'Mary the mother of James and Joseph' is described in Mark as 'the mother of James the Little and Joses'; and Matthew's 'mother of the sons of Zebedee' replaces Mark's 'Salome'. In Mark, it is said that 'they did him service when he was in Galilee'; Matthew alters this to the effect that they gave their services on the journey.

How large a company is supposed to accompany Jesus from Galilee to Jerusalem, along with his immediate disciples? 'Large crowds' are mentioned as he leaves Galilee—19:2; 'a great crowd', as they leave Jericho—20:29; are these the 'crowd' of 21:8 also? In Luke, we hear that at one point of the journey 'tens of thousands of the crowd had gathered, so that they were treading on one another' (12:1)—this can hardly have been continuing all along the way! Much earlier, Luke mentions in the company 'some women who had been healed of evil spirits and infirmities'. Here again the first to be mentioned is Mary Magdalene 'from whom seven devils had gone out', but the other names are otherwise not known— 'Joanna the wife of Chuza, Herod's steward, and Susanna, and many others, who provided for them out of their means' (Lk.8:2f.).

The Burial 27:57–61

57 In the evening there came a wealthy man from Arimathaea, Joseph by name, who had also become a disciple of Jesus. 58 This man made an approach to Pilate and asked for the body of Jesus. Pilate ordered it to be given him. 59 Having received the body, Joseph wrapped it in a clean linen shroud 60 and laid it in his own new tomb which he had cut out in the rock; he rolled a large stone against the entrance of the tomb and went away. 61 Mary Magdalene was there, and the other Mary, sitting over against the sepulchre.

Matthew again revises the wording of Mark. His 'wealthy' replaces Mark's 'a respected councillor'; and he interprets Mark's description of Joseph as one 'who was waiting expectantly for the kingdom of God' to mean that 'he had become a disciple (ἐμαθητεύθη) of Jesus'. He omits Mark's statements that Pilate 'was surprised to hear that [Jesus] was already dead', that he summoned the centurion to confirm this, and only then gave permission to Joseph to remove the body (Mk.15:44f). Minor changes are made also in the account of the act of burial and in the mention of the two women.

In Luke, Joseph is not described as 'wealthy' but as 'good and righteous', and that, although a member of the Sanhedrin (βουλευτής), he 'had not consented to their purpose and deed' (Lk.23:50f.). He notes that it was 'the day of Preparation' (Friday), 'and the sabbath was beginning'. This prepares the way for the failure to take any further action until the Sunday. The women 'saw the tomb, and how his body was laid' (there is no mention of a stone placed at the entrance, which would have made it impossible to see 'how his body was laid'; but the stone is mentioned in 24:2, as rolled away from the tomb). 'Then they returned and prepared spices and ointments, and on the sabbath they rested according to the commandment' (vv.55f.). John's account has some elements in common with Luke, but in distinction from all the others, he brings Nicodemus in to help Joseph with the burial, and to provide 'a mixture of myrrh and aloes weighing about a hundred pounds' (λίτρα, the Roman pound, weighed about twelve ounces), and he and Joseph wrap these spices in with the shroud about him (Jn.19:39f.). He is embalmed at the time of burial, and there is no need for the women to come with spices (Mk.16:1; Lk.24:1; not in Matthew, where they go only 'to see the sepulchre').

Joseph of Arimathaea has not previously been mentioned. A considerable legend grows around him in time, even to the extent of bringing him to Glastonbury in Britain, carrying with him the Holy Grail, and founding there the first Christian church in the country. A much earlier legend tells us that he took care of the Virgin Mary until her death. The apocryphal *Gospel of Nicodemus* makes him the founder of a church at Lydda. The story of his part in the burial is probably to be regarded as the first element in the legend, and quite as legendary as the later stories. It is doubtful if Jesus received any more distinguished burial than the criminals who were crucified with him; their bodies would be put in a trench and covered with earth by soldiers. Even this was better than the usual treatment of executed men; the Romans commonly left the bodies on the crosses to be devoured by vultures. In Judaea, however, it would have been a serious affront to Jewish law and custom to leave a corpse over night after crucifixion without burial (cf. Deut.21:22f.).

Sequel: The Guard at the Tomb 27:62—66

[62] On the next day, which follows the Preparation, the chief priests and the Pharisees came together to Pilate. [63] 'Sir,' they said, 'we remember that this deceiver said, while he was still living, "After

three days I shall rise." [64] Give orders, then, for the sepulchre to be made secure until the third day, so that his disciples may not go and steal his body and say to the people, "He has risen from the dead", and the last deception will be worse than the first.' [65] Pilate said to them, 'You have your body of guards; go, take such measures of security as you can.' [66] They went and made the sepulchre secure by setting a seal on the stone and posting the guard.

Surely one of the most extravagant of inventions. Nothing like it is found in any of the other Gospels. The Pharisees appear for the first time in the entire Passion story. Here it is they who accompany the chief priests, while up to this point Matthew has spoken of the elders of the people, or of the scribes and the elders, as leading the action against Jesus. But since the disciples themselves do not appear to remember that Jesus predicted that he would rise on the third day—as far as the Gospel story goes there is no suggestion that he ever made such a prediction in public—how could it be supposed that 'the chief priests and the Pharisees' know of it, and remember it so vividly? It would seem, for that matter, that if they really suspected that the disciples would attempt a tomb robbery, they would need to take measures to secure the tomb on the first night as well as the second. Again, the 'next day' would be the sabbath—Matthew avoids pointing this out by saying that it was the day 'after the Preparation'. (Is it natural to speak of Saturday as 'the day after Friday'?) The Pharisees would surely be violating their strong sabbatarian principles if they chose that day to send a deputation to Pilate, in company with the chief priests, for any purpose. We must also doubt whether the prefect would take enough stock in the wild fancy of which they speak to provide them with a detachment of soldiers to keep guard over the tomb, to make it impossible for the corpse to be stolen.

The whole story is given here to pave the way for the allegation that 'the Jews' of Matthew's day alleged that the disciples stole the body away while the guards were sleeping (28:15). Something like this may well have circulated as Jewish propaganda against the Christian proclamation of the resurrection of Jesus; but that the chief priests and the Pharisees actually took measures to make such an attempt at deception is improbable—this can only be regarded as a Christian fabrication devised to counter the current Jewish assertion that Jesus was not raised from the dead.

Epilogue:
The Resurrection of Jesus

Mt. 28:1-20

The proclamation of the resurrection of Jesus was a cardinal element of the apostolic gospel from the start. Paul could say with perfect justice: 'If Christ has not risen, our preaching is vain, and your faith is also vain . . . if Christ has not risen, your faith is vain, you are still in your sins' (1 Cor.15:14,16f.). It was among the 'first things' (ἐν πρώτοις) which he himself received and in his turn delivered to his hearers (1 Cor.15:3–8). Yet nothing is clearer than that all our *narratives* of resurrection appearances are relatively late in formation, and it is significant that none of our Gospels give any account of the appearance to Peter, though the tradition holds that he appeared first to Peter (1 Cor.15:5; Lk.24:34). Mark tells the story of the finding of the empty tomb, and this is taken up in different ways by all the other evangelists, but even that appears to be unknown to Paul. It was not part of the early Passion narrative. Mark recounts no appearances at all.

In the Matthaean version, the resurrection story falls into three parts:

1 The Discovery of the Empty Tomb and Jesus' Appearance to the Women 28:1–10
2 The Bribing of the Guard 28:11–15
3 Reunion in Galilee: The Commission to Evangelize the World 28:16–20

1 THE DISCOVERY OF THE EMPTY TOMB AND JESUS' APPEARANCE TO THE WOMEN *28:1–10*

[1] Late on the sabbath, as it was dawning towards the first day of the week, Mary Magdalene and the other Mary came to see the tomb. [2] Now there was a great earthquake; an angel of the Lord coming down from heaven approached and rolled away the stone, and seated himself upon it. [3] His appearance was like lightning, and his clothing white as snow, [4] and for fear of him the men on guard quaked and became like dead men. [5] But the angel said to the women, 'Do not be afraid. I know that you are looking for Jesus the

Crucified. ⁶ He is not here; he has risen, as he foretold. Come see the place where he lay. ⁷ Now go quickly and tell his disciples that he has risen and is going to Galilee before you. There you will see him. This is my message to you.'

⁸ They went quickly away from the tomb, in fear and great joy; and ran to bring word to his disciples.

SUPPLEMENT: JESUS APPEARS TO THE WOMEN

⁹ Now Jesus met them and said, 'Greetings!' They made approach, took hold of his feet, and worshipped him. ¹⁰ Then Jesus said to them, 'Do not be afraid. Go tell my disciples to go back to Galilee, and there they will see me.'

Matthew has radically revised the Markan story. He omits the mention of a third woman (in Mark, Salome), and the statement that 'when the sabbath was over . . . they bought spices . . . to anoint him' (Mk.16:1). As the Jewish day began at sunset, that would mean that they bought the spices as soon as the shops opened in the evening, planning to do the anointing in the morning when it was light. Matthew cuts away their conversation on the way, about the problem of finding someone to roll away the stone. He adds the note about the earthquake, and the description of the angel and his descent from heaven, and the rolling away of the stone (Mark says nothing about how the stone was rolled away; simply that the women found the entrance clear and went directly into the tomb). As Mark knows nothing of a guard posted at the tomb, it is Matthew who must supply the information about their fright. Matthew has the angel speak to the women outside the tomb; in Mark they see a 'young man clothed in white seated to the right' after they have entered it; no doubt Mark thinks of him as an angel, but he does not call him that. Matthew omits the phrase 'the Nazarene' of Mark, and the mention of Peter individually. Otherwise, the message is substantially in the same words.

The supplement, however, is a much greater departure from Mark, for in Mark there is no appearance of Jesus at all. The women receive the message, indeed, but they are so terrified that they do not even carry the news to the disciples. Mark ends his Gospel on the strange note, 'They said nothing to anyone, for they were afraid.' (There are two Markan supplements, but these are found only in late and inferior witnesses, and there is every reason to believe that Mark deliberately ended his Gospel on this note of mystery.)

It should be observed that the earliest tradition of appearances of the risen Christ that has come down to us (1 Cor.15:4—8) has no relationship with any of the accounts in the Gospels. The appearances listed by Paul (fifteen years or so before Mark was published) are not echoed in the Gospels in any shape or form. There is nothing to show that Paul had any acquaintance with the story of the empty tomb, and it is questionable whether it is even compatible with his conception of resurrection from the dead. Elsewhere, he suggests that he thinks of the 'spiritual body' which is raised (1 Cor.15:44), not as a reanimated physical body, but as 'a building from God, a house not made with hands, eternal in the heavens' (2 Cor.5:1).

VERSE 1: The expression of time is very awkward; the circumlocution is perhaps an attempt to combine Mark's 'when the sabbath was over' with his 'after the sun had risen'. Perhaps he thinks of them arriving in the half-light before the breaking of dawn. But 'late on the sabbath' would mean just before sunset, not shortly before dawn. The Jewish day began and ended at sunset.

'To see the tomb'—there is no suggestion that they are coming to anoint the body with spices. Probably Matthew thought that the anointing had already taken place at Bethany (26:12).

VERSES 3—4: The description of the angel and the phenomena is no more than an haggadic elaboration of Mark; there is no need to postulate an independent tradition.

VERSE 8: 'Fear and great joy' replaces Mark's 'trembling and astonishment'. It paves the way for the vision that is to follow.

Neither here nor in Mark are the women reported as giving the message to the disciples. In Luke, we are told that they 'reported all this to the eleven and to all the rest . . . but these words seemed to them an idle tale, and they did not believe them' (Lk.24:9,11). In John, Mary Magdalene comes alone to the tomb and finds it empty. She runs to tell Peter and the mysterious disciple 'whom Jesus loved', drawing the natural conclusion, 'They have taken the Lord out of the tomb, and we do not know where they have laid him' (Jn.20:1f.).

VERSE 10: The risen Jesus has nothing to say that has not been said in virtually the same words by the angel.

2   THE BRIBING OF THE GUARD *28:11—15*

[11] As they were on their way, some of the guard went into the city and reported to the chief priests all that had happened. [12] When they had met in assembly with the elders and discussed the matter, they gave the soldiers an ample sum of money, [13] telling them, 'You are to say that his disciples came by night and stole his body while we were

asleep; [14] if this comes to the ears of the prefect, we will reason with him and keep you out of trouble.'

[15] They took the money and did as they were instructed; and this report spread widely in Jewish communities, and continues to this day.

VERSE 11: If a guard of Roman soldiers was put at the disposal of the Sanhedrin, they might conceivably report to the chief priests; but normally they would make their report to one of their own officers or directly to the prefect.

VERSE 12: The phrasing of Matthew seems intended to suggest that the Sanhedrin is called into session.

VERSE 13: It would of course be a serious breach of discipline for soldiers to go to sleep at their post. It is asking a good deal of them that they should spread the word of such a dereliction to the general public.

VERSE 14: They were promising more than they could perform in undertaking to persuade Pilate to overlook such a breach of duty. But we need not quibble over the details of a story that is so completely incredible as a whole.

VERSE 15: This is probably the only touch of fact in it all, that such a story was widely believed among the Jews by the time of Matthew—not, of course, the bribing of the guard by the chief priests, but the report that the disciples of Jesus stole his body from its tomb and then pretended that it had been raised from the dead by supernatural power. Justin (*c*.150) and Tertullian (*c*.200) say that such a report was current among Jews in their time.

3 REUNION IN GALILEE: THE COMMISSION TO EVANGELIZE THE WORLD *28:16–20*

[16] The eleven disciples went their way to Galilee, to the mountain which Jesus had appointed for them. [17] When they saw him they worshipped him, but some doubted. [18] Jesus approached and spoke to them in these words: 'All authority has been committed to me, in heaven and on earth. [19] Go, therefore, make disciples of all the nations, baptizing them in the name of the Father and of the Son and of the Holy Spirit, [20] teaching them to observe all the commandments that I have given you. I am with you always, until the end of the age.'

VERSE 16: 'Which Jesus had appointed'—possibly, 'where Jesus had instructed them' (delivered the 'Sermon on the Mount'—McNeile); but the verb διατάσσω nearly always means 'give directions, commands', etc., not to give teachings. The difficulty is that Jesus has given instructions to them to go to Galilee, but there has been no indication that he would meet them in a particular place. In any case, the 'mountain' is not to be located on a map—it is the place of revelation.

VERSE 17: 'Some doubted'—there has been no suggestion that any others were on the scene besides the eleven. The words seem to reflect an early tradition that even the appearances of the risen Jesus were not enough to convince all the remaining disciples that he had actually risen from the dead. This tradition is given specific shape in the Johannine story of the doubts of Thomas (Jn.20:24—29).

VERSE 18: This is only the second time that Jesus 'approaches' them (or anyone), out of fifty-two instances of the use of this verb (προσέρχομαι) in Matthew. In all the remaining fifty, it is others who 'make approach' to him. It is significant that in the only other instance it is the Jesus whom they have just seen in glory, 'trans-figured', who approached them (17:7).

'All authority'—Matthew goes far beyond any Messianic categories in his claims for Jesus. No king of Israel ever claimed, no future 'Messiah' was ever promised, any kind of authority in heaven. Jesus now proclaims that sovereignty over the entire universe has been committed to him—by God, of course. In the Temptation story, Satan had tried to allure him by offering to give him 'all the kingdoms of the world and the glory of them,' if Jesus would 'fall down and worship him' (4:8f.). Now he who was content to be servant of all is given prerogatives far higher than the rule of all earthly kingdoms (cf. Phil.2:9—11).

VERSE 19: As Israel's Messiah, Jesus had limited his mission on earth to 'the lost sheep of the house of Israel', and had charged his disciples not to go to Gentiles or to Samaritans, but only to Israel (10:5f.; 15:24). The Sovereign of the universe sends them to make disciples of 'all the nations'. The Gentile mission of the church is not merely authorized but commanded.

Obviously enough, if any such command had been known to the apostles, and to the early church, they would not have debated about the legitimacy of such a mission, and the 'pillars' of the mother church in Jerusalem could hardly have agreed to restrict themselves to 'the circumcision' while it was left to Paul and Barnabas—two men who had not been among the eleven who received the command —to go to the Gentiles. This alone would be enough to demonstrate that this charge of the risen Jesus is a relatively late formulation. The controversy over the admission of Gentiles is long over, and indeed forgotten.

'Make disciples'—the verb is formed on the noun μαθητής, 'disciple'. Matthew has shown clearly enough what it means to be a 'disciple'. It means renunciation of all earthly ambition, the denial of self, the bearing of the cross, the following of Christ, the willingness to be a servant to all, the commitment to doing the will of the heavenly Father.

'Baptizing them'—it is evident that converts were admitted to the church by baptism, from the very beginning, but up to this point there has been no mention of any baptism other than that of John, which Jesus and his first disciples had received. There was, of course, the prediction of John—in his mouth, probably much more threat than promise—that his greater successor would baptize 'with wind [taken by the evangelists to mean "spirit"]—and fire'. The phrase seems to indicate that John thought of this 'baptism' as something quite different from his baptism with water, rather than as something accomplished in association with water baptism, or following it.

'In the name of the Father and of the Son and of the Holy Spirit' —this became the classic form used in Christian baptism; this verse is our earliest evidence for it. From Acts and the Pauline epistles, we gather that in the earliest days, converts were baptized 'in the name of Jesus Christ' (Acts 2:38), or of 'the Lord Jesus' (Acts 8:16); 'into Christ Jesus' (Rom.6:3), or 'into Christ' (Gal.3:27). But in these earliest baptisms, it was promised that they would receive the gift of the Holy Spirit, and those who were Gentiles 'turned to God from idols to serve a God living and true' (1 Thess. 1:9); through Jesus they learned to be 'faithful to God who raised him from the dead and gave him glory' (1 Pet.1:21). The triple formulation found here is not early, but it corresponds to the realities of Christian experience. It is not, properly speaking, 'trinitarian'; there is no element of speculation about the divine essence or the relations between Father, Son, and Holy Spirit. It reflects the modes in which the divine is manifested in Christian faith.

VERSE 20: 'Teaching them to observe . . .'—the teaching which they are to give to their converts is not primarily doctrinal, but ethical. It consists of commandments which are to be kept. This is undoubtedly the central emphasis in Matthew. It is so strongly emphasized as to bring with it the danger of a new legalism, as if what Christ brought were a 'new law' (Tertullian's phrase—*nova lex*, over against the *antiqua lex* of the Mosaic commandments). Matthew gives no indication that he appreciates the great distinction between Law and grace; 'the law was given through Moses; grace and truth came through Jesus Christ' (Jn.1:17). Matthew gives the impression, much of the time, that he thinks of the Christian life as simply a more faithful keeping of more rigorous commandments than was known to Pharisaic Judaism. Does he not come close to imposing the 'yoke of slavery' against which Paul warned his converts so earnestly? (Gal.5:1.)

The promise of Christ's return in power and glory, attended by hosts of angels, is more than supplemented (though not entirely superseded) by this assurance of his constant presence. The future anticipation is still suggested by the concluding phrase, 'until the end of the age'. For Matthew, the 'end of the age' was not far off; but the length of the interval is reduced in importance. The constant presence of Christ in spiritual experience here and now leaves us with no great desire to see some triumphant manifestation in the future— whether it come sooner or later.

Index